GREAT HISTORIANS FROM ANTIQUITY TO 1800

Great Historians from Antiquity to 1800

AN INTERNATIONAL DICTIONARY

LUCIAN BOIA, Editor-in-Chief

Ellen Nore, Keith Hitchins,
and Georg G. Iggers, Associate Editors

Sponsored by the Commission on the History of Historiography of the International Committee on the Historical Sciences

GREENWOOD PRESS
New York • Westport, Connecticut • London

Library of Congress Cataloging-in-Publication Data

Great historians from antiquity to 1800 : an international dictionary / editor-in-chief, Lucian Boia.
p. cm.
"Sponsored by the Commission on the History of Historiography of the International Committee on the Historical Sciences."
Bibliography: v. 1, p.
Includes index.
ISBN 0–313–24517–7 (lib. bdg. : v. 1 : alk. paper)
1. Historians—Biography—Dictionaries. I. Boia, Lucian. II. International Committee on the Historical Sciences. Commission on the History of Historiography.
D14.G74 1989
907'.2022—dc19 88–25089

British Library Cataloguing in Publication Data is available.

Library of Congress Catalog Card Number: 88–25089
ISBN: 0–313–24517–7

First published in 1989

Greenwood Press, Inc.
88 Post Road West, Westport, Connecticut 06881

Printed in the United States of America

The paper used in this book complies with the Permanent Paper Standard issued by the National Information Standards Organization (Z39.48–1984).

10 9 8 7 6 5 4 3 2 1

CONTENTS

PREFACE

Great Historians from Antiquity to 1800 is the result of an extensive international collaboration facilitated through the International Commission on the History of Historiography. In choosing the entries, two criteria were used: the "absolute" merit of these individuals in the development of universal historiography and their significance within each national culture.

Historiography is simultaneously international (as are most disciplines aspiring to be scientific) and national. Although the world has known very great historians who have shaped the general course of historiography, each nation has also recognized its own acclaimed historians. Undoubtedly, some lacunae remain; all cultures were not able to be represented in this work, but our goal was to insure the presence of the greatest possible number of national historiographies. We live in a world of nations, and the heritage of each is precious for the common future of humanity.

Entries are arranged by countries or geographical areas and alphabetized within these divisions. The editors have provided both an index of historians and a general subject index. Cross-references are indicated by "q.v." following the name of the individual mentioned in the text who is the subject of a separate entry. English translations of books and articles in non-Western languages appear in parentheses. The authors, who represent many nations of the world, used various systems of transliteration, but within areas (for example, Chinese or Arabic) they used the same system.

The geographic scope of this volume is the entire world, and chronologically, the book includes historiography from its beginnings to approximately 1800. Despite the differences that separate historians of antiquity from their counterparts in the Middle Ages, the Renaissance, or the Age of Enlightenment, they share a common characteristic in having written their works before the professionalization of history. They were less concerned with the scientific side of history, if they were aware of this at all, and more ambitious regarding literary and moral goals.

A separate volume is composed of great historians of the nineteenth and twentieth centuries, representing historiography that aspired to be more and more professional, specialized, methodical, and scientific.

INTRODUCTION

A dictionary of great historians begins with an injustice: there is history well before there is historiography. This history is oral and anonymous, told by nameless "great historians," but nevertheless has as its mission the recording of traditions of preliterate peoples, those situated on the first rung of the ladder of civilizations. Reconstruction of the past for Black Africa, Pre-Columbian America, or Oceania, would be unthinkable without the contribution of oral traditions.[1] The beginnings of European historiography also rest on a foundation of orally transmitted memory; thus the *Iliad* and the *Odyssey* led Heinrich Schliemann to the discovery of the civilizations of Troy and Mycenae.

Historiography, that is, the writing of history, began almost simultaneously in Mesopotamian towns and in Egypt around 3000 B.C. More advanced political structures (a state or cities interested in recording essential events for the community), a calendar and the invention of writing were factors decisive in the evolution of historiography. Yet the great historians were always invisible. For two or three millennia, the Orient produced only "annals," the simplest form of historiography, an impersonal testimony, a listing of memorable political, religious, or military events. This was a purely official historiography. Counting for little, the historian hid himself behind the facts and remained no more than a simple servant of established institutions.

The liberation of history and of the historian occurred in Greece during the fifth century B.C. In this epoch, as a consequence of their diversity and freedom, the Greeks invented history, just as they invented almost all of the other sciences. Free Greek men were not only subjects but also citizens. An extremely dense citizenly life propelled these men to another political and intellectual level from which they faced a vast oriental world essentially rural and under authoritarian direction. Diverse cities emulated each other, each desiring to promote its own traditions. But above all, the democratic regime of Athens and other Greek cities nourished the bloom of history. Historical work ceased being official and anonymous. Historians rendered personal judgments on men, deeds, and public affairs. The epoch of great historians commenced.

By no accident do the first great names of history belong to writers born on the Greek coast of Asia Minor: Hecataeus of Miletus (q.v.) and, above all,

Herodotus of Halicarnassus (q.v.). Through this region passed the line of separation and confrontation between Greek and oriental civilizations. Differences and antagonisms between the two types of civilizations inspired political and historical questions; the historians' role was to attempt explanations.

Herodotus' *Histories*, the first properly to bear that name, investigated known civilizations engaged in conflict in the first half of the fifth century B.C. In fact, history had two fathers: the first was Herodotus, and the second, no less important, was Thucydides (q.v.) The latter's *Peloponnesian War* proposed a type of history different from that of Herodotus. Whereas Herodotus practiced a sort of "reportage," grouping, without a grand system, the most diverse elements of geography, ethnography, and history, Thucydides carefully defined and limited the domain of historiography. This became a "scientific" thought process seeking to establish, in a rigorous way, through analysis and criticism of sources, the facts within a sensible interpretation. This necessary limitation arose in relation to the global ambitions of Herodotus and was alone capable of insuring coherence and precision in historical writing. For the next 2,500 years, historians wrote essentially within the scheme established by Thucydides. But the modern epoch witnesses the revenge of Herodotus. The movement away from narration of events and the present preoccupation with global history and a history of civilizations, places the first of history's fathers in the precursor's position as an originator of the most modern historiographical tendencies.

Did the Greeks, and in particular Thucydides, invent "scientific" history? To suggest this would be an exaggeration. From the beginning, history was and remains an ambivalent study, at once science and literature, a reconstruction of the past but always within the subjective perspective of the present, a search for the truth but an exercise in style and the derivation of moral lessons. History is a drama constructed with materials drawn from real life. History, *magistra vitae* and *opus oratorium maxime* (teacher of lives and sublime work of oratory), said Cicero, illustrating thus the double face of this discipline as not "pure" science. Polybius (q.v.), among the ancients, went the furthest toward a history more "scientific" than literary. A mediocre narrator, he applied himself diligently to discovering the causes of the great restructurings of history, in his case, the triumph of the Roman Republic.

The Romans invented no new formulas for history. Adopting methods of their great Greek predecessors, they weighted the balance in their writings toward the literary and moral side. Criticism of sources and objective research were less important. In contrast with the diversity of the Greek world, the Roman state sought to imprint a single political and historical consciousness, and historiography served this end by highlighting uncritically the glorious Roman traditions. For Titus Livy (q.v.), Tacitus (q.v.), and all of the great Roman historians, history was an epic or drama and, in that capacity, could serve as a lesson in civic duty and patriotism. Tacitus proclaimed a wonderful motto: *sine ira et studio*, without hatred or partiality, but he himself was hardly capable of applying his fine precept. How can one write history in a detached manner?

Historiography embraces two principal formulas that developed independently. The first mode, Greco-Roman, continues in European and thus in world history into the present. The second mode was invented in China by Si-ma Qian (q.v.) about 100 B.C. and was continued by Ban Gu (q.v.) in the first century A.D. In China's historiography and, generally in the Far East, an essential role was played by Confucius's (q.v.) philosophic system; he insisted on the moral role of history in which the facts speak for themselves, with the least possible intervention of the author. While European historians made homogeneous reconstructions of definite form, their Chinese colleagues conceived of history more as a mosaic of facts and problems and juxtaposed the most diverse categories of information within annals of their sovereigns as well as in monographs dedicated to institutions or to social and cultural topics. Favoring the art of composition and presupposing the individual mark of each historian, the European mode contrasted with the Chinese method, whereby the historian was secreted among his sources. For two thousand years, until the time of Western influences, this manner of writing history continued in China and, under Chinese influence, in the Far East.

As antiquity drew to a close, Greco-Roman historiography underwent a major transformation due to the impact of Christianity. Between A.D. 300 and 430, Eusebios of Caesarea (q.v.) and Saint Augustine (q.v.) introduced a new notion of the structure of history. Time became the decisive factor. In the minds of ancient Greeks and Romans, history had been a matter of cycles or a temporal succession somewhat vaguely defined. With the advent of Christianity, everything changed: history became rectilinear; time was rigorously defined, or confined, with the parameters of the creation of the world, as told in Genesis, and the Last Judgment, foretold in numerous sources. In a stroke, chronology became central to history, and the historian was swallowed by theology. History was no longer an affair appropriate for human efforts; it was now the reflection of a divine plan.

For a long time the Middle Ages were viewed as an epoch of regression at all levels in the history of Europe, including historiography. In fact this period is one of a new synthesis, a time neither inferior nor superior to antiquity, simply different. Moreover, there exists a certain continuity between the historiography of antiquity and that of the Middle Ages. Latin and Greek were the scholarly languages, and Greco-Roman works were copied and used as models. There was no general medieval feeling of having been cut off from any past: the Roman Empire continued, or gave the impression of continuing, through the emperors of Constantinople, through Charlemagne, and through the germanic Holy Empire. Christianity was also a bridge between antiquity and the Middle Ages. The historiographic mode was that established by the Church fathers at the end of the classical period.

Medieval historiography served mainly as an auxiliary to theology. The critical spirit was reduced to modest proportions, reflecting the status of this sort of thinking. The authority of sources assumed primary importance and none could envisage a critical examination of the Bible or commentaries by the fathers of the Church. On the other hand, this history possessed a meaning lacking in Greco-Roman history. This history pictured humanity in the ascendant, a unitary and progressive evolution. Thus it valued time. For centuries the *Universal Chronicle* was the genre most cultivated. Preoccupied by the two limits of history, creation of the world and its end, historians of the Middle Ages were thus obsessed with chronology and applied themselves to establishing dates as precisely as possible. Despite their naivete, they laid a foundation for modern erudition.[2]

Doubtless, there were several Middle Ages. Literate culture receded in the early centuries. Intellectual life took refuge behind the walls of monasteries. Copied and recopied by monks, the few exemplars of historical manuscripts circulated with difficulty. A medieval "best-seller" meant a "diffusion" of some tens or at best hundreds of manuscripts during the space of several centuries. Yet from the beginning, the Middle Ages also produced some masterpieces, such as those of Gregory of Tours (q.v.) or Bede (q.v.). The Carolingian Renaissance revitalized the imperial ideal, reunited writers with Latin sources, and allowed Eginhard (q.v.) to write the life of Charlemagne following the classical model of Suetonius (q.v.).

A true evolution and diversification of history manifested itself especially from the eleventh through the twelfth centuries. The rapid expansion of towns, a growing population, new technologies, the assertion of political power by states, and the far-ranging Crusaders' expeditions created for Europe a new social and intellectual framework. Historiography was no longer exclusively a matter for ecclesiastics. Royal power, nobility, towns, and the bourgeoisie were already supporting their own medium of historiographical expression. Otto von Freising (q.v.), a church leader, with his universal history of Augustinian inspiration; Villehardouin (q.v.), feudal lord, author of an account of the fourth Crusade written not in Latin but, for the first time, in the national language, French; Froissart (q.v.), this bourgeois who knew so well how to paint a reproduction of feudal society; the Villani family of Florence, bourgeois writing a bourgeois history of a town—all enhanced the variety of a historiography that never again came down to a single, obligatory pattern.

There was also a rich historiography in Eastern Europe, Orthodox Europe, where the model was Byzantine. A theological outlook did not prevent the Byzantine historians, for example, Prokopios (q.v.) of Caesarea, Psellos (q.v.), or Anna Comnena (q.v.), from maintaining some narrow connections with the classical Greek tradition and an acute awareness of the role of the state in public affairs.

While Chinese historiography continued during the Middle Ages without essential changes in its ancient traditions, there was, between this and European historiography, a third historiographical type taking form in the Islamic world. This historiography brought new horizons because of Arab historians' interest in biography, genealogy, and geography. An exceptional historian of the fourteenth century was Ibn Khaldūn (q.v.), a man ahead of his times, who attempted a science of history, a sociology, or a science of society.

The Renaissance, during the fifteenth and sixteenth centuries, opened the mind of the West to new historiographical perspectives. The invention of printing marked a fundamental shift in the fortunes of humanity. Historical research, a more general diffusion of history, and the debate of historical questions all gained momentum from the introduction of presses. Whereas the hand-copied manuscripts of the Middle Ages had been necessarily limited in number and their circulation difficult, the presses of Europe, between 1450 and 1500, circulation difficult, the presses of Europe, between 1450 and 1500, some 20 million copies of books and, from 1500 to 1600, 200 million.[3] At the the same time, geographical discoveries enlarged the known world and posed questions of a moral and historical nature, questions concerning the questions of a moral and historical nature, questions concerning the humankind and of civilizations.
humankind and of civilizations.

Renaissance humanism did not set itself against religion, but discovered a history belonging to humanity, a history they tried to separate from holy or ecclesiastical history. History broke its bond with theology and became an autonomous study. As interpretation developed, so also did historical method. Criticism of sources replaced the ancient notion of authority. (An historian such as Lorenzo Valla (q.v.) challenged the authority of the Pope himself.) Historians aspired at the same time to uncover human causes, rationales, a logical interpretation of events and historical processes.

Such enterprise needed a model, a point of reference. Disassociating itself from the Middle Ages, the Renaissance sought out, from the culture of antiquity, Greco-Roman historiography, which limited for a time the trend toward writing in the national languages. Historians wrote in Latin, imitating classical texts and producing massive editions of ancient writers. An inventory of books published between 1450 and 1700 shows no less than 2,355 editions of ancient historians, with a total of some 2.5 million copies.[4]

Italy was a radiant center of humanist historiography. Along with Valla, Leonardo Bruni (q.v.) and Flavio Biondo (q.v.) wrote learned, critical histories that were inspired by classical models. Machiavelli (q.v.) and Guicciardini (q.v.), at the beginning of the sixteenth century, raised the new formula to perfection within a synthesis in which history confronted political problems within Italy and Europe in the midst of a crisis of reconstruction. From being the ancient auxiliary of theology, historiography more and more became an instrument of political analysis and civic education.

One very interesting historiographical development occurred in France. About 1500 medieval elements coexisted with humanism in the work of Commynes (q.v.), but less than a century later, Jean Bodin (q.v.), Etienne Pasquier (q.v.), and La Popelinière (q.v.) launched a fascinating new historiographical venture through a new historical form, "perfect" history (*histoire accomplie*), a type of global history involving the analysis of problems and the interpretation of the achievements of civilization. Even though they had no immediate successors, the amplitude and the modernity of their approach could lead to the conclusion that truly modern history, the science of history, would have commenced in France at exactly that time.[5]

But the Renaissance also displayed another side. Along with the liberation of humanity and human judgment came fanaticism. Commencing under the sign of humanism, the epoch ended under that of religious conflict. Theology, Catholic or Protestant, reasserted its rights during the sixteenth and seventeenth centuries. The German Flacius (q.v.) and the Italian Baronio (q.v.) reflected the two antagonistic tendencies within a similar ecclesiastical interpretation of history.

During the same epoch, the New World made its historiographical debut, offering to history novel civilizations and studying the consequences of their contact with Europe. Las Casas (q.v.) was the historian and defender of the Native Americans, while the Peruvian Garcilaso de la Vega (q.v.) emerged as the first great historian born under the sun of that continent.

Between the intense times of the Renaissance and the historiography of the Enlightenment, the seventeenth century offers a sort of parenthesis, in any case a less coherent historiographical image. The creative and free spirit of the Renaissance arrived at a terrain less favorable and had to operate within a troubled political, social, and economic context marred by religious, political, and intellectual intolerance. While the century turned instead toward philosophy and the exact sciences, history principally exhibited two tendencies: (1) a literary approach, which one might call "baroque," more concerned with style and dramatic effects than with seeking the truth (finished for the moment were the philosophic and scientific ambitions of an *histoire accomplie*);[6] (2) an erudite history absolutely distinct from previous trends, a history preoccupied with deciphering and critically analyzing sources. This type of history was brilliantly represented by the Jesuit Jean Bolland (q.v.) and the Benedictines Jean Mabillon (q.v.) and Bernard de Montfaucon (q.v.). Illustrating the spirit of the seventeenth century, at once conventional and innovative, is the fact that, in the same year, 1681, appeared Jacques Bossuet's (q.v.) *Discours sur l'histoire universelle* (Discourse on Universal History), a traditional ecclesiastic interpretation, and *De re diplomatica* (On Diplomatics) by Mabillon, which marks a date in the construction of the modern method of historical research.

The eighteenth century, especially the second half, is the epoch of the Enlightenment, an essential turning point in the history of humanity. The scientific, technological, and industrial revolution; the demographic revolution; and the great social and political revolutions of the modern age find here their point of departure. From this moment, history accelerated. Progress and the future were discovered, two notions that became inseparable from all human undertakings.

In that climate, the historian willed himself to be mainly a philosopher and a man of science. The mission would be to produce a scientific treatment of history, to outline both causes of events and the laws of development. The philosophy of history was born in the work of Vico (q.v.), Voltaire (q.v.), and Herder (q.v.). The accent fell more and more often on the analysis of civilizations with the goal of unveiling a universal history, a history alone capable of explaining entirely the human phenomenon. Structure and problems were preferred to simple narrative. Voltaire's *Le siècle de Louis XIV* (Century of Louis XIV) and the *Essai sur les moeurs et l'esprit des nations* (Essay on the Customs and Spirit of Nations) were masterpieces of the rationalist school, to which are appended the great Scottish and English historians: David Hume, William Robertson, and Edward Gibbon (qq.v.).

Searching for rational explanations, the historian–philosophers of the Enlightenment destroyed the last bridges linking history with theology. For divine influence Montesquieu (q.v.) substituted the natural environment, whereas Voltaire, Hume, Robertson, and Gibbon offered moral, social, and political orders as causative factors in history. Scientific history, rationally explicable, eventually governed by laws, was even thought by Condorcet (q.v.) to be capable of revealing the future.

In Germany another development originated fraught with consequences: the professionalization of history, which became there an autonomous discipline within the university. Until this moment, the historian had been more an "amateur" than a member of a rigorously standardized profession. Founded in 1737, the University of Göttingen set history apart and gave chairs to several prominent historians, among them Gatterer (q.v.), Schlözer (q.v.), and Heeren. By 1800 nearly a dozen chairs of history existed in German universities. After 1800 this practice accelerated and spread to other countries. One may thus propose that the beginning of the nineteenth century was the frontier between the old historiography, practiced by erudites, writers, philosophers, politicians, and churchmen, and the new history, a history of professionals, members of a well-defined profession, following a body of generally accepted rules and methods.

To those ancient historians, those who wrote before the professionalization of history, is dedicated this volume of *Great Historians*.

NOTES

1. The historical value of oral tradition was discussed at the Fifteenth International Congress of Historical Sciences (Bucharest, August 1980). See especially the study by E. J. Alagoa, "Oral Tradition," in the *Reports* of the Congress, vol. 1 (Bucharest, 1980), pp. 529–535.

2. On the subject of medieval historiography, see particularly Bernard Guenée, *Histoire et culture historique dans l'Occident médiéval* (Paris, 1980).

3. Lucien Febvre and Henri-Jean Martin, *L'apparition du livre* (Paris, 1958).

4. Peter Burke, "A Survey of the Popularity of Ancient Historians, 1450–1700," *History and Theory* 5 (1966): 135–152.

5. George Huppert, *The Idea of Perfect History* (Urbana, Ill., 1970).

6. Charles-Olivier Carbonell, "Retour baroque à une histoire narrative. Les théoriciens de l'histoire en France au XVIIe siècle (1599–1681)," in *Etudes d'historiographie*, under the direction of Lucian Boia (Bucharest, 1985), pp. 83–95.

REGIONAL EDITORS

E. J. Alagoa (University of Port Harcourt, Nigeria)
African Section

Stelian Brezeanu (University of Bucharest, Romania)
Byzantine Section

Charles-Olivier Carbonell (University of Montpellier, France)
French Section

Eugen Cizek (University of Bucharest, Romania)
Roman Section

Cornell Fleischer (University of Illinois, Urbana)
Ottoman Section

William H. Frederick (Ohio University)
Southeast Asian Section

Constant Georgescu (University of Bucharest, Romania)
Greek Section

Antonia Gransden (University of Nottingham, Great Britain)
English Section

Nikita Harwich Vallenilla (Universidad Santa Maria, Venezuela)
Latin American Section

William Salomone (University of Rochester)
Italian Section

Samir Saul (University of Quebec, Canada)
Islamic Section

Hans Schleier (Central History Institute of the Academy of Sciences of G.D.R., Berlin)
German Section

Ronald P. Toby (University of Illinois, Urbana)
Far Eastern Section

CONTRIBUTORS

E. J. Alagoa, University of Port Harcourt, Nigeria

V. A. Arutyunova-Fidanyan, National Committee of Historians of the Soviet Union, Moscow, USSR

Hans-Joachim Bartmuss, Martin Luther Universitat Halle-Wittenberg, Moritzburgring, German Democratic Republic

Werner Berthold, Karl-Marx-Universität, Leipzig, German Democratic Republic

Ragnar Björk, University of Uppsala, Sweden

Lucian Boia, University of Bucharest, Romania

Stelian Brezeanu, University of Bucharest, Romania

Peter Burke, Emmanuel College, Cambridge, Great Britain

Cang Xiu-liang, Institute of History of the Chinese Academy of Social Sciences, Beijing, China

Charles-Olivier Carbonell, University of Montpellier, France

Chen Guang-chong, Institute of History of the Chinese Academy of Social Sciences, Beijing, China

Chen Qian-jun, Institute of History of the Chinese Academy of Social Sciences, Beijing, China

Yŏng-ho Ch'oe, University of Hawaii, Honolulu, Hawaii

Paloma Cirujano, Centro de Estudios Históricos del Consejo Superior de Investigaciones Cientificas, Madrid, Spain

Eugen Cizek, University of Bucharest, Romania

Stuart Clark, University College of Swansea, Swansea, Great Britain

Radu Constantinescu, Institute of History ''Nicolae Iorga'' and State Archives, Bucharest, Romania

Vittorio Conti, University of Florence, Italy

Phillip Corina, Emmanuel College, Cambridge, Great Britain

Cui Wen-yin, Institute of History of the Chinese Academy of Social Sciences, Beijing, China

John F. D'Amico, George Mason University, Fairfax, Virginia

Lajos Demény, Institute of History "Nicolae Iorga", Bucharest, Romania

Dimitrije Djordjevic, University of California, Santa Barbara

Nadezda Dragova, Institute of Balkan Studies, Sofia, Bulgaria

Jean-Michel Dufays, Institut d'Enseignement Supérieur Social de l'Etat, Bruxelles, Belgium

Maria Teresa Elorriaga Planes, Centro de Estudios Históricos del Consejo Superior de Investigaciones Cientificas, Madrid, Spain

Fritz Fellner, University of Salzburg, Austria

Cornell Fleischer, University of Illinois, Urbana, Illinois

William H. Frederick, Ohio University, Athens, Ohio, USA

Constant Georgescu, University of Bucharest, Romania

Ferenc Glatz, Institute of History, Budapest, Hungary

Elisabeth G. Gleason, Tiburon, California

Jean Glénisson, Institut de recherche et d'histoire des textes, Paris, France

Antonia Gransden, University of Nottingham, Great Britain

S. Groenveld, Rijksuniversiteit, Leiden, The Netherlands

Nikita Harwich Vallenilla, Universidad Santa Maria, Caracas, Venezuela

Milan Hauner, University of Wisconsin-Madison, Madison, Wisconsin

Denys Hay, University of Edinburgh, Great Britain

Keith Hitchins, University of Illinois, Urbana, Illinois

Siegfried Hoyer, Karl-Marx-Universitát, Leipzig, German Democratic Republic

Georg G. Iggers, State University of New York at Buffalo, New York

Johannes Irmscher, Zentralinstitut für Alte Geschichte und Archae ologie, Berlin, German Democratic Republic

Arlette Jouanna, University of Montpellier, France

T. M. Kalinina, National Committee of Historians of Soviet Union, Moscow, USSR

R. A. Kireyeva, National Committee of Historians of Soviet Union, Moscow, USSR

Jonathan B. Knudsen, Wellesley College, Wellesley, Massachusetts

M. D. Kurmachev, National Committee of Historians of Soviet Union, Moscow, USSR

Lai Chang-yang, Institute of History of the Chinese Academy of Social Sciences, Beijing, China

Rudi Paul Lindner, University of Michigan, Ann Arbor, Michigan

Maria Lordkipanidze, Institute of History, Tbilisi, Georgia, USSR

Luo Shi-lie, Institute of History of the Chinese Academy of Sciences, Beijing, China

Krikor H. Maksoudian, Harvard University, Cambridge, Massachusetts

Jens Chr. Manniche, Institute of History, University of Aarhus, Denmark

Mian Yue, Institute of History of the Chinese Academy of Sciences, Beijing, China

Min Zhao-wen, Institute of History of the Chinese Academy of Sciences, Beijing, China

Günter Mühlpfordt, Martin-Luther-Universität, Halle-Wittenberg, German Democratic Republic

Rhoads Murphey, Columbia University, New York

Maria Beatriz Nizza da Silva, University of Sao Paulo, Brazil

Emiliana Pasca Noether, University of Connecticut, Storrs, Connecticut

A. H. de Oliveira Marques, Universidade Nova, Lisbon, Portugal

Juan Sisinio Pérez Garzón, Centro de Estudios Históricos del Consejo Superior de Investigaciones Cientificas, Madrid, Spain

Eluggero Pii, University of Florence, Italy

Qu Ling-dong, Institute of History of the Chinese Academy of Sciences, Beijing, China

Peter Hanns Reill, University of California, Los Angeles, California

Gary A. Rendsburg, Canisius College, Buffalo, New York

Johanna Roelevink, Zoetermeer, The Netherlands

V. A. Rzhanitsina, National Committee of Historians of Soviet Union, Moscow, USSR

Masayuki Sato, Yamanashi University, Kofu, Yamanashi, Japan

Samir Saul, University of Quebec, Canada

Conrad Schirokauer, Chinese Academy of Social Sciences, Beijing, China

Kevin, Sharpe, Southampton University, Southampton, Great Britain

Y. N. Shchapov, National Committee of Historians of Soviet Union, Moscow, USSR

Shi Ding, Institute of History of the Chinese Academy of Sciences, Beijing, China

Peter Stadler, University of Zürich, Switzerland

Edward C. Thaden, University of Illinois at Chicago, Illinois

Jerzy Topolski, University of Poznan, Poland

Winfried Trillitzsch, Friedrich-Schiller-Universität, Jena, German Democratic Republic

Francesco Turvasi, Cardinal Newman College, St. Louis, Missouri

Michel de Waha, University of Bruxelles, Belgium

Wang Zheng-yao, Institute of History of the Chinese Academy of Sciences, Beijing, China

L. H. M. Wessels, Instituut voor Nieuwe Geschiedenis, Nÿmequen, The Netherlands

David J. Womersley, Jesus College, Oxford, Great Britain

Wu Huai-qi, Institute of History of the Chinese Academy of Social Sciences, Beijing, China

Xiao Jiefu, Institute of History of the Chinese Academy of Social Sciences, Beijing, China

Xie Bao-cheng, Institute of History of the Chinese Academy of Social Sciences, Beijing, China

Ye Tan, Institute of History of the Chinese Academy of Social Sciences, Beijing, China

Zeng Yi-fen, Institute of History of the Chinese Academy of Social Sciences, Beijing, China

Zhang Cheng-zong, Institute of History of the Chinese Academy of Social Sciences, Beijing, China

Zhuang Zhao, Institute of History of the Chinese Academy of Social Sciences, Beijing, China

Walter Zöllner, Martin-Luther-Universität, Halle-Wittenberg, German Democratic Republic

GREAT HISTORIANS FROM ANTIQUITY TO 1800

Great Historians: African

AFRICANUS, Leo (Al-Hassan ibn Muhammad al-Wazzan Al-Zayyati Al-Fasi) (Granada, c. 1494–Tunis? 1552), Moroccan travel historian. Born after the Spanish victory over the Arabs, Africanus and his family moved to Fez in Morocco; he was thus brought up in Africa. He was captured on a voyage to Constantinople by Italian pirates about 1520 and taken to Pope Leo X, who freed and converted him to Christianity and became his godfather and patron. Africanus apparently returned to Africa after the death of the pope and reverted to Islam. A celebrity as a scholar and teacher of Arabic in Italy, he became famous for his *History and Description of Africa*, first written in Arabic and translated into Italian by the author in 1526. It was quickly adopted as the standard authority on North and Negro Africa in Europe. It was recognized as the most important piece in the Italian compendium of voyages and travels by Ramusio (1550). The work of Leo Africanus was translated into French (1556), English (1600), and German (1806). He was subsequently plagiarized, cited, and used by later European travelers, geographers, and cartographers of Africa until the nineteenth century. Africanus impressed Europe as a representative of Arab scholarship in Africa writing in a European language from a Christian point of view and speaking directly to Christian readers. He had the additional advantage over other Arab sources available to Europe during this period of writing from personal observation and eyewitness informants. Accordingly, his credit and authority for objectivity and accuracy rose with the increase of European knowledge of Africa. However, since he did not, apparently, know Berber, his rendering of non-Arab place names, transliterated in succeeding European texts, has led to confusion in identification. Leo Africanus exercised a significant influence on European consciousness of Africa for nearly four centuries.

Bibliography: Robert Brown, ed., *The History and Description of Africa and of the Notable Things Therein Contained, Written by Al-Hassan Ibn-Mohammed Al-Wezaz Al-Fasi, a Moor, Baptised as Giovanni Leone, but Better Known as Leo Africanus, Done into English in the Year 1600, by John Pory*, 3 vols. (London, 1896).

E. J. Alagoa

AHMAD BĀBĀ (Abu'l-'Abbās Ahmad Bābā b. Ahmad b. al-Hajj Ahmad b.'Umar b. Muhammad Aqīt al-Sinhājī, al-Timbuktī) (Araouane/Arawān, 1556–Timbuktu, 1627), Malian scholar. Deported to and imprisoned in Marrakush, Morocco (1594), Ahmad Baba was later released and became a teacher (1596). He returned to Timbuktu in 1607. Ahmad Baba was the last of the outstanding Aqit family of Timbuktu who were virtually a ruling dynasty in the city throughout the sixteenth century until the Moroccan conquest in 1591. His fame rose during the period of his exile in Morocco where he was prolific in his writing and taught some of the most influential local scholars, including the historian and jurist Ahmad al-Maqqari. Legal and academic questions were referred to him for answers from as far away as Egypt. A total of fifty-six titles of his works are known, of which about thirty-two are extant. The majority were on legal subjects, including commentaries on the works or views of established scholars and a few on grammar and historical biography. His most important historical works were *Nail al-Ibtihāj* (The Obtaining of Pleasure), completed in 1596; and *Kifāyat al-Muhtāj* (The Sufficiency of the Needy), written in 1603. Ahmad Baba's writing provides the clearest evidence that Timbuktu was equal, if not superior, in Islamic scholarship to the Maghrib at the time and that it derived its inspiration directly from Egypt and the Middle East. His *Kifāyat al-Muhtāj*, for example, was acknowledged to be a major historical source on Maliki Islam based on twenty-three biographical works and numerous oral testimonies. Timbuktu does not appear to have had public libraries, even in the famous Sankore mosque, but private libraries were well stocked. Thus Ahmad Baba is reported to have lost up to sixteen hundred books on his deportation. The *Nail al-Ibtihāj* was aimed at an international readership and included the biographies of Maliki scholars throughout the Islamic world. The section devoted to Timbuktu was restricted mainly to members of the Aqit family and its associates. The work attracted the attention of scholars in North Africa and the Middle East. Ahmad Baba believed that learning benefited a community more than saintliness, which was of benefit mainly to the seeker. A Sanhaja Berber, he loved Timbuktu and took the first opportunity to return, in spite of his successes in Morocco. He was faithful to his teachers and assiduous in compiling the *sanad*, or line of transmission, of the knowledge he acquired to its sources in Mecca and the Middle East, and he eventually declared his principal teacher in Timbuktu, Muhammad Baghayughu, a *mujaddid*, or renovator of the faith. He himself achieved recognition from scholars in the western and central Sudan, North Africa, and the Middle East. Biographical notices of him exist in works from all of these places, including al-Sa'di's *Tarikh al-Sudan* (History of Sudan) and the *Infāq al-Maisūr* (Giving of What Is Available) of Muhammad Bello, sultan of Sokoto in Nigeria.

Bibliography: "Further Light on Ahmad Baba al-Timbuktī," *Research Bulletin* (Centre for Arabic Documentation, Ibadan) 2, no. 2 (1966): 19–31; J. O. Hunwick, "Ahmad Baba and the Moroccan Invasion of the Sudan (1591)," *Journal of the Historical Society of Nigeria* 2, no. 3 (1962): 311–328; "A New Source for the Biography of Ahmad Baba al-Timbukti (1556–1627)," *Bulletin of the School of Oriental and African Studies* 27, no. 3 (1964): 568–593; Elias N. Saad, *Social History of Timbuktu: The Role of Muslim Scholars and Notables, 1400–1900* (Cambridge, Eng., 1983).

E. J. Alagoa

Al-SA'DI, 'Abd al-Rahmān (Timbuktu, 1596–Timbuktu, 1656?), Malian historian. Al-Sa'di was celebrated for his book *Tarikh al-Sudan* (History of Sudan), completed about 1655. Although he was of Berber origin, *Tarikh al-Sudan* represents the first surviving example of a local West African history in the Islamic tradition of historiography. Timbuktu became the center of Islamic scholarship in this region of Africa south of the Sahara and north of the tropical forest, and its university mosque and quarter of Sankore became famous. The *Tarikh al-Sudan* has been called the official history of Timbuktu, recounting as it does, in detail, the activities and lives of its scholars and rulers and providing information on the history of the Songhay Empire through the period of its defeat by the Moroccans in 1591. The *Tarikh al-Sudan* is approached in importance only by the *Tarikh al-Fattash fī akhbār wa'l-juyush wa-akābir al-nās* (The Chronicle of the Researcher into the History of Countries, Armies, and Principal Personalities). The *Tarikh al-Fattash* is subject to controversy about its authorship and because of emendations and additions to the texts. It was, apparently, put together by Ibn Mukhtar Qunbulu around 1664 from texts and/or notes from his maternal grandfather Mahmud b. al-Hajj al-Mutawakkil Ka'ti and his uncle Isma'il Ka'ti. Since the Ka'ti family was of Soninke origin, living in the Tindirma community near Timbuktu, the *Tarikh al-Fattash* represents the spread of Islamic learning among the local groups of the western Sudan. This is further confirmed by references in *Tarikh al-Fattash* to a lost chronicle of an even earlier date than *Tarikh al-Sudan*, entitled *Al-Durar al-Hisān fi Akhbār Muluk al-Sūdān* (The Good Abundance in the News of the Sudanese Kings) and written by Bābā Guru al-Hajj Muhammad of the al-Amin Kānu family, apparently immigrants from the Nigerian city of Kano. Al-Sa'di's *Tarikh al-Sudan* cites another great scholar of Timbuktu, Ahmad Bābā (q.v.). These historical works, then, used the methods of Islamic historiography to synthesize oral traditions, chronicles of contemporary events, and biographies and genealogies of scholars and of notable men. Al-Sa'di avoided controversy and presented reconciliations of current traditions.

Bibliography: O. Houdas and E. Benoist, eds., *Tarikh es-Sudan, par Abderrahman es-Sadi* (Paris, 1898, 1900, 1964); O. Houdas and M. Delafosse, eds. and trans., *Tarikh el-Fettach, par Mahmoud Kati et l'un de ses petits fils* (Paris, 1913, 1964); N. Levtzion, "A Seventeenth-Century Chronicle by Ibn Al-Mukhtar: A Critical Study of *Tarikh al-Fattash*," *Bulletin of the School of Oriental and African Studies* 34, pt. 3 (1971): 571–593; Elias N. Saad, *Social History of Timbuktu: The Role of Muslim Scholars and Notables, 1400–1900* (London, 1983).

E. J. Alagoa

ATHANASIUS, Saint (Alexandria, A.D. 295–Alexandria, A.D. 373), Egyptian Church historian; archbishop of Alexandria (A.D. 328). Athanasius' life and writing were conditioned by his defense of the decisions of the Council of Nicaea called by Emperor Constantine in A.D. 325 and of the theological canons enshrined in the resulting Nicene Creed against assaults on it by the Arians. The Arians taught that Christ had the nature of a creature of God, rather than being "of one substance" with the Father as agreed at Nicaea. Athanasius was ousted from his office more than once by his opponents and became a refugee among the monks of the Egyptian desert for a while after A.D. 356. He took great pains to record the events of his life and, therefore, of the history of the early Christian Church and the development of the monastic movement in Egypt. His most important historical works were the following: *Epistola Encyclica* (Encyclical or Circular), A.D. 340; *Apologia contra Arianos* (Treatise against the Arians), A.D. 350; *Epistola ad Episcopos Aegypti et Libyae* (Letter to the Bishops of Egypt and Libya), A.D. 356; *Apologia ad Constantium* (Apology for Constantius), A.D. 356; *Apologia de Fuga* (Apology for My Flight), A.D. 357; *Epistola ad Serapiones de morte Arii* (Letter to Serapion on the Death of Arius), A.D. 358; *Epistola ad Monachos et Historia Arianorum* (Letter to the Monks and History of the Arians), A.D. 358; and *Epistola de Synodis Ariminensi et Seleuciana* (Discourse on the Councils Held at Ariminum and Seleucia), A.D. 359. Athanasius is also credited with a book on the biography of the founder of the monastic movement in Egypt, *The Life of Saint Anthony*, which influenced Saint Augustine (q.v.) of Hippo at the point of his conversion. Athanasius, "the great champion of the Nicene Creed," also surpassed his contemporaries as historian of fourth-century Christianity in Egypt and of the doctrinal controversies of the Church in the Eastern Roman Empire.

Bibliography: W. Bright, ed., *Historical writings of St. Athanasius according to the Benedictine Text* (Oxford, 1881).

E. J. Alagoa

IBN BATTUTA, Shams al-Din Abu Abd Allah Muḥammad (Tangier, 1304–Marrakush, 1368), Moroccan travel historian. Ibn Battuta left on his first pilgrimage to Mecca in 1325 and eventually traveled through the Middle and Near East, East Africa, India, China, and Spain. On his return, the Marinid sultan, Abu Inan, commissioned him to visit the kingdom of Mali in West African Sudan (1352–1353) in the reign of Mansa Sulaiman. He completed the dictation of the account of his travels at the end of 1355. Since he was, apparently, not a great literary scholar, the sultan's scribe, Abu Abdallah ibn Juzayy, was instructed "to put the work into elegant literary style." Although born a Luwata Berber, Ibn Battuta was a full member of the Arab Islamic culture of the Maghrib or Muslim West and felt at home in all of the Muslim lands he visited, in several of which he served as a *qadi*, or judge. He was undoubtedly the greatest traveler of his time throughout the Muslim world, following his own rule, "never, so far as possible, to cover a second time any road." Ibn Khaldūn (q.v.) recorded that Ibn Battuta's account of his travels, especially those concerning India, were received with skepticism in Morocco. Yet these accounts have been acknowledged by scholars as being in the main honest and reliable, especially those about West Africa at the end of his travel career. The western Sudan was known to Moroccans, and Ibn Battuta would not risk exposure by falsifying what he saw. In addition, the West African account was written relatively soon after his visit. However, it is possible that the literary editor embellished the account by adding details from the accounts of earlier Arab visitors to western Sudan, such as al-Umari. Ibn Battuta, as a young traveler to East Africa and a mature one to West Africa, provided some of the earliest internal African accounts on which the history of Africa is now being reconstructed and interpreted.

Bibliography: H.A.R. Gibb, ed. and trans., *The Travels of Ibn Battuta, A.D. 1325–1354* (Cambridge, Eng., 1958); Said Hamdun and Noel King, *Ibn Battuta in Black Africa* (London, 1975).

E. J. Alagoa

IBN FARTUWA, Ahmad (Ngarzargamo, sixteenth century), Nigerian historian. Nothing is known about the life of the first Nigerian historian in the local Islamic tradition apart from the fact that he was the *imam* of the famous ruler of the Kanem-Borno Empire, Mai Idris Alooma (1569–1619). His surviving historical works are *Tarikh Mai Idris* (History of the First Twelve Years of the Reign of Mai Idris Alooma) and *Tarikh Mai Idris wa ghazawatihi* (Kanem Wars of Mai Idris Alooma), both of which were brought to Europe by Heinrich Barth in 1853. In *Tarikh Mai Idris* he described himself as "the Imam ul Kabir Ahmad ibn Fartua of the tribe of Muhammad ibn Mani." In that work he disavowed all display of learning or pride of spirit and wished only to use "the materials from the past, even though our work may be poor and of no account." He despaired of his ability to give "a thorough and full account" of the life and work of Mai Idris, a task he thought beyond the capacity even of "a council of the learned." Even such a group could not possibly achieve certainty, because of the "many wars" Mai Idris fought and the magnitude of his exploits. Nontheless, Al-Imam Ahmad ibn Fartuwa al-Barnawi carried out his main objectives in the two chronicles "to narrate the mode of life of our Sultan and what he did in a history of his reign and of his wars and encampments and of his clearing the roads for merchants." The major concerns of modern historians in using his material lie in making allowances for the extent of his adulation for Mai Idris Alooma and in the absence of systematic dating of events.

Bibliography: A.D.H. Bivar and M. Hiskett, "The Arabic Literature of Nigeria to 1804: A Provisional Account," *Bulletin of the School of Oriental and African Studies* 25 (1962): 104–148; *Kanem Wars of Mai Idris Alooma*. Vol. 1: *Sudanese Memoirs* (Lagos, 1928; London, 1967); H. R. Palmer, ed. and trans., *History of the First Twelve Years of the Reign of Mai Idris Alooma of Bornu, 1571–1583, by His Imam, Ahmad Ibn Fartua* (Lagos, 1926; London 1970).

E. J. Alagoa

MANETHO (Sebennytus, now Samannûd, third century B.C.), ancient Egyptian historian. High priest in the temple at Hêliopolis, Manetho introduced the cult of Serapis to Alexandria. He is credited with writing between three and six books, mainly for the education of the Greek population of Alexandria. The best known of them were the *Aegyptiaca* (The History of Egypt) and *The Sacred Book* dealing with Egyptian mythology and antiquities. Manetho wrote the *Aegyptiaca* partially to correct the errors of earlier Greek histories of Egypt by Hecataeus of Abdera and Herodotus (q.v.). Although Manetho's history has many parallels with the *Aegyptiaca* of Hecataeus, which has been described as "a philosophical romance" and "an ethnographical Utopia," rather than a critical history, he made no direct attack on Hecataeus. Rather, he criticized Herodotus for errors of fact. Manetho's *Aegyptiaca* also has similarities with the *Chaldaîca* of Berosus (q.v.), priest of Marduk in Babylon, which was also written for the Greek rulers of Chaldaea. It appears that Manetho was commissioned by Ptolemy Philadelphus of Alexandria in competition with the ruler of the neighboring Greek territories. The original text of Manetho's history is no longer extant. It survives in the excerpts preserved in the writings of Josephus and in the *Epitome* made at an early date, in the form of Lists of Dynasties with short notes on important kings and events. The existing texts have been altered by Jews who wished to prove their antiquity with reference to Egyptian history and chronology and by later Christian writers such as Sextus Julius Africanus and Eusebius of Caesarea (q.v.). As high priest, Manetho had access to authentic sources. In the temple at Heliopolis, stood "the sacred tree" on which "the goddess Seshat, the Lady of Letters, the Mistress of the Library," was believed to have recorded the names and actions of Egyptian rulers. There were also papyri containing annals, liturgies and poems, hieroglyphic tablets, wall sculptures, and inscriptions on monuments and pyramids. Manetho also used oral traditions current in his time. From these diverse sources he wrote a history in three books dealing with periods of the gods, demigods, and spirits of the dead, and the period of mortal men until the time of Darius the Persian. The fragments have, accordingly, become the basis for the construction of the dynastic chronology of Egypt, in spite of the fact that it is recognized to be less than a critical and scientific study. Manetho stands out as the first Egyptian, and African, historian writing in Greek for the contemporary world of letters.

Bibliography: W. Helck, *Untersuchungen zu Manetho und den aegyptischen Königslisten, Untersuchungen* 18 (Berlin, 1956); W. G. Waddell, *The Aegyptiaca of Manetho: Manetho's History of Egypt* (Cambridge, Mass., and London, 1940, 1971).

E. J. Alagoa

Great Historians: Armenian

AGATHANGELOS (Armenia, A.D. fifth century), Armenian historian. According to his own testimony, Agathangelos was secretary to King Tiridates III (A.D. 298–330) and a man of Roman origin proficient in Latin and Greek and skilled in writing history. He was commissioned by King Tiridates to write the history of the events that transpired in Armenia during the third and the beginning of the fourth century. Modern scholarship, however, has shown on the basis of linguistic and stylistic evidence and historical as well as literary analysis that Agathangelos was not a contemporary of King Tiridates III and that the historical work attributed to him, namely, the *Patmut'iwn Hayoc'* (History of the Armenians) is a composite work consisting of a life of Saint Gregory the Illuminator, of which there are versions in several medieval languages and various hagiographical as well as epic elements and historical recollections. The work covers the history of Armenia from A.D. 220 to about 430. It is intended for a milieu struggling to maintain its Christian faith and to assert the importance of its religious center at Vałaršapat, the former capital of the Armenian Arsacids and a place closely associated with the name of Saint Gregory the Illuminator. The author of the *History* was not so much worried about historical accuracy as he was concerned about attaining his goal. Despite the legendary nature of the *History*, Agathangelos's work contains a great deal of factual material and is very valuable for the historian of late antiquity. The historical narrative is interrupted by a lengthy section, which is an early catechism bearing the title *The Teaching of St. Gregory* and which was probably not a part of the original work.

Bibliography: *Agathangelos: History of the Armenians*, trans. and commentary by R. W. Thomson (Albany, N.Y., 1976); Gérard Garitte, *Documents pour l'étude du livre d'Agathange*, Studi e Testi 127 (Vatican City, 1946); idem, "La vie grecque inédite de saint Grégoire d'Arménie," *Analecta Bollandiana* 83 (1965); Michel Van Esbroeck, "Un nouveau temoin du livre d'Agathange," *Revue des études arméniennes*, n.s., 8 (1971): 13–167.

K. H. Maksoudian

Č'AMČ'IAN, Mik'ayēl (Constantinople, 1738–Constantinople, 1823), Armenian historian and a member of the Armenian Mekhitarist Order. He received his education at the Mekhitarist monastery on the island of San Lazzaro in Venice.

In 1762 he was ordained a priest and from 1769 to 1775 he served as the pastor for the Armenian Catholic community of Basra, Iraq. He spent 1775 to 1789 in the Mekhitarist monastery in Venice teaching and at the same time writing and publishing his three volume *Patmut'iwn Hayoc'* (History of Armenia). Č'amč'ian spent the remaining thirty-four years of his life in Constantinople where he founded a parochial school. In 1820 he was involved in a movement that had set as its goal the unity of the Armenian Catholic and Armenian Orthodox communities. Besides his ecclesiastical duties and teaching, Č'amč'ian was a prolific writer, a grammarian, profound theologian and an exegetist. Č'amč'ian is considered to be the first modern Armenian historian. The first volume of his book, which was published in 1784, covers the history of Armenia from the time of creation to the year A.D. 441. The second volume, published in 1785, is about the period of Persian, Byzantine and Arab domination and the Bagratid kingdom, ending with the year 1080. The third volume, published in 1786, covers the events from the end of the eleventh century to the time of the author. Č'amč'ian's *History* is an encyclopedic work covering the entire breadth of the Armenian experience and is still useful to the modern student of Armenian history, especially since he occasionally uses sources about which we do not know. Č'amč'ian generally indicates his sources and has a critical approach in evaluating their information. His philosophy of history and point of view, however, are not very progressive, and he is forever trying to show that the fathers of the Armenian Church were not in disagreement with the doctrinal formulations of the Roman Church. Although Č'amč'ian used the general historical methodology of western scholars of his time, he was apparently little influenced by the ideas of the Enlightenment.

Bibliography: M. Chamchian, *History of Armenia, from B.C. 2247 to the year of Christ 1780*, trans. J. Avdall (2 vols., Calcutta, 1827); Mesrop Čamašian, *Patmut'iwn ardi hay grakanut'ean* ("History of Modern Armenian Literature ") (Vol.1, Venice, 1953); Sahak Čēmčēmian, "H. Mik'ayēl Č'amč'ian ew ir Hayoc' Patmut'iwno" (Fr. Mik'ayēl Č'amč'ian and his History of Armenia), *Pazmaveb* 139 (1981), no. 3–4.

K. H. Maksoudian

EŁIŠĒ (Armenia, c. A.D. fifth to sixth century?), Armenian historian who implied that he was an eyewitness to the events that transpired in Armenia during the period from about A.D. 440 to 458. Later tradition elaborated on this and presented Ełišē as secretary to Vardan Mamikonean, the commander-in-chief of the Armenian armies and the leader of the great insurrection against the Sasanian state. Although certain modern scholars still accept Ełišē as a contemporary of the events that he described, the majority of Western scholars reject the medieval tradition and the implication of the author and place him toward the middle or the end of the sixth century. Among the exegetical and homiletical works attributed to him, *Vasn Vardanay ew Hayoc' paterazmin* (History of Vardan and the Armenian War) is the only historical work. It opens with a letter that is addressed to a priest, David Mamikon, presumably a member of the Mamikonean clan that Ełišē favored. Modern scholars have shown the dependence of Ełišē on Łazar P'arpec'i's (q.v.) History for factual material. Ełišē, however, has used the historical facts to provide his patron and readers with an opportunity to examine "the heavenly providence which in its foreknowledge dispenses the compensations" of the valorous and the cowards and "by visible means presages the invisible." This philosophical approach prevails throughout the work.

Bibliography: Nerses Akinian, *Elisaus Vardapet und seine Geschichte des armenischen Krieges*, vols. 1–3 (Vienna, 1932–1960); Ełišē, *History of Vardan and the Armenian War*, trans. and commentary by Robert W. Thomson (Cambridge, Mass., and London, 1982).

K. H. Maksoudian

KHORENATSI, Movses (Moses of Khoren) (A.D. fifth century). Khorenatsi belonged to the younger generation of pupils of Mesrop Maštoc' and Sahak Partev, who created the Armenian written language. He, together with other of Mesrop's pupils, worked in the Edessa archives around the year A.D. 435 and studied in Palestine and Alexandria (Egypt). Alexandria then was a center of the rising Christian Ecumenical Church while remaining the hub of Hellenistic culture. As one of the founding fathers of the school for Hellenophiles in Armenia, he was granted the rank of *kerdolahayr*, head of grammarians and poets. Among works ascribed to him are *Epistle to Sahak Artsruni, Ripsimyan* (History of Holy Virgins from Ripsime), *On the Transfiguration*, and *The Book of Rhetoric, Geography* collected in *Works by Moses of Khoren* (Venice, 1843). His basic work, however, was *History of Armenia* for the writing of which he used monuments of the pre-Christian Hellenic epoch of Armenia in the Greek and Aramaic languages that have not reached us; classical Byzantine and Syrian sources; works by his elder contemporaries Koryun, Faustus of Byzantium, and Agathangelos; and biblical traditions and Armenian folklore. It was a grandiose enterprise for his time to span the history of the Armenian people from their legendary forefathers to A.D. 428 (the year when the monarchy in eastern Armenia was abolished). The book was later supplemented with chapters on the death of Mesrop Maštoc' and Sahak Partev and *Lament on Discontinuation of the Armenian Kings from the House of Arshakuni and the Patriarchate from the House of St. George*. Later interpolations found in the manuscript of the book led historians erroneously to relate the book and its author to the sixth, seventh, eighth, and even ninth centuries. The *History* was prompted by the complicated political situation in Armenia in the fifth century and by the need for a patriotic-minded work depicting love of country and calling for its liberation against the backdrop of anti-Iranian uprisings in the years A.D. 450–451 and 482–484. The book is permeated with the idea of Armenian unity. It was the first attempt ever to present a systematized history of the Armenians and a most important historical source providing valuable information on Armenia and contiguous countries. It is likewise a work of art. *History of Armenia* in many respects has no equal in

Armenian historiography: generation after generation were brought up on it, and its author was awarded the honorary title of Father of Armenian Historiography.

Bibliography: M. Abegyan, *Istoriya drevnearmyanskoi literature* (History of the Early Armenian Literature) (Yerevan, 1975), pp. 135–162; Moses Khorenatsi, *History of the Armenians*, ed. R. W. Thomson (London, 1978); G. Kh. Sarkisyan, *Chronological System of Moses Khorenatsi's "History of Armenia"* (Yerevan, 1965), in Armenian.

V. A. Arutyunova-Fidanyan

KORIWN (Armenia, c. A.D. 390–? c. A.D. 448), Armenian historian. Koriwn was a pupil and associate of Maštoc', the inventor of the Armenian alphabet. There is almost no information about his life, and what there is derives from his biography of Maštoc'. About A.D. 430 he and another associate, the presbyter Łewond, went to Constantinople where they joined two others, Eznik of Kołb and Yovsēp', and turned their energies to literary pursuits, gathering and translating the works of the early fathers. Soon after the Council of Ephesus in A.D. 431 he and his associates returned to Armenia with the Nicaean canons, an authoritative copy of the Scriptures, and several patristic works. It is assumed that Koriwn spent the period until the death of Maštoc' in A.D. 440 in close association and collaboration with the latter. The last recorded event in the *Life of Maštoc'* refers to the construction of a martyrium on the tomb of Maštoc' which was completed in A.D. 443. Koriwn wrote the *Life* soon after that date. He probably died shortly before the rebellion of the Armenians against the Sasanian state in A.D. 451, since his name is not mentioned among the other members of his circle who played a very active role during those events. Koriwn's only known work is *Vark' Maštoc'i* (Life of Maštoc') written between A.D. 443 and 448. Modern scholars attribute to him the translations of certain books of the Armenian version of the Bible and two other works, the *Histories* of Agathangelos (q.v.) and P'awstos Buzand (q.v.). Their arguments, however, are not very convincing. The *Life* is a hagiographical work. The author is deeply influenced by the Scriptures, the lives of the early Christian saints, and Eusebius of Caesarea's (q.v.) historical works. His approach to Christian biography is that of an apologist, since his is the first attempt in Armenian reality to provide convincing arguments to justify the sanctification of a man who died a natural death.

Bibliography: Nerses Akinian, *Der hl. Maschtotz Wardapet*, mit einer deutschen Zusammenfassung (Vienna, 1949); Koriwn, *Vark' Maštoc'i* (Life of Maštoč') critical edition, English translation, concordance and with a new introduction by Krikor H. Maksoudian (Delmar, N.Y., 1985); Joseph Marquart, *Über das armenische Alphabet in Verbindung mit der Biographie des hl. Maštoc'* (Vienna, 1917).

K. H. Maksoudian

LASTIVERTSI, Aristakes (Lastivert, near Artsn, c. 1022–? pre–1087), Armenian historian. There are no data on Lastivertsi's biography. It is known that he was a priest *(vardapet)* who lived in Artsn. He wrote *Narration of Vardapet Aristakes Lastivertsi about the Misfortunes Brought upon Us by the Neighbouring Barbarians* and other works on Church dogmata. His *Narration* encompassing the years from 1000 to 1071 was written in the 1070s. It is one of the chief sources on the eleventh century history of Armenia and its neighbors. The book deals with three main problems: Armenian-Byzantine relations, the Seljuk conquest, and activization of the Tondrak heresy. His account of Byzantine history shows that he was well versed in the empire's political life, court intrigues, and local terminology. In describing the Seljuks' invasion, he charted the routes along which they entered his country, their military organization, and their lifestyle and customs. These chapters on the invasion are an invaluable source for studying the history of the Seljuks. Two chapters examine the Tondrak movement, the heresy of which was closely related to that of the Paulicians. His account of the Tondrakians referred to the turn of the eleventh century and disrupts the chronology of his *Narration*. The Byzantine government, jointly with the Armenian feudal lords, crushed the Tondrakian communities. His philosophical digressions show that he was concerned with the destiny of all Armenian people. In this sense he can be regarded as a historian of the entire nation. The earliest historical writings posed the idea of Armenian unity, which, to a large extent, was conditioned by the struggle against foreign invasion. His *Narration* ranks high among other historical works of medieval Armenia because he furthered the idea of unity. This book can be regarded as a work of great historical, moral, and artistic merit.

Bibliography: *Narration of Aristakes Lastivertci* (Yerevan, 1963), in Armenian; Aristakes Lastivertsi's work is discussed in prefaces to the following editions: *Histoire d'Arménie, comprenant la fin du royaume d'Ani et le commencement de l'invasion des seldjoukides par Arisdaques de Lastiverd'*, trans. Evarite Prud'homme (Paris, 1964); G. Manukjan, *Narration of Aristakes Lastivertci* (Yerevan, 1977), in Armenian; *Povestovovaniye Aristakesa Lastivertsi* (Narration of the Vardapet Aristakes Lastivertci), trans. and commentary by K. N. Yuzbashyan (Moscow, 1968).

V. A. Arutyunova-Fidanyan

ŁAZAR P'ARPEC'I (P'arpi, c. A.D. 440–? c. A.D. 500), Armenian historian. Łazar was a pupil of Ałan Arcruni; a disciple of Mesrop Maštoc', the inventor of the Armenian alphabet; and the maternal uncle of Vahan Mamikonean, who became the governor of Sasanian Armenia in A.D. 485. Łazar grew up in the court of the prince of Gugark' with Vahan and the cadets of the Mamikonean and Kamsarakan feudal families. Subsequently, following the example of his teacher, he became a priest and a solitary. Probably after the rise of Vahan to power in A.D. 484 or 485, Łazar became the prior of the monastery of the cathedral of Vałaršapat (now Ējmiacin). Controversies of unknown nature within the congregation forced Łazar to flee his abode and take refuge in Amida. It is assumed that the controversies had something to do with the division in fifth-century A.D. Armenia between pro-Greek and pro-Syrian clergy, Łazar himself being a supporter of Greek culture, since he was educated at an unspecified school somewhere "in the land of the Greeks." There are two important works attributed to Łazar, the *Patmut'iwn Hayoc'* (History of Armenia) and the *T'ułt'* *ař Vahan Mamikonean* (Letter to Vahan Mamikonean), both written either at the end of the fifth or the beginning of the sixth century. The *History* is Łazar's major work. It covers the history of Armenia from A.D. 387, when the kingdom was partitioned between the Byzantine and the Sasanian empires, to A.D. 485, the date of Vahan Mamikonean's appointment as *marzpan*, or governor, of Sasanian Armenia. He wrote the *History* at the request of Vahan Mamikonean and was definitely biased in favor of Vahan and the Mamikonean clan. If one sets aside the interpolations in the first section of the *History*, the book is either based on the accounts of eyewitnesses or is the direct testimony of Łazar himself, who was an eyewitness to some of the events he described. The general structure and composition of the *History* are heavily influenced by hagiography.

Bibliography: C.J.F. Dowsett, "The Newly Discovered Fragment of Lazar of P'arp's History," *Le Muséon*, 89 (1976): 97–122; Lazare de Pharbe, *Histoire d'Arménie*, trans. and ed. P. S. Ghésarian, intro. by V. Langlois, in *Collection des historiens de l'Arménie* vol. 2 (Paris, 1869); M. Minassian, "Remarques inédites de Meillet sur les textes des historiens arméniens Lazare de P'arpi et Elisée," *Revue des études arméniennes*, 4 (1967); F. Müller, "Lazer Parpetsi und Koriun," *Wiener Zeitschrift für die Kunde des Morgenlandes* 36–38 (1891); C. Sanspeur, "Trois sources byzantines de *L'histoire des Arméniens* de Lazare de P'arpi," *Byzantion* 44 (1974).

K. H. Maksoudian

ŁEWOND (Armenia, A.D. eighth to ninth century), Armenian historian. Although we have absolutely no information about Łewond, the title of his only work, *Patmut'iwn Łewandeay Meci Vardapeti Hayoc'* (History of Łewond the Eminent Vardapet of the Armenians), suggests that he was a priest. From the colophon of this work we learn that Łewond composed it at the order of Prince Šapuh Bagratuni, who is identified with a late eighth-century A.D. personality of the same name. The author was definitely biased in favor of the Bagratid feudal family. The *History* covers the events that transpired in Armenia during the years A.D. 632–788, the period of Arab domination. Chapters 13 and 14 in the present text, comprising one-fifth of the entire work, contain the correspondence between the Byzantine emperor Leo III and the caliph ᶜUmar II. Since the style of this section is different from that of the *History*, certain scholars believe that the correspondence was interpolated into the text by a medieval editor. Łewond's *History* consists of a factual account of the events; the author occasionally claimed that he derived his information from eyewitnesses. One may challenge this claim by citing the fact that none of the Armenian historians living in the ninth and tenth centuries knew Łewond's work or used it for information on the Arab period. He is first mentioned by a historian living at the end of the tenth century. Łewond's purpose of writing the *History* was mainly to register the disasters that befell the Armenians as a result of the coming of the Arabs. Like the seventh-century Armenian historian Sebeos, he thought that the Arabs came as a punishment from God and that the Christian princes as well as nations deserved to be struck by the Divine wrath because of their manifold sins.

Bibliography: *History of Łewond the Eminent Vardapet of the Armenians*, trans. intro.

and commentary by Zaven Arzoumanian (Philadelphia, 1982); Arthur Jeffrey, "Ghewond's Text of the Correspondence between ᶜUmar II and Leo III," *Harvard Theological Review* 37 (1944); J. Laurent, *L'Arménie entre Byzance et l'Islam depuis la conquête arabe jusqu'en 886*, nouvelle édition revue et mise à jour par M. Canard (Lisbon, 1980); Aram Ter-Ghewondyan, *The Arab Emirates in Bagratid Armenia*, trans. Nina G. Garsoïan (Lisbon, 1976).

K. H. Maksoudian

MOVSĒS DASXURANC'I (Caucasian Albania?–eleventh century?), Armenian historian. Although we have no firm information about Movsēs' identity, according to the *Albanian Chronicle* of Mxit'ar Goš, which was compiled at the end of the twelfth century, Movsēs was the author of a *History of the Caucasian Albanians*. The thirteenth-century historian Kirakos Ganjakec'i, who was a pupil of Mxit'ar Goš, identified the author of the same work as Movsēs Kałankatuac'i. The consensus among the modern scholars is that Kirakos was misled by a reference in the *History of the Caucasion Albanians* to the village of Kałankatuk in the province of Uti to which the author referred as the place "where I too am from" (ii). The author was probably referring not to Kałankatuk but to the province of Uti. An otherwise unknown historian named Movsēs, either from Dasxuran or Kałankatuk, is cited as the author of an extant historical work bearing the title *Patmut'iwn Ałuanic' ašxarhi* (History of the Land of [Caucasian] *Albania)*. Modern scholars have shown that this *History* is a medieval compilation, parts of which were in circulation earlier than the tenth century, and that Movsēs Dasxuranc'i is the last editor and not the author. The *History* consists of three books and is written in classical Armenian. There is no evidence that the work is a translation from Albanian. Although the title of the book suggests that it is the history of the Caucasian Albanians, it is actually about the eastern provinces of Armenia—Utik' and Arc'ax and the Armeno-Albanian marchlands—and the Armenian elements living in these areas. The first book of the *History* covers the period from the creation to the end of the fifth century A.D. In the second book the concentration is mostly on the events of the sixth and seventh centuries A.D. The third book covers the history of the period of Arab domination from the mid-seventh to the ninth century and the events until the 1180s. This *History* is a compilation of historical documents, legendary material, hagiographical writings, and even poetry. Some of these works are of great historical value.

Bibliography: *The History of the Caucasian Albanians by Movsēs Dasxuranc'i*, trans. C.J.F. Dowsett (London, 1961); Hakob Manandian, *Beiträge zur albanischen Geschichte, Untersuchungen über Moses der Utier (Kalankatuaci)* (Leipzig, 1897); A. Sh. Mnatsakanian, *O Literature Kavkazskoi Albanii* (Yerevan, 1969); K. V. Trever, *Ocherki po istorii i kult'ure kavkazskoi Albanii* (Leningrad, 1959).

K. H. Maksoudian

MOVSĒS XORENAC'I (Armenia, A.D. fifth to eighth century), Armenian historian. Movsēs claimed to be a pupil of the fifth-century A.D. Armenian monk Mesrop Maštoc', the inventor of the Armenian alphabet. *Xorenac'i*, the second part of the name, indicates a person's place of origin, suggesting that Movsēs was presumably from the village of Xoronk' in Taron (now Mush in eastern Anatolia). According to his own testimony, Movsēs was first educated in Armenia and then sent to Alexandria where he spent a few years studying at the Neo-Platonic school. On his way back, adverse winds took his ship to Italy and Greece where he spent some time. After his return to Armenia, presumably after A.D. 440, he discovered that his teachers were dead and Armenia as well as the Armenian Church were in a pathetic state. According to the medieval tradition, Movsēs devoted his life to teaching and writing. His tomb was located in the courtyard of the Aṙak'eloc' Monastery in Taron. Among the numerous works attributed to Movsēs, the most renowned is *Patmut'iwn Hayoc'* (History of the Armenians). The time of composition of this work, as well as the veracity of Movsēs' statements about himself, have been seriously challenged by certain nineteenth-century Armenian and contemporary Western scholars. There is, however, no agreement among them about the time; some place Movsēs in the sixth century A.D., whereas others put him in the seventh, eighth, or even the ninth century. The *History* consists of three books, the first of which is a genealogy of the royal dynasties and feudal families of Armenia. The second book covers the history of the Pagan Arsacid kings of Armenia, and the third is about the Christian Arsacids until their fall in A.D. 428. Movsēs continued his narrative until the death of Maštoc' in A.D. 440. The *History* ends with a "lament" about the situation in Armenia. The work was commissioned by Smbat Bagratuni, who is generally identified with the *marzpan* (governor) of Armenia (A.D. 481–482). The *History* as it has reached us is the work of an author who was biased in favor of the Armenian Bagratid clan that acquired full political power in Armenia in the eighth century and was ultimately established as a royal dynasty in A.D. 884. Even if one were to accept that the *History* was written at an earlier date, one cannot deny that it was extensively edited or reworked during the Bagratid period in order to serve as an official history of the Armenians. Movsēs Xorenac'i was recognized as the "Father of [Armenian] history" because of the political importance of the *History of the Armenians*. The purpose of the *History* was to present a glorified picture of political life in Armenia under the rule of early Armenian dynasties. The intention was to arouse in the heart of the contemporary reader a national feeling for the revival of the kingdom of Armenia and the maintenance of the feudal social order in the country. Movsēs used history and a beautiful elevated style to achieve this end. From his point of view, history is a record of "manly deeds" worthy of being committed to writing.

Bibliography: August Carriére, *Nouvelles sources de Moise de Khoren* (Vienna, 1893); Grigor Khalatiants, *Armianskie Arshakidy v "Istorii Armenii" Moiseia Khorenskago*, 2 pts. (Moscow, 1903); Moses Khorenats'i, *History of the Armenians*, trans. and commentary on the literary sources by Robert W. Thomson (Cambridge, Mass., and London, 1978); H. Lewy "The Date and Purpose of Moses of Chorene's History," *Byzantion* 11 (1936): 81–96.

K. H. Maksoudian

P'AWSTOS BUZAND (Armenia, A.D. fifth century), Armenian historian. Although we have no detailed information, since the early sixth century A.D. it has been assumed that *Buzand*, the second part of the name of the historian, actually stands for *Biwzandac'i* ("from Byzantium") and that the person known as P'awstos ("Faustus") was of Greek origin and originally wrote in Greek. This view has been seriously challenged, since the only work by this author, known as *Buzandaran patmut'iwnk'* (Epic Histories) does not appear to be a translation but an original work composed in the A.D. 460s or 470s. The name of the author is probably fictional, P'awstos being an actual personality mentioned in the work and Buzand being an abbreviated form of "Buzandaran." The *Buzandaran patmut'iwnk'* roughly covers the period of Armenian history from A.D. 330 to 387, the date of the partition of Armenia between the Byzantines and the Persians. The work is not a history or a chronology but a medley of saga, epic tales, legends, memoirs of actual historical events and lives of saints, and even an extensive excerpt from a liturgical text. These items are arranged according to the reigns of the Armenian Arsacid kings, even though there is absolutely no trace of chronology in the book. This medley was probably intended for a lay audience of an aristocratic origin since it contains bawdy expressions and anecdotes and has the characteristic features of Märchen. Because of this, the majority of the medieval historians avoided using the *Buzandaran patmut'iwnk'* as a source for the events of the fourth century. Yet the *Buzandaran* contains some information that is substantiated by the testimony of non-Armenian sources. The purpose of the author seems to be directed toward emphasizing the role of the chief bishops of Armenia (who were later called catholicoi) and that of the Mamikonean feudal family (hereditary commanders-in-chief of the Armenian armies) when the Armenian Church, the Mamikoneans, and the major feudal families were oppressed by the Sasanian court.

Bibliography: F. Feydit, "L'histoire de Fauste de Byzance comprenait-elle deux livres aujourd'hui perdus?" *Pazmaveb* 124 (1966); Joseph Markwart, "Zur Kritik des Faustos von Byzanz," *Philologus* 60 (1886): 212–224; *Ps. P'awstos, Buzandaran patmut'iwnk'*, a facsimile reproduction of the 1883 St. Petersburg edition with an introduction by Nina G. Garsoïan (Delmar, N.Y.), 1984; E. Stien, "Fauste de Buzanta a-t-il écrit en Grec?" *Histoire de Bas Empire*. Vol. 2: Excursus U., ed. J. R. Palanque (Paris, 1949).

K. H. Maksoudian

SEBĒOS (Armenia c. A.D. 600–? c. A.D. 665), Armenian historian who is usually identified with Sebēos, bishop of the Bagratuni clan, a participant as well as a signatory of the council of Dvin in A.D. 645. Certain modern scholars assume that Sebēos was the Monophysite bishop who refused to take communion with the Byzantine emperor Constans II in the Cathedral of Dvin in A.D. 652. According to the medieval sources, Sebēos is the author of a historical work, *Patmut'iwn i Herakln* (History of Heraclius). A work bearing that title was first published in the nineteenth century, and despite questions raised by a few scholars about its authenticity, the majority of modern Armenian specialists consider it to be the *History* of Sebēos. It consists of two sections; the longer second section covers the period from A.D. 500 to 662. The first section has two parts; the first is a primary history of Armenia, probably put in its present state in the eleventh century but based on very ancient sources. This is followed by a second part that is drawn from the histories of Movsēs Xorenac'i (q.v.) and Step'anos Asołik (q.v.). The majority of modern scholars consider Sebēos the author of only the second section, which is a chronologically arranged narrative of the political events that transpired in and around Armenia in the seventh century A.D, namely, the wars between the Sasanians and the Byzantines, the fall of the Sasanian kingdom, and the Arab raids into Armenia. The author was for the most part an eyewitnesses to the events that he described or drew his information from the testimony of others who were eyewitnesses. His philosophy of history was that of a pious Christian who wanted to show that the princes of this world rise against and destroy one another "by the order of God who is angry at the entire world" and that everything is perishable except for the words of God, which are eternal.

Bibliography: G. Abgarian, "Remarques sur l'Historie de Sébéos," *Revue des études arméniennes*, n.s., I (1964); N. A. Adontz, "Nachal'naia istorii Armenii' v Sebeosa v' eia otnosheniiakh' k' trudam' Moiseia Khorenskago i Fausta Vizantiiskago" (Primary History of Armenia in Sebeos in Connection with the Works of Moses of Khoren and Faustus of Byzantium), *Vitzantiiskii Vremmenik* 8 (1901); Sébéos, *Histoire d'Héraclius*, trans. from Armenian and annotated by F. Macler (Paris,1904).

STEP'ANOS ASOŁIK (Taron, 935?–? 1015?), Armenian historian. Although we have little information about Step'anos Asołik, the second part of his name, Asołik, is thought to be an epithet given to him for his talent in music. Tradition as well as his own testimony indicate that he was a *vardapet*, or doctor (of theology). Asołik seems to have been well acquainted with the monasteries and monastic life in the tenth century. He was appointed by Catholicos Sargis of Armenia to some kind of a position of supervision that involved him in touring the monasteries. Asołik died at a very old age, according to the testimony of an eleventh-century source. His only known work is the *Patmut'iwn tiezerakan* (Universal History), which begins with the creation and ends with the year A.D. 904. He composed the *History* at the request of Catholicos Sargis (992–1029). The work is divided into three books or sections. The first is ancient history until the time of Tiridates III (A.D. 298–330), the first Christian king of Armenia; it contains lists of dynasties, both Armenian and non-Armenian. The historical information on Armenia is based mostly on the *History* of Movsēs Xorenac'i (q.v.). The second book is the history of Christian Armenia from the time of Tiridates to that of the first Bagratid king Ašot I, who was crowned in A.D. 884. The third book is about the reign of the Bagratid dynasty. The information in the second and third sections, to the year A.D. 925, is derived from earlier sources. For the period from 925 to 1004 Asołik is an original and an indispensable source for the history of Armenia, the Caucasus and Byzantium. The derived as well as the original sections of the *History* form a single unit. Asołik's outlook on the past and present reflects the views of the late tenth-century hierarchs of the Armenian Church. The role of the Christian historian is compared by him with that of Moses and the prophets of Israel. Asołik underscored the point that the historian wrote about the events of the past as a "showing" or a "demonstration" or perhaps even a "testimony" for posterity. Since the goal of a Christian is to reach God through Christ, it is important that a person have a knowledge of the past—of historical events and figures, both good and bad—to see how God bestows honor on the good and punishes the bad, and, consequently, to make the right choice in life. Asołik is the first Armenian historian who made a systematic use of chronology and arranged the facts in a strictly chronological order.

Bibliography: M. Dedurand, "Citations patristiques chez Étienne de Taron," in *Armeniaca* (Venice, 1969); *Histoire Universelle, par Étienne Açoghig de Daron*, pt. 1, trans. and annotated by Éd. Dulaurier (Paris, 1883); pt. 2, trans. and annotated by F. Macler (Paris, 1917).

K. H. Maksoudian

T'OVMA ARCRUNI (Vaspurakan, A.D. second half of eighth and first quarter of ninth centuries), Armenian historian. Although there is little available biographical information, T'ovma Arcruni was commissioned by Prince Grigor Derenik of Vaspurakan, who died in A.D. 888, to write the history of the Arcruni feudal clan. T'ovma undertook the task, which he continued during the reign of Gagik Arcruni, Grigor's son, who ruled first as prince from A.D. 904 to 908 and then as king until about 946. The medieval sources refer to him as a *vardapet*, or doctor (of theology), meaning that he was a priest and a teacher. The only work attributed to T'ovma is the *Patmut'iwn tann Arcruneac'* (History of the Arcruni House), of which the exact date of composition is difficult to establish, since the work as it has reached us is incomplete, with a section missing at the end. The last event in the work can be dated to about A.D. 905. There are four other shorter texts attached to T'ovma's work that belong to other authors. The first book of T'ovma's *History* begins with the creation of the world and ends with the death of Mesrop Maštoc', the inventor of the Armenian alphabet, in A.D. 440. This section is an epitome of Movsēs Xorenac'i's (q.v.) *History*. The second book covers the period from the fifth to the middle of the ninth century A.D., and the third book covers the events of the contemporary period from the middle of the ninth century. Unlike the earlier Armenian historians, T'ovma is a family historian who was officially commissioned to write the history of a single dynasty. His purpose was to glorify the ancestors of the Arcruni princes and praise the achievements of his patrons. Like the other medieval Armenian historians, T'ovma thought that political adversities take place as a result of sin and the wrath of God.

Bibliography: T'ovma Artsruni, *History of the Artsruni House*,, trans. and commentary by R. W. Thomsom (Cambridge, Mass., 1986); V. Vardanyan, *Vaspurakani Arcrunyac' t'agavorutyuna, 908–1021* (The Kingdom of the Arcruni of Vaspurakan, 908–1021) (Yerevan, 1969).

K. H. Maksoudian

VARDAN AREWELC'I (Ganjak, c. 1200–Xor Virap, 1271), Armenian historian. Vardan was a pupil of Vanakan Vardapet and was educated in eastern Armenia. In 1240 he went to Jerusalem on a pilgrimage and on his way back visited Cilicia where he remained from 1241 to 1246 at the invitation of King Het'um I and Catholicos Constantine. In 1243 the catholicos officially designated him to take the canons of the Council of Sis, which had met in the same year, and bring them to Greater Armenia so that the prelates and the priors of the major monasteries would give their consent and sign the document. Vardan carried out this undertaking with success. In 1264 he went to Tabriz to meet the Mongol Il-khan Hulagu from whom he acquired an edict that alleviated the condition of the Armenians in Armenia living under Mongol rule. Vardan was a renowned teacher who founded several schools. In the prime of his life, from 1235 to 1239 and from 1251 to 1255, Vardan founded and taught at the Monastery of S. Andrē in Kayēnaberd. He also taught at Hałbat, one of the most renowned monasteries in Armenia, and at Ałǰoy Vank'. The greater part of his life as a teacher, however, was spent at Xor Virap, where he founded a school and taught several pupils, many of whom became well known as scholars. Vardan was a prolific author and a polymath with interests in law, biblical exegesis, grammar and rhetoric, geography, and other fields. He has one historical work, the *Hawak'umn patmut'ean* (Compilation of History), which is a compendium covering the events from the time of the creation of the world to 1267 when Catholicos Constantine passed away. In the earlier chapters of the *History* Vardan gave numerous lists of dynasties, including those of Armenian kings, and in a sense it is a "universal history." From A.D. 298 he dealt exclusively with the history of Christian Armenia, still drawing his information from earlier sources. Some of his information is very valuable, since we do not always know who his source was. For the events of the thirteenth century, Vardan himself was the original source. The events are arranged in a chronological order and are narrated under each year. It is difficult to state what Vardan's philosophy of history was since he did not have any discussions of that nature; the facts are given in a straightforward manner, with no interpretation. It seems that the *History* is a general compilation put together either for personal use or for educational purposes.

Bibliography: M. Brosset, *Deux historiens arméniens*, vol. 1 (St. Petersburg, 1870); M. Canard, "À propos de la traduction d'un passage de l'Histoire Universelle de Vardan sur les luttes entre Mongols d'Iran et Mongols de la Horde d'Or," *Revue des études arméniennes*, n.s., 5 (1968); J. Muyldermans, *La domination arabe en Arménie, extrait de l'Histoire Universelle de Vardan, traduit de l'arménien et annoté, étude de critique textuelle et littéraire* (Louvain and Paris, 1927).

K. H. Maksoudian

YOVHANNĒS DRASXANAKERTC'I (Drasxanakert, Armenia, c. A.D. 850–Vaspuraken, A.D. 925). Yovhannēs received his education with his relative Maštoc' Vardapet probably in the monastery of Sewan. He became a priest and was later elevated to the rank of bishop. As the resident bishop in the patriarchate of Dvin, in A.D. 894 he was delegated with the task of raising funds to liberate Catholicos George who had been incarcerated by Afshīn, the emir of Azerbaijan. In A.D. 898 Yovhannes succeeded his teacher Maštoc' as catholicos of Armenia, a position he held until his death in 925. Yovhannes's pontificate coincided with the reign of the Bagratid Kings Smbat I (A.D. 890–914) and Ašot II Erkat' (A.D. 915–929). It was a most difficult period. The Bagratids were still trying to set on a firm foundation their newly founded kingdom, which was threatened by the Byzantines, by the Sādjids of Azerbaijan, and by internal strife. Yovhannēs played a very active political role. He himself was incarcerated by the Sādjid emir Yūsuf in A.D. 908 and was forced to spend a few years away from his see. In A.D. 914 he opened negotiations with the Byzantine emperor to have Ašot II recognized as the head of the Armenian state. He spent his energies to strengthen the position of a political and ecclesiastical central authority in a country torn asunder among feudal clans. Under the constant stress of Sādjid harassment, he was forced to abandon the patriarchal residence in Dvin and even his own fortress at Biwrakan, taking flight and ultimately seeking asylum with king Gagik of Vaspurakan in A.D. 924. Yovhannēs is the author of a historical work, *Patmut'iwn Hayoc'* (History of Armenia), which begins with the deluge and ends with his own escape to Vaspurakan in 924. The earlier section is based on the *History* of Movsēs Xorenac'i (q.v.) and other early sources. In the second section, which covers the period from the beginning of the ninth century A.D. to 924 and is very detailed, Yovhannēs is an original source of exceptional value, since as catholicos of Armenia he had access to the patriarchal archives and had firsthand knowledge about contemporary issues. The *History* was written over a long period; this is evident from the present text. Parts of it were probably written as memoirs, but the final edition was not compiled until Yovhannēs went to Vaspurakan. According to the epilogue of the *History*, Yovhannēs considered putting together his opus at the request of the kings who ruled in Armenia in A.D. 924, namely, Ašot II Erkat', Ašot son of Šapuh who ruled in Dvin and Bagaran, and Gagik of Vaspurakan. The purpose of the work was to provide the readers—who were the kings, princes, bishops, and leaders of the period—with a "mirror" so that they would end their centrifugal policies and face the common enemy with a united front.

Bibliography: N. Adontz, *Études Arméno-Byzantines* (Lisbon, 1955); *Histoire d'Arménie, par le Patriarche Jean VI, dit Jean Catholicos*, trans. M. Saint-Martin (Paris, 1841); *Hovhannēs Draskhanakertets'i, Patmut'iwn Hayots'*, a facsimile reproduction of the 1912 Tiflis edition with intro. by Krikor Maksoudian (Delmar, N.Y., 1980); Aram N. Ter-Gewondian, *Armeniia i Arabskii Khalifat* (Yerevan, 1977).

K. H. Maksoudian

Great Historians: Austrian

SCHMIDT, Michael Ignaz (Arnstein/Würzburg, 1736–Wien, 1794), German-Austrian historian. Schmidt's place in the history of historiography is based on his *Geschichte der Teutschen*, the first two volumes of which were published in 1778 but which remained unfinished, ending with the death of Ferdinand III. Schmidt was educated by the Jesuits but did not join the order and became a secular priest. His first scholarly works as well as the beginning of his academic career fell into the field of theology, but when Schmidt was made head of the library at the University of Würzburg in 1771, he was at the same time appointed professor at the theological faculty of the same university. In 1780 Schmidt was appointed director of the Haus und Staatsarchiv in Vienna and became history teacher of the future Emperor Franz II; Schmidt's *Geschichte der Teutschen* shows influence by the ideas of Johann Herder (q.v.) and Justus Möser (q.v.), but the emphasis given to world history and to cultural details can be traced to the impact of the Enlightenment and of Voltaire's (q.v.) historical writing. Schmidt wanted to present "Germany by describing her customs, laws, arts and sciences and especially her excellent constitution of state and church." A great admirer of enlightened absolutism as represented by Joseph II, Schmidt was close to Jansenism and was an outspoken critic of papal power policy in the Middle Ages, which made him an apologist for the political aims of the emperors in the late Middle Ages. In dealing with the modern centuries, Schmidt, who had based his account on sources in the Viennese archive, took the side of the Habsburg emperors in their rivalry with the princes of German territories.

Bibliography: A. Berney, "Michael Ignaz Schmidt," *Historisches Jahrbuch* 44 (1924); H.v. Srbik, *Geist und Geschichte vom deutschen Humanismus bis zur Gegenwart*, vol.1 (Munich, 1950).

Fritz Fellner

Great Historians: Baltic Region

HENRY OF LIVONIA (Henricus de Lettis) (Saxony, c. 1178–Papendorf, Livonia, c. 1259), Roman Catholic priest and missionary in Livonia. The evidence contained in Henry's *Chronicon Livoniae* indicates that he was born and educated in northern Germany, arrived in Livonia around 1205, and took holy orders in 1208. He spent the remainder of his life principally as a parish priest in the village of Papendorf, which was located on the northern edge of the language frontier in Livonia that separated the Latvians from the neighboring Livs and Estonians. He participated as a translator and missionary in a number of the major military campaigns that brought Livonia into the Roman Catholic Church during the first three decades of the thirteenth century; in 1225–1227 Henry accompanied William of Modena on trips that this papal legate made throughout Livonia. Henry apparently decided to record the events that had led to the establishment of the Livonian Church in connection with William's visit, for the *Chronicon* was written during and shortly after the papal legate's stay in Livonia.

Written in Latin, Henry's work is the oldest and most valuable of the medieval Livonian chronicles. Based mainly on his own personal experience in Livonia, the *Chronicon* offers a detailed account of the military campaigns and missionary expeditions in which Henry participated. He clearly identified himself with the Germans who imposed their rule and the Roman Catholic Church on the indigenous Estonian and Latvian population, but he was a parish priest and missionary and knew very little about the ambitions and high politics of the bishops of Riga and Sword-Brothers (*Fratres Militiae Christi de Livonia*). He was well disposed to Baltic converts to Christianity, and he recorded approvingly the admonition of papal legate William of Modena to the Livonian Germans that they should impose no "harsh and unbearable burden upon the shoulders of the converts, but rather the sweet and light yoke of the Lord" (Bk. 29, 3). Henry obviously did not consider it his task to preserve knowledge about the heathen past of the Baltic peoples, whose alleged vices and criminal and unnatural acts are described in the *Chronicon* with images taken from the Vulgate Bible and the liturgical and missionary literature of his time. Yet Henry was a good and trustworthy observer and well informed about the peoples of Livonia; his chronicle is by far the most important written source for the early history of the Estonians and Latvians.

Bibliography: *The Chronicle of Henry of Livonia*, trans. and ed. J. A. Brundage (Madison, Wisc., 1961); *Geschichte der deutschbaltischen Geschichtsschreibung*, ed. G. v. Rauch (Cologne, 1986); *Heinrichs Livländische Chronik*, Scriptores rerum Germanicarum in usum scholarum, Bd. 31, ed. L. Arbusow and A. Bauer (Hanover, 1955); P. Johansen, "Die Chronik als Biographie: Heinrich von Lettlands Lebensgang und Weltanschauung," *Jahrbücher für Geschichte Osteuropas*, N.F. 1 (1953): 1–24; *Livländische Chronik*, trans. and ed. A. Bauer (Wurzburg, 1959).

Edward C. Thaden

RUSSOW, Balthasar (Reval, now Tallinn, c. 1535–Reval, 1600). The son of an Estonian teamster, Russow studied in Germany and then was the pastor of the Estonian-speaking Lutheran congregation in his native city. He was a respected figure in Reval and wrote the *Chronica der Provintz Lyfflandt* at the urging of prominent local citizens who thought that the notable events that had taken place during the Livonian War deserved to be recorded. Russow outlined in his work the history of Livonia since the time that German merchants and missionaries first appeared in the valley of the Western Dvina River in the second part of the twelfth century but paid particular attention to the war between the Livonians and Ivan Groznyi in the latter part of the sixteenth century. Russow wrote the *Chronica* in Middle Low German and divided it into four parts. He based the first two parts on a compilation of earlier chronicles and oral tradition In writing about pre–1561 Livonia, he provided colorful and vivid detail about how the Livonian knights, Roman Catholic churchmen, German landowners, and Estonian peasants and townsmen lived and conducted themselves. He judged severely the leaders of old Livonian society for their sins and vices, oppression of the Livonian peasants, and failure to build schools and to look out for the religious and spiritual needs of the common people. But he also disapproved of the unchristian way of life of a large part of the peasantry and town population. For all of his Lutheran moralizing, Russow was a master of the Low German language and offered his readers graphic, Breughel-like tableaux depicting the life of all social classes in old Livonia. The *Chronica* was published in Germany in three editions between 1578 and 1584 and quickly became a sort of best-seller in Livonia and northern Germany. Russow based parts three and four of the *Chronica* on what he had personally observed, on the study of printed or manuscript materials available to him, and on interviews with contemporaries. He was especially well informed about events that took place in Estland, that is, in Reval and the districts of northern Estonia that placed themselves under Sweden in 1561. Being a Lutheran pastor, Russow thought well of Protestant Sweden, and in his chronicle he often referred favorably to the benefits resulting from Swedish naval, military, and commercial activities in Estland, Reval, and the Gulf of Finland. He was, however, above all a Reval patriot who portrayed movingly how the common efforts of townsmen of all classes, peasants from the surrounding countryside, and the small Swedish garrison worked together, demonstrated remarkable courage and resourcefulness, kept open vital lines of supply, and successfully defended Reval against overwhelming enemy forces during the two Russian sieges of 1570–1571 and 1577. Ivan Groznyi personally led armies against Reval, giving Russow an opportunity to observe the Russian tsar firsthand. Russow commented perceptively concerning the policy, motives, and objectives of Ivan in Livonia. The *Chronica* is important, then, not only for the history of Reval and Estland but also for the study of the reign of Muscovite Tsar Ivan IV.

Bibliography: *Geschichte der deutschbaltischen Geschichtsschreibung*, ed. G. v. Rauch (Cologne, 1986); B. Russow, *Chronica der Provintz Lyfflandt*, 3d ed. (Barth, 1584); E. Thaden, "Ivan IV in Baltic German Historiography," *Russian History* 12 (1985): 377–394; W. Urban, "The Nationality of Balthasar Russow," *Journal of Baltic Studies* 12 (1981): 160–172.

Edward C. Thaden

Great Historians: Belgian

BOLLAND, Jean (Julémont, province of Liège, 1596–Antwerp, 1665). Belgian hagiographer. In 1607 Héribert Rosweyde (1569–1629), a Jesuit living in Antwerp, announced in his *Fasti sanctorum* (Fasti of the Saints) the forthcoming publication, in eighteen volumes, of a collection of *Acta Sanctorum* (Acts of the Saints), but he died before the work was even begun. In 1630 Bolland, then master of studies at the College of Malines, was appointed ordinary confessor and director of the "Latin" congregation in Antwerp. Born on August 13, 1596, at Julémont, in the former duchy of Limbourg, he had entered the Jesuits on September 12, 1612. His superiors assigned him the task of carrying out the enterprise projected by Rosweyde. Bolland then made two changes to the original plan. First, he expanded the official Roman martyrology by adding the numerous saints venerated by various Christian communities. Second, when no *Life* was available for a particular saint, he compiled an entry using information based upon original sources. Moreover, each *Life* was accompanied by a complete philological commentary. In 1635 Bolland found a collaborator in Godefroid Henschens (1601–1681), who contributed to the definition of the project. The team was joined in 1660 by Daniel Papebroch (q.v.). The first two volumes containing the *Acta sanctorum* of January did not appear until 1643; the three volumes pertaining to February followed only in 1658. Between the two dates, Bolland also established the archives and library of the museum that was later to carry his name. But drawing up lists of all of the Christian saints and compiling a complete dossier for each of them meant not only corresponding with scholars throughout Europe but also traveling in search of new sources. It was with this intention that Bolland accepted the invitation extended by Pope Alexander VII (1599–1667) to inspect the valuable documents of the Vatican library. Too old and infirm to travel, Bolland dispatched instead his two collaborators, Henschens and Papebroch, but he nevertheless planned the details of their itinerary, which took them to Germany (Bolland himself accompanying them as far as Cologne), Italy, and France, from 1660 to 1662. He died on September 12, 1665. Even today, his work is carried on by a small group of Bollandists at the Jesuit College of Saint Michael in Brussels.

Bibliography: The basic source is Daniel Papebroch's *Tractatus praeliminaris de vita, operibus et virtutibus Johannis Bollandi* (Preliminary Treatise concerning the Life, the Works, and the Qualities of B.) in *Acta sanctorum martii*, vol.1 (Antwerp, 1668), pp. i–xlvii; see also the notices by J.-J. Thonissen in *Biographie nationale (de Belgique)*, vol. 2 (Brussels, 1868), cols. 630–641, and by J. Van den Gheyn in *Dictionnaire de théologie catholique*, vol. 2, pt. 1, (Paris, 1923), cols. 950–951; on the history of the Bollandists, see Hippolyte Delehaye, *A travers trois siècles. . L'oeuvre des Bollandistes, 1615–1915* (1st ed., Brussels, 1920; 2d ed., Brussels, 1959); and Paul Peeters, *L'oeuvre des Bollandistes* (1st ed., Brussels, 1942; new ed. Brussels, 1961).

Jean-Michel Dufays

PAPEBROCH, Daniel (Van Papenbroeck) (Antwerp, 1628–Antwerp, 1714), Belgian hagiographer. Born in Antwerp on March 17, 1628, the Jesuit Daniel Papebroch was invited in 1660 by Jean Bolland (q.v.) to collaborate in publishing the *Acta Sanctorum* (Acts of the Saints). From July 22, 1660, until December 21, 1662, Papebroch journeyed through Germany, Italy, and France, accompanied by Godefroid Henschens (1601–1681), and he kept a day-by-day account of their travels in his *Iter Romanum* (Journey to Rome). In particular, they spent nine months in Rome and three and a half months in Paris. From the various libraries that they visited they brought back many unpublished documents, including fourteen hundred Lives of Saints or Passions of Martyrs, in Latin and Greek. It was with the first volume of the *Acta Sanctorum* for March, published in 1668, that Byzantine texts began to be used as sources. Three years later, Papebroch confronted Russian hagiography during a stay of several months in Amsterdam. Another journey that started in August 1668 took him, together once again with Henschens, to the abbeys along the Meuse and the Mosel. During a forced stop in Luxembourg, while examining a fake charter reputedly granted by Dagobert I in A.D. 646 in favor of the monastery of Oeren (now in Northrhine–Westphalia in West Germany), Papebroch attempted to formulate a critical apparatus for testing the authenticity of medieval charters. The criteria appeared in his famous *Propylaeum antiquarium circa veri ac falsi discrimen in vetustis membranis* (A Scholarly Introduction concerning the Distinction between Truth and Falsity in Ancient Parchments), published in 1675 as the preface to volume 2 of the *Acta Sanctorum* pertaining to April. His conclusions were too severe and cast doubt on the authenticity of most Merovingian monastic diplomas, in particular those kept by the monastery of Saint Denis. The Benedictines thus felt threatened. Dom Vincent Marsolle, then in charge of the Congregation of Saint Maur, conferred the task of refuting the Jesuit's arguments on Dom Jean Mabillon (q.v.) (1632–1707), who performed the assignment admirably in his famous *De re diplomatica* (On Diplomatics), published in 1681. This debate, carried out in the best scholarly tradition, reinforced the esteem that Papebroch and Mabillon already held for each other. However, another debate was soon to take a very different tone, bordering on fanaticism. Although the Carmelites maintained that they could trace their origins directly to the prophet

Elijah, Papebroch proved, albeit with tact, that these claims had no historical basis, first in volume 1 of the *Acta Sanctorum* for April (the entry for April 7 about Saint Albert) (1675), then in volume 1 of the *Acta Sanctorum* for May (1680), and finally in the *Propylaeum maii* (Introduction for May) (1685). Among the numerous attacks on these texts, the most important was made in 1693 by Sebastian de Saint Paul, the Carmelite provincial of the Flemish-Belgian Province. To undermine the whole Bollandist enterprise, he refuted the so-called errors of Papebroch (*Exhibitio errorum*) [Presention of Errors]), and as a result, fourteen volumes of the *Acta Sanctorum* (March, April, and May, including the May *Propylaeum*) were condemned for heresy by the Toledo Inquisition on November 14, 1695. Papebroch replied to the Carmelite's arguments in three texts: first in the two parts of his *Responsio ad Exhibitionem errorum* (Reply to the Presentation of Errors), published in 1696 and 1697, and then in his *Elucidatio historica* (Historical Clarification), published in 1698. He was supported by several highly regarded scholars including Charles Du Cange (q.v.) (1610–1688), Dom Jean Mabillon, Antonio Magliabechi (1633–1714), Benedetto Bacchini (1651–1721), Dom Bernard de Montfaucon (q.v.) (1655–1741), and Ludovico A. Muratori (q.v.) (1672–1750). But all was for naught, since on December 22, 1700, a decree was issued by the newly elected Pope Clement XI (1649–1721) condemning the *Propylaeum maii*. This decree was not abrogated until January 1715, shortly after Papebroch's death on June 28, 1714. Papebroch had spent his last years writing, among other works, the *Annales Antverpienses* (The Annals of the City of Antwerp), of which seven out of the original eleven volumes were later found and published between 1845 and 1848. Papebroch was thus the principal author of the eighteen volumes of the *Acta Sanctorum* published between 1668 and 1709 (from volume 1 for March to volume 5 for June).

Bibliography: The basic source is Jean Pien's *Historia de vita, gestis, operibus ac virtutibus R. P. Danielis Papebrochii* (History concerning the Life, the Deeds, the Works, and the Qualities of P.) in *Acta sanctorum junii*, vol. 6, pt. 1 (Antwerp, 1715), pp. 3–21; see also Hippolyte DeLehaye's notice in *Biographie Nationale (de Belgique)*, vol. 16 (Brussels, 1901), cols. 581–589; among the most recent works on Papebroch, see especially Ildefonso Tassi, "La corrispondenza letteraria di D. Benedetto Bacchini col P. Daniele Van Ban Papenbroeck bollandista" (The Literary Correspondence between B. and P.), *Benedictina*, vol. 6 (Rome, 1952), pts. 1–2, pp. 123–149, containing thirty-one letters addressed to Bolland by Papebroch, 1693–1700; Maurice Coens, "Du Cange et les *Acta Sanctorum*," *Académie royale de Belgique, Bulletin de la Classe des lettres et des sciences morales et politiques*, 5th ser., 41 (Brussels, 1955), pt.10, pp. 551–570, reprinted in idem, *Recueil d'études bollandienneses* (Brussels, 1963), pp. 325–343; Andrea-M. Dal Pino, "Agiografia Servitana nell'opera dei Bollandisti dal 1660 al 1701" (Servit Hagiography in the Works of the Bollandists), *Studi storici dell'Ordine dei Servi di Maria*, vol. 12 (Rome, 1962), pp. 140–201; Baudouin de Gaiffier, "Hagiographie et critique. Quelques aspects de l'oeuvre des bollandistes au XVIIe siècle," in *Religion, érudition et critique à la fin du XVIIe siècle et au debut du XVIIIe* (Paris, 1968), pp. 1–20; María Asunción Vilaplana, "Correspondencia de Papebroch con el marqués de Mondéjar (1669–1697)'' (Correspondence between Papebroch and the Marquis of Mon*déjar), Hispania sacra* 25 (1972); (Barcelona–Madrid), 26 (1973), pt. 2, pp. 293–349, containing twenty-six letters addressed to Mondéjar by Papebroch.

Jean-Michel Dufays

SIGEBERT OF GEMBLOUX (Liège, c. 1030–? 1112), teacher, ecclesiastical advisor, and chronicler. During his life Sigebert enjoyed a notable fame, reaching the heights of ''Belgian'' medio-Latin literature. Trained at the school of Olbert of Gembloux, Sigebert taught in Metz from 1050 to around 1070–1075. Returning to Gembloux, he was a highly regarded intellectual and advisor to important churchmen. In this time of conflict between Henry IV and the popes, Sigebert became the spokesperson of the imperialistic clerics of the diocese of Liège. His great universal *Chronicle*, the first attempt of this kind in the region, must be considered as the main history placing the diocese of Liège in a wider cultural context. Basing his works on varied sources of information and ordering the elements, Sigebert was most concerned with chronology. His *Chronicle* is concise and close to that of the ''annals manuscripts.'' At the end of his work, Sigebert condemned the Gregorians. He developed the thesis of moral warnings to be tendered to the sovereign who deviated from his counselors and from spiritual authority. No human authority may willingly judge the sovereign, only God would do so. Thus Sigebert opposed history to the interventionist politic of the Gregorians. Generally, the *Chronicle* is balanced, but the historical ''ordinatio'' nevertheless fixes firmly the eminent rights of the secular power. In polemic works—the *Apology* and the *Response* to Pascal the II's letter—as in the *Chronicle*, Sigebert built his case on historical precedents, on the repetition of historical events, which thus create tradition. He attacked opponents' views by calling them unprecedented novelties without any roots in the past. Therefore, history was the basis of political science, even the origin of law, because it registered and justified custom. History as knowledge of the past becomes a guide to actions of the present. The legitimacy of power presupposes the respect for some kind of a code about which Sigebert gave us little information. He seemed to reject the conception of a control on the prince and did not grant the pope this power. Yet he used the idea to criticize Henry IV. Sigebert was a ''historian'' because he thought that the past gave examples that could be used as arguments in his own times. This conception of history is not clearly different from our own. He regarded history as a profound respect for, interest in, and knowledge of the past and, thus, as the strongest basis for any culture.

Bibliography: S. Balau, *Etude sur les sources de l'Histoire du Pays de Liège au Moyen Age* (Brussels, 1902); W. Buchwald, A. Hohlweg, and O. Prinz, *Tusculum-Lexikon griechischer und lateinischer Autoren des Altertums und des Mittelalters*, vol. 3 (Munich, 1982), pp. 726–727; M. de Waha, ''Sigebert de Gembloux faussaire? Le chroniqueur et les sources anciennes de son abbaye,'' *Revue belge de philologie et d'histoire*, 55, no. 3 (1977), 989–1036; L . Genicot and P. Tombeur (dir.), *Index Scriptorum Operumque Latino-Belgicorum Medii Aevi*, pt. 2: P. Fransen and H. Maraite, *Le XI siecle* (Brussels,

1976), pp. 87, 89, 91, 93, 95, 97, 179, 181, 189, 191, 193, 197, 199, 217, 219, 221, 223, 239; J. Schumacher, "L'oeuvre de Sigebert de Gembloux. Etudes philologiques," (Doctoral diss., Université catholique de Louvain, 1975); R. Witte, *Catalogus Sigeberti Gemblacensis monachi de viris illustribus. Kritische Ausgabe* (Frankfurt, 1974).

Michel de Waha

Great Historians: Bulgarian

PAISSI HILENDARSKI (? 1722/1723–? 1773/1798) founder of the Bulgarian national historiography. Only one of Paissi's writings, the short book entitled *Istoriya slavianobolgarskaya* (A Slavonic-Bulgarian History), has been preserved; it comprises eighty-three handwritten pages. It is known that the book was finished in 1762 in Aton, in the Bulgarian Zograf monastery. It did not appear in print during Paissi's lifetime. For more than a century, it was copied by hand and distributed. More than fifty copies are available at present. The first publication appeared in 1844 under the title *Zarstvenik ili istoriya bolgarskaya* (A Book of Kings or a History of Bulgaria). The copying and distribution of the *History* have played an important role for the introduction and dissemination of historical knowledge among the Bulgarian people during the eighteenth and nineteenth centuries. The kinship of the Bulgarians and the other Slavic people, especially the Russians, is emphatically stressed, against the background of the important political role Russia assumed with regard to the enslaved Balkan peoples. A Slavic consciousness is obvious in Paissi's work, with respect to the content and the form of the history. This is manifested even in the title, and the *History* was written in the language, which according to Paissi had to become the spoken language. In many cases, Paissi preserved the Slavonic-Russian language of his sources. The *History* became the first national program of the Bulgarian people and introduced the historical approach as an important component of the Bulgarian national psychology in the age of the national revival. It has also established the tradition of a significant and active impact of the historical sciences on social life in Bulgaria.

Bibliography: M. Arnaudov, *Paissi Hilendarski, licnost, delo, epoha* (Sofia, n.d.); "Istoriya na Bulgaria," *Ban 5* (1985): 127–149; 218–219; Vladimir Topencharov, *Paissi Hilendarski, Portret na Paissi* (Sofia, 1962).

Nadezda Dragova

Great Historians: Byzantine

AKROPOLITES, Georgios (Constantinople, 1217–? 1282), Byzantine historian. When Akropolites was a teenager, his parents sent him from the Latin-ruled Constantinople to Nicaea, cradle of the Greek resistance, where he studied with the greatest scholars of that time, such as Nikephoros Blemmydes. Received at the imperial court, he made a brilliant career—imperial secretary under Ioannes III Vatatzes and high chancellor under Theodoros II Lascaris and Michael VIII Palaiologos—to become one of the outstanding personalities of Byzantine political life. He headed the most important diplomatic missions in his capacity as high chancellor. He was also on the Byzantine legation that signed the Union of Lyon (1274). His work *Chronikē syngraphē* (Chronological Exposition) covers the years of the Nicaean exile (1203–1261) and was drafted in the Constantinople liberated from the Latins in 1261. Representative of the Byzantine nobility, Akropolites opposed the antiaristocratic policies pursued by Theodoros II Lascaris and was a staunch supporter of the social policies of Michael Palaiologos, whom he saw as the predestined emperor. But Akropolites' support of Michael Palaiologos' policy concerned only its domestic facets. Although his historical work was written in the years when the anachronical Western policy promoted by his sovereign was in full progress, the political vision of the Nicaean historian departed from the Byzantine traditional imperial idea to advocate a Greek national empire. The space beyond the borders of the empire ruled by the Byzantine emperors is, in Akropolites' work, populated by independent South Slav and Turkish states. The historian relied on his own experience and contemporaries' testimony. Although modern historians give him much credit, his subjectiveness is most conspicuous in the last part of his work where he described the reign of Theodoros II and the early rule of Michael VIII Palaiologos. The largest part of his work describes foreign policy, military campaigns, and court life. There are numerous realistic scenes and details in which the modern reader takes a particular interest. Miracles and prophecies that abound in the work of other Byzantine authors are fewer in Akropolites' work and render the atmosphere of the epoch. The style of the historian with *termini technici*, ethnical and geographic names picked from the vernacular, is free of precious atticisms. The narration is sober and balanced with optimistic undertones.

Bibliography: A. Heisenberg, *Studien zu Akropolites*, in "Sitzungberichte Bayer. Ak. Wiss.," *Philos.-hist. Kl.* 2 (1899): 463–558; idem, "De vita scriptoris," in G. Acropolitae, *Opera*, vol. 2 (Leipzig, 1903), pp. iii–xv; H. Hunger, *Hochsprachliche profane Literatur der Byzantiner*, vol. 1 (Münich, 1977), pp. 443–447.

Stelian Brezeanu

ATTALEIATES, Michael (Constantinople, c. 1030–? c. 1085), Byzantine historian. An imperial judge, Attaleiates took part in the military campaigns of Romanos IV Diogenes (1067–1071). The climax of his career was during the reign of Nikephorus Botaneiates (1078–1081), when he was promoted to patrikios, magistros, and proedros. His work, *Historia* (History), written between 1080 and 1085, covers the 1034–1079/1080 period, but almost one-third of it reports the first two years of the reign of his protector, Botaneiates. The author was partial to Isaak Comnenos and Romanos Diogenes whose reigns are extensively dealt with in the book. The main emphasis of the book falls on the tragic decade of Byzantine history between the disaster of Mantzikert (1071) and the accession to the throne of Alexios Comnenos (1081). The historian was aware that the fate of the empire was decided in the East where the fights with Seljuk Turks were fought. Although he criticized Romanos Diogenes for some tactical mistakes during his campaigns, the author was well aware that the loss of the oriental provinces was, above all, due to the policy of savings at the expense of the army pursued by the senatorial party and the Dukas clan with their short-sighted policies. He was also aware of the decline in the qualities of the Byzantine army and of its commanders as compared to ancient times. But the historian's objectivity in reporting events and their causes stopped when Nikephoros Botaneiates's person and reign were involved. The book may be regarded as a true panegyric to Botaneiates. Attaleiates's hero had all the military, political, and moral virtues and was a born master. The historic value of the book is incontestable. Crucial events for the history of the eleventh century are described in a vision that differs from that of Michael Psellos (q.v.), Anna Comnena (q.v.), and N. Bryennios. The author wrote in a classicized language. However, *termini technici* and words from the spoken language can also be traced in the book.

Bibliography: H. Hunger, *Hochsprachliche profane Literatur der Byzantiner,* vol. 1 (Munich, 1977), pp. 382–389. E. Th. Tsolakis, "Das Geschichtswerk des Michael Attaleiates und die Zeit seiner Abfassung," *Byzantina* 2 (1970): 251–268.

Stelian Brezeanu

CHALKOKONDYLES, Laonikos (Athens, ca. 1423–? ca. 1490). In 1435 Chalkokondyles was forced to flee his native city and take refuge in Mistra, capital of Moreea despotate, after the abortive coup against the Acciaiuoli seigneurs with whom his father had been involved. There, he was taught by the great Renaissance scholar and philosopher Gemistos Plethon, and he acquired a thorough classical and Byzantine culture. Apparently, he discharged diplomatic missions for the despots of Mistra. His work *Apodeixeis historiōn* (Historical Exposés), in ten books, does not concentrate on the history of the Byzantine state but on the ascent of the world empire of the sultans (1288–1463). Taking Herodotus (q.v.) as a model, whose book is based on the opposition between the Hellens and the Barbarians, Chalkokondyles made the substance of his book from the Christianity-Islam rivalry. In that confrontation, Byzantium and the European Christian powers vied with the Turks, Moors, and Tartars. Although he described the decline and fall of the Byzantine Empire, the author was no pessimist. He believed in the destiny of his people and was proud of their cultural and historic prestige. As such, Chalkokondyles appeared as one of the first representatives of neohellenism. It is very interesting that the Athenian author is the only Byzantine historian for whom the sovereigns of Constantinople were "basileis of the Hellens" and not "basileis of the Romans," a term applied to the Western emperors. True intellectual of the Renaissance, he displayed a universal interest in things. The book contains ethnographic, geographic, and cultural-historical data on the peoples in Southeastern Europe and even on Western Europe that are remarkably extensive, comprehensive, and highly documented. Most of his work relies and dwells on events the historian himself experienced. For the first part of the book, the sources of the historian are Gregoras (q.v.) and an unknown historical writing. He also used information provided by Turkish and Latin sources, most of them oral. The speeches he wrote for his heroes are an imitation of his ancient models Herodotus (q.v.) and Thucydides (q.v.). His language is archaic, with ancient ethnic and geographic names. A certain stylistic monotony does not render the reading of the book any easier.

Bibliography: E. Darkó, "Zum Leben des Laonikos Chalkokondyles," *Byzantinische Zeitschrift* 24 (1923–1924): 29–39; H. Ditten, "Bemerkungen zu Laonikos Chalkokondyles' Nachrichten über die Länder und Völker an den europäischen Küsten des Schwarzen Meeres," *Klio* 43–45 (1965): 185–246; A. Pertusi, *La caduta di Constantinopoli*, vol. 2 (Verona, 1976), pp. 194–227.

Stelian Brezeanu

CHONIATES, Nicetas (Chonai, c. 1155–Nicaea, c. 1215), Byzantine historian. Choniates grew up as an intellectual in Constantinople where he had been brought by his brother Michael Choniates, the future metropolitan of Athens. He began his career in the imperial administration in the last years of Manuel Comnenos' rule. Imperial secretary, then governor of the theme Philipopolis in the Balkans, he became one of the highest dignitaries of the empire under Alexios III Angelos. After the fall of Constantinople under the Latins in 1204, he took refuge in Selymbria, on the Thracian Pontic shore; early in 1207 he managed to reach the court of Theodoros I Lascaris of Nicaea, that had already become the most important center of the Greek resistance against the Latin aggression. His work *Chronikē Diēgēsis* (Chronological Exposition), one of the masterpieces of Byzantine historical literature, a work in twenty-one books, covers the 1118–1206 period. It was written in several stages. The first part of his work, which covers the period spanning 1118 to 1202, was written before 1204. In Selymbria he continued his work with the events that had preceded the Latin conquest of Constantinople and the 1205 events. In Nicaea he rewrote his historical work, mostly the part devoted to the period after 1180. The bitter experience of the 1203–1204 years marked the last version of the book since the author felt the need to blame and criticize the representatives of the Angeloi dynasty for the Byzantine tragedy of 1204. Choniates wrote an imperial history par excellence. The political universe of the author was that of the ecumenic empire of the basileis with the capital in Constantinople. In the light of that ideal, the political emancipation movement of the peoples in the Balkans (Vlachs, Bulgarians, Serbians), in a space considered by the basileis as their legitimate dominion, was viewed by Choniates as a ''rebellion'' against the ''cosmic order'' embodied by the Constantinople Empire. Criticisms of the policy of some emperors, from Manuel Comnenos to Alexios Angelos, refer to the emperors themselves and not to the imperial institution.

More than ever before in Byzantine history, ''the political theology'' or the ''imperial religion'' left deep marks in Choniates' work: hence, the biased character of his work with its flagrant deformations of facts, selected and viewed in the light of a conservative ideology that advocated the conservation of an empire that had become anachronistic under the new historical circumstances of that time. Dedicated to the traditional medieval conception, Choniates saw the divine will as the ultimate cause of events. However, human action was largely autonomous in his work. Constantinople's Latin conquest, the event that is preponderant in the *History* of Choniates, appears as divine retribution that befell the ''chosen people'' for their sins. But the natural causes of the 1204 disaster appear as an outcome of the mutual Byzantine-Latin resentments, of the political errors made by Manuel Comnenos, and of the bad management of the empire by the emperors of the Angeloi family. The foreign policy, the military events, and the court intrigues are in the foreground of Choniates' historical work. He also gave interesting details on the social and cultural daily life, and his exquisite esthetic sense and understanding for arts show in the final chapter, ''De signis'' (On Signs), where he described the statues of Constantinople broken by the Latins in 1204. Remarkable are the vigorous and plastic portrayals of the leading figures of the Byzantine political scene (Manuel Comnenos and Andronikos Comnenos). The style is rhetorical and full of atticisms, with many quotations and examples from the Bible and the works of ancient authors (Homer, Lucian, Plutarch [q.v.], and Euripides).

Bibliography: H. Hunger, *Hochsprachliche profane Literatur der Byzantiner*, vol. 1 (Munich, 1977), pp. 429–441; G. Stadtmüller, ''Zur Biographie des Niketas Choniates (um 1150-um 1214),'' Byzantinische Forschungen 1 (1966): 321–328; J.–L. van Dieten, *Niketas Choniates. Erlaüterungen zu den Reden und Briefen nebst einer Biographie* (Berlin, 1971).

Stelian Brezeanu

COMNENA, Anna (Constantinople, 1083–Constantinople, c. 1153), Byzantine historian. Porphyrogenete, daughter of emperor Alexios I Comnenos (1081–1118) and of his wife, Irena, of the Dukas family that had given two emperors to the empire. The firstborn of the imperial couple and betrothed to Constantine Dukas, Comnena was seen as the legitimate successor to the throne and was to become basilissa. After her fiancé died (ca. 1094), she was married to Nikephoros Bryennios, descendant of one of noblest families of the empire. She acquired an encyclopedic knowledge: history and geography, rhetoric and grammar, theology and mythology, medicine and philosophy. In her ardent ambition for power, she wanted the scepter of the empire for her husband. But Alexios bequeathed the crown to his son Ioannes II Comnenos (1118–1143) in spite of Anna's and her mother Irena's maneuvers. Yet Anna did not give up. Supported by her mother, she plotted two times to overthrow her brother. But she failed and was forced to a nunnery where she would remain for more than thirty years. There, she became the sponsor of a circle of literary men and philosophers also involved in politics.

Her work *Alexias* (Alexiad) is titled in Homeric style reflecting the taste of the Byzantine feudal aristocracy to which the clans Dukas, Comnenos, and Bryennios belonged. In fifteen books, the work is devoted to Alexios Comnenos. The work records the beginnings of the political career of Alexios before he had acceded to the throne and continues with the story of her father's efforts partially to restore the power of Byzantium (1069–1118) almost shattered after the Mantzikert disaster (1071). Her historical work is also conceived as a continuation of her husband N. Bryennios's work, as announced in the *Prooimion*, which covered the 1070–1079 period and had been left unfinished at his death (1137/1138). The *Alexiad*, written between 1138 and 1148, is both a political manifesto and a political program. The pride she took in her imperial origin and mostly her unquenched ambition for power and the bitter taste of failure underlay her political attitude. The work is an assertion of her claims to the crown, sprung from her betrothal with the legitimate heir to the imperial throne and the right of the firstborn, and it questions the legitimate succession to the throne of her brother Ioannes and her nephew Manuel. She appears as a representative of the Dukas clan, not of the Comnenoi: hence, the leniency and sympathy for their father's enemies, all Dukai, that were aspiring to overthrow Alexios. But the *Alexiad* is also the highest expression of the Byzantine political ideology. The Constantinople Empire was "by nature master over the other peoples." The superiority complexes of the Byzantines toward the "barbarians" are openly stated. The work shows hostility for the West and the refusal of dialogue with the Latins, fruit of Anna's experience with the participants in the First Crusade. She criticized the policy of rapprochement to the Western world pursued by Ioannes and even more by Manuel Comnenos. Alexios was described by Anna as an ideal that fit her political program. He gave credit to her opposition to her brother's and nephew's rules. The *Alexiad* rests on impressive research. It is the fruit of the author's personal experience, of her talks with veterans who fought under her father, and of the investigation of imperial archives from which she reproduced many official documents. As for the Latin world, she seemed to have read an unknown Italian source in addition to acquiring oral information. The Comnenian princess observed the promise to write sine ira et studio mostly where details were concerned, which were, however, handled so as to impose her own vision of facts. The ostensibly subjective portraits of her mother, husband (N. Bryennios), and brother (Ioannes II Comnenos) are revealing. Foreign relations, military events, and court life drew Anna's attention as these activities demonstrated the exceptional military, political, and moral traits of her hero. Written in classical style—she quoted from Homer and Thucydides (q.v.), from other ancient writers, and from Michael Psellos (q.v.), the Byzantine—the *Alexiad* is mainly a realistic book. Its literary value is remarkable, and it contains pages that are among the best in the entire Byzantine literature.

Bibliography: G. Buckler, *Anna Comnena. A Study* (Oxford, 1929); H. Hunger, *Hochsprachliche profane Literatur der Byzantiner*, vol. 1 (Munich, 1977), pp. 400–409; J. N. Liubarskij, "Ob istočnikach 'Aleksiady' Anny Komninoj," *Vizantijskij Vremennik* 25 (1964): 99–120.

Stelian Brezeanu

CONSTANTINE Porphyrogennetos (Constantinople, A.D. 905–Olympus, Bithynia, A.D. 959), Byzantine historian. The only child to the imperial couple of Leon VI the Wise and Zoe, Constantine became an emperor at a young age (A.D. 913), under a regency also including his mother. In A.D. 920 Romanos Lekapenos assumed power and proclaimed himself emperor; Constantine, married to Lekapenos's daughter, was a mere associate to the throne. It was only in A.D. 945, after Lekapenos's removal and his sons' abortive attempt to dethrone the lawful emperor, that Constantine claimed power for himself (A.D. 945–959). Not needing to concern himself with ruling the state, he was able until A.D. 945 to dedicate himself to cultural and scientific activities, which he continued also in the years when he was the only ruler, as a result of the peace that reigned along the frontiers of the empire.

Constantine's cultural and scientific preoccupations were numerous, and two of their facets largely illustrate Constantine's personality as a historian. One of them is the elaboration of scientific works. The first, in chronologic sequence, is known conventionally as *De thematibus* (On Themes), written in his youthful years, possibly soon after A.D. 930. It is a geographic description of the empire, comprising data related to administration, population, and area of the state. Although one finds in this work incorrect ethymologies of some names of provinces and mythologic and even imaginary events and characters, it comprises information of outstanding historical value related to the genesis and organization of the system of themes. The main sources are, besides the author's personal experience and oral information gathered by him, Stephanos Byzantinos and Hierokles of the sixth century A.D. Constantine's second and most valuable work is known as *De administrando imperio* (On the Administration of the Empire). Written for didactic purposes, for the political guidance of Romanos, heir to the throne, as Constantine announced in the *Prooimion*, the work belongs to the "Mirror for Princes" genre, widely disseminated in the medieval historical literature. But the author did not mean to give here the image of an ideal prince, just practical advice about how to rule the empire. It was written during a period of several years, probably between A.D. 948 and 952, which explains the repetitions and even annoying contradictions from one chapter to another and the absence of a general scheme of the work. Conceived as an extension of the work *On Themes, De administrando imperio* describes the external horizon of the empire and the Byzantine political relations with foreign peoples. The author produced information of outstanding value about the populations living by the northern frontiers of the empire, in the states in the West. The main written sources of his ethnographic and geographic data are Theophanes, Georgios Monachos, and Stephanos Byzantinos. But the most valuable pieces of information came from oral sources, collected by the imperial writer from foreigners. The historian's third work, too, has a conventional name, *De ceremoniis aulae byzantinae* (On the Ceremonies of the Byzantine Court) and was written in his last years (A.D. 952–959). The work, composite in structure, has the same didactic purpose, standing for a guide of conduct of the heir to the throne, at the imperial court, on the most varied occasions: crowning, wedding, promotion of high dignitaries to offices, reception of foreign messengers, and so on. It includes information about daily life in the Byzantine metropolis and at the imperial court and data of cultural history. These three books by Constantine can be considered as a set, given both their didactic intention and the nature of the information. Constantine's fourth book is *Vita Basilii* (Basileios's Life), written around A.D. 950 and dedicated to the career and reign of the author's grandfather, Basileios I (A.D. 867–886), the founder of the Macedonian dynasty. A panegyrical work in the mode of Polybius (q.v.) and Plutarch (q.v.) *Vita Basilii* has a political function. It tries to justify for posterity the usurpation by Constantine's grandfather of the imperial power through the removal and assassination of basileus Michael III, his benefactor.

The second facet of Constantine Porphyrogennetos' historical activity is his role as a guide and sponsor of the activity of a circle of scholars at his court. The circle's literary plans are impressive. The whole ancient and Byzantine historical literature was to be systematized in fifty-three thematic sections for the benefit of posterity. Unfortunately, most of the work of the scholars' circle is lost, the only section preserved integrally being that dealing with the reception of messengers. Preserved also was the text of the medical (*Iatrika*) and agronomic (*Geoponika*) encyclopedias, developed by the same group of scholars. The cultural and scientific movement around Constantine was the apex of what P. Lemerle has called "the first Byzantine humanism," a concern to conserve a legacy for future generations rather than to follow new creative impulses. In this way the movement, as well as Constantine's own works, are distinguished from intellectual trends of the ancient world.

Bibliography: P. Lemerle, *Le premier humanisme byzantine. Notes et remarques sur l'enseignement et la culture a Byzance des origines au X-ème siècle* (Paris, 1971); Gy. Moravcsik, *Byzantinoturcica*, vol. 1 (Berlin, 1958), pp. 356–390.

Stelian Brezeanu

DUKAS (New Phocaea, c. 1400–c. 1470), Byzantine historian. Dukas lived in the Greek world of the micro-Asian littoral powerfully imbued with Italian influences. He performed numerous diplomatic missions at the service of the Genoese aristocratic family of Gattilusio, masters of Lesbos Island. He headed a few missions to Sultan Mehmet II, gathering on the occasion fresh intelligence from Constantinople recently conquered by the Turks. His work, whose title remains unknown since the title page of the only manuscript left of it is lost, is a genuine continuation of the historical works of Gregoras (q.v.) and Kantakuzenos (q.v.) of the fourteenth century. It begins in the style of the universal chronicles, with the events since the creation of the world, and continues with the reigns of the Byzantine sovereigns. With the reign of Ioannes V Palaiologos, the information becomes more and more substantial, but only with the year 1402 does the work gain depth, accounting for one of the most valuable sources of Byzantine history for the next sixty years (1402–1462), with extensive references to Turkish, Serbian, Hungarian, Romanian, Venetian, and Genoese history. A supporter of the union with Rome and conversant with political realities in the islands, the author focused his narration on the events in the archipelago and on the western coast of Asia Minor. The fact that the historian depicted events of which he had firsthand knowledge, or knew from eyewitness experience, lends great documentary value to the work. For instance, the pages devoted to the fall of Constantinople are remarkable owing to the heartfelt and dramatic rendition. The style of the work is lively and colorful; the language, although dominated by archaic tendencies, includes numerous elements of common language in style and grammar.

Bibliography: V. Grecu, "Istoricul bizantin Duca. Omul si opera," *Bulletin Academica Roumania, Sect. Hist.* 29 (1947): 591–662; idem, "Pour une meilleure connaissance de l'historien Doukas," in *Memorial Louis Petit* (Paris, 1948), pp. 128–141; H. Hunger, *Hochsprachliche profane Literatur der Byzantiner*, vol. 1 (Munich, 1977) pp. 490–494.

Stelian Brezeanu

EUSEBIOS, Bishop of Caesarea (? c. A.D. 265–? c. A.D. 340), Christian historian. Eusebios grew up as an intellectual in Caesarea, in Palestine, where Pamphilos built upon Origenes's literary legacy. A disciple and collaborator of Pamphilos, Eusebios was imprisoned with him during the anti-Christian persecutions of Diocletian and his associates (A.D. 303–311). Set free after the edict of toleration of Galerius, Eusebios became bishop of Caesarea (A.D. 313). He was a close adviser to Emperor Constantine, after the latter became the only sovereign of the Roman Empire (A.D. 323). In the Arian dispute, he supported the Emperor in the efforts to maintain the unity of the Church and of the empire by compromise. However, dogmatically, he was partial to Areios. Henceforth, he helped rehabilitate Areios and banish Athanasios (A.D. 335). His literary work impresses one by its extent and variety. Most important are three of his historical works that laid the foundations of the medieval Christian historiography. *Chronikoi kanones* (Chronological Canons), written in A.D. 303, marked a turning point in the evolution of ancient historiography. Eusebios left behind a historiography where rhetoric had prevailed to inaugurate a time-oriented historiography. In the first part, the book surveys the major chronological systems of antiquity: Chaldean, Assyrian, Hebrew, Egyptian, Greek, and Roman. In the second part, Eusebios gives synchronous tables in parallel columns of the major events of the world history. The book covers the period between Abraham's birth and the onset of Diocletian's anti-Christian persecutions (c. 2016 B.C.–A.D. 303). Data on the history of Christianity held a prominent place in the last part of the book. Thus Eusebios integrated the sacred history into humankind's history and placed the Hebrew history in the center of world history. The book is based on the chronography of Iulius Africanus in which the world was six thousand years old and the birth of Jesus Christ was placed at the beginning of the sixth millennium. But Eusebios emulated only his model's effort to give history a rigorous chronologic framework and completely gave up the latter's eschatological concerns. Only fragments of Eusebios' original chronology survived. Its complete form is known only from an Armenian version compiled after the historian's death. At the end of the fourth century, Hieronymus produced a Latin version of the book and continued with the succession of events until A.D. 378. As a result of this last version, Eusebios was to exert an overwhelming influence on Latin medieval historiography in an attempt to place events in time.

Eusebios's second historical work is titled *Ekklēsiastikē historia* (Ecclesiastic History) and has ten books. The author did not mean to write a systematic history of the Christian Church but to offer an apologetic standpoint on the succession of apostles, the Christian writers, the gnostics, the heretics, anti-Christian persecutions, and the martyrs. Its first version had only eight books and was written in A.D. 311. The ensuing events—the disputes of Constantine and Licinus with Maxentius and Maximianus and then the conflict between Licinus and Constantine and the latter's triumph (A.D. 324)—compelled him to add Book 9 (A.D. 313) and Book 10 (A.D. 325) and even to alter the initial project of the book. In *Ecclesiastic History* Eusebios departed from the Greco-Roman historiography by his method of work. The ancient historians' main emphasis fell on rhetoric, and documentation was given lesser attention. On the contrary, out of the need to impose the historic authority of the Christian Church, the bishop of Caesarea gave pride of place to documents and thus set a pattern for Byzantine historiography and also for Western medieval historiography, owing to the Latin version of Rufinus (A.D. 403). Eusebios' last book was *Eis ton bion tou makariou Konstantinou basileōs* (Life of Most Serene Emperor Constantine), best known under its Latin title of *Vita Constantini*. The book is mostly an encomiastic work and to a lesser extent a historical one. Written after Constantine's death, the book dwells on the emperor's care for the Christian Church and not on his biography. But in this book, too, the facts are presented in a chronological sequence and show the historian's effort for documentation. *Vita Constantini* and the treatise *Triakontaeterikos*, written in A.D. 336, lay the foundations of the Byzantine "political theology." In Eusebios' vision, Constantine was the

Roman emperor under divine protection, the new Moses who brought the salvation of God's new chosen people. The historian depicted the Christian Roman Empire as an earthly replica of the celestial kingdom; the earthly order repeats the cosmic one, and the emperor is the representative of God on earth. Eventually, the Christian Empire, being the last of the world empires, would have no spatial and temporal successors in the world history.

Bibliography: N. H. Baynes, "Eusebios and the Christian Empire," in *Mélanges Bidez*, vol. 1 (Brussels, 1934), pp. 13–18; Ed Schwartz's article in Pauly-Wissowa, *Real-encyclopedia*, vol. 6 (Stuttgart, 1907), col. 1370–1440; J. Sirinelli, *Les vues historiques d'Eusèbe de Césarée durant la période prénicéenne* (Paris, 1961).

Stelian Brezeanu

GREGORAS, Nikephoros (Heraclea Pontica, c. 1295–Constantinople, c. 1359), Byzantine historian. Gregoras studied philosophy and theology in his native town and then logic and rhetoric in Constantinople. Significant in his intellectual development were his contacts with the great humanist scholar Theodoros Metochites. Because of Metochites, Gregoras became one of the favorites of old Emperor Andronikos II Palaiologos. At that time, he wrote several scientific works and was the master of a private school. After the fall of Andronikos II (1328), he managed to win the favor of the new emperor, Andronikos III, by winning the friendship of grand domestic Ioannes Kantakuzenos (q.v.), the would-be historian. In the political and religious conflicts that started after the death of Andronikos III (1341), Gregoras took a stand against the party of Kantakuzenos, proclaimed emperor, and against Palamism. Because of the energetic attacks pursued by Gregoras against the Palamite party, Kantakuzenos forced him into a monastery. Freed from the monastery after the abdication of Kantakuzenos (1354), Gregoras continued the dispute with the Palamite party until his death. His work *Historia Rhomaikē* (Roman History) is one of the most important of all Byzantine historical literature. The thirty-seven volume work covers the events between 1204 and 1358. However, the coverage is uneven. The first eleven volumes comprise the events from 1204 to 1341. The following eighteen volumes span only fourteen years (1341–1355). Volumes 30–35 are in fact two bulky treatises of theology, produced in the struggle against the Palamites from 1355 to 1357. Finally, the last two volumes narrate the events of 1355–1358. For the 1204–1308 period, his sources were the histories of Akropolites (q.v.) and Pachymeres (q.v.), as well as an unknown source. The narration of the next fifty years (1308–1358), covered in thirty volumes, has as a main source the author's own experience. The first eleven volumes were probably written before 1351, the following eighteen during his stay in the monastery and soon after his leaving it, and the last two in 1357–1358. His work, close to the genre of memoires, is a stand taken on the dramatic events in the fifth and sixth decades of the fourteenth century, when the empire was caught between the invading Ottoman power and Dushan's Serbian state. Gregoras, a humanist scientist, was aware that the very existence of the Byzantine Empire was at stake. He was aware that the dismantlement of the imperial army and fleet, institutions that had formerly insured the grandeur of Byzantium, and the relinquishing of the centralizing political traditions spelled a deadly threat to the empire. An actor and observer of the political scene of the midfourteenth century, Gregoras managed to keep his objectivity with regard both to the main personalities of the lay and ecclesiastic life of the time and to the problem of religious union. He was critical about the interference of the Athonite monks in political life and of the Zealots' movement in Thessalonica. His preoccupations with internal policy and even with economic life were remarkable. Just like all Byzantine historians, he announced the astronomic events, but his interest in sciences prevailed. Following in the steps of his ancient models, Gregoras included in the narration addresses by the leading characters and numerous digressions of a historical-geographic nature, the most valuable being reference to the peoples of the steppes.

Bibliography: H. Hunger, *Hochsprachliche profane Literatur der Byzantiner*, vol. 1 (Munich 1977), pp. 453–465; J. L. van Dieten, *Entstehung und Überlieferung der Historia Rhomaike des Nikephoros Gregoras* (Diss., University of Köln, 1975); idem, *Nikephoros Gregoras, Rhomäische Geschichte*, vol. 1 (Stuttgart, 1973), pp. 1–41.

Stelian Brezeanu

KANTAKUZENOS, Ioannes (?1295/1296–Athos, 1383), Byzantine historian. Coming from an aristocratic family with military traditions, Kantakuzenos was promoted great domestic and commander of the imperial army, under Andronikos II Palaiologos. He joined young Andronikos Palaiologos in the civil war between the latter and his grandfather Andronikos II. As a result of the military support given by Kantakuzenos, young Andronikos emerged as victor (1328), and under his rule the great domestic was the most outstanding personality of the Byzantine political scene. After the death of Andronikos III (1341), his widow and her partisans started the fight against the great domestic that turned into a long and tragic civil war. Kantakuzenos proclaimed himself emperor (1341). After many years of fighting, he occupied Constantinople (1347) and imposed his recognition as coemperor, one of his daughters marrying the lawful emperor Ioannes V Palaiologos. Soon, the war between Kantakuzenos and the party of the Palaiologoi started again. The two parties applied to the Turks and Serbians, respectively. Defeated in 1354, Ioannes VI Kantakuzenos abdicated and retired from political life. He spent the last thirty years of his long life in monasteries in Constantinople and Athos, at the court of his son Manuel, despot at Mistra, or in jail at Pera. His work, *Historiai* (Histories), in four volumes, belongs to the genre of memoires par excellence. It covers the events between 1320 and 1356, when the author was one of the leading characters of the Byzantine political scene. Unlike most of the Byzantine historical works, his work has a logical and well-balanced structure: the first volume deals with the civil war between Andronikos II and Andronikos III (1320–1328), the next with the rule of Andronikos III (1328–1341), the third with the period between the death of Andronikos III and Kantakuzenos's march on Constantinople (1341–1347), and the last one with the rule of Ioannes VI Kantakuzenos and the years after his abdication (1347–1356). The work was written in the seventh decade of the fourteenth century, probably between 1362 and 1369, while he was in a monastery. It is the fruit of Kantakuzenos' own experience as an observer and actor of the Byzantine political scene. The author also included in the work documents, chancellory papers, and letters such as the famous epistle of the sultan of Egypt to Ioannes VI Kantakuzenos. Kantakuzenos, too, was one of the historians who promised to respect the "truth." But his "memoires" were meant to blame the starting of the civil war of 1341–1354 on his political enemies and to dismiss the guilt of having craved the imperial crown and having brought to Europe the Ottoman Turks, the fiercest enemies of Byzantium. Therefore, Kantakuzenos' interpretation of the events spanning the 1320–1356 period must be taken *cum grano salis* and compared with Nikephoros Gregoras' (q.v.) information all the way especially considering the fact that the imperial author employed special procedures to give the impression of objectivity: speaking of himself he used the third person and attributed to other personalities of the political life eulogistic appreciations of himself. But the historian's subjectiveness also resided in skipping some of his failures or of his friends' deeds that could have cast a shadow on his figure. However, the value of his memoires as a historical document cannot be questioned. Together with the work of Gregoras, his friend and, later, his political opponent, they make a comprehensive picture of the Byzantine political and religious life in the first half of the fourteenth century. The home political events, culminating with the two civil wars, and the diplomatic relations with the two military powers of the time—the Serbians and the Ottoman Turks—are conspicuously in the focus of the historian's work. However, one can also find in it interesting details about the hectic everyday life of the Byzantine society, dominated by economic crisis and grave external threats.

Bibligraphy: J. Dräseke, "Zu Johannes Kantakuzenos," *Byzantinische Zeitschrift* 9 (1900): 72–84; H. Hunger, *Hochsprachliche profane Literatur der Byzantiner*, vol. 1 (Munich, 1977), pp. 465–476; V. Parisot, *Cantacuzène, homme d'état et historien* (Paris, 1845).

Stelian Brezeanu

KINNAMOS, Ioannes (? c. 1143–? c. 1200), Byzantine historian. Imperial secretary under Manuel Comnenos, Kinnamos participated in the conquest of the Semlin city on the Danube (1165) and, probably, in the battle at Myriokephalon (1176). His work, written between 1180 and 1183, known by the concise and improper title of *Epitomē* (Resumé), has every feature of an imperial history. The work deals with the period between 1118 and 1176 and is a continuation of Anna Comnena's (q.v.) work. But the period of the rule of Ioannes II Comnenos (1118–1143) remained a mere introduction to the rule of his son Manuel Comnenos (1143–1180). It may be inferred that not all of the work was preserved; he must have narrated the events at least until Manuel Comnenos' death. As for the sources, the work relies first on the historian's own experience and on information gathered from contemporaries. For Ioannes Comnenos' rule, he referred to older written and oral sources. The work also includes official documents—imperial diplomata, letters, peace treaties—that he, however, did not reproduce to the letter. A historian and imperial functionary, Kinnamos viewed Constantinople as the center of the then political world from which he perceived the events. These events he selected and interpreted in the light of a conservative ideology, as champion of the maintenance of an anachronistic political order. The history of the young ''national'' European monarchies and of the Italian cities, the live forces of the twelfth century, is confined to their relations with the empire of Constantinople and presented in the light of the latter's interests. Frederick Barbarossa's questioning of the political doctrine embittered him. He felt the same when he found out that the Byzantine military strategy and the imperial fleet were then declining compared to older times. The narration is focused on Manuel Comnenos, the perfect hero. He embodies every merit: powerful and handsome, courageous and righteous. Despite the fact that Kinnamos idealized his hero and that he was the representative of a conservative ideology, he retained objectiveness and accuracy in rendering the facts. The empire's political failures and the Western emperors' objecting to the doctrine were not overlooked. Manuel's deeds of arms and the life at the court with the same imperial hero in its center are given pride of place in the historian's narration. But the work also includes events of the Byzantine society's everyday life and ethnographic, geographic, and historical-cultural data. The atticized language, imitating Prokopios (q.v.), is nevertheless distinguished by simple and clear expression.

Bibliography: F. Chalandon, *Les Comnène*, vol. 2 (Paris, 1912): pp. xiv–xxii; H. Hunger, *Hochsprachliche profane Literatur der Byzantiner*, vol. 1 (Munich, 1977), pp. 409–416; G. Moravcsik, *Byzantinoturcica*, vol. 1 (1958), pp. 324–328.

Stelian Brezeanu

KRITOBULOS, Michael (Imbros, c. 1400–Athos, c. 1470), Byzantine historian. Born to a Greek family and reared in the Byzantine intellectual traditions, Kritobulos placed himself at the service of the Turkish conquerors. Attached to the Ottoman functionaries, in favor with the sultan, he was appointed governor of his native island, Imbros (1456). After the Venetians conquered the island (1466) he took refuge in Constantinople. He probably spent the last years of his life in a monastery in Athos. His work, *Historiai* (Histories), in five volumes, is devoted to the first sixteen years of the reign of Sultan Mehmet II, conqueror of Constantinople (1451–1467). The author, who wrote a little before 1470, justified his action of writing the history of the conqueror of his own people, invoking the theory of imperial translation, a singular theory in the Byzantine history. He maintained that empires are not eternal, that they pass from one people to another: by turn, they passed to the Assyrians, Medes, Persians, Greeks, Romans, and, then, to the Turks. To him, the conquest of Constantinople was the Asian world's revenge for the destruction of Troy by the Greeks. He was, however, moved by the tragedy of 1453. The conquest of Constantinople had the dimensions of the fall of Troy, Babylon, Carthage, Jerusalem, and Rome; the Byzantine disaster was, however, greater than all of the others. Panegyrical and biased, his work includes many inexact statements and many facts are omitted. The Ottomans' acts of plundering and conquest are caused by the victims; the conqueror's failures are turned into victories. The Turkish angle of the historian's writing is only too obvious. The Albanians' and Romanians' wars of liberation are viewed as acts of ''apostasy'' vis-à-vis Mehmet II, ''emperor of emperors,'' compared to Alexander the Great and the Roman caesars. His model was Thucydides (q.v.), whom he slavishly imitated. The plague in Constantinople, in 1467, is depicted in the same terms as the famous plague depicted by his model, the portraits of his characters are lifeless because of phrases borrowed from the same model. The ethnic and geographic names were atticized, which makes them difficult to identify. The style of the work is archaic and colorless.

Bibliography: V. Grecu, ''Kritobulos aus Imbros,'' *Byzantinoslavica* 18 (1957): 1–17; A. Pertusi, *La caduta di Constantinopoli*, vol. 2 (Verona, 1976), pp. 228–251.

Stelian Brezeanu

LEON, Diakonos (Kaloe, c. A.D. 950–? A.D. post–992), Byzantine historian. A deacon with the palatine clergy, Leon accompanied Emperor Basileios II in A.D. 986 in the campaign against Czar Samuel. His work *Historia* (History) covers the A.D. 959–976 period, that is, the reigns of emperors Romanos II, Nikephoros II Phokas, and Ioannes Tzimiskes. The narration, dominated by the military campaigns, covers the events in the East, Crete, and the Balkans that redeemed the world hegemony of the empire. Memorable is the description made by Leon of the regaining of Crete by Nikephoros Phokas and, especially, Tzimiskes's Danubian campaign, conducted impressively against the great Russian Sviatoslav. A representative of the traditional imperial ideology, Leon regarded the conquests made by Phokas and Tzimiskes in the East, the Mediterranean, and the Balkans as an action of redemption of territories formerly usurped by the ''barbarians.'' The work was written after A.D. 992, probably at a time when Leon had retired from the court of Basileios II. This explains the historian's critical position vis-à-vis Romanos II, father of Basileios II, and his leniency to the two soldier emperors Phokas and Tzimiskes, considered as ''usurpers'' at the new basileus' court. Leon's *Historia* rests on the author's personal experience and on testimonies gathered from participants in the events. The consonance of description of certain events in the first part of the narration with the relevant parts in Skylitzes' chronicle leads to the inference that both historians used an unknown written source. The documentary value of Leon's work is remarkable, and it stands for the main source of the beginning of the ''Byzantine epopée.'' The style of the work is markedly classical, with numerous direct speeches, according to the ancient manner. His models were Homer, Agathias, and Theophylaktos Simokattes.

Bibliography: G. Moravcsik, *Byzantinoturcica*, vol. 1 (Berlin, 1958), pp. 398–400; G. Wartenberg, "Das Geschichtswerk des Leon Diakonos," *Byzantinische Zeitschrift* 6 (1897): 106–111.

Stelian Brezeanu

PACHYMERES, Georgios (Nicaea, 1242—? c. 1310), Byzantine historian. In Constantinople, freed of Latin domination, Pachymeres studied philosophy, rhetoric, mathematics, and physics, and then he dedicated himself to an ecclesiastic career. His work *Syngraphikai historiai* (Composed Histories), in thirteen books, comprises events of the 1260–1308 period, continuing Akropolites' (q.v.) work. Pachymeres lived through the progress of the Turkish expansion in Asia Minor, where the empire retained only the coast, and the fall of the Byzantine military power in the first years of the fourteenth century, when Andronikos II Palaiologos unfortunately volunteered for the Catalan campaign. The two events that dominate a good deal of his narration set the pace for the historian's narration. Akropolites' optimism yields to the pessimism of Pachymeres, who viewed the proaristocratic social work and the occidental policy of Michael Palaiologos as the origin of Byzantium's decline. Contemporaneous with the events, Pachymeres relied on his own experience in writing his book. He proved remarkably objective in reporting the facts, and his promise to write *sine ira et studio* became his real creed. Dedicated to the traditions of the Byzantine historical literature, Pachymeres made the military and foreign policy events and the theological disputes the basis of his work. The modern reader, however, also finds data related to the economic life, prosopographic data, and ethnographic, geographic, and cultural-historical facts. Pachymeres is viewed by modern researchers as one of the first "humanists" of the Renaissance of the palaiologoi. His "humanism" appears in his general spiritual attitude, in his deep knowledge of the Hellenic antiquity from which he often quoted (Homer, Plato, Pindar), and in the language and style of his work.

Bibliography: G. Arnakis, "George Pachimeres: A Byzantine Humanist," *The Greek Orthodox Theological Review* 12 (1966–1967): 161–167; H. Hunger, *Hochsprachliche profane Literatur der Byzantiner*, vol. 1 (Munich, 1977), pp. 447–453.

Stelian Brezeanu

PROKOPIOS (Caesarea, c. A.D. 500–? c. A.D. 562), Byzantine historian. Born to an aristocratic family, Prokopios received, in his native city on the Palestinian coast, a classical education, with rhetoric and law in the forefront. General Belisarios' *consiliarius* as early as A.D. 527, Prokopios accompanied the great general in his most important military campaigns: in the wars against the Persians (A.D. 527–531), in the expeditions to Vandal Africa (A.D. 533–534), and in the battles against the Ostrogoths in Italy (A.D. 536–540). After A.D. 540 his biographic data are uncertain. In A.D. 542 he was in Constantinople where, probably, he remained longer. Late sources state that he might have held the high titles of *patrikios* and *illustrios* in the last part of his life. His chief work, *Tōn polemōn* *logoi* (On Wars), with the Latin title of *Bella* (The Wars), is made up of eight books. Books 1–2 cover Belisarios's battles against the Persians, the next two the African campaigns; Books 5–7 deal with the wars against the Ostrogoths from A.D. 535 to 540, and the last book covers the history of A.D. 551–553. The first seven books were written between A.D. 545 and 550, the last one probably in 553. The work, with panegyrical tendencies, focuses its narration on General Belisarios. But the historian did not spare Justinian, criticizing him for his negative role in the wars in Ostrogothic Italy. The work also presents domestic policy events, most important of which is the Nika uprising, and extensive information of a geographic, ethnographic, and cultural-historical nature in which the classically educated historian excelled. Prokopios' second work, *Peri ktismatōn* (On Constructions), with the Latin title of *De aedificiis*, is made up of six books. Written around A.D. 557, the work eulogizes Justinian's activity as an aedile. Everything that had been built, from the St. Sophia church to the fortifications on the limes, is attributed to the emperor who has no peer in history.

His third work, *Anekdota* (Unknown Work), known by the Latin title of *Historia arcana* (Secret History) and written around A.D. 550 or, maybe, around A.D. 558, somewhat negates the first two works of the historian. The work, singular in the whole Byzantine literature, contrasts with the two previous ones through a critical, sarcastic reference to the regime of Justinian as characterized by incompetence and abuses, corruption and vice. The emperor and his wife, Theodora, are blamed not only for the tares of the regime but also for the natural catastrophes: earthquakes, drought, and floods. Even Belisarios, the hero of *Bella*, is criticized. Those features of the *Secret History* made many experts question Prokopios' authorship. More recent research into its style and language, however, attests to his authorship. His critical attitude towards Justinian must be taken in the light of his class position. The author lived in the society of the "happy ones" (*eudaimones*) and of the great landlords from among whom the senatorial order was recruited, and it is their political aspirations that he expressed. Prokopios, in the name of senatorial opposition, did not attack the system but only Justinian's rule. Actually, he criticized only the measures that harmed the interests of the senatorial order: the abolition of some institutions of the Roman Principate, the consolidation of the autocratic character of the imperial power and the diminution of the Senate's influence, the fiscal policy, and so on. Otherwise, he proved to be a partisan of the emperor's policy of conquests, regarded as a drive for redeeming for the empire some territories usurped by the barbarians. Prokopios's historical work rests on the author's tremendous experience, on the notes taken during the long military campaigns in which he participated, on pieces of information gathered from witnesses, and military reports. He also employed written sources from the fourth to the fifth centuries, among which there must surely have been the now lost historical work of Priskos. His model was Thucydides (q.v.), where structure of the work, way of writing history, and style and language are concerned, but Homer, Herodotus (q.v.), Xenophon (q.v.), Polybios (q.v.), and others also had their influence on his style. For geographic and ethnographic information he applied to Strabo (q.v.) and Arrian (q.v.). Known to many Byzantine historians, he influenced most of them.

Bibliography: H. Hunger, *Hochsprachliche profane Literatur der Byzantiner*, vol. 1 (Munich, 1977), pp. 291–300; H. Mihăescu, in *Procopius din Caesarea, Războiul cu gotii* (Bucuresti, 1963), pp. 5–22; Gy. Moravcsik, *Byzantinoturcica*, vol. 1 (Berlin, 1958), pp. 489–500.

Stelian Brezeanu

PSELLOS, Michael (Constantinople, 1018–? 1078), Byzantine historian. In the imperial metropole Psellos acquired encyclopedic culture with illustrious teachers. He then started a bright career in administration, first as a functionary in the province. In 1041 he became imperial secretary in Constantinople. He was then promoted to the highest stages of the Byzantine administration: vestarches, protoedros, prime minister under Constantine X Dukas, and private imperial adviser under Michael VII Dukas. Under Michael VII Dukas Psellos also tasted disgrace shortly before his death. Upon instruction from Constantine IX Monomachos (1042–1055), he also handled the reorganization of higher learning in Constantinople, together with the then greatest scholars. Psellos, the most famous of them all, had the title of "chief of the philosophers." An admirer of Aristotle and Plato, he wrote a work that was impressive through its dimensions and diversity. His historical work, *Chronographia*, was probably titled by the copyists. The author called his work *historia* and confessed that he intended "to keep the balance right between ancient Rome's historians and our modern chroniclers." In other words, aware of the purpose and nature of history, he selected the events according to the rules of history instead of simply narrating them chronologically. The work is, therefore, rather a memoir, as proved by its structure. The author began his narration with events that occurred under the rule of Emperor Basileios II and thus continued the work of Diakonos Leon (q.v.). But the long reign of the great emperor is presented in a brief introduction to the work. Just as cursorily are the reigns of the next four emperors presented. But the reign of Constantine IX, under whom the author started his career with the metropolitan administration, is amply described, covering almost one-third of the whole work. Extensive details are given about the reigns of Michael VI and Isaak Comnenos. This first part of the *Chronographia*, dealing with the 976–1059 period, with special stress on the events between 1042 and 1059, was probably written during 1059–1063. It seems that the author intended to stop there with his work. Urged by the Dukas emperors, under whom Psellos knew the greatest honors, he continued the work with the events up to 1078. But this last part (1059–1078) is very brief. It actually is a mere panegyric dedicated to Constantine X and Michael VII rather than a systematic narration of the events. It was written shortly before the author's death (c. 1078).

Chronographia, as a memoir, does not present all events of the epoch, especially the external ones. The author was not concerned with the glorious deeds of arms of Basileios II or the events in the tragical decade of the eleventh century that resulted in the loss of Italy and of the oriental provinces. Courtier Psellos' attention was focused on the political scene in Constantinople, where he knew eleven emperors. He proved to be a matchless master of description of court life, with imperial intrigues and usurpations, but also of the popular movements in the metropole. Remarkable are the portraits of the leading characters of his narration, Constantine IX, Empress Zoe, Isaak Comnenos, and others, portraits that have color and relief. Psellos often revised his portraits, adjusting them in keeping with the sequence of events, presenting their physical and moral features. But the author himself is in the center of his narration. His portrait results from the many pages he dedicated to himself. Psellos, a great scholar and courtier, blended like nobody else in the Byzantine world the greatest qualities and defects—an encyclopedic science and profound knowledge of the people along with boundless ambition, lack of scruples, servilism, and boundless conceit. In *Chronographia* the ultimate cause of events is the divine will, but as a humanist, Psellos left to the people the responsibility for their actions. Most of the work is the result of the author's own experience. Psellos was perfectly informed and interested in everything, in tune with his encyclopedic education, hence also the remarkable documentary value of the work, where the realities of eleventh-century Byzantine society are concerned. In style and language, its models were Homer, Herodotus (q.v.), Plutarch (q.v.), and, above all, Thucydides (q.v.).

Bibliography: J. Hussey, "Michael Psellos, the Byzantine Historian," *Speculum* 10 (1935): 81–90; E. Renaud, in Michel Psellos, *Chronographie ou histoire d'un siecle de Byzance (976–1077)*, vol. 1 (Paris, 1926), pp. ix–lxxxviii.

Stelian Brezeanu

SPHRANTZES, Georgios (Lemnos, 1401–Corfu, c. 1478), Byzantine historian. Serving from the beginning under emperors Manuel II Palaiologos and Ioannes VIII Palaiologos, Sphrantzes then became, for more than twenty years, the confidant of Constantine Palaiologos, despot of Moreea (1427–1448) and then emperor at Constantinople (1448–1453). In that latter capacity, he discharged several diplomatic missions to the Christian princes in Trapezunt and then in Armenia, to the Italian aristocrats in the Archipelago, and even to the sultan and high Ottoman functionaries. When he was in Constantinople in 1453, the Turks made him and his family prisoners. Freed a few months after that, he wandered until the end of his life in Peloponesus, in the service of the despots there; then in Corfu; in Italy; and again in Corfu, where he spent the last ten years of his life in a monastery. His work *Memoires*, which holds a singular place in the whole Byzantine historical literature, covers his lifetime. The author recorded in a genuine memoire the daily events in which he held the leading place. The diary was considerably extended in rewriting by the author in his last years of life, probably in the years spent in monastery. A private diary, Sprhantzes' work is very sincere, and it betrays the author's great sorrow about the tragedy lived by his people. His work, the fruit of the experience gained at the service of the last three Byzantine emperors and as an eyewitness to the dramatic events of 1453, is one of the most valuable of the whole Byzantine historical literature of the fifteenth century. The clear style and language, an intermediary between the spoken language and the literary one, enhance the value of Sphrantzes' work. His *Memoires* form the substance of the *Chronicle* by Metropolitan of Monembasia Makarios Melissenos, written around 1573–1575. The latter enlarged the chronological frame of the narration (1258–1481), giving his work considerable scope.

Bibliography: V. Grecu, "Das Memoirenwerk des Georgios Sphrantzes", in *Actes XIIème Congrès International des Etudes Byzantines*, vol. 2 (Belgrad, 1964), pp. 327–341; idem, "Georgios Sphrantzes. Leben und Werk. Makarios Melissenos und sein Werk. Die Ausgabe," *Byzantinoslavica* 26 (1967): 62–73; A. Pertusi, *La caduta di Constantinopoli*, vol. 1 (Verona, 1976), pp. 214–225.

Stelian Brezeanu

THEOPHANES, the Confessor (? c.A.D. 752–Samothrace, A.D. 818), Byzantine chronicler. A descendant of a rich family himself, Theophanes married a rich young lady. Soon after the wedding, he donated his entire fortune to the poor and went to a monastery together with his wife. He was an opponent of the financial policy conducted by Nikephoros I (A.D. 802–811) that harmed the interests of the aristocratic class, and he openly stood against Leon V's icon hunting. That latter position brought him a two-year confinement in prison (A.D. 815–817) and then exile to Samothrace island, where he died. His work *Chronographia* was written upon the request of his friend Georgios Synkellos (d. c. A.D. 810), who had written a universal chronicle, from the creation of the world to A.D. 284. Theophanes continued that work with the events starting from Diocletian's rule to the beginning of Leon V's reign (A.D. 284–813). Written from A.D. 810 to 814, *Chronographia* employed several systems of dating, probably borrowed from its sources: the Alexandrian era, the Christian era, the sequence of events following the sequence of the Byzantine emperors, Persian kings, Arab califs, Orthodox patriarchs, and Roman pontiffs. The problem of Theophanes' sources is one of the thorniest of his work. For the first part (the fourth-sixth centuries A.D.), the basic sources were the Church historians (Sokrates, Sozomenos, and Theodoretos), Priskos, Prokopios (q.v.), Agathias, Malalas, Theophylaktos Simokattes, and Georgios Pisides. It is, however, not clear whether the chronicler applied to their works directly or to a late compilation of them. For the most important part of the work, covering the "dark centuries" of the Byzantine history (seventh-eighth centuries A.D.), the sources remain unknown. Among the possible sources is the so-called *Megas chronographos*, an iconoclastic writing from the late eighth century A.D., used also by Nikephoros Patriarcha, and a chronicle by Traianos Patrikios, now lost, that covered events until A.D. 813. For the last part, the chronicle relies upon the author's own experience and upon oral information gathered from contemporaries. The differences of style and language from one chapter to another of the chronicle point to his work method. He took over the pieces of information, with no personal compilation, retaining the peculiarities of style and language of his sources. Theophanes' chronicle is the most important source for the seventh-eighth centuries A.D., hence also its remarkable documentary value. The work was largely known in Byzantium and was used by most of the Byzantine chroniclers (Giorgios Monachos, Symeon Logothetes, Skylitzes-Kedrenos, and Zonaras). Through Anastasius Bibliothecarius's Latin version, it also reached Western medieval historical literature.

Bibliography: H. Hunger, *Hochsprachliche profane Literatur der Byzantiner*, vol. 1 (Munich, 1977), pp. 334–339; K. Krumbacher, *Geschichte der byzantinischer Literatur* (Munich, 1897), pp. 342–347; Gy. Moravcsik, *Byzantinoturcica*, vol. 1 (Berlin, 1958), pp. 531–537.

Stelian Brezeanu

Great Historians: Chinese

BAN Gu (An-ling, Fu-feng) (east of modern Xian-yang, Shanxi, A.D. 32–Luoyang, Henan, A.D. 92), Chinese historian in the later Han (A.D. 26–220) dynasty. In his youth Ban Gu entered the higher imperial academy in Loyang, the capital, and studied various doctrines proposed by competing philosophical schools. Later, he began to edit the manuscript of *Shi-ji hou-zhuan* (Later Traditions of the Historical Records, Continued) by Si-ma Qian (q.v.), begun by his father Ban Bian. He then joined the staff of the imperial library, where he was in charge of collating the collection, and also worked at writing history. He was promoted to be the emperor's attendant in charge of secretarial affairs and was ordered to write the official history of the former Han dynasty (206 B.C.–A.D. 8), entitled upon its completion the *Han Shu* (History of the Han). Methodologically, Ban Gu based himself on Si-ma Qian's *Shi-ji*, whose former Han chapters he largely copied. But Si-ma Qian attempted to cover all of human history, whereas Ban limited himself to the history of a single dynasty. The former Han had been overthrown in A.D. 8 and was followed by an interregnum of 117 years. But Ban Gu included the interregnum and effectively commenced a practice that later became standard—the responsibility of each Chinese dynasty to compile the official history of its predecessor. In A.D. 79, Ban was ordered to compile the results of the White Tiger Hall debates, discussions comparing the five classics, which he completed as *Bai-hu tong-yi* (The Summary of Bai-hu-guan Discussions). This work is a vulgar combination of classism and theology. He advocated that the emperors and kings were determined by the mandate of Heaven. During the beginning of the A.D. 80s, he completed *Han Shu* (one hundred volumes), which covers a period of 230 years from the founding of the former Han to the end of the Wang Mang dynasties. But eight biographies and a monograph on astronomy in it were completed by his sister Ban Zhao (A.D. 49–120) after his death. The purpose of Ban Gu in writing this work was different from that of Si-ma Qian. Ban wanted to show that the history of Han was directly inherited from the (mythic) sage emperor Yao and to use history as indoctrination to justify and consolidate the Han's rule.

The core of Ban's historical thinking is the outlook of theological history, that is, the extension of the idea of "Heaven's mandate" developed in the middle years of the former Han dynasty. He thought that the founding of the former Han and the restoration of the later Han were both arranged by the will of Heaven (*tian ming*). He studied history through the arrangement of historical events and interpreted and linked historical events by means of Confucianism of the Han. This method was conservative at that time. But *Han Shu* inherited the tradition of the *Shi Ji* in content and expressions and developed them further. *Han Shu* consists of four parts: the chronicles focused on emperors; the chronological tables, on the influential historical personalities such as nobles, officials with merits, and imperial relatives; the comprehensive articles, on social institutions and important subjects; and the biographies, on the representative personalities of different groups in the former Han dynasty. The third part is also divided into ten categories: calendar and system of measures and weights, rites and music, criminal laws, worshipping, astronomy, abnormal natural phenomena, geography, irrigation, and culture. It not only reflected the nature and society comprehensively but also encouraged the development of some disciplines in the late ages. *Han Shu* made an important contribution to the Chinese historiography. This was the first work to use a biographical style to write dynastic history, and it thus became the model for writing the later feudal "dynastic histories." Moreover, *Han Shu* has been highly regarded by scholars of the past and the present for its care and comprehensiveness. After the fifth century A.D., the study of *Han Shu* became a special branch of learning. Ban Gu's other writing and poems were later collected in *Ban Gu Ji* (The Collected Works of Ban Gu).

Bibliography: Bai Shou-yi, "*Si-ma Qian yu Ban Gu*" (Si-ma Qian and Ban Gu), *Shi-xue-shi zi-liao* (Historiographical Materials), no. 2 (1979); Ban Gu, *The History of the Former Han Dynasty*, 3 vols., trans. H. H. Dubs (Baltimore, 1938); Hans A. A. Bielenstein, "The Restoration of the Han Dynasty," *Bulletin of the Museum of Far Eastern Antiquities* (Stockholm), no. 21 (1954); H. H. Dubs, "The Reliability of Chinese Histories," *Far Eastern Quarterly* 4 (1946–1947): 22–43; Hou Wai-lu et al., *Zhong-guo si-xiang tong-shi* (General History of Chinese Thought), vol. 2, Ren-min chu-ban-she (Beijing, 1957); M.A.N. Loewe, "Some Recent Editions of the Ch'ien-Han-Shu," *Asia Major* 10, no. 2 (1963): 162–172; C. S. Sargent, "Subsidized History: Pan Ku and the Historical Records of the Former Han Dynasty," *Far Eastern Quarterly* 3 (1943–1944): 119–143; O. B. Van Der Sprenkel, *Pan Piao, Pan Ku, and the Han History* (Canberra 1964).

Qu Ling-dong

CHEN Shou (Anhan prefecture, Baxi commandery, modern Nanchong, Sichuan, A.D. 233–Loyang, A.D. 297), Chinese historian who rose to the rank of censor for Administration of Documents during the Western Jin dynasty (A.D. 265–317). Continuing the tradition of Si-ma Qian's (q.v.) *Shi Ji* and Ban Gu's (q.v.) *Han Shu*, Chen composed the *Sanguo zhi* (Chronicles of the Three States), a monument of Chinese annalistic and biographical historiography. Starting from the closing years of the later Han, *Sanguo zhi* relates the history of the three states of Wei, Shu, and Wu, in three separate books, totaling sixty-five chapters. Chen drew on Wang Chen's *Wei shu* (History of Wei), Yu Huan's *Wei Lue*

(Outline of Wei History), and Wei Yao's (Wei Zhao's) *Wu shu* (History of Wu), among other works, yet went beyond them to use a wealth of information from a variety of other sources in order to record even hearsay and historically unreliable reports. For example, in composing the "Biography of Zhuge Liang" chronicling the life of one of the great political figures of the Three States period, the subject of numerous legends, Chen exercised great probity in selecting and excluding materials, rejecting both the fantastic tales about Zhuge Liang capturing and releasing Meng Huo seven times during his southern military expedition and the story about Zhuge, on his northern campaign, single-handedly driving back Sima Yi's great army from the city of Yangping, which was at the time undefended by troops. Chen also struck from the record any reference to *Huo Chu Shi Piao* (Later Memorial on Leading Out the Army), a work fabricated by an Eastern Wu (A.D. 222–280) author and attributed to Zhuge. As circumstances required, Chen accorded an individual biography to or treated in appended sections virtually every figure who left his mark on the political, economic, or military history of the Three States period or who made a contribution to the scholarly thought, literature, art, or science and technology of the times. His concern for national minorities is evidenced by his "Biographies of the Wuhwan, Xianbei, and Eastern Yi Peoples." But Chen failed to create a separate biography for the Western Di and Qiang peoples and the states of the Western Regions. The lack of treatises (*zhi*) to complement the annals and biographies is a further defect of the work. *Sanguo zhi* was favorably received on its completion. Contemporaries who saw the manuscript "praised (Chen's) excellence in narrating events and his talents as a fine historian." The fact remains, however, that Chen's treatment of the Si-ma clan, the unifiers of the Western Jin, verges on apology at times. *Sanguo zhi* has been justly acclaimed for its mode of historical narration and its prose style, both of which may be characterized as spare, crisp, and flawlessly uncluttered. Traditionally, the work has been grouped with *Shi Ji*, *Han Shu*, and Fan Ye's (q.v.) *Hou Han Shu* (History of the Later Han) as one of the "Former Four Histories" that are viewed as the crowning achievements of Chinese annalistic and biographical historiography. Nevertheless, *Sanguo zhi*, which is succinct, sometimes fails in being overly laconic. It remained for Pei Songzhi in the Liu Song dynasty (A.D. 420–279) to annotate *Sanguo zhi*. By supplementing, providing different accounts, correcting errors, and arguing issues in the work, Pei made up for the deficiencies of the *Sanguo zhi*.

Bibliography: Lu Bi, *Sanguo zhi jijie* (Beijing, 1957); Ryusaku Tsunoda and L. Carrington Goodrich, eds., *Japan in the Chinese Dynastic Histories* (Pasadena, 1968), containing a translation of the section on the "Wo" people, generally agreed to be somewhere in Japan, from the "Biographies of the Dong-yi peoples" in the *Weizhi* section of the *Sanguo zhi*.

Mian Yue

DU You (Wan-nian County, Jing-zhao Prefecture, now Chang-an County, Shanxi, A.D. 735–? 812), Chinese scholar, official and historian. Du You's *Tong dian* (Comprehensive Institutions, two hundred volumes) is the first Chinese history to deal specifically with institutions. Du held posts in the offices of land and water transportation, tax collection, and financial affairs, and he served as governor in the regions of De-zong, Shun-zong, and Xian-zong. The monumental *Tong dian* (A.D. 801) took Du thirty-six years to complete and has had great influence on subsequent Chinese historiography. It established the fundamental model for Chinese institutional history and created a new genre for historical works. *Tong dian* influenced Zheng Qiao's (q.v.) composition of *Tong Zhi* (The Comprehensive Monographs), for example, and Ma Duan-lin's (q.v.) *Wen-xian tong-kao* (An Encyclopedia of Institutions). *Tong dian* is divided into eight sections: *shi-huo* (economy), *xuan-ju* (selection), *zhi-quan* (posts and officials), *li* (rites), *yue* (music), *bing-xing* (military affairs and criminal punishments), *zhou-jun* (prefectures and commanderies), and *bian-fang* (border defense). Each section is in turn subdivided into several subject headings. For example, the section on economics, *shi-huo*, covers eighteen subjects, including the land system and taxation. Du selected these eight sections according to their importance in governing the country and arranged them according to their relationships to each other. Du believed that the most important task in governing a country is to educate the people and convert them into cultured beings, but the basis of that is to let the people live in plenty. Consequently, he broke with traditional Chinese historiography, which ranked the ethical components of government highest, and was the first historian to place his treatment of the economy (*shi-huo*) first, before his other sections. This revealed his foresight, attaching first importance to the material factors. Under *shi-huo* he also paid attention to the demographic data of the preceding dynasties and problems of the circulation of commodities, in addition to the land system and tax collection—hence his treatment differed from, and surpassed, preceding historical works.

Du naively believed that, compared to institutions, human society had developed continuously. He said: "In ancient China, many places were just like the present backward ones." For this reason he opposed the practice "to praise the past and criticize the present." Some ancient institutions might be good, but with the passage of time, they could not survive or function in the present, so one could not follow them blindly. But he did not oppose learning from the past; on the contrary, he valued the lessons of the past as guides for present government. This was his purpose in writing *Tong dian*. He proposed that the government should "learn from the past in order to catch up with time" and that proper institutions should be worked out to suit current conditions. If there was something wrong with contemporary institutions, they should be reformed. Du valued highly those who had advocated reforms in history. Shang Yang and Li Kui have been criticized by many historians as iron-fisted politicians, but Du praised their reforms and called them men of virtue. He also had a good opinion of the tax reform in the Tang and regarded the reforms of Yang Yan (A.D. 727–781) as "the proper measures, in accord with [his] contemporary conditions, and the right way to eliminate social abuses." In regard to the relationship between people of ancient times and Heaven, Du apparently paid much attention to human affairs. He vividly recorded the story of Yao Chong's opposition to the idea of regarding a locust blight as an omen of human affairs and praised Yao's accomplishment in mobilizing people to eliminate locusts. Du emphasized that no historical event could be separated from human activities. Human activities created "situations," which in turn created the historical events. He noted that although An Lu-shan did feel compelled to rebel at first, the expansionist wars waged continuously by Emperor Xuan-zong in the Tang increased the tax burden of starving people all the more, so the "situation" for An's rebellion (A.D. 755) matured. This "situation" was created by "human affairs," not by "Heaven's will." Du believed that human activities could not only create the "situations" but also could change them. This idea to attach more importance to human affairs and the aggressiveness of human efforts was progressive and had positive value at that time. *Tong dian* records many classics and documents before the Tang and current writing and also preserves a large amount of valuable historical materials and fragments of ancient books that are no longer extant. More than nine hundred entries from lost ancient texts are found in *Tong dian*. Du also wrote *Li-dao yao-jue* (Key to Regulating the Way), but it is not preserved.

Bibliography: Etienne Balazs, "L'histoire comme guide de la practique bureaucratique (Les monographies, les encyclopedies, les recueils de statuts)," in W. G. Beasley and E. G. Pulleyblank, eds., *Historians of China and Japan* (Oxford, 1961); Ssu-yu Teng and Knight Biggerstaff, *An Annotated Bibliography of Selected Chinese Reference Works, Revised* (Cambridge, Mass., 1950), pp. 148–149.

Zeng Yi-fen

FAN Ye (Shun-yang, now Xi-chuan, He-nan A.D. 398–Jian-kang, now Nanjing, A.D. 446), Chinese historian in the Liu Song dynasty. Fan Ye was well versed in poetry and literature and was assigned to the private secretariat (confidential?) works, but he also commanded the army for the northern expedition. He dared to criticize government maladministration and the abuses of enfeoffment of princes and was involved in the factional struggles at court. After his first failure in the political struggles in A.D. 432, he was determined to collate the histories of the later Han by different authors into a standard one. He made comments in his work to identify the successes and failures of that period. In the fifteen years after A.D. 432, while taking part in the political struggles in the ruling groups, he completed his compilation of *Hou Han Shu* (History of the Later Han). This is his only extant work. It originally had one hundred volumes, in which there were ten volumes of *ben-ji* (imperial annals), eighty volumes of *li-zhuan* (biographies) and ten volumes of *zhi* (treatises). But after he was punished, the manuscripts of his treatises were destroyed; later generations replaced them with thirty volumes of treatises from the *Xu Han Shu* (History of Han, Continued). Fan Ye modeled this work on Ban Gu's (q.v.) *Han Shu*. In internal affairs, Fan advocated national consolidation and the unification of the North and South; in foreign relations, he favored friendly contact rather than predatory wars. In his studies, he proposed that history should be separated from the classics and differentiated from literature as well. He emphasized that the essays should "regard the meaning as essentials, the essays pass on essentials," and that there should be the "law of sound" in essays. *Hou Han Shu* speaks frankly of the events of the later Han, recording the greed and extravagance of the less scrupulous rulers. It adds the category of *Li-zhuan* and supplements events with the biographies of individuals such as factional politicians, eunuchs, conjurers and alchemists, persons independent of customs and fashions, hermits, and men of letters. It classifies people into categories so that the narration can be clearer and more convenient. Moreover, the narrations are brief and precise, their central ideas clear and glaring. For example, the story of Wu Han's defeat of Gongsun Shu in the biography of Wu Han is not repeated in the biography of Gongsun Shu. *Hou Han Shu* breaks the rules of feudal hierarchy and also writes of people of the lower classes. Fan especially praised those who would suffer or even sacrifice themselves for friendship. He recommended Ban Gu's *Han Shu* and described his *Hou Han Shu* as "comprehensive and meticulous," so the compilation of dynastic histories gained more importance thereafter. His *Hou Han Shu* and *Shi Ji* by Si-ma Qian (q.v.), *Han Shu* by Ban Gu (q.v.), as well as *San Guo Zhi* by Chen Shou (q.v.), have been called "the four former histories," and have become outstanding representative works of biographical history.

Bibliography: Hans A. A. Bielenstein, "The Restoration of the Han Dynasty," *Bulletin of the Museum of Far Eastern Antiquities* (Stockholm) 21 (1953): 20–81; A.F.P. Hulsewe, "Notes on the Historiography of the Han Period," in W. G. Beasley and E. G. Pulleyblank, eds., *Historians of China and Japan* (Oxford, 1961).

Chen Qian-jun

GU Zu-yu (Wan-xi, Wuxi Prefecture, Jiangsu Province, 1631–? 1692), Chinese historical geographer. Gu Zu-yu worked as a private school tutor as a teenager because of poverty. In 1659 he began his *Du shi fang yu yao* (Geographical Summaries for Reading History), a comprehensive and systematic historical geography on the evolution of the Chinese territories. In 1687 when Xu Quianxue compiled *Da ging yi tong zhi* (The Chinese General Geography in the Great Qing Dynasty) under imperial auspices, Gu was invited with other noted scholars to join this project, but he refused to accept Xu's recommendation and was unwilling to be listed among the authors after the book was completed. For more than thirty years he concentrated on compilation of his *Geographical Summaries*, which ultimately comprised 130 volumes of text and 4 volumes of appendix under the title of *Essential Maps*. The first 9 volumes describe the terrain of the various historical provinces and prefectures, the next 114 volumes describe the two capitals and thirteen provinces, with their subordinate prefectures and counties, and the last 7 volumes describe in detail the similarities and differences of the mountains and rivers with their dividing lines. The volumes are put in such an order as to realize his aspirations. In the volumes, discussion of each province is preceded by an introduction discussing its most important historical features to make clear its situation and circumstances. Discussion of each prefecture follows the same format but in more detail. For each county he recorded the main mountains and rivers, passes and bridges, posts and towns. An outline opens each volume, and then notes are made for it. This book is distinguished for its great military value, giving a minute description of the strategical defiles and the battles in history with their successes and failures. As Gu pointed out, topographical advantages provide the basis for military successes. Attention was drawn to exhaustive accounts of geographical features one needed to know to be well versed in the art of war. But Gu considered a commander's subjective initiative more important for success in war. This is why the same place had played different roles at different times. In the final analysis war is conditioned by actions of the commander himself with his troops. The foundation of the capital must be determined not only by its position or transport facilities but also by its productivity or advantageous position against the enemy.

Bibliography: J. Gray, "Historical Writing in Twentieth-Century China: Notes on its Background and Development," in W. G. Beasley and E. G. Pulleyblank, eds., *Historians of China and Japan* (Oxford, 1961).

Cang Xiu-liang

HUANG Zong-xi (Yu-yao of Zhejiang, 1610–? 1695). Chinese historian and philosopher; Ming loyalist. Huang was the son of a prominent late Ming dynasty scholar–official, and his early education was that of an orthodox Neo-Confucian. He passed the *ju-ren* provincial examinations in 1623, but later, under his teacher Liu Zong-zhou, he turned to the philosophy of Wang Yangming. During the southern expedition of the Manchus he recruited soldiers to fight against the invaders and became deputy superintendent to the prince of Lu of the Southern Ming dynasty. After the defeat of the Ming, he retired to the countryside, applying himself assiduously to academic research, teaching, and writing for thirty years. He wrote more than sixty works in more than thirteen hundred volumes. His one-volume *Ming-yi-dai-fang-lu* (A Plan for the Prince [translated in de Bary, 1957]) is among his most influential works, informed by his wide learning and profound insight. His remark that keeping the country in order does not depend on the rise or fall of an imperial family but on whether the people enjoy security or not is not only the thesis of the book but also a vivid reflection of his conception of history. It took unusual courage and insight to point out that the feudal emperors were "the greatest calamities of the world." His conclusion was based on a great quantity of historical facts, reviewed in the light of his personal experience, as he learned from the fall of the Ming dynasty. It illustrates strikingly his theory of learning as a tool for statecraft. In regard to historiography, he held that historians must value objective historical facts, reflect on their own practices, and carefully collect, examine, and verify historical data before making generalizations. Besides, they must study other related disciplines thoroughly, especially original texts. Historical writings must be well organized and unified. To appraise historical figures, historians must rely on their analysis of historical realities, repudiating sectarian bias. His major work, *Ming-ru-xue-an* (Records of Ming Philosophers), classified Confucian scholars into nineteen schools according to their different doctrines, including two hundred and more scholars with pithy expressions. It is the fruit of his academic labor and the first complete and systematic monographic study of the academic and ideological history. In his incomplete manuscript *Song Yuan xue-an* (History of Scholarship in the Song and Yuan Dynasties) he blazed new trails in compilation by introducing statistical forms and appendices. His *Xing-chao-lu* and *Nan-lei-wen-ding* have left us many valuable materials. He also made great contributions by compiling the *Ming-shi* (History of the Ming Dynasty). Huang Zong-xi was the founder both of the science of history in the Qing dynasty and of the influential Eastern Zhejiang school.

Bibliography: William Theodore de Bary, "Chinese Despotism and the Confucian Ideal: A Seventeenth-Century View," in J. K. Fairbank, ed., *Chinese Thought and Institutions* (Chicago, 1957), pp. 163–203; idem, "A Plan for the Prince: The Ming-i tai-fang lu of Huang Tsung-hsi" (Ph.D. diss., Columbia University, 1953); Huang Qi-hou, *A Chronicle of Huang Zong-xi's Life* (Yu-yao, 1873); Huang Tsung-hsi, *The Records of Ming Scholars*, ed. Julia Ching, with Chaoying Fang (Honolulu, 1987); Tu Lien-che, "Huang Tsung-hsi," in Arthur W. Hummel, ed., *Eminent Chinese of the Ch'ing Period, 1644–1912* (Washington, D. C., 1943) pp. 351–354; Frederic Wakeman, Jr., *The Great Enterprise: The Manchu Reconstruction of Imperial Order in Seventeenth-Century China* (Berkeley, Calif.; Los Angeles; and London, 1985), pp. 1080–1093.

Wang Zheng-yao

KONG-ZI (Confucius) (Zuo, now in Shandong Province, 552 B.C.–? 479 B.C.). Kong-zi (Mr. Kong) is widely known as Confucius, a Latinized version of Kong Fu-zi (Master Kong). He was a Chinese historian, philosopher, political theorist, and educator whose thought has profoundly influenced the development of East Asian society and culture until the present. In East Asia (China, Korea, Japan, Vietnam), where classical Chinese served as a common literary language in the manner of Latin in Europe, the Chinese language was spread largely through the Confucian classics, especially the *Lunyu* (Analects), and Confucius's ideas, especially as interpreted by later theorists, formed the dominant discourse informing philosophy and historiography throughout the region. Born to a family of impoverished peers, Kong-zi studied in the state of Lu, a center of learning in late Zhou times. He took the duke of Zhou (Zhou-gong), a son of the founder of the Zhou dynasty, as his ideal hero and tried through education, writing, and polemics to develop the duke of Zhou as a model for his own contemporary ruler, the duke of Lu. China was then in a feudal age, only nominally united, as various states including Lu competed with each other for dominance. Kong-zi failed in his attempts at administrative reform and fled Lu with his pupils in 498 B.C.. He spent the next fourteen years in exile, seeking a ruler who would accept his advice. In 484 B.C. he managed to return to Lu and spent the remainder of his life there, devoted to teaching, writing, and editing the classics. Kong-zi was a great mind in search of the truth behind practicality. His key concepts are *li* (propriety) and *ren* (benevolence). *Propriety* is the foundation of social order secured by correct maintenance of the fundamental human relationships that form the basis of community: sovereign and subject, father and son, elder and younger, husband and wife. *Benevolence* refers to that human virtue which allows the individual to recognize that people are social beings and to conform to the social order by restraining selfishness. Kong-zi sought the essence of these concepts not by speculation or meditation but by careful study of prior human experience, especially the actions of great and respectable men. Knowledge of the acts of great men of the past, moreover, could be obtained only through written records, hence the centrality of history and historical scholarship in the Kong-zi's thought and the Confucian tradition. The two key historiographical issues stemming from Kong-zi's attitude toward the past are, first, that annotation as a style, essential to comprehend correctly the meaning of the Five Classics, constituted the core of Chinese scholarship until the early twentieth century. Second, the study of history was tantamount to learning directly from the past, so that historiography was thought to be founded first on moral judgment. Kong-zi's concerns were with practical affairs of the world: He based his ideas on real conditions rather than ideals: he held great store in humaneness and urged the rule of "propriety" rather than of "law." Therefore, it follows that Kong-zi spoke "neither about transcendence nor about eternity" (*Lunyu*), which also had an enduring influence on Chinese historiography; there are correspondingly few works on philosophy of history, that is, speculative and metaphysical interpretations of history, in traditional China. Kong-zi has become synonymous with conservatism and the evils of the past, but it should be remembered that his thought was "revolutionary" in his own age, when the affairs of state were governed by mediums using scapulimancy and other forms of divination.

Confucianism was first adopted as an official state ideology by Emperor Wu (reigned 140–87 B.C.) of the Han dynasty (206 B.C.–A.D. 9; A.D. 23–220) and developed into the dominant orthodoxy among Chinese scholars and historians until the early twentieth century. In Confucianism, the Five Classics are regarded as the central canon, which every cultivated person should master: *Yi jing* (classic of changes), *Shu jing* (classic of documents, also called the Book of History), *Shi jing* (classic of poetry), *Li ji* (Book of Rites), and *Chun giu* (Spring and Autumn Annals). *Jing* (classic) implies a book that describes how to conduct one's life properly, and tradition ascribes the compilation of the Five Classics to Kong-zi. Although modern Chinese historians have challenged the ascription of the Five Classics to Kong-zi, historiographic priority should be placed not on whether Kong-zi actually edited them but on the very tradition of ascribing them to him, a tradition that survived for two thousand years. Among the Five Classics, the *Shu jing* (classic of documents) and *Chun giu* (spring and autumn annals) are of major historiographical significance. Even in the Zhou period (1122–408 B.C.), the office of astrologer, chronicler, or historian had become institutionalized, one chronicler recording what the king said; the other, what he did. The former is the *Shu jing*, and the latter is the *Chun giu*. These two classics formed the basic styles of traditional Chinese historiography that were synthesized by Zuo Qiu-ming (q.v.) and Si-ma Qian (q.v.) and later elaborated by other historians (see Ban Gu, Si-ma Guang, and Yuan Shou). Selection and compilation of the *Shu jing* is traditionally ascribed to Kong-zi, who is said to have seen them as models for proper ethics and benevolent government. In fifty-eight chapters, in its present form, it covers seventeen centuries until 630 B.C. under categories such as "canons," "counsels," "instructions," "announcements," "oaths," and "charges." Twenty-five chapters, however, were later shown to be forgeries of Yan Ruo-qu (1636–1704), one of the founders of the "Kao-zhong zhi xue" school of historical study based on textual criticism of historical documents (see Huang Zong-xi, Wang Fuzhi, Gu Zu-yu, and Qian da-xin). The *Shu jing* was originally called, simply, *Shu* (book; document), which signified an orthodox history. This was a model for Ban Gu's *Han Shu* (Classic of Documents of the Han dynasty), and more than half of the twenty-four standard histories were called "shu" (see Fan Ye, Qu-yang Xiu). The *Book of Documents* evolved in the Han dynasty into a classic symbol of authority in the view of Confucians who idealized the Zhou period; the book itself, however, was changed in their hands, as they added chapters and deleted material. Yet it was here that the work became scriptural in force, losing its position as a history; it came to be called the *Shang shu* (Ancient Documents) in the Han period and the *Shu jing* (Classic of Documents) in the Song (960–1279) dynasty.

The *Spring and Autumn Annals* covers major events in the reigns of the twelve dukes of Lu from 722 to 481 B.C. (hence this period is called the Spring and Autumn era) and was also said to be compiled by Kong-zi on the basis of Lu court records. He is traditionally thought to have exercised his judgment of good and evil by his selection of actual historical events, using the events of the 240-year period to illustrate the moral standard to which he would hold the ideal ruler and his vision of the ideal society. The *Spring and Autumn Annals* consists of extremely terse narrative statements; Kong-zi was thought to have taken full advantage of the ideographic content of Chinese characters to convey his moral judgment on historical figures. It has since been shown that such an analysis cannot be sustained (see Kennedy 1942), but it follows from this belief, nearly universal in traditional China, that it is necessary to elucidate the moral judgments Kong-zi sought to convey with such subtle verbal distinctions. Thus soon after Kong-zi's death began a tradition of commentaries on the *Spring and Autumn Annals*. The *Gong-yang zhuan* and *Gu-liang zhuan* (Gung-yang's and Gu-liang's Commentaries) attach particular importance to these verbal distinctions and Kong-zi's moral judgments. By contrast, the *Zuo-zhuan* (Zuo [Qiu-ming]'s Commentary) employs a "historical method" in explaining Kong-zi's intent, exposing circumstances not mentioned in the *Annals* to explain events. Although the *Annals* were quickly invested with scriptural authority, Chinese historians came to regard the *Zuo-zhuan* as a paragon of historiography.

Kong-zi's attitude toward historical writing can be summarized in one sentence: "Writing down all the abstract words is not as clear as seeing [their meaning] in action [as historical fact]'' (*Shi-ji*). Kong-zi's idea of learning as ''a transmitter, not a creator, a votary and a devotee of antiquity'' *(Analects)*, laid the foundations of a historiographical ideal of history as an inviolable record of events recorded exactly as they happened, later developing into a style of history in which the historian separated his judgments from his description of events (see Zuo Qiu-ming, Si-ma Qian, Ban Gu). Kong-zi's central idea is to resolve matters on the level of human affairs; the authority for judgment derives not from divine words but from the words and acts of humans of the past. History, therefore, required a style that let the ''facts speak for themselves.'' This fostered the ideal of historical objectivity over two millennia ago. Institutionally, this ideal was reflected in the office of the state historiographer and in the royal library, where historians worked on state papers, archives, and other documents gathered from the entire country as early as the beginning of the Han period (206 B.C.–A.D. 220). That is why historiography, particularly the ''standard histories'' each dynasty compiled of its predecessor, occupied a position next in importance to the classics in traditional Chinese learning. There is no denying that most Chinese historians were government officials and therefore not free of their role as accessories to the state. Yet it should be recalled that history clearly distinguished itself from politics and administration, standing as the basis for judgment. It is thus due to Kong-zi's idea of history that China led the world in producing and preserving historical writings; it is also a large part of the reason that China produced fewer works of metahistory. However, it should be recalled that Chinese historiography had already produced by the eighth century A.D. an extended discussion on historical knowledge and historical method, the *Shi-tong* of Liu zhi-ji (A.D. 66–721), which discusses selection and criticism of materials, historical judgment and objectivity, historical causality, and so on. Although this necessarily led Liu to criticise Kong-zi, it was a constant companion of the Chinese historian until the nineteenth century, and it gave rise to the metahistorical traditions of Chinese historiography in the Qing dynasty (1644–1911; see Zheng Qiao; Zhang Xue-cheng). The modernization of Chinese historiography after the nineteenth century was, in a way, an emancipation from the world of Kong-zi: it was when the classics began to be read as ancient records rather than as classics and the object of historical study expanded from *historia rerum gestarum* to *res gestae*. It was an indication of the dawn of modern historical scholarship in China and East Asia, a process in which the introduction of Western learning played a crucial role. Yet it is the thought of Kong-zi that enabled China to lead the world in the art of historical writing, although in a way very different from the historiography of the Western tradition.

Bibliography: F. S. Couvroeur, trans., *Tch'ouen T'siou et Tso Tchouan*, 3 vols. (?1914); Herlee G. Creel, *Confucius, the Man and the Myth* (?1949), reprinted as *Confucius and the Way* (? 1960); W. Theodore de Bary, Wing-tsit Chan, and Burton Watson, comps., *Sources of Chinese Tradition* (?1960); James Legge, trans., *The Chinese Classics*, 2d ed., 5 vols., (?1893–1895; repr. Hong Kong, 1960); Bernard Karlgren, trans., *The Book of Documents* (?1950); George A. Kennedy, ''Interpretation of the *Ch'un-ch'iu*,''

Journal of the American Oriental Society 62 (1942): 40–48; Harold Hakwon Sunoo, *China of Confucius: A Critical Interpretation* (?1985); Arthur Waley, trans., *The Analects of Confucius* (?1937); R. Wilhelm, *Kung-tse, Leben und Werk* (?1956).

Masayuki Sato

LIU Zhi-ji (Pen-cheng, Xu-zhou in the Tang, now Xu-zhou, A.D. 661–Anzhou, now Anlu, Hubei, A.D. 721), famous Chinese historian. Liu arrived in Changan, the capital, in A.D. 669 and passed the state literary examinations, which governed entrance into the civil service, in 680, receiving the *jin-shi* degree. He then embarked on a career as a civil servant, serving in a provincial post for nearly twenty years while also pursuing his interest in history. He returned to the capital in A.D. 699 under princely patronage and assisted in the compilation of the *San-jiao ju-ying* (Gems and Blossoms of The Three Doctrines), an encyclopedia of Buddhism, Taoism, and Confucianism. In A.D. 701 he was appointed to the staff of the History Office and took part in writing official histories, daily records of the emperor, and veritable records. But he was dissatisfied with the compiling system of the office, so he resigned in A.D. 708 and compiled his *Shi Tong* (The Comprehensive Historiography) to express his own views on historiography. He was promoted or demoted at times thereafter, but he kept on writing history. Liu wrote many books and essays, but except for some essays, poems, and prose poems (*fu*), *Shi Tong* is his only surviving work representing his accomplishment in historiography. He compiled this work for more than ten years. After completion it was still to be revised by him. *Shi Tong* is the first work that systematically sums up Chinese historiography; it consists of twenty volumes and is divided into the parts of *nei-pian* and *wai-pian*. Because some of them were already lost in circulation, the present *Shi Tong* contains thirty-six sections in ten volumes of *nei-pian* and thirteen sections in ten volumes of *wai-pian*. In *nei-pian*, the first four volumes deal with historical forms and styles, the next two volumes with methods of historical compilation and the arts of expression, volumes seven and eight with historical views, and volumes nine and ten with general comments and miscellaneous subjects. In the *wai-pian*, the first two volumes deal with the development of ancient historiography, the two middle volumes express Liu's doubts about the Confucian sages and classics, and the last six volumes deal by and large with historical views and also refer to the methods and skills needed in compiling histories. Liu summed up the development of historiography of the feudal society of China, referring to the purposes of writing history, historical outlooks, historical thoughts, the self-cultivation of historians, the methods and systems of writing history, the compilation of histories, the styles of history, and the origins of historiography.

First, *Shi Tong* claims that the role of historiography is not only to exhort good and punish evil but also to serve as a means for governing the country. Second, *Shi Tong* displays a progressive historical outlook and criticizes the theological superstition that had penetrated into the historical sphere since the third century A.D. as "deceiving, absurd" ideas. The rise and fall of dynasties and the successes and failures of the people are not determined by Heaven's mandate, Liu argued, but by"human affairs." History is not static, because situations cause it to change. Third, Liu proposed that the fundamental principle of compiling histories and the basic quality of a historian should be "frankness and honesty." Fourth, a historian must possess the qualities of *shi-cai, shi-xue*, and *shi-shi*. *Shi-cai* means the ability to select, discriminate, and organize the historical data. *Shi-xue* means the historical data, historical knowledge and other learnings grasped by a historian. *Shi-shi* means the historical views and opinions of a historian. Of the three, *shi-shi* is the most difficult to be attained. Fifth, it describes the writing of histories before the Tang and analyzes their orgins, styles and categories. It divides historical works into dynastic histories and other histories. The origins of dynastic histories are in turn divided into "six schools," and the forms into "two styles," the style of chronicles and the style of biographies. At the same time, *Shi Tong* makes systematic generalizations and comments on the different parts of the historical works of the biographical style, so the compilation of biographical works became more standard and meticulous. The miscellaneous histories are also divided into ten classes, according to their contents. Finally, *Shi Tong* sets forth the system of the official compilers and their establishment and development, admitting the importance of establishing historical bureaus but also pointing out their shortcomings. Liu's historical outlook was clearly connected with his views on historiography. He regarded the purpose of writing history and historical outlook as the basic starting points, so his views were more advanced than the theories of earlier feudal historians. But he did not touch upon feudal ethics in historiography, so his historical outlook still contained elements of conservatism. Consequently, there must be contradictions in his comments on historiography. For example, he criticized Si-ma Qian's (q.v.) biography of Chen She in the *Shi-ji* and approved of Ban Gu's (q.v.) criticism of "She jia" (noble families). There are numerous studies and commentaries on the *Shi Tong*, among which *Shi-tong tong shi* (Comprehensive Commentary on *Shi Tong*, 1752) by Pu Qi-long, a Qing scholar, incorporates previous studies, and is now the standard text.

Bibliography: Byongik Koh, "Zur Werttheorie in der chinesischen Historiographie auf Grand des Shih-t'ung des Liu Chih-chi (661–721)," *Oriens Extremus* 4 (1957): 5–51, 125–181; Fu Jenlun, *Liu Zhiji nianpu* (Chronological Biography of Liu Zhiji) (Beijing, 1963); Guy Gagnon, *Concordance combinée du Shitong et du Shitong xiaofan*, 2 vols. (Travauz d'index, du bibliographie et de documentation sinologiques publiés par l'Institut des Hautes Etudes Chinoises College de France), vol. 7 (Paris, 1977); Williams Hung, "A T'ang Historiographer's Letter," *Harvard Journal of Asiatic Studies* 29 (1969): 88–163; Tsuneo Masui, "Liu Chih-chi and the *Shih-t'ung*," *The Memoirs of the Toyo Bunko* 34 (1976): 113–162; E. G. Pulleyblank, "Chinese Historical Criticism: Liu Chih-chi and Ssu-ma Kuang," in W. G. Beasley and E. G. Pulleyblank, eds., *Historians of China and Japan* (Oxford, 1961): 134–151; Yin Da, ed., *Zhong-guo shi-xue fa-zhan-shi* (History of The Development of Chinese Historiography) (Henan, China, 1985).

Xie Bao-cheng

MA Duan-lin (Le-ping of Raozhou, now Le-ping of Kiangsi, 1254–? 1323), Chinese historian. Ma Duan-lin's *Wen-xian tong-kao* (Comprehensive Survey of Historical Resources) in 348 volumes is a monument of historiography in medieval China. After the overthrow of the Song dynasty by the Yuan in 1279, he declined any government official post but taught and directed academies such as Ci-hu and Keshan and became an instructor at Taizhou. About age thirty, he began to compile his *Wen-xian tong-kao*, completing it after more than twenty years' work. The *Wen-xian tong-kao* is among the most influential of works after *Tong-dian* of Du You (q.v.) in the Tang dynasty and *Tong-zhi* of Zheng Qiao (q.v.) in the Song dynasty, narrating and studying the historical developments of the decrees, regulations, and institutions from ancient times to A.D. 1224. The *Tong-kao* has twenty-four sections, of which eight on taxation and coins treat economics, three on feudal election and academic schools treat government structure and selection of officials; and four on *Li* and *Yue* (rites and music, a euphemism for proper government) treat feudal ceremonies in relation to social strata. Two sections treat the armed forces and the penal system, and a large section of seventy-six volumes on *Jing-Ji* discusses ancient books and records, attempting to resolve questions of their existence. Two sections on imperial and feudal genealogies cover imperial reigns and the organization of the state. The remaining four sections treat celestial phenomena, natural disasters, geography, and the minority nationalities. Whereas the *Tong-dian* mainly discusses economic and political institutions, *Wen-xian tong-kao* pays attention to culture and the organization of the feudal state. The latter has a wider scope, showing clearly a cross-section of feudal China. Ma Duan-lin carried forward the best traditions of the ancient Chinese historians. First, like Du You, he stressed material factors in a scientific way, putting emphasis first on the study of economic institutions. Next, he greatly minimized attention to *Li* but had fine sections on *Jing-ji* and the like, which are not covered in *Tong-dian*. He thought highly of the achievements of earlier historians but was not bound by conventions like Du You and Zheng Qiao; he stood against the superstitious theory of the five elements, which he considered sheer nonsense. But he did recognize that some things in nature are difficult to explain. Notwithstanding the mixture of strained interpretations and far-fetched analogies in the ancient records, Ma still preserved these materials, thus revealing his objective attitude toward natural history. Like Du You, Ma held that history must be an authentic and objective record. He opposed passing arbitrary judgement on historians, since tendentious records can hardly reproduce historical realities. Yet he greatly advanced the traditional method of generalization through the ages, initiated by Si-ma Qian (q.v.), in the study of history. Yet Ma has his own characteristics; that is, he paid attention not only to the totality of historical developments but also to historical stages. *Wen-xian tong-kao* drew its materials from the ancient classics and histories and commented on former ministers and scholars. Ma referred to the former as *Wen* (writings) and to the latter as *xian* (documents), and thus his work was titled as *Wen-xian tong-kao*.

Bibliography: Bai Shou-yi, *Ma Duan-lin's Historical Thoughts, in Xue-bu-ji* (Beijing, 1978); Ssu-yu Teng and Knight Biggerstaff, *An Annotated Bibliography of Chinese Reference Works, Revised* (Cambridge, Mass., 1950), pp. 150–151.

Cui Wen-yin

OU-YANG Xiu (Yong-feng, Ji-zhou in the Northern Song, now Yong-feng Jiangxi, 1007–Ying-zhou, now Fu-yang, Anhui, 1072), Chinese official, poet, essayist, philosopher, and historian. A child prodigy, Ou-Yang received the *jin-shi* degree, the highest degree, at the age of twenty-four and immediately began his official career. He was well known for his literary talents and also as a daring and upright official and scholar, with the courage to initiate reforms. In 1043 he was appointed to the Censorate and supported the prime minister Fan Zhong-yan (989–1052) in starting a major political reform movement. After the failure of the reforms, he was demoted to a local post for ten years. He returned to the capital in 1054 and was assigned to several official posts, from the Hanlin Academy to political positions in government. Ou-yang spoke and acted for the benefit of the country and people, so he accomplished many things in his posts. He wrote prodigiously, but two of his works are especially important. One is the *Xin Tang Shu* (New History of The Tang Dynasty) of which he was the chief compiler. This official dynastic history was completed in 1060, recording in 225 volumes the 290-year history of the Tang dynasty (A.D. 618–907). The *Xin Wu-dai-shi* (New History of The Five Dynasties) in 74 volumes records the histories of five dynasties—Liang, later Tang, Jin, Han, and Zhou—that rose and fell in the decades of disunity (A.D. 907–960) separating the Tang from the Song dynasty. The *Xin Wu-dai-shi* records a wide range of historical material about politics, military affairs, the economy, culture, national minorities, and foreign countries. Ou-yang paid great attention to the collection of historical data (including documents and relics). His *Xin Tang Shu* was written on the basis of *Jiu Tang shu* (History of The Tang Dynasty), completed in A.D. 945, but made many important supplements to the history of the Tang, especially the waning years of the dynasty. The *bing-zhi* (monograph on military matters), for example, is one of Ou-yang's innovations. The biographies of late Tang personalities such as Huang Chao (?-A.D. 884) were more vivid and thorough in *Xin Tang Shu* than in *Jiu Tang shu*. Ou-yang also added valuable historical tables absent from the previous historical works, and he thus restored and developed the traditional historiographical style. He paid special attention to the veracity of historical records, arguing that history "should not conceal the truth." He also corrected distortions and omissions of the historical truth about certain dynasties and personalities. He plainly criticized the theological superstitious ideas found in earlier histories. From ancient times, many historians had regarded Heaven as the supreme force controlling nature and human society and had believed that human activities were determined by Heaven's will. But Ou-yang maintained that Heaven was merely an objective existence, not the supreme force that commanded everything. He proposed that "it is man, not Heaven, that brings order from disorder,'' and he argued that ''human affairs'' are the dominant factor in political activities.

In the *Xin Tang Shu* monographs dealing with the Five Elements and astronomy and the *Xin Wu-dai-shi* monograph on astronomy, he discriminated between natural phenomena, such as eclipses, earthquakes, and the appearance of curious animals, and the fortunes and misfortunes of social phenomena; he therefore eliminated from his histories records that associated natural phenomena with social phenomena. Based on this understanding, he said that ''a country will be strong and prosperous if it implements benevolent rule; if, on the contrary, it does not, it will fail.'' The rise and fall of a country has nothing to do with ''Heaven's mandate'' or ''good or bad omens.'' He also opposed the superstitious ideas of Buddhism and Taoism and the extravagent customs of building temples and worshipping gods, thus expressing his inclination toward materialist atheism. Ou-yang made important contributions to the ancient Chinese historiography and also deeply influenced the later generations.

Bibliography: James T. C. Liu, *Ou-yang Hsiu: An Eleventh-Century Neo-Confucianist* (Stanford, Calif., 1967).

Chen Guang-chong

QIAN Da-xin (Jia-ding, Jiangsu, 1728–Suzhou, Jiangsu, 1804), Chinese official and historian. Qian was an outstanding student, earning the *xiu-cai* degree at the exceptionally young age of fifteen. He began his teaching career at seventeen as a tutor and continued his studies in his employer's private library. It was there that he first became familiar with the new school of historical scholarship known as *kao-ju* (search for evidence), laying the foundations for his later work as a historian. In 1749 he was invited to study at the Zi-yang Academy in Suzhou, and in 1751 he was one of six successful competitors in a special examination held at Nanjing on the occasion of an imperial tour of the South. Called to the capital in 1752, he passed the metropolitan and palace examinations, attaining the *jin-shi*, the highest degree. While in the capital, he also studied mathematics. From 1752 until 1775, when he was forty-seven, he held a series of posts in central government, principally in the departments of culture and education, where he was frequently called on to serve as editor of officially sponsored histories and gazetteers, as a cartographer on the Imperial Board of Astronomy, and as a teacher and official examiner. Thus even in his bureaucratic capacity, he never abandoned study of the Confucian classics and history. On the pretext of staying home for the funeral of a parent, he resigned his posts in 1775 and began to teach in the academies of Zhong-shan in Nanjing, Zon-dong in Suzhou, and Zi-yang in Jiangsu. He was the first, during the reigns of the Qianlong (1736–1796) and Jiaqing (1796–1821) emperors, to apply the method of textual criticism *(kao-cheng)* of the Confucian classics to the study of history, further enhancing his reputation for erudition, prudence, and impartiality. He finished his most important work, *Nian-er-shi-kao-yi* (Verification of the Text of the Twenty-two Histories), in 1782, in which he examined and corrected the characters and language, dates and places, genealogies and institutions, in the texts of the twenty-two official dynastic histories. The *Verification* enabled later generations of scholars to pursue further study on the basis of more reliable historical records. For example, Qian demonstrated that the account in "Huo zhi lie-zhuan" in Si-ma Qian's (q.v.) *Shi Ji* is erroneous, for it was impossible that Bai Gui applied Shang Yang's methods of production management since, as Qian properly pointed out, Bai Gui was a contemporary of Marquis Wen of the state of Wei, and yet Shang Yang started his reform twenty-five years after Wen's death. Another of Qian's works, a collection of his reading notes, *Shi-jia zhai-yang xin-lu*, was completed in 1799 and included most of his appraisals of the histories and historical figures, as well as expositions of scholarship methodology. He recommended the practical and realistic study of history, holding that historical textual criticism must be based on facts and that historical texts must be verified as thoroughly as possible. He confirmed historical records by reference to the Confucian classics, official and unofficial histories, and anecdotes. He also verified the historical documents by use of epigraphy and archaeological discoveries. All of them would later inspire Wang Guo-wei to develop the method he called "twofold evidences." Qian was especially interested in the study of the history of the Yuan dynasty, like the Qing, a conquest dynasty from the north, because he believed that knowledge of the Yuan might be conducive to a better understanding of the Qing dynasty. He aspired to recompile the history of the Yuan, but he only completed the *Yi-wen-zhi* (Bibliography of [Yuan] Belles Lettres) and *Shi-zu-biao* (Guide to [Mongol] Clan and Family Names), leaving a draft history (Yuan-shi-kao) in manuscript. His other papers were collected and edited by his son Qian Dong-bi and his students under the title *Qian Yan-tang wen-ji*.

Bibliography: Arkhimandrit Palladii, trans., "Si iu tsi ili opisanie puteshestviia na Zapad," in *Trudy chlenov Rosiiskoi dukhovnoi missii v Pekinie*, vol. 4. (St. Petersburg, 1866), pp. 259–434; Tu Lien-che, "Ch'ien Ta-hsin" (Qian Daxin), in Arthur W. Hummel, *Eminent Chinese of the Ch'ing Period* (Washington, D.C., 1943).

Zhang Cheng-zong

SI-MA Guang (Shaan-zhou, in the Northern Song, now Xia-xien in Shanxi, 1019–Bian-jing, now Kaifeng, Henan, 1086), one of the greatest Chinese historians and Confucian theorists. Si-ma received the *jin-shi* degree, the highest scholarly degree, at twenty and then began a long official career, assuming the office of prime minister in his old age. A man of profound knowledge, he was well versed in the classics, histories, music, calender, and astronomy. He wrote thirty-two major works in 886 volumes, but only sixteen titles in 557 volumes are extant. His major historical works are *Zi-zhi tong-jian* (hereafter, *Tong jian*; The Comprehensive Mirror for Aid in Government), *Ji-gu-lu* (A Chronicle of Ancient Practices), and *Su-shui ji-wen* (The Notes of Su-shui). Si-ma's *Tong jian* is his most important and widely influential work, establishing him as one of traditional China's most important and influential historians. The *Tong jian* served as a model for historians throughout East Asia for several centuries after Si-ma's death (see, for example, Hayashi Razan). He was deeply concerned that the large amount and variety of historical works created difficulties for rulers seeking to draw lessons from historical events and, consequently, was determined to write a brief and concise general history in chronological form. In 1066 the Song emperor Ying-zong ordered Si-ma to establish a bureau and select assistants for compiling "The Careers of The Emperors and Ministers of The Successive Dynasties." The following year, after the enthronement of the Shen-zong, the new emperor entitled this work *Zi-zhi tong-jian* and wrote a preface himself. The historical bureau was first established in Bian-jing but later moved to Lo-yang when Si-ma retired there because he had been at odds with Wang An-shi. Si-ma spent nineteen years with his assistants Liu Shu, Liu Ban, Fan Zu-yu, and others and finally completed the *Tong jian* in 1084. The compilation of the *Tong jian* was extremely careful, being divided into preparing the catalogue of events intended for inclusion, collecting data, and writing the manuscripts. It is a great chronicle modeled consciously on Zuo Qiu-ming's (q.v.) *Zuo Chuan*, covering the period from 403 B.C. to A.D. 959. It narrates the history of the rise and decline of sixteen dynasties over 1,362 years and is extremely rich in reliable materials. It includes dynastic histories, chronicles, biographies, unofficial histories, and miscellaneous data, even including material from some 330 novels. Since most of the sources cited in the *Tong jian* are no longer extant, it is of especially great historical value, even beyond its importance as a methodological model. In historiography, *Tong jian* concentrates more on recent periods and also pays special attention to the identification of historical truth; its narration is clear and comprehensive, its style careful and complete.

Si-ma's main purpose in writing *Tong jian* was to study thoroughly the cycles of order and chaos during the successive dynasties; hence he concentrated on "the rise and fall of the successive dynasties, as well as the people's joys and sorrows, taking the good and avoiding the bad" *(Tong jian)*. He did not believe that everything was determined by Heaven, nor did he believe in the Yin-yang and Five Elements theories. The doctrines of Buddhism and Taoism he dismissed as absurd, as they were no help in governing and stabilizing the country. He opposed making distinctions between "legitimate" and "usurper" dynasties in the manner proposed by his contemporary Ou-yang Xiu (1007–1072), because it would falsify history arbitrarily. Hence he narrated history more objectively and faithfully. Si-ma Guang was an orthodox feudal historian, and his *Tong jian* was written from a strongly Confucian viewpoint. This led *Tong jian* to advocate a historical outlook of heroism centered on emperors, princes, and high-ranking generals and ministers, to sustain people in their "proper places" in the hierarchy of feudal society, to favor the Confucian ideal of rule by rites, and to encourage restorationism and conservatism as against change and reform. But Si-ma Guang was still a great historian in the feudal era. After it was published, *Tong jian* revived the position of chronicles, which had been in low repute as a historical mode. *Xu zi-zhi tong-jian zhang bian* (Collected Data for a Sequel to The *Tong jian*) and *Xu zi-zhi tong-jian* (Sequel to The *Tong jian)*, written after the style of *Tong jian*, were published one after another. After publication of the *Tong-jian chi-shi ben-mo* (Topical Arrangement of The *Tong jian)* and Ju Xi's *Zi-zhi tong-jian gang-mo* (The Outline of The Comprehensive Mirror for Aid in Government), there appeared in China a new outline style for writing history. There are various commentaries and supplements of the *Tong jian* that make the study of *Tong jian* a special discipline, of which the most outstanding and influential example is the commentary by Hu San-sheng. Not long after the completion of *Tong jian*, Song Sheng-zong died, and the empress dowager, who opposed the reforms of Wang An-shi, assumed regency. Si-ma Guang was appointed prime minister. Within a year after he took the office, he abolished all reforms. Consequently, the Northern Song was weakened all the more. Si-ma Guang, though a giant among men of letters, was a political conservative.

Bibliography: Chen Qing-quan and Su Shuang-bi et al., eds., *Zhong-guo shi-xue-jia ping-zhuan* (Critical Biographies of Chinese Historians) (Henan, China, 1985); Rafe de Crespigny, *The Last of the Han* (Canberra, 1969), including translations of Chs. 58–68 of *Zi-zhi tong-jian*; Achilles Fang, trans., *The Chronicle of the Three Kingdoms*, 2 vols. (Cambridge, Mass., 1952, 1965), including translations of Chs. 69–78 of *Zi-zhi tong-jian* and analyses of its methodology; Otto Franke, "Das Tse Tschi T'ung Kien und das T'ung Kien Mu," *Sitzungsberichte der preussischen Akademie der Wissenschaften: philosophisch-Historische Klasse* (Berlin, 1930): 103–156; Liu Jie, *Zhong-guo shi-xue-shi gao* (A Draft History of Chinese Historiography) (Henan, China, 1982); E. G. Pulleyblank, "Chinese Historical Criticism: Liu Chih-chi and Ssu-ma Kuang," in W. G. Beasley and E. G. Pulleyblank, eds., *Historians of China and Japan* (Oxford, 1961) pp. 151–166.

Zhuang Zhao

SI-MA Qian (Long-men, Xia-gang district in the Han dynasty, now Han-cheng, Shanxi province, 145 B.C.–? ? B.C.), the greatest Chinese historian and writer in the Han and also one of the few great historians in the world. At twenty Si-ma Qian visited the Middle and Lower Yangtze and some places in present Shandong and Henan. As a senior secretary and attendant of the emperor, Si-ma had visited Si-chuan and Western Yunnan and had inspected many places in Northwest China. In 108 B.C. he succeeded his father as the *Tai-shi-ling* (grand historian) and thus had the opportunity to read widely in the vast imperial and libraries' archives. In 104 B.C., after taking part in the work of revising the calendar ordered by the court, he spared no effort to write history to carry out his father's will. In 98 B.C. Si-ma was castrated as punishment for offending the emperor, but he became *Tai-shi-ling* again after being released from jail. He endured this ruthless insult and continued his unfinished work, finally completing his historical work *Tai-shi-gong-shu* (The Book of The Grand Historian), which is also called *Shi Ji* (The Historical Records). This work consists of 130 volumes and more than 520,000 words. Intended as a record of all human history, it starts with the Huang-di dynasty and continues through the Xia, Shang, and Zhou dynasties; the Spring and Autumn *(Chun-qiu)* and Warring States periods;

the Qin dynasty; and Si-ma's own era, the Han dynasty, to the reign of the emperor Wu-di, recording historical events over more than three thousand years. It covers regions far beyond the bounds of Chinese territory, referring to Central Asia, South Asia, and many countries to the east. This was the first time that Chinese knowledge about time and space was applied to the records of history. In this sense, it is China's first world history. *Shi Ji* is rich in historical materials and preserves many valuable documents. It served for two millennia as a model of historical method and organization not only in China but also in Korea (see Kim Pu-sik's [q.v.] *Samguk sagi)* and elsewhere in the Confucian world. Various aspects of the lives and activities of people of various social strata are fully reflected in this work.

Si-ma Qian's originality can be seen in the organization of the *Shi Ji*. It consists of five parts: "Ben chi" (annals, twelve volumes), "Biao" (tables, ten volumes), "Shu" (treaties, eight volumes), "Shi-jia" (noble houses, thirty volumes), and "Lie-chuan" (memoirs, seventy volumes). "Ben chi," or imperial annals, focuses on key figures who influenced events in order to narrate the important political affairs in China. "Biao," or tables, narrates the main events of the successive dynasties chronologically and systematically but concentrates on the main points. "Shu" provides the special records on development of institutions. "Shi jia," using both methods of writing chronicles and biographies, records feudal states, nobles, and events and personalities exerting great influence on society. "Lie-chuan" consists mainly of biographies of the famous personalities but also includes some special articles on national minorities and events in neighboring countries. These five forms of narration, supplementing one another, constitute an integral system that offers a fuller image of the social history of the time. The texts are vivid, the persons described distinctive. *Shi Ji* is also one of the important works in the history of world literature. The author's outlook on history and life can be seen clearly in his comments on historiography in the *Shi Ji* and in a letter to his friend Ren An. He said that his main purpose in writing the *Shi Ji* was to propose his own idea on the principles underlying the rise and fall of successive dynasties by using the materials in his possession and identifying as well as possible the historical truth.

Si-ma's main approach was the relation between Heaven's will and the history of society and the changes of history from the past to the present. He criticized the contemporary view that Heaven determined everything and believed that human history was not a mixture of heavenly and human affairs. The testing of the individual and historical events and developments were not determined fundamentally by Heaven. The personal interests of individuals were the axes around which the whole society revolved. No forces could thwart individuals in their search for spiritual and material livelihood, no matter what changes took place in history. The relation between the commanding and the commanded was determined by the amount of property the individuals possessed. The individual's thinking and ethical value were dependent on his own economic position. Historical changes followed a clear process from emergence to development to sudden change. Everything developed toward its own opposite. In explaining the causes of "changes from the past to the present," Si-ma sometimes emphasized analyzing the "situation" and "military strength," sometimes personal popularity and strategy, but frequently he linked these factors with economic ones. On the whole, his outlook on history is the outlook of naive materialism. Si-ma and his *Shi Ji* have exerted much influence on historiography and literature of later generations, both in China and throughout East Asia. Even those who were opposed to his views had to admit that the *Shi Ji* was a "veritable record," and the "lie-chuan" style became the model for biographical writing. The style adopted by the *Shi Ji* was later called the biographical style and became the main form for writing and compiling histories. All "official histories" adopted this form without exception. There are several commentaries on the *Shi Ji*, of which *Shi-ji ji-jie* (The Collected Commentaries of *Shi Ji*) by Pei Yin in the Southern Song dynasty, *Shi-ji suo-yin* (Index to the *Shi Ji*)), and *Shi Ji* *** (The Correct Explanations of Shi Ji) are called the "Three commentaries."

Bibliography: Bai Shou-yi, "*Si-ma Qian yu Ban Gu*" (Si-ma Qian and Ban Gu), *Beijing Shi-fan da-xue* (The Bulletin of Beijing Teachers University), no. 4. (1963); Hou Wai-lu, "Ssuma Chion: Great Ancient Historian," *People's China* 12 (June 16, 1956): 36–40; A.F.P. Hulsewé, "Notes on the Historiography of the Han Period," in W. G. Beasley and E. G. Pulleyblank, eds., *Historians of China and Japan* (New York, 1961), pp. 31–43; F. Jäger, "Der heutige Stand der *Shi-ki*-Forschung," *Asia Major* 9 (1933): 21–37; Si-ma Qian, *Les mémoires historiques de Se-ma Ts'ien*, trans. Edouard Chavannes (Paris, 1898); Si-ma Qian (Syma Tsian), *Istoricheskie zapiski*, vol. 1, trans. R. V. Viatkin and V. S. Taskin; gen. ed. R. V. Viatkin; intro. by M. V. Kriukov (Moscow, 1972); idem, *Records of the Grand Historian*, 2 vols., trans. Burton Watson (New York, 1961); Wang Guo-wei, "*Tai-shi-gong xing-nian-kao*" (The Life of Tai-shi-gong), *Guan-tang*, Ji-lin; Burton Watson. *Ssu-ma Ch'ien: Grand Historian of China* (New York, 1958); Yi Da, ed., *Zhong-guo shi-xue fa-zhan-shi* (History of The Development of Chinese Historiography) (Henan, China, 1985.)

Lai Chang-yang

WANG Fuzhi (Hengyang Prefecture, Hunan, 1619–?1692). Chinese philosopher and historian. Wang lived during the dynastic turmoil and civil war of the late Ming and early Qing periods. In his youth he took part in the activities of progressive societies and passed requirements for the *ju-ren* degree in the provincial examination of 1642, only two years before the Qing conquest. After the fall of the Ming dynasty, he organized people to resist the Qing army in Hengshan but was defeated by the Qing forces. He continued to be active in the Ming loyalist resistance until 1650, when he acknowledged the futility of hoping to restore the dynasty. From then on, he spent the rest of his life as a recluse on the desolate hillside of Mt. Shichuan and devoted himself to scholarship and writing. His writings were posthumously edited and compiled into nearly four hundred volumes under the title *Chuan-shan i-shu* (Bequeathed Writings of Chuan-shan), "Chuan-shan" being one of Wang's pen names. His historical works, such as *Du Tong-jian lun* (Comments on Reading The *Zi-ji tong-jian*

[Comprehensive Mirror for Aid in Government of Si-ma Guang, q.v.]) and *Song lun* (Comments on The Song Dynasty). In these works Wang Fuzhi expounded his political and philosophical thought through a historical analysis and review. By doing so, he created a new style of historical research in which the historian not only records but also comments on and criticizes the past in relation to the present. In his writings on contemporary history, including *Yong-li shi-lu* (The Veritable Records of the Yong-li Reign), and *Tuo shi* (The History of Tuo), he defied the threat of literary inquisition under the early Qing government with his honest and frank recording of the historical facts of the Southern Ming and of the heroic deeds of Li Dingguo, Li Laihen, and others, the leaders of the armies of the peasant uprisings. His outstanding contribution is the unprecedentedly progressive historical outlook that he proclaimed in these works and in his other academic writings as well. Supported by his field investigations of the social customs and conventions of minority peoples and his study of ancient historical documents, he broke with the traditional superstition about the ancient history of Xia (legendary), Yin (1766?–1122 B.C.) and Zhou (1122–407 B.C.) dynasties by convincingly refuting both antiquarianism and various theories of historical cycles. He interpreted human history as an evolutionary process from the savage to the civilized and very properly compared the dukedoms of the Tang and the Xia, Yin and Zhou dynasties to the chieftains and tribes of his own times. He is famous for his pronouncement that our ancestors are "erect-walking beasts."

Wang carried on the idea of "historical tendency" found in works by Liu Zhi-ji (q.v.) and Liu Zonyuan and advanced the new concept that "historical rationality coexists with historical tendencies" to rebut the fallacy that "Providence/order/fate," "Divine power/Heaven's will," and "Confucian tradition/Moral orthodoxy" are the controlling forces of history. Thus he strongly affirmed that history has its own innate logic. He introduced a new concept claiming that the logic of history and the tendency of history are complementary and that "the logic of history is found in the necessity of historical tendency." In his ingenious analysis of historical facts, such as transformation of the lordship and enfeoffment system of the Zhou dynasty 1122–403 B.C. into the prefecture and county system of the Qin dynasty (221–207 B.C.) and Cao Cao's (d. 220 B.C.) unification of Northern China, he integrated historical necessity with historical rationality and concluded that "while historical tendency is dependent upon the times, historical logic is dependent upon the tendency" and that "the logic will change as the tide of events turns." He adopted the traditional category of "Heaven" as the symbol of the dominating forces in historical development while stressing that "Heaven exists only through close contact with the people." Thus he attributed Heaven to the united will of the people and was fully aware of the tremendous significance of the popular will in history. Besides, he never lacked originality in historical methodology. He held that the purpose of historical study lies in "interpreting the past and setting up models for the future." To him, history should be a mirror for humans, and historians should apply themselves vigorously to historical facts to acquire the model for better rule. He advocated maintaining a serious attitude toward historical study, "seeking calm and satisfaction in one's mind, seeking conformity with reason, and seeking relevance of application." The method of research should also be objective and realistic, any rashness and flippancy must be rigorously avoided, and the assessment or review of historical figures must not be confined to only a single event or deed but made part of an overall consideration of their times. Only in this way can a "fair and just history" be written. Wang Fu-zhi's view on historical study has now become a treasured intellectual heritage for progressive humanity.

Bibliography: S. H. Ch'i, "Wang Fu-chih," in Arthur W. Hummel, ed., *Eminent Chinese of the Ch'ing Period (1644–1912)* (Washington, D.C., 1943), pp. 817–819; Ian McMorran, "The Patriot and the Partisans: Wang Fu-chih's Involvement in the Politics of the Yung-li Court," in Jonathan D. Spence and John E. Wills, Jr., eds., *From Ming to Ch'ing: Conquest, Region, and Continuity in Seventeenth-Century China* (New Haven, 1979), pp. 133–166; idem, "Wang Fu-chih and the Neo-Confucian Tradition," in William T. de Bary, ed., *The Unfolding of Neo-Confucianism* (New York, 1975), pp. 413–467; Hou Wailu, *The Summary of Chuan Shan's Doctrine* (Hunan, China, 1982); S. Y. Teng, "Wang Fu-chih's Views on History and Historical Writing," *The Journal of Asian Studies*, 27, no.1 (1968): 111–123; "Wang Fu-chih," in Wm. Theodore de Bary et al., eds., *Sources of Chinese Tradition* (New York and London, 1960), pp. 597–606.

Xiao Jiefu

XUN Yue (Ying yang, Ying-chuan, now Xu-chang, Henan A.D. 148–Lo-vang, A.D. 209), Chinese historian. Xun was an official of the later Han dynasty who took the political line to help Cao Cao (d. A.D. 220) assist the weakening Han dynasty. He wrote *Shen jian* (A.D. 197), a five-chapter history of the Han dynasty, in an attempt to make the history of the dynasty serve as a mirror (*jian*), reflecting the past for the edification of current and future emperors. Thinking that the text of *Han Shu* by Ban Gu (q.v.) was too prolix to be readily grasped, Emperor Xian (reigned A.D. 190–220, the last emperor of the Han dynasty) ordered Xun to reedit it after the style of *Zuo Zhuan*. Xun compiled thirty volumes of *Han Ji*: two to set up formalities and rites; three to grasp the past and present; four to propagate merit; five to praise the wise and able. In the meantime, he pointed out its contents in sixteen respects, so *Han Ji* became the historical work of "reference" and "broadening knowledge" for the rulers. It provided historical lessons for rulers, concentrating mainly on two points, "to develop to the utmost the principles of government and the proper behavior of rulers and ministers". However, the work emphasizes Heaven's will and mandate, not only attributing natural disasters to Heaven's mandate but also advocating that even phenomena apparently created by human efforts and social conditions are caused by Heaven's mandate. Xun's main purpose was to assert the Han to be the only legitimate dynasty, determined by Heaven's mandate. *Han Ji* is an innovation in compiling chronicles. In recording important dated historical events and figures, it also rearranges those political events, personalities, and institutions as well as national minorities that are similar and relevant to the above-mentioned events and figures but undated or unfit to be categorized under different chronological entries, so as to enlarge the narration of chronicles. The comments of *Han Ji* on the Chinese ancient history also have influenced the writing of history, and by means of omitting, recording, supplementing, correcting, and commenting, *Han Ji* expresses the author's ideas on historiography. The innovation in compilation of *Han Ji* and the author's ideas have made the historical work's chronicle style and biographical style two of the major forms of Chinese ancient historiography that influenced the writing of chronicles in later generations.

Bibliography: Chi-yun Chen, *Hsün Yüeh* (A.D. *148–209): The Life and Reflections of an Early Medieval Confucian* (Cambridge, Eng., 1974); *Shen jian tong jian, Jong Fa Han Xue-Yan-jiu-so tong-jian cong-kan.* Vol. 8: comp. Centre franco-chinois d'etudes sinologiques (Paris, 1947), including a summary of the *Shen jian* in French.

Min Zhao-wen

YUAN Shu (Jian-an, Jian-zhou in the Southern Song, now Jian-ou, Fujian, 1131–? 1205), Chinese historian. Yuan started his official career at thirty-three, and devoted his entire life to the work of education and writing history. During the period of hostilities between the Song and Jin dynasties although full of royalism and patriotism and detesting the world and its ways, he was left out in the cold. He was appointed to teach in Yan-zhou (now Jian-de, Zhe-jiang), and during that period (1173–1176) he concentrated his political enthusiasm on writing history. He appreciated *Zi-zhi tong-jian* (The Comprehensive Mirror for Aid in Government; see Si-ma Guang), but he tired of its comprehensiveness, and arranged its contents according to the development of events. Each event was narrated in chronological order, and the major events occuring in the 1,362 years covered were classified into 239 topics. At last, he completed *Tong-jian ji-shi ben-mo* (Topical Arrangement of The Comprehensive Mirror) in forty-two volumes. This style guided "one to know its end after an event just occurred and to understand the omens of its development before it became clear," so "the words of this style are fewer than that of biographical style but its narration is broader than that of chronicle style" (*Tong-jian ji-shi ben-mo*). The *Tong-jian ji-shi ben-mo* is only half as long as the *Zi-zhi tong-jian*, but because Yuan Shu "arranged the topics according to the events and was not confined by the common rules," this work can hardly explain the relations between the contemporaneous historical events and narrate the whole historical development. Yuan's aim in writing this work was to provide a historical mirror for the rulers, and this is his unique contribution. He paid attention to the history of "turbulent times," especially to periods of disunion, and to disasters and chaos in "peaceful times." So he selected military and political topics and focused on the narration of the relationship with minority nationalities, peasant uprisings, and internal struggles within the ruling groups. He included only two topics concerning economics, and he completely neglected thought and culture. His style of writing also reflected his thinking on historiography, so this work was highly praised by the Song emperor Xiao-Zong (reigned 1163–1190), who said that the ways of government had all been included in this work and distributed many copies to the frontier commanders. Yuan initiated the topical style of arrangement in writing history. This style, the chronicle style, and the biographic style have become the three major styles of traditional Chinese historiography, which have exerted great influence on Chinese historiography in later generations. There are many later historical works with the title of "ji-shi ben-mo," modeled on Yuan's and narrating one or several events, so this style of historical writing developed considerably. In his late years, Yuan Shu studied *Yi-jing* (Book of Changes) and wrote *Yin-jing jie-yi* (Annotations of Book of Changes) and *Zhou-yi bian-yi* (Discrimination of Book of Changes).

Ye Tan

ZHANG Xue-cheng (Guiji, now Shaoxing, Zhejiang province, 1738–? 1801), noted Chinese historian. Zhang gave lectures in the academies of Ding-wu, Qing-zhang, and others and compiled numerous local chronicles and gazetteers, such as *He-zhou-zhi* and *Hubei-tong-zhi*, emphasizing especially the study of historical theories. In an age when the ideal of "Ji-gu-you-wen," investigating the past (the classics), and preferring the civil over the martial spirit dominated scholarship, and the historical world was flooded with official histories, Zhang declined to join the official historical bureau and contribute to the compilation of history. He also refused to follow the dominant school of so-called Han scholars, who indulged themselves in textual criticism or the empty talk of the "Song scholars" in order to pursue personal fame as learned scholars or experts in neo-Confucianism. He worked for several decades on his historio-theoretical monograph *Wen-shi-tong-yi* (General Survey of Literature and History, published in 1920 in Zhang's posthumous papers), in which he aimed both to rebut the bad style of study among the literati because of their *Wu-kao-suo* (indulging in textual criticism) and *Tang-kong-yan* (indulging in empty talk) and also to hold conservative officials up to ridicule. He emphasized making use of history in statecraft, denying the study of history only as an end in itself. He refused "to attend to the past to the neglect of the present, or to attend to Nature to the neglect of human affairs." He held the view that historians must integrate the past and the present and make the past serve the present. In his opinion the meaning of studying history is to get to the essence of things. It should not be just a record of events or an exercise in phrase mongering. Historians must not become mere textual researchers or literati, a trend prevalent in Zhang's day, but must grasp the idea of "the integration of events, writings and truth," and also the idea of "the integration of ways and implements." They must learn to discriminate and let narration present historical theories and viewpoints so that they can be unique in their historical writings. Zhang put forward an idea of *shi-de*, historical ethics, or the writers' good intentions, emphasizing that historians must take bearings between nature and human affairs, exhausting nature but adding little of their own feelings and wishes. Historians, in other words, must handle correctly the relationship between the subjective and the objective. They must value historical events without regard to their own inclinations, even though their pens are splendid and emotional. The subjective must conform to the objective. But Zhang's concept of *jing-shi* means maintaining feudal politics, his *ming-dao* means more or less to elaborate feudal ideology, and his *shi-de* never breaks away from traditional ethics. With respect to prose style in history, he urged conveying actuality through simplicity of style. He opposed showing off one's writing talents, demanding that writings must mirror events and historical personages and must be written realistically and vividly.

His historical theories were combined with practices polished through long years of compiling local gazetteers. The local gazetteers, chronicles, and histories already had a long tradition in China, but they forged rapidly ahead in the Qing dynasty. Yet scholars had been slow to develop a theory of local history. Gazetteers had been classified as geography until Zhang succeeded in reclassifying them as a branch of history. He stressed that local chronicles cover local histories, including all aspects of local politics, economics, culture, and customs. They may be written as complete, local historical annals, they may be handed down to posterity as local records, and the dynastic histories may draw materials from them. Moreover, he formulated new stylistic rules and layouts for the compilation of local chronicles and recommended ways to preserve local sources in good condition. His *Jiao-chou-gong-yi* (General Textual Criticism) is a major contribution in its field. He also compiled a *Shi-ji-kao* (Survey of Historical Sources) in more than three hundred volumes, but it did not survive.

Bibliography: P. Demieville, "Chang Hsueh-cheng and his Historiography," in W. G. Beasley and E. G. Pulleyblank, eds., *Historians of China and Japan* (New York, 1961), pp. 167–185; Hiromu Momose, "Chang Hsüeh-ch'eng," in Arthur W. Hummel, ed., *Eminent Chinese of the Ch'ing Period* (Washington, D.C., 1943); *History of The Development of The Chinese Historiography*, ed. Yin Da (Henan, China, 1985); David S. Nivison, *The Life and Thought of Chang Hsüeh-ch'eng (1738–1801)* (Stanford, Calif., 1966); Shih-chia Chu, "Chang Hsüeh-ch'eng: His Contributions to Chinese Local Historiography" (Ph. D. diss., Columbia University, 1950).

Shi Ding

ZHENG Qiao (Xing-hua, now Pu-tian County, Fujian, 1104–? 1162), Chinese historian. Zheng studied hard and made friends with country folk and elders, learning from them much practical knowledge. His academic interests were diverse; he studied subjects such as classics, rites, music, scripts, astronomy, geography, insects and fishes, plants, and textual criticism. After the end of the Northern Song dynasty (1126), Zheng presented a memorial to the throne expressing his determination to resist the Jin but did not receive any attention. He presented his works twice to Emperor Gao-zong of the Southern Song dynasty (reigned 1127–1162). Zheng wrote many books, but the only works that survive are *Tong Zhi* (Comprehensive Monographs, two-hundred volumes), *Jia-ji yi-gao* (Manuscripts Left by Zheng Qiao, three volumes), *Er-ya zhu* (Commentary on the *Er Ya*, three volumes), and *Shi-bian-wang* (Discrimination of Absurdity in Poetry), which was compiled later. *Tong Zhi* is the pinnacle of Zheng's lifetime of scholarly accomplishments. It is a general history in biographical style, in which the "twenty lue" (classifications) are the most important. Zheng emphasized the continuity of historical development. He said that thousands of rivers, although they flow in different directions, must finally flow into the great sea. Only in this way could China be spared from suffering the disaster of flood. "Thousands of foreign countries," although they develop in different ways, must link with the peoples of Middle Kingdom (China). Only in this way will the various distant places not suffer the miseries of isolation. "Linking" was too important to be ignored. He thought that Kong Zi (q.v.) (Confucius) and Sima Qian (q.v.) had conceived the idea of "linking" in writing histories. Zheng criticized Ban Gu (q.v.) for breaking the continuity and writing a history of the single dynasty of the former Han only, because this would ultimately lead to the loss of the idea of "linking" with adverse effects for the development of historiography in later generations. Scholars in the Han period, like Dong Zhongshu and Ban Gu, believed that the rise and fall of dynasties were determined by "Heaven's will." The cyclical order arranged by Heaven's will determined the dynastic cycle. Zheng rejected their beliefs as groundless nonsense. The natural phenomena had nothing to do with human fortunes, good or ill. The erroneous interpretation of natural phenomena as indicative of human affairs was a kind of *Yao xue* (weird learning). Zheng also maintained that the duty of the historian was to keep detailed record of historical events but not to make any praise or criticism of them. He rejected the common theory that every word in the histories contained an implication of either praise or criticism of its subject. Zheng held that history should have practical value and that the *Zhi* (monographs), a regular part of standard histories, should be especially carefully written. There should be illustrations and tales in a historical work. A historical work, no matter how carefully compiled, would be useless if were written without regard for its practical value; such a history Zheng likened to an eloquent housewife who could not do her household duties. Zheng also held that a historian should write his own achievements in order to make his work "distinctive"; the way of studying and making textual criticism of books, just like that of commanding an army, was to keep the work in good order and proper classification. This was the method of "classification" that he proposed.

Wu Huai-qi

ZHU Xi (Chu Hsi) (Yuqi, Fujian, 1130–Kaoting, Jianyang county, Fujian, 1200), Chinese philosopher. Zhu received the highest civil service examination degree, the *jin-shi*, in 1148 and assumed his first official post in 1151, but spent only nine years in active official service, mostly on the local level. In 1194 he became lecturer-in-waiting at court but was soon dismissed as part of a partisan political campaign conducted under the guise of an attack on "false learning." He died in disgrace but received the first of a series of posthumous honors in 1209. Subsequently, his version of Neo-Confucian philosophy became accepted as orthodox, and his commentaries on the *Four Books* were required reading for all civil service examination candidates until the examination system was abolished in 1905. He was responsible for establishing four texts: The *Lun Yu* (Analects); *Mencius*; *Da Xue* (The Great Learning); and *Zhong Yong* (The Doctrine of the Mean), as the core curriculum for the education of the elite. Although none of these books is a history and Zhu Xi was primarily a moral metaphysician and philosopher of self-cultivation, he lived in a period of heightened historical consciousness and was keenly concerned with history, both in the sense of the human past and of written accounts of that past. For Zhu the *li* (principle or pattern, singular or plural) that structure human events and physical reality, past and present, are timeless and are best grasped by studying the classics, repositories of eternal truth. Without prior comprehension of the *li*, the study of history is apt to lead men astray, as it had some contemporary utilitarians. At its most unhistorical this attitude is exemplified by the *Zi Zhi Tong Jian Gangmu* (1172) (Outline and Details of the Comprehensive Mirror for Aid in Government), a reworking of Si-ma Guang's masterpiece by Zhu's disciples according to rules he laid out but did not himself implement. This work, often attributed to Zhu Xi himself, became enormously influential not only in China and East Asia in general but also in Europe where its translation by J.A.M. de Moyriac de Maille (1669–1748) under the title *Histoire Generale de la Chine, ou Annales de cet Empire* (Paris, 1777–1783) helped perpetuate a moralizing, Neo-Confucian vision of Chinese history until Otto Franke demonstrated its shortcoming as history. Today most historians would agree with the Japanese scholar Ogyu Sorai (1666–1728) that the book's arguments are like "the application of a rubber stamp." More highly regarded is Zhu Xi's *Bachao mingzhen yanxing lu* (1172) (Words and Deeds of Eminent Ministers of Eight Courts), a collection of anecdotes about Northern Song statesmen although the principles for selection are unclear. Zhu provided accounts of his immediate intellectual predecessors in another book, the *I-Lo yuan-yuan lu* (1173) (Records of the Origins of the School of the Two Chengs). These and other writings demonstrate his conviction that history is made by men; but for his further ideas on history reference must be made to his recorded conversations (*Yu-lei*) as well as letters and other not strictly "historical writings" included in his collected writings (*Wenji*). Here his views on specific historical personages and policies are often quite critical, nuanced and judicious, and his practical recommendations are often informed by history. Zhu Xi does not have a fully articulated philosophy of history, convinced that the accurate historical record can speak for itself, and that what it says will have moral significance: "Confucius [in compiling the *Chunqiu* (Spring and Autumn Annals)] simply described things as they were, and right and wrong became apparent of themselves." Underlying this position is the Neo-Confucian view that principle (*li*) is both descriptive and prescriptive. However, in actual life, past and present, right and wrong are not self-evident. Men fail to apprehend what is right because in human beings, as in all things, the *li* never appears apart from *qi*, the material energy which in all but sages obstructs principle. Unfortunately, sagely wisdom has been absent from the world since high antiquity and its attainment has become ever more difficult, though by no means impossible, because of the long-term deterioration of *qi*. Without such wisdom, even the greatest leaders were unable to regain the perfection of high antiquity when the world was ruled by sages. Thus Zhu faulted even the founders of the great dynasties, the Han, Tang, as well as his own Song for having overcompensated for the defects of their predecessors. Thus he holds that the Song founders, aware of the ultimately fatal Tang decentralization, had gone too far in the opposite direction. If this is an essentially pessimistic outlook on history, it should also be noted that Zhu has his optimistic side, for sagehood remains distinctly attainable. There is also a strong note of optimism in his claim that his own immediate predecessors had repossessed the *Dao*, the Way, lost ever since the death of Mencius more than a thousand years earlier.

Bibliography: Wing-tsit Chan, ed. *Chu Hsi and Neo-Confucianism*, Honolulu, 1986; Ch'ien Mu, *Zhuzi xin xuean*, 5 vols., Taipei, 1971; Otto Franke, "*Das Tse tschi t'ung kien* und das *T'ung kien kang mu* ihr Wesen, ihr Verhältnis zueinander und ihr Quellenwqert," *Siytzungsberichte der Preussischen Akademie der Wissenschaften. Phil.-Hist. Kl* (1930): 103–144; Yves Hervouet, *A Sung Bibliography*, Hong Kong, 1978; Miura Kunio, *Shushi*, Tokyo, 1979.

Conrad Schirokauer

ZUO Qiu-ming (the *gu-meng*) (Lu, fifth-sixth centuries B.C.), blind official historian, perhaps master of oral lore, living a little earlier than Confucius (see Kong-zi); author of the ancient Chinese annals and literary work *Zuo-shi Chun-qiu*, or *Zuo Chuan* (Zuo's Commentary on The Spring and Autumn Annals). Chinese historiography was in its embryonic stages in the Eastern Zhou dynasty (also known as the Chun-qiu, or Spring and Autumn period, 722–481 B.C.), when the *Chun qiu* (The Spring and Autumn Annals, attributed traditionally to Kong-zi) was compiled by official historians; it dealt chronologically with major events from 723 to 497 B.C. The events were supplemented with vivid stories told by the *gu-meng* and with legends of extreme antiquity. These stories from the oral tradition enriched and supplemented the written records, creating a vivid work of history. What Zuo despised were exaggeration, obsequious flattering, and hiding one's hatred in order to pretend to be friendly. When listening to Zuo's narratives, Confucius was deeply impressed and fully agreed with Zuo's evaluation of leading historical figures. This shows that Zuo was a brilliant historian, whom Confucius himself recognized, and also the first historian to leave a large number of stories taken from oral tradition. But there has been a continuing controversy during the past two millennia as to the connections between *Chun-qiu* and *Zuo Chuan*. Current opinion suggests that *Chun-qiu* was the original record written by official historians of the time but that its contents were very brief, just outlines of events. These outlines had to be supplemented by the narratives of the *gu-meng*, among whom Zuo was the most prominent. Later-recorded contents told by the *gu-meng* are called *Yu* (Discourses). It is said that Zuo's *Guo yu* (The Discourse on The States) is one of these discourses.

The *Chun-qiu* and *Yu* became part of the standard Confucian curriculum. Zi Xia, a student of Confucius, who taught in the fifth century B.C. in the state of Wei, was a famous master in teaching *Chiu-qiu*. During the fourth century B.C., the Confucianists in Wei, taking *Chun-qiu* as their guide and *Yu* and other historical documents as their basis, compiled this earliest and most comprehensive ancient history of China, *Zuo-shi Chun-qiu*. Judging from its contents, it is most likely that the work was completed more than a hundred years after the death of Confucius and could not have been written by Zuo himself, who lived earlier than Confucius. It's main contents, however, must be the historical events narrated by Zuo. For this reason, this work bears his name as its title in accord with the tradition of ancient Chinese works.

Zuo-shi Chun-qiu records the important historical events in the Spring and Autumn period (722–481 B.C.) and earlier legends. It is an important work for studying ancient Chinese culture; it already displays the embryo of later Chinese rationalism. It states that "the people are the masters of Heaven, so the wise kings must take care of the people's affairs before worshipping Heaven." "The truth of Heaven is remote, but the people's affairs are very close; there is no connection between them." It emphasizes that kings should be faithful to their subjects and diligent in handling the national affairs. If they neglected their duties at the expense of the people's interests, they were doomed to fail. The kings of the state of Lu indulged themselves in luxuries and extravagances while the ministers of the state of Ji worked diligently for the national good generation after generation, so the people forgot the kings of Lu. "There is no fixed master in a state. The positions of king and ministers can be changed. It is a rule from ancient times." These were the characteristics of political thought at that time, which did not acknowledge any single autocratic monarch. "The kings regard their feudal princes as their subjects; the feudal princes regard their officials as their subjects; the officials regard the scholars as their subjects." Inferiors should obey their immediate superiors. If the scholars were loyal to the feudal princes against their officials, they were regarded as rebels.

Bibliography: Hsu Zhong-shu, "The Author of Zuo Chuan and the Date of Its Completion," *Historical Teaching*, no. 9 (1962); K.B.J. Karlgren, "The Early History of the Chou li and Tso chuan Texts," *Bulletin of the Museum of Far Eastern Antiquities* (Stockholm) 3 (1931): 1–59; idem, "On the Authenticity and Nature of the Tso chuan," *Göteborg Högskolas Arsskirift* 32, no. 3 (1926): 1–65; idem, *Zuo Zhuang zhen-wei kao*, trans. Lu Kan-ru (On The True or False of Zhu Chuan) (Xin-yue shu-dian, 1927); James Legge, trans., *The Chinese Classics*. Vol 5: *The Ch'un Ts'ew with the Tso Chuen* (Hong Kong, 1960); Henri Maspero, "La Composition et la Date du Tso tchuan,"in *Mélange Chinois et Bouddhiques, Institut Belge des Hautes Etudes Chinoises* 1 (1931–1932): 137–215.

Luo Shi-lie

Great Historians: Croatian

LUCIUS, Ivan (Croatian Lucić or Lučić, Italian Lucio) (Trogir, Dalmatia, 1604–Rome, 1679), historian. Descendant of an old noble family, Lucius started education in his native Trogir. He studied law in Padua and humanistic sciences in Rome and obtained doctoral degrees in both. In 1625 he returned to Trogir and took an active part in the city's communal affairs. In Rome Lucius became attracted to history and acquainted with the works of Cesare Baronius, Raynaldi, Ughelli, Mascardi, and other famous historians. Having returned to Dalmatia and being familiar with the both the Italian and Croatian languages, Lucius began research in the communal archives of Trogir and started collecting documents, charters, and statutes relevant to the history of Dalmatia. He engaged a team of researchers in Zadar, Split, and Rab. Supplied with a significant number of collected sources, he returned in 1654 to Rome where he lived and worked for the rest of his life. In Rome Lucius was appointed head of the College of St. Hieronimus and lived surrounded with prominent countrymen including the scholar Stjepan Gradić (Gradi, now Dubrovnik, 1613–Rome, 1683), the representative of Dubrovnik and the curator of the Vatican Library (from 1661). It was in 1657 that Lucius published the important contribution to Croatian history of the eleventh and twelfth centuries *Vita beati Ioannis episcopi Traguriensis*, about the bishop who administered the Trogir Church the reign of Croatian rulers Petar Krešimir, Slavac, Zvonimir, and Stjepan II. With additional sources collected in Rome, Lucius was able to enlarge and correct the draft already written in Trogir and to proceed to the final version of his major work *De regno Dalmatiae et Croatiae libri sex*. The manuscript was finished about 1661 and published in Amsterdam in 1666. The second edition appeared in the third volume of J. Schwandtner's *Scriptores rerum Hungaricarum, Dalmaticarum, Croaticarum et Slavonicarum ceteres ac genuint* (Vienna, 1748). Translated into Italian, it was published in Trieste in 1896. It included six volumes (*libri*) subdivided into chapters. The first volume dealt with the history of Roman provinces Illiricum and Dalmatia, followed in the second volume by the history of the coming Croats and Serbs and the formation and development of the Croation State. In the third volume Lucius described the joining of Croatia to Hungary and the Venetian penetration in Dalmatia. The fourth and the fifth volumes referred to the struggle of Venice and Hungary over Dalmatia and its joining to Venice. The last volume discussed the political life in Dalmatia and Croatia after they had lost their independence. The entire study is objective, realistic, and based on a cautious and critical use of documents. As a supplement to his major work, Lucius published in Venice, in 1673, *Joannis Lucii inscriptiones dalmaticae, notae et memoriale Pauli di Paulo, note ad Palladium Fuscum, addenda vel corrigenda in opere de regno Dalmatiae et Croatiae, variae lectiones chronici ungarici manuscripti cum editis*, which contained Roman and other inscriptions concerning Dalmatia. Collecting a large number of primary sources, Lucius was able to write the history of his native Trogir entitled *Memorie storiche di Tragurio, ora detto Trau* (1673), which described its history from the foundation until it came under Venetian rule. Preserved in its Italian translation, the study is also important for the history of Croatia. Lucius distinguished himself as the best Croatian historian of the epoch. He is accurate, analytical, and well informed. In that manner he represents the precursor of Croatian critical historiography. His work is still valid. Lucius saved for posterity a wealth of historical sources.

Bibliography: Ivan Kukuljević, Izvorna pisma Ivana Lučića, *Arkiv za povjestnicu jugoslavensku* (Zadar, 1899, 1900, 1904); Franjo Rački, *Povjestnik Ivan Lučić, Trogiranin*, vol. 4, Rad Jugoslavenske akademije znanosti i umjetnosti (Zagreb, 1879), pp. 65–102.

Dimitrije Djordjevic

ORBINI, Mavro (Dubrovnik, middle of the sixteenth century–Dubrovnik, 1611), historian of the South Slavs and of the city of Dubrovnik. Orbini was ordained in the Benedictine monastery in Mljet, of which he became abbot. After spending some time as abbot in Bacs (Hungary), he returned to Dubrovnik where he spent most of his life. In Dalmatia and Dubrovnik, humanism stimulated studies concerning the origins and history of the Slavs, as a response to pan-Romanism and pan-Germanism of Italian and German writers. Dubrovnik was close to the events that took place in its adjacent as well as larger Balkan hinterland. In its archives and libraries were stored manuscripts and charters. Orbini's predecessor, Vinko Pribojevic (middle fifteenth-middle sixteenth century), a Dominican who lived for three years in Cracow (Poland), published in 1532, in Venice, *De origine successibusque Slavorum* in which he stressed the greatness and unity of the Slavs. Attracted to the same idea, Orbini published in 1601, in Pesaro, his major work, *Il regno degli Slavi*, in which he glorified the antiquity, fame, and territorial expansion of the Slavs. An ardent Slavic patriot, impressed by the similarity of Slavic languages, Orbini equated, in the first part of his history, old legends with his pan-Slavic feelings and tried to prove the autochtonal origin of the Slavs. Thus he Slavicized the Illyrians and the Thracians as well as all of the Roman emperors born on the eastern side of the Adriatic. Orbini became the forerunner of later pan-Slavists. The second part of his history contains a general account of the South Slavic states until their fall under the Turks. It is based on more reliable sources. Orbini was the first to write Serbian history in its continuity and from a standpoint of a Westernized humanist. The city of Dubrovnik was especially dear to him, and that prompted his attempts to combine its history with the existing histories of Italian cities. Orbini based his study on a variety of sources (which are quoted at the beginning of his work) but largely relied on uncritically reproduced popular traditions, legends, and chronicles. However, Orbini's endeavors, inspired with warm patriotic feelings that blurred the historical accuracy, are more important for the impact thay had on further historiography and national awakening of the South Slavs than for the correctness of his statements. Charles du Cange (1610–1688), the founder of modern Byzantology, and Louis Fernand Marsigli (1658–1730) were acquainted with his writings. His history had great influence on Serbian and Croatian historians Sava Vladislavić (1660–1670?–1738), who translated Orbini's work into Russian in 1772, and Count Djordje Branković (q.v.) (1645–1711), Jovan Rajić (q.v.) (1726–1801), and Andrija Kačić Miošić (1704–1760). Orbini had an immense influence on Father Paisii (q.v.), the founder of Bulgarian historiography. When the Balkan peoples were enslaved and forgotten in the vast Ottoman Empire, Orbini's history opened new perspectives and encouragement, which were more important for the national revival than was its historical accuracy.

Bibliography: N. Radojčić, *Srpska istorija Mavra Orbinia* (Beograd, 1950); L. Rava, *Mavro Orbini, Primo storico dei popoli Slavi* (Bologna, 1913); R. Samardžić, "Mavro Orbini, Kraljevstvo Slovena u razvitku srpske istoriografije," in *Pisci srpske istorije*, vol. 1 (Beograd, 1976).

Dimitrije Djordjevic

VITEZOVIĆ, Ritter Pavao (Senj, Croatia, 1652–Vienna, 1713), historian, poet, printer, publisher, and lexicographer. Offspring on his father's side of a German family from Alsace and of a Croatian mother, he translated his last name Ritter into Croatian Vitezović. He studied grammar and rhetoric in a Jesuit school in Zagreb. After graduating, Vitezović traveled to Rome and several European countries, living as a scholar and researcher without a steady job. Most influential to his development were the two years he spent in Krain (Slovenia) in the library of Ivan Weikhard Valvazor (1641–1693). Valvazor, a polyhistor himself, was the author of *Die Ehre des Herzogthums Krain* (1689), a study in which he described the history, geography, and ethnography of his native land and its neighboring parts of Istria and Croatia. Collector of antiquities and historical sources, Valvazor was elected a member of the British Royal Society in London (1687). In Valvazor's library Vitezović learned the art of making copperplates and was stimulated in historical research. After returning to his native Senj (1679), he entered politics and was elected the city's deputy in the Diet of Sopron (Hungary) and representative at the imperial Court in Vienna, where he acted as *agens regni* on behalf of Croatian interests. This activity brought him the title of court councellor and baron. After several years of commuting between Vienna and Senj, Vitezović was appointed director of the newly founded Metropolitan Library and printing works in Zagreb. As an emissary of the Croatian estates, Vitezović became a member of the committee appointed to fix the frontiers between Venice and Turkey. Rewarded by Vienna with a land estate belonging to an insane canon from Zagreb, Vitezović met the opposition of the Croatian estates, was evicted from the estate, and was forced to flee to Vienna, where he died in poverty.

Among various scholarly activities, that of historian was the area in which Vitezović distinguished himself, and he wrote in both Latin and Croatian languages. Already in his first study in which he tried to prove the alleged noble origins of the Slovenian family Gušić (Gussich), published in 1681 in Ljubljana, Vitezović relied on historical sources. The didactic *Kronika aliti spomen vsega svieta vikov* (Chronicle or Recollection of All World's Centuries), published in 1696, dealt with Croatian history. In 1700 Vitezović published *Croatia rediviva* in which he tried to prove that the names Illyrian, Slavic, and Croatian are synonymous and that in fact all of the South Slavs are Croatians. He intended to produce a large encyclopedic work, *De aris et focis illyricorum*, and to offer a history of the South Slavs from prehistory until his time but was able to finish only the *Stemmatographia sive armorum illiricorum delineatio, descriptio et restitutio* (Vienna, 1701) in which he reproduced fifty-six coats of arms that, according to him, belonged to the Illyricum. The work was later translated into Serbo-Croatian by Hristifor Žefarović (end of seventeenth century–1753) and had a large influence on the national revival of the South Slavs. Vitezović also wrote a history of Serbia (*Serbia ilustrata*) but the manuscript was not published due to lack of money. In the study *Bosnia captiva*, published in 1712, Veitzović deplored the fate of Bosnia under Turkish rule and expressed the hope of its liberation. Concerned with the destiny of the South Slavic peoples who were partitioned under foreign rule, Vitezović assigned to Austria the role of their unifier and liberator. In *Plorantis Croatiae saecula duo* Vitezović described in verses the events and battles in Croatia during the sixteenth and seventeenth centuries. In the poem *Odiljenje sigetsko* (1684, The Resistance of Szigetvar) he described in hexametres the 1566 battle for the city. The *Banologia sive de banatu Croatiae* is preserved only in manuscript form. As a polyhistor, Vitezović was the author of two dictionaries (*Lexicon latino-illyricum* and *Lexicon illyrico-latinum*) of which only one manuscript was saved containing twenty-three thousand words. He also published calendars, epistles, and tracts. By his linguistic attempts to simplify the orthography and establish a literary language, as well as by his writing about Slavdom, Yugoslavdom, and Croatianism, Vitezović became the predecessor of Ljudevit Gaj (1809–1872) and the Illyrian movement in Croatia in the nineteenth century.

Bibliography: V. Klaić, *Život i djela Pavla Ritera Vitezovića* (Zagreb, 1914). See the list (with a description) of Vitezović's works, published and unpublished, with commentaries in the catalog *Isložbe djela Pavla Vitezovića* (Zagreb 1952).

Dimitrije Djordjevic

Great Historians: Czech

BALBÍN, Bohuslav (Hradec Králové, 1621–Prague, 1688), Jesuit priest; major Czech historian of the seventeenth century. Although in favor of rapid re-Catholicization of the Czech kingdom in the aftermath of the Hapsburg victory over the Protestants, Balbín nevertheless devoted most of his life to the defense of the Czech language, as can be testified by his most eloquent work, *Dissertatio Apologetica Pro Lingua Slavonica, Praecipue Bohemica* (composed in 1672, published in 1775 by F. M. Pelcl). For his devotion to Czech uniqueness, Balbín was persecuted by the church hierarchy, and his major work, *Epitome Rerum Bohemicarum* (Survey of Czech History), suffered from censorship. Completed in 1688, *Epitome* was prevented from publication by the intervention of the general of the Jesuit Order and allowed to appear in press only in 1677 after Balbín had agreed to make extensive changes. Heuristically, Balbín represents a certain advancement over previous Czech chroniclers, whose works he quoted. He used historical documents, especially diplomatic treaties, among his sources. Endowed with an encyclopedic capacity to collect materials in archives and libraries, Balbín's lifelong ambition was to produce a major *historia bohemica universalis* and to realize his plan for a monumental historical encyclopedia of no less than thirty volumes, divided into three series with ten volumes each, of which a mere torso, *Miscellanea Historica Regni Bohemiae*, appeared during his lifetime. Conceived as an introduction to the encyclopedia (Vol. 1., 1679), it was followed by eight volumes of the first series and two volumes of the second. During the era of Enlightenment the remaining volumes 9 and 10 of the first series were published by K. R. Ungar under the title *Bohemia Docta* (1776–1780), and *Liber Curialis*, was published by J. A. Riegger (in *Materialien zur Statistik von Böhmen*, 1787–1793). The first volume can be regarded as the first attempt to present the history of Czech literature; the second is an extremely useful compendium of Bohemia's administrative, legal, and military history. Although his place in premodern Czech historiography is secure, Balbín remains a controversial author because of his extreme and overenthusiastic Catholic bias. After all, he is a typical representative of baroque historiography with a large proportion of his writings on devotional subjects. He wrote, among other things, the histories of holy places in Silesia (*Diva Vartensis*, 1655), Moravia (*Diva*

Turzanensis, 1658), and Bohemia (*Diva Montis Sanctis*, 1665), a monograph about the first archbishop of Prague (*Vita venerable Arnesti*, 1664), and numerous other hagiographies and genealogies of Czech nobility. These works are the least serious among Balbín's rich production, inspired by the muse of poetry and the Catholic zeal to combat Protestantism rather than by considering history as a serious science. On the other hand, Balbín paid attention to the advance of historiography on the Continent. He was familiar with Jean Mabillon's (q.v.) work on historical diplomacy and contributed to the major international history project organized by Catholic historians, the *Acta Sanctorum* (edited by Jan Bolland from 1643), for which Balbín wrote the life of the Czech patron saint Jan (Johann) of Nepomuk.

Bibliography: W. Bobek, *Bohuslav Balbín* (Bratislava, 1932); Josef Hanuš, "Bohuslava Balbína, *Bohemia Docta*," *Český časopis historický* (December 1906); Kamil Krofta, *O Balbínovi dějepisci* (Prague, 1938); Jan P. Kučera and Jiří Rak, *Bohuslav Balbín a jeho místo v české kultuře* (Prague, 1983); Antonin Rejzek, *P. B. Balbín*, S. J. (1908).

Milan Hauner

DALIMIL (?–?), assumed author of the oldest chronicle of Bohemia written in the Czech language at the beginning of the fourteenth century. The unknown author, who presumably belonged to the lower Czech nobility, must have completed the chronicle between 1308 and 1314, because he commented on the election of Jan of Luxemberg as the king of Bohemia. The rhymed chronicle carries a clear nationalistic message reflecting the dramatic upheavals during the interregnum that followed the murder of the last Bohemian king, Václav III of the Přemysl dynasty. It is highly nationalistic and directed against all foreigners, especially Germans. Although the identity of the true author is unknown, he seemed to have belonged to the gentry and possibly served in an ecclesiastical order since he knew several earlier chronicles, including *Chronica Bohemorum* by Kosmas (q.v.), and oral histories. Even the name of "Dalimil" is not certain, since it is based on the erroneous judgment of Tomáš Pěšina z Čechorodu, a seventeenth-century historian, who attributed the chronicle to a certain Dalimil Meziříčský, a dean in the city of Boleslav; other interpreters speculated that the name Dalimil might refer to prominent Church dignitaries such as Hynek Žák z Dubé, the bishop of Olomouc, or the Prague bishop Jan IV of Dražice. The first printed edition of the Dalimil chronicle was prepared in 1618 by Pavel Ješín z Bezdězí, but two years later, following the end of Czech independence after the Battle of the White Mountain, the remaining copies of the chronicle were destroyed. It was not until 1786 that F. F. Procházka published Dalimil's work in the new Czech transliteration. When Václav Hanka prepared a new edition of Dalimil's work in the 1830s, the Austrian censors interceded again, and the edition had to wait until 1849. Significantly, it was reprinted again during the Nazi occupation, 1939–1945.

Bibliography: The chronicle was published with a German translation in *Fontes Rerum Bohemicarum*, vol. 3, by Josef Jirecek (1882); see also Hohuslav Havránek and Jiří Daňhelka, eds., *Nejstarší česká rýmovaná kronika tak řečeného Dalimila* (Prague, 1957).

Milan Hauner

KOSMAS (? 1045–? 1125), author of *Chronica Bohemorum*, first chronicle of Bohemia written in Latin. Kosmas served as canon, later dean, in St. Guy's chapter of the Prague Cathedral. Kosmas acquired an impressive education having studied at cathedral schools in Prague, in Lutych in today's Belgium, and in France. As a member of the Prague's bishop delegation he traveled widely and knew Germany and Italy. The *Chronica* was written in the traditional style of the epoch, opening with a survey of the mythical origins of the Czech nation. Kosmas started to write his chronicle in 1119, using a highly ornate style. As it was customary for medieval chroniclers to do, Kosmas put the main emphasis on describing the deeds of the monarchs but mentioned only those events he wanted to present. The chronicle is divided into three parts, the first up to the death of Prince Jaromir in 1038, the second up to the death of King Vratislav I in 1092, and the third up to the death of Prince Vladislav I in 1125. Kosmas combined Latin rhetoric with an extensive use of oral history, folk tales, and legends. He defended the Latin liturgy against the Eastern Orthodox rite, which he rejected as semibarbarian; he sided with Episcopal authorities against secular encroachments by the Přemysl dynasty; on the other hand, Kosmas also advocated strong prerogatives for the monarchy as the best means for maintaining the unity of the Czech state against German and Polish claims. Kosmas' *Chronica Bolhemorum* occupies the same place in Czech history as *Historia Francorum* by Gregory of Tours (q.v.).

Bibliography: First critical edition of *Chronica Bohemorum* was edited by F. M. Pelcl (1734–1801), the first professor of Czech language and literature at the Charles University of Prague, and Josef Dobrovský (1753–1829), the founder of modern Slavic philology, for the collection *Scriptores Rerum Bohemicarum*, vol. 1 (1783). The main critical edition was undertaken by Josef Emler for *Fontes Rerum Bohemicarum*, vol. 2 (1874). Since then Kosmas' chronicle was published several times in Czech as *Kosmova kronika česká*, trans. Karel Hrdina (Prague, 1929; republished, Prague, 1975); the Latin and German text (*Die Chronik der Böhmen des Cosmas von Prag*) was edited by Berthold Bretholz for the *Monumenta Germaniae Historica*, n.s., 2 (1923); see also F. Palacký, *Würdigung der alten böhmischen Geschichtsschreiber* (Prague, 1830).

Milan Hauner

STRÁNSKÝ, Pavel (1583–1657), Czech anti-Catholic historian; director (rector) of schools in Litoměřice before his exile; professor of history at the Protestant university of Toruń (Thorn). Together with the religious historian Pavel Skála ze Zhoře (1583–1640) and the noted educationalist Jan Amos Komenský, known as Comenius abroad (1592–1670), Stránský belongs to the generation of prominent Czech exiles who had to leave their country because of religious persecution after the Battle of the White Mountain. His major work is *Respublica Bojema*, published several times in Leyden, Holland, by the famous publishing house of Elzevir Brothers (1634, 1643, 1648, and 1713 in Amsterdam). It was conceived as a polemical response to the views of Melchior Goldast, the Catholic adviser of Emperor Ferdinand II (*Commentarii de Bohemiae incorporatorumque provinciarum juribis et privilegiis*), who defended the Catholic counterreformation in Bohemia and tried to prove the dependence of the Czech kingdom on the German Empire headed at the time by the Hapsburgs. Stránský's work is a comprehensive survey of Czech institutions, such as laws, estates (social classes represented in the Bohemian Diet), and finances. Translated into German during the Enlightenment and expanded with the inclusion of updated materials, it was edited by the historian Ignacius Cornova as *Paul Stranskýs Staat von Böhmen*, vols. 1–7 (Prague, 1792–1803).

Milan Hauner

Great Historians: Danish

GRAM, Hans (Bjergby by Hjørring, 1685–Copenhagen, 1748), Danish historian, professor (of Greek) at the University of Copenhagen (1714–1748), royal historiographer, librarian, and archivist (from 1730). Gram was known as a very learned man, "a living library," almost in a polyhistoric way, and he took the initiative to found the Royal Danish Society of the Sciences (1742). In the field of history he belonged to the erudite tradition with its growing insight in the nature and the problems of the sources, inspired by the school of rigorous critical research founded by the French Benedictines. As royal archivist he founded what later became the Danish State Archives as a historical collection. He is a good example of the dividing line that existed then between historical erudition and historical writing; his most important works were the edition and analysis of texts. In the introduction to his edition of *Niels Krag's Annales Christierni III*, from c. 1600 (1737; Danish trans. 1776), he gave a modern critical study of the work. His notes and commentaries to the edition of *Johannes Meursius: Historica Danica* (in *Opera* 9 [1746]) is a thorough critical treatment of Denmark's ancient and medieval history. His work has since been looked upon as epochmaking in Danish historical research with its critical analysis of every detail and its meticulous study of the sources and their reliability.

Bibliography: Ellen Jorgensen, "Hans Gram," *Historisk Tidsskrift* 9.r. III (1924): 165–191; R. Paulli, "Gram, Hans," *Dansk Biografisk Leksikon* (Danish Biographical Dictionary), 3d ed., vol. 5 (Copenhagen, 1980), pp. 259–263; *Vita Johannis Grammii*, ed. Th. A. Muller and B. Kornerup (Copenhagen, 1942).

Jens Chr. Manniche

HUITFELDT, Arild (Bergen, 1546–Herlufsholm, 1609), Danish historian. Of noble birth, Huitfeldt was a public servant in the Danish State Chancery, from 1586 lord chancellor and member of the Privy Council. Like many other members of the aristocracy in the sixteenth century, he collected historical sources, and his duties gave him special opportunities for copying documents and records in central and local archives in the country. He published some medieval chronicles, but his main work was *Danmarks Riges Krønike*, 1595–1603 (Chronicle of the Kingdom of Denmark). Working backwards he covered the history of Denmark from the first mythological kings to 1559. Because it was a yearbook, it was a collection and edition of an enormous amount of material rather than the well-organized composition of a historian. He did, however, prefer contemporary sources when possible. His interpretation of the sequence of events and his conception of history in general was pragmatic. History to him was a mirror from which the reader could learn from others' experience; history repeats itself, men are alike throughout the ages, and the same events happen again and again. Consequently, the intention of the work was, moreover, to educate the young king Christian IV politically. This view of the present and the past playing together and Huitfeldt's free interpretation of this interplay probably makes his work unique in North European historiography in this period. Huitfeldt was influenced especially by Philippe de Commynes (q.v.) whom he regarded as a model of an unlearned nobleman with political experience who had been able to create a wise and intelligent work of history. For many generations Huitfeldt's chronicle constituted the image of Denmark's past, and it is still of value because it contains material otherwise lost.

Bibliography: Harald Ilsøe, "Huitfeldt, Arild," *Dansk Biografisk Leksikon* (Danish Biographical Dictionary), 3d ed., vol. 6 (Copenhagen, 1980), pp. 598–602; Jan Kanstrup, "Huitfeldts fremstilling af Christoffer II's tilbagekomst til Danmark" (Huitfeldt's Account of the Return of Christoffer II to Denmark)," *Historisk Tidsskrift* 12. r., 6 (1972–1973): 93–121; H. F. Rørdam, *Historieskriverren Arild Huitfeldt* (The History Writer, Arild Huitfeldt) (Copenhagen, 1896).

Jens Chr. Manniche

SAXO GRAMMATICUS (probably post–1160–post–1210), Danish historian. Little is known of Saxo. He was a clerk in the service of Archbishop Absalon of Lund (d. 1201) and must have received a thorough education, probably at European universities. He wrote *Gesta Danorum*, one of the greatest works of history in the European Middle Ages (first published in Paris in 1514). It deals with the history of Denmark from the foundation of the kingdom in the age of legends to around 1185 and was the first full account of the history of that country. Most of the work was probably done between 1190 and 1210. Saxo named as his models Bede (q.v.), Dudo, and Paulus Diaconus, but other medieval historians and writers from antiquity also evidently provided him with themes, motives, and examples. In addition, he used a rich variety of sources (of which many are still accessible), including other medieval chronicles, the Norse tradition of myths, heroic poems and sagas, diploma, and oral tradition. He worked thoroughly with his material and interpreted it in the light of his own general conception. For this reason, the work as a source of Danish history in the early Middle Ages is now obsolete, but up to this century he was considered the main authority on this period and had a profound influence on historical consciousness in Denmark. His work gives, moreover, much information of his own time, even if it is colored by his political views. But now it is primarily regarded as evidence of a highly educated man's view of the history of his country around 1200 and as an important source of ideology, mentality, and culture in Denmark at that time.

The work is organized in sixteen books, the first nine dealing with legendary kings, the last seven with historical kings from the tenth century and onward. The list of kings constitutes the main theme, and Saxo saw no difference in the relations between king and his advisors, housecarls, and the Danish people from time immemorial to his own days. His loyalty is with the national monarchy, where king and Church cooperate for the benefit of the country. In a sense his most literal concern is to be a propagandist for Danish imperialism and to praise positive moral values and warn against vices. But at the same time, as modern analysis seems to show, the composition is patterned to convey central parts of the twelfth-century universe of ideas. The sixteen books can be divided into four parts that give a picture of the necessary development of people and society from pagan times via the time of the birth of Christ to the christening of Denmark and the establishment of the archbishopric. Another interesting organizing principle seems to be the four cardinal virtues *fortitudo*, *temperentia*, *justitia*, and *prudentia*, which dominate each quarter of the work. Other interpretations of the work have suggested, for instance, that it may be read as an allegory of human language and the liberal arts. These are just a few of the many interpretations that this extraordinary and original work, written in ornate Latin of the Silver Age, seems to offer and that still makes it the subject of research and discussion.

Bibliography: K. Friis-Jensen, ed., *Saxo Grammaticus: A Medieval Author between Norse and Latin Culture* (Copenhagen,1981); Saxo, *Danorum regum heroumque historia*, Bks. 10–16, ed. with trans. and commentary by Eric Christiansen (Oxford, 1980–1981); Saxo Grammaticus, *The History of the Danes*, Bks. 1–9, trans. and commentary by Peter Fisher and Hilda Ellis Davidson (Cambridge, Eng., 1979); Inge Skovgaard-Petersen, *Da Tidernes Herre Var nær: Studier i Saxos historiesyn* (When the Lord of the Times Was Near: Studies in Saxo's Conception of History), with an English Summary (Copenhagen, 1987). Inge Skovgaard-Petersen, ''Saxo,''*Dansk Biografisk Leksikon* (Danish Biographical Dictionary), 3d ed., vol. 12 (1983), pp. 638–642.

Jens Chr. Manniche

Great Historians: Dutch

GROTIUS (De Groot), Hugo (Delft, 1583–Rostock, 1645), Dutch historian. Public prosecutor at the court of Holland (1607). Pensionary of Rotterdam (1613) and member of the executive commission of the States of Holland. His controversial political involvement resulted in his arrest (1618) and imprisonment. He escaped in 1621 and went to Paris where he was nominated ambassador of Sweden (1634). A very precocious youth, Grotius wrote many poems, dramas, religious tracts and published editions of the classics during his long and productive life, but above all he made his name as the author of works of jurisprudence. His historical works form only a small part of his oeuvre and are strongly influenced by his patriotism and the memory of the difficult struggle of the Dutch provinces against Spain. In his *Parallelon rerum publicarum liber tertius: de moribus ingenioque propulorum Atheniensium, Romanorum, Batavorum* (written at the age of 19, but published in 1802–1803) he compared the characters and habits of the people of Athens, Rome and Batavia. Grotius concluded from his evidence that the inhabitants of the Low Countries were to be considered superior to those of Athens and Rome because they had tempered freedom with government by notables. In his less polemical *De antiquitate respublicae Batavicae* (The antiquity of the commonwealth of the Batavians, 1610), which may be regarded as the sequel, Grotius again used the past to bolster the present. The Batavians, "now called Hollanders," had been independent of any foreign power since Roman times. They had always been governed by states, composed of the optimates and the best qualified representatives of the people. At a later stage of his life Grotius rejected his political-historical treatise as a product of youthful enthusiasm but at the time he sincerely believed in this Batavian myth. For a long period his interpretation of the past was highly influential in Holland, where its role was in some respects analogous to Hotman's *Francogallia* in France in that it enabled the new Dutch state to appropriate a convenient history. These works were predominantly of an antiquarian character.

In the same years, however, Grotius with government support was working on his *Annales et historiae de rebus Belgicis* (Annals and History of the Low Countries, 1657, published by his sons). This was intended to be a grand history of the revolt to 1609, following in style and conception all prescriptions of contemporary humanist historiography. But when the book was finished in 1612 the authorities were not prepared to publish it. The fierce controversies in the country during the twelve-year truce with Spain probably account for this setback. Grotius did not succeed in getting it into publication although he adapted the text in later years during his exile in France. The *Annales et historiae* as they have come down to us are thus the result of much editing, and as a consequence the sense of chronology and the link between political and military action are sometimes lost, submerged under the mass of details. Written in a tacitean latin the overwhelming concern of the book was to explain to foreigners the nature of the Dutch struggle by extensive presentation and discussion of sieges and battles. Regularly, as was fitting in this kind of historiography, the moral implications of procedures were made clear. It is remarkable that Grotius ignored the religious factor that played a central part in the revolt and treated the internal disputes that resulted from it in exclusively political terms. On the other hand, he tried to draw attention to any foreign development that could have a bearing on the Dutch situation and discussed the Dutch voyages of exploration and the manners and customs the explorers encountered in foreign countries. This work, intended to be the first complete history of the Dutch Revolt for an international public, became more or less like the career of Groitus himself, a victim of political circumstances. However, along with his contemporary Hooft (q.v.), Grotius remains the greatest and last heir of Renaissance historiography in the Dutch Republic.

Bibliography: Eco O. G. Haitsma Mulier, ''Grotius, Hooft and the Writing of History in the Dutch Republic,'' in A. C. Duke and C. A. Tamse, eds., *Clio's mirror, Historiography in Britain and the Netherlands*. Britain and the Netherlands VIII, papers delivered to the eighth Anglo-Dutch historical conference, Zutphen, 1985, pp. 55–72; H.C.A. Muller, *Hugo de Groot's 'Annales et Historiae,'* Utrecht, 1919.

Eco Haitsma Mulier

HOOFT, Pieter Corneliszoon (Amsterdam, 1581–The Hague, 1647), Dutch regent, poet, and historian. Hooft, son of a merchant family, travelled through France, Italy, and Germany (1598–1601) and was educated at Leyden University (1606–1607). In 1609 he was appointed bailiff of Muiden and of Gooiland, posts he held until his death. As a regional governor, Hooft wrote political poems and a play, *Geeraerdt van Velsen* (1613), to justify revolt against Spain and to promote the aristocratic republic as opposed to a monarchy under the House of Orange. Yet Hooft had been influenced by Tacitus (q.v.), who had preferred aristocratic republicanism to monarchy but who had also thought that peace was more likely achieved by a prince in times of trouble. Hooft's second historical drama, *Baeto* (1617), reflects these themes. In 1618 he abandoned drama for history. Tacitus remained his model, and Hooft chose the yearbook as his form. Instead of writing in Latin, he opted for Dutch, the vernacular, in which he wrote tersely and vividly. Rejecting the study of older periods, Hooft settled on contemporary history, which, he noted in 1626, offered the great advantage that readers could understand the lessons of this part of the past very well by knowing the contexts of events. Hooft's first prose work, *Henrik de Grote* (Henry the Great), appeared in 1626. It was a biography of Henry IV of France but was intended as a didactic piece for the benefit of the new stadtholder, Frederick Henry of Orange. By now, Hooft supported close cooperation of the artistocratic states with the Prince of Orange. On the problems of such cooperation, he wrote *Rampsaligheden der verheffinge van den Huize van Medicis* (Disasters of the Rise of the House of Medici) in 1636, although it was not printed until 1649, after his death. Hooft's masterwork, *Nederlandsche Historiën* (Dutch Histories), describing the Dutch Revolt from 1555 to 1584, appeared in 1642; a sequel, up to 1587, remained unfinished at Hooft's death and appeared in 1654. (Between 1628 and 1636 Hooft also translated the works of Tacitus into Dutch.) The *Historiën* was not the first book on the Dutch Revolt, but Hooft's theme, the Dutch fighting for their liberty, is displayed in magnificent style and with some structure given to the facts, although Hooft, like other seventeenth-century historians, lacked the notion of a process of linear development. Hooft used mostly printed sources although also a few manuscripts and some interviews with eyewitnesses. Unfortunately, he embellished many documents and speeches printed in his text. He was also too credulous toward his sources. Yet until the end of the eighteenth century, when his methods were criticized, Hooft's *Historiën* was considered great history. Nowadays, even though his techniques are out of date and his research is seen as insufficient, the *Historiën* is considered unquestionably to be the *magnum opus* of Dutch historiography of the seventeenth century.

Bibliography: J. C. Breen, *Pieter Corneliszoon Hooft als schrijver der Nederlandsche Historiën* (Amsterdam, 1894); J. D. Cornelissen, *Hooft en Tacitus* (Nijmegen, Utrecht, 1938); S. Groenveld, *Hooft als historieschrijver. Twee studies* (Weesp, 1981); E.O.G. Haitsma Mulier, "Grotius, Hooft and the Writing of History in the Dutch Republic," in A. C. Duke and C. A. Tamse, eds., *Clio's Mirror: Historiography in Britain and the Netherlands* (Zutphen, 1985), pp. 55–72; H. W. van Tricht, *Het leven van P. C. Hooft* (The Hague, 1980).

S. Groenveld

KLUIT, Adriaan (Dordrecht, 1735–Leyden, 1807), Dutch historian. Kluit, a scholar caught up in the political conflict between Orangists and Patriots, was able to make a decisive contribution to the interpretation of Dutch history. He belonged to the partially antiquarian, partially enlightened tradition that set great store by factual analysis of the medieval and early modern development of the state and its institutions. Endowed with a critical sense, driven by a keen interest in the Dutch language and a deep respect for original documents, firmly committed to the cause of the Orangists, Kluit set out to study the history of Holland, the province that dominated the Dutch Republic. His pioneering *Historia critica comitatus Hollandiae et Zeelandiae ab antiquissimis inde deducta temporibus* (Critical History of the Counties of Holland and Zeeland from the Earliest Times) (1777–1782) was both a full edition and an incisive appraisal of the chronicle of Egmond and of many documents pertaining to it. Thereafter, Kluit published a number of minor studies devoted to what he rightly considered to be the pivotal problem, the growth of the power of the medieval counts of Holland. Finally, deprived of his professorship by the Patriots, he wrote his famous *Historie der Hollandsche Staats-Regeering* (History of the States' Government of Holland) in 1802, underpinning his views with a wealth of evidence. Kluit described the development of institutions and of political thought, trying to relate both to economic growth and the welfare of the nation. He attacked the traditional view, eloquently stated by Hugo Grotius, that it was not the count of Holland but the people, that is, the ruling classes united in the states, who had been the sovereign rulers in medieval times. Kluit maintained that the power of the count, within a weak German Empire, had developed into nearly absolute sovereignty. Although attaching too much importance to this power, Kluit justly stressed the fact that the states of Holland were nonexistent before the fifteenth century. According to him, the Dutch Revolt and the abjuration by the states of the then count, King Philip II of Spain, were acts of self-preservation and of defense of property, justified in the light of privileges and natural law. From then on the states were the legitimate sovereign representatives of the whole people. Kluit's conservative view, calculated to safeguard the position of the prince of Orange as "stadhouder" within the existing political structure, did not endear him to the Patriots who considered the people themselves to be sovereign. In 1795 he lost his position as professor of antiquities and "diplomatic" history of the United Provinces at Leyden university, but political changes made it possible for him to resume his task in 1802. He was an inspiring teacher, the first in the Netherlands to deal systematically with the complexities of medieval sources. Kluit also taught "Statistik" as developed by Gottfried Achenwall and August von Schlözer (q.v.). His studies, supported by meticulous study of original documents, mark both the culmination and the end of a predominantly legal approach to Dutch history. His knowledge of the subject's medieval and modern sources was unsurpassed in his time.

Bibliography: George A Boutelje, *Bijdrage tot de kennis van A. Kluits opvattingen over onze oudere vaderlandsche geschiedenis* (A Contribution to the Knowledge of A. Kluit's Ideas concerning Dutch History) (Groningen and The Hague, 1920); Frederik W. N. Hugenholtz, "Adriaan Kluit en het onderwijs in de mediaevistiek" (Adriaan Kluit and The Teaching of Medieval History), *Forum der Letteren* (1965): 142–160; I. Leonard Leeb, *The Ideological Origins of the Batavian Revolution: History and Politics in the Dutch Republic, 1747–1800* (The Hague, 1973); Arie Th. van Deursen, *Geschiedenis en toekomstverwachting. Het onderwijs in de statistiek aan de universiteiten van de achttiende eeuw* (History and Hopes of the Future: The Teaching of Statistics at the Universities in the Eighteenth Century) (Kampen, 1971).

Johanna Roelevink

WAGENAAR, Jan (Amsterdam, 1709–Amsterdam, 1773), Dutch historian; since 1758, officially appointed "historiographer" of Amsterdam. Descended from a lower middle-class family, Wagenaar lacked the usual academic background. While working for his living in a trade office, he acquired most of his intellectual schooling on his own. He studied different languages—Hebrew, Greek, Latin, French, and English—which assured him of access to the classical authors as well as to the fruits of modern and contemporary thinking. Apart from revealing an interest in history, Wagenaar constantly displayed an active interest in natural sciences, theology, philosophy, and literature. In law and government he took note of the opinions of Grotius (q.v.), Locke, and Montesquieu (q.v.). Besides reading, he translated a number of discourses of men like Tillotson, Benjamin Hoadly, De Réaumur, Boerhaave, and Barbeyrac. Being a member of a dissenting church, he advocated an optimistically Christian-inspired, commonsense philosophy, combined with a clear preference for the empirically based, inductive approach to method. So he read with approval Samuel Clarke and Isaac Newton on science while rejecting pure Cartesianism. Tolerance and broad-mindedness were in general the most important characteristics of his attitude in religious affairs. Judging by his intellectual activities, Wagenaar may be considered a true representative of the Christian-inspired Enlightenment, especially in that he managed to reconcile *Ratio* and *Revelatio*. In 1747 he published *De Patriot* (The Patriot), a weekly review in which he commented upon topical issues. Occasionally, he turned to polemics, in particular in 1747–1748 and 1756–1757, when he was forced to defend his political and historical views. In politics he moderately supported a conservative, aristocratically based form of government. The most important of his discourses were collected and republished posthumously as *Historiesche en Politike Tractaaten* (Historical and Political Treatises, 1776, 1780). The first important result in the historical field was his contribution (in seven volumes, 1738–1758) to the *Tegenwoordige Staat*. . . (Present State of the United Netherlands, an extension of the English equivalent by Salmon). Between 1749 and 1759 his *Vaderlandsche Historie* (History of the Fatherland) appeared in twenty-one volumes, in which the first easily accessible overall survey of Dutch history "from the earliest times" to 1751 was presented, based on a thorough knowledge of manuscripts and of historical sources and writings published previously. Besides noting the profound research, contemporaries admired the elegance of the author's style. Wagenaar's *History*, which was to become the leading historical work of the era, was reprinted, revised, and continued several times and, moreover, was translated into German and French.

The Amsterdam magistrate honored the successful historian. In 1758 he got the title "historiographer of the city" and in 1760 he became first clerk of the muncipial secretary. Moreover, he received permission to investigate the city archives. Thus Wagenaar was in a unique position to study the history of Amsterdam in greater detail than ever before, which resulted in his second opus magnum: *Amsterdam in zyne Opkomst . . . geschetst* (Amsterdam in Its Origins, Growth, Histories, Privileges, Commerce, Buildings, etc.), published between 1760 and 1768 in two editions. Wagenaar gave evidence of critical reflection concerning the position and treatment of history on several occasions. As time progressed, he revealed himself increasingly as susceptible to the attainments of Enlightenment historiography. In contrast with, for example, the traditional approach of the *History*, in which he predominantly presented political history, he opted in *Amsterdam* for a thematic representation, paying separate attention to the political, social, economical, religious, and cultural significance of the citizenry. In general, the Enlightenment's influence emerges, in part, from his search for causal and comparative explanations or from his resolve to write the "history of the people" (in practice, usually the middle class) and of the "nation's freedom." However, Wagenaar did not appreciate all aspects of the contemporary developments. Historical writing in the spirit of Voltaire's (q.v.) adage "en philosophe," often not free from speculation, in which the character of the past was frequently weighed and judged against the background of universal principles or eighteenth-century norms, could not, in his opinion, do justice to the past's own intrinsic value or to his admittedly imperfect notion of change and development in history. Although Wagenaar was a scrupulous historian, he also was a party man. A main point of criticism concerns his "hidden bias" and his interpretation of the concept of "freedom," both corresponding with his political and religious views described above, which have left unmistakable traces in his historical works. Despite this, both Wagenaar's *History* and his *Amsterdam* are useful today as reliable works of reference.

Bibliography: P. Huisinga Bakker, *Het leeven van Jan Wagenaar. Benevens eenige Brieven*... (Life of J. W. including Some Letters...) (Amsterdam, 1776); R. J. Castendijk, *Jan Wagenaar en zijn "Vaderlandsche Historie"* (J. W. and His "History of the Fatherland") (Schiedam, 1927); L.H.M. Wessels, "Jan Wagenaar (1709–1773). Bijdrage tot een herwaardering" (Jan Wagenaar [1709–1773]. Contribution to a Reevaluation), in P.A.M. Geurts and A.E.M. Janssen, eds., *Geschiedschrijving in Nederland*... (Historiography in the Netherlands...), vol. 1 (Den Haag, 1981), pp. 117–140; idem, "Jan Wagenaar's 'Remarques' (1754): A Reaction to Elie Luzac as a Pamphleteer. An Eighteenth-Century Confrontation in the Northern Low Countries," *LIAS: Sources and Documents Relating to the Early Modern History of Ideas* XI, no.1 (1984): 19–82.

L.H.M. Wessels

Great Historians: English

BACON, Francis (London, 1561–London, 1626), English lawyer, politician, and philosopher of science. Bacon began his public career as a professional lawyer, entered Parliament in 1584, but waited until 1607 for high political office as solicitor-general to James I. He became lord chancellor in 1618, was disgraced in 1621 following accusations of corruption, and spent his last years working on a huge scientific enterprise, the *Instauratio Magna*, and various literary projects. One of these projects was a history of the Tudors, of which he completed only the *History of the Reign of King Henry the Seventh* (1622). This eventually small output belied an interest in history that took Bacon to the theory of the discipline as well as back in time to the sixteenth century. Built into the survey of knowledge attempted in *The Advancement of Learning* (1605) and in its expanded Latin version of 1623 was an *ars historica* in which he focused on the character of "civil history" in what he called its "perfect" form—that is, the history of political affairs written according to the literary standards of late Renaissance historiography. Essentially, Bacon's ideal was the conventional one in which the narrative techniques perfected by the Florentine humanists and by Machiavelli and Guicciardini were made to serve didactic purposes. Scholarship, in the sense of source criticism and accurate documentation, was assumed to be much less important than skill in distilling moral and political wisdom from the study of the "counsels, acts, and events" that made up the flow of public engagements. But Bacon also had the unusual idea of subordinating civil history to scientific needs (as he conceived them). The data of human experience could be used to construct a science of humankind in the same way that the facts of nature produced physics. Like an early positivist, Bacon said that the logic of scientific inquiry extended to studies of disposition, behavior, self-advancement, and statecraft. Exact studies of personality and policy would emerge, once the psychological and political insights offered by "lives" and "times" had been harnassed by induction. The attraction of the Tudor period was that it offered an unusually wide "variety of strange events," like an especially revealing specimen from the natural world. The *History of Henry VII* had great contemporary relevance as the story of a very critical period in recent English history handled by a prominent political figure seeking a return to office. It is also regarded as a consummate example of Bacon's powers as a stylist. But in many respects it is best seen as an example of the sort of history on which Bacon hoped to found his science of humankind. Borrowing the narrative he found in the accounts of Polydore Vergil and Edward Hall and paying little attention to erudition or accuracy of fact, Bacon jettisoned their interpretive frameworks and freely elaborated his own. In this, the king's character came to be at the forefront of analysis. The *History* is, in effect, a case study in historical psychology. The portrait that emerges is of a king of considerable political skill, courage, industry, and wisdom who was nevertheless susceptible to wilfulness, overcautiousness, and distrustfulness and whose judgment was marred by a tendency to think only of the occasion and clouded by a natural cupidity.

Bibliography: Sydney Anglo, "Ill of the Dead: The Posthumous Reputation of Henry VII," *Renaissance Studies* (Society for Renaissance Studies), no. 1 (1987); Stuart Clark, "Bacon's *Henry VII*: A Case-Study in the Science of Man," *History and Theory*, no. 2, (1974): 97–118; B. A Haddock, *An Introduction to Historical Thought* (London, 1980), pp. 19–31; F. J. Levy, ed., *The History of the Reign of King Henry the Seventh* (New York, 1972), introduction; George H. Nadel, "History as Psychology in Francis Bacon's Theory of History," *History and Theory*, no. 3 (1966): 275–287.

Stuart Clark

BEDE, the Venerable (Northumbria, A.D. 672/673–Jarrow, Northumbria, A.D. August 15, 735), monk of Wearmouth/Jarrow (c. 680-). Bede was a Father of the Church and one of the greatest Dark Ages historians. Among the luminaries of the Northumbrian renaissance his intellectual achievements were unrivaled. He combined speculative faculty, acute judgment, and profound learning with literary talent and an excellent command of the Latin language. By the standards of his age Bede was a polymath: he wrote on theology, geography, science, and chronology; he composed homilies, hagiographies, chronicles, and histories; and he compiled schoolbooks and translated Latin works into English. In his own day Bede was famous mainly as a theologian, but today we know him as a historian. He composed two *Lives of St. Cuthbert*, one in prose (*Two Lives of St. Cuthbert*, ed., with an English translation, Bertram Colgrave [Cambridge, Eng., 1940], pp. 142–307) and one in verse (*Bedas metrische Vita Sancti Cuthberti*, Palaestra no. 198, ed. Werner Jaager [Leipzig, 1935]), which, although hagiographies, are of considerable historical value. He compiled two world chronicles, to A.D. 703 and 725, respectively (ed. Theodor Mommsen, *Monumenta Germaniae Historica, Auctores Antiquissimi*, vol. 13, *Chronica Minora*, vol. 3 [Berlin, 1898], pp. 223–327). He also wrote a history of his own monastery of Wearmouth/Jarrow, the *Historia Abbatum* (*Venerabilis Baedae Opera Historica*, ed. Charles Plummer, 2 vols. [Oxford, 1896], 1: 364–387). But his reputation rests primarily on the *Historia Ecclesiastica Gentis Anglorum* (vol. 1, ed. Charles Plummer [Oxford, 1896] pp. 5–363), which he completed in A.D. 731, a history of the English people and Church from the Anglo-Saxon invasions until his own time. Bede's environment favored his historical enterprises. The library of Wearmouth/Jarrow had a rich collection of history books and saints' *Lives*, which provided historiographical and hagiographical models and source material. For past history Bede had access to, among other works, Eusebios' (q.v.) *Historia Ecclesiastica*, Orosius' (q.v.) *Adversus paganos*, Gregory of Tours' (q.v.) *Historia Francorum*, and Gildas' *De Excidio Britanniae*. Also in the library were Constantius' *Life of St. Germanus* and a now-lost *Life of St. Alban*. For recent history, saints' *Lives* again came to his aid, because the hagiographical tradition was already well established in Northumbria. Available, for instance, were the anonymous *Life of Abbot Ceolfrid* (vol. 1, ed. Charles Plummer [Oxford, 1896], pp. 388–404), *Two Lives of St. Cuthbert* (pp. 60–139), and Eddius' *Life of Bishop Wilfrid* (*The Life of Bishop Wilfrid by Eddius Stephanus*, ed., with an English translation, Bertram Colgrave [Cambridge, Eng., 1927]). For recent history Wearmouth/Jarrow offered other advantages. The monastic archives supplied useful documents—and the example of record keeping. Bede was also indebted to Wearmouth/Jarrow's close contacts with the outside world through visitors and the travels of its own monks. Thus he acquired documents and, above all, oral information, so essential for writing recent history, from elsewhere in England and from the Continent.

The *Historia Ecclesiastica* shares the edificatory and theological outlook of Bede's literary sources. He stated in the preface that he hoped, by providing an example of the sayings and doings of virtuous men and, conversely, of those of wicked men, to encourage the "listener or reader . . . to imitate what is good . . . and eschew what is harmful and perverse." He included much hagiographical material for this purpose. Salvation, indeed, was his central preoccupation, but since the way to Heaven was narrow, it was only likely within the Roman Church. Bede wrote his account of the conflict between the Roman and Celtic churches over the correct method of calculating the date of Easter as a partisan of the Roman cause. He described the Synod of Whitby (A.D. 664) in detail, rejoicing at the ultimate triumph of the Roman party. But the *Historia Ecclesiastica* also reflects Bede's love of Britain and of the Anglo-Saxon people. It begins with a brief geographical description of Britain and proceeds with the history of the Roman occupation and of the Anglo-Saxons before their conversion to Christianity. Insofar as Bede wrote a national history, he resembled Gregory of Tours. But his deepest loyalty was to the Northumbrians in particular. In places the *Historia Ecclesiastica* reads like a panegyric on Northumbria. Bede regarded the reign of Edwin (A.D. 616–632), the first Christian king of Deira, as a golden age. Edwin's power, he claimed, extended over all England except Kent; "It is related that there was so great a peace in Britain, wherever [his] dominion reached, that, as the proverb still runs, a woman with a new-born child could walk unharmed throughout the island from sea to sea." Undoubtedly, Bede as a historian was circumscribed by the presuppositions of his age and by the embryonic state or total absence of the sciences ancillary to history. Nevertheless, his achievements were remarkable. Although he described numerous miracles, he was not blind to natural causation. He had a sense of geography (as shown, for example by his demarkation of the continental homes of the Anglo-Saxon tribes before their migration and of their areas of settlement in England) and an interest in place names (thus he gives an acceptable derivation of "Ely"). He was an assiduous collector of information, whether from written records or by word of mouth, and the scholarly preface to the *Historia Ecclesiastica*, setting forth many of his sources, foreshadowed modern methodology. But most important was his contribution to chronology, a subject in which he was profoundly interested, as the account of the Paschal controversy in the *Historia Ecclesiastica* and his works on time, the *De Temporibus* and *De Temporum Ratione* (*Bedae Opera de Temporibus*, ed. C. W. Jones [Cambridge, Mass., 1943]), testify.

The *Historia Ecclesiastica* was of supreme importance in the evolution of a viable chronological system. Admittedly, it dates events in various ways, but often it uses the era of the Incarnation, and it was because of its influence that the practice of dating A.D. and B.C. gradually spread throughout Western Europe. Indeed, the success of the *Historia Ecclesiastica* was immediate. More than one hundred and fifty medieval manuscripts survive, the earliest two written in Northumbria within a decade of Bede's death, and a number of continental provenance. It was the first English history book to be printed (Strasburg, 1475), was repeatedly published thereafter, and is today available in paperback. Its success is not surprising. In England it served Bede's generation as a *pièce justificative* of the Roman Church, while the love of the English people that it expresses has a perennial appeal. Its popularity not only in England but also in Western Europe during the Dark and Middle Ages was insured by its piety and stories about saints. Always, it has had universal recognition as the principal source for early Anglo-Saxon history, as a product of intellectual genius, and as a masterpiece of Latin prose.

Bibliography: G. Bonner, ed., *Famulus Christi* (London, 1973); J. Campbell. "Bede," in T. A. Dorey, ed., *Latin Historians* (London, 1966), pp. 159–190; C. W. Jones, "Bede as Early Medieval Historian," *Mediaevalia et Humanistica*, fasc. 4 (1946): 26–36.; idem, *Saints' Lives and Chronicles in Early England* (Ithaca, N.Y., 1947) ; M.L.W. Laistner, *A Hand-List of Bede Manuscripts* (Ithaca, 1943); R. A. Markus, *Bede and the Tradition of Ecclesiastical Historiography* (Jarrow, 1975); A. H. Thompson, ed., *Bede: His Life, Times, and Writings* (Oxford, 1935).

Antonia Gransden

BURNET, Gilbert (Edinburgh, 1643–London, 1715), Scottish historian. Educated at the University of Aberdeen, Burnet then entered the Church. He was a man of wide interests, an early member of the Royal Society, and an observant traveler to many parts of Europe who led an active literary and political life. A fervent Whig, he supported the Revolution of 1688 and was rewarded with the bishopric of Salisbury. Burnet began his career as a historian with the *Memoirs of the Dukes of Hamilton* (1677) but made his reputation with his *History of the Reformation* (3 vols., 1679–1714). The first volume was an immediate success, for reasons mainly political. Written "to awake the nation" to the danger of Catholicism, it happened to appear a few months after the rumors of the "Popish Plot"; Burnet received the official thanks of the houses of Parliament, not to mention an invitation from Louis XIV to "write on his side." Written in a hurry, often inaccurate on points of detail, and grossly unfair to the medieval Church, as some contemporary critics were quick to point out, this first volume was to a considerable extent based on documents in the Cottonian Library and the State Paper Office. The work is not only the first important example of Whig history—in the most literal sense—but also, as Sir George Clark put it, is "the first English book which told the story of a great historical change as a coherent whole." Toward the end of his life, Burnet wrote his memoirs, which turned into a history of Britain from 1660 to 1713. Inspired by the example of Jacques-Auguste de Thou, and written to reply to the recently published Tory history of Clarendon and to justify the Revolution of 1688, Burnet's *History of His Own Time* was first published posthumously, in two parts, in 1723 and 1734. It remains of interest as a work of history more or less in the traditional grand manner, as well as a useful source. However, it was his *History of the Reformation* that really earned Burnet his place in the history of historical writing.

Bibliography: Peter Burke, "The Politics of Reformation History: Burnet and Brandt," in *Clio's Mirror: Historiography in Britain and the Netherlands*, ed. Alasdair Duke and Coenraad Tamse (Zutphen, 1985), ch. 4; John Kenyon, *The History Men* (London, 1983), pp. 33–38.

Peter Burke

CAMDEN, William (London, 1551–Chislehurst, 1623), English historian. In several respects, Camden stands at a crossroads of English historical scholarship. He was brought up in the traditions of antiquarian scholarship, of William Lambarde, Laurence Nowell, and John Leland, that flourished after the dissolution of the monasteries. Yet Camden was also in contact with continental scholarship, with Abraham Ortelius and the French philological scholars Jean Hotman, Nicholas Peires, and Jacques Auguste de Thou. The proceedings of the Society of Antiquaries founded by Camden in 1586 illustrate these dual influences and the new interest in philological methods of inquiry. Camden's *Britannia*, published in Latin in the same year, paying novel attention to the history of Roman Britain, brought England into the world of humanist historical scholarship. *Britannia* was a tremendous success abroad and at home. Freed from the chores of a schoolmaster by his appointment in 1597 as Clarenceux king at arms, Camden continued to tour England and collect and study for several subsequent editions, culminating in a folio in 1607. The 1607 edition (translated into English in 1610) pointed to another development: Camden's increased interest in relatively recent history. While working on the *Britannia* and the *Remains* that emerged from it, he also had turned his attention to a history of Queen Elizabeth's reign, written in the fashion of "politic" histories, such as Francis Bacon's *History of Henry VII*. After the early years of the seventeenth century, Camden appears to have attached greater importance to the role of history as *magister vitae*: the *Annals of Elizabeth's Reign* touched on sensitive and topical subjects; Camden prepared for a history of James I's reign. In 1623 he founded a history lectureship at Oxford and instructed his first lecturer, Degory Wheare, to lecture on Florus. Wheare stressed the value of history as "practick philosophy" and the "moral and political" dimension of historical studies. Writing to approve the lectures just before his death, Camden described Wheare as the man for his age. While never quite freeing himself from the myths and polemics of Tudor antiquarian studies (he criticized but never denied the Brutus legend), Camden may be regarded as a father of critical historical scholarship in England and of new etymological and archaeological methodologies that were greatly to influence historical studies for the rest of the century and beyond.

Kevin Sharpe

CLARENDON, Lord (Edward Hyde) (Wiltshire, 1609–Rouen, 1674). A gentleman lawyer, Hyde belonged to the intellectual circle around Lord Falkland and his house at Great Tew, admirers of the *via media* in religion advocated by Erasmus, Hooker, and Grotius. A member of the Long Parliament, he advised and supported Charles I once the civil war had begun; followed the prince of Wales into exile in the Scilly Islands Jersey, and France; and returned to England with him at the Restoration, when he was made earl of Clarendon and lord chancellor. In 1667 he fell from power and went into exile once more, in France. Clarendon began his *History of the Rebellion* during his first exile, carrying the story to 1644. During his second exile he began by writing his memoirs, but when his son brought him the manuscript of his *History*, he used the memoirs to continue it. This history was published posthumously in 1702, making considerable profits for Oxford University Press; a critical edition was published in 1888. Clarendon began writing his history as a way of advising Charles I and to answer the *History of the Parliament of England* (1640), written by the poet Thomas May as propaganda for the Parliamentarians. He wrote his memoirs to justify his own conduct. What he produced was Tory history; that is why the book sold so well on publication. As a historical source, his work needs to be treated with extreme caution, allowing for both unconscious bias and for deliberate attempts to deceive. However, the *History of the Rebellion* is a historical as well as a literary masterpiece, one of the last great works of humanist history in the manner of Thucydides (q.v), Tacitus (q.v.), Guicciardini (q.v.), and Davila, excelling in the character sketch in particular (among the most memorable are the portraits of the dukes of Buckingham, Strafford, and Cromwell). It makes considerable use of documents (such as the journals of the House of Commons) as well as the author's firsthand knowledge of events. The history also embodies a subtle and complex view of historical explanation. At the most immediate level, Clarendon has much to say about individual motives, especially the more selfish ones. He suggested that religious zeal was often a "pretence" or a "cloak" for the king's opponents to cover their ambitions, hence Charles Firth's (1938) description of the book as "a history of a religious revolution in which the religious element is omitted." At the most profound level, Clarendon couched his explanation in terms of Providence, the "hand of Heaven." However, this emphasis on the role of God did not exclude "natural causes." Although he appeared to reject structural explanations of the civil war with his famous confession (a shaft aimed at May) that he was "not so sharp-sighted as those, who have discerned this rebellion contriving from (if not before) the death of Queen Elizabeth," Clarendon was interested in social conflict at the county level, allowing Christopher Hill to speak of his "interpretation of the civil war in class terms." In fact, the author made the analysis with concepts of his own, and he was at his most original when analyzing collective behavior (that of the court, the Parliament, the army, and so on), in terms of the "temper" or "spirit" or "disposition" of the time, in a way that David Hume (q.v.) and others would develop a century later.

Bibliography: Charles Firth, "Clarendon," in *Essays* (London, 1938); Christopher Hill, "Clarendon and the Puritan Revolution," in *Puritanism and Revolution* (London, 1958), Ch. 6; Hugh Trevor-Roper, "Clarendon and the Practice of History," in F. R. Fogle and Hugh Trevor-Roper, *Milton and Clarendon* (Los Angeles, 1965), pp. 21–52; Brian Wormald, *Clarendon* (Cambridge, Eng., 1951).

Peter Burke

DICETO, Ralph De (Diss, Norfolk? c. 1125–St. Paul's, London, 1201), English chronicler. Diceto was canon of St. Paul's and archdeacon of Middlesex from 1152 or 1153. He visited Paris in the 1140s, perhaps to study at the university, and was dean of St. Paul's from 1180 to 1181. Diceto's principal works were the *Abbreviationes Chronicorum*, which briefly covers the period from the creation of the world to 1148 (2 vols., *The Historical Works of Master Ralph de Diceto, Dean of London*, ed. William Stubbs [London, 1876], 1: 3–263), and the *Ymagines Historiarum*, covering the years from 1148 to 1200 (ibid., 1:291–440; 2: 3–174). His residence at St. Paul's in London meant that he was at the center of affairs. He himself took part in public life and was acquainted with many of the leading men of his time, both lay and ecclesiastical. His chronicles, therefore, are very well informed about the government of, and events in, England and also about the continental components of the Angevin Empire. He showed a marked interest in the latter, giving, for example, a graphic description of the bridge with houses on it over the Loire at Angers and of the culinary practices of the people at Poitou. He was an able historian, and his work was to be one of Matthew Paris's (q.v.) sources and also apparently methodological models. He adopted novel means of organizing his mass of information to make it more readily comprehensible to his audience; since Paris used similar methods, it is likely that Diceto influenced him in this respect. Diceto's methods were twofold. Using the *Ymagines* as a source, he produced an epitome, the *Capitula Ymaginum Historiarum* (ibid., 1:267–287), and a number of *opuscula* on individual subjects; an example is the short history of the counts of Anjou (ibid., 2:267–268). He applied to both the *Abbreviation* and the *Ymagines* his second aid to easy reference: he put twelve distinguishing symbols in the margins by entries about particular topics, prefixing a list of the symbols to the *Abbreviationes*. Diceto was, therefore, more than a competent, knowledgeable chronicler; he was also a historian of some originality.

Bibliography: Antonia Gransden, *Historical Writing in England*, [i], *c. 550–c. 1307* (London, 1974), pp. 230–236 and Plate VII; John le Neve, *Fasti Ecclesiae Anglicanae, 1066–1300. Vol. 1: St. Paul's London*, comp. D. E. Greenway (London, 1968), pp. xiv, 5–6, 15–16, 79, 90.

Antonia Gransden

EADMER (Kent, c. 1060–Christ Church Cathedral priory, Canterbury, c. 1130), English biographer and historian; monk of Christ Church, Canterbury. Eadmer's principal work was the *Vita Sancti Anselmi* (ed., with an English translation, R. W. Southern [London and Edinburgh, 1962]) and the *Historia Novorum in Anglia* (ed. Martin Rule, [London, 1884]). Eadmer was the constant companion of Saint Anselm, archbishop of Canterbury, 1093–1109, and until about 1100 the *Vita* is based on Eadmer's contemporary notes. It is remarkable for its intimate touches and apparently authentic record of the saint's talk; it provides a more convincing, comprehensive portrait of a man than any biography previously written in England. Eadmer conceived the *Vita* as complementary to the *Historia Novorum*. It concerned Saint Anselm's private life and miracles, whereas the *Historia* dealt with his public life, especially his relations with William Rufus and Henry I. However, the *Historia* exceeds the bounds of a biography. It starts before Saint Anselm's time and ends after his death and contains a detailed account of Church and state relations, with many supporting documents cited *in extenso*. In addition, it has a conceptual structure: Eadmer regarded the Danish invasions of England in the eleventh century and the Norman Conquest as divine punishments for sin, in fulfillment of a prophecy made by Saint Dunstan; William the Conqueror's seizure of power was justified because King Harold was a perjuror and because William and Archbishop Lanfranc reformed the corrupt and degenerate Anglo-Saxon Church. Eadmer was in fact the first man since Bede (q.v.) to write a full-scale history in literary form. His incentives were his affection for Saint Anselm and indignation at royal encroachments on ecclesiastical privilege. But he was also influenced by the hagiographical tradition at Christ Church, which had been revived shortly after the Norman Conquest by the monk Osbern. Eadmer was especially interested in the saints associated with Christ Church because he was keeper of the relics. He, like Osbern, wrote the *Lives* to defend the saints against aspersions cast on their reputations in the Anglo-Norman period and so to preserve Christ Church's ancient religious tradition. His consequent research into written records helped train him as a historian. Nor did he neglect visual evidence. He was eager to demonstrate the exact locations of individual shrines in the old cathedral before its destruction by fire in 1067 to prove that Christ Church had owned the relics in question in Anglo-Saxon times. This led him to study the cathedral's architectural history; his research bore its best fruit in the description of the pre–1067 cathedral, which he included in his tract on the relics of Saint Ouen (André Wilmart, "Edmeri Cantuariensis cantoris nova opuscula de sanctorum veneratione et obsecratione," *Revue des Sciences religieuses*, 15 [1935]: 362–370); as a detailed architectural description, this was unprecedented in England and remained unique for another century. Eadmer's love of Christ Church was accompanied by unquestioning support for the archbishop of Canterbury's primacy over the Church in England. Unfortunately, his loyalty to Christ Church and to the archbishop's office resulted in flaws in his biographical and historical work. The *Vita Sancti Anselmi* and the *Historia* have distracting digressions on saints and relics, but worst damage was done by the primacy issue. Eadmer became increasingly obsessed with the controversy between Canterbury and York. He added two books to the *Historia* to support the Canterbury case and included copies of documents that he must have known were forged. Nevertheless, despite these faults, Eadmer deserves much praise for his important contribution to the development of biographical and historical writing in England.

Bibliography: R. W. Southern, *St. Anselm and His Biographer* (Cambridge, Eng., 1963).

Antonia Gransden

GEOFFREY OF MONMOUTH (Monmouth? c. 1100–St Asaph's? 1155?), pseudo-historian. Geoffrey had settled in Oxford by 1129 and was bishop of St. Asaph's by 1151. He wrote his immensely successful *Historia Regum Brittaniae* (ed. Acton Griscom and R. E. Jones [New York, 1929]), a (legendary) history of the Britons from prehistoric times until the late seventh century A.D., probably in 1136. He dedicated individual copies to various people, including King Stephen, Robert Earl of Gloucester, and Alexander Bishop of Lincoln. Geoffrey claimed that the *Historia* is a true account of the period it covers; it is, he stated, a translation of "a certain very old book written in the British language," which Walter archdeacon of Oxford had given him, having brought it "ex Britannia" (probably meaning from Brittany). However, there is no evidence confirming that any such book ever existed. Geoffrey also cited sources that are well known today, and his treatment of them does not inspire confidence in his integrity as a historian. For example, he attributed information to Gildas that occurred only very briefly in the latter's *De Excidio Britanniae* or not at all. Geoffrey possibly made some use of oral folk legend and of a few now lost written sources. However, his work must primarily be regarded as the product of his fertile imagination and outstanding literary talent. He was, indeed, the first man in England to write a history wholly in the romance tradition. He told tales of bloody battles, feats of chivalry, and courtly love and is most famous as the originator of the Arthurian legends in elaborate literary form. The historicity of Geoffrey's work was challenged by a few writers within a generation of his death; William of Newburgh in particular subjected the *Historia* to devastating criticism. (But its reputation survived apparently unscathed.) Although the *Historia* is valueless as an authority on British prehistory, it throws interesting light on the politics and institutions of Geoffrey's own day, since these things provided the backcloth against which his *personae dramatis* performed. Moreover, it illuminates aspects of twelfth-century mentality. It shows, for example, the preoccupation with national origins: Geoffrey asserted that the ancestor of the Britons was Brutus, an exile from the fall of Troy; in this way he put Britain on a par with France, since the French claimed Antenor, another Trojan exile, as their ancestor. Without doubt Geoffrey correctly gauged the tastes of his audience. The *Historia* was soon translated from Latin into English and French, which made it more accessible to the laity. More than two hundred medieval copies survive, more even than of Bede's (q.v.) *Historia Ecclesiastica*. It exerted a momentous influence on English historiography, partially bad but partially good. A bad effect was that it preempted early British history, blocking further research; henceforth until the sixteenth century historians almost invariably relied on Geoffrey for that period. A good effect was that the vernacular versions provided the stock from which useful annalistic continuations grew. Some of these so-called *Brut* chronicles continued beyond the midfifteenth century, and a version covering events to 1461 was the first book to be printed in England (1480). In general, the *Historia* fostered an interest in the British past among clergy and laity alike.

Bibliography: J.S.P. Tatlock, *The Legendary History of Britain: Geoffrey of Monmouth's Historia Regum Britanniae and Its Early Vernacular Versions* (Berkeley, Calif., 1950; repr., New York, 1974); Lewis Thorpe, trans., *Geoffrey of Monmouth: The History of the Kings of Britain* (Harmondsworth, Eng., 1966); Neil Wright, ed., *The Historia Regum Britanniae of Geoffrey of Monmouth*. Vol. 1: *Bern, Burgerbibliothek, MS. 568*, John S. Brewer (Cambridge, Eng., 1985); see pp. lx–lxv for an up-to-date bibliography.

Antonia Gransden

GERALD OF WALES (Maenor Pyr, Pembrokeshire, Wales, 1146–Lincoln, 1223), professional writer, autobiographer, and journalist, with a penchant for history, anthropology, and topography. A member of a powerful Cambro-Norman family, the de Barris (or "Geraldines"), Gerald studied in Paris until about 1175, was appointed archdeacon of Brecon in 1175, and was elected bishop of St. David's in the same year. However, his election was never confirmed because it was unacceptable to the king and to Hubert Walter, archbishop of Canterbury, and in 1203 Gerald, after a long struggle, abandoned his claim. In 1184 he entered the employment of Henry II. He accompanied John, count of Poitou, on his Irish expedition in 1185 and Baldwin, archbishop of Canterbury, when he toured Wales in 1188 to preach the Crusade. In 1194 Gerald, tired of court life and disillusioned with the Angevins, left royal service. Despite his ability and industry and the fact that he had dedicated a number of his books to royalty, he had failed to win sufficient favor to procure confirmation of his election to the bishopric of St. David's. He retired to Lincoln to write. As a writer Gerald was prolific and had outstanding talent. He was a product of the twelfth-century renaissance and his works show traces of classical influence. For example, he liked to put rhetorical speeches into the mouths of his protagonists and to describe people's characters and appearances in convincing detail in the style of Suetonius (q.v.). Moreover, he was self-revelatory to a degree rare even in the twelfth century. Although the complete text of his autobiography, the *De Rebus a se Gestis*, written in 1208, is now lost, it has been reconstructed from passages scattered throughout his other works (*Giraldi Cambrensis Opera*, 8 vols., ed. J. S. Brewer, J. F. Dimock, and G. F. Warner [London, 1861–9], vol. 1). Gerald emerged as a vain, boastful, paranoic man, who became bitterly obsessed by his failure over St. David's. His obsession increasingly warped his judgment of any person or matter connected with the controversy. However, although untrustworthy in that respect, his writings are in general of great value to the historian today.

Gerald was an excellent journalist; he left, for example, two eyewitness accounts of the excavation in Glastonbury in 1191 of (allegedly) King Arthur's body (*Giraldi Cambrensis Opera*, 4: 47–51; 8:126–129). A number of his works contain historical material. The *Expugnatio Hibernica* (ibid., vol. 5), written in 1188, relates the history of the Norman Conquest of Ireland (with particular emphasis on the de Barrises' participation) and includes a long pen portrait of Henry II. The last two of the three sections comprising *De Principis Instructione* (ibid., vol. 8) of 1218 is an account of Henry II's reign and of his sons, told as a homily on the fate of a sinful king; Henry's fortunes rise on the Wheel of Fortune but fall because of God's anger at the murder of Thomas Becket. Some of Gerald's works concern local history. The *De Invectionibus* (ibid., vol. 3) of 1216 is a well-documented but self-justificatory account of the St. David's controversy, to which subject Gerald reverted in *De Jure et Statu Menevensis Ecclesiae* (ibid., vol. 3). While at Lincoln, Gerald also wrote biographies of the bishops of Lincoln (ibid., vol. 7). However, Gerald is most famous for his *Topographia Hibernica* (ibid., vol. 5) of 1188, *Itinerarium Cambriae* (ibid., vol. 5) of 1191, and *Descriptio Cambriae* (ibid., vol. 6) of 1194. Besides legend and folklore, they contain realistic descriptions of the native people and their customs and of animals, antiquities, and the like. These decriptions are based on firsthand observations made by Gerald on his travels in Ireland (1185) and Wales (1188)). Many of them are unique contributions to our knowledge of historical anthropology and topography, and all demonstrate the originality of Gerald's mind, the acuteness of his perception, and his literary talent.

Bibliography: Robert Bartlett, *Gerald of Wales, 1146–1223* (Oxford, 1982); H. E. Butler, *The Autobiography of Giraldus Cambrensis* (London, 1937); Antonia Gransden, "The Growth of the Glastonbury Traditions and Legends in the Twelfth Century," *Journal of Ecclesiastical History*, 27 (1976): esp. 350–356; idem., "Realistic Observation in Twelfth Century England," *Speculum* 47 (1972): esp. 48–51; J. J. O'Meara, *The First*

Version of the Topography of Ireland (Dundalk, Ire., 1951); Brynley F. Roberts, *Gerald of Wales* (Cardiff, Wales, 1982); Lewis Thorpe, *Gerald of Wales, The Journey through Wales and the Description of Wales* (Harmondsworth, Eng., 1978).

Antonia Gransden

GIBBON, Edward (Putney, 1737–London, 1794), English historian. Born into a well-to-do family, Gibbon was educated at Westminster School and Magdalen College, Oxford. While at Oxford he became a Roman Catholic, an apostasy to which his father responded by sending him to Lausanne, and it was in Switzerland that Gibbon laid the foundations of his intellectual life through extensive and methodical study under the guidance of Daniel Pavillard. Reconverted to Protestantism, he returned to England in 1758, lost his literary maidenhead with the *Essai sur l'Étude de la Littérature* (1761), and, after some distasteful service with the militia, went on an abbreviated version of the Grand Tour (1763–1765). Gibbon reported that it was during this tour, in Rome in 1764, that the idea of writing *The History of the Decline and Fall of the Roman Empire* (1776–1788) first came to mind. The death of his spendthrift father in 1770 forced him to sell some of the family estate, but his circumstances were still sufficiently easy for him to lead a gentlemanly life in London and to begin work on *The Decline and Fall*. He entered Parliament in 1774 and acquired a lucrative sinecure by becoming a commissioner of trade. But when, through political vicissitudes, he lost both of these positions, he was forced from motives of economy to retire to Lausanne (1783), where in 1788 he completed *The Decline and Fall* and devoted his remaining years to the composition of his *Memoirs*, which were published posthumously with his *Miscellaneous Works* by Lord Sheffield in 1796.

The Decline and Fall has traditionally been viewed as a masterpiece of successful structure and as the crowning example of "philosophic history." Gibbon's periods of residence on the Continent had exposed him to the work of the *philosophes*, many of whom he knew personally. But his relationships with them were never cordial, and intellectually as well as socially, he kept a careful distance. The first volume of *The Decline and Fall* (1776) seems closest to the historiography of the *philosophes* in its ironic stance toward Christianity and in its subscription to the *philosophe* tenets of a constant and universal human nature and a regular historical causality. But as Gibbon moved further away from the Age of the Antonines and deeper into less thoroughly documented areas of the past, he uncovered material that was less amenable to those *philosophe* assumptions and that obliged him in the two final installments (1781 and 1788) to discover and adopt a new idiom in which irony is tempered by a willingness to admire and faith in causality by an acknowledgment of how the past may fruitfully elude our attempts to discover in it a constant and proportionate causation. In these final volumes, Gibbon appeared not as a whole-hearted spokesman for Enlightenment values but as a historian wrestling with a cross-grained subject that eventually unsettled the assumptions with which he had set out and that led him in some measure to anticipate historism.

Bibliography: M. Baridon, *Edward Gibbon et le Mythe de Rome* (Paris, 1977); J. W. Burrow, *Gibbon* (Oxford, 1985); G. Giarrizzo, *Edward Gibbon e la Cultura Europea del Settecento* (Naples, 1954); L. Gossman, *The Empire Unpossess'd* (Cambridge, Eng., 1981); A. Momigliano, "Gibbon's Contribution to Historical Method," in *Studies in Historiography* (London, 1966), pp. 40–55.

David Womersley

HENRY OF HUNTINGDON (Cambridgeshire or Huntingdonshire? c. 1085–Lincoln? c. 1157), English historian; archdeacon of Huntingdon about 1120 until his death. Henry was probably the son of Nicholas, archdeacon of Cambridge. He entered the household of Robert Bloet, bishop of Lincoln, as a boy and served his successor, Alexander of Bloir, bishop from 1123 to 1148. He wrote his *Historia Anglorum* (ed. Thomas Arnold [London, 1879]), a history of England from the Anglo-Saxon invasions until 1154, undertaken at the request of Bishop Alexander, to whom he dedicated the work, in stages between 1124 and 1154. In its final form the *Historia* contained ten books; two of them, Books 8 and 9, are extraneous to the historical narrative. Book 8, *De Summitatibus*, comprises three letters, which Henry certainly wrote for publication, addressed to Henry I; Warin, "a Briton"; and Walter, possibly the archdeacon of Leicester of that name. This last letter, entitled *De Contemptu Mundi*, is a valuable source for the history of Lincoln cathedral; to illustrate the theme that all people die, Henry cited the lives, among others, of the cathedral's past and present clergy. Book 9, *De Miraculis*, concerns the miracles of English saints. Since Henry advised those who want to know more about the saints in question to visit their shrines personally, he was in effect providing a guidebook for pilgrims. As a historian, Henry wrote in a strongly edificatory, homiletic vein. He attributed a number of disasters to divine vengeance. God punished the degeneracy of the Britons and Anglo-Saxons with plagues and invasions; the perjury of Roger, bishop of Salisbury, with capture and a miserable death; and the sacrilege of Geoffrey de Mandeville, likewise with death. Henry emphasized the transitory nature of all earthly glory—the theme of the *De Contemptu Mundi*. He wrote under the influence of Bede (q.v.), whose *Historia Ecclesiastica* provided the model for his introductory chapter on the geography of Britain. For later Anglo-Saxon and early Anglo-Norman history, Henry derived information from the *Old English Chronicle*. But he was also a product of the twelfth-century renaissance, and the *Historia* shows the influence of classical literature. It contains citations from classical authors such as Ovid and abounds in formal rhetorical speeches. Henry related the legend that the French nation originated with Antenor, an exile from the fall of Troy. To attribute classical origins to a nation was a feature of romance literature. The latter clearly was another strong influence on Henry. He was interested in King Arthur and loved describing battle scenes. His taste for such matters was augmented when in 1139 a copy of Geoffrey of Monmouth's (q.v.) *Historia Regum Britanniae* came into his hands. He was delighted with this (largely legendary) history and summarized some of its contents in his letter to

Warin. Henry's work had immediate success. It owed its popularity partially to his literary talent—his gift for graphic narrative and as a storyteller. He was the first authority for the now time-honored story of Henry I's death from eating a surfeit of lampreys, and he was one of the two earliest authorities to present the tale of Canute's attempt to turn back the tide.

Bibliography: Introduction to Thomas Arnold, ed., *Historia Anglorum*, Rolls Series (London, 1879); Antonia Gransden, *Historical Writing in England* [i], *c. 550–c. 1307* (London, 1974), pp. 193–201; Nancy F. Partner, *Serious Entertainments: The Writing of History in Twelfth-Century England* (Chicago and London, 1977), p. 1.

Antonia Gransden

HIGDEN, Ranulf (? c. 1280–St. Werburgh's Abbey, Chester, c. 1360), English historian and encyclopedist. Little is known about Higden's life. He took the habit at St. Werburgh's in 1299 and later probably held the office of *armarius* or keeper of the monastic library and head of the scriptorium. He is not known to have traveled from St. Werburgh's except on one occasion: on August 21, 1352, he was summoned by the king's council to come "with all your chronicles and those in your charge to speak and treat with the council concerning matters to be explained to you on our behalf." This summons shows that by that time Higden enjoyed a nationwide reputation as a historian—a reputation that rested on his great work, the *Polychronicon*, which he wrote in a number of recensions between 1327 and 1352 (9 vols., ed. Churchill Babington and J. R. Lumby, [London, 1865–1886]). The *Polychronicon* is a universal history of encylopedic scope. Starting with the creation, it describes the geography of the world before proceeding with the history of humankind from pagan times until Higden's own time. (The final recension ends in 1352.) It deals with all aspects of history; besides enjoying geography, Higden was interested in social anthropology, cultural history, and natural history. No previous writer in England had treated history in such depth and breadth. It is true that Matthew Paris's (q.v.) *Chronica Majora* is a universal history insofar as it begins at the creation and interprets its subjects widely, but Paris, unlike Higden, was mainly interested in the recent, not the distant, past. Higden's immediate forerunner in England was Nicholas Trevet, but the latter's *Historia ab orbe condito ad Christi Nativitatem*, although a universal history, did not compare in scale and comprehensiveness with the *Polychronicon*. Again, although Gerald of Wales (q.v.) was interested in social anthropology and natural history, he did not write about them in primarily historical context. For an obvious precedent we have to look abroad, to France—to Vincent of Beauvais, whose *Speculum Historiale* was, indeed, one of Higden's sources. Hidgen assembled his information from numerous standard authorities, using some directly and others by means of compendia. Among his classical sources were Pliny's *Natural History* and Suetonius' (q.v.) *Lives of the Caesars*, and among his early Christian sources were Eusebios (q.v.), Saint Augustine (q.v.), and Isidore of Seville. For the Dark and Middle Ages he used most of the well-known English writers, including Bede (q.v.), William of Malmesbury (q.v.), Geoffrey of Monmouth (q.v.), and Gerald of Wales (q.v.). The result of his extensive reading was a mass of miscellaneous material. The *Polychronicon* might well have been a jumble of disconnected information. But it is not. This is because Higden imposed order on it in masterly fashion. He adopted a number of structural devices, most of them new to English historiography (certainly no previous or subsequent historian in medieval England expended such care on the arrangement of his work). Higden employed the ancient concept of humans as the microcosm of the world in a novel way, employing it to link the geographical section of the *Polychronicon* to the historical narrative; since God created the greater world first, its geography should be described before the history of the lesser world, humankind. Higden elaborated on this theme and also used various numerological conceits that further synthesized his disparate material. Among them was the (fairly commonplace) device of dividing the work into seven books, "after the example of the Creator, who made all things in six days and rested on the seventh" (*Polychronicon*).

Higden was the first historian in England to stamp his name on his work by means of an acrostic (contrived from the first letter of the first word of each book). Nevertheless, despite his historiographical innovations, both Higden's choice of material and the methods he adopted to organize it show him to have been a typically medieval scholar. The *Polychronicon*'s contents can be seen as a celebration of God's creation, and its structure was determined by religious symbolism. Moreover, it includes many edificatory stories, *exempla* that belong to the homiletic tradition. (Higden, in fact, wrote two books on preaching, the *Ars componendi Sermones* and the *Speculum Curatorum*). His treatment of his sources was in general uncritical. He transmitted with evident relish the time-honored legacy of fictions—myths, marvels, and miracles—that he found in his authorities, rarely questioning their historicity. He presented his audience, using considerable literary skill, with traditional learning and lore. It is not surprising that the *Polychronicon* was an immediate and immense success; among historians in medieval England only Bede and Geoffrey of Monmouth excelled beyond Higden as authors of best-sellers. More than one hundred and twenty copies of the *Polychronicon* still survive. It was translated into English by John Trevisa in the 1380s and was again translated in the fifteenth century. Trevisa's translation formed the basis of William Caxton's printed edition of 1482, which gave the *Polychronicon* the distinction of being the second book to be printed in England. To the historian today, the value of the *Polychronicon* is limited as a source of concrete facts because of the large proportion of fiction it contains. However, its popularity shows that Higden correctly gauged the tastes of many of his contemporaries. Their vision was widening to include a great variety of places and peoples, in preparation, as it were, for the expansion of Western Europe.

Bibliography: V. H. Galbraith, "An autograph MS. of Ranulph Higden's *Polychronicon*," *Huntington Library Quarterly*, 24 (1959–1960): 1–18; Antonia Gransden, *His-*

torical Writing in England, [ii], *c.1307 to the Early Sixteenth Century* (London, 1982), Ch. 2; idem, "Silent Meanings in Ranulf Higden's *Polychronicon* and in Thomas Elmham's *Liber Metricus de Henrico Quinto*," *Medium Aevum* 46, (1978): 231–233; John Taylor, *The Universal Chronicle of Ranulf Higden* (Oxford, 1966).

Antonia Gransden

HUME, David (Edinburgh, 1711–Edinburgh, 1776), British historian and philosopher. Aside from his international reputation as the founder of modern analytical philosophy, Hume was a distinguished historian. The first volume of *The History of England*, otherwise known as *The History of Great Britain*, covering the reigns of James I and Charles I was published in 1754, followed by a second volume surveying the Commonwealth and the reigns of Charles II and James II in 1756. After the publication of the two-volume *House of Tudor* in 1759, he completed the history with two further volumes, on the period between Julius Caesar and the accession of Henry VII in 1762. Although often interpreted as a "Tory" historian, Hume is more satisfactorily viewed as an "establishment" historian who replaced Rapin de Thoyras in his capacity as a historian suited to the political requirements of a stable, limited monarchy under the Hanoverians. Rejecting the basic ideas of traditional Whig history, especially the interpretation of English history in terms of the reaffirmation of a timeless ancient constitution, he demonstrated the modern nature of political liberty, based on the recent revolution of 1688. Hume interpreted the preceding centuries of English history as a period when the constitution was in a state of continuous change, such that it was impossible to define the regal power as either limited or absolute. Hence it was possible to extenuate the policies of James I and Charles I, precisely because they were based on as much precedent as their antagonists. If anything, the protagonists for parliamentary liberty were the innovators who challenged the status quo. Hume's account of the preceding century, which he saw as an age of almost oriental despotism on the part of the Tudor monarchs, strengthened his belief that the first two Stuarts were on the defensive. His account of the Saxon and medieval period also undermined naive "Whig" assumptions by pointing out the unrepresentative nature of the Anglo-Saxon constitution, the dramatic effects on property and power of the Norman Conquest and its tyrannical aftermath, and also the late arrival of the Commons in the medieval period. Hume's fascination with religious motivation, also expressed in an essay on the "natural history" of religion (proving the historical priority of polytheism to monotheism) was revealed in his account of the Civil War and Commonwealth, and part of his explanation for the seventeenth century rise of a "spirit of liberty" can be accounted for in terms of the concept of "enthusiasm," which he had outlined in a separate essay. Indeed, Hume believed that he was writing a "history of the human mind," and he explained the desire for "a new plan of liberty" in terms of a " revolution" of "manners" that had occurred during the opening years of the seventeenth century. However, he was also aware of the economic origins of the Civil War, such as the peculiar financial situation of the monarchy at that period and the consequences of the new balance of property in Parliament achieved during the sixteenth century. Hume also added a set of appendices to his chronological narrative dealing with issues such as the standard of living or the "manners" and "customs" of a period, which earned him the title of social historian.

Bibliography: Duncan Forbes, *Hume's Philosophical Politics* (Cambridge, Eng., 1975); Giuseppe Giarrizzo, *David Hume, politico e storico* (Turin, 1962); David Fate Norton and Richard Popkin, eds., *David Hume: Philosophical Historian* (Indianapolis, 1965); Victor G. Wrexler, *David Hume and the "History of England"* (Philadelphia, 1979).

Phillip Corina

MATTHEW PARIS (? c. 1200–St. Albans, Hertfordshire, 1259), English chronicler. A monk of the Benedictine abbey of St. Albans from 1217, Matthew Paris attended the feast of St. Edward in Westminster abbey in 1247, and Pope Innocent III sent him to the abbey of St. Benet Holm, on the island of Nidarholm, Norway, in 1248; otherwise, as far as is known, he spent his life at St. Albans, writing history. His great work was the *Chronica Majora* covering the period from the creation of the world until 1259 (7 vols., ed. H. R. Luard [London, 1872–1883]), which he began about 1240. In 1250 he compiled a book of documents relevant to the narrative of the *Chronica Majora*, the *Liber Additamentorium* (ibid., vol. 6). He used the *Chronica Majora* as the main source for three shorter works: the *Historia Anglorum*, a chronicle of England from the Norman Conquest, ultimately to 1255 (3 vols., ed. Frederick Madden [London, 1866–1869]); the *Abbreviatio Chronicorum* (ibid., vol. 3); and the *Flores Historiarum* (3 vols., ed. H. R. Luard [London, 1890]). He also wrote a history of St. Albans' abbey from its (supposed) foundation in 793 to 1255, the *Gesta Abbatum Monasterii Sancti Albani* (3 vols. ed., in *Thomas Walsingham's* version, H. T. Riley [London, 1867–1869]); Paris' own text is *Vitae Duorum Offarum sive Offanorum, Merciorum Regum, Coenobii Sancti Albani fundatorum; et viginti trium Abbatum Sancti Albani* . . . (ed., William Wats [London, 1639]). Besides being a chronicler, Paris was a biographer. He wrote two biographies in Latin, one of Archbishop Stephen Langton, *Ungedruckte Anglo-Normannische Geschichtsquellen* (ed. Felix Lieberman [Strasburg, 1879]) and the other of Archbishop Saint Edmund Rich (*St. Edmund of Abingdon*, ed. C. H. Lawrence, [Oxford, 1960], pp. 73–100). In addition, he wrote a number of hagiographies in Anglo-Norman verse, including one of St. Alban (facsimile ed. W.R.L. Lowe, E. F. Jacob, and M. R. James [Oxford, 1924]). Paris' principle work was indisputedly the *Chronica Majora*. It was the most comprehensive chronicle yet written in England and remains the most important contemporary narrative source for thirteenth-century English history. For the period 1235 Paris relied on the *Flores Historiarum* a chronicle from the creation to 1235 (3 vols., ed., from 1154, H. G. Hewlett [London, 1886–1889]) by Roger of Wendover, his predecessor as chronicler at St. Albans. From the point in 1235 where Wendover ended, the *Chronica Majora* is independent of all known literary authorities.

For this section Paris amassed numerous documents and acquired information verbally. He was well situated for obtaining such source material. St. Albans lay within twenty miles of London, on one of the principal roads north, and, through its cells at Tynemouth, Belvoir, Binham, and Wymondham, was in touch with northern England, the Midlands, and East Anglia. The king was a frequent visitor at St. Albans, and so were many royal officials and magnates besides innumerable lesser people who might bring news. Paris exploited his opportunities to the full. The *Chronica Majora* and *Liber Additamentorum* have copies of documents not otherwise known, and Paris' narrative contains much information that cannot be found elsewhere. Particularly remarkable was the wide range of his interests.

Paris was the first chronicler to treat European history as a subject in its own right, not just as an adjunct to English history. His curiosity, indeed, was omnivorous. His descriptions of buildings and works of art were not without precedent (notably in the works of William of Malmesbury [q.v.]), but he was also interested in some subjects that had not hitherto attracted a chronicler's attention. He studied heraldry, and the paintings of shields that illustrate the *Chronica Majora*, the *Liber Additamentorum*, and the *Historia Anglorum* are among the earliest evidences for this topic. His interest in natural history appears, for example, in his realistic description and paintings of the elephant acquired by Henry III. Examples of his interest in cartography are his maps of the British Isles, the first-known maps to treat Britain as an entity and to be based on thought and research rather than tradition. Many of Paris's interests were undoubtedly fostered by his excellent visual sense. He was an accomplished artist. The surviving holographs of his works are notable for the pictures, mostly in the margins, with which Paris (and his pupils at St. Albans) illustrated and enlivened the texts. Although the pictures and Paris' literary style insure that the *Chronica Majora* is never tedious, Paris was aware that its great length and vast amount of information tended to make it cumbersome. For this reason he produced three shorter chronicles (the *Historia Anglorum* concentrates particularly on English history) and relegated many documents to the *Liber Additamentorum*. To link such documents with the relevant parts of the *Chronica Majora*, he developed a system of marginal *signa* for cross-referencing. Moreover, he adopted Ralph De Diceto's (q.v.) practice of using pictorial symbols in the margins to indicate entries on specific topics. He also used *signa* and pictorial symbols in the *Historia Anglorum*, which, although shorter than the *Chronica Majora*, is a very substantial work.

All Paris' chronicles have a distinctive flavor. They are pervaded by his strong opinions, expressed forcefully in colorful, eloquent prose. He was bitterly critical of the king, his advisers, and officials; of the papacy and its agents, and, indeed, of anyone who encroached upon the autonomy of religious houses—especially St. Albans. However, later in life Paris revised both the *Chronica Majora* and the *Historia Anglorum* to modify his invective. Perhaps this revision was the result of his acquisition of fame. He became well known to Henry III. When he attended the feast of Saint Edward at Westminster in 1247, Henry told him to record the occasion in his chronicle and asked him to dine. When Henry visited St. Albans in 1259 Paris was his "constant companion" and dined at his table, and Henry gave him information for his chronicle. Meanwhile, Paris wrote his saints' *Lives* for royal and noble patronesses. He may, therefore, have altered his opinions about the "great" and revised his chronicles accordingly. But he may also have considered it expedient not to offend those in power. No chronicle subsequently written in England equaled the scale and eloquence of the *Chronica Majora*; no chronicler rivaled the breadth of Paris' interests or the variety of his talents; and no one, except Thomas Walsingham (q.v.) a century later, aspired even to try to emulate his achievements. Although the *Chronica Majora* can be seen as representing the high-water mark of chronicle writing in England, one of Paris' lesser works, the *Flores Historiarum*, enjoyed more widespread success in the Middle Ages. After Paris' death, the *Flores* was continued at St. Albans to 1265. Then a copy went to Westminster, where a further continuation was added to 1306. Copies of this Westminster version went to numerous religious houses and elsewhere, and a few were continued in their new homes.

Bibliography: V. H. Galbraith, *Roger Wendover and Matthew Paris* (Glasgow, 1944), reprinted in idem, *Kings and Chroniclers* (London, 1982), no. 10; Antonia Gransden, *Historical Writing in England*, [i], *c. 550–c. 1307* (London, 1974), Ch. 16; J. C. Holt, "St. Albans Chroniclers and Magna Carta," *Transactions of the Royal Historical Society*, 5th ser., 14 (1964): 67–88; Richard Vaughan, *Matthew Paris* (Cambridge, Eng., 1958).

Antonia Gransden

MILLAR, John (Shotts, Lanarkshire, 1735–Millheugh, Lanarkshire, 1801), British historian; professor of civil law at Glasgow University. Millar is best known for two published works. *The Origin of the Distinction of Ranks* (1771) is a notable example of eighteenth-century "natural history," a technique delineating a universal stage theory of development for any social phenomenon. Millar's version of this genre is remarkable for its concentration on political authority and the social status of women, and he related the stages of their development to an economic and technological base. The *Historical View of the English Government* (1787) is one of the great precursors of nineteenth-century constitutional history. An application of his "natural history" of political authority, the *Historical View* situates constitutional change in an economic context, covering the period from the Saxon settlement until 1603. His emphasis on social and economic forces in constitutional history forced him to reject the Whig myths of Saxon political wisdom and liberty, as well as the belief that the great pillars of the free constitution arose from liberal intentions, while enabling him to reveal the naivety of the "Tory" view of the Norman Conquest. His views on the later periods, mostly published posthumously, constitute a strong rebuttal to David Hume (q.v.), emphasizing the continuity of a liberal constitution since the Norman Conquest, the existence of parliamentary liberty during the supposed Tudor despotism, and the constitutional innovations of the first two Stuart monarchs.

Bibliography: John Craig, *Life*, prefixed to *Origin of Ranks* (Edinburgh 1806); Duncan Forbes, "Scientific Whiggism: Adam Smith and John Millar," *Cambridge Journal* 7 (1954): 643–670; W. C. Lehmann, *John Millar of Glasgow* (Cambridge, Eng., 1960).

Phillip Corina

MORE, Thomas (London, 1478–London, 1535), English lawyer, politician, and humanist author. More divided his early career between the bar, diplomacy, and humanistic letters. Entering the Council of Henry VIII in 1517, he became lord chancellor in 1529 but was eventually executed for opposing the creation of the royal supremacy over the English Church. He was a virile controversialist on many subjects but is best known for *Utopia* (1516). His reputation as a historian rests on the incomplete *History of King Richard the Third*, composed in Latin and English between 1513 and 1522, pirated in other chronicles of 1543 and 1548, and first published in a reliable version in 1557. The work has become notorious for depicting its subject in the blackest terms and is held mainly responsible for the later Shakespearian stereotype. But to concentrate on its myth-making quality or its supposed infidelity to the "real" Richard III is to miss the point. More wished to tell the truth, but like all humanist historians, he measured this in ways other than by factual accuracy. In part, he was aiming, for virtually the first time in England, at the rounded Ciceronian interpretation of a major political episode—the usurpation of the throne—which anatomized its origins, motivations, and consequences in the course of telling a plausible story. This involved a good deal of imaginative, but brilliantly effective, reconstruction of oral testimony. Here, the conception of the historian's task was essentially literary, even dramaturgical, and the purpose was to teach (and in More's case, to learn) general truths about political life. In particular, the work applied to English history a model of tyranny that More derived from the ancient historians, notably Sallustius (q.v.), Suetonius (q.v.), and Tacitus (q.v.). In this context, Richard's actions were like those of Tiberius—essentially symbols of the timeless politics of dissimulation and injustice. Above all, More could not have divorced his history from the purposes of a Christian province that, allowing for human as well as demonic evil, brings both retributive punishment and hope for the countermanding actions of just men. In these various ways, and principally for his own benefit, he sought to inject meaning into the most disquieting events of the recent English past. The result is so true to this aim that it genuinely transcends any (essentially modern) concern for mere veracity to facts.

Bibliography: Alistair Fox, *Thomas More: History and Providence* (Oxford, 1982); Alison Hanham, *Richard III and His Early Historians, 1483–1535* (Oxford, 1975); R. S. Sylvester, ed., *The History of King Richard III*, Yale Edition of the *Complete Works of St. Thomas More*, vol. 2 (New Haven and London, 1963), Introduction; R. S. Sylvester and G. Marc'hadour, eds., *Essential Articles for the Study of Thomas More* (Hamden, Conn., 1977).

Stuart Clark

ROBERTSON, William (Borthwick/Midlothian, 1721–Edinburgh, 1793), British historian. Minister of Old Greyfriars Edinburgh, principal of Edinburgh University, moderator of the Scottish Assembly, and member of the Select Society, Robertson was acknowledged as one of the "triumvirate" along with David Hume (q.v.) and Edward Gibbon (q.v.). Of the three, Robertson is considered a leading exemplar of "philosophical history." His abilities to generalize about history and to integrate social theory with political narrative have secured him a reputation as one of the most theoretically aware historians in the eighteenth century. His first publication was a sermon entitled *The Situation of the World at the Time of Christ's Appearance* (1755). It is of importance to Robertson's later historical work because he used the concept of "Providence" working through the unintended consequences of human action to explain why the Gospel was made public at so late a time in antiquity; the concept of Providence, or God's plan for human history, being traced through the "natural" causes of "civil history" exerts a profound influence as a causal explanation in his later works. His first major historical study was *The History of Scotland* (1759). In the opening pages he revealed a characteristic skepticism about the possibility of writing the story of the origins of nations. Viewed in the context of the polemical disputes on the ancient Scottish constitution and the guilt or innocence of Mary Queen of Scots, Robertson showed "philosophical" detachment. Ten years later, he published *The History of the Reign of the Emperor Charles V*. His talent for delineating broad historical trends is expressed in the first volume, which contains a remarkable survey, partially indebted to Voltaire (q.v.), of the progress from the "barbarism" of the Dark Ages to the "refinement" of the sixteenth century. The survey is notable for its analysis of the European feudal system and for its emphasis on the role of the Italian city-states in destroying feudalism and on the rise of a new international system of diplomacy, founded on the principle of the balance of power that made sixteenth-century history of peculiar revelance to the present.

Robertson's last two historical works *The History of America* (1777) and *Historical Disquisition concerning the Knowledge Which the Ancients Had of India* (1791) reveal the influence of the histories of commerce by Raynal and Adam Anderson. The *History of America* is famous for its narrative of the Spanish discovery and conquest of the New World, but it also provides an important contribution to eighteenth-century social theory in the form of a study of the savage "manners and customs" of the North American Indian tribes and a similar analysis of the more sophisticated societies of the Aztec and Inca empires. Robertson rejected the theory that cultural similarities could be explained by tracing the influences of one people upon another. Instead, like Robert Turgot and Adam Smith, he suggested that any society could be related to a particular social stage in a finite choice of usually three or four social models; cultural similarities were evidence that societies had reached the same social stage rather than an indication of direct links. Thus his last two works demonstrate in particular the theoretical bent to his history, which he successfully combined with narrative skills.

Bibliography: J. B. Black, *The Art of History* (London, 1926); Manfred Schlenke, "Aus der Frühzeit des englischen Historismus William Robertsons Beitrag zur methodischen Grundlegung der Geschichtswissenschaftim 18 Jahrhundert," *Saeculum* 7 (1956): 107–125; idem, "Kulturgeschichte oder politische Geschichte in der Geschichtsschreibung des 18. Jahrhunderts, William Robertson als Historiker des europäischen Staatensystem," *Archiv für Kulturgeschichte* 37 (1955): 60–97; Dugald Stewart, *Account of the Life and Writings of William Robertson* (London, 1801).

Phillip Corina

ROGER OF HOWDEN (Yorkshire, midtwelfth century?–Howden, Yorkshire? c. 1201), English chronicler. The identity of Roger the chronicler is not certain. He was no doubt the royal clerk of that name who appears in the public records in various official capacities between 1174 and 1190. Less certain, but not unlikely, is that he was also the "Roger of Howden" who became vicar of Howden sometime between 1173 and 1176 and was at the siege of Acre in 1191. His *Chronica* (4 vols., ed. William Stubbs) [London, 1868–1871]) covers the period from 732 to 1201. To 1148 it is compiled from well-known, mainly north-country, sources. From 1148 to 1169 it is almost totally independent of known chronicles but from 1170 to 1192 is based on the chronicle that goes under the name of *Benedict of Peterborough* (2 vols., ed. William Stubbs [London, 1867]). From 1192 to the end it is an original account written fairly close in time to the events it records. There is evidence suggesting that Roger himself wrote *Benedict*. If so, certain marked differences between the *Chronica* and *Benedict* need explaining. The *Chronica* devotes more space to north-country affairs and less to those of the central government than does *Benedict*. These variations would be accounted for if Roger wrote *Benedict* while in royal service and the *Chronica* during retirement late in life at Howden. Whatever the truth, both *Benedict* and the *Chronica* are remarkable for their quasi-official character. They reflect the increasing activity and institutionalization of royal administration under the Angevin kings. They are excellently informed about the central government and cite numerous official documents *in extenso* (some of the texts they preserve do not apparently survive elsewhere). They also contain a valuable account of the Third Crusade, including an itinerary of Richard I derived from a journal of someone, perhaps Roger himself, who accompanied the king; the version in the *Chronica*, although based on that in *Benedict*, adds a few graphic touches. In fact, *Benedict* and the *Chronica* are sources of primary importance for the reigns of Henry II and Richard I.

Bibliography: Frank Barlow, "Roger of Howden," *English Historical Review* 65, (1950): 352–360; Antonia Gransden, *Historical Writing in England,* [i], *c. 550–c. 1307* (London, 1974), pp. 222–230; J. C. Holt, "The Assizes of Henry II: The Texts," D. A. Bullough and R. L. Storey, eds., *The Study of Medieval Records: Essays in Honour of*

Kathleen Major (Oxford, 1971), pp. 85–106; D. M. Stenton, "Roger of Howden and Benedict," *English Historical Review* 68 (1953): 574–582; William Stubbs, *Benedict of Peterborough*, 2 vols., Rolls Series (London, 1867), Introductions.

Antonia Gransden

SELDEN, John (West Tarling, 1584–London, 1654), English historian. The son of a Sussex Yeoman, Selden was educated at Oxford and the Inns of Court and practiced law for a time before devoting himself to scholarship and politics (he was a member of Parliament before and during the civil wars). Selden was a friend of William Camden (q.v.) and of the poets Ben Jonson and Michael Drayton, whom he advised on matters of history. He had a fine library (now in the Bodleian, Oxford) and a collection of antiquities. Selden can be seen as a late example of legal humanism, a philologist in the style of William Budé and Jacob Cujas. As a scholar he led two lives, as an orientalist and a medievalist. In the former field his most famous work was his book on Syrian mythology, *De deis syriis* (1617); he also wrote a series of studies on Jewish law (concerning property, marriage, divorce, and so on) and institutions (the calendar, the high priest, and so on). As a medievalist he specialized in English legal history, editing a series of texts, from Eadmer (q.v.) in the eleventh century to Fortescue in the fifteenth century, as well as writing studies of his own. His most important as well as his most controversial work was his *History of Tithes* (1617), an example of "problematic" or institutional history over the long term that claimed to be a "mere narrative" but was interpreted otherwise, doubtless with justice, since it points out that the Church did not levy tithes until about A.D. 400. Selden had to appear before the Court of High Commission in 1618 and acknowledge his error in offering any "occasion of Argument" over the clergy's claim to a divine right to tithes. His *Titles of Honour* (1614), which is also concerned with the history of rituals, such as coronations, was another work with political implications; his section on the title of baron, for example, included a discussion of medieval parliaments. Selden practiced and preached a history based on sources ("I ever loved the fountain"), notably the records then preserved in the Tower of London. However, he was no mere antiquarian; he contrasted "the too studious Affectation of bare and sterile Antiquitie" with the study of what "gives necessarie light to the Present in matter of state."

Bibliography: F. Fussner, *The Historical Revolution* (London, 1962), Ch.11; D. Ogg, Introduction to his edition of John Selden's *Dissertation on the Fleta* (Cambridge, Eng., 1925).

Peter Burke

VERGIL, Polydore (Urbino, c. 1470–Urbino, 1555), Italian humanist historian. Vergil went to England in 1502 as the deputy to Adriano Castellesi, the bishop of Hereford, collector of papal taxes, and future cardinal and spent the intervening years mainly in England. He had little in the way of taxes to remit but made himself useful in various ways as an intermediary between Englishmen and the papal curia; he was patronized by the new dynasty of the Tudors, managed to keep out of serious political trouble, and after other promotions was finally made archdeacon of Wells. When he arrived in 1502 he was already the author of two works destined to be popular: the *Adagia* (1498), eclipsed by Erasmus's collection of proverbs; and the *De inventoribus rerum* (1499), an antiquarian survey of "first begetters" that was widely read and translated into most European languages. Besides the *De inventoribus rerum*, Vergil's most celebrated and influential book was the *Historia Anglica*. The manuscript of this was written in 1512–1513 and is now in the Vatican Library. The book was first published as a handsome folio at Basel in 1534. After a chapter describing England and sections dealing with early government, the narrative then devoted a book to each reign until the death of Henry VII (1509), a pattern followed by narrative historians almost to our own day. Revised in detail, it was reprinted in 1546; in 1555 after further revision the author added another book covering events to 1538. Other reprints followed to 1603. Intended to appeal to the literati of Europe, the *Anglica Historia* remained for a long time the standard reference book for continental scholars. Although no English translation was published, portions of a midsixteenth-century version came out in two volumes of the Camden Series in 1844 and 1846; in 1960 the same series published an edition and translation of the Vatican manuscript from 1485 to 1513, followed by a text and translation of the 1555 edition covering the period 1513–1537. Vergil's history was contemporary with Thomas More's (q.v.) *Richard III* and, like it, defended the new Tudor dynasty against its critics. They were both absorbed into Hall's *Chronicle* and so came to influence the historical dramatists, notably Shakespeare. Vergil followed his main texts faithfully, depending on standard accounts such as Matthew Paris and the St. Albans chroniclers, the London town chroniclers, and, where they were relevant, ancient authorities such as Caesar. He also produced an edition of the sixth-century work of Gildas, *De calamitate, excidio et conquestu Britanniae*, to reinforce his skeptical attitude toward the Authurian legend. This came out, probably at Antwerp, in 1525.

Bibliography: Denys Hay, *P. V. Renaissance Historian and Man of Letters* (Oxford, 1952); see suggested corrections in C. H. Clough, *English Historical Review* 82 (1967): 772–783. For the *De inventoribus*, see Brian P. Copenhaver, "The Historiography of Discovery in the Renaissance," *Journal of the Warburg and Courtauld Institutes* 41 (1978): 112–214.

Denys Hay

WALSINGHAM, Thomas (Walsingham, Norfolk?, midfourteenth century–St. Albans, c. 1432), English chronicler; monk of St. Albans, Hertfordshire. In the fourteenth century St. Albans was an important intellectual center. Its most famous scholar was Abbot Richard de Wallingford (1328–1336), mathematician and astonomer. Abbot Thomas de la Mare (1349–1396) built studies and a new library (for which he amassed books) and scriptorium. Nevertheless, the historiographical tradition, which had achieved such excellence in the thirteenth century, with Matthew Paris (q.v.), languished until Thomas Walsingham revived it. In 1380 Abbot de la Mare appointed Walsingham precentor, which office gave him charge of the scriptorium. Almost immediately Walsingham, who saw himself as Paris's successor, started writing chronicles. His first was a continuation to 1377 of Ranulf Higden's (q.v.) *Polychronicon*. Soon afterwards he began his best-known work, a continuation to 1392 of Matthew Paris's *Chronica Majora*, which he wrote more or less contemporaneously with the events he recorded. About the same time he started to continue Paris's history of St. Albans' abbey, the *Gesta Abbatum Monasterii Sancti Albani*, which, ultimately, he carried on to 1393 (3 vols., ed. H. T. Riley, [London, 1867–1868]). In addition, he composed a short chronicle of the world, from the creation to 1392 (which roughly corresponds to Paris's *Abbreviatio Chronicarum*). He stopped writing the *Chronica Majora* and *Gesta Abbatum* probably in 1394, when the abbot appointed him prior of Wymondham (Norfolk), one of St. Alban's cells, an office that he held until 1396. While at Wymondham he composed a short version of his *Chronica Majora*, the *Historia Anglicana* (which can be compared with Paris's *Historia Anglorum*). On his return from Wymondham in 1396 Walsingham turned his attention to classical studies and composed the *Archana Deorum*, a commentary on Ovid's *Metamorphoses*, besides two works on ancient history. However, he resumed writing chronicles in the late fourteenth or early fifteenth century, after Henry Bolingbroke's usurpation of the throne in 1399. He continued the *Chronica Majora* to 1420 and the shorter chronicle to 1422. Sometime between 1419 and 1422 he wrote the *Ypodigma Neustriae*, a chronicle from 911 to 1419, which he dedicated to Henry V (ed. H. T. Riley [London, 1876]). Ostensibly, it was a history of Normandy, but in fact it was a brief history of England (which has been compared with Paris's *Flores Historiarum*).

Although Walsingham did not have Paris's variety of talents and interests, he shared his gift for eloquent prose and, conversely, for exact descriptive writing; above all, like Paris, he was a brilliant reporter of recent events. In places, Walsingham's chronicles have a homiletic tone. He expatiated on the sins of contemporary individuals, exhorting them to repentance in rhetorical style. He also attributed many catastrophes to divine vengeance. Nevertheless, he was capable of rational thought. Sometimes he attributed an event both to God's intervention and to natural causes. For example, he regarded the Peasant's Revolt as a punishment for the sins of the English but also exasperation at the poll tax (the immediate cause) and at servile obligations (the long-term cause). The challenges of Walsingham's own times must have fostered his taste for reportage. His life coincided with the dramatic events of the Peasant's Revolt and Richard II's deposition, besides the rise of England's first heretical sect, the Lollards, and the beginning of the Great Schism. Walsingham left detailed accounts of all of these landmarks in history. As a reporter he enjoyed great advantages at St. Albans. The town itself was the scene of violent disturbance during the Peasant's Revolt, and its neighbourhood witnessed considerable Lollard activity. (Indeed, Sir John Oldcastle himself, Walsingham related, took refuge for several days in 1417 "in the house of a rustic" on the abbot's demesne.) Nor was St. Albans remote from more distant events. It was within twenty miles of London (where the abbot had a residence) and the frequent venue of king, magnates, and many other potential newsbearers. Among the latter were the abbey's benefactors, some of them important men of affairs, for example, Richard II's uncle, Thomas of Woodstock, duke of Gloucester, a leader of the opposition to the king, and Sir John Philpot, mayor of London, 1378–1379, a key figure in London politics. (Walsingham's interest in the abbey's benefactors is testified to by his first-known book, the *Liber Benefactorum*, which commemorated them and recorded their donations.) It is not, therefore, surprising that Walsingham is an invaluable authority for Richard II's reign, but he is a biased one.

In his first phase of chronicle writing his attitude to king and government was similar to Paris's. Although during Richard's minority, Walsingham wrote of the king with some respect, he was bitterly hostile to those in power, notably to John of Gaunt. After Richard gained his majority, Walsingham became severely critical of him and even more so of his ministers and favorites, while his opinion of Gaunt gradually rose. Conversely, Walsingham was an ardent supporter of the opponents of the government, men such as Sir Thomas de la Mare, spokesman of the commons in the Good Parliament (1376), and the Appellant lords, who led the opposition in the Merciless Parliament (1388). But in his last historiographical phase Walsingham was influenced by the propaganda that Bolingbroke used to strengthen his position when he seized the throne to become Henry IV. Walsingham wrote the account of Richard II's "tyranny" (1396–1399) after the usurpation; his denigration of Richard is partially drawn from the official record of the deposition "parliament," which stated the case against the king. The same source provided Walsingham with material for the deposition itself. Meanwhile, Walsingham revised the earlier part of his chronicle to modify or remove his abuse of John of Gaunt, Henry IV's father. Although Walsingham in his first phase as chronicler could claim to share Paris's "constitutional" views, in his second phase he can be accused of timeserving. Nevertheless, Walsingham had outstanding merits as a chronicler—intelligence, curiosity, an accute eye, and immense industry that enabled him to give full coverage of whatever recent history came within reach of his knowledge. These merits far outweigh his demerits, his rhetorical flights, his occasional superstition, and his political bias. He has the distinction of being the last great chronicler of medieval England.

Bibliography: *Chronicon Angliae ab Anno Domini 1328 usque ad Annum 1388, auctore monacho quodam Sancti Albani*, Rolls Series, ed. E. M. Thompson (London, 1874); Antonia Gransden, *Historical Writing in England*, [ii], *c. 1307 to the Early Sixteenth Century* (London, 1982), Ch. 5; *Johannis de Trokelowe . . . Chronica et Annales*, Rolls Series, ed. H. H. Riley (London, 1866), pp. 155–424; *The St. Albans Chronicle, 1406–1420*, ed. V. H. Galbraith (Oxford, 1937); (the complex relationship of these printed editions to the texts of the *Chronica Majora* and *Historia Anglicana* is explained by

Galbraith p. xlvi; *Thomae Walsingham, quondam Monachi S. Albani, Historia Anglicana*, Rolls Series, 2 vols, ed. H. T. Riley (London, 1863–1864).

Antonia Gransden

WILLIAM OF MALMESBURY (Wiltshire, England, c. 1093–Malmesbury, Wiltshire, 1153) probably the best known of the Anglo-Norman historians; monk of Malmesbury (c. 1100-?). William was of mixed parentage, part Norman and part English, and as a scholar was a product of the renaissance of religious life, culture, and learning that distinguished the Severn basin in the late eleventh and early twelfth centuries. His environment, indeed, favored his intellectual studies. He entered Malmesbury as an oblate when Godfrey, founder of the monastic library, was abbot (c. 1090–c. 1105). Early in life William helped him in the library; later he became librarian and successfully continued Godfrey's work. William, therefore, had access to a rich collection of books, which could be augmented by loans from neighboring monasteries. Malmesbury was in close touch with houses such as Evesham and Worcester, both important centers of the renaissance. William was a polymath, a student of the Scriptures, theology, canon and civil law, the classics, and hagiography, besides history, but it is on his work as a historian that his reputation primarily rests. His productive life in this capacity had two phases. During the first phase, which lasted for a year or two, about 1125, he wrote his two longest and most ambitious works: *The Gesta Regum Anglorum* (2 vols., ed. William Stubbs [London, 1887–1889]), a history of England from the Anglo-Saxon invasions until 1120; and the *Gesta Pontificum Anglorum* (ed. N.E.S.A. Hamilton [London, 1870]), an ecclesiastical history of England from the Conversion to 1125. William's second phase of productivity lasted from about 1130 until 1143, the year of his death. During that period he revised the *Gesta Regum* and the *Gesta Pontificum* and wrote the *Historia Novella* (ed., with English trans., K. R. Potter [London and Edinburgh, 1955]); the *De Antiquitate Glastoniensis Ecclesiae* (ed., with English trans., John Scott [Woodbridge, 1981]), history of Glastonbury abbey from its Celtic origins until William's own time; and the *Vita Sancti Dunstani* (ed. William Stubbs, *Memorials of St Dunstan* [London, 1874], pp. 250–324).

The *Gesta Regum* and *Gesta Pontificum* are witness to William's omnivorous reading of literary sources. The influence of continental models is apparent. He broke away from the annalistic tradition of historiography that was so well established among the Anglo-Saxons. He probably derived the idea of calling his works *Gestae* from continental examples (such as William of Poitiers' *Gesta Guillelmi Ducis Normannorum et Regis Anglorum*). His treatment of the reigns of individual kings in the *Gesta Regum* shows the influence of Suetonius' (q.v.) *Lives of the Caesars,* and his biographies of saints in the *Gesta Pontificum* were deeply indebted to the Anglo-Saxon hagiographical tradition. But the most remarkable feature of the *Gesta Pontificum* is the use William made in it of visual evidence; he used it to an extent unprecendented in English historiography and thus foreshadowed the antiquaries of the fifteenth and sixteenth centuries. To acquire such data, as well as to examine written sources, William traveled widely, visiting numerous monasteries. The *De Antiquitate* is based on similar sources and, indeed, contains a good example of William's observation of the physical remains of the past—the graphic description of the two Celtic stone crosses in the cemetery at Glastonbury. The two *Gestae* and the *De Antiquitate* are all primarily concerned with past history, and the *Vita Sancti Dunstani* is exclusively so. William, who saw himself as the successor of the Venerable Bede (q.v.), aimed to demonstrate the continuity of the past with the present, a continuity threatened by the new Anglo-Norman regime. In the *Gesta Pontificum,* the *De Antiquitate,* and the *Vita Sancti Dunstani* he concentrated on the ancient glories of the Church in England, since its tradition was in particular jeopardy. But during the last phase of his historical activity he also responded to the disturbed politics of his time. Malmesbury abbey could not afford to have enemies among the powerful. This was especially true after the outbreak of sporadic civil war following the death of Henry I, when King Stephen and Empress Matilda were in dispute over the succession to the throne. William revised the *Gesta Regum* and *Gesta Pontificum,* which had contained criticism of the Anglo-Norman kings and of various magnates, to make them less offensive. He also wrote a contemporary history, the *Historia Novella,* at the request of a leading magnate, his patron Robert, earl of Gloucester. Since Robert was Matilda's uncle, the *Historia* not only eulogized him but also gave an account of the civil war strongly biased in favor of the empress. Undoubtedly, as a historian William had some of the faults characteristic of historians in his day. Although not incapable of assessing evidence critically, he sometimes, whether knowingly or not, treated fiction as fact (he loved good stories) and the inauthentic as authentic (for example, he used forged charters to support the claim of Canterbury against York in his discussions of the primacy controversy). Again, he only occasionally attributed events to natural, not divine, causes. Nevertheless, he deserves an important place in the history of English historiography. He had a rare understanding of the value of original sources, including "antiquities" and had thought about the historian's task to an unusual degree. But above all he was the first man since Bede to produce a substantial corpus of historical works.

Bibliography: Hugh Farmer, "William of Malmesbury's Life and Works," *Journal of Ecclesiastical History* 13 (1962), 39–54; Antonia Gransden, *Historical Writing in England,* [i], *c. 550–c. 1307* (London, 1974), Ch. 6; J. Armitage Robinson, "William of Malmesbury 'On the Antiquity of Glastonbury,' " in *Somerset Historical Essays* (Oxford, 1921), pp. 3–25; R. M. Thomson, "William of Malmesbury's Carolingian Sources," *Journal of Medieval History* 7, no. 4 (1981): 321–337; idem, "William of Malmesbury as Historian and Man of Letters," *Journal of Ecclesiastical History* 29 (1978): 387–413.

Antonia Gransden

WILLIAM OF NEWBURGH (Yorkshire, 1135/1136–Newburgh, Yorkshire, 1198?), English chronicler; canon of the Augustinian priory of Newburgh, Yorkshire. Besides his chronicle William wrote some sermons and a commentary on the Canticles. An attempt has been made to identify him with "William, canon of Newburgh," who was the son of Ellis, brother of Bernard, and prior of Newburgh, who married Emma de Peri about 1160. If this identification is correct he must have become a canon late in life, after Emma's death. However, other evidence weighs against it. William began his *Historia Rerum Anglorum* (in Richard Howlett, ed., *Chronicles of the Reigns of Stephen, Henry II, and Richard I,* 4 vols. [London, 1884–1889], 1:11–408; 2:416–583) about 1198 at the request of Ernald, abbot of Rievaulx. Ernald was interested in history but was prevented from commissioning one of his own monks to write a chronicle by the regulations of his order. The *Historia* is a history of England from the Norman Conquest until 1198. William used a number of well-known histories as sources (for example, the *Historia Regum* ascribed to Symeon of Durham and Henry of Huntingdon's [q.v.] *Historia Anglorum*). His work is of value to the historian today partially because William added material of his own to that derived from preexisting histories. But even those portions of the *Historia* that are derivative are of interest. One of his sources, a biography of Richard I, is lost; the *Historia,* therefore, provides evidence of its contents. Moreover, since William treated his sources selectively and paraphrased his borrowings, the whole of the work reflects his mentality. As a historian William had outstanding merits. He combined unusual critical acumen and independence of mind with wide-ranging curiosity and a talent for descriptive and narrative prose. His critical faculty appears at its best in his prologue, where he demolished the credibility of Geoffrey of Monmouth's (q.v.) *Historia Regum Britanniae*: how, he asked, can all of these tales about King Arthur be true when Bede (q.v.) and Bede's early source, Gildas, made no mention of any British king of that name? He also impugned the legends on historical grounds. For example, he accused Geoffrey of attributing to Arthur the conquest of more kingdoms than existed in his day. William's objectivity appears in his judicious handling of the controversy between Henry II and Thomas Becket; he could see right and wrong on both sides. Even more remarkable is his attitude to the Jews. He did not share his contemporaries' dogmatic intolerance, or condone the violence against Jews that followed the accession of Richard I and the revival of crusading zeal. He condemned the massacre of the Jews of York on humanitarian grounds and accused the perpetrators of base motives—the desire for loot and to destroy the bonds binding debtors to Jewish moneylenders. William's interests spread far afield, to East Anglia and London and abroad (he gave, for instance, a brief account of recent Norwegian history). The *Historia* abounds with colorful narrative and good stories. Particularly notable are stories that show Scandinavian influence and so demonstrate the close cultural contacts between Yorkshire (part of the ancient Danelaw) and the Scandinavian countries. However, the *Historia* exerted little influence on subsequent chroniclers, and it was not until the sixteenth century that a historian turned William's criticisms of Geoffrey of Monmouth to good effect. Then Polydore Vergil (q.v.) used it as the basis for his own exposé of the legendary British history.

Bibliography: Antonia Gransden, ''Bede's Reputation as an Historian in Medieval England,'' *Journal of Ecclesiastical History* 32 (1981): 416–419; idem, *Historical Writing in England*, [i], *c. 550–c. 1307* (London, 1974), pp. 263–268; Rudolph Jahncke, *Guilelmus Neubrigensis, ein pragmatischer Geschichtsschreiber des zwölften Jahrhunderts* (Bonn, 1912); Nancy F. Partner, *Serious Entertainments: The Writing of History in Twelfth-Century England* (Chicago and London, 1977), p. 2; H. E. Salter, ''William of Newburgh,'' *English Historical Review* 22 (1907): 510–514.

Antonia Gransden

Great Historians: Finnish

PORTHAN, Henrik Gabriel (Viitasaari, 1739–Turku, 1804), Finnish philologist and historian. Porthan was a professor of Latin literature at the University of Turku from 1777 to 1804. Of encyclopedic spirit, he treated all aspects of Finnish culture and civilization in his works and was among the first to draw attention to the original aspects of Finnish folklore in a period when the elite of his country were almost entirely Swedish. He studied popular poetry (*De poësi fennica,* 1766–1778), showing the value of this source to historians and inaugurating thereby a most important research method, which led to the restoration of *Kalevala* by Elias Lönnrot (1802–1884) between 1835 and 1849. Porthan also directed himself to study Finnish mythology and Finnish language (*De praecipius dialectis linguae Fennicae,* 1801). As a historian, he displayed great erudition in his critical edition of Paulus Juusten, *Chronicon Episcoporum Finlandesium* (1784–1800). In 1770 Porthan founded Aurora, a cultural society and edited *Tidningar,* the first newspaper published in Finland. He was both an inventor of historical methodology, through his emphasis on folklore, language, and mythology, and one of the architects of Finnish national consciousness.

Bibliography: *Brockhaus's Konversations- Lexikon* (1901-), vol.17, p. 782; *Enciclopedia italiana,* vol. 27, p. 970.

Lucian Boia

Great Historians: French

BODIN, Jean (Angers, 1529/1530–Laon, 1596). Son of a rich master couturier, Bodin was first trained as a Carmelite novice in Angers and then in Paris. (It is possible that he took vows and was subsequently released from them about 1548.) He then studied at the Law Faculty in Toulouse and gave independent lectures before settling in Paris to become a lawyer at the Parlement of Paris about 1561. He was entrusted with various missions by Charles IX, was Third Estate deputy at the States General of Blois in 1576, and entered the service of the Duc d'Alençon; he thus acquired varied political experience. He finished his career as prosecutor at the Presidial Court in Laon, not without having had to join the league—doubtless for reasons of prudence since the ups and downs of his life show that he was at least sympathetic to the Reformed Church, and his last work, *Heptaplomeres,* reveals the attraction that he felt for Judaist Neo-Platonism. Bodin's work reflects his life: it is complex, full of a variety of curiosities and involvements that sometimes appear to be contradictory. Philosopher, political theorist, economist, and demonologist, he was interested in history less as a historian than as a reader of the "histoires" available in the sixteenth century. He published *Methodus ad facilem historiarum cognitionem* in 1566 to show how it was possible to find a key thread running through the disconcerting variety of facts reported by historians. Bodin wanted to "*connaître*" history, that is, to perceive the hidden meaning contained in the geographical distribution of peoples over the surface of the world and the chronological evolution of their power and civilization; he wanted to seize the sequence of the most significant facts in a convenient way and finally to construct a theory of individual and collective action. Knowledge of history thus had a triple purpose: "scientific," didactic, and political. To achieve this, Bodin first selected the most reliable historians, whom he listed at the end of his book. This is how he approached the question of historical criticism. He considered history to be "rerum ante gestarum vera relatio": the facts had to be rigorously established to serve as a basis for theorizing that would be acceptable to everybody. Thus Bodin took a stand both against fables accepted without any critical sense and also against rhetorical history more concerned with formal elegance than with accuracy, as practiced by Paolo Giovio (q.v.).

The reading of histories should be comparative to detect the similarities and differences between the various peoples. The facts thus assembled are analyzed and classified in categories formed by time, geography, and natural history. Three large zones, each with 30 degree axes, divide the earth into hot, temperate, and cold regions. The simplicity of this triple division is modified however by the existence of physical relief that results in a dominant cold feature in the hot regions and by opposition between the East, which has analogies with the South, and the West, which is similar to the North. A specific combination of elements, humors, and properties of matter correspond to each of the units defined in this way. For example, southern people are cold, dry, smooth skinned, small, and have weak constitutions; however, they possess an inventive spirit and are given to contemplation. Northerners are hot, damp, hairy, pale, big, with vigorous bodies, but are brutal and barbarian. In the intermediate regions, men display a balance between physical features and moral and intellectual qualities, which results in their excelling in the art of politics. The order thus detected with regard to geometry and space is mathematical; to this is added political order, making the universe a vast universal Republic in which the northerners are the soldiers and artisans, and the southerners are the pontiffs and wise men, and the folk in the center are the magistrates. Even the influence of heavenly bodies must be taken into account. Bodin discussed this factor at the end of Chapter 5 in terms that reveal much about the spirit of his method: he affirmed that it would be enough to carry out systematic comparison of memorable events, the regions in which they took place, changes in political regime, and the astral conjunctions in order to advance the study of the customs and nature of peoples (''scientiam de moribus et natura populorum'') and to make more reliable assessments of all types of histories (''de omni genere historiarum''). Nevertheless, Bodin did not believe that humans are completely a slave to the effects of place, temperament, or the stars. It is necessary to know natural laws to use them profitably through the appropriate institutions. Knowledge of history is thus of direct benefit to political science. Jean Bodin made the historian the adviser of the powerful; it was in this spirit that in *Oratio de instituenda in Republica juventute ad Senatum Populumque Tolosatem* (1559) he used his knowledge of history to encourage the *capitouls* of Toulouse to practice a bold cultural policy; in the same way *Les six Livres de la République* (1576) urged the king to find a balanced form of government that would enable him to weather the storms of his time. Jean Bodin has been considered as the precursor of historical sociology and of ethnology. However, his classification categories are still medieval. His originality lies in his determination to apply the idea of method to the comparative history of peoples and in the scope of his attempt to organize human events into an intelligent synthesis.

Bibliography: Claude-Gilbert Dubois, *La conception de l'histoire en France au XVIe siècle* (Paris, 1977), p. 668 (pp. 94–113 on Jean Bodin); colloquys on Jean Bodin (Munich, 1971, published 1973), papers by Girolamo Cotroneo, Julien Freund, and Donald R. Kelley; (Angers, 1985), papers by Philippe Desan, Frank Lestringant, and John L.

Brown; Julian H. Franklin, *Jean Bodin and the Sixteenth-Century Revolution in the Methodology of Law and History* (New York, 1963) pp. xi–163.

Arlette Jouanna

BOSSUET, Jacques Bénigne (Dijon, 1627–Paris, 1704). Born into a parliamentary family that directed him very early on toward an ecclesiastical career, Bossuet became canon of Metz in 1640 and was ordained priest in 1652; he was awarded a degree of doctor of theology in the same year. Bossuet was appointed bishop of Condom in 1669 but resigned shortly afterwards to devote more of his efforts to educating the Dauphin, having been appointed tutor by the king in 1670. When he had completed this task he was appointed bishop of Meaux in 1681. Preacher, theologian, and moralist, Bossuet was very much a historian in many of his sermons and writings. For example, his funeral orations and eulogies of the saints contain historical parts. However, this aspect of his talents can be seen above all in his works of controversy and in those written for the education of the Dauphin. The former category includes *Histoire des Variations des Eglises Protestantes* (1688) and *Défense de l'Histoire des Variations* (1691) in which he concentrated on showing, using documentary evidence, that the doctrinal uncertainties of the reformed churches proved that they were mistaken. The historical works produced from Bossuet's teaching experience comprise first his *Abrégé de l'Histoire de France,* written about 1677 and published in 1747, and *Discours sur l'Histoire Universelle,* which was published in 1681 (republished with fresh material in 1700 and then published with additions from unpublished manuscripts in what is known as the "Versailles" edition of Bossuet's *Oeuvres* in 1818). The first of these books was compiled from the notes taken by the Dauphin during his lessons, which were put into shape, revised, and corrected by Bossuet; the French text was then to form material for translation into Latin. It is a somewhat disparate chronicle, although the reigns of Francis I and Charles IV are covered fairly extensively, and was intended to teach the prince about his country's past and give him lessons in ethics and politics as well.

Discours sur l'Histoire Universelle is on a completely different scale. The work has three parts. The first, *Les Epoques,* is a chronological summary that attempts to find the line running through human history ("tenir, pour ainsi dire, le fil de toutes les affaires de l'univers") by embracing with a single glance "les deux points sur lesquels roulent les choses humaines," that is, religion and political government. To do this, the historian's eye halts (the word *epoch* comes from a Greek word meaning to stop) at one of the landmarks chosen in the sequence of time since they mark important events and represent steps forward for the whole of humankind. There are twelve such landmarks, the first being the creation of the world and the last the founding of Charlemagne's empire. In the second part, *La Suite de la Religion,* Bossuet studied the history of the Hebrews until the birth of Christ. The third part, *Les Empires,* describes the destinies of great civilizations: those of Egypt, the Chaldeans, the Persians, the

Greeks, and finally the Romans. Bossuet thus began by combining sacred and profane history in a vast synthesis before separating them later. However, this distinction between points of view in the last two parts has, above all, a pedagogical purpose. There was only one sort of history for Bossuet: the history of all people. For him, this history has a religious meaning to the extent that it is the slow gestation of a saved humankind. Divine will and human action collaborate in time: divine will because the hidden design of Providence lies behind the sequence of causalities and human action because God has enough respect for the inventiveness of each people to leave it free to create rich and original civilizations. The *raison d'être* of historians stems precisely from the mystery of this collaboration. Bossuet's faith convinced him of both the existence of finality from above and a certain autonomy allowed to humankind by God, whose signs history attempts to discover: "La vraie science de l'histoire est de remarquer dans chaque temps les secrètes dispositions qui ont préparé les grands changements et les conjonctures importantes qui les ont fait arriver" (*Discours*, III, 2). Thus to rediscover the features of civilizations that have disappeared, Bossuet carefully chose the witnesses that he considered to be the most reliable: ancient philosophers and historians, chroniclers, and memorialists. He applied to them the critical methods that he had seen used in the 1650s by the Dupuy brothers and by the scholars of the Congregation de Saint Maur and attempted to form a reasonably well-based opinion. Thus the exacting nature of his very methods meant that history could help the faithful to gain better knowledge of God's purpose.

Bibliography: Raymond Darricau, "De l'histoire théologienne à la grande érudition: Bossuet (XVIe–XVIIIe siècles)," *Historiographie du Catharisme,* Cahiers de Fanjeaux (1979): 85–117; Thérèse Goyet, "Autour du Discours sur l'Histoire universelle. Etudes critiques," *Annales littéraires de l'Université de Besançon* (Paris, 1956); idem, *L'Humanisme de Bossuet,* 2 vols. (Paris, 1965); Jacques Truchet, Préface to *Discours sur l'Histoire Universelle* (Paris, 1966).

Arlette Jouanna

COMMYNES, Philippe de (Renescure, c. 1447–Argenton, 1511), French chronicler. Commynes, Flemish by birth, was the scion of a well-to-do bourgeois family of Ypres. His surname was Van den Clyte, but he traditionally went under the name of the lordship (now Comines, a Belgian town near the frontier with France) that had been in his family since the fourteenth century. In 1464 he entered the service of the count of Charolais, the future duke of Burgundy (Charles the Bold, 1467–1477). Promoted chamberlain and counselor to this prince, he was employed, in particular, on diplomatic missions. During a trip to Spain (1471), he got as far as the French court where in 1472, betraying his former master, he openly entered the service of the king of France whom he had been aiding secretly since 1468. He became French, was laden with riches, received the principality of Talmont, seized from the house of Amboise, and was married to a wealthy heiress. A member of the king's inner circle, he dealt with important diplomatic affairs. His influence diminished beginning about 1477, and following the death of Louis XI (1483) it ended completely. He took to plotting, was imprisoned (1486–1489), and then was exiled to one of his castles. But he seems to have regained his position beginning in 1492 and was charged, in 1494–1495, with negotiating missions at Venice and Milan, in which he failed. His principality was restored, after long litigation, to the Tremoille who were recognized as the legitimate heirs. He retired to his castle of Argenton and there occupied his forced leisure in writing his *Mémoires*. These have been divided by their modern editors into eight books, the first six of which concern the history of Louis XI from 1464 to 1483 and the last two, the Italian expedition of 1494–1495. They were composed in several stages: (1) the first five books in 1489–1490; (2) the sixth in 1492; (3) the seventh toward the end of 1495 and in 1496; and (4) the eighth in 1498. Commynes began his *Mémoires* at the request of Angelo Cato, a Neapolitan, the doctor and astrologer of Louis XI who became archbishop of Vienne in 1482 but later took a personal interest and continued the *Mémoires* even after the death of the archbishop. It is legitimate to assume that the author strove from the beginning to the end of his work to justify his defection of 1472 by insisting on the shortcomings of his first master, Charles the Bold, and by looking for signs of betrayal even among those of his contemporaries who were considered the most loyal. The princes are not dealt with any more gently: the petty and sordid motives of their actions are revealed. War is a misfortune and victory, as a rule, a matter of luck. Statesmen have discovered in the *Mémoires* a sort of bible of their craft. It was in this sense that he was esteemed by the Emperor Charles V, and Commynes himself claimed to address his work "to princes and courtiers." He has often been compared to Machiavelli (q.v.) for playing the philosophizing moralist at every turn and multiplying the maxims. His *Mémoires*, which place him in the ranks of major writers in the French language, were first published in 1524 and have gone through an impressive number of editions since that time.

Bibliography: Karl Bittmann, *Die Memoiren des Philipps de Commynes als historische Quelle*, 3 vols. (Gottingen, 1964–1970); Philippe de Commynes, *Mémoires* (Classiques de l'histoire de France au Moyen Age), 3 vols., ed. Joseph Calmette and Georges Durville (Paris, 1924–1925); Jean Dufournet, *La vie de Philippe de Commynes* (Paris, 1969); Charles Whibley, *The History of Comines, englished by Thomas Danett, anno 1596*, in *Tudor Translations*, 17, 18 (London, 1897).

Jean Glénisson

CONDORCET, Marie-Jean-Antoine de Caritat, Marquess de (Ribemont, 1743–Bourg-la-Reine, 1794), French mathematician, philosopher, and politician. From 1769 Condorcet was a member, then permanent secretary (1776), of the Academy of Sciences in Paris. During the Revolution he was the president of the Legislative Assembly (1792) and then a deputy in the convention. He was arrested as a Girondin and committed suicide in prison. Condorcet was interested in the history of the sciences, which he believed were closely interrelated (*Eloges* *des Académiciens*, 1773). He advocated "a unified mathematical science, in principle applicable to all aspects of human action and existence" (Baker 1975). In 1793 he wrote *Esquisse d'un tableau historique des progrès de l'esprit humain* (published in 1795 after his death). This work can be compared with Anne-Robert Turgot's discourse *Sur les progrès succesifs de l'esprit humain*, 1750 (Condorcet also published *Vie de Turgot*, 1786). The two works, however, differ in that Condorcet accepted the idea of revolution and looked not only to the past but to the future. His conception of humankind's evolution was one of a continuing progress along the path of civilization. He distinguished nine phases in history and believed the tenth phase began with the French Revolution. In his opinion, a regularity exists in history, and thus it is possible to foretell the future along general lines. With Condorcet, the idea of progress in history reached a fullness of expression unknown before then. Through his effort to create a science of social evolution, he preceded the philosophy of Auguste Comte.

Bibliography: Keith Michael Baker, *Condorcet: From Natural Philosophy to Social Mathematics* (Chicago and London, 1975); Rolf Reichardt, *Reform und Revolution bei Condorcet: Ein Beitrag zur späten Aufklärung in Frankreich* (Bonn, 1973).

Lucian Boia

DU CANGE (Sieur), Charles du Fresne (Amiens, 1610–Paris, 1688), French historian. Born into a family of royal judges, Charles Du Cange became a barrister at the Parlement of Paris in 1631 and then *Trésorier de France* in the *généralité* of Amiens in 1645. He left his native town—besieged by the plague—in 1668 and moved to the parish of St. Gervais in Paris and thereafter led the life of a scholar entirely devoted to study, visiting Paris libraries and attending the meetings organized by the St. Maur Benedictines at the abbey of St. Germain des Près. In 1676 his reputation was such that Colbert admitted him to a commission of scholars charged with assembling a series called *Historiens de France*, for which Du Cange drew up the detailed plan. His relations with French and European scholars, whom he received in his home with a degree of courtesy that has remained legendary, together with the interest created by his works, gave him uncontested authority in the learned circles that were working on the perfecting of methods of historical criticism, under the patronage of Colbert and Guillaume de Lamoignon, first President of the Parlement of Paris. Charles Du Cange's curiosity led him to three fields: the history of the Crusades and the Byzantine Empire, the history of Picardy, and the history of France. His research on the Latin East during the Crusades led to an important manuscript on the nobility of the Christian kingdoms and to his first publication: *Histoire de l'Empire de Constantinople sous les Empereurs français* (1657); then toward the end of his life, he devoted his *Historia Byzantina* (1680) to the genealogical study of the families of the Byzantine emperors and the description of Constantinople. In the preface to this work, he described what were for him the four parts of history: "*pragmatique*," or narration of facts; "*chronique*, " to unravel time;

"*généalogique*," which examines people and their descendants; and "*topique*," or the portrayal of places in which action has taken place. In parallel, he contributed to the publication of the Louvre's Byzantine series with Cinname's *Histoires* in 1670, Zonaras' *Annales* in 1686, and *Chronique Pascale* in 1688 (the last book was published after his death). Research on his native province, resulting in numerous manuscripts on the history of Amiens and its counts and bishops together with a collection of original documents and copies, led to only one publication: *Traité historique du chef de Saint Jean-Baptiste* (1665), which was intended to support favorable presumptions with regard to the relic kept in Amiens cathedral. His desire to base the history of France on reliable sources led him to publishing Jean Joinville's (q.v.) *Histoire de Saint Louis* enriched with unpublished fragments and thirty essays (1668). He also made notes for the drawing up of a vast historical and genealogical *Nobiliaire* of France, which remained at manuscript stage.

Charles Du Cange's contribution to the historical work of his time lies in the number and variety of documents, handwritten and printed sources, coins, and archaeological remains examined and in the rigor of his criticism of texts and the breadth of his scholarship. His working methods astonished his contemporaries. "He works," wrote the Benedictine monk Dom Paul Bonnefont in 1658 "not on pages but on loose half-sheets." This habit of working on cards and noting his observations on the language of medieval authors and on the customs and laws that they described enabled him to complete the monumental work that established his reputation: the three folio volumes of *Glossarium ad scriptores mediae et infimae latinitatis,* which appeared in 1678. In it, Du Cange listed approximately five thousand Low Latin authors and provided biographical and bibliographical details; the list was followed by examination of the meanings of some one hundred forty thousand words in notes, which are sometimes veritable literary and historical essays. The glossary is followed by a treatise on the coins and medals of the lower empire. This work was republished in 1681 and 1710 and then complemented by the Benedictines of St. Maur and by Dom Carpentier of the Order of Cluny in the eighteenth century. Du Cange published a Greek glossary ten years after his Latin one. Entitled *Glossarium ad scriptores mediae et infimae graecitatis*, it was published in two folio volumes in Lyons in 1688 and contained analysis of variations in meaning and neologisms that had appeared in Greek since ancient times. Du Cange's publications form only part of the immense volume of his work. In addition to his notes on the great noble families of France, England, and Germany, his *Traité du droit et comportement des armes*, in which he laid down the scientific bases of heraldry, remained in manuscript form, as did treatises on the geography of the ancient provinces of Gaul, showing the importance that he accorded to geographical background. The variety of the fields that he became involved in reveals the extent of Charles Du Cange's erudition, which was accompanied by an exemplary pursuit of accuracy and rigor.

Bibliography: Catalogue de l'exposition organisée à l'occasion du tricentenaire du *Glossarium mediae et infimae latinitatis* par la Bibliothèque Nationale, in *La Lexicographie du Latin médiéval* (Paris, 1981), pp. 509–547; Leon Feugère, *Etude sur la vie et les ouvrages de Du Cange* (Paris, 1852).

Arlette Jouanna

EGINHARD (Maingau, c. A.D. 775/780–Seligenstadt, A.D. 840), Frankish historian. *Einhardus* (from which the alternative form Einhard), native of Maingau, studied at the monastery of Fulda where his intellectual qualities proved so outstanding that he was dispatched to the court of Aix-la-Chapelle. He resided at the palace in the emperor's entourage beginning in A.D. 796 at the latest. He distinguished himself there for his literary gifts. He played a prominent role in the accession of Louis the Pious (A.D. 814) whose secretary he became. The recipient of numerous favors, abbot of Fontenelle, he was entrusted in A.D. 817 with the education of Lothair, Louis' eldest son. He retired to Fontenelle in A.D. 828 and then to the monastery of Seligenstadt (Mülheim-on-Main), which he had founded and where he died. Around A.D. 830 he wrote the *Vita Karoli* (Life of Charlemagne)—the first medieval biography—in a refurbished classical Latin in the manner of Suetonius (q.v.). The biography opens directly with an account of the war of Aquitaine (A.D. 769), Charles' childhood being deliberately ignored in the absence of information. The work is of exceptional quality: the author had been a member of the sovereign's inner circle, sometimes his confidant. His duties under Louis the Pious had given him access to documents conserved in the palace archives. The history of events (wars, political questions in general) is based on the Royal Annals, but a large part of the account (physical and moral description, political behavior, private conduct of the emperor) is founded on personal observation and is reliable. The *Vita* was a great success (about eighty manuscripts of it are known to exist). "Its influence on medieval historical literature has been considerable" (Ganshof 1924).

Bibliography: Eginhard, *Vie de Charlemagne*, 4th ed., ed. and trans. L. Halphen, (Paris, 1967); F.L. Ganshof, "*Notes critiques sur Eginhard, biographe de Charlemagne,*" *Revue belge de philologie et d'histoire* 3 (1924); O. Holder-Egger, *Einhardi Vita Karoli Magni*, Scriptores Rerum Germanicarum in usum scholarum (Hanover and Leipzig, 1911).

Jean Glénisson

FROISSART, Jean (Valenciennes, Nord, 1337–Chimay, post–1404), historian in the French language. Froissart's historical work, which made him so famous, was only one of the literary activities of this tonsured cleric who was "above all a minstrel who occupied the idle hours in the life at court. He used his gifts as a poet and story teller to entertain the lords and ladies whose company he kept. It was for them that he composed his long allegorical poems, his songs and ballads, his *virelays*, his rounds and the four books of his chronicle"(Guenée). The stages of his life are known because of the personal data that he himself scattered throughout his work. Doubtless from a bourgeois background, he was already embarked on a literary career when he appeared in

London in 1361 and offered Queen Philippine de Hainaut, the wife of Edward III, a historical work in verse, composed in 1353 and now lost. He had the gift of ingratiating himself with the great lords, and he lived henceforth in their entourage—and at their expense. Following the death of the queen of England (1369), he was successively the table companion of Wenceslas of Bohemia, duke of Brabant; of Gui de Blois (who made him his chaplain and obtained for him the curacy of Lessines in Hainaut in 1373 and a canonicate of Chimay in 1384); of Aubert of Bavaria; and of his son Guillaume d'Ostrevant. Generally, as a member of a princely retinue, he visited France (1364), Scotland (1365), and Italy (1368) and returned on several occasions to Paris and for the second and last time to England in 1395. He was an intimate of Robert Bruce, king of Scotland; the Black Prince in his Aquitaine possessions; Gaston Phébus, count of Foix and of Béarn, at Orthez; and Richard II, whose birth he had witnessed at Bordeaux.

An inquiring spirit, he interviewed the actors and witnesses of great events and composed, between voyages, in his "forge" of Valenciennes, the monumental historical work that we know as the *Chroniques*. It includes four books whose composition, covering thirty years of the author's life, was complex. The *Premier Livre* (from 1325 to 1377) exists in three versions: (1) The first version, completed in 1373, covering the period 1325–1369, is based very closely on the *Chronique* of Jean le Bel (before 1290–1370); it was soon revised and continued to 1377. (2) The second version, composed between 1375 and 1383, contains developments that are missing in the first. (3) The third version, composed around 1399–1400, constitutes a total revision (from 1325 to 1350) of the preceding versions. The *Deuxième Livre* (from 1377 to 1385), written in 1387, contains an account of the wars of Flanders and has not been revised. The *Troisième Livre* (1386–1388), exists in two versions, the first written between 1390 and 1391, the second after 1392. The author has inserted the account of his trip to Orthez and has corrected and enriched his text with information obtained at Middelburg in Zeeland from the Portuguese knight Fernando Pacheco. The *Quatrième Livre* (1389–1400) was written in Hainaut in several stages between 1390 and 1400. The account is concerned essentially with the conflict between France and England, later known as the Hundred Years War, but related or contemporary conflicts (in Scotland, Flanders, Spain) are also recounted. At the start, closely inspired (to the point of plagiarism, a practice perfectly admissible at that time) by his predecessor Jean le Bel, who had written between 1351 and 1362, Froissart himself admitted he had no personal knowledge of events before the battle of Poitiers (1356). However, he freed himself almost completely from his model in the third version of the *Premier Livre*. His purpose was "to witness the marvels of this world, to hear and take stock of 'nouvelles,' to write and chronicle other histories:" hence the revisions of the chronicles progressively enriched with new information but also influenced by the circles—sometimes pro-French, sometimes favorable to the English—in which the author moved. Brilliant passages abound in this enormous work, which recreates the life of a particular social milieu, that of the warring nobility and soldiers of fortune, when their deeds of derring-do failed to dissimulate the perfidy, the cruelty, and the avidity of the great personages or the misery of the populace, which seems to have escaped Froissart's attention. Critics deplore the too literary tone, the obvious exaggerations, and the untimely nature of the variations that mark the transition from one version to the next.

Bibliography: *Chroniques de Froissart*, 15 vols. in print, ed. S. Luce, G. Raynaud, et al. (Paris, 1869–1975); Kervyn de Leltenhove, *Oeuvres de Froissart*, 28 vols. (Brussels, 1867–1877; reissued, 1967); F. S. Shears, *Froissart,Chronicler and Poet* (London, 1930).

Jean Glénisson

GRANDES CHRONIQUES DE FRANCE. Historical compilation in French retracing the history of France from its beginnings to 1328, first composed at the Benedictine abbey of St. Denis and then continued in various ways and published, in 1477, by the editor Pasquier Bonhomme with additions leading to the year 1461. It finally received the traditional title "Grandes Chroniques de France" in the edition of Antoine Vérard, printed in 1493. The stages of this collective work, carried out over two centuries, are the following: (1) The Benedictine abbey of St. Denis, closely tied to the French monarchy since the early seventh century, final resting place of kings, had devoted itself to historical research and compilation, especially since the abbotcy of Suger (1081–1151), himself a historian, author of the life of Louis VII. The monks worked at composing a history of the princes who had ruled France since the beginning of the Merovingian dynasty. In the thirteenth century, Saint Denis disposed of two Latin compilations recounting the history of France from the beginnings, in one case to the death of Louis VI, the Fat (1137), and in the other to the death of Philip Augustus (1223). (2) Louis IX (1226–1270) commissioned the monk Primat, who lived at St. Denis under the abbotcy of Mathieu de Vendôme (1253–1286), to produce a French version of the Latin chronicle composed in his monastery. This task was achieved in 1274. Primat translated the authors successively copied in the Latin compilation until 1223. But he added personal touches of his own with the intent of composing a continuous history that he called "The Romance of the Kings" ("romance" or *roman*, that is, a work written in French). At the same time he conferred a "national" character to his work by taking into account the legend according to which the French, a people of noble Trojan origin, had first lived without a king and had freely chosen Pharamond as their first sovereign.

(3) The historiographical work continued in the same spirit at St. Denis. One monk composed, first in Latin, a little after 1285 a life of Louis VIII (1223–1226). Guillaume de Nangis (the monastery's archivist from 1285 to 1300) followed with the life of Saint Louis (1226–1270), also in Latin, and then a life of Philip III (1270–1285). These works, translated into French, constituted a first sequel to the work of Primat, revised by the monk Richard Lescot (at St. Denis since 1329) and enriched by the same author with numerous additions.

Around 1350 a second modified version of that sequel was copied at the end of the original work of Primat, in the very manuscript that the latter had presented to the king in 1274, assuming in this way an "official" character. About this time the decision was taken to continue the task of prolonging the chroncile, first to 1344 and then to 1350. It was at this time that certain manuscripts containing the entire work had for the first time the title "Chroniques de France" or "Chroniques de France as composed in the Church of Saint Denis in France." (4) King Charles V (1364–1380), a man of letters, conscious of the usefulness of "propaganda," had the work—to this time effected by the abbey—continued by a layman, his chancellor Pierre d'Orgement, who recounted, not without a certain dryness but from a point of view that was very favorable to the Capetian dynasty, at that time engaged in a struggle with its English rivals, the history of the reign of John the Good (1350–1364) and that of the reign of Charles himself from 1364 to 1377. (5) From this time on, the work no longer depended on the initiative of the abbey and the monarchs. It was more and more diffused among a growing public by the Parisian booksellers who first commissioned rich illustrated copies for wealthy readers and then, in the second half of the fifteenth century, less expensive versions intended for a more modest public of men of law and merchants. At the close of the century the chronicle was carried forward, doubtless at the behest of a bookseller, to 1461, as a result of supplements of various origins, and published for the first time in this last version in 1477. After 1518 (date of the last edition) it was largely forgotten. "In the development of French national sentiment at the end of the Middle Ages, the knowledge of the French past played a fundamental role. French national sentiment possesses an historical component which is essential. The 'Chroniques de France' were without question the most developed, the most prestigious and perhaps the best known history of France."

Bibliography: B. Guenée, *Les Grandes Chroniques de France. Le roman aux roys* (1274–1518) in *Les lieux de mémoire*, ed. Pierre Nora, tome II, *La Nation*, 1, pp. 189–214; *Les Grandes chroniques de France. Chroniques des règnes de Jean II et de Charles V.*, 4 vols. ed. R. Delachenal (Paris, 1910–1920); J. Viard, ed., *Les Grandes chroniques de France*, 10 vols. (Paris, 1920–1953).

Jean Glénisson

GREGORY OF TOURS (Georgius Florentius Gregorius; sometimes known as "the French Herodotus" or "the Father of French History") (Clermont-Ferrand, A.D. 538/539– Tours, A.D. 594), bishop of Tours (A.D. 573). Canonized by the Church. Gregory was extremely proud of his aristocratic origins. Connected with the Auvergne on his father's side and Burgundy on his mother's side, he was related to Saint Nizier, bishop of Lyons, and Saint Gregory, bishop of Langres. Following his elevation to the bishopric, he was deeply involved in the political and religious life of Frankish Gaul, maintaining sometimes friendly and often difficult relations with the kings who shared and vied for power over the country. Charitable and courageous, he defended the faithful of his diocese against the brutality and cupidity of the Frankish princes; he raised a new basilica to Saint Martin. He was very representative of the bishops of his day "who enjoyed at that time the rare privilege of being educated, of being able to dispose of excellent libraries and of being, by virtue of their position, involved in the great affairs of the day" (Guenée). He was the author of an important body of writings: (1) numerous lives of the saints, not all of which have survived, including *Liber in gloria martyrum, Liber de virtutibus sancti Juliani martyris, De virtutibus sancti Martini libri quatuor, Liber vitae Patrum*, and *Liber in Gloria martyrum*—rich in details concerning the mores, beliefs, and ideas of the sixth century, these writings "constitute a veritable guide through the hagiographic literature which is so difficult to interpret" (Rouche); (2) a historical work, the *Historia Francorum* (also called *Historia ecclesiastica, Gesta Francorum*), divided into six parts ("books") and written purposely in simple Latin (*sermo rusticus*) to reach a broad public. The first part (Bks. 1–4), completed about A.D. 576, is a universal history covering the time until the death of King Sigebert (A.D. 575) that ends with a chronological recapitulation. The second part (Bks. 5–10), preceded by a special prologue addressed to the Frankish princes, exists in two versions for Books 5 and 6. It takes us to A.D. 591. Based on oral testimony as well as the personal recollections of the author, it resembles "memoirs" in form and is rich in picturesque details that supplied the French romantic historian Augustin Thierry (1795–1856) with the substance of his celebrated *Récits des temps mérovingiens* (2 vols., Paris, 1840). Until the time that Gregory's recollections are first-hand rather than second-hand (c. A.D. 550), the chronology is vague and confused, but the *Historia* is the principal source of Merovingian historiography.

Bibliography: In *Monumenta Germaniae Historica. Scriptores rerum Merovingicarum,* I, *Gregorii Turonersis Opera. Vol. 1: Historia Francorum,* ed. B. Krusch and W. Leninson (1951); *Vol. 2: Miracula et Opera minora,* ed. B. Krusch (1885); O. M. Dalton, *The History of the Franks by Gregory of Tours*, 2 vols. (Oxford, 1927); G. Monod, *Études critiques sur les sources de l'histoire mérovingienne*. Intro. by Marius d'Avenches, Bibliothèque de l'Ecole Practique des Hautes Études, 8 (Paris, 1972).

Jean Glénisson

GUIBERT DE NOGENT (Clermont, 1053–Nogent-sous-Coucy, 1124), French historian. Born near Clermont in the diocese of Beauvais into a family of the minor nobility, Guibert, in 1064, entered the Benedictine abbey of St. Germer de Flay (Oise) where he followed the teaching of Saint Anselm. In 1104 he was elected abbot of the monastery of Nogent-sous-Coucy (Aisne) and remained there until he died. He was very prolific. Among his works (in large part theological), three are of great interest to historians. *De sanctis et pignoribus sanctorum* (On Saintly Relics), a treatise in four books dedicated to Eudes, abbot of St. Symphorien of Beauvais, has survived in a single manuscript. It was composed in 1119 to combat a tract (lost today) in which the monks of St. Médard of Soissons boasted of the miraculous qualities of a relic (a baby tooth of Jesus Christ) among the treasures of their monastery. Guibert challenged the genuineness of the tooth and demonstrated a real critical spirit with regard to relics, visions, and miraculous occurrences in general. *De vita mea* (History of My Life), composed in 1115, mingled autobiography in the manner of Saint Augustine (q.v.) and chronicle. Book 1 is autobiographical (childhood, education, and family; reminiscences of the lords of Beauvais, the abbey of St. Germer, and so on). Book 2 is a history of the abbey of Nugent-sous-Coucy, enriched with very pertinent considerations on the archeological remains to be found there. Book 3 is a history of the struggles in 1112 between the bishop and the commune ("Commune, non nouveau, hom detestable!") of the town of Laon. The whole is highly original and of inestimable value as social history, the history of mental attitudes, and historical pyschoanalysis. A lively account of the birth of the commune of Laon was the inspiration for one of the *Letters* of Augustin Thierry (1795–1856) on the history of France. *Gesta Dei per Francos* (On the Action of God Through the Intermediary of the Franks) is a history of the First Crusade, written before 1112, relating the events of the years 1095–1104. It is a composite work (certain parts are in verse) in what is considered a confused style, but Guibert demonstrated a critical spirit and declared, before beginning a description of events, his intention of revealing the "motives," the "reasons," and "the considerations that rendered this expedition so urgent" (*Gesta Dei per Francos*). The book is very important for the large number of moral traits revealed therein that one encounters nowhere else. The picture that it paints of the preaching of Peter the Hermit and of the departure of the crusaders is of special interest.

Bibliography: Guibert de Nogent, *Histoire de sa vie (1053–1124)*, (Collection de texts pour servir à l'étude et a l'enseignement de l'histoire), ed. G. Bourgin (Paris, 1927).

Jean Glénisson

JOINVILLE, Jean, Sire de (? 1224– ? 1317), French chronicler. Born into a great noble family of Champagne, Joinville bore the hereditary title of "seneschal of Champagne." An orphan, he was reared at the court of Count Thibaut IV. After being married and the father of two children, he departed on the Crusade (April 1248) at the head of a troop of vassals. He joined Louis IX, king of France, at Cyprus in September and was a member of the king's retinue in Egypt and in Syria until his return to France in 1254. Although he continued to frequent the French court and remained a friend of the king, he refused to follow him on a new Crusade in 1267. He testified at Louis' canonization proceedings (1282) and personified, in the last years of a long life, a throwback to the age of chivalry. In 1305 (?), at the request of Jeanne de Navarre, countess of Champagne and queen of France, he began a book on Saint Louis, which he completed after the queen's death and presented, in 1309, to her son, the future Louis X of France (1315–1317). This *Livre des saintes paroles et des bons faits de notre saint roi Louis* today goes under the title *Vie de Saint Louis* or *Histoire de Saint Louis*. It is a hybrid genre. Written in the first person, the account is at once "memoirs" and "documentary": "what I saw and heard during the six years when I accompanied him on the overseas pilgrimage and since we returned" (ce que je vis et ouïs par l'espace de six ans que je fus en sa compagnie au pélerinage d'Outre mer et depuis que nous revînmes). It "includes the essential elements of historical chronicle, epic poetry and hagiography" (Corbett). The work is divided into two very unequal parts. The main part is concerned with the account of the Crusade, from 1248 to 1254 (557 paragraphs in the edition of N. de Wailly [1868]), consisting above all of personal recollections and in which the king only figures in connection with his relations with the author. The narration of the last sixteen years of the life of Louis IX is much shorter (103 paragraphs) and includes certain repetitions as well as extracts from the *Grandes chroniques de France,* the text of an ordinance of justice, and one on the *Enseignements* of the king to his son Philippe III. It is the work of an eighty-year-old ex-solider and administrator without any literary pretensions who proposed that the king he had attended was a model of saintly virtue. He wrote in a language that is considered "an example of the best prose style of that age," offering posterity, at the same time, "the first and the most distinguished specimen of the first-hand account (littérature de témoignage) in the history of French literature."

Bibliography: H.-F. Delaborde, *Jean de Joinville et les seigneurs de Joinville* (Paris, 1894); *Histoire de Saint Louis, par Jean sire de Joinville,* ed. Natalis de Wailly (Paris, 1868; New York, 1965); *La vie de Saint Louis. Le témoignage de Jehan, seigneur de Joinville. Texte du XIV siècle,* Collection "Études," ed. Noël Corbett (Sherbrooke, 1977).

Jean Glénisson

LA POPELINIÈRE, Henri Lancelot Voisin, Sieur de (La Popelinière de Sainte-Gemme) (Poitou, 1541–Paris, 1608), French historian. After extensive studies in Paris and Toulouse, this Protestant gentleman took part in the fighting during the Wars of Religion and then withdrew to devote himself to intellectual life. *La vraye et entière histoire de ces derniers troubles advenus tant en France qu'en Flandres et pays circonvoisins* was published in Cologne in 1571; the work was republished with additions and under a slightly different title in Basel in 1572 and in La Rochelle in 1573. In 1581 a rewritten and expanded version of the book was published, again in La Rochelle, under a new title: *L'Histoire de France enrichie des plus notables occurances survenues es provinces de l'Europe et pays circonvoisins, depuis l'an 1550 jusques à ces temps.* However, his impartiality with regard to the two opposing faiths led to condemnation by his fellow Protestants at the Synod of La Rochelle, which was held in the same year. In 1599 La Popelinière's *L'histoire des Histoires, avec l'Idée de l'Histoire accomplie. Plus le dessein de l'Histoire nouvelle des François* was published in Paris by Marc Orry. As can be seen from the title, this history assembles three works in a single volume: the first, *L'histoire des Histoires,* is a critical catalogue of historical works arranged by period and country; the second, *L'Idée de l'Histoire accomplie,* is a theoretical reflection on the methods used by historians and on the objectives they should have; the third work, *Le dessein de l'Histoire nouvelle des François,* contains a number of concrete examples of the way in which the general principles already described can be applied.

According to La Popelinière, who has been influenced by Jean Bodin (q.v.), history should be encyclopedic and form "la représentation de tout"; that is, it should not concentrate on just one particular aspect of the past but attempt to describe the spirit and movement of a whole period. For this, the historian should select a chronological and geographical framework that is neither too large, since the task would be too great for one person, nor too small; in this respect, the history of France is a subject of suitable dimensions. He must then seek out documents and verify the authenticity of the sources, In *L'Idée de l'Histoire accomplie,* La Popelinière set out very clearly the questionnaire to which sources should be subjected before they can be used: date and circumstances of writing, religion and beliefs of the author, and aims. Faced with a disorganized mass of facts, the historian must choose among them and select the most "notable" ones, guided by another questionnaire dictated by the requirements of the research. For instance, in *Dessein de l'Histoire nouvelle des François,* La Popelinière listed a series of questions about the Franks covering their geographical origin, their social and political customs, the way they came into Gaul, and their conversion to Christianity. The historian would thus be able to detect the links of causality that would make order emerge from apparent incoherence. According to La Popelinière, the explanation of this order does not lie in theology, which is outside the field of history, but in an overall rationality of the human phenomenon. Finally, the results obtained, however imperfect, must be expressed in clear, simple language since embellishments of style risk distorting the reality of facts. While laying the theoretical and practical foundations of a true national history, La Popelinière wondered why there had not been a historian worthy of the name since antiquity. He vehemently rejected the easy explanation that held that men had degenerated since then. On the contrary, he revealed his support of the idea of the intellectual and moral progress of humanity: he thought that the time that had elapsed since the ancient authors should mean that his contemporaries were superior to them. He considered that there were political and social reasons for this lack of historians. The political reasons were that since the time of the Greeks and Romans there had not been any collective awareness of the need for appropriate subsidizing of a body of scholars—including historians—in such a way as to provide them with the economic independence they needed to enjoy freedom of opinion. Henry III's creation of the post of historiographer financed by the king for Bernard de Girard, sieur du Haillan, was only a preliminary step in this direction. The social reasons were that this negligence had left history in the hands of clerks and hack writers who did not have it in them to carry out the work satisfactorily. Only gentlemen and, more generally, those whose conduct depended on honor and not profit, were cut out to be historians. This statement reveals how La Popelinière, who claimed proudly to be a gentleman, was attached to the values of his own social order. This led him to hold views on the structures of societies that contrast curiously with his idea of a general forward movement of humanity: he considered that the hierarchy of nobles and commoners had eternal value since it could be seen everywhere and always: "in all states, in all times" ("en tous etats, de tous temps," *Idée de l'Histoire accomplie* [G. Huppert, 1973, p. 246]). These contradictions between a static vision and a dynamic conception of history in La Popelinière's thought reflect the birth pangs of what he himself called *La Nouvelle Histoire*.

Bibliography: C. G. Dubois, *La conception de l'Histoire en France au XVIe siécle (1560–1610)* (Paris, 1977), pp. 124–153 on La Popelinière; G. Huppert, *The Idea of Perfect History* (Urbana, Ill., 1970) French translation entitled *L'Idée de l'Histoire parfaite* (Paris, 1973), Ch. 8 on La Popelinière; C. W. Sypher, "La Popelinière's Histoire de France," *Journal of the History of Ideas* 24 (1963): 41–54; M. Yardeni, "L'Histoire dans l'oeuvre de La Popelinière," *Revue d'Histoire Moderne et Contemporaine* 11 (1964): 111–126.

Arlette Jouanna

MABILLON, Jean (St. Pierremont near Reims, 1632–St. Germain des Prés, 1707), Benedictine and French historian; member of the Academy of Inscriptions (1701). Eleven years after Mabillon entered the Congregation of St. Maur, home of Catholic erudition during the seventeenth and eighteenth centuries, he was asked to collaborate in the publication of the *Acta sanctorum* by the Abbey of St. Germain des Prés. From 1668 to 1702, he wrote the nine volumes of the *Acta sanctorum ordinis sancti Benedicti,* certainly a work of apology but also a work that, using the model of the *Acta sanctorum* of Jean Bolland (q.v.), freed the *Lives of the Saints* from the edifying fables imposed on them through credulous centuries. In accomplishing his task, Dom Mabillon laid down the rules of a direct method in his famous *De re diplomatica,* published in 1681, the year seen by Marc Bloch as "a great moment in the history of the human spirit." Responding to the Bollandist, Daniel Papebroch (q.v.), who had declared fraudulent the Merovingian diplomas conserved in the Abbey of St. Denis, Mabillon in an article, "On the Discernment of the True and the False in the Old Parchments" (1675), demonstrated the authenticity of the Merovingian parchments by examining two hundred documents in the context of a very meticulous external critical analysis of ink, writing, language, and form. He proved irrefutably that his adversary was wrong, and thus, nearly a half-century after Descartes' *Discourse on Method* (1637), historians received from Mabillon a method, the art of distinguishing the true from the false: the textual critique. Dom Mabillon eventually published six volumes of the *Annales ordinis Sancti Benedicti* up to 1657. Unquestionably a collection of solidly authenticated documents arranged in a rigorously chronological order, the *Annales* reveal Mabillon as first among scholars if not the greatest historian of his rich period.

Bibliography: E. de Broglie, *Mabillon et la société de l'Abbaye de Saint Germain-des-Prés à la fin du 17e siècle* (Paris, 1888); J.-B. Vanel, *Les Bénédictins de Saint-Maur à Saint Germain-des-Prés* (Paris, 1896).

Ch.-O. Carbonell

MÉZERAY, François Eudes, Sieur de (Houay, Lower Normandy, 1610–Paris, 1683), French historian. Army commissioner in 1635, Mézeray was appointed historiographer to the king after the publication of the first volume of his *Histoire de France* in 1643. However, he lost this post when Jean Baptiste Colbert found some passages of his *Abrégé de l'Histoire de France,* published in 1667–1668, too critical of the monarchy's fiscal policy. He was elected to the *Académie Française* in 1648 and became its perpetual secretary in 1675. Mézeray's ambition was to write a complete history of France from the earliest times to the end of the Wars of Religion that would both meet the needs of scholars and please a vast public of nonspecialists. This target corresponded to a real need, as can be seen from the success of his historical works. The first, *Histoire de France depuis Pharamond jusqu'a maintenant,* was published in three folio volumes between 1643 and 1651. Mézeray took up the work again a few years later and added fresh research; the result was published as *Abrégé chronologique ou extrait de l'Histoire de France* (three quarto volumes); a new edition was published in 1672 containing additional material and also corrections designed to rectify the passages that Colbert had disapproved of. This set of works was completed by the publication of a study of the origins of France: *Histoire de France avant Clovis. L'origine des François et leur établissement dans les Gaules* (1682). Mézeray also took an interest in the history of the Near East; he published Chalkokondyles' (q.v.) history of the decline of the Greek Empire with its continuation by Thomas Artus, which he himself continued to 1649 (1st ed., 1650) and then to 1661 (2d ed., 1662). Finally, the various notes gathered during a lifetime of study provided the material for *Dictionnaire historique,* published only in 1732 with additions by the publisher Camusat under the title *Mémoires historiques sur divers points de l'Histoire de France et plusieurs autres sujets curieux.*

Mézeray's works are mainly compilations of earlier works. Although he did not neglect personal research, and carried it out seriously, using the unpublished documents that he had managed to collect either as originals or in the form of copies of material from Paris archives and libraries, he mainly used it to provide complementary information or to decide between the authors used. The whole of Mézeray's talent thus lies in the skillful popularization of the contribution of a century of scholarly historiography. He used the classic devices of the humanist historian to place historical discoveries within the reach of the cultivated public: reconstitution of the speeches of the main protagonists, boldly drawn psychological portraits and heroic and edifying anecdotes. In a more innovative way, he also made systematic use of illustration to hold the attention and arouse the curiosity of lazy or even illiterate readers. Thus the works devoted to the history of France are illustrated with the portraits of kings and queens taken to a great extent from a collection of work by the engraver Jacques de Bie, with reproductions of medals copied from *La France Métallique* by the same author. Mézeray's publication and continuation of the history of the Turks are decorated by engravings of the sultans, the main social types, and a plan of Constantinople.

He did not even consider that he had done enough in this respect, and in *Dessein d'une parfaite Histoire de France,* which has remained in a manuscript form, he outlined the plan for an ideal book that he would have liked to have produced, and which would have been a "histoire des François, non pas de la France ny des Roys de France ny de la Monarchie de France." In this he would have liked to include not only the medals and portraits of great men but also "des figures des machines et des bastions de guerre et des armeures," pictures of "habits et de semblables gentillesses," and finally, "quarante cinq ou cinquante plans d'autant des plus mémorables sièges et batailles." "L'Histoire de France parfaite" as dreamed of by Mézeray would have been the synthesis of some ten thousand works that he considered it necessary to go through, written in a lively, colorful style and illustrated with numerous engravings.

Mézeray thought that history should fulfill three purposes. The first was to perpetuate the memory of "*belles actions*," that is, valorous military and civilian deeds and also to record progress in science and art, to which he also wanted to devote a literary and scientific journal. The second was to amuse. The third was to provide instruction, particularly for young nobles who were to have important posts. This educational role for the governing elite was very close to being a political one. In his works, Mézeray frequently addressed the reader to give his opinion of the facts described, and he did so with a freedom of tone that earned him the reputation of being a *républicain*, in the sense that the word had then—not of being against the monarchy but of having a mind with too much freedom of judgment. Pamphlets written during the Fronde and signed under the name Sandricourt were attributed to him, as was the *Histoire de la Maltôte,* which remained unpublished and was prudently burned by his heir. This theory of three functions of history corresponded perfectly to what was wanted by the public, if not by the authorities, and Mézeray had the merit of applying it in a lively and attractive manner.

Bibliography: Wilfred Hugo Evans, *L'historien Mézeray et la conception de l'histoire en France au XVIIe siècle* (Paris, 1930); Orest Ranum, *Artisans of Glory: Writers and Historical Thought in Seventeenth-Century France* (Chapel Hill, N.C., 1980); Michel Tyvaert, "Recherches sur les histoires générales de la France au XVIIe siècle (domaine français)," 2 vols. (Thesis, troisiéme cycle, Université of Paris, 1973).

Arlette Jouanna

MONTESQUIEU, Charles de Secondat, Baron de (La Brède, Bordeaux, 1689–Paris, 1755), French philosopher, writer, jurist, political theoretician, and historian. Montesquieu exercised several judicial functions: a councillor in the Bordeaux Parliament (1714–1716) and then its president (1716–1726). He gave up his career in law and between 1728 and 1731 traveled to several European countries: Germany, Austria, Italy, Switzerland, Holland, and especially England, whose political institutions so impressed him that he remained there between 1729 and 1731. Later, he lived in his castle in La Brède, where he wrote his major works. Montesquieu made a name for himself in literature in 1721 with his *Lettres persanes*. A literary fantasy, it nevertheless contains a series of historical and political ideas that were elaborated in his later works. In 1734 he published *Considérations sur les causes de la grandeur des Romains et de leur décadence,* a history of ancient Rome conceived in a philosophical spirit; it is the interpretation of facts that is considered essential, not their narration. Providence is set completely aside; the author is searching for the key to the historical process in a combination of factors (political and institutional structures, ways of governing, military organization, customs, foreign relations, personalities, and so on) that would condition one another mutually and combine strictly into a network of causes and effects. The influence of natural science is felt in Montesquieu's interest in experimental methods, his approach to history in the Cartesian spirit, his attempt to treat it scientifically. However, the documentation is limited and his approach is insufficiently critical: he accepted the information found in Livy (q.v.) without examining it. Moreover, Montesquieu had a tendency to generalize starting from a single fact, which itself was not always certain.

His major work, *De l'Esprit des lois* (1748), is more than a manual of political science; it is a true encyclopedia that sets forth, not very systematically, the whole of the author's knowledge and ideas. In this work, Montesquieu studied the origin, character, and development of political institutions and of laws, during which he frequently touched upon political, social, and economic history. Society is seen as an organism, the functioning of which is determined by objective laws that can be learned and studied scientifically. Among the fundamental causes taken into consideration, Montesquieu put first the geographic factor, especially climate; thus in a more complex and rigorous manner, he expanded on Jean Bodin's (q.v.) ideas. The human physical and spiritual aspect, and as a result the various civilizations and the differences among them, and the specific laws that can be applied to them are essentially conditioned by climatic differences ("L'empire du climat est le premier de tous les empires"). Montesquieu's approach to this kind of determinism is more subtle (and to a certain extent contradicts it) because it takes into account other factors, too, such as religion (although it, too, is seen as influenced by climate), laws, types of government, commerce, historical tradition, customs, manners. On the one hand, he believed that laws are the objective products of a certain environment and, on the other hand, that they themselves can become determining factors in influencing the customs and character of a nation; a legislator, therefore, can impose a new direction on the development of a nation. His preference tended toward the English political system, toward constitutional or limited monarchy. The climate theory has exercised a notable influence on historiography and provoked a lively debate, both pro and con. The same can be said for Montesquieu's preoccupation with the history of laws, institutions, and commerce (Book 21 of *L'Esprit des lois* is a synthesis of the history of commerce). In certain respects, historians like Heeren or Tocqueville can be considered his disciples. Voltaire (q.v.) had a superior critical spirit but was too much of a skeptic to construct a true system.

Montesquieu tried to work out a complete sociological system, open to discussion as is any system, but one that offered the prospect of looking at history as a science of society.

Bibliography: Louis Althusser, *Montesquieu, la politique et l'histoire* (Paris, 1959); Henri-Auguste Barckhausen, *Montesquieu, ses idées et ses oeuvres* (Paris, 1907: Geneva, 1970); Jean Starobinski, *Montesquieu* (Paris, 1979).

Lucian Boia

MONTFAUCON, Bernard de (Soulage, Languedoc, 1655–Paris, 1741), French historian. Born into a family of gentlemen, Montfaucon left home at eighteen and served in de Turenne's army for two years. Then in 1676 he entered the congregation of the Bénédictins de St. Maur. After several years in the provinces he was called to Paris to work on the publication of the Greek Fathers; for this he traveled in Italy from 1678 to 1701 to collect manuscripts. When he returned to St. Germain des Près, he assembled information and iconographical documents for two large works: the ten folio volumes of *L'Antiquité expliquée* and its *Supplément* (1719–1724) and the five volumes of *Les Monumens de la Monarchie françoise* (1729–1733), which, among his numerous publications, gave him the reputation of a historian. These two works are collections of plates accompanied by a learned commentary. The first is a vast encyclopedia of *antiquity*. Montfaucon gave the latter word a very broad meaning and devoted considerable space to prehistoric discoveries reported to him by his correspondents. He thus described megalithic monuments, considering that their purpose was funerary, and dated them from a period when metals were still unknown. Like the scholar Peiresc before him, he used a comparative method to obtain better understanding of the customs of ancient European peoples, setting them against the American Indians.

Les Monumens de la Monarchie françoise is the continuation of *L'Antiquité expliquée*. Montfaucon wished to draw up a catalogue of archaeological and artistic items dating from the Middle Ages in France. His documents were from three sources: first, the compilations assembled by the collector Roger de Gaignières and which mainly concerned Northwest France and the Paris area; second, the drawings that he had made of the buildings and objects that he had seen or had copied from the works of Jean Mabillon (q.v.), Etienne Baluze, and Jules Chifflet; his third source was the information supplied by correspondents scattered throughout France and whom he had asked to collaborate in a prospectus sent in 1725. The drawings were made by Antoine Benoist, whose accurate and elegant work is unfortunately often marred by the quality of the engraving. The work met a certain amount of success but not enough to make Montfaucon's publishers bring out the sequel that he had prepared and which he wished to devote to religious buildings and to iconographic documents in civil and military life in medieval France. The cultivated public able to show interest in what was commonly referred to as "gothic barbarism" was still small. Montfaucon himself sometimes described the taste of earlier centuries as coarse; however, he told his draftsman to copy material accurately since, he said, the evolution of the arts was an aspect of capital importance in human history: "the decline or the restoration of the arts is of considerable historical significance" ("la décadence ou le rétablissement des arts faisant à mon avis un point considérable de l'Histoire"). Thanks to the records he made, the memory of certain works that were later destroyed has been kept, for example, the statues of the main door of St. Denis. Montfaucon's commentaries are often penetrating in their shrewdness and good sense; however, he did make mistakes in dating and judgment because of the difficulty in covering the whole of the vast field that he had selected. The range of his curiosity was prodigious and helped to open up many lines of research.

Bibliography: Emmanuel de Broglie, *Bernard de Montfaucon et les Bernadins,* 2 vols. (Paris, 1891); J. Mommeja, "Dom Bernard de Montfaucon et l'archéologie préhistorique," *Revue de Gascogne,* 39 (1898): 5–22, 73–88; André Rostand, "La documentation iconographique des Monumens de la Monarchie françoise de Bernard de Montfaucon," *Bulletin de la Société d'Histoire de l'Art français* (1932): 104–149; Jacques Vanuxem, "The Theories of Mabillon and Montfaucon on French Sculpture of the Twelfth Century," *Journal of the Warburg and Courtauld Institutes* 20 (1957): 45–58.

Arlette Jouanna

NITHARD (? c. A.D. 800–? A.D.845), Frankish historian. The illegitimate son of Angilbert, poet and man of letters in the entourage of Charlemagne, and of the latter's daughter Berthe, Nithard received a thorough literary education. At the death of Louis the Pious, he participated in the fratricidal struggles between the sons of the emperor: Lothair, Louis the German, and Charles the Bald. He rallied to the latter, fought at his side, and remained constantly faithful to him. Named lay abbot of St. Riquies (845), he died in combat against a Norman force defending the region of the Somme. At the request of his cousin, Charles the Bald, he composed, in Latin, a work conserved in a single manuscript and known, since the edition of G. H. Pertz (1829), by the title *Historiarum libri IIII*. It is a history of the sons of Louis the Pious. Book 1 recounts the reign of that emperor in such a way as to explain the origins of the civil wars, the account of which (from A.D. 840 to 843) is contained in Books 2 to 4. Perhaps discouraged by the unhappy events he had lived through, Nithard failed to terminate a work that can be considered nonetheless "as the most remarkable historical product of the Carolingian Renaissance at its apogee" (Ganshof). The firsthand information (the author participated in the negotiations and was one of the principal advisors of King Charles) is rich and sure. Despite his partisanship, the tone is measured. Nithard has inserted some famous documents in his account, the "Oaths of Strasburg" (A.D. February 14, 842), that provide, on the one hand, the oldest text in the French language and, on the other hand, one of the oldest Germanic texts in existence.

Bibliography: P. Lauer, *Histoire des fils de Louis le Pieux,* Classiques de l'Histoire de France au Moyen Age (Paris, 1926); E. Müller, *Nithardi Historiarum libri IIII*, Scriptores Rerum Germanicarum in usum scholarum (Hanover, 1907).

Jean Glénisson

PASQUIER, Etienne (Paris, 1529–Paris, 1615), French historian; lawyer at the Parlement of Paris; crown prosecutor at the Chambre des comptes (until 1604). Pasquier was raised to nobility by letters patent in 1574. With his friends Claude Fauchet, Pierre Pitou, and Jean du Tillet, he established the bases of a national history using carefully cross-checked and criticized sources. His main publication, on which he worked for the whole of his life, has the revealing title *Les Recherches de la France*. Book 1 was published in 1560, Book 2 in 1565, Books 3–6 in 1596, Books 7–8 in various editions in 1607, 1611, and 1617; Book 9 was published posthumously in 1621. In this work, Pasquier undertook a real quest for the identity of France. Its originality lies in the fact that Pasquier did not stop at a chronological, factual approach but covered a great number of very varied subjects ranging from the Gallic and Frankish origins to the history of the University of Paris and the College of France, with documented studies of the relations between the kings of France and the popes, printing and artillery, French language and literature, games like chess and tennis, customs in dress, and so on. This variety was taken to such a degree that *Les Recherches* took the form of a collection of historical essays assembling the conclusions of an inquisitive, rigorous mind that wanted to fix the identity and individuality of the kingdom of France through its history, institutions, customs, language, and literature. Etienne Pasquier aimed at carrying out solid work that would serve as reference: "Je me suis résolu de ne rien dire qui importe, sans en faire preuve," he wrote at the beginning of Book 1, that is, without basing each statement on original sources that he did not hesitate to quote at length for the reader. For Pasquier, the work of historian thus started with the search for documents of the most varied kinds, manuscripts, coins, and architectural remains; he then compared all of this material and criticized it using the methods devised by classical philologists like Lorenzo Valla (q.v.) or Guillaume Budé and taught by the jurists whose lectures he had attended in Paris, Toulouse, and Pavia: Baudouin, Hotman, Cujas, and Alciat. He formed an opinion with as much objectivity as possible while remaining aware of the difficulty of the task, particularly when sources were not sufficiently numerous. He thus attempted to give history the dignity of a science. Nevertheless, his reconstruction of origins was influenced by his political and social opinions. For example, he wrote that victors and vanquished intermingled after the conquest of Gaul by the Franks, and the French people thus acquired unity. This was to take up a conciliatory, peacemaking position in the controversy between two concepts of state and society: one based on military values and upheld by the gentlemen—who identified their ancestors in the conquering Franks—and the other on peaceful values more defended by nobles in the legal profession and who had judicial functions. Likewise, the desire to prove that the power of the throne had always been limited in France led Pasquier to exaggerating the age of the *parlements,* which he considered as forming protection against the arbitrary.

Etienne Pasquier was also the historian of his own times in his *Lettres,* first published in 1586 in a volume consisting of ten books reprinted four times between 1590 and 1607; a further twelve books were added in the two-volume posthumous edition published in 1619. The letters are extremely varied, comprising critical reviews of literary works, philosophical and moral dissertations, theories about spelling and language, political controversies, and his first responses to contemporary events. Pasquier made an effort to be impartial; although he was a devout Roman Catholic, he gave unprejudiced opinions on the responsibility of the adversaries in the religious wars. He was careful to check the facts he reported if he had not witnessed them himself, and he analyzed them with acuteness that provoked the admiration of contemporary readers. Nevertheless, there is a subject about which Pasquier, as a staunch Gallican, is partial: the activities of the Jesuits, against whom he defended the University of Paris (1565) and whom he attacked in his book *Le Catéchisme des Jésuites* (1602). In addition to writing historical works, Pasquier published many anonymous pamphlets and satirical sonnets in which his contemporaries took pleasure in recognizing his hand. He also wrote poetry, love letters, and *Dialogues* on love that revealed the extent of his curiosity and the breadth of his culture.

Bibliography: Paul Bouteiller, "Un historien du seizième siècle," *Bibliographie d'Humanisme et Renaissance* 6 (1945); Leon Feugère, *Essai sur la vie et les ouvrages d'Etienne Pasquier* (Paris, 1848); George Huppert, "Les Recherches d'Etienne Pasquier," in *L'Idée de l'Histoire Parfaite* (Paris, 1973), translated from *The Idea of Perfect History* (Urbana, Ill., 1970); Donald R. Kelley, *Foundations of Modern Historical Scholarship: Language, Law, and History in the French Renaissance* (New York and London, 1970); Dorothy Thickett, *Etienne Pasquier (1529–1615) The Versatile Barrister of Sixteenth-Century France* (London and New York, 1979).

Arlette Jouanna

RAOUL GLABER (Raoul the Bald) (? c. 985–? c. 1046), French historian. Glaber Rodulfus entered the monastery of St. Germain d'Auxerre, where he was educated when he was very young. A troubled spirit and unstable character, intolerant of monastic discipline, he remained throughout his life a wandering monk, passing from one monastery to the next. A capital event in his existence was his encounter at St. Bénigne of Dijon with Guillaume de Volpiano (961–1031), abbot of that monastery in 990 and tireless apostle of religious reform, who exercised a profound influence on Raoul and included him in his suite on a trip to Italy (c. 1025). Around 1031–1033 he was at Cluny under the abbot Odilon. He died at St. Germain d'Auxerre. Raoul has left a history of the "Roman Empire" (Western Christendom) from the beginning of the tenth century known as *Historiarum libri quinque*, which was written at the behest of Guillaume de Volpiano (of whom he composed la "Vita") and dedicated to the abbot Odilon about 1044. Begun at Cluny, the work was no doubt completed at St. Germain. Indifferent to chronology, informed about events in Burgundy and the kingdom of France, less sure in matters concerning the papacy and the empire, it is a history profoundly marked by its author's personality with regard to which judgments differ. At the time of "positivist" history it was condemned for its inexactitudes, its aberrations, its propensity for recounting calamities, its obsession with ''funereal and satanic'' visions. ''It is a bizarre work, written in an incorrect and pretentious style wherein the author reveals himself for what he was; superstitous even for that age'' confused, prolix'' (Auguste Molinier 1902). Today it is conceded that his work should not be judged in terms of our own mental attitudes and logic. ''If one takes the trouble to enter into the spirit of his work, he immediately appears as one of the very best witnesses of his age'' (Georges Duby 1967). In fact, the historians of the nineteenth and twentieth centuries have drawn from Raoul Glaber some colorful images: concerning the double millennia that he lived through (the year 1000 and the millennium [1033] of the passion of Christ) about which he enumerated the signs and prodigies ''which accord with the prophecy of Saint John according to whom Satan would be unleased at the end of one thousand years''; concerning the wave of religious building ''at the time when the third year after the Year One Thousand was about to begin, it seemed that the world shook itself and cast off its villainies in order to clothe itself anew in a white robe of churches.'' This visionary was at the same time an excellent epigrapher employed by several monasteries to decipher and restore their ancient inscriptions worn away by time.

Bibliography: Raoul Glaber, *Les cinq livres de les histoires (900–1044),* Collection de texte pour servir à l'ètude et à l'enseignement de l'histoire, ed., M. Prou (Paris, 1886).

Jean Glénisson

THOU, Jacques-Auguste de (Paris, 1533–Paris, 1617). French historian. Like his father, Christophe de Thou, president in the Parlement of Paris, Jacques-Auguste de Thou followed a career in the high magistrature: he became president in the same parlement in 1587, councilor of state in 1588, and then grand-master of the royal library from 1594 until his death. A moderate Catholic, a Gallican, and a supporter of a strong royal power, he was one of the active members of the *Politiques* conciliatory movement. Henry IV and the then queen-mother Marie de Médicis entrusted him with numerous tasks of negotiation with the Protestants. His incessant struggle to calm the religious and political conflicts of his time inspired in him the desire to encourage people to forget their passions and to strengthen national feeling by establishing the truth of the facts obscured by hatred in a history that would be as impartial as possible. He started to collect documents in 1578 and began writing in 1593. The first part of the history of his time, *Historiarum sui temporis pars prima,* was published in 1604 by Veuve Mamert Patisson. The work contains a general introduction that summarizes the events of the first half of the sixteenth century and then covers the years 1546 to 1560. Geographically, it covers not only France but also the whole of the known world. De Thou wrote a total of 138 books covering events to 1607, but he allowed publication of only the first 80 books during his lifetime, postponing that of the remaining 58 until a period when the truth would be less dangerous. His work was accused of being too favorable to the Protestants and too critical of the papacy; it was in fact condemned by Rome and put on the Roman Catholic Index in November 1609. He also offended sensibilities at court and in neighboring countries, and much pressure was put on him to water down the text in successive editions. That is why he wrote in Latin and was opposed to any translation that would have resulted in stirring up feelings even more. The whole set of 138 books was not published until after his death; this was carried out in Geneva in 1620 by his friend Georg Lingelsheim, who added to this edition the *Commentariorum de vita sua libri sex* in which de Thou defended his history against calumny and explained how he came to write it. The vicissitudes of the writing and publication of the work, the number of corrections, deletions, and additions made by the author, make it difficult to propose an accurate statement of the development of his thinking. The best edition of the Latin text is the one assembled by Thomas Carte and published in London in 1733 by Samuel Buckley. In addition, there is no really satisfactory translation. These difficulties should not detract from the importance of J. A. de Thou in the history of historiography. He set himself the task of writing a book about his times that would not be simple memoirs but a true history; he thus came to pay special attention to the criticism of his sources, which were listed at the beginning of each book from the fifth edition (1618). He expressed his ideas on his method in the *Preface to Henri IV,* which was immediately translated into French by Jean Hotman de Villiers on the orders of the king and published separately in 1604, and in the *Préface au lecteur,* which appeared in the fourth edition published in 1609 and in a modified form in the fifth edition in 1618.

De Thou believed that the major quality for a historian was the absence of passion, which affects freedom of judgment; he must thus imperatively stand back from prejudices and accepted ideas of his time. To achieve this, de Thou constantly submitted himself to the scrutiny of posterity, considering this to be the only truly impartial judge. This procedure was for him a methodical principle and intellectual technique in order to be in the best emotional and psychological condition and thus to be able to see the truth. The ideal historian possesses detachment and discernment, prudence and courage; moreover, he should use a simple, concise style with no useless formal affectation. The truth that de Thou sought to detect beneath the apparently disorganized unleashings of passions was the recognizable presence of general laws of human psychology. He hoped to show that the religious conflicts were only a pathological state that could be cured; this evidence should enable former adversaries to recognize the need to obey common laws, guaranteed by royal authority and unanimously accepted, in spite of differences in faith, while waiting for the latter to fade away by the grace of God. The ideal of the good historian thus finally rejoined that of the good citizen, master of himself, facing events with reasoned serenity. This convergence made the success of de Thou's rich, varied work in which there were both equitable narration of the facts and the constituents of a theory of the methodical detachment of the historian.

Bibliography: Claude-Gilbert Dubois, *La conception de l'Histoire en France au XVIe siècle (1560–1610)* (Paris, 1977); Samuel Kinser, *The works of Jacques-Auguste de Thou* (The Hague, 1966); Abbé A. J. Rance, *J. A. de Thou, son Histoire universelle et ses démêlés avec Rome* (Paris, 1881); Alfred Soman, *De Thou and the "Index" Letters from Christophe Dupuy (1603–1607)* (Geneva, 1972).

Arlette Jouanna

VILLEHARDOUIN, Geoffroi de (Villehardouin, c. 1150–? c. 1213), French chronicler. Hereditary marshal of Champagne, this noble lord took the cross with his suzerain, the count of Champagne, in 1199. With five other barons, he negotiated, at Venice, for the transportation of the expedition. Following the capture of Constantinople by the crusaders in 1204, he distinguished himself as counselor to Boniface de Montferrat and to the emperor Baudouin. His soldierly qualities manifested themselves during the retreat from Adrianople (1204). Named marshal of Romania and rewarded with important fiefs in Thrace, he remained in the East. He "dictated" (which can also signify in the French of that period "composed"), during the last years of his life (from 1207 to 1212), his political and military memoirs for the benefit of his family and his compatriots in Champagne. Known today by the title *Conquest of Constantinople*, this account, covering the period 1198–1207, is considered an adroit attempt to justify in the eyes of contemporaries the inexplicable deviation of an expedition intended to liberate the Holy Sepulchre in Jerusalem but which ended, after the capture of Zara in the Adriatic on the Venetians' behalf, by overthrowing the Basileus and substituting a Latin empire on the Bosphorus for the Greek Empire. Considering the rich historiography on the Fourth Crusade, the prestige of these very clever and biased "memoirs" depends above all on their literary qualities.

Bibliography: J. Dufournet, *Les écrivains de la quatrième croisade. Villehardouin et Clari*, 2 vols. (Paris, 1973); *La Conquête de Constantinople*, 1st ed., 2 vols., Les Classiques de l'Histoire de France au Moyen Âge, 18 and 19; ed. and trans. E. Faral (Paris, 1969).

Jean Glénisson

VOLTAIRE (Pseudonym of François-Marie Arouet) (Paris, 1694–Paris, 1778), French writer, philosopher, and historian. Voltaire was the most productive and influential cultural personality of the eighteenth century. The principal episodes of his life unfold first in Paris, where he established, at a very young age, his reputation as a poet and playwright and where, although of bourgeois origin, he penetrated the highest circles of the aristocracy (although he was also twice imprisoned in the Bastille, in 1717–1718 and in 1726). He was exiled in England from 1726 to 1729, an important period when he came under the influence of English liberal thinking and scientific spirit (John Locke, Isaac Newton, Henry Bolingbroke). He lived on the Cirey Estate of the Marquise Emilie du Châtelet (1706–1749), his friend and inspiration, staying there, with interruptions, between 1734 and 1749. He also lived at Potsdam at the court of Frederic II, king of Prussia, between 1750 and 1753 and on his own estate and castle, in Ferney, between 1758 and 1778. Voltaire first approached history through his epic *La Henriade* (1723), a reconstruction of the age of Henri IV. His first historical monograph is *Histoire de Charles XII* (1731), a biography of the renowned Swedish king; a well-documented work written with talent, it marked the transition from traditional historiography to the rationalist and philosophic historiography of the eighteenth century. Voltaire himself was to be the promotor of this current. *Le Siècle de Louis XIV*, begun between 1732 and 1734 and published in 1751, marks a milestone not only in Voltaire's works but also in the evolution of all modern historiography; Eduard Fueter considered it "the first modern book of history." For the first time the strictly chronological order of facts was broken up and an attempt was made at a new complete picture of an epoch. Voltaire presented political events, the life of the king and of the court, the system of government and administration, law, economy, trade, finance, military organization, the sciences, the arts, literature, ecclesiastical matters, and religious conflicts. He was moving toward a history of material and spiritual civilization; political and military events continued to be significant, but they were presented from a philosophical perspective in an attempt to draw meanings and lessons from them. Voltaire was often reproached for his unsystematic treatment of material in chapters insufficiently tied together, "a history with drawers"; such an approach, however, was natural once historical problems were placed before chronology in order of importance.

After *Annales de l'Empire* (1753), a modest compilation without any special value, came his second fundamental historical work: *Essai sur les moeurs et l'esprit des nations* (1756, definitive edition 1769). It is a world history that continued, though in a new secular and liberal spirit, Jacques Bossuet's (q.v.) work; it presents, following an introduction on antiquity, the development of the historical process from the epoch of Charlemagne to his own times. Voltaire also coined the phrase "philosophy of history" (in an introduction published in 1765 under the title *La Philosophie de l'histoire*), by which he meant, in fact, a history of the human spirit, of civilizations, explained rationally, without the intervention of Providence. It is the first general history of civilizations; special importance is accorded to social, intellectual, and material life and the customs and spirit of nations and epochs (90 chapters out of 197 are concerned with these problems). At the same time, Voltaire put before himself the task of going beyond the traditional European-centered view; several chapters are devoted to the countries and peoples of Asia (China, India, Japan, Persia, Arabia, and so on), Africa, and America. Wars and intolerance are the main evils he condemned; progress can only be insured through the development of the sciences and the arts and freedom of thought. Many details and judgments are wrong or unfair; the Middle Ages are too little understood and too harshly judged by a man who saw everything through the prism of the rationalism of his age. Through its totally new approach and the incomparable critical spirit that permeates it, however, the work represents a remarkable historiographic achievement.

Other historical works were *Histoire de la Russie sous Pierre le Grand* (1759–1763), an idealized presentation of the rule of the great czar; *Précis du siècle de Louis XV* (1768), which like the former is inferior to the monograph on Louis

XIV; and *Histoire du Parlement de Paris* (1769), an attempt at constitutional history. Voltaire renewed the fundamental concept and method of history. With his relentless critical spirit he caused many false authorities, prejudices, and traditions to fall, and he proved the need for a firm and permanent control of the sources. An adversary of systems, he did not propound a rigorous or systematic philosophy of history. He opposed theological or biblical interpretations and admitted divinity only as a first cause of the universe and the laws that govern it. Humans are subject to ''destiny,'' an objective historical development that results from certain strict causal connections. He accorded some importance to climate but opposed Montesquieu's (q.v.) exaggerations and considered as much more important the influence of government and religion. He also invoked the ''spirit of the times'' or the ''spirit of nations.'' Chance, seemingly trifling events, can have significant repercussions, hence his skepticism about the possibility of a logical prediction of historical development. ''Great men'' as opposed to ''heroes'' (who, like Charles XII, not only do not create anything that lasts but are even capable of provoking the ruin of their country) were accorded an essential role. Great men are those who contribute to the progress of civilization. Enlightened monarchs occupy a special place: through Louis XIV and Peter the Great, Voltaire became the principal ideologue of enlightened despotism. He conceived of history as a political weapon to be used against injustice, fanaticism, and ignorance and was in favor of reforms that open the way to progress. Through the triple dimension of his historical work—critical history, history of civilization, militant political history—Voltaire greatly stimulated historical research and thought in the whole of Europe in the second half of the eighteenth century.

Bibliography: Theodore Besterman, *Voltaire* (New York, 1969); J. H. Brumfitt, *Voltaire Historian* (London, 1958); Furio Diaz, *Voltaire storico* (Torino, 1958); Gustave Lanson, *Voltaire* (Paris 1906); Haydn Mason, *Voltaire* (Baltimore, 1981).

Lucian Boia

Great Historians: Georgian

BAGRATIONI, VAKHUSHTI (Tbilisi, 1696–Moscow, 1757), Georgian historian. His major work, *The History of Georgia*, covering the period from earliest times to the eighteenth century, is a systematic exposition of the history of Georgia, the first attempt at a critical study of the past of the Georgian people. The history of Georgia is considered in interrelationship with and against the background of world history. The historical narration is in the style of a chronicle; mainly, developments of the country's political history are described; an attempt is made by the author to account for the historical facts through a cause-and-effect relationship. The *History of Georgia* is divided into two periods: that of the unity of Georgia, to the 1460s, and the period following the breakup of the kingdom. The author paid special attention to the substantiation of the political and ethnic unity of Georgia. The first part of Bagrationi's work is based on *Kartlis Tskhovreba*, a corpus of annals (History of Georgia), which had been supplemented from time to time. The second part of the work is largely an original historical study based on sources in different languages (Greek, Armenian, Turkish, European, and so on) and other evidence (so-called general histories, family chronicles, documents, inscriptions, numismatic data, remains of material culture, and so on) Bagrationi introduced new, hitherto unknown, methods into Georgian historiography; he enriched historical facts, starting the historical narration with geographic and ethnographic descriptions; he expanded the subject matter by introducing ecclesiastical history, law, mores, and so on, with reference to original sources; the work is supplied with a critical-historical introduction, notes, chronological and genealogical tables, maps, and indexes.

Bibliography: Bagrationi's work was published in 1973 *(Kartlis Tskhovreba*, vol. 4, ed. S. Qaukhchishvili); portions of the work had been published several times; separate Russian translations of the geographical and historical parts are available (Vakhushti Bagrationi, *The History of the Kingdom of Georgia*, trans N. T. Nakashidze [Tbilisi, 1976]). The maps compiled by Bagrationi were translated into Russian and French, being widely used in Russia and Europe. The work was translated into French by M. Brosset.

M. Lordkipanidze

GEORGIAN Anonym (? seventh century). The work *Moktsevai Kartlisai* (The Conversion of Georgia) comprises three major parts. The history of the emergence of the kingdom of Kartli (eastern Georgia), from the fourth century B.C. to the fourth century A.D. and lists of pre-Christian kings are presented, with very brief information about their activities (mainly constructional). The chronicle devotes more space to the rule of the first Christian king Mirian (second half of the fourth century) and to Nino, the illuminatrix of the Georgians. This first part is believed to have been compiled by Grigol the Deacon very soon after the Christianization of the Georgians. The chronicle was updated in the seventh century, the narration reaching the events of the A.D. 640s. This part, too, contains lists of the kings and catholicoi, as well as brief information on the building of churches, monasteries, strongholds, and cities. The chronicle gives a relatively more detailed account of the activities of King Vakhtang Gorgasali (second half of the fifth century), the establishment of the Catholicosate, and the campaigns of Byzantine Emperor Heraclius (A.D. 610–664) in the East. The anonym shares the medieval conception of the periodization of world history according to the four major monarchies. Since the Farnavazid dynasty in Kartli commenced in the fourth century, the formation of the Kartlian kingdom is related to the campaigns of Alexander the Great. In the ninth century the chronicle was edited; it was supplemented with lists of high secular and ecclesiastical officials and with an extended version of the ''Life of Saint Nino.''

Bibliography: Ivané Javakhishvili, *Moktsevai Kartlisai* (The Chronicle of the Conversion of Georgia), in Javakhishvili, *Works* (in Georgian) 12 vols., vol. 8 (Tbilisi, 1977), pp. 112–116; Korneli Kekelidze, *A History of Georgian Literature* (in Georgian), vol. 1 (Tbilisi, 1941), pp. 485–492; G. A. Melikishvili, ''Old Georgian Historical Works: 'Moktsevai Kartlisai' and 'Kartlis Tskhovreba' as Sources for the History of Georgia,'' in G. A. Melikishvili, *Towards the History of Ancient Georgia* (in Russian) (Tbilisi, 1959), pp. 23–62; *Monuments of Old Georgian Hagiographic Literature* (in Old Georgian), Bk. 1 (Tbilisi, 1963), pp. 81–163; *The Shatberdi Corpus of the 10th Century* (Tbilisi, 1979), Russian translation: E. Taqaishvili, ''Sources of Georgian Annals: Three Chronicles,'' in *Sbornik materialov dlya opsaniya mestnostei i plemen Kavkaza*, issue 28 (Tiflis, 1900), pp. 1–50; German translation: G. Pätsch, ''Die Bekehrung Georgiens 'Mockcevay Kartlisay,' '' in *Bedi Kartlisa, Revue de Kartvelologie* (Paris, 1975), pp. 288–337.

M. Lordkipanidze

HISTORIAN OF DAVID (anonymous, known under this name) (Tbilisi, first half of the twelfth century), Georgian historian. The historian's work *The Life of the King of Kings David* was written in the 1130s and consists of two major parts: the first part (a relatively long manuscript of twenty-seven pages) deals with the military activities of King David IV, the Builder (1089–1125); the second part (a manuscript of twenty pages) gives an account of the king's civilian, ecclesiastical, and ethical activities. The historian advocated the king's strong centralist policy, the entire work being infused with a polemical spirit against the feudal rulers opposed to David's reforms. Conceding the great personal talent and capacity of the king, the historian accounted for David's military victories and the defeat of the strong internal opposition as being largely due to God's favor and aid. Thus the historian's outlook was providential. In his narration the author frequently had recourse to the comparative method, citing examples from Hebrew, Greek, and Persian history; he compared David with Alexander the Great. The work of David's historian forms part of the corpus entitled *Kartlis Tskhovreba* (History of Georgia). The first composition (Leonti Mroveli's "The Life of the Kings") sets forth Georgian history from the biblical Adam to the fifth century A.D. Subsequently, *Kartlis Tskhovreba* was supplemented from time to time, the updating lasting until the fourteenth century. King David's history was added in this manner. The continuation of *Kartlis Tskhovreba* was resumed in the eighteenth century. The work of David's historian has been published several times, the last being *Kartlis Tskhovreba*, vol. 1 (Tbilisi, 1955), pp. 318–364.

Bibliography: A. Bogveradze, "Concerning the Date and Character of the History of David the Builder," in *Georgian Historiography*, vol. 2 (in Georgian) (Tbilisi, 1971), pp. 70–83; M. Brosset, *Histoire de la Georgie*, pt. 1, book 1, SPB (1849), pp. 346–381; Ivané Javakhishvili, "The Historian of David the Builder," in Ivané Javakhishvili, *Works* (in Georgian), 12 vols., vol. 8 (Tbilisi, 1977), pp. 210–220; M. Sabinin, *Complete Lives of the Saints of the Georgian Church*, vol. 3 (St. Petersburg, 1873), Russian translation.

M. Lordkipanidze

MROVELI, Leontii (? A.D. eighth century/eleventh century), Georgian historian. Mroveli is assumed to be the author of the *Lives of the Karthvelian Tsars*, which opens the saga of Georgia's history from the earliest times to the fifth century A.D. The author sought to establish the origins of the Caucasian peoples, specifically, the Georgians, their language and religion, and the rise of royal power in Georgia and social inequality. Along with using written sources, Mroveli made extensive use of oral legends and myths with their peculiar reflection of past events. The work emphasizes close historical relations and kinship of Georgian tribes and is permeated with a political trend consistent with the demands of the movement for unity in Georgia in the eleventh century. In addition to writing the *Lives of the Karthvelian Tsars*, Mroveli is also thought to have been the author of the following works in the *Karthlis Tskhoveba* collection: "Karthli's Conversion to Christianity by St. Nina" and "The Martyrdom of St. Archill, Tsar of Kartli."

Bibliography: M. Brosset, *Histoire de la Géorgie* (St. Petersburg, 1849); I. Djavakhishvili, *Historical Literature of Old Georgia from the Fifth to Eighteenth Centuries* (Tbilisi, 1945), Georgian language edition; P. Ingorokva, "Leontii Mroveli," *Moalbe* 10 (1941): 93–151 (in Georgian); G. V. Tsulaya, *Vvedeniye k izdaniyu texta "Letopis Kartli"* (Introduction to the Karthvelian Chronicle) (Tbilisi, 1982).

V. A. Rzhanitsina

Great Historians: German

ADAM VON BREMEN (near Bamberg, c. 1040–Bremen, post–1085), North German cleric, chronicler, and geographer. About 1066 Adam Von Bremen came from the eastern part of Franconia to Bremen; received promotion by Archbishop Adalbert, a close party supporter of the Saliers; and in 1069 was named in a document as "magister scholarum," the headmaster of the cathedral school. As was proved by a great number of classical and postclassical writers, he acquired a high level of education in Bamberg. Soon after his arrival at Bremen, he began writing the *Gesta Hammaburgensis ecclesiae pontificum* (Church History of Hamburg) in four volumes, the first two volumes being devoted to the development of the archdiocese until the assumption of office by his patron Adalbert in 1043, the third being his pontificate, and the fourth being "Descriptio Insularum Aquilonis" (Description of the Islands of the North) with the perspective of the envisaged missionary activities, prompting him personally to collect information at the Court of the Danish King Svend Estudsen. He made a careful selection, using many presently unavailable documents, hagiographies, and chronicles; for part 4 he also used the fables of classical writers and stories of seafarers, turning out a comprehensive history on the northern German part and on the missionary activities to the north and northeast, irrespective of some slight errors. About 1075 he handed over the first version of his work to Archbishop Liemar but continued to work on the text until his death. In the Middle Ages it was especially the fourth book that drew great attention. In 1917 Bernhard Schmeidler published the first critical edition in the *Monumenta Germaniae Historica in usum scholarum*.

Bibliography: Rudolf Buchner, "Die politische Vorstellungswelt Adams von Bremen," *Archiv für Kulturgeschichte* 46 (1963): 15–59; Anne Katerine Gade Kristensen, *Studien zur Adam von Bremen Überlieferung* (København, 1975); Bernhard Schmeidler, "Zur Entstehung und zum Plan der hamburgischen Kirchengeschichte Adams von Bremen," *Neues Archiv für ältere deutsche Geschichtskunde* 50 (1933): 221–228.

Siegfried Hoyer

ADELUNG, Johann Christoph (Anklam, now Pomerania, 1732/1734–Dresden, 1806), German philologue and historian. An outstanding representative of Middle German Enlightenment, an encyclopaedic genius, and conspicuous in linguistics (mainly Germanic) and historiography, Adelung began by writing political *Zeitgeschichte*, later turned to *Kulturgeschichte*—philosophy, didactic pedagogics of all disciplines, and scientific journalism. This distinguished "Aufklärer" is still well known as a lexicographer of German but is almost forgotten as an innovator in historiography of culture (civilization, including science) and in philosophy of history. Adelung studied at the University of Halle, where he became an adherent of Christian Wolff's rationalism and was secretary to the masonic lodge. Persecuted while a high school teacher in Erfurt, he then lived as a private scholar in Leipzig and from 1787 as a librarian in Dresden. Contested for his enlightened views, Adelung published many works anonymously. Because of his frank utterances against suppression by orthodoxy, by nobles and princes, as well as against militarism, and in favor of the middle class and of the people, he did not get a professorship in a university. He was the second German historian that founded, next to August Schlözor (q.v.), critically enlightening, "pragmatic" general historiography of culture. He was the first historical thinker in Germany who fathomed comprehensively the material and mental causes of cultural and scientific progress. He stressed the demographic and socioeconomic reasons for cultural development, without neglecting the intellectual, political, and geographical factors. He simplified some problems and overestimated the importance of density and increase of population in the development of civilization. The single cultures, he argued, are transitory, in a biological cycle (with rise, development, stagnation, decline, and ruin), while the culture of humankind as a whole makes continual progress. According to him, progress in culture is the most important content of history. Adelung sought the sense of history in the advance of humankind to prosperity and to a high civilization. Schlözer and Adelung, the first German *kulturhistorikers* of a critical modern type, mark the beginning of the liberal-democratic current in German historiography.

Bibliography: Günter Mühlpfordt, "J. C. Adelung als Wegbereiter der Kulturgeschichtsschreibung," in *Storia della Storiografia* (Milan, 1987); Karl-Ernst Sickel, "Johann Christoph Adelung. Seine Persönlichkeit und seine Geschichtsauffassung" (Diss., University of Leipzig, 1933); *Spreche und Kulturentwicklung in Blickfeld der deutschen Spätaufklärung. Der Beitrag Johann Christoph Adelungs, herausgegeben von Werner Bahner* (Berlin, 1984), Abhandlungen der Sächsischen Akademie der Wissenschaften zu Leipzig. Philologisch-historische Klasse, Band 70, Heft 4 (28 studies); Margrit Strohbach, *Johann Christoph Adelung. Ein Geitrag zu seinem germanistischen Schaffen. Mit einer Bibliographie seines Gesamtwerkes* (Berlin and New York, 1984). Reprints: Allgemeines Gelehrtenlexikon, 2 vols. (Hildesheim, 1960), Letters A–J; *Alteste Geschichte der Deutschen* (Hildesheim, 1973); *Versuch einer Geschichte der Kultur des menschlichen Geschlechts* (Königstein and Taunus, 1979).

Günter Mühlpfordt

FLACIUS ILLYRICUS, Matthias, prop. Vlačić (Labin, near Rijeka, 1520–Frankfurt on the Main, 1575), Istrian historian and theologian. Flacius Illyricus studied at Venice, Basle, Tübingen, and Wittenberg and became a Lutheran. In 1544 he was appointed professor of Hebrew at Wittenberg University. The

Interims of Augsburg and Leipzig produced his stiff opposition. He left Wittenberg on Easter 1549 and went to Magdeburg. From 1557 to 1561 he was engaged as professor of the New Testament at the University of Jena and transformed the Thuringian Academy into a center of orthodox Lutheranism (so-called Gnesio-Lutherans). Persecuted by the elector of Saxony and local magistrates, he stayed until his death, in various European towns, always disputing the Protestant dogma (against Melanchthon and his followers George Major, Andrew Osiander, and Caspar Schwenckfeld). The historiographic work of Flacius cannot be separated from his theological intentions. It served to promote the struggle against the Catholic Church. Flacius intended to demonstrate by means of historical documents that Luther was not a theological newcomer. Good Christians always attacked the papal empire. He attempted to destroy the historical background of the Catholic Church, doubting the authenticity of documents. He thus can be regarded as the founder of Protestant ecclesiastical historiography. He focused on the historical origin and development of the two confessions and stimulated further scientific research. His most important works were the *Catalogus testium veritatis* (Catalogue of Truth Testifiers [1st ed., Basle, 1556; 2nd augmented ed., Basle, 1562]) and the *Magdeburg Centuries* (the original title is *Ecclesiastica historia* [Church History] [1st vol., Basle, 1559; 13th and last vol., Basle, 1574]). The *Catalogue* tells about some hundred opponents (persons and institutions) to papal supremacy; the other work is written by centuries (therefore the name), each century divided into sixteen chapters, and reports ecclesiastical history until the thirteenth century. For this Flacius organized a team of learned men and received financial aid given by noblemen and public officers. He also edited the *Frankish History* of Gregory, Bishop of Tours (q.v.) (1568).

Bibliography: Johannes Burkhardt, *Die Entstehung der modernen Jahrhundertrechnung* (Göppingen, West Germany, 1971); Pontien Polman, ''Flacius Illyricus, historien de l'eglise,'' *Revue d'histoire ecclésiastique* 27 (1931): 27–73; Wilhelm Preger, *Matthias Flacius Illyricus und seine Zeit,* 2 vols. (Erlangen, West Germany, 1859–1861, with index of writings in vol. 2, pp. 539–572); Heinz Scheible, ''Die Entstehung der Magdeburger Zenturien,'' *Gütersloh* (1966); S. L. Verheus, *Zeugnis und Gericht. Kirchengeschiechtliche Betrachtungen bei Sebastian Franck und Matthias Flacius* (Nieukoop, West Germany, 1971).

Walter Zöllner

GATTERER, Johann Christoph (Altdorf, 1729–Göttingen, 1799), German historian. Gatterer played an important role in the development of history as a professionalized, ''scientific'' discipline in eighteenth-century Germany. His contribution was primarily programmatic, but it helped to effect the turn to historical reasoning that took place during the Enlightenment. Along with other colleagues at Göttingen, Gatterer helped make Göttingen the leading German center for the professional study of history. Gatterer's program consisted of four interlocking concerns: (1) to determine history's object of inquiry and to reflect upon the nature of historical representation; (2) to evolve an adequate epistemology that could validate the scientific nature of historical understanding; (3)

to expand and perfect the methodological tools necessary for historical research; and (4) to create institutions to regularize and facilitate the professional study of history. Guiding these endeavors was Gatterer's belief that all aspects of life were interconnected: each event was part of the general connection of things (*nexus rerum universalis*) and hence could not be studied in isolation. For this reason, Gatterer believed that it was fruitless to rely upon simple mechanical formulas or to restrict one's scope to the traditional categories of political and diplomatic history. Like his colleague August Schlözer (q.v.), Gatterer called for an expansion of the historical field of inquiry to encompass those fields we today would call social, economic, and cultural history. To accomplish this without falling into a labyrinth of unconnected empirical data, the historian was to discriminate the important from the unimportant, to organize this material in a comprehensive pattern, and to portray change over time as well as relations across time (diachronic and synchronic representation). These basic tasks were spelled out in his article "Vom historischen Plan" (1765), a plan that he attempted to realize, though with limited success, in his numerous manuals on universal history. In addition to these pragmatic concerns, Gatterer was convinced that the new history required an epistemologic base that would justify it as a science.

In his two important articles, "Von der Evidenz in der Geschichte" (1767) and "Abhandlung vom Standort und Gesichtspunkt des Geschichtsschreibers" (1768), Gatterer evolved an epistemology that was original and important. He emphasized the relativistic nature of historical understanding, argued that it was an individualizing science, not a generalizing one, and claimed that it employed forms of understanding different from those used in the "abstract sciences." Historians, though required to uncover causal connections, had to recreate past life through an act of intuitive understanding (*anschauende Erkenntnis*), which because of its immediacy was a truer, more "evident" form of apprehension than that provided by mere ratiocination. Here Gatterer helped establish a strategy of argument that was to justify the scientific nature of history for much of the nineteenth century. Gatterer's theoretical concerns were enhanced by his desire to expand the methodological arsenal of the historian and to institutionalize its systematic study. He expended a great deal of energy in developing the ancillary sciences as evidenced by his manuals on chronology, diplomatics, geography, numismatics, and heraldry. Although not a pioneer in these fields, he established them firmly within the university curriculum and perfected their use. The call to institutionalize historical studies found expression in his founding of an Historisches Institut at Göttingen in 1764 and with the introduction of a general introductory program for the study of history called the "Historische Encyclopädie." Not only was the institute a place for the exchange of scholarly information, it successfully published two successive journals, the *Allgemeine Historische Bibliothek* (1767–1771) and the *Historische Journal* (1772–1781). In general, Gatterer envisioned a thoroughgoing revolution of historical understanding that he strove to implement. In this sense, he played a vital role in the formation of the modern conception of history.

Bibliography: Herbert Butterfield, *Man on His Past: The Study of Historical Scholarship* (Cambridge, Eng., 1955); Notkar Hammerstein, *Jus und Historie* (Göttingen, 1972); Luigi Marino, *I Maestri della Germania* (Turin, 1975); Peter Hanns Reill, *The German Enlightenment and the Rise of Historicism* (Berkeley, Calif., and Los Angeles, 1975).

Peter Hanns Reill

HERDER, Johann Gottfried (Mohrungen, 1744–Weimar, 1803), German representative of the Enlightenment movement; philosopher of history; theorist of Sturm and Drang movement. Herder studied theology and philosophy at Königsberg (1762–1764), was a teacher and preacher in Riga (1764–1769), took educational journeys and was a teacher of princes (1769–1771), and held high religious posts in Bückeberg (1771–1776) and Weimar (1776–1803). His important works were *Ideen zur Philosophie der Geschichte der Menschheit* (1784–1791), *Briefe zur Beförderung der Humanität* (1792–1797), and *Auch eine Philosophie der Geschichte der Bildung der Menschheit* (1774). His complete works were titled *Sämtliche Werke. Historischkritische Ausgabe* (33 vols., Berlin, 1877–1913). Especially under the influence of the French and German Enlightenment, notably Gotthold Lessing, Benedict de Spinoza, Gottfried Leibniz, and Giovan Vico (q.v.) and others, he developed the most important philosophy of history of the German Enlightenment, an image of history and a perspective of humankind, with the essential content of a contradictory, yet incessant, progression to ever higher forms of humanity. The characteristics of his humanistic concept are the increasing rule of people over nature; the development of science, technology, and art; the liberation from all forms of rule obstructing people in their full development; and ultimately, the abolition of the state. This was the way for an orientation to cultural history. But the lack of conceptual precision corresponded with a logically controversial mixture of Spinozist-materialist and Christian-idealist views. This determined also his view on the driving forces of history. In his *Ideen zur Philosophie der Geschichte der Menschheit* he outlined a comprehensive picture of history that was essentially determined by pantheism. The history of humankind where all peoples enjoy equal rights emanated from the history of the universe and nature. From prehistory and early history he followed the stages in the history of humankind via the former Orient and antiquity to the feudal Middle Ages until the end of the fourteenth century. There was no depreciative description of the Middle Ages, compared to that of the other representatives of Enlightenment. Rather, the idea was to portray the Middle Ages, as any other epoch, as a necessary stage of development in the history of humankind. According to his democratic understanding, his sympathy belonged to the popular masses of the oppressed peoples, especially the Slavs. He strongly condemned any colonial policy. His antifeudal position applied also to enlightened absolutism. He saw in revolutions an indispensable instrument for achieving progress. In an effort to honor the Great French Revolution, he began in 1791 with his work *Briefen zur Beförderung der Humanität*, which can be viewed as a continuation of his *Ideen*. Like most German intellectuals, he followed the development of the revolution with great sympathy until the execution of Louis XVI and the establishment of the Jacobin dictatorship. But he was an opponent of the wars of intervention, which he also expressed in his peace program. In 1799 he outlined a positive all-out assessment of the revolution and its worldwide effects on the historical process of the progress of humanity. Herder exerted a great effect on history, reaching into the present time.

Bibliography: Werner Berthold, ''Herder, Kant und die GroBe Französische Revolution—Versuch eines Vergleichs,'' *Wissenschaftliche Zeitschrift der Karl-Marx-Universität Leipzig,* Gesellschaftsund Sprachwissenschaftliche Reihe, no. 3, (1981): 287–288; Robert T. Clark, *Herder: His Life and Thought* (Berkeley, Calif., and Los Angeles, 1955); Wolfgang Förster, ''Geschichts philosophie und Humanitätsbegriff Herders,'' *Jahrbuch für Geschichte* 19 (1979): 7–59; A. S. Gulyga, *Johann Friedrich Herder. Eine Einführung in seine Philosophie* (Leipzig, 1978).

Werner Berthold

LAMPERT VON HERSFELD (Franconia, 1028–Hasungen, pre–1085), a monk and chronicler. Lampert Von Hersfeld received a good education, probably in Bamberg, and in 1058 he became a monk, entered the monastery Hersfeld, and was ordained. In Hersfeld he ran the monastery school. He died as the abbot of the monastery in Hasungen near Kassel, where before 1080 he had established the rules of the monastic reform of Hiersau. Around 1070 he began his activity as a historiographer with the *Vita Sancti Lulli* (The Life of Saint Lullus), the disciple of Boniface and founder of Hersfeld. A poem written around 1073 on the problems of his monastery against the background of the Hersfeld dispute on tithe was lost. Another work, *Libellus de institutione Herveldenses ecclesiae* (Hersfeld Monastic History), is preserved only in fragments. *The Annals,* written about 1078, are his most important and most comprehensive work. He began with the creation of the world; from 1040 the information is richer and continues to intensify after the onset of the conflict of Heinrich IV with the German princes or the pope. *The Annals* are written in a fascinating style, yet are strongly subjective in their judgment and deeply prejudiced in favor of the opponents to King Heinrich IV. As to the degree of truth of *The Annals*, there was a protracted controversy in German historiography in the second half of the nineteenth century; the reproach of deliberate falsification has to be rejected today. *The Annals* were printed first in Tübingen in 1525. In 1894 Otto Holder-Egger published a critical edition in the Monumenta Germaniae Historica.

Bibliography: Wolfgang Eggert, ''Lampertus scriptor callidissimus,'' *Jahrbuch für Geschichte des Feudalismus* 1 (1977): 89–120; Joself Semmler, ''Lampert von Hersfeld und Giselbert von Hasungen,'' *Studien und Mitteilungen zur Geschichte des Benediktinerordens und seiner Zweige* 67 (1956): 261–270; Tilman Struve, ''Lampert von Hersfeld. Persönlichkeit und Weltbild eines Geschichtsschreibers am Beginn des

Investiturstreits,'' *Hessisches Jahrbuch für Landesgeschichte* (1969): 1–123; 20 (1970): 23–143.

Siegfried Hoyer

MÖSER, Justus (Osnabrück, 1720–Osnabrück, 1794), German publicist and historian. The dominant political and cultural figure in the bishopric of Osnabrück through the late 1780s, Möser combined numerous administrative and legal responsibilities, especially after 1763, with a prolific career as a journalist of local affairs. These writings, collected during his lifetime in four volumes as the *Patriotische Phantasien* (1774, 1775, 1778, 1786), made him a central figure in the German Enlightenment and form one basis for later historiographers (E. Fueter, M. Ritter) judging him to be Germany's first ''social historian.'' These writings cannot be easily summarized or interpreted, since they considered so many specific issues and since Möser, like Kierkegaard, adopted numerous voices and often advanced mutually antagonistic perspectives. In orientation, Möser was a convinced perspectivist, arguing in an early essay (''Von dem moralischen Gesichtspunke'' [From the Moral Standpoint, 1767]), for instance, that ''jede Sache [hat] *ihren Gesichtspunkt,* worin sie *allein* schön ist'' (''everything has its own perspective within which alone it is beautiful).'' In some essays he considered the craft of historical writing, comparing it in one essay to the writing of epic; in others he pursued aesthetic issues, articulating in later life a doctrine of ''*Total-Eindrücke*'' that expressed an intuitionist view of history and recognized limits to human understanding before the complexity of experience. Such essays became linked by later readers to nineteenth-century doctrines of historical intuition and empathy. His views regarding historical method in the *Patriotische Phantasien,* however, are fragmentary; their real significance rests on their historically tempered analysis of the eighteenth-century world of the German estates. Drawing upon his substantial administrative expertise, Möser used them to explore the social and economic underpinnings of that world: for example, the relations between overpopulation and the political system, the development of the rural textile industry, the survival of the guilds, and the economic improvement of the peasantry. Möser's fame as a historian also rests on his multivolume *Osnabrückische Geschichte,* first published in a compressed form (1765) and then revised and expanded during his lifetime, but remaining unfinished at his death. In this work he adapted the older historiographical traditions of Reichspublizistik, Reichshistorie, and Latin civic humanism to the study of Osnabrück's social, economic, and political constitution. Unlike his essays in which he remained committed to perspectivism, here he explored the social and material continuities that had created the world of the estates in Osnabrück. He consciously sought to subordinate dynastic narrative to the history of ''Freiheit und Eigentum,'' by which he meant the cultural evolution of landholding and communal property rights. This led him to examine the climate, the crops, the settlement of the land, and their combined influence on the evolution of the political and military institutions that eventually became the foundation of his own pluralistic society. Although unfinished and uneven, this vision of a total history linked to the world of the estates and its social orders had significant influence on German letters, inspiring among others Johann Herder (q.v), Goethe, the Baron vom Stein, and Berthold Niebuhr.

Bibliography: Jonathan B. Knudsen, *Justus Möser and the German Enlightenment* (New York, 1986); Friedrich Meinecke, *Die Entstehung des Historismus,* 4th ed. (Munich, 1965); Peter Schmidt, *Justus Möser als Historiker* Göppingen, West Germany, 1975).

Jonathan B. Knudsen

OTTO VON FREISING (? c. 1114–Morimund, 1158). Von Freising was the grandson of Heinrich IV, and the Hohenstaufen king Konrad III was his half-brother from the first marriage of his mother, Agnes. Already as a child he became provost of the convent Klosterneuburg. He studied in Paris, where he was influenced by the Augustine Hugo von Saint Victor and, gripped by the ideals of the ascetic-monastic reformative movement, he entered the monastic Cistercian order in 1133. About 1137 he was abbot of the monastery Morimund and after that, bishop of Freising. He fought together with Konrad III against the Guelphs and in 1147 took part in the Second Crusade and celebrated Easter in 1148 in Jerusalem. Under the reign of Friedrich I (from 1152) he was also involved in the affairs of the Reich. On the way to the general chapter of his order he died in Morimund in 1158. In continuation of the idea of history by Saint Augustine (q.v.) and Paulus Orosius (q.v.), he set about writing, in 1143, his *Chronica sive Historia de duabus civitatibus* (Chronicle or the History of the Two States). Three years later (1146) he had almost concluded the work. On account of the great internal conflicts, he expected the arrival of the Antichrist as the first stage for the establishment of the kingdom of God on Earth. In 1157, at a time of peace, he handed the *Chronicle* over to Emperor Friedrich I and began to record the *Gesta Friderici* (The Deeds of Friedrich) on the basis of documents that were made accessible to him. It covered the years to 1156. In it the Hohenstaufens were entrusted with the task of halting the end of the world by the government of the Reich. The *Gesta* was continued to 1160 by the Freising canon and notary Os Rahewin. Both works are first-rate sources of the early period of Hohenstaufen, the *Chronicle* additionally being the most important document of historical thought in the High Middle Ages.

Bibliography: Hans Martin Klinkenberg, "Der Sinn der Chronik Ottos von Freising," *Aus Mittelalter und Neuzeit,* Festschrift für Gerhard Kallen (Bonn, 1957), pp. 67–76; Walter Lammers, *Weltgeschichte und Zeitgeschichte bei Otto von Freising* (Wiesbaden, 1977).

Siegfried Hoyer

PUFENDORF, Samuel (Dorfchemnitz, 1632–Berlin 1694), German natural rights philosopher and court historian. Pufendorf was tutor to the Swedish minister in Denmark (1658–1660), professor at the Universities of Heidelberg (1660–1668) and Lund, Sweden (1668–1676), secretary of state and historian to the

Swedish court (1677–1688), and, finally, historian to the Brandenburg-Prussian court (1688–1694). He was noted for the development of history in three areas: as a natural rights theorist examining the bases of law and human culture, as an analyst of the German political system, and as a practicing historian of Europe, Sweden, and Brandenburg–Prussia. He was deeply influenced by the writings of Descartes, Grotius, Hobbes, and Galileo, as they had been introduced to him by his Jena teacher, the Cartesian mathematician Erhard Weigel (*Arithemetische Beschreibung der Moralweisheit,* 1674). His values and problems were formed in the wake of the Thirty Years War, giving him a lasting commitment to discovering universal legal norms for controlling political behavior and for shaping the ethical development of the individual. The major works from his period as a natural rights philosopher were his *Elementa jurisprudentiae universalis* (Elements of Universal Jurisprudence, 1660); his monumental *De jure naturae et gentium* (On the Law of Nature and Nations, 1672); the abbreviated introduction to *De jure*, *De officio hominis et civis juxta legem naturalem* (On the Duty of Man and the Citizen According to Natural Law, 1673); and a collection of polemics against his critics, *Eris Scandica* (Scandinavian Polemics, 1686). In these works Pufendorf emancipated the study of law from Lutheran orthodoxy and late medieval scholasticism. He developed basic notions regarding the moral autonomy of the individual and of a society of rights based on contract, freedom, equality, and basic toleration. These works were fundamental to the intellectual formation of the European Enlightenment; they also proved important to the development of the speculative philosophy of history conceived as the history of civil society. Methodology was central to his work. He made basic distinctions between rational and experiential knowledge while also accepting the traditional Aristotelian view that the human world was subject to a different kind of certainty than the physical world. In his articulation of the notion of "moral individuals" (*entia moralia*), Pufendorf has been seen (Welzel 1958) as the first to focus on the uniqueness of the cultural world and its constructs. Indeed, he was perhaps the first to use the term *culture* in a modern sense. Although Pufendorf himself remained essentially a taxonomist, never examining legal reality but merely describing an analytical approach, his position led logically to the sociocultural study of law, and Montesquieu and Rousseau appear to have read him in this light. Pufendorf's famous study of the Holy Roman Empire, *De statu imperii Germanici* (On the Constitution of the German Empire, 1667), was also a powerful polemic within the literature of imperial legal reform (*Reichspublizistik*). Its contribution to the development of history rests in its subordination of legal and historical detail to an analytical argument based on Aristotelian political categories. Late in life, Pufendorf turned exclusively to writing history and produced four main works—*Einleitung zur Historie der Vornehmsten Reiche und Staaten so itziger Zeit in Europa sich befinden* (1685), *Commentariorum de rebus Suecicis libri XXVI ab expeditione Gustavi Adolphi Regis in Germaniam ad abdictionem usque Christinae* (Commentaries on Swedish Affairs in Twenty-six Books from the Expedition of King Gustavus Adolphus into Germany to the

Abdication of Queen Christina, 1686), *De rebus a Carolo Gustavo Sueciae Rege gestis commentariorum libri VII* (Commentaries on the History of King Charles Gustavus of Sweden in Seven Books, 1696), and *De rebus gestis Friderici Wilhelmi Magni Electoris Brandenburgici commentariorum libri XIX* (Commentaries on the History of Frederick William, Great Elector of Brandenburg in Nineteen Books, 1695). These works, written under the perspective of "reason of state," belong to traditions of political chronicle and were partisan accounts of the monarchies who employed him. In spite of their political bias, they remain noteworthy for their use of archival materials and for Pufendorf's willingness to render forthright judgments on the past failures of the actors in his account (Rödding 1912). Pufendorf's works were translated and printed in every major European language in the eighteenth and early nineteenth centuries, and they became part of the cultural inheritance of later generations.

Bibliography: Horst Denzer, *Moralphilosophie und Naturrecht bei Samuel Pufendorf (Munich, 1972); Leonard Krieger, The Politics of Discretion: Pufendorf and the Acceptance of Natural Law* (Chicago, 1965); Hans Medick, *Naturzustand und Naturgeschichte der bügerlichen Gesellschaft* (Göttingen, 1973); Hans Rödding, *Pufendorf als Historiker und Politiker in den "Commentarii de rebus gestis Frederici Tertii"* (Halle, 1912); Hans Welzel, *Die Naturrechtslehre Samuel Pufendorfs* (Berlin, 1958); Erik Wolf, "Samuel Pufendorf," in his *Grobe Rechtsdenker der deutschen Geistesgeschichte*, 4th ed. (Tübingen, 1963), pp. 311–70.

Jonathan B. Knudsen

RHENANUS, Beatus (Schlettstadt, 1485–Strasbourg, 1547), German humanist. Rhenanus descended from a prosperous family of craftsmen with the name "Bild." In 1503 he studied at the University in Paris and received editorial suggestions from Henricus Stephanus. In Basle from 1511 to 1526, he got acquainted with Erasmus von Rotterdam with whom he formed a close friendship lasting throughout his life. From 1526 he lived in Schlettstadt until his death, concerned with humanistic and historical studies. The result of his philological concerns, and of his contact through Erasmus with classical, humanistic, and patristic authors, was that many carefully made editions appeared, among them especially those of the ancient historians (Tacitus, [q.v.], Livius, Velleius Paterculus). These works are of interest even today and draw attention to his own historical work, *Rerum Germanicarum libri III* (German History in Three Books [Basle, 1531]). Starting with Tacitus' *Germania* (First Commentary, 1519), he adopted the plan devised by K. Celtis on a description of Germany from the view of cultural history (*Germania illustrata*) and gave an unparalleled portrayal of early German history. The point of departure was the description of Roman Germania with the versatile movements of Germanic tribes before and during the migration of peoples; this was followed by a history of the various tribes, notably the ascendency and decline of the Frankish Empire. In the preface Rhenanus outlined his view of history: history is conceived as development; ancient times and Middle Ages are to be separated; ancient Germany and contemporary Germany require a different approach; time of origin and historical preconditions of sources have to be taken into account; the "monastic tradition" of clerical historiography of the Middle Ages has to be critically considered and, if necessary, rejected. Rhenanus was a careful historian without any patriotically panegyrical exaggerations of the humanistic style.

Bibliography: Paul Adam, *Der Humanismus zu Schlettstadt,* Schlettstadt o. J. (c. 1978); Karl Hartfelder, "Rhenanus," *Allgemeine Deutsche Biographie* 28 (1889), with former literature; Paul Joachimsen, *Geschichtsauffassung und Geschichtsschreibung in Deutschland unter dem Einfluss des Humanismus* (Leipzig 1910); Richard Newald, "Beatus Rhenanus," *Neue Deutsche Biographie* 1 (1953).

Winfried Trillitzsch

SCHLÖZER, August Ludwig von (Jaggstadt, Würtemberg, 1733–Göttingen, 1809); German historian. A professor at the University of Göttingen from 1769 until his death, Schlözer more than any other German historian of the eighteenth or nineteenth century combined a rigorous commitment to critical method with a broad interest in political, social, and anthropological aspects of universal history. Born as the son and grandson of Protestant pastors, he studied theology in Wittenberg but then turned to philology, Orientalistics, and medicine at the new University of Göttingen. His stay as a tutor in Sweden resulted in a history of Phoenician trade. At the Academy of Sciences in St. Petersburg he turned to an edition of Nestor's (q.v.) *Russian Annals*, in which he applied strict methods of philological criticism to an Old Slavonic text and laid the basis for his *Nordic History,* published in 1771 as a continuation of the English *Universal History*. In this work he replaced chronological narrative with an ethnological and linguistic approach to the histories of the various peoples of Northern and Eastern Europe. Schlözer avoided the pitfalls of later German academic historians who concentrated narrowly on politics although he at all times was deeply interested in the study of politics and saw in it the thread that gave history its unity. In an essay, "Vorstellung seiner Universalhistorie" (1771), sharply attacked by Johann Herder (q.v.), he argued for a history that went beyond an "aggregate" of facts to a "systematic" view of human history. He was interested not only in the "chronological" course of events but also in a "synchronic and analytical" approach to history. He saw history as a sequence of "revolutions" among which he understood not only political upheavals but fundamental changes in the economy, technology, social relations, and manners.

In his *World History* of 1792 Schlözer stressed the importance of the "discovery of fire and glass, brandy and potatoes on our continent." "The history of tobacco," he wrote elsewhere, "is at least as interesting a subject as the history of the great Tamerlane . . . provided that these inventions are seen in their world-historical context." Schlözer was an admirer of enlightened absolutism—Czar Alexander ennobled him for his contributions to Russian history—and at the same time a staunch defender of intellectual freedom and due process of law. In 1776 he founded a political and historical journal, the *Briefwechsel,* that was succeeded in 1782 by the influential *Staatsanzeigen,* forbidden in 1794 because of its critical attitude. The *Staatsanzeigen* in 1791 had published the first full German translation of the French "Declaration of the Rights of Man and of the Citizen." The journal included an impressive amount of data on social conditions and articles on the "revolution of the diet in Europe" and drinking habits. Schlözer did not succeed, however, in writing a connected social history of the modern world. His *Staatsanzeigen* was more statistical in the sense of the Enlightenment than historical, and the historians of the nineteenth century questioned his sense of historical development although his history of the Germans in Transylvania (1795) possesses a superb sense of historical continuity and change.

Bibliography: U. A. J. Becher, *Politische Gesellschaft. Studien zur Genese bürgerlicher Öffentlichkeit in Deutschland* (Göttingen, 1978); Joan Theresa Karle, "August Ludwig von Schloezer: An Intellectual Biography"; B. Warlich, "A. L. von Schlözer, 1735–1809, zwischen Reform und Revolution" (Diss, Friedrich-Alexander- Universität, Erlangen, 1972).

Georg G. Iggers

SLEIDANUS [or Sleidan], Johannes (father's name, Philippi or Philippson) (Schleiden near Aachen, c. 1506–Strasbourg, 1556), German historian. Sleidan studied law in Paris and Orléans and received the licentiate's degree (1536). From 1537 he served under the French King Francis I as a diplomat, handling the relations between France and the Schmalkaldic League. In 1545 he became a diplomat, interpreter, and historian in service of the Schmalkaldic League. During the years 1551–1552 the municipal council of Strasbourg sent him to the Council of Trent. Sleidan began his historiographic activity by translating the chronicle of Jean Froissart (q.v.) (1537) and the memoirs of Commines (1545–1548). His chief work, however, was the history of 1517 to 1555, divided into twenty-five books and based on numerous original documents that he had collected over the years. Sleidan published this work in 1555 under the title *De statu religionis et reipublicae, Carolo Quinto, Caesare, Commentarii* (Commentaries on the Religious and Secular Events under Charles V, at Strasbourg: Wendelin Rihel). Soon translations into French (1557) and English (1560) appeared. Sleidan left the rhetoric of the humanists and intended to give an objective, well-documented description of political events that was not colored by polemics against Catholicism. Contemporary opinion was negative, but posterity appreciated the *Commentaries* as a most valuable treatise and source and considered Sleidan to be the greatest historian of the Reformation age. Finally, he composed a small compendium of world history entitled *De quattuor summis imperiis* (The Four World Monarchies, at Strasbourg: Wendelin Rihel, 1556, in three books). Later revised and augmented, it became one of the most effective historical works of German Protestantism (English translation in 1563). The remaining correspondence of Sleidan was edited by Hermann Baumgarten in 1881.

Bibliography: A. G. Dickens, "Johannes Sleidan and Reformation History," *Refor-*

mation, Conformity, and Dissent. Essays in Honor of Geoffrey Nuttall, ed. R. Buick Knox (London, 1977), pp. 17–43; Walter Friedensburg, *Johannes Sleidanus. Der Geschichtsschreiber und die Schicksalsmächte der Reformationszeit* (Leipzig 1935); Donald R. Kelley, "Johann Sleidan and the Origins of History as a Profession," *Journal of Modern History* 52 (1980): t573–598; Walter Siebel, "Johannes Sleidanus, der Geschichtsschreiber der Reformation," *Monatshefte für Evangelische Kirchengeschichte des Rheinlandes* 6 (1957): 1–21.

Walter Zöllner

THIETMAR VON MERSEBURG (Walbeck? 975–Merseburg, 1018), German historian. Thietmar came from the Saxon noble family of the counts of Walbeck. He was educated in the monastery of Quedlinburg and in the cloister of Berge near Magdeburg. In 990 he was accepted into the cathedral monastery of Magdeburg; after about 1000 he became a member of the cathedral chapter there. At the death in 997 of his mother who was descended from the noble Saxon family of the counts of Stade, he inherited considerable landed property including one-half of the family monastery of Walbeck of which he became provost. In 1009 he became bishop of Merseburg. Between 1012 and 1018 he wrote his chronicle (*Thietmari Merseburgensis episcopi chronicon*) in eight books. Originally, it was supposed to deal only with the history of the bishopric of Merseburg, which had been founded in 968 and between 981 and 1004 temporarily abolished. But because of the close relations to the Saxon Ottonian kings and to the empire it became a genuine imperial history. Books 1 to 4 deal with the time of Henry I (919–936), Otto I (936–973), Otto II (973–983), and Otto III (983–1002); Books 5 to 8, with the time of Henry II. Thietmar relied in part on records with which he was acquainted: the history of Saxony by Widukind of Corvey; the *Annales Quedlinburgenses*; documents from Magdeburg, Merseburg, and Walbeck; and other sources for the last decades of the tenth and eleventh centuries but, above all, on his own perceptions. As a member of the high Saxon nobility and as bishop of Merseburg, he had excellent insights into the conditions of his time, particularly among the Saxons, Bohemians, and Poles. In his chronicle he loosely linked all occurrences that he held noteworthy and expressed his judgments of them very frankly. For historical scholarship Thietmar's chronicle with its great abundance of facts is indispensable for the illumination of the history of the Saxon imperial period.

Bibliography: Albert Brackmann, "Widukinds von Korvei Sachsengeschichte und die Chronik des Thietmar von Merseburg in neuer Ausgabe und die letzten Forschungen über ihren Quellenwert," *Deutsches Archiv für Landes und Volksforschung* 5 (1941); *Die Chronik des Bischofs Thietmar von Merseburg und ihre Korveier überarbeitung*, Thietmari Merseburgensis episcopi chronicon, ed. Robert Holtzmann, Monumenta Germaniae Historica Scriptores rerum Germanicum n.s., 9 (?1935); Erich Donnert, "Die frühmittelalterlich-deutsche Slawenkunde und Thietmar von Merseburg," *Zeitschrift für Slawistik* 9 (1964); Robert Holtzmann, "Über die Chronik Thietmars von Merseburg," *Neues Archiv der Gesellschaft für ältere deutsche Geschichtskunde* 50 (1935); E. Kessel, "Thietmar und die Magdeburger Geschichtsschreibung," *Sachsen und Anhalt* 9 (1933); Friedrich

Kurze, "Bischof Thietmar von Merseburg und seine Chronik," *Neujahrsblätter. Historische Kommission für die Provinz Sachsen und das Herzogtum Anhalt* 14 (1890); H. Lippelt, "Thietmar von Merseburg, Reichsbischof und Chronist," *Mitteldeutsche Forschungen* 72 (1973); Annerose Schneider, "Thietmar von Merseburg über Kirchliche, politische und ständische Fragen seiner Zeit," *Archiv für Kulturgeschichte* 44 (1962).

Hans-Joachim Bartmuss

WIDUKIND VON KORVEY (Westphalia, c. A.D. 925–Korvey, post–A.D. 973). Widukind came from Saxon nobility, in A.D. 940 entered the monastery Korvey, and soon began his literary activities. The *Passion of the Virgin Thekla* and the *Vita of the Hermit Paulus of Thebes* were lost. His main work, *Rerum gestarum Saxonicarum libri tres* (The Three Books of Saxon History), written in a vivid style adopted from classical authors, begins with the tribal legend of the Saxons and the rule of Heinrich I. The second book deals with the first decade of Otto I (until (A.D. 946); the third, the period until A.D. 958. After realizing the interest of the imperial family in his work, he continued it to the death of Otto I (A.D. 973) and dedicated it to Mathilde, Otto I's daughter who in A.D. 966 had become abbess of Quedlinburg. Widukind drew upon written sources in writing the first part but also used legends and popular songs as well as oral traditions available in Korvey on the history of his time. His education, influenced by Roman authors, prompted him occasionally to transfer the classical pictures to the tenth century. He described the history of the Reich from the position of a Saxon nobleman, with enjoyment of fighting and heroic deeds, rather than from that of a monk. The last critical edition of the Saxon history was published by Paul Hirsch in 1935 for the *Monumenta Germaniae Historica in usum scholarum*.

Bibliography: Helmut Beumann, *Widukind von Korvey, Utersuchungen zur Geschichtsschreibung und zur Ideengeschichte des 10. Jh.* (Weimar, 1950); Paul Hirsch, "Einleitung zu Widukind von Korvey," in *Rerum Gestarum Saxonicarum Libri Tres* (1935); Marin Lintzel, "Die Entstehungszeit von Widukinds Sachsengeschicte," in *Ausgewählte Aufsätze*, vol. 2 (Berlin, 1961), pp. 302–311.

Siegfried Hoyer

WINCKELMANN, Johann Joachim (Stendal, 1717–Triest, 1768), German classical scholar; founder of classical archaeology and historiography of art. The son of an impoverished shoemaker, Winckelmann learned the classical languages, studied Protestant theology, worked as a private tutor and teacher, and from 1748 was the librarian of Graf Heinrich v. Bünau at Nöthnitz near Dresden. In 1755 he published, in Dresden, his programmatic work *Gedanken über die Nachahmung der griechischen Werke in der Malerei und Bildhauerkunst,* which he used, while rejecting the "modern style" of baroque and rococo, to substantiate the concept of art of the classical period. His (formal) change to Catholicism brought him in 1755 to Rome, where he worked his way up to the Prefetto delle Antichitá di Roma and Scrittore at the Vatican. His *Geschichte der Kunst des Altertums* (1764) replaced the former antiquarian collection of facts by an integrated description, well ordered according to historical principles in the spirit of Enlightenment and on the basis of comprehensive correlations providing a background for the theory of the beautiful developed by the author. The work was soon translated into French, Italian, and English. The other works of Winckelmann are *Sendschreiben über die herkulanischen Entdeckungen* (1762), which drew attention to the beginning exposure of settlements destroyed by the eruption of the volcano Vesuvius in A.D.79, and the incomplete work *Monumenti anti chi inediti* (1767), which tried to identify systematically the classical monuments. His four-volume corpus of letters (edited 1952–1967) is a unique contemporary document. His death at the hand of a murderer, the causes of which are still unknown today, provoked a great response throughout Europe. In 1805 Goethe published the collection of Winckelmann's letters and articles in *Winckelmann und sein Jahrhundert*. The international Winckelmann Society has been active in the German Democratic Republic; in 1955 a memorial museum was opened in Stendal.

Bibliography: Berthold Häsler, ed., *Beiträge zu einem neuen Winckelmannbild* (Berlin 1973); Carl Justi, *Winckelmann und seine Zeitgenossen,* 5th ed., 3 vols. (Cologne 1956); Max Kunze and Johannes Irmscher, *Johann Joachim Winckelmann. Leben und Wirkung* (Stendal 1974); Arthur Schulz, *Winckelmann und seine Welt* (Berlin 1962).

Johannes Irmscher

WOLF, Friedrich August (Hainrode bei Nordhausen, 1759–Marseilles, 1824), German archaeologist. Wolf, the son of a teacher, entered the university in Göttingen in 1776 as a student of philology to demonstrate the independence of his subject vis-à-vis theology, which he tried to put into practice as a teacher in Ilfeld and Osterode, as a professor in Halle (from 1783) and Berlin (from 1810), and as coworker of Wilhelm v. Humboldt. With his *Prolegomena ad Homerum* (1795) he posed the Homeric question that, proceeding from the view that at Homer's time presumably no script existed and from the contradictions in both works, denied the common authorship of Homer for the *Iliad* and the *Odyssey* and attributed their dramatic form to an unknown editor. Inspired by Goethe, Wolf in 1807 published his *Darstellung der Altertumswissenschaft nach Begriff, Umfang, Zweck und Wert* (newly edited by J. Irmscher [Berlin, 1985]), which provided the foundations for the image of antiquities of the German classical period. He cleared the way for the Greco-Roman studies on the basis of the unity and common features of the special disciplines of classical studies to be an integral part of a large discipline.

Bibliography: Johannes Irmscher, "Friedrich August Wolf als Vertreter aufklärerischen Geschichtsdenkens," *Jahrbuch für Geschichte,* vol. 25 (Berlin 1982), pp. 7–22; Otto Kern, *Die klassische Altertumswissenschaft in Halle seit Friedrich August Wolf* (Halle, 1928).

Johannes Irmscher

Great Historians: Greek

APPIAN(US) (Alexandria, c. A.D. 90–Rome, after A.D. 165), Greek historian. A rich provincial, Appian had several important functions in the administration of Alexandria. Transferring to Rome, he became *advocatus fisci* and *procurator Augusti*. In his old age he wrote the *History of Roman Conquests* in twenty-four books, of which Books 13–17 dealt with the civil wars, embracing the period from Aeneas to Appian's own time. His work followed an original criterion, namely, the ethnographical. A sober and loyal imperial official, Appian was, at the same time, in history, a disciple of Polybius (q.v.) inasmuch as he limited himself to facts, reduced the number of speeches, and gave up rhetorical and stylistic ornaments. His experience in the administrative system perhaps stirred his interest in the economy of the first centuries of the empire and made him see a parallel with the Republican period. He concluded that economic reasons determine political and historical events. This is the idea that made an original historian of him. Although he praised "the amazing deeds" that had created the Roman Empire, he did not cease to be critical. His history has an objective tone. The Roman world of his time, he wrote in his *History*, "spends for some of the subjects more than it receives"; the plebs' parasitism and the tendency to annihilate the differences of costume between various social classes were characteristic: "If you undress a Senator of his toga, the rest of the clothes are that of a servant." "The Romans who would suffer none to be called king now make gods of their emperors after death." Appian condemned—by Brutus's own mouth—the unjust Roman military colonies "on some other land and house" in the year 44 B.C. Because of his objectivity toward both winners and losers in the civil wars, readers can estimate with more impartiality characters such as Pompey, Brutus, or Marcus Antonius. The social contrasts and the features of the antegracchian slaveowning economy based on increasing numbers of captives were portrayed with acute understanding. The latifundia brought to the rich "a good income because of the great number of their slave children whose number increased, for they did not take part in military expeditions." As a direct result, "the powerful grew excessively rich, while the slave population increased throughout the country. The Italians decreased in number and the lack of men was felt ever more." Original as a historian, Appian was not an ordinary compiler. He chose his sources with care and applied to them his own method. For two remarkable events considered essential in Roman history—the dictatorship of Sulla and Octavian's victory at Actium followed by the annexation of Egypt—Appian's sober history remains the main source.

Bibliography: E. Gabba, *Appiano e la storia delle guerre civili* (Firenze, 1956).

Constant Georgescu

ARRIAN (Nicomedia, c. A.D. 95–Nicomedia, c. A.D. 175), Greek historian and philosopher. Like Appian (q.v.), a Romanized provincial, Arrian attended the courses of the Stoic Epictetus during Trajan's reign. He became, in his mature years, a senator under Hadrian and spent his last years in his native Bithynia, where he had been appointed a lifetime priest of Demeter and Cora, the goddesses of agriculture and fertility. He claimed Xenophon (q.v.) as his model and was called "the new Xenophon" by his successors. Arrian's literary products, rich and varied, included philosophy, history, geography, and military advice, and most of his work survives. Epictetus' influence pervaded his early books. His *Dissertations* (in eight books of which four are preserved) and *Handbook* are important, as they recreate in their orality the lectures of a philosopher. Other geographical and military treatises were written in spare time while he served as an official. The historical and biographical series began with the *Alexander Expedition* (*Anábasis Alexándrou*) in seven books, which was considered by his contemporaries and successors to be the best work written on the great Macedonian. Living five centuries after the events, Arrian united the whole corpus of previous historians of Alexander and created, for later historians, a new source as well as an ornament to accompany Xenophon's *Anabasis*. In contrast to that of Plutarch (q.v.), Arrian's military experience served him well when he wrote with competent precision about battles. He tried to be objective by citing the reproachable acts and admiring the great exploits. Alexander, he wrote, "always wanted more, something one never saw before" and was characterized by a "thirst for adventures and a pleasure in involving others in adventure" (Bk. 7, 1, 4–5). The minor histories on Timoleon of Corinth, Dion of Syracuse, as well as a life of "the brigand" Tilliborus, the latter probably on a social movement of his age, have all been lost except for fragments. Arrian completed his *Anabasis* with an informative work about the most fabulous conquest of the Macedonian king *Indiké*, in forty-three chapters, written in Ionic dialect, a successful pastiche much like that of the logographers and Herodotus (q.v.). Unfortunately, only fragments of his most important historical work, *History of Alexander Successors*, have survived. Arrian was not a mere compiler. He was original in his selection and critical appreciation of sources. He was an honest, creative imitator of Xenophon and was less successful than the latter in regard to language. His writing interested Cassius Dio (q.v.), who wrote a lost biography of Arrian, the philosopher.

Bibliography: A. B. Breebart, *Einige historiographische Aspekten von Arrians Anabasis Alexandri*, Leyden, 1960.

Constant Georgescu

BEROSUS (Babylon, c. 335 B.C.–? ?), Babylonian historian of Greek language. Berosus was a priest in the temple of the god Bel-Marduk in Babylon. As a Hellenized native and as part of the Seleucid policy, he wrote, about 280 B.C. in Greek a local chronicle entitled *Babylonian* or *Chaldean History* (*Babyloniaká* or *Chaldaiká*) in three books, dedicated to the Seleucid king Antiochus I Soter.

The first two books gave us a chronology of the Assyrian Empire, merely enumerating kings, their names, and their reigns. With the last book began a detailed historical story from Nabonassar to the death of Alexander, about 323 B.C. Berosus adopted the Babylonian system of chronology, calculating by solar years with the conversion into Greek years, taking as reference point "the era of Nabonassar" (747 B.C.). Scientific Assyriology thus begins with Berosus. He explained the concept of "conflagration" in the Greek philosophy (*ekpýrosis*) by astrology; on the other hand, he interpreted in a Greek manner the cosmogonic mythical version in the first book of Mesopotamian origin. His famous fragment 1 is simultaneously a cosmogony, a physiogony, and an anthropogony. From *water*, the primordial element, he asserted, were brought forth fabulous creatures: first, the mythical fishman Ocannes, a civilizing hero and initiator of men; then, primordial hermaphrodite monsters; finally, Tiamat, the goddess of primordial Chaos, who, being divided in two parts by the god Bel, conceived Heaven and Earth. Berosus's well-known version of the Great Deluge in the second book—the oldest we know—already included many elements later familiar in the Bible.

Bibliography: P. Schnabel, *Berossos und die babylonisch-hellenistische Literatur* (Leipzig, 1923).

Constant Georgescu

CASSIUS DIO. See Great Historians: Roman

DIODORUS SICULUS (Agyrium, c. 104? B.C.–? c. 20 B.C.), Greek historian from Sicily. Diodorus lived for a long period in Rome and traveled along Asia and Europe. Starting from the necessity of gathering his heterogeneous informative materials—obtained with difficulty—within one corpus, he wrote a massive universal and encyclopedic history entitled, in a moment of inspiration, *The Historical Library* (*Historiôn bibliothéke*) in forty books, of which more than a quarter have been preserved (books 1–5, 11–20, from mythical times to 302 B.C.). Although the hypercritical historiographers of the nineteenth century considered him a compiler void of originality, a mirror of his sources, his image today has been substantially modified. A serious compiler endowed with critical spirit, he knew how to select the most informative sources. His common method was to use, with precision, a main source within which he included excerpts from other sources that complemented each other and his own interpretations as well. A general introduction (Bk. 1, 1–15) sets forth a clear and unitary plan of the work. Deliberately rejecting the pre-Trojan chronology (Castor of Rhodes) as unscientific, Diodorus began his history proper with the seventh book and about the year 1184 B.C. He adopted a double reference system: the annalistic one corroborated with the synchronistic: consuls-archons with Olympiads. Diodorus justified writing a universal history in a pragmatic-utilitarian version with ethical implications. An implicit conception of history can be found in the same general introduction and in Book 32, 27, 3, as well. Through a heroic self-surpassing act (*hyperoché*) the individual, subject to physical extinction, Diodorus argued, aspires to eternity and can achieve immortality. Only heroes can perform acts of self-transcendence: Alexander the Great, Epaminodas, Caesar. The seventh and eighth chapters of the first book also include a cosmogony and a theory of the appearance of culture based on the ordinary ideas of his fellow intellectuals of the time. Although a compilation, *The Historical Library* is the greatest universal history handed down to us in Greek literature, and thus it is a main source for the history of Sicily and the Orient, for the fourth century B.C. and the beginnings of Rome, as well as for Greek mythology (Books 4, 6, 7).

Bibliography: M. Pavan, ''La teoresi storica di Diodoro Siculo,'' *Rendiconti dell'Accademia dei Lincei*, f.1–2, 16 (1961): 19–52; f. 3–4, 16 (1961): 117–151; W. Spoerri, *Späthellenistische Berichte über Welt, Kultur und Göter*, Untersuchungen zu Diodor von Sizilien (Schweitzer Beiträge, 29) (Basel, 1959).

Constant Georgescu

DIONYSIUS OF HALICARNASSUS (Halicarnassus, c. 75 B.C.–Rome? c. 7 B.C.), Greek historian and rhetorician. In 30 B.C. Dionysius went to Rome, where he taught rhetoric and prepared his great historiographical work. Of the twenty books of *Roman Antiquities* (*Rhomaike archaialogía*) relating events to the beginning of the Punic Wars (264 B.C.), only the first eleven books survived. Dionysius was convinced that he had priority in the oldest history of Rome. As seen by him, history was a form close to poetry; thus he added another name to the rhetorical historiography. His interest and originality lie in his attempt to justify, following Polybius (q.v.) and Cato (q.v.) especially, a common Greco-Latin universe, seeing in Rome's civilization, as did his contemporary Vergilius, a transformation worked by Greek emigrants. Thus he applied the investigative criteria of Greek science to the realities of Roman history. In Dionysius' conception, Rome was an *apoikia* (colony) of her *metrópolis* Alba, and her *oikistés* (founder) was Romulus (Bk.1, 9, 2). The great history of Italy appeared to him as a work of Greek *apoikiai*. The concept of *barbarization* was added to the concept of *apoikia*: Greeks, populating Italy, blended with the barbarian natives, Umbrians, and Tyrrhenians; the resulting Romans, due to their prodigious faculty of assimilation and helped by ''Providence'' (*prónoia*), even if they had a mixed language, preserved the traces of Greek origins (Bk.1, 89–90). This attractive idea, wrong from the historical point of view, usefully served Augustan political propaganda and endured for a long time. In his rhetorical work, which is rich, varied and valuable, only part of Dionysius' concerns as a historian reappear. He criticized Thucydides' (q.v.) forerunners, whose works were often characterized by a fabulous tone, irrational content (*anóeton*), and "adventures similar to those at the theatre" (*tragodeîn*). He also condemned all historians after Alexander the Great, those of the Hellenistic age, as bearers of Asiatic decline, competitors, and destroyers of the wise Attic rhetoric. But, said Dionysius in the preamble to his treatise, "On the old rhetoricians" (*Perí ton archáion rhetóron*, 1–3), "our time (the age of Augustus) gave back to the old and wise rhetoric the right honor." This literary fact he explained by a political fact: the universal empire of Rome, center of the world, had reestablished the Attic rhetoric. The text definitely recorded the victory of atticism over Asianism, an event implying consequences of maximum importance. It also marked the affirmation of classicism as an act of culture. Unfortunately, Dionysius substituted the great historiographical problems for the problems of formal imitation of some "classical" writer. Dionysius is a name in ancient rhetoric, criticism, and literary theory bringing, in each of these branches, some capital contributions.

Bibliography: S. F. Bonner, *The Literary Treatises of Dionysius of Halicarnassus: A Study of The Development of Critical Method* (Cambridge, Eng., 1939); E. Gabba, *Dionigi e la storia di Roma arcaica*, Actes IXe Congrès (Paris, 1974), pp. 218–229.

Constant Georgescu

EPHORUS (Cumae, c. 380 B.C.–? c. 317 B.C.), Greek historian. A disciple of Isocrates, Ephorus imposed himself as the most famous representative of rhetorical historiography in the fourth century B.C. with his historical writing *Historíai* (Histories), the twenty-nine books of which narrated events from the Heraclidae returning in Peloponnesus (*Herakleidôn káthodos*, 1069 B.C.: Dorian invasion) to the Sacred War (357–356 B.C.). Ephorus wrote a rhetorical history that was a universal history as well. He innovated in a revolutionary way, eliminating from his *Histories* the mythical period by opposing the present to the myth, and he preferred recent history to antique history, which meant a considerable critical progress. In chronology, he chose as a fixed reference point Alexander passing to Asia (*diábasis*, 335–334 B.C.), with the return of the Heraclidaes 735 years before (1069 B.C.) and the Trojan War 120 years before (1189 B.C.). For him, the ideal past society was Sparta under Lycurgus, a society governed by a perfect legislation similar to that of Crete and characterized by liberty (*eleuthería*), implying concord (*homónoia*), wisdom (*sophia*), frugality (*eutéleia*), and moderation (*enkráteia*) "between equals." The encomium of Sparta's original constitution (*politéia*) in the fourth book of the *Histories* tacitly includes the idea of Sparta's moral decay in his time. The deliberate heroism of Leonidas and his Spartans at Thermopylae pointed out a very important new concept, the "*proháiresis*" (aim intended; see Diod, Bk. 11, 11). Attributing the invention of the coin to the inhabitants of Aegina, Ephorus opened a new road for the study of economic and monetary history in archaic Greece. The crisis of historical ideas in the fourth century B.C., including Ephorus' dilemma, was solved by Ephorus himself in favor of history: genealogies were meant for the amateur of antiquities and the founding of cities; the story of historical gests (*práxeis*) was meant for the political person. Ideally, the historian would participate in the events of his history. In Ephorus' opinion, the best form of knowledge for the historian was the knowledge based on personal experience (*autopsĭa,* Plb. 12, 27, 7), which offered him an undisputable methodological principle.

Bibliography: G. L. Barber, *The Historian Ephorus* (Cambridge, Eng., 1935).

Constant Georgescu

HECATAEUS (Miletus, c. 550 B.C.–Miletus? c. 476 B.C.), Greek geographer, logographer, and genealogist. In his youth, Hecataeus traveled to Microasia, Western Europe, and Egypt. Afterwards, he played a prominent political role in his native town. His first important work, *Perihégesis*, or *Gês perĭhodos* (Earth Description), a literary echo of the great Greek colonization, was a systematic geoethnographical inquiry (*historíe*) in two books (1: Europe; 2: Asia), including a geographical map (*pínax*). At this inceptive stage of development, his writing did not distinguish between historiographic inquiry and geographical research. With his *Perihégesis*, Hecataeus rose above the common preoccupations of the logographers, poetical works and maps. He seems to be the first who transcended a limited national horizon, admitting the importance and value of other peoples' historical traditions. *Perihégesis* soon became a reference book all over Greece. Still more important, the other work, *Genealogies*, or *Histories*, has a predominantly historical character. As a historiographer setting his "seal" (*sphragís*, "So speaks Hecataeus the Milesian"), he offered a model for the future. The rationalist reform he introduced in history established the critical background of historiography. Both people and gods' deeds are judged by the criterion of verisimilitude (*to eikós*). Hecataeus tried to reduce the mythical traditions to rationalistic elements without destroying the myth itself (for example, Cerberus was a snake). Thus a new anthropological vision and universe was opposed to the old mythical vision and universe. Human inventive action was pointed out even in heroic times ("Danaos introduced the writing"). Some called him the first rationalist among the Greeks. In the evaluation of historical facts, the idea of justice (*dike*) was essential. With the theoretic approach in the *Genealogies*, the explanation of the past grew emancipated from the myth, taking a laic form and opening the way for historiography. A superior continuer of epic tradition, a *historikós* rather than a *logopoiós*, Hecataeus can be considered the great forerunner of Herodotus (q.v.).

Bibliography: G. Nenei, *Hecataei Milesii fragments* (Firenze, 1954); P. Tezzi, "Studi su Ecateo di Mileto," *Athenaeum* 44 (1966): 41–76.

Constant Georgescu

HERODIAN (Antiochia? c. A.D. 175–Rome? c. A.D. 250), Greek historian. A Romanized provincial of oriental origin, Herodian was an enfranchised slave or an imperial slave at Court, perhaps a *procurator*, living in Rome in the age of Commodus, of the Severes, and some time afterwards. Having the correct feeling of contemporary crisis and aiming at didactic-moral purposes in a fictionalized biography of the "paradoxical" emperor, he wrote the *History of the Empire after Marcus Aurelius* (*Tes metá Márkon basiléias historíai,* in eight books), including the turbulent period at the end of Marcus (A.D. 180) up to Gordian's third ascension (A.D. 238). The title itself and the motivation in the preface mark two epochs: a long one of relative stability and normality, from Augustus to the "good" and wise Marcus Aurelius, considered to be a crucial point, and another of chronic instability, sixty to seventy years of an unusual agglomeration of monstrous and ephemeral princes. Unlike Cassius Dio (q.v.), who wrote from a senatorial perspective, Herodian introduced a plebeian vision of events. He demonstrated a certain psychologizing tendency in investigating the motives for some political acts, which also separated him from Cassius Dio. However, modern critics have judged Herodian severely for his sacrifice of some important events (for example, Edict of Caracalla) in favor of sensational details. In a manner worthy of Thucydides (q.v.) and in a way that makes him as readable as Cassius Dio, Appian (q.v.), and Arrian (q.v.), Herodian tried to penetrate the psychology of the world masters. Thus he honorably concluded the list of remarkable Greek authors before the affirmation of the Christian and Byzantine historiography.

Bibliography: L. F. Piper, "Why Read Herodian?" *Classical Bulletin* 52 (1975): 24–28.

Constant Georgescu

HERODOTUS (Halicarnassus, c. 484 B.C.–Thurii, post–420 B.C.), Greek historian. Of distinguished origin, as a young man, Herodotus was expelled with his family to Samos. Between 455 and 447 B.C. he travelled farther away than all of his logographer predecessors and considerably enlarged the extent of the earth as known by Greeks. In 444/443, B.C. he took part in the founding of the Panhellenic colony at Thurii. From there he travelled to Magna Graecia and Sicily, returning to spend his last years at Thurii. His life's work, *Historíes apódeixis* (The Result of My Inquiry), published after 430 B.C., was written in three stages: in Samos, Athens, and Thurii. Originally a compilation of twenty-eight isolated *lógoi* (narratives), the work was later reorganized by Alexandrians in nine books under the title of *Moúsai* (Muses). On the whole, it was a general survey of "the great deeds worthy of esteem," a history dealing with both barbarians (non-Greeks) and Greeks during a two hundred-year period from King Gyges of Lydia to the conquest of Sestos by Athenians in 478 B.C. The information is vast and certifies to the abundance of Herodotus' sources. As he stated in Book 7, 152, "I am obliged to reproduce what oral tradition says, but I am not at all obliged to believe it as well." This was the spirit in which Herodotus approached his work, conceiving the investigative act (*historíe*) as a liberation from myth (*mýthos*) and tracing an essential distinction between a mythical time and a historical time. Thus he passed from the historical-poetical narrative to history proper. His aim was to confront the contrasts and reveal the transient character of human phenomena (Bk. I, 5). Under the influence of Presocratic ideas, Herodotus turned his attention to the investigation of causes in a way never known before him. Cause, meaning also culpability (*aitíe*), pretext (*próphasis*), and event (*arché*), provided the concepts that Thucydides (q.v.) systematically used. Herodotus thought of three main explanations for events: first, in this world everything happens according to a providential plan (*tou théiou he prónoia*) that is fulfilled in spite of impediments and whose hidden aims are lost to the mortals. Fate resides at the top of the hierarchy of power over gods and people. Second, any mean and reprimandable deed (*adíkon érgon*) springing from reckless arrogance (*hýbris*) on the part of persons or nations is judged by divinity according to a moral code. In fact, the unity of the *Histories* comes from the dialectic alternation between culpability (*aitíe*) and punishment (*tísis, áte*). Notions of *hýbris* and *Némesis* are the governing law (*despótes nómos*) of empires and people and give to his work a dramatic dimension. Third, history's vicissitudes are partially explained by the jealousy of gods (*tou théiou phtonerón*). Therefore, there is a theodicaea (*dĩke*, or justice) and an anthropodicaea (*dikaiosýne*, or equity). Thus divine revenge coexists with human revenge.

For Herodotus, the Persian colossus symbolized despotism fascinated by the dream of universal domination. The Athenian coalition symbolized citizen liberty and human equality. Despite previsions, disproportion, and logic itself, the colossus had been defeated and stopped from expanding. The Athenian triumph had confirmed the superiority of liberty (*eleuthería*) over slavery and that of moral force over rough force. Among individuals, the cases of the Lydian king Croesus and the Persian kings Cambyses and Xerxes offered characteristic instances for his anthropological dialectic, which considered self-confidence as a cause of misfortune. In fact, as Solon said, "nobody can consider himself happy before the end of life" (Bk.1, 37). Croesus performed for Herodotus a key function as source of the Persian-Greek conflict. Yet Herodotus argued most importantly that, after the end of the glorious struggles for liberty, Athens, rescuer of Greece, led by Pericles, made itself guilty (see Bk. 8, 3) of an imperialist policy not differing from that of the Persians. This permanent cycle—guilt, punishment, equilibrium restored—summarizes the whole philosophy of history in the work of Herodotus. He used only one sort of chronological measure, namely, the equation of three generations with one hundred years, but he did not always respect this standard. Cicero's title for Herodotus, "Father of History" (*De legibus*, Bk.1, 1) is fully justified. Herodotus gave the first known classification of political regimes by structure: democracy (*dêmos*), aristocracy (*oligarchíe*), and monarchy (*monarkhes*) (Bk. 3, 80–82). He was the first to describe oriental despotism, to mention or describe a great number of works of art. He innovated in the "history of culture," plainly asserting the "ego," his personal opinion (*gnóme*). He first introduced speeches in his work, using them not as simple ornaments but to explain events to readers (see esp. Bks. 7 and 9), and thus he prefigured Thucydides. The speeches set in contrast opposite theses and added to Herodotus' prose other remarkable examples. Herodotus detached himself from the logographers by surpassing "coherent style" (*léxis eireméne*) and systematically using the hypotaxis, but, above all, by his incomparable narrative talent. His work, placed between the Ionian narrative of the logographers and the masterpieces of Attic literature, has the same value for prose as the Homeric epos had for poetry.

Bibliography: J. A. Evans, *Herodotus* (Boston, 1982); J. Hart, *Herodotus and Greek History* (New York, 1982); H. G. Immerwahr, *Form and Thought in Herodotus* (Cleveland, 1966); J. Myres, *Herodotus, Father of History* (Oxford, 1953); M. Pohlenz, *Herodot, der erste Geschichtsschreiber des Abendlandes*, 2d ed. (Leipzig, 1937, 1961).

Constant Georgescu

PLUTARCH (Chaeronea, c. A.D. 46–Chaeronea, c. A.D. 127), Greek philosopher and historian. Plutarch united family life with public and literary activities. By his efforts, the dying Apollonic oracle temporarily revived. He was favored by the emperors Trajan and Hadrian, and he spent his last years in Chaeronea teaching and studying and being held in universal esteem. Most of his vast and multiform work has been preserved. Of these 132 works, a group of 82 are philosophical-moral works (some of them not authentic), which the monk Maximos Planudes, in an edition of 1296, entitled, not very exactly, *Ethiká* (Latin, *Moralia*), while others more suitably called them *syngrámmata miktá* (various writings). In these works, Plutarch appears as a representative of popular philosophy. According to form, the works belonging to this group can be divided into lectures, or diatribes (apologetical, doctrinal, polemical) and dialogues, which were inspired by Plato's dialogues without ever reaching his magnificence. As to content, they deal with various fields: (1) rhetorical and demonstrative works; (2) some important works of Platonic philosophy revealing the anti-Stoic and anti-Epicurean preoccupations of the New Academy. Plutarch dealt with ethics proper only in several treatises. Other pedagogical works reveal his vocation as an educator; (3) political treatises, the majority of which were written in the years of maturity; (4) theological writings called "Delphian" or "Pythian" dialogues; (5) scientific works; (6) many writings on literature and antiquities. Plutarch was not an original thinker. He elaborated the Platonic doctrine with large openings to oriental influences and the syncretism of his epoch. He tried to reconcile everything: the great unique god with popular divinities, Plato with Aristotle, Chrysippus with Pythagoras, the great philosophical doctrines with the cult of state. His Delphic concept admitted a transcendent god helpful to people. Between divinity and humans, he saw demons, intermediate creatures of mixed nature, which, by their divine nature, continually try to rise but are always threatened, by their human aspect, with the fall and the cycle of birth. Humans themselves, by their ambivalent nature, are similar to these demons.

Plutarch's religion was equidistant from atheism and superstition. In the very middle of his ethics and politics stood the notion of ''humanity'' or ''humanitarism'' (*philanthropía*).

The second great category of works includes the ''Parallel Biographies'' (or ''Lives''), in at least thirteen books out of which only fifty ''Lives'' survive, now grouped in twenty-three pairs (forty-six ''Lives''), the Greek and Roman in each pair usually forming a basis for comparison (*sýnkrisis*). The twenty-three parallel pairs covered the history of the Greeks and Romans from Theseus and Romulus to Dion and Brutus. An additional four isolated ''Lives'' make a total of fifty. Although biographies of politicians were not new, Plutarch had all of the qualities that made him the creator of biography as a literary genre. As he wrote in the preface to the ''Life of Alexander,'' ''Here we do not write history but we tell about the life of some people. The nature of a man is often revealed not by his greatest deeds but, many times, by one insignificant thing—a word, a certain joke.'' Plutarch brought out the striking features of his personages, and, in addition to his moralizing intention, the ''Lives'' of Greeks and Romans in parallel had the aim of bringing together the two cultures and thus preparing the future Greco-Latin synthesis. The political person described by Plutarch is alive and tragically full of contradictions, a mixture of good and evil, a pendant of demonology in Moralia. The reader is impressed not only by the vivid narrative but also by the author's humanism, an active attitude in front of evil that is described in its crudity and opposed to good examples. Main themes in the ''Lives'' are the importance of education and the problem of the good king (the problem of power). Not deification but virtue and justice bring glory to the sovereign. Read from generation to generation in the East, the West rediscovered Plutarch in 1559 through the masterly translation of J. Amyot, *Vie des hommes illustres*. Plutarch's formative role as a constructor of modern humanism is not yet ended.

Bibliography: C. J. Gianakaris, *Plutarch* (New York, 1970); C. Theander, ''Plutarch und die Geschichte,'' *Bulletin de la Société des Lettres de Lund* 1 (1950–1951): 1–86; Yv. Vernière, *Symboles et mythes dans la pensée de Plutarque* (Paris, 1977).

Constant Georgescu

POLYBIUS (Megalopolis, c. 201 B.C.–Megalopolis, c. 120 B.C.), Greek historian. Polybius was the son of Lycortas, a strategist of the Achaean League, by whose side he gained experience of political and military life. About 170 B.C., he was elected *hipparchos* of the league in a moment critical for Greece. After the victory of L. Aemilius Paullus at Pydna (June 6, 168 B.C.) over the Macedonians, Polybius was among one thousand Achaeans suspected of philo-Macedonism and transported to Italy as hostages. Charged with the education of the victor's sons, especially Publius (Cornelius Scipio Aemilianus), Polybius remained in Rome, became a member of the Scipion's society, became acquainted with the Roman aristocracy, and studied attentively, *de visu*, the orders of the State through documents from protagonists and the archives. Gradually, he became an enthusiastic admirer of Roman power. In 150 B.C., after seventeen years in exile, the living Achaeans (about three hundred, mostly elderly) returned to their country, among them Polybius, who was often afterwards called back to Rome as a military adviser. He often accompanied Scipio to the battlefield as an observer. He also undertook documentary and exploratory travels. His masterpiece, *Histories*, in forty books, of which Books 1–6 are extant and the rest in fragments, minutely described, as had Thucydides (q.v.), the epoch in which he lived, beginning with the accession of Philip V of Macedonia (221 B.C.) and ending in 144 B.C. His purpose, clearly stated in the preface, was to make his fellow citizens understand how, when, and why Rome had become master of the world. Polybius alternated the story of Rome's confrontation with Carthage, Macedonia, and Syria with general methodological digressions. He exhibited a profoundly original conception of history. In his view, once Rome had imposed its control between 220 and 168 B.C., events could not be treated separately any longer but had to be presented within a universal or ecumenical history. His treatise (*pragmatéia*) conceived of the world of events as a unitary whole (*somatoeidés*) whose center was Rome. He felt the historian should gather documentary evidence on the spot (*autopátheia*) with the experience of a political and military man (XII, 25, 28); thus, he could offer a pragmatic or factual history (*pragmatike historia*, IX, 2) whose morals were not harmful for the reader. He also wanted history to be didactic (or epidictical) as a means of correcting and instructing people (I, 1; III, 31). Revealing his ideas, Polybius polemicized with the historical school in the service of rhetorical education and the oratorial profession. His criticism was against peripatetic dramatizing (Phylarchus) and captivating historiography (Theopompus [q.v.]), as well as against "cabinet" discursive historiography (Timaeus [q.v.]), all of them falsifying the reality. On the contrary, a historian should be engaged in the steady search for the truth, impartiality, the immediate political experience, direct documentation, *de visu*, the practical knowledge of geography as an auxiliary science and the investigation of economic factors. In his concept of causality, the irrational (*to parálogon*) disappeared and supernatural intervention was not embraced. The most important cause of historical reality is the state organization, the political constitution (*politéias sýstasin*), and only in a secondary way the psychological factor and the role of individuals. There are six possible constitutional forms (*politéumata*): three of them are good and three corrupted. After a good form follows a corresponding corrupted form in a perpetual motion like the heavens. Each of the six constitutional forms has—in its turn—three moments: rising (*anábasis*, *áuxesis*), apogee (*akmé*), decline (*kátabasis*), as in a biological process. This kind of becoming, acting as a law, is known as "constitutional rotation" (*anakýklosis* V, 1, frg. II, 9). Schematically, the cycle of constitutions takes an ascending-descending road: primitive monarchy or royalty leads down to tyranny leads up to aristocracy leads down to oligarchy leads up to democracy leads down to ochlocracy, after which the cycle is repeated to infinity. History reveals laws, the practical consequence of which is the prognostication of the next phase once a certain phase has been located. This doctrine of the "anacyclosis" affirmed, however, the progress in a closed circle with the permanent danger of regression. The only remedy against regression was seen to be the linking of the three good constitutional forms within a so-called "mixed" constitution (VI, 11; 18) which is the best. This doctrine was of Peripatetic inspiration but Polybius was unique in applying it to a particular case. Rome had been successful because of the tripartite structure of its constitution (consuls = monarchy, senate = aristocracy, people = democracy). Rome of the Punic Wars, the Rome of Polybius, was passing through a period of maximum prosperity, after which, according to the objective laws, decline would follow. The confrontation between Rome and Carthage, between a "mixed" constitution and a democratic one, between Hannibal and Scipio, exemplified, to Polybius, the truth of his doctrine. Some have seen a contradiction between Polybius's cyclical thinking and his emphasis on mixed constitutions as a means to prevent regression. Yet they might be seen to complement each other. Polybius did see Roman imperialism and opportunism. He saw Rome through Greek eyes, as a derivative community, without cultural, religious or political originality. Thus he implicitly raised the prestige of Hellenic culture. We could state that he was the Greek who gave the Romans the idea of Rome. His most audacious innovation was to break with the tradition of fictitious speeches (Timaeus); he limited himself to an insignificant number of authentic speeches, such as the one of Agelaos (Bk. 5, 104) uttered before King Philip V at Naupactus, a speech that can be considered the oldest document attesting to a political opposition in Greece against the danger coming from the West. Polybius, participant and witness of Roman expansion, wrote from a Panhellenic point of view and not as an Athenian. He authored the conception of history as pragmatic science. Because of his objectivity, exactitude and lucidity, he is preferred by some to Thucydides.

Bibliography: K. V. Fritz, *The Theory of Mixed Constitutions: A Critical Analysis of Polybius' Political Ideas* (New York, 1954); E. Mioni, *Polibio. Problemi d'oggi* (Padova, 1949); "Polybe," Discussions prepared and presented by E. Gabba, Entretiens Hardt XX, V and oeuvres (Geneva, 1974); F. W. Walbank, *A Historical Commentary on Polybius* (1st ed., Oxford, 1957; 2d ed., 1967); idem, *Polybius* (Beverly Hills, Calif., and Los Angeles, 1972).

Constant Georgescu

STRABO (Amaseia, B.C. 64–Amaseia? c. A.D. 26), Greek geographer and historian. Strabo traveled throughout much of the Roman domains, from Armenia to Sardinia and from the Euxine Pontus to the Ethiopian frontiers. The result was a treatise of grandiose vision meant for study by statesmen. He carried on the histories of Polybius (q.v.) with forty-seven books, *Historical Commentaries (Historiká hypomnémata)*, almost completely lost, reaching the year 27 B.C. and using as a main source the *Histories* of Poseidonius (fifty-two books). Strabo's masterwork was the *Geography*, written in seventeen books, wholly preserved. In this work, a real *summa* of ancient ideas, the four branches of geography (mathematical, physical, descriptive, and politico-historical) merge successfully. A masterpiece of scientific maturity, his *Geography* revealed the universalistic influence of Polybius as well as the author's own historical vocation, which influenced the structure. Unlike the majority of his predecessors, Strabo paid much attention to history (in general), to the migration of peoples, and to ethnogenesis. Strabo had an evolutionary point of view. Space and time are in close interdependence, as they were in Hecataeus' (q.v.) work as well. Thus in writing of physical geography, Strabo deduced the existence of great earthly changes in the past before the insignificant changes that he could observe. He was the first to divide the evolution of life on the planet into eras, according to the rocks: azoic, proterozoic, palaeozoic, mezozoic, cainozoic. His descriptive and political geography made him "The Geographer" above all for his accuracy, scientific probity, and overwhelming impression of absolute authority and greatness. Strabo understood with acuity the principles of historical geography when he noticed, contrary to geographical determinism, that the influence of terrain and climate over a nation should not be explained as a direct effect of nature on humans but as an influence that varied with the levels of industrial and political techniques. Trained in the school of Polybius, he was the most critical among the scholars of his age. Writing on Amazons, he distinguished between the mythical and the historical: "All mythical and miraculous events in the past are called legends or myths, while history is looking for the truth" (Bk. 11, 5, 3/504). Considering geography to be the study of the whole populated world, including the political life and the practices of government, Strabo brought this science up to a higher level and proved to be the genuine successor to Polybius.

Bibliography: G. Aujac, *Strabon et la science de son temps* (Paris, 1966).

Constant Georgescu

THEOPOMPUS (Chios, c. 378/377 B.C.–? ?), Greek historian. A brilliant representative of rhetorical historiography in the fourth century B.C. and a disciple of Isocrates, Theopompus lived an itinerant life from one royal court to another. After preparing some rhetorical small treatises, he wrote a continuation of Thucydides' (q.v.) *Greek History* (*Helleniká*), in twelve books exposing events from 411 to 394 B.C. With *The History of Philip* (*Philippikái historíai*) a masterpiece, in fifty-eight books dealing with the years 360–337 B.C., for the first time a historian placed a character in the center of his history, demonstrating a remarkable understanding of the historical moment. The personality's ascension is closely connected to the fall of the old *polis*. Praise of Philip did not stop Theopompus from denouncing the vices of this prince in a lucid way; he, an aristocrat, noticed with disgust the presence of some humble people, even slaves, in the king's entourage, in fact a new bourgeoisie. His interest in social problems and especially the problem of slavery reflected the debates in his epoch as to the best forms of slavery (for example, Plato in his *Republic*). Theopompus was also the Greek who offered the first historical interpretation of slavery by distinguishing between the *old slavery*—slaves by conquest, in his opinion a reprovable system, and the *new slavery*—slaves bought for money, a type of slavery initiated by the inhabitants of Chios and accepted because it meant progress. Noticing the customs of peoples and individuals, he also initiated a moral approach to history and is considered the creator of psychological history and Tacitus' (q.v.) remote forerunner by scrutinizing the secret causes of statesmen's actions. A certain feeling of progress made him consider the new writers to be superior to the old ones. Looking for an explanation of the end of Greek liberty, Theopompus wrote a satirical work, *The Three-Headed Monster* (*Trikáranos*), which, following Isocrates' ideas, denounced the bankruptcy of the three hegemonic powers in Greece—Athens, Sparta, Thebes—implying the triumphant presence of Macedonia's hegemonic power. Criticized by Cornelius Nepos, he was praised by the subtle critic Dionysius and much used afterwards by Diodorus (q.v.), Plutarch (q.v.), Athenaeus (q.v.), and Pompeius Trogus (q.v.).

Bibliography: W. R. Conner, *Theopompus and Fifth-Century Athens* (Washington, D.C., 1968).

Constant Georgescu

THUCYDIDES (Athens, c. 460 B.C.–Athens, post–400 B.C.), Greek historian. Through his father, Thucydides was a descendant of the royal Thracian family. As commander of the Athenian fleet in Thasos, he failed to rescue the besieged Amphipolis, was exiled, and retired to his dominions in Skapte Hyle (Thrace). Recalled from exile in May 404 B.C., he was killed several years later, perhaps by a political enemy. His life's work, *Prose (Xyngraphé)*, or *Histories (Historíai)*, related contemporary events, twenty-one of the twenty-seven years of the Peloponnesian War to 411 B.C., ending because of the author's death. The plan of the eight books is simple: Books 1–4, the Ten Years' War (the Archidamic War, 431–421 B.C.); Book 5, 25–116, the years of false peace (Nicias' peace, 421–415 B.C.); Books 5–6, the war in Sicily (415–413 B.C.); Book 8, the beginning of the Decelean War (413–411 B.C.). As a rule, Thucydides never mentioned his sources. His main concern was to delimit himself from his predecessors (Homer, Herodotus [q.v.], the logographer Hellanicus), adopting a polemical attitude toward them. But he was strongly influenced by the Sophists, by Pericles' political ideas, and, certainly, by grave contemporary events. Unlike Herodotus, Thucydides used a unique chronological system to calculate years of war and summer and winter time for each year. Therefore, he produced an annalistic and seasonal history. His two prefaces (Bk.1, 1–2, 21–23; Book 5, 25–26) formulated, in a scientific way, his real program and historical method. In the historical happening (*auxethénai*, Book 1, 2, 6), where the miraculous is not to be found (*to me mythödes*), there is an eternal datum, human nature (*to anthrópinon*), the correct study of which confers utility (*ophélima*) on history as a "work of permanent value [*ktēma es aiéi*, Book 1 22, 4], a usufruct for posterity, not for a moment's hearing only." The Persian Wars, limited in time and space, were contrasted with the Peloponnesian War, a real world war, "the greatest and most important of all," which had overturned the political and moral equilibrium. Thucydides saw it as only one war, the peace of Nicias being only a "false peace," an *entr'acte* full of hostilities. The real cause of the broken agreements and the return to war was Athenian expansion and the disruption of the balance of forces. Thucydides presented the whole war, a narrative of facts (*érga*) in the spirit of exactitude and without partiality (*eunóias*), alternating the narrative with speeches (*lógoi*) of the characters in the drama, not rendered literally but created as closely as possible to their general meaning. By his deliberate impassivity, rising above the passions of both city and individuals, Thucydides offered, in most cases, a literary pendant to the calmness of Pericles and a model in historiography. In his writing, historical events evolve in three distinct moments: starting point (*arché*), explanation (*próphasis*), and the real cause, or the real motive (*áition, aitía*). Thucydides revealed all of the specific problems of the war: genocide, suppression of political enemies, executions, even cases of cannibalism. He also paid attention to economic factors (*ta chrémata*), including some data about social unrest. In a famous digression, the "archaiologia" (Bk.1, 1–21), Thucydides studied the law of historical continuity and explained the present through the past. In the "Pentekontaetia"(Bk.1, 89–117) he described the development of Athenian power in "the 50 years" from Xerxes' withdrawal (480 B.C.) to the beginning of the Peloponnesian War (430 B.C.). The descriptions are not simple ornaments: the well-known discussion of the plague in Athens (Bk. 2, 47–54) was perhaps a medical metaphor applied to an imperialistic state and also a pathetic symbol of the human condition. In a sober and clear style, he described the battles and also gave geographical information.

In the forty-four direct speeches, Thucydides revealed his political ideas. Meant as food for the thoughts of politicians and inserted at key moments in the narrative, the speeches commented on the problems of both individual and collective political action. Presenting the most probable substance (*élexan toiáde*), Thucydides made the speeches into authentic pieces by offering to the orators (for example, Pericles) ideas they already had in their minds. In the spirit and in the name of a purely Attic mental discipline marked by experience with the Sophists, Thucydides eliminated from his work religion (Herodotus), mythology, (logographers), and poetry (Homer, Mimnermus). He explained everything by humans themselves, their ideas and deeds. In the future, because human nature is the same, the same events will take place. Human nature *(he anthropéia physis, physis anthrópon)* was given the value of a law. It was simultaneously seen as destructive, put into action by three possible causes: thirst for prestige (*timé*), fear (*phóbos, déos*), and interest (*ophelía*). Thucydides' philosophy of power was asserted in Pericles' funeral speech in honor of those who died in the first year of war (known as "*epitáphios lógos*," Bk.2, 35–46) and in the Melians dialogue. Relations between states and individuals are based, Thucydides argued, on the iron law of power, a law as eternal as human nature. The power (*dýnamis*), indispensable for political actions, becomes corrupted during war, converting into force (*ischýs*) and violence (*bía*). The crisis of the city of Athens after Pericles' death had been caused by the decay of custom, by the corruption of democracy, by the discord among citizens, by the lack of a personality able to rule, and by the human losses resulting from war. To break the crisis, the solution was Athenian expansion westward, but this had been only an expedient. The "plague" in Athens (430–429 B.C.) and the expedition to Sicily are two general repetitions and at the same time two premonitions of the final disaster in 404 B.C. (*panolethría*). The quarries in Syracuse where Athenian prisoners were thrown (Bk.7, 87) appear to us as antiquity's extermination camp and the grave of Athenian democracy. All of these ideas were organized, as were the speeches, in antithetical pairs: word (*lógos*)–deed (*érgon*), rational prevision (*gnóme*)–hazard (*Týche*), convention (*nómos*)–nature (*phýsis*), force (*ischýn*)–law (*díkaion*), Ionians–Dorians—and expressed in percussive and profound sentences. In the beginning of his work, which has a tragic unity of tone, Thucydides, under the influence of Anaxagoras, associated the historical "becoming" with the qualitative oppositions between nations and cities facing one another. Later, under the influence of Democritus, he explained historical becoming by the quantitative differences of the material forces in combat. After Hecataeus and Herodotus imposed history as literary genre, Thucydides instituted history as science. He has had imitators but no equals.

Bibliography: F. E. Adcock, *Thucydides and His History* (Cambridge, Eng., 1963); G. B. Grundy, *Thucydides and the History of His Age*, 2d ed., 2 vols. (Oxford, 1948); J. de Romilly, *Histoire et raison chez Thucydide* (Paris, 1956); idem, *Thucydide et l'impérialisme athénien* (Paris, 1947); E. Schwartz, *Das Geschichtswerk des Thucydides*, 2d ed. (Bonn, 1929); H. D. Westlake, *Individuals in Thucydides* (Cambridge, Eng., 1968).

Constant Georgescu

TIMAEUS (Tauromenium, c. 357 B.C.–Tauromenium or Syracuse? c. 261 B.C.), Greek historian from Sicily. Timaeus spent fifty years as an exile in Athens. Then he returned to his country. His masterpiece is *The History of Sicily* (*Sikelikái historíai*) in at least thirty-eight books, beginning in ancient times and concluding at the outbreak of the Punic Wars (264 B.C.). A companion work, *The Winners at the Olympic Games* (*Olympioníkai*), presented his principles of chronology. Among other things, he brilliantly dealt with a new problem untouched in classical historiography: slavery. Timaeus outlined a history of slavery in Greece: "the Locrians and Phocaeans had no slaves (men or women) till recent times: the Phocaean Mnason purchased a thousand slaves and thus deprived of wages (*anankáian trophén*) the same number of free citizens." This idea of competition between free and unfree labor expresses with acuity the essence of free labor-servile labor dialectics. Timaeus was also the first to make use of mythology to suggest that Sicily and Italy were once Greek countries. Timaeus brought a special contribution in the field of chronology by establishing synchronisms between the kings and ephors in Sparta, the archons in Athens, the priestesses in Argos, and the Olympic winners, with the latter being taken for a normative chronological reference point; thus the beginning of the first olympiad was placed in 776 B.C. For the first time in Greek historiography, a unique chronological system was used, and it was adopted by all subsequent historians. By establishing a synchronism between Rome's foundation and that of Carthage, Timaeus was the first to anticipate Roman greatness. Polybius (q.v.), Diodorus (q.v.), Strabo (q.v.), and Plutarch (q.v.) drew inspiration from Timaeus. His solid erudition, his objectivity, his sharp critical spirit, and his common sense make of his work the main source for the ancient history of Sicily and recommend him as the most outstanding historian from the end of the fourth century B.C. to the time of Polybius.

Bibliography: T. S. Brown, *Timaeus of Tauromenium* (Berkeley, Calif., 1958); G. Mansuelli, *Lo storico Timeo di Tauromenio* (Bologna, 1958).

Constant Georgescu

XENOPHON (Athens, c. 430 B.C.–Corinth, c. 354 B.C.), Greek philosopher and historian. In 404 B.C. Xenophon became a disciple of Socrates. In 401 B.C. he joined Greek mercenaries in the famous Asian expedition known as the "Retreat of the Ten Thousand." Rewarded by Sparta for his services, he retired to Scillus near Olympia, where he lived for many years. Later, he was constrained to take refuge in Corinth. His nineteen works, wholly preserved, can be classified according to subject: Socratic, historical, or didactic. Of all of the Socratic Works, in which the figure of the beloved master appears, the most important is the so-called *Memorabilia* (Latin for *Apomnemonéumata Sokrátous*, Memoirs on Socrates) wherein Socrates talks to his young disciples on moral subjects using his well-known method. In his *Oeconomicus* (*Oikonomikós*), Xenophon had Socrates develop the main ideas of economy: market laws, the connection between certain economic phenomena and their social consequences, the importance of slaves in agriculture, and the place of woman. In the *Banquet* (*Sympósion*), Xenophon presented, through dialogue of Socrates, a discussion of the separation in Athens of wealth and power, the last being in the hands of the majority. The historical works include a work of military memoirs, the first of its kind in the world: *Cyrus' Expedition* (*Anábasis Kýrou*) also known under the name *Retreat of the Ten Thousand*, in seven books, describing the campaign of 401–399 B.C. This autobiographical work is generally held to be Xenophon's masterpiece because of its narrative clarity and drama, its perfection of form, and its fascinating quality of adventure. But the work suggests much more, for example, a turning away from the particularism of the polis to an almost Hellenistic cosmopolitanism. Xenophon tried to eliminate the barrier separating the Greeks from the Barbarians and the Spartans from the Athenians. He attempted to study social and military organization of the contacted peoples as well. This gives his work a remarkable documentary interest.

In the seven books of *Greek History* (*Helleniká*), Xenophon dealt with history proper. These books continued the narrative of Greek history from the point at which Thucydides had stopped, 411 B.C., to the Battle of Mantinea, 362 B.C.

Xenophon warned at the end of this history that, after Mantinea, "the disorder (*akrisía*) and trouble (*taraché*) in Greece were greater than before" (Bk.7, 5, 27). Choosing contemporary history, as Thucydides had, often striving for objectivity, Xenophon tempered his philo-Laconism by pointing out some things in the history of fourth-century Sparta unworthy of eulogies. Since Xenophon sometimes omitted important events and had no conception of historical development, he was still far from his model Thucydides (q.v.). However, his work is an important historical source. In the didactic work *Cyrus' Education* (*Kýrou Paidéia, Cyropaedia*), eight books with real historical background, Xenophon outlined the figure of an ideal monarch and military commander who was a representative product of a good education. This work is considered to be a predecessor to the Greek novel. Among the smaller treatises, *On Income* (*Póroi e perí prosódon*) certified the crisis of production at that time and suggested that the economy of the polis could be made healthy by the expansion of trade in conjunction with use of the silver mines in Laurium. *The Cavalry Commander* (*Hipparchikós*) was a handbook of advice to the superior officers of this body in Athens. Xenophon was the first writer on military matters to stress the value of cavalry. For the common cavalry man, he wrote *On Equitation* (*Perí hippikés*), the first book on riding horses. In the last in this series of small treatises, *On Hunting* (*Kynegetikós*), he discussed hunting with dogs and urged young men to leave the Sophists' empty talk for this sport. Strongly marked by Socratic learning and yet influenced by the Sophists he criticized, Xenophon was also a religious man who defended his faith with philosophical arguments. By vocation a moralist, he admired four virtues—temperance (*enkráteia*), courage (*andréia*), justice (*dikaiosýne*), and practical science (*sophrosýne*)—which made, he urged, the perfect man (*kalokagathós*). The remarkable quality of this military man, memoirist, philosopher, historian, and pedagogue remains his inborn humanism, which, together with his qualities of language and style, recommend him as a preeminently classical author.

Bibliography: J. K. Anderson, *Xenophon* (London, 1974); H. R. Breitenbach, "Historiographische Anschauungsformen Xenophons" (Diss., Basel, 1951); G. B. Nussbaum, *The Ten Thousand: A Study* (Leyden,1967).

Constant Georgescu

Great Historians: Hungarian

ANONYMUS (? Twelfth-thirteenth century?), medieval Magyar chronicler. The one who signed his work *P. dictus magister quondam Bele regis Hungarie notarius* was, in all probability, the secretary of King Bela III (1172–1196). Hence he lived in the second part of the twelfth century and the first decades of the thirteenth century. When he wrote, the former *notarius regalis* was a clergyman, probably a bishop called Petrus or Paulus. He gave few positive data in his chronicle. In his youth he had studied rhetoric, history, grammar, and calligraphy in Paris. He had been there when the epic poem and the chivalry romance were in fashion. He also admitted to some knowledge of Greek and even Turkish. His work *Gesta Hungarorum,* probably written between 1200 and 1220, contains fifty-seven chapters of various lengths. It reports the conquest of Pannonia by the Hungarian tribes headed by Arpad, the campaigns for plunder in the first half of the tenth century, and the events of Hungarian history until Duke Geza, father of Saint Stephen. The chronicle was not finished or perhaps the last part was lost. The major source of the anonymous secretary was *Gesta Ungarorum,* a chronicle written by another anonymous clergyman toward 1091–1092, lost today, which had drawn from Regino's chronicle and the Annales Altahenses. Other sources for Anonymus were Justinus and mostly the oral family traditions of Hungarian kings and nobles. The value of Anonymus's chronicle as a historic document is highly controversial. Some scholars see in it a most reliable source for the ninth and tenth centuries. Other scholars take it for a chivalry romance with no history value. It is obvious that Anonymus, just like many other medieval chroniclers, was a historian as much as he was a politician. Therefore, he viewed the history of the ninth and tenth centuries in the light of the interests of the Arpadian society of 1200. The political intention of the work shows clearly in the author's obvious anti-imperial attitude and mostly in the effort to legitimate the Hungarian tribes' rule in Pannonia on the basis of the "historic right" conferred by the myth of the Magyars' Hun origin and Arpad's descendance from Attila. Arpad's conquest of Pannonia, populated by "Slavs, Bulgarians, and Vlachs," was for Anonymus a "reaffirmation" of the legitimate heir's earlier rights, and Arpad's rule over territories that had not been part of the "Hun kingdom" was justified in terms of feudal law. In Transylvania, for instance, the "Romanians and the Slavs," inhabitants of the region, took an oath of allegiance to a chieftain of Arpad after the death of the Romanian duke Gelu. Considering the militant aspect of his work, the thesis of anachronism some modern historians uphold, accusing Anonymus of having mentioned populations that would not have lived in Pannonia, Slovakia, or Transylvania in the nineth and tenth centuries, is completely groundless. The historian expressed his conviction and that of the society he lived in that the Slovaks were Slovakia's first inhabitants, just as the Romanians, "shepherds and colonists of the Romans," had been living in Transylvania ever since the end of antiquity.

Bibliography: S. Brezeanu, "Romani" si "Blachi" la Anonymus. Isterie si ideologie politica," *Revista de istorie* 34, no. 7 (1981): 1313–1340; Gy. Gyórffi, "Abfassungszeit, Autorschab und Glaubwürdigkeit der Gesta Hungarorum des Anonymen Notars," *Acta Antiqua Academiae Scientiarium Hungaricae* 20 (1972): 209–229; B. Hóman, "La premiere période de l'historiographie hongroise," *Revue des études hongroises et finno-ougriennes* 3 (1925): 125–164.

Stelian Brezeanu

BÉL, Mátyás (Ocsova, 1684–Pozsony/Bratislava, 1749). Hungarian and Slovak scholar and historian. He studied at the Halle university between 1704 and 1707, where he was among the close friends of August Hermann Francke, the prominent representative of German pietism. Back home, Bél was rector of the high schools in Besztercebánya/Banská Bystrica and Pozsony/Bratislava, and from 1719 was vicar of Bratislava. Following in the German polyhistors' steps, Mátyás Bél worked out a vast program of economic, historical, geographic, ethnographic, political, linguistic, and medical description of Hungary's counties, published in Nürnberg in 1723 under the title, *Hungariae antiquae et novae prodromus*. The first five tomes covering ten counties were edited in Vienna between 1735 and 1742 under the title, *Notitia Hungariae novae historico-geographica*. The second part of the work remained in manuscript until recently. Conceived in the pietistic spirit by Staatskenntnis and achieved with wide collaboration, *Notitia* is an interdisciplinary work and a most valuable source, augmented by historical-geographic maps. Mátyás Bél also produced the first edition of Latin-Hungarian narrative sources that claimed to be scientific. In his publication of sources, *Adparatus ad historiam Hungariae* (1735–1746), he published the works of twelve Hungarian chroniclers of the fourteenth to sixteenth centuries. Mátyás Bél then joined his pupil, Austrian historian Johann Georg Schwandtner, in Vienna, and between 1746 and 1748 edited three volumes of the most important Hungarian chronicles written in Latin. In studies accompanying Schwandtner's series, *Scriptores Hungaricarum veteres et genuini*, Mátyás Bél analyzed and commented on some chronicles, including *Gesta Hungarorum* by Anonymus (q.v.), opening the two-and-a-half-century-long dispute about the author's identity. Besides school books, Mátyás Bél also wrote and published works on agriculture and peasantry, grammar, literary history, and religion. He also edited the weekly *Nova Posoniensia* between 1721 and 1722. Mátyás Bél enjoyed wide international recognition, was a founding member of the Austrian scientific society *Societas eruditorum incognitorum in terris Austriacis,* and was a member of other academies and scientific societies in various countries.

Bibliography: Haan Imre, *Bél Mátyás*, Budapest, 1879; Wellmann Imre, "Bél Mátyás és a magyar tudós társaság terve 1735-ben" (Mátyás Bél and the Plan of Founding the Hungarian Scientific Society of 1735), *Magyar Tudomány,* 1965, no. 11, pp. 738–741.

Lajos Demény

BETHLEN, Miklós (Bunea Mică, 1642–Vienna, 1716). Hungarian statesman and memorialist. Miklós Bethlen was the most outstanding representative of the pleiad of Hungarian chroniclers and historian memorialists of the seventeenth century and the beginning of the eighteenth century, a pleiad made up of János Kemény, János Szalárdy, Farkas and János Bethlen, Mihály Cserei, and István Wesselényi. A pupil of Transylvanian Cartesian János Apáczai Csere, Miklós Bethlen returned to Transylvania after studies at Heidelberg, Utrecht, and Leyden and after a trip to England, France, and Italy to perform various political functions, including the office of chancellor of the country. He wrote a number of proclamations denouncing the abuses committed by the rule established in Transylvania by the Hapsburgs, campaigning in the end for the restoration of Transylvanian autonomy under a German protestant prince. Put under arrest because of the last memoire, he was placed under the hand of the English and Dutch peace negotiators in Vienna. Miklós Bethlen wrote his chief oeuvre, *Önéletírás (Autobiography)*, between 1708 and 1710 while he was detained. In it he narrated extensively and with a rare literary talent the events and realities in Transylvania from 1650 to 1700. Thc work of a politician of vast European culture, Miklós Bethlen's autobiography, for all its subjective shades, is a very important source of the political restructuring of central and southeastern Europe during the decline of the Ottoman Empire and the growth and development of the Hapsburg Empire. Its author was a direct participant in the events narrated and therefore it has not only literary value but also historical informative importance, with respect both to local realities and to what the author saw during his trip to western European countries.

Bibliography: After two earlier editions, Miklós Bethlen's autobiography was published in a critical edition by Éva V. Windisch, *Bethlen Miklós Önéletirása*, 2 vols., Budapest, 1955, with an introductory study on the author's life and work by Gábor Tolnai.

Lajos Demény

BONFINI, Antonio (Ascoli, c. 1427–Buda, 1503). Italian humanist historian at the Hungarian royal court. After studies taken at the universities in Florence, Padua, and Ferrara, Bonfini was a teacher in Ascoli and Recanati. In 1486, at the invitation of Hungary's King Matthias Corvinus, he arrived at the royal court, bringing with him some of his lesser works: *De Corvinae domus origine* and *Historia Asculana* (both of them lost by now); *Synopsion de virginitate et pudicitia coniugali*; *Epigramma* (it too almost entirely lost); Latin translations from

Herodianus (*Historiarum libri VIII*) and Hermogenes (*De arte rethorica*). At the king's court he translated from Greek into Latin some of Philostratos's works (*Heroica et Icones et Vitae sophistarum*) and from Italian into Latin, Antonio Verulino's famous work of architecture (*Architectura*). Bonfini's chief work however remains *Rerum Hungaricarum Decades,* written on the king's request. It comprises the first humanist compilation of Hungarian history from its origins to 1496. Bonfini followed the method and editing technique of Flavio Biondo's (q.v.) work *Historiarum ab inclinatione Romanorum decades III*, printed in Venice in 1483. Of the fifth-three books that make up Bonfini's writing, twenty-seven deal with the period between 1458 and 1496. Whereas the first part of the work is a compilation of various authors (János Thúróczi (q.v.), István Hartvik, Rogerius, Paul the Deacon (q.v.), Aeneas Sylvius Piccolomini (q.v.), Callimachus Expericus, Andrea Navagero, and others), the events between 1458 and 1496 were reported relying on information checked or even lived by the author himself. In a wider context, Bonfini's writing contains lavish information on the history of the peoples in central and southeastern Europe, and that is why the chronicle was used as a source not only by the Hungarian chroniclers and historians that followed, but also by the German, Czech, Romanian, Russian, and Polish historians as early as the sixteenth century. *Rerum Hungaricarum Decades* has had several editions starting in 1543, including a German translation and a free Magyar rendition, with the 1568 Basel edition considered the most complete of all by the end of the eighteenth century. The critical edition of this work was made between 1936 and 1976 in four tomes, by József Fogel, Béla Iványi, László Juhász, and Margit and Péter Kulcsár in the series *Bibliotheca Scriptorum Medii Recentisque Aevorum*.

Bibliography: Giulio Amadio, *La vita e l'opera di Antonio Bonfini primo storico della nazione ungherese in generale e di Mattia Corvino in particolare,* Monalto Marche, 1930; Péter Kulcsár, *Bonfini Magyar Történetének forrásai és keletkezése* (The Sources and Genesis of Bonfini's Hungarian History), Budapest, 1973.

Lajos Demény

ISTVÁNFFY, Miklós (Kisasszonypa, 1538–Vinica, 1615), Hungarian historian. He was born into a landowning family in southern Hungary. His father had studied in Italy and was one of a number of humanist writers of no more than average ability. Miklós Istvánffy studied at the universities in Padua and Bologna under the patronage of the leading humanist politicians and scholars in Hungary. Later, he made his way to the chancellery of the royal court in Vienna. In 1578 he became a royal councilor and in 1581, a vice-palatine. He was a wholehearted supporter of the house of Hapsburg and a sworn enemy of the rapidly spreading Reformation in Hungary. He was a true Renaissance man: a diplomat who spoke several languages, a soldier renowned for his bravery, and a cunning politician who would not shrink from intrigue.

Having written several smaller dissertations on historical subjects, among them *De sigillis regis Hungariae,* in 1590 he started to write the history of Hungary after 1490, that is, a continuation of Antonio Bonfini's (q.v.) history. This became the monumental, 900 folio-page *Historiarum de rebus Ungaricis libri XXXIV,* which was published in Cologne in 1622. He spent many years collecting his material. For his history of 1490 to 1550, he referred to the popular and widely read books of the Hungarian humanist historians, comparing them not just to each other but also to a wide range of documents. For the second part of his history, 1550–1606, he relied instead on personal experiences and information. Istvánffy wanted his history to be an example to the politicians of his day by recalling the time when the divided Hungary was united under the strong, centralized monarchy of Matthias (1458–1490) and fulfilled its duty to the rest of Europe by protecting Christianity from the Turkish threat. According to Istvánffy, the decline in the fortunes of Hungary was directly related to a decline in religious morals: *disciplina et religio*. He wanted to mobilize the nation and chase the Turks out of Hungary once and for all. Istvánffy wrote according to the rhetorical principles laid down by historians in Padua: a narration along the lines of *Annales* is colored by vivid scenes and historical characters described in detail. These character sketches particularly show Istvánffy's outstanding writing ability. Although he does allude to Hungary's (Pannonia's) relationship with Rome and to Roman archeological monuments, he did not portray his heroes in the same way as did the Italian humanist historians of the previous century. His extremely lengthy work, was published by Péter Pázmány, the founder of Hungarian Catholic national culture, who was one of Istvánffy's supporters. The work ran into four editions in Western Europe and was the definitive source on sixteenth-century Hungarian history until the end of the eighteenth century.

Bibliography: Béla Vargyas, "The Development of Humanist Historiography (A humanista történetirás virágzása)," in *The History of Hungarian Literature* (*A magyar irodalom története*), ed. Tibor Klaniczay (Budapest, 1964), pp. 425–437.

Ferenc Glatz

OLAHUS, Nicolaus (Sibiu, 1493–Trnava, 1568), Transylvanian prelate, politician, and historian. Of Romanian origin, Olahus studied at the chapel school of Oradea, was a page at the royal court of Buda, and became a priest in 1518. He served the Hungarian king Louis II (1516–1526) as a secretary. After the king's defeat and death in battle against the Turks at Mohacz, Olahus accompanied the widowed queen Marie, a sister of Charles V, to Germany and the Netherlands. A friend of Erasmus, Olahus became bishop of Zagreb in 1543 and chancellor of Hungary under the Hapsburgs, archbishop of Esztergom and primate of Hungary in 1553, and regent of Hungary in 1562. In these offices, he proved an obstinate adversary of both the Turks and the Lutheran reformers. To nurture patriotism after the Hungarian defeat at Mohacz, he wrote a history of Attila (1536), whom he viewed as an ancestor of Hungarians. *Hungaria,* written in 1536 and edited in 1735 by Mátyás Bél (q.v.) in his *Adparatus ad historiam Hungariae*, was a historical, geographical, and ethnographic description of Hungary; *Chronicon* traced events in Hungary from 1464 to 1558.

Bibliography: Stefan Bezdechi, *Nicolae Olahus: Primul umanist de origine română* (Aninoasa-Gorj, 1939); I. S. Firu and Corneliu Albu, *Umanistul Nicolae Olahus* (București, 1968).

Lucian Boia

SIMON, Kézai (? thirteenth century), medieval Magyar chronicler. A priest holding the title of magister, probably in the chapter of the bishopric of Oradea, Simon lived in the second half of the thirteenth century. He traveled in Italy and France. His work *Gesta Hunnorum et Hungarorum* was written between 1282 and 1285 and was dedicated to King Laslo the Kuman (1272–1290). The book has two parts, the first describing the ''dismounting'' of the Huns in Pannonia and the last the ''dismounting'' of Arpad and of the Hungarian tribes as well as the events of Magyar history until the thirteenth century. The chronicle also contains an appendix with valuable social and demographic historical data in a survey of the populations in the Arpadian kingdom. The main sources of the chronicle are *Gesta Hungarorum,* the second archetype of the medieval Magyar historiography, written in the second half of the thirteenth century and lost today, Jordanes' *Getica,* the *Roman History* by Paulus, and the chronicle of Gotfried de Viterbo. Like Anonymus (q.v.), the other great name of the medieval Hungarian historiography, Simon wrote a militant work, supporting the interests of the Hungarian kings and mostly those of the Hungarian nobles. The myth of the identity of the Hungarians and the Huns and of Arpad's descendance from Attila in Simon's work had an obvious sociopolitical significance—to justify the Magyar domination in Pannonia. He clearly distinguished the ''pure Hunno-Hungarian nation'' *(natio pura Hungarica*), assimilated into the Magyar aristocracy, from the ''foreign nations'' (*advenae*) that had penetrated the kingdom and had put into jeopardy the class domination of the former. By the ''foreign nations'' he meant the recent ''foreigners''—Germans, Italians, Frenchmen, Spaniards, Greeks, Kumans, Czechs, Poles, and others—promoted to noble ranks and who threatened the ''purity'' of the Hunno-Hungarian nation, hence his open hostility toward them; he also meant the ''Slavs, Vlachs, Greeks, and Teutons'' who had been present in the Danube basin before Arpad's ''dismounting'' or even before the Hun ''dismounting,'' as was also the case of the Romanians. Toward the Romanians, ''ordinary subjects'' of the Arpadian crown, he displayed no xenophobic feelings. Subsequently, his chronicle served as a source for the entire medieval Hungarian historiography of the fourteenth and fifteenth centuries.

Bibliography: S. Brezeanu, '' 'Romani' si 'Blachi' la Anonymus. Istorie si ideologie politică,'' *Revista de istorie* 34, no. 7 (1981): 1313–1340; J. Szücs, ''Társadalomelmélet, politikai teória és történetszemlétet Kézai Simon Gesta Hungarorum,'' *Századok* 107, no. 3 (1973): 569–643; no. 4 (1973): 827–878.

Stelian Brezeanu

THURÓCZY, János (? c. 1430–? c. 1490), Hungarian historian. Born into the lower nobility, Thuróczy worked in the legal profession. At first living in the country as a procurator, by 1467 he could be found among the scribes and clerks of the chief justice of the royal high court. He continued his life as an "official" working as a notary clerk at the Ság monastery in Hont County, although by 1475 he again could be found in the royal high court. From 1486 to 1489 he was a prothonotary in the royal court and assistant chief justice. Thuróczy was the first Hungarian historian who was not a Church official. Rather, he was a member of the rising middle class of lower nobility and secular government officials that developed in the fifteenth century.

Thuróczy, a newcomer to the royal court, was given the job of writing down Hungarian history after 1382. Thuróczy handled the task like any other medieval historian. He reworked Lorenzo de Monacis' rhymed work on the years between 1382 and 1386, spicing it up a little with things he had heard in the royal court. Next, he wrote a Hungarian history from its beginnings until 1382. Here, too, he borrowed from the texts of those chronicles that were at his disposal. In this section he emphasized the oneness of the Hungarians and the Huns, drawing a parallel between the two great commanders, Attila the Hun and King Matthias of Hungary. The political strength of the Hungarian lower nobility was symbolized by the growth in the tradition of a connection between the Huns and the Hungarians: the military prowess of the Huns was the basic trait of Hungarian nobility, and the lower nobility's exceptional military abilities should therefore entitle them to be regarded as the equals of the barons, the aristocracy. After completing this section, Thuróczy wrote the history of the years 1387 to 1487. In this section he made use of documents from the royal chancellery and to such an extent that the forms and phraseology of the documents in places intrudes upon his own style. Naturally, he also built upon the accounts of those who had lived through the events he was writing about. Thuróczy's approach to historiography is a transition point between the writers of the medieval chronicles and the humanist approach. He made use of earlier texts by freely rewriting long passages from them into his own work like a chronical writer; even so, he dressed his heroes as Renaissance men. From the Attila he found in early Church chronicles, he created a fifth-century ruler whose characteristics and personality traits agree with those advocated by Italian Renaissance writers on political science: ambition, courage, and shrewdness to name a few. He broke away from the tendency of the chronicles to concentrate on the royal dynasties, although he praised the character of the Hunyadi family and of King Matthias in particular in a most uncritical fashion. By making use of his everyday experiences in the field of law, Thuróczy was able to expand the thematic range of his work beyond that of the chronicles and even beyond that of the contemporary humanist historians. He gave accounts of everyday society, of the ins and outs of political and legal life, of the relationship between the different social strata, and of clashes between different interest groups within the aristocracy.

Thuróczy's *Chronica Hungarorum* was published in 1488 in Brno in Bohemia, then under the rule of King Matthias, and later that same year in Augsburg. Because of its exceptionally readable style and use of dialogue, the work became immensely popular and widely read. For half a century, it was accepted in Central and Western Europe as the standard work on the history of Hungary. That would change later with the appearance of an out-and-out humanist work following the fashion of the age. That work was Antonio Bonfini's (q.v.) *Hungaricarum rerum decades*.

Bibliography: Elemér Mályusz, *The Thuróczy Chronicle and Its Sources* (A Thuróczy krónika és forrásai) (Budapest, 1967).

Ferenz Glatz

Great Historians: Icelandic

MAGNÚSSON, Árni (Kvennabrekka, Iceland, 1663–Copenhagen, 1730), Icelandic historian and collector; professor, University of Copenhagen, 1701, first of philosophy and Danish antiquities and later of history and geography. Magnússon started early collecting ancient books and Nordic manuscripts, especially Icelandic ones. He acquired medieval Icelandic parchment-books and on the whole everything he could find. From 1702 to 1712 he was a member of a government fact-finding commission in Iceland (then a part of the Danish Monarchy), and in his lifetime Iceland was practically cleared of its medieval literary relics. He carefully investigated the history of the collected material but published very little. His contribution to history consisted above all in saving for posterity a great many sources of the medieval history of Iceland. The collection was kept in Copenhagen, but a substantial part was given back to Iceland after 1965, following mutual agreement between the governments of Denmark and Iceland.

Bibliography: H. Bekker-Nielsen and O. Widding, *Arne Magnusson: The Manuscript Collector* (Odense, Denmark, 1972).

Jens Chr. Manniche

SNORRI STURLUSON (Hvamm at Breidefjord, 1178/1179–Reykjarholt, 1241), Icelandic historian. From a distinguished family, Snorri became one of the mightiest men in Iceland, elected "lawspeaker" (president of the Alting, the highest public office in the Free State), 1215–1218 and 1222–1231. His works include the *Prose Edda* (completed c. 1223), a handbook of Scaldic poetry, in which he illustrated his points with stories from Norse mythology. According to many scholars, around this time he also wrote *Egils Saga*, the life of Egil Skallagrimson, the greatest of the Scalds, one of the most stirring and adventurous of the sagas about Icelandic heroes. His fame as a historian, however, rests on two works on Norwegian history (he visited Norway 1218–20 and collected manuscript sources and oral traditions that he used in his works). *The Saga of St. Olaf of Norway* (d. 1137), completed in the 1220s, was based on earlier manuscripts, but in addition, he made systematic use of the Scaldic epics as sources. This was done with a critical sense and a rational attitude toward what were earlier seen as miracles. Instead of trying to write as a hagiographer or annalist, his intention was to describe the king's spiritual development from Viking to saint. The saga was incorporated in a revised and shortened form in Snorri's main work, later named after the first words, *Heimskringla* (The Orb of the World), completed in the beginning of the 1230s. It is a carefully composed history of the Norwegian kings from the earliest mythological origins to 1177. As in the *Saga of St. Olaf*, his sources were a rich variety of earlier works—Latin chronicles, collections of sagas, individual sagas, the records of others, Scaldic poems, and oral tradition. He sometimes copied his sources directly, but generally he treated them with an independent critical sense. The work is furthermore characterized by exact chronology, vigourous delineation of character, and firm coherence, bearing the stamp of the writer's personality. In the historiography in the vernacular of the Middle Ages, this is probably the masterpiece. He saw the relation between royal power and the magnates as the decisive element in the development of history and represented the many conflicts in his history as the outcome of a rich variety of differences of character. Snorri was killed in one of the many conflicts in Iceland at this time, in which the Norwegian king also interfered. *Heimskringla* became especially important in Norway where it later became perhaps the most important book for the self-consciousness of the Norwegian people, in particular in the nineteenth century. But in Iceland, too, it played an important role in the Icelandic struggle for independence.

Bibliography: A. Ya. Gurevich, "Saga and History: The 'Historical Conception' of Snorri Sturluson," *Medieval Scandinavia* 4 (1971): 42–53; *Heimskringla*, 4 vols., trans. W. Morris and E. Magnússon (1893–1905), including a life of Snorri; Halvdan Koht, "Snorre Sturlason," *Norsk biografisk Leksikon* (Norwegian Biographical Dictionary), vol. 14 (1962), pp. 107–120; Eirik Øverås, *Snorre Sturlason* (Oslo, 1941); Sigurdur Nordal; *Snorri Sturluson* (Reykjavik, 1920).

Jens Chr. Manniche

Great Historians: Islamic (Arab, Egyptian, Persian)

IBN ‘ABD AL-ḤAKAM, ‘Abd al-Raḥmān (Fusṭāṭ, Egypt, c. A.D. 803–Fusṭāṭ, A.D. 871), religious scholar and historian. Ibn ’Abd al-Ḥakam was the author of the oldest historical work on Egypt in the Arabic language. In the fifteenth century the pleiad of historians known as the Egyptian school still relied on it. Variously entitled *Futūḥ Miṣr wa’l-Maghrib* (The Conquest of Egypt and North Africa), *Futūḥ Miṣr wa Akhbāruhā* (The Conquest of Egypt and Its History), or *Futūḥ Miṣr wa Akhbāruhā min Qadim al-Zamān* (The Conquest of Egypt and Its History from Earlier Times), this text was significant in a number of respects. It inaugurated a new type of Islamic historiography whereby the history of the Muslim community as an entity was supplemented by works focusing on a single area or province. What Ibn ‘Abd al-Ḥakam did for Egypt and the Maghrib would later be followed by others for neighboring Islamic regions or countries. Local history lent itself particularly to a historiographic genre known as *khiṭaṭ* (districts). According to that approach, the history of a country was presented in the form of a topographical study of its major cities and towns, their noteworthy inhabitants, and their monuments. Ibn ‘Abd al-Ḥakam became the first to employ the *khiṭaṭ* method in a long line of historians, which included al-Kindī (q.v.), Ibn Zūlāq (919–997), al-Masbaḥī (977–1029), al-Qaḍā‘ī (d. 1063), Ibn ‘Abd al-Zāhir (1223–1292), Ibn Duqmāq (1349–1406), al-Awḥadī (1360–1408), al-Maqrīzī (q.v.) (1364–1441), al-Ṣadīqī (1596–1650), ‘Alī Mubārak, (1823–1893), and Kurd ‘Alī (1876–1953). Ibn ‘Abd al-Ḥakam’s book was also noteworthy as an early document demonstrating the emergence of historiography from the crucible of the religious disciplines. Being a *muḥaddith* (religious traditionist) and *faqīh* (religious jurist), the author applied to history the procedure of *isnād* to support information with the chain of transmitters on whose credentials rested the authenticity of a report. So extensive were the *isnād*—and sundry digressions—that at times they occupied inordinate space relative to the historical account proper. Where the author displayed critical faculties or exercised judgement, it was more often about the origins of a testimony than about its substance. *Isnād* was less necessary for periods closer to the author’s lifetime and especially for the *khiṭaṭ* sections. Ibn ‘Abd al-Ḥakam’s sources included selections from basic fields of early Islamic literature such as *sīra* (biographies), *riwāya* (stories), *maghāzī* (tales of battles), *ṭabaqāt* (biographies grouped by generation), and books on *ansāb* (genealogies). *Futūḥ* was divided into seven parts, of which the first five were arranged chronologically. It covered the ancient history of Egypt; the Muslim conquest; the *khiṭaṭ* of Fusṭāṭ and the taxation system; the Muslim administration of Egypt; the conquest of North Africa and Spain to A.D. 743; the judges of Egypt to A.D. 860; and the traditions surrounding fifty-two companions of the Prophet who entered Egypt. Each part comprised several sections. The unit of inquiry was delimited topically, not annalistically (as *al-Ṭabarī*) or in terms of the succession of reigns (as with *al-Ya'qūbī*). Ibn 'Abd al-Ḥakam deserved credit for his concern with the history of ancient and Coptic Egypt, although the dearth of material led him to give credence to fables and legends. On the other hand, his book remains an indispensable source on the Muslim organization of Egypt and its financial structure.

Bibliography: Muḥammad 'Abd Allah 'Inān, *Miṣr al-Islāmiyya wa Ta'rīkh al-Khiṭaṭ al-Miṣriyya* (Islamic Egypt and the History of the Egyptian Khiṭaṭ), Dār al-Kutub (Cairo, 1931), on the *khiṭaṭ* genre; Ibrahīm A. al-'Adawī, *Ibn 'Abd al-Ḥakam, Rā'id al-Mu'arrikhūn al-'Arab* (Ibn 'Abd al-Ḥakam, Pioneer among Arab Historians), (Cairo, 1963); R. Brunschvig, "Ibn Abdalhakam et la conquête de l'Afrique du Nord par les Arabes," *Annales de l'Institut des Etudes Orientales*, no. 6 (1942–1947): 108–155; *Dirāsāt 'an Ibn 'Abd al-Ḥakam* (Studies on Ibn 'Abd al-Ḥakam), al-Hay'a al Miṣriyya al-'Āma li'l-Kitāb (Cairo, 1975); Muḥammad Jabr Abū Sa'da, *Ibn 'Abd al-Ḥakam al-Mu'arrikh wa Kitābuh Futūḥ Miṣr wa Akhbāruhā* (Ibn 'Abd al-Ḥakam the Historian and His Book "The Conquest of Egypt and Its History") (Cairo, 1979).

Samir Saul

IBN AL-ATHĪR, 'Izz al-Dīn . . . (Jazīra, north of Mosul, Iraq, 1160–Mosul, 1232), Iraqi historian. Ibn al-Athīr was one of three brothers who devoted themselves to learned pursuits. Their father, the chief officer of the administrative council (*mutawallī diwan*) of Mosul, was a landowner who also engaged in the trade between Iraq and Syria. 'Izz al-Dīn traveled widely and frequented leading scholars in Mosul, Baghdad, Damascus, Aleppo, and Jerusalem. He developed a special interest in history and went on to become one of the most important medieval Muslim historians. His central contribution was the monumental *al-Kāmil fi'l-Ta'rīkh* (The Complete Book of History), a universal history starting with the creation and ending in 1230. The last eleven volumes of the twelve-volume compendium constituted a year-by-year relation of the development of the Islamic community from its birth to 628 H. (A.D. 1230). The first volume dealt with the creation, the Hebrews, Christianity, Persia, and the Arabs before the advent of Islam. The author acknowledge his debt to al-Ṭabarī (q.v.), whose work he often reproduced. He also relied on the writings of al-Bayḥaqī (q.v.), Ibn Kalbī, al-Balādhurī (q.v.), al-Mas'ūdī (q.v.), and others for material not supplied by al-Ṭabarī. Ibn al-Athīr provided original information mainly for matters he knew firsthand or was told about by eyewitnesses, and he is one of the best Arabic sources on the later Crusades. Having borrowed al-Ṭabarī's annalistic mode, he brought it to its acme. Nevertheless, although he excerpted passages from and imitated the method of his predecessor, Ibn al-Athīr proved to be more than a mere anthologist and mechanical chronicler. There lay the novelty of *al-Kāmil*. In fact, as the author stated in his preface, he was moved to compose it because he enjoyed reading about history and found that information was usually scattered in many works. They were either too elaborate or too condensed and ignored certain periods or regions. *Al-Kāmil* was the first book to include the history of the eastern and western Islamic countries. As he set about providing a comprehensive text, Ibn al-Athīr went further than al-Ṭabarī and strove to achieve a synthesis of material often culled from his predecessor.

Ibn al-Athīr could not be content with the reproduction of various accounts, each supported by a number of authorities. Rather, he was led to adopt a critical approach, read widely, weigh his sources, choose among them, compare, edit, and complete them, and, most notably, blend his information in a single narration. He thus succeeded in mitigating the disconnectedness inherent in the dominant historiographic approach based on the juxtaposition of different versions of facts or on the annalistic form. Not only was the *isnād* (chain of authorities) less prominent than in the past, but important events were rendered in an unbroken fashion, overcoming the discontinuity imposed by the annalistic construction. Less important events and obituaries of scholars and notables were dealt with year by year. The result was a balanced text, combining a great wealth of information with a broad vision on history. Judicious and lucid, inclined to take into account the overall context, the author perceived the mechanism of causation and sensed the phenomenon of change. An earlier and shorter work by Ibn al-Athīr, entitled *al-Ta'rīkh al-Bāhir fī 'Al-Dawla al-Atābakiyya* (The Splendid History of the Atābak Empire, 1211) did not demonstrate the same qualities of impartiality or depth. Relying on his memory and that of his father, but also on Ibn 'Asākir, Ibn al-'Adīm, and others, he recorded the history of the Zangid dynasty in Mosul from 1127 to 1212. Perhaps for reasons of local patriotism, he was strongly favorable to it and hostile to its adversary, Saladin. Moreover, in contrast with the clear, unadorned idiom of *al-Kāmil*, the style of *al-Bāhir* was weakened by rhetorical devices, the search for embellishments, and the frequent use of verse and rhymed prose (*saj'*). Ibn al-Athīr earned distinction in two classical genres of Muslim historiography. *Al-Lubāb fī Tahdhīb al-Ansāb* (The Essence of the Manner of Condensing Genealogies) was an abridged and corrected edition of Sam'ānī's genealogies. In *Usd al-Ghāba fī Ma'rafat al-Ṣaḥāba* (Lions of the Jungle concerning Acquaintance with the Companions of the Prophet), he wrote biographies of 7,554 companions of Muhammad and the traditions they transmitted. Both were substantial dictionaries, arranged alphabetically. In both cases, the author took pains to collate facts from many sources, compare them, and provide compact and coherent entries.

Bibliography: Sayyid al-Bāz al-'Arīnī, *Mu'arrikhū al-Ḥurūb al-Ṣalībiyya* (Historians of the Crusades), Dār al-Nahḍa al-'Arabiyya (Cairo, 1962), pp. 204–234, Salah al-Dīn al-Munajjid, *A'lām al-Ta'rīkh wa'l-Jughrāfiā 'ind al-'Arab* (Noted Arab Historians and Geographers), Dār al-Kitāb al-Jadīd, vol. 3 (1959, repr. Beirut, 1978) pp. 57–96; C.

Brockelmann, "Das Verhaltinis von Ibn el Atirs Kamil fit-Tarikh" (Doctoral diss., University of Strasbourg, 1890).

Samir Saul

AL-BALĀDHURĪ, Aḥmad Ibn Yaḥya Ibn Jābir (? ?–? A.D. 829), Arab historian, court official, and poet. Al-Balādhurī's work remains one of the most useful sources for the early period of the Arab expansion. Although he was a close friend of the 'Abbasid caliph al-Mutawakkil, he managed to approach the 'Umayyads with relative freedom from partisanship. In general, his writings have been considered accurate and reliable, if not profound. Early Arab historiography fell within three broad categories: descriptions of military campaigns (*maghāzī*), biography (*sīra*), and genealogy (*ansāb*). The lives of individuals were often combined into classes or generations (*ṭabaqāt*). Practical considerations were not foreign to the interest in lineages and the lives of important personalities, sincc kinship to the Prophet or his companions determined the distribution of land or state pensions. Al-Balādhurī's books could be classified under one of the basic genres, despite the fact that he did introduce some modifications. Two of his manuscripts are extant. He never finished the *Ansāb al-Ashrāf* (Genealogies of the Nobles), but what survived was considerable. Authors such as al-Madā'inī (d. A.D. 840?) and al-Wāqidī (d. A.D. 822) probably served as his models, and he referred to them as authorities. The book opened with the lives of Muḥammad and his companions, but the principle of selection thereafter was not that of religious status. *Ansāb al-Ashrāf* consisted of the biographies of Arabs who were of noble descent, so it represented in effect the family tree of the Arab aristocracy. Although the arrangement was genealogical, the author inserted information on various individuals and provided accounts of current events, traditions, and so on. Moreover, he altered the traditional system of *isnād* (chain of authorities) by combining and abridging the reports that he transmitted. Al-Balādhurī's other volume was a shortened version of a work that has not come down to us. Entitled *Futūḥ al-Buldān* (Conquests of Countries), it recounted the expansion of Islam from the first battles in Arabia to the entry into Syria, Mesopotamia, Armenia, Egypt, North Africa, Andalusia, Nubia, Iraq, and Persia. This was indeed *maghāzī* literature, but the author did not confine himself to military affairs. He tried, albeit unevenly, to give descriptions of the social organization, administration, and economic or fiscal (for example, the land tax) aspects of the various countries at the time of their conquest. Al-Balādhurī's writings were put to use by later Muslim historians, such as al-Mas'sūdī (q.v.) and Yāqūt (q.v.).

Bibliography: Ṣalāḥ al-Dīn al-Munajjid, *A'Alām al-Ta'rīkh wa'l-Jughrāfia 'ind al-'Arab* (Noted Arab Historians and Geographers), Dār al-Kitāb al-Jadīd, vol. 1 (1959; repr. Beirut, 1978), pp. 11–57; S. D. Goitein, "The Place of Baladhuri's Ansab al-Ashraf in Arabic Historiography" (*Nineteenth International Orientalists' Congress,* 1935), pp. 603–606; Muhammad Hamidullah, "Le Livre des généalogies d'al-Balādurīy," *Bulletin d'Etudes Orientales,* no. 14 (1952–1957): 197–211.

Samir Saul

AL-BAYHAQĪ, Abū'l-Faḍl Muḥammad Ibn al-Ḥusāyn (Hārith̲ābād, Bayhaq district, 995–Ṣafar, 1077), Persian historian. After undergoing a traditional religious and literary education in Nīs̲hāpūr, al-Bayhaqī entered the service of the G̲haznawid rulers of Persia. He was employed by the chancery (*Dīwān al-Ins̲hā'*, or Office of Correspondence) first as secretary and then as assistant to the director. His functions brought him in direct contact with official documents that he had to copy or even draft. He was, therefore, well acquainted with the intricacies of government and court life when he retired in 1056 to write the history of the G̲haznawid kings. The result was a massive work of thirty volumes of which only six, numbered from 5 to 10, have been recovered. Entitled *Tārīk̲h-i Bayhaqī* (Bayhaqī's History), the surviving portion covered the years 1030 to 1040. The author's focus of interest was the dynasty; his perspective appeared to be that of a close observer telling a story about the events he experienced and the personalities he encountered. Early in volume 5, al-Bayhaqī declared that he would not be content, like other historians, with stating the bare facts. Instead, he wanted to be exhaustive and leave nothing untold. He strove to attain that objective, often sacrificing relevance in the process. The voluminous text contains digressions and long stories, interspersed with poetry, as well as valuable information. Al-Bayhaqī resembled other medieval historians in that he was more reliable with regard to contemporary events or ones that he witnessed than with regard to those of the past. As befitted a state official, influenced by chancery tradition, he used an ornate and labored prose. Al-Bayhaqī wrote a manual of literary style in the genre of the *ādāb al-ins̲hā'* (epistolary art) and reminiscences related to him by the director of the G̲haznawid chancery.

Bibliography: Mujtaba Minovi, "The Persian Historian Bayhaqī," in B. Lewis and P. M. Holt, eds., *Historians of the Middle East* (London, 1962), pp. 138–140.

Samir Saul

AL-D̲HAHABĪ, Muḥammad Ibn Aḥmad . . . (Mayyāfāriqīn, or Damascus, 1274–Damascus 1348), Syrian Arab religious scholar and historian. Al-D̲hahabī's early education at Damascus was greatly developed by travels to various centers of learning in Syria, such as Ba'albakk, Ḥims, and Aleppo in Egypt, and in the Ḥijāz. His teachers were the leading authorities of their time and were believed to number no less than thirteen hundred. A special emphasis in al-D̲hahabī's studies was placed on *ḥadīth* (religious traditions), *fiqh* (religious jurisprudence), and history. When he later became a professor in Damascus, he taught *ḥadīth*. More than one hundred titles are attributed to him, most of them in the domain of tradition. Al-D̲hahabī produced many abridgements of the works of other authors. His chief historical work, completed in 1314 after about fourteen years of preparation, was entitled *Ta'rīk̲h al-Islām* (History of Islam). The subject, a universal history of Islam from its inception to 1300, was developed in annalistic form in twenty-one large volumes. However, following the biography of Muhammad, the years were grouped in decades, at the end of which appeared *ṭabaqāt* (generations or classes) of corresponding obituaries. Hence there were seventy *ṭabaqāts* for the seven hundred years the book covered. The author used older works thoroughly and relied on them. He contributed to editing them as well as supplementing elements they had not taken into account. *Ta'rīkh* was noteworthy for having paid attention to the history of the entire Muslim world, both East and West. But the most striking feature of the book remains the far greater weight al-Dhahabī accorded to the biographies as opposed to historical events. The outlook of the *muḥaddith* (traditionist) undoubtedly influenced the author, in contrast to that of the secular historians who tended to favor chronicles of events. Equally discernible were the views he expressed on people and events in accordance with his personal beliefs. Although al-Dhahabī belonged to the Shāfiʻī school of Islam, he had befriended the proponent of Ḥanbalī fundamentalism, Ibn Taymiyya, and leaned toward a literal interpretation of the Qur'ān. Other authors wrote continuations of the *Ta'rīkh,* bringing it to 1388.

Al-Dhahabī prepared several abstracts or abridgments of the Ta'rīkh, which, in fact, can more correctly be described as different but shorter versions for they omit some of the content of the *Ta'rīkh* and include new material. *Kitāb Duwal al-Islām* (The Dynasties of Islām), also known as the *Tarīkh al-Ṣaghīr* (The Concise History), as opposed to the *Ta'rīkh al-Kabīr* (The Great History), was based on the portions of the *Ta'rīkh* dealing with historical events. It covered Islamic history from its beginning to 1344 in an annalistic framework. *Al-'Ibar fī Khabar man Ghabar* (Examples in the Chronicles of the Departed), completed in 1315, contained the biographies arranged according to year of death from the Hijra to 1330. Ibn 'Imād in *Shadharāt al Dhahāb fī Akhbār man Dhahāb* (Particles of Gold in Chronicles on Those Who Passed Away) claimed that *al-'Ibar* was really an abridgment of another important biographical dictionary entitled *Siyar A'lām al-Nubalā'* (Biographies of Outstanding Men among the Highborn, 1339). Even if the author used the *Ta'rīkh* as a source, he did not extract the *Siyar* from it. Starting with that of the Prophet, al-Dhahabī proceeded to the biographies of the caliphs, the companions, and so on. The fourteen large volumes included outstanding individuals from all domains, and the material was organized in the form of forty *ṭabaqāt*. The extensive use of *isnād* (chain of authorities) was carried over from the methodology of *ḥadīth*. *Siyar* was one of the sources of *al-Wāfī bi' l-Wafayāt* (The Complete Book of Obituaries) prepared by al-Dhahabī's student, Ṣafadī. In *Tajrīd Asmā' al-Ṣaḥāba* (Bringing to Light the Names of the Companions of the Prophet), the author presented alphabetically the lives of about eight thousand of Muḥammad's companions until A.D. 632. It was mainly based on Ibn al-Athīr's (q.v.) *Usd al-Ghāba*. Other biographical or genealogical dictionaries included *Tadhkirat al-Ḥuffāẓ* (Memoir on the Qur'ān Experts), *Tadhhīb Tadhhīb al-Kamāl fī Asmā' al-Rijāl* (Setting Out to Achieve Perfection in the Biographies of Traditionists), *Mizān al-I'tidāl fī Naqd al-Rijāl* (Balance of Equilibrium in the Criticism of the Traditionists), and *al-Mushtabih fī Asmā' al-Rijāl* (The Skeptic in the Matter of Biographies of the Traditionists).

Bibliography: Ṣalāḥ al-Dīn al-Munajjid, *A'lām al-Ta'rīkh wa'l-Jughrāfia 'ind al-'Arab* (Noted Arab Historians and Geographers), Dār al-Kitāb al-Jadīd, Vol. 3 (1959; repr., Beirut, 1978), pp. 97–154; idem, "Taṣḥīḥ al-Juz' al-Awal min *Siyar al-Nubalā'*" (Editing the First Part of *Siyar al-Nubalā'*) *Majallat Ma'had al-Makhṭūṭāt al-'Arabiyya* (Journal of the Institute of Arabic Manuscripts) 3, pt. 1 (May 1957): 176–181; Joseph de Somogyi, "A Qaṣīda on the Destruction of Baghdād by the Mongols," *Bulletin of the School of Oriental Studies* 7 (1933): 41–48; idem, "Adh-Dhahabī's Record of the Destruction of Damascus by the Mongols in 699–700/1299–1301," in Samuel Lowinger and Joseph de Somogyi, eds., *Ignace Goldziher Memorial Volume* (Budapest, 1948), pt. 1, pp. 353–386; idem, "Ein Arabisches Kompendium Der Weltgeschichte: Das Kitāb Duwal al-Islām Des Ad-Dahabī," *Islamica* (Leipzig) 5 (1931–1932): 334–353; B.'A. Ma'rūf and S. al-Arna'ūṭ, Introductions to the latest edition of *Siyar A'lām al-Nubalā'* (Beirut, 1981), pp. 5–159.

Samir Saul

IBN ḤAJAR AL-'ASQALĀNĪ (Cairo, 1372–Cairo, 1449). Egyptian religious scholar, judge, and historian. Ibn Ḥajar al-'Asqalānī was one of the leading *'ulamā'* (men of learning) and the most famous scholar of *ḥadīth* (religious tradition) of his age. His interest in history stemmed from his background and training as a *muḥaddith*. He was very active as a teacher in several schools and earned the profound respect of his students. One of them, al-Sakhāwī (q.v.), wrote a lengthy and admiring, but generally accurate, biography of his master, *al-Jawāhir wa'l-Durar fī Tarjamat Shaykh al-Islām Ibn Ḥajar* (The Gems and the Pearls in the Biography of Shaykh al-Islām Ibn Ḥajar). Ibn Ḥajar also achieved notoriety in the discipline of *fiqh* (religious jurisprudence), became a judge, and was eventually appointed to the office of Shāfi'ī grand judge (*qāḍī*) of Egypt. In addition to following his career as a scholar and judge, he engaged in commerce, thus pursuing the profession of his forefathers. His frequent journeys in Egypt and abroad combined studies and trade. Born into a wealthy family, he was always part of the upper strata of Egyptian society. As a *'ālim* and merchant, he straddled the two social groups that ranked immediately behind the ruling Mamlūk military aristocracy. Like other learned men of his age, Ibn Ḥajar proved to be a prolific author–compiler in many disciplines. His four most important historical works are considered here. The connection between Muslim historiography and *ḥadīth* studies was nowhere closer than in the domain of biography, for the authenticity of a tradition rested on the reliability of those who transmitted it from the early years of Islam. It was the function of the biographer to judge the men and ascertain their value as transmitters. In *al-Iṣāba fī Tamyīz al-Ṣaḥāba* (The Aim of Distinguishing the Ṣaḥāba), Ibn Ḥajar wrote not only about the Prophet's companions (the *ṣaḥāba*) but about his contemporaries in general. Divided in four parts, the work was set in the form of a dictionary and arranged alphabetically. *Raf' al-Iṣr 'an Quḍāt Miṣr* (Removing the Burden about the Judges of Egypt) represented a biographical dictionary of judges in Egypt since the Muslim conquest. The author relied on the works of predecessors like al-Kindī (q.v.), Ibn Zulāq, and al-Maqrīzī (q.v.). At first organized by generations (*ṭabaqāt*) of judges, it was recast in alphabetical order by one of his students. Ibn Ḥajar inaugurated the type of biographical dictionary concerning a single century in *al-Durar al-Kāmina fī A'yān al-Mi'a al-Thāmina* (Hidden Pearls among Eminent Individuals of the Eighth-Century H.). He covered all countries of Islam, using as sources the collections of al-Ṣafadī, Abu Ḥiyān, al-Dhahabī, Ibn Rāfi‘, and al-Maqrīzī. He adopted an alphabetical order in that work also. Accompanying biography in medieval Muslim historiography was annalistic history. *Inbā' al-Ghumr bi-Anbā' al-'Umr* (Information of the Novice about Events of the Epoch) described the events of 1372 to 1447, year by year and month by month, with obituaries at the end of each year. Intended as a complement to Ibn Kāthīr's history, it was not limited to Egypt but dealt with all Islam. The writings of Ibn al-Furāt, Ibn Duqmāq, al-Maqrīzī, al-Fāsī, and others were used as sources for events the author had not witnessed. *Inbā'* contained valuable information on political, economic, social, and cultural matters, as well as biographies of noteworthy men from various walks of life. Ibn Ḥajar had been taught history by Ibn Khaldūn (q.v.), Ibn Duqmāq, al-Awḥadī, and al-Maqrīzī. Yet in *Raf' al-Iṣr* (pt. 2) he was the initiator of the critiques that his student al-Sakhāwī (q.v.) formulated against Ibn Khaldūn and al-Maqrīzī.

Bibliography: Muḥammad 'Abd al-Ghanī Ḥasan, "Tarājim al-Qarn al-Thāmin wa Ibn Ḥajar al-'Asqalānī" (Biographies of the Eighth Century and Ibn Ḥajar al-'Asqalānī), *al-Thathqāfa* (Culture) 14 (1952): 14–16; Shākir Maḥmūd 'Abd al-Mun'im, *Ibn Ḥajar al-'Asqalānī: wa Dirāsāt Muṣannafātih wa Manhajih wa Mawāridih fī Kitābih al-Iṣāba* (Ibn Ḥajar al-'Asqalānī: A Study of His Composition, Method and Sources for His Book *al-Isāba*), Dār al-Risāla li'l-Tibā'a (Bāghdād, 1978); Sayyid Abul Fazl, "Ibn Ḥajar: His Times and His Life," *Islamic Culture* 32, no. 1 (January 1958): 28–46; Sabri Khalid Kawash, "Ibn Ḥajar al-'Asqalānī (1372–1449 A.D.): A Study of the Background, Education and Career of a 'Alim in Egypt" (Doctoral diss., Princeton University, 1969); Maḥmūd Rizq Salīm, "Ibn Ḥajar al'Adīb" (Ibn Ḥajar, the Man of Letters), *āl-Risāla* (The Message) 16 (1948): 198–200.

Samir Saul

IBN ISFANDIYĀR, Bahā'al-Dīn Muḥammad Ibn Ḥasan (? early thirteenth century), Persian historian. What little is known about the author was provided by himself. Like al-Narshakhī (q.v.), he wrote a local history, namely, that of his native Ṭabaristān. Ibn Isfandiyār had the support of the rulers of that region. His book *Tārīkh-i Ṭabaristān* (History of Ṭabaristān) constituted an important compendium of the information available on the subject. For the early history, the author accepted some legendary accounts and related many anecdotes. He then presented biographical material that he arranged by professional categories before resuming his narration of events of the Islamic period. His interest was mainly in dynastic, political, and military history. Quotations of verse abound throughout.

Bibliography: Richard W. Bulliet, "City Histories in Medieval Iran," *Iranian Studies*, 1, no.3 (Summer 1968): 104–109.

Samir Saul

IBN IYĀS, Muḥammad Ibn Aḥmad (Cairo, 1448–Cairo, 1524), Egyptian chronicler-historian. Ibn Iyās studied under al-Suyūṭī (q.v.) and was the last of the historians who wrote in Egypt in the fifteenth century. He was also the last important one to emerge in that country until al-Jabartī at the end of the eighteenth century. Ibn Iyās belonged to the governing Mamlūk families. The fief he held in usufruct insured his livelihood and allowed him to devote his time to intellectual activity. Security of income seemed to reinforce his independence of mind, for his chronicles revealed the critical stance he took toward the ruling circles of *amīrs*. Five of the six titles he authored were of a historical character, and one concerned cosmography. *Nuzhat al-Umam fi'l-'Ajā'ib wa'l-Ḥikam* (The Excursion of Nations into Wonders and Wisdom) was a short universal history, and *Marj al-Zuhūr fī Waqā'i' al-Duhūr* (Meadow of Flowers about Happenings over the Ages) was a history of prophets. Ibn Iyās wrote a brief synopsis of the history of Egypt known as *'Uqūd al-Jumān fī Waqā'i' al-Azmān* (Necklaces of Pearls about Happenings of the Times). But he is remembered primarily for his major chronicle *Badā'i' al-Zuhūr fī Waqā'i al-Duhūr* (Wondrous Blossoms among Happenings over the Ages). Ibn Iyās started this history of Egypt from the earliest times, relying, as he stated, on about thirty-seven sources, among them al-Ṭabarī (q.v.), al-Mas'ūdī (q.v.), and al-Maqrīzī (q.v.). The book was original only for the period that the author witnessed. It remains one of the basic reference works on the final years of the Mamlūk era and, especially, on the Ottoman conquest of Egypt in 1516. After the general survey on the remote past, Ibn Iyās adopted the annalistic manner and arranged his material year by year and, near the end, month by month or day by day.

Finally, the dryness inherent in a chronicle was relieved somewhat by the author's frequent employment of the vernacular and even of colloquialisms. Such a predilection also signaled, from another standpoint, the incipient corruption of classical written Arabic. Terminating in A.D. 1522 (928 H.), the book was particularly valuable because the author's connections with the prominent clans gave him privileged access to information. Ibn Iyās drew a vivid picture of the internal situation of Egypt on the eve of the Ottoman conquest. His descriptions of the political system and accounts of the contention among Mamlūk factions were detailed. He paid attention not only to military and administrative affairs but also to economic (such as levels of prices and the Nile), social (such as popular feasts and epidemics), and cultural life. The text contained biographies or obituaries of many contemporaries. A product of careful observation, the chronicle was a painstaking effort to achieve accuracy, if not historical depth or penetration. The author strove to be equitable without forsaking criticism. He attributed defeat at the hands of the Ottomans to administrative corruption and the perpetual feuding among the Mamlūks. By no means a supporter of Ottoman rule, he showed his discontent at the destructions it wrought. That was perhaps the reason, suggested the historian Muḥammad Muṣṭafa Ziyāda (1954, p. 55), for his exclusion from subsequent biographical dictionaries.

Bibliography: Muḥammad 'Abd Allah 'Inān, *Mu'arrikhū Miṣr al-Islāmiyya wa Maṣādir al-Ta'rīkh al-Miṣrī* (Historians of Islamic Egypt and Sources of Egyptian History), Maṭba'at Lajnat al-Ta'līf wa'l-Tarjama wa'l-Nashr (Cairo, 1969), pp. 152–168; *Ibn Iyās (Dirāsāt wa Buḥūth)* (Ibn Iyās [Studies and Research]), al-Hay'a al-Miṣriyya al-'Āma li'l-Kitāb (Cairo, 1977); Symposium held on December 17–21, 1973, in Cairo and presided over by Aḥmad 'Izzat'Abd al-Karīm; Muḥammad Muṣṭafa Ziyāda, *Al-Mu 'arrikhūn fī Miṣr fi'l-Qarn al-Khāmis 'Ashr al-Milādī (al-Qarn al-Tāsī' al-Hijrī)* (Historians in Egypt in the Fifteenth Century A.D. [Ninth Century H.]), 2d ed., Maṭba'at Lajnat al-Ta'līf wa' l-Tarjama wa'l-Nashr (Cairo, 1954), pp. 46–55.

Samir Saul

JUVAYNĪ, 'Alā' al-Dīn 'Ata-Malik (Azadvar, Khurāsān, 1226–Arrān, 1283), Persian historian and governor of Baghdad. Juvaynī belonged to a leading family of Persia, several members of which held high government office. His grandfather filled the post of *Ṣāḥib Dīwān* (equivalent to minister of finance). Juvaynī lived during the era of the Mongol invasion, which devastated medieval Islam. In about three decades, Muslim Asia was overwhelmed, and the Caliphate of Baghdad was terminated in 1258. Juvaynī was the principal historian of the great cataclysm. He wrote from a unique vantage point, for, continuing the family tradition, he entered the service of the Mongol Il-Khāns of Persia. His father had become their *Ṣāḥib Dīwān*; his brother was later named by them to the same position and, for twenty-two years, to that of grand vizir of Persia. Juvaynī was secretary to the Mongol governor of Persia and Asia Minor for nearly fifteen years. He also accompanied Hülagü in 1256 on his campaign to overthrow the Ismā'īlīs (the "Assassins") of Alamūt (Northern Persia) and the Caliphate. In 1259, one year after the capture of Baghdad, he was appointed by the Mongol conquerors as governor of Baghdad, Lower Iraq, and Khūzistān. He enjoyed the confidence of the Mongol overlords and remained at his post for twenty-four years. Juvaynī began writing his *Tārīkh-i Jahānkushāy* (History of the World-Conqueror) in 1252 or 1253 and stopped in 1260. This work is particularly valuable as a basic source of information on the Mongols. The author traveled to Mongolia on his official duties and was able to learn much about the history and customs of the new masters of Asia. He was an eyewitness to or a participant in many of the events that he described. Divided in three parts, the work set forth the origins of the Mongols and the conquests of Chingiz-Khān, the history of the Khwarazm-Shāhs and the Mongols in Khurāsān, and the destruction of the Ismā'īlīs. Juvaynī carried his account to the year 1257 and, by all appearances, may have intended to continue it. Composed during the author's journeys, the manuscript was unrevised and contained some inaccuracies. Juvaynī treaded carefully between his sorrow over the calamities that befell Islam and the necessity of avoiding the displeasure of the Mongols for whom he was working. Recognizing the latter's military and social qualities, he did not shrink from expatiating upon the disastrous consequences of the invasion. His criticism was indirect, mainly in the form of quotations from the poets, the Qur'ān, and the *Shahnāma*, the great Persian epos. He went to great lengths to explain and justify the invasion as the punishment meted out by God on the Muslim community. As a representative of the traditional style of officialdom, Juvaynī produced a florid and complicated prose. Although one of his successors, Rashīd al-Dīn, expressed himself plainly, another, Vassaf, made excessive use of inflated rhetoric and recondite words.

Bibliography: J. A. Boyle, Introduction to his translation of *Tārīkh-i Jahānkushāy: The History of the World-Conqueror*, 2 vols. (Cambridge, Mass., 1958); idem, "Juvaynī and Rashīd al-Dīn as Sources on the History of the Mongols," in B. Lewis and P. M. Holt, eds., *Historians of the Middle East* (London, 1962), pp. 133–137; E. G. Browne, "Note on the Contents of the Tārīkh-i-Jahān-Gushā," *Journal of the Royal Asiatic Society of Great Britain and Ireland* (January 1904): 27–43; V. Minorsky, "Caucasia III: The Alān Capital *Magas and the Mongol Campaigns," *Bulletin of the School of Oriental and African Studies* 14, pt. 2 (1952): 221–238.

Samir Saul

IBN KHALDŪN, 'Abd al-Raḥmān (Tunis, 1332–Cairo, 1406), Arab historian, statesman, and judge. A uniquely profound and original figure, Ibn Khaldūn is generally considered to be the first historian anywhere to attempt to raise the discipline of history to the level of a science. The two sides of his personality, the man of action and the man of learning, appeared to correspond to different periods of his life but in fact intertwined and gave his works a remarkably novel stamp. Out of a tumultuous political career came the urge to seek explanations and understand the forces that operated within society. Ibn Khaldūn left a factual autobiography entitled *al-Ta'rīf bi-Ibn Khaldūn* (Knowing Ibn Khaldūn). He was educated in the classical Muslim tradition and trained in philosophy under al-Ābilī. In the throes of perpetual warfare between the Ḥafṣīds of Tunis, the Marīnids of Fās, and others, the Maghrib was entering a period of deep turmoil during which no claimant to any throne seemed capable of bringing about unification or even staying in power. In 1350 Ibn Khaldūn embarked upon a career of service to the contending chieftains, characterized by sudden changes of fortune, hurried departures, and ceaseless intrigue. Having learned and practiced the methods requisite for survival in court politics, he nevertheless suffered setbacks and disappointments. From 1375 to 1378 he withdrew to prepare the *Muqaddima* (Introduction) and settled permanently in Cairo in 1382. His fame had reached the East; he became a professor at al-Azhar and was appointed grand Mālikī judge. Ibn Khaldūn's principal historical work, *Kitāb al-'Ibar* . . . (Book of Instructive Example . . .), was a universal history, arranged according to dynasties. Although it was the equal of any other contemporary account, it has been considered less than a masterpiece in view of the intentions expressed in the *Muqaddima*. *'Ibar* was largely overshadowed by the *Muqaddima*, its celebrated introductory treatise exposing the foundations and methodology of the science of history. This essay has been justly hailed as a major landmark in the development of historical thought. For the first time, history was perceived as the analysis of all social phenomena, the investigation of their interrelations, the discovery of the complex web of cause and effect underlying them, and the formulation of the laws governing them. Going beyond history as it was understood by his contemporaries, the author was led to widen the focus of study to include the whole *'umrān* (civilization or social life) and to posit the necessity of a "new science," autonomous and endowed with its own concepts. All aspects of organized social life, material and spiritual, came within its purview. The object of history, as a new science, was to analyze society and to elucidate the factors operative in its evolution. It was oriented toward the notion that the root cause of events lay in the transformation of social structures. There emerged from the *Muqaddima* a decidedly original conception of the historical process and the way to approach its study, indeed of the epistemological substratum of thought in general. Not only had Ibn K̲h̲aldūn envisioned society as a structured totality, he had discerned the mechanisms of its inner conflicts. Society was not only an intelligible part of objective reality admitting of explanation, it was a natural entity in a constant state of motion and unavoidable change. Never before had such a rigorously scientific outlook on history been articulated, much less applied. Ibn K̲h̲aldūn himself clearly grasped its novel character.

In his interpretation of social life, the author concluded that a never-ceasing state of tension existed between the *'umrān badawī* (primitive civilization, pastoral or agricultural) and the *'umrān ḥaḍārī* (urban civilization). Only those tribes possessing *'aṣabiyya* (a central concept for Ibn K̲h̲aldūn, variously translated as group spirit, group solidarity, esprit de corps, collective conscience, and so on) could found a state. Upon achieving that, they would settle as townsmen, become decadent, lose their *'aṣabiyya*, and witness the disintegration of the state as a result of internal disorder and the blows of tribal attacks. Yet the consolidation of the state was inconceivable in the absence of an advanced level of civilization, which only cities could foster. Ibn K̲h̲aldūn arrived at a coherent interpretation of the birth, growth, and dissolution of collective life, one in which an inherent structural deficiency seemed to lie at the core of social development. The conditions obtaining at the time of the establishment of the state quickly came to naught but were not replaced by new ones required to maintain the state. Ibn K̲h̲aldūn's concept of history derived from an approach to knowledge profoundly at variance with the epistemology of his epoch. Contemporary historians described concrete phenomena but not in a comprehensive manner. Never did they consider them as an autonomous, all-encompassing totality to be explained as a single dynamic process obeying the rules of causality. Interpretation of the general scheme of life was the task of theologians or speculative philosophers who started either from revelation and dogma or from metaphysics, abstract reason, and deductive logic. A priori thinking, as opposed to actual observation that remained fragmentary, was the hallmark of prescientific rationalism. In contrast, Ibn K̲h̲aldūn, relying on an integral empiricism, studied social organization as a natural phenomenon. Unlike other historians, he searched for explanations; unlike theologians and philosophers, he intended to find them solely in real life. A leap so momentous in the history of epistemology, making Ibn K̲h̲aldūn the forerunner of the modern social sciences, inevitably raised the central issue of the genesis of such a revolution. "Modernist," and often anachronistic, interpretations disregarded historical conditions. Recently, the tendency has been to place the author in the context of his culture and his times, whether as a continuator of rationalism (Mahdi 1957) or in relation to his own historical production (Oumlil 1982) or that of his contemporaries (Shatzmiller 1982). An attempt has been made to show that the religiosity of the fourteenth-century Maghrib, in which Ibn Khaldūn partook, neutralized his training in speculative philosophy and opened the way to empiricism (Lacoste 1966). Explanations would stand on firmer ground if they were not confined to the domain of thought. Ibn Khaldūn was painfully aware of the Maghrib's engulfment in a deep crisis entailing decline and decomposition. The hopes he cherished in his political career of restoring the power of the state had been dashed, and he perceived the chasm between reality and the models of the ideal polity.

When Ibn Khaldūn retired in 1375, he attempted to comprehend the events he had lived by turning to history instead of philosophy. Thus on the basis of his political experience, he opted for empirical investigation. Moreover, he broached history from a peculiar angle not just to record facts like contemporary historians but to elucidate the problem uppermost in his mind, that of the rise and fall of the state. Both the preference he accorded history over philosophy and the thematic approach testify to a new outlook, born of the fusion in one individual of the man of action and the scholar at a specific historical juncture of great change. Confronted with the poverty of the historiography prevalent in the Maghrib—in the *Muqaddima* he castigated its uncritical spirit, superficiality, imitativeness, vapid rhetoric, and disregard of causal links—he was obliged to devise a "new science" to enable him to draw meaning from the welter of facts. Under the impetus of the *'ilm al-'umrān* the projected history of the Berbers grew into a universal history. But *Kitāb al-'Ibar* . . . fell short of the methodology set forth in the *Muqaddima*. The author lacked evidence to substantiate his insight, and the "new science" had to await advances in historiography in the nineteenth century to be supplied with material from the systematic criticism of sources. This could account for the fact that Ibn Khaldūn remained for so long without successors. He was historically circumscribed in other respects. His theory was suited to the Maghrib but not necessarily to other areas. Furthermore, from his standpoint, social change seemed repetitive and cyclical. Development was not cumulative and irreversible over an extended period. Motion did not imply forward movement toward a qualitatively new society but eventual relapse to original primitive forms. The author could only analyze the history of the Maghrib as it was until his time; he could not transcend his time. Although they made possible the fundamental questions Ibn Khaldūn posed, historical conditions then did not allow him to answer them.

Bibliography: Aziz al-'Azmeh, *Ibn Khaldūn: An Essay in Reinterpretation* (London, 1982); Fuad Baali and Ali Wardi, *Ibn Khaldun and Islamic Thought-Styles: A Social Perspective* (Boston, 1981); Walter J. Fischel, *Ibn Khaldun in Egypt: His Public Functions and His Historical Research, 1382–1406* (Berkeley, Calif., 1967); Yves Lacoste, *Ibn Khaldoun: Naissance de l'Histoire, Passé du tiers-monde* (1966; repr., Paris 1981); Muhsin Mahdi, *Ibn Khaldun's Philosophy of History: A Study in the Philosophic Foundation of the Science of Culture* (Chicago, 1957); 'Ali Oumlil, *L'histoire et son discours:*

Essai sur la méthodologie d'Ibn Khaldun, 2d. ed. (Rabat, 1982); Maya Shatzmiller, *L'historiographie mérinide: Ibn Khaldun et ses contemporains* (Leiden, 1982).

Samir Saul

IBN KHALLIKĀN, Muḥammad Ibn Ibrāhīm... (Irbil, Syria, 1211–Damascus, 1282), Syrian biographer–historian, judge, and teacher. Ibn Khallikān studied *ḥadīth* (religious traditions) and *fiqh* (religious jurisprudence) in Aleppo under Ibn Shaddād from 1229 to 1234, *tafsīr* (exegesis) under Ibn Salāḥ in Damascus, history under Ibn al-Athīr (q.v.) in Mosul, and grammar and literature under Ibn al-Ṣāyigh. In Egypt, where he had resided since 1239, he was appointed judge in 1249 but was then promoted to the position of chief judge of Syria in 1261. Following his removal ten years later, he became a teacher in Cairo. Called back to his former post in Damascus in 1278, he was dismissed and reappointed several times by the sultan until 1281. While discharging his official functions, Ibn Khallikān proved to be an accomplished scholar, greatly drawn to poetry, even if his own verse was more pedestrian than profound. In 1257 he conceived of the project for which he achieved fame. An admirer of Ibn al-Athīr, he considered the latter's historical work difficult to improve upon. Instead he set himself the task of preparing a great biographical dictionary concerning the lives of eminent personalities. Only individuals whose year of death he could determine—hence have some evidence of their renown—were included. In view of their easy availability, biographies of Muḥammad's companions (the *ṣaḥāba*), his followers of the next generation (the *tābi'ūn*), and the caliphs were left out. Ibn Khallikān read widely and made use of material from his teachers as well as his own experience to produce *Wafayāt al-A'yān wa-Anbā' Abnā' al-Zamān* (Obituaries of Illustrious Men and Information on Contemporaries). Completed in 1274, it was continuously revised by the author. The acclaim it earned caused it to be supplemented later by Ibn Shākir al-Kutubī's *Fawāt al-Wafayāt* (Omissions from the Obituaries), al-Ṣuqā'ī's *Tālī Kitāb Wafayāt al-A''yān* (Continuation of the Obituaries of Illustrious Men), al-Ṣafadī's *al-Wāfī bi'l-Wafayāt* (The Complete Book of Obituaries), Ibn Taġhrī Birdī's (q.v.), *al-Manhal al-Ṣāfī* (The Clear Spring), and others. What set Ibn Khallikān's dictionary apart from previous biographical works was its ecumenical character. It was not confined to persons belonging to a single city or profession but was aimed at universality. Moreover, although the accuracy of the author has been generally recognized, his approach in the 855 notices further enhanced the value of his dictionary. Conscious that other works already contained biographical information, Ibn Khallikān strove to depict each subject by quick strokes, anecdotes, and piquant details. In addition to being agreeable to read, *Wafayāt* thus furnished valuable insights on contemporary mores.

Bibliography: Salāḥ al-Dīn al-Munajjid, *A'lām al-Ta'rīkh wa'l-Jughrāfia 'ind al-'Arab* (Noted Arab Historians and Geographers), Dār al-Kitāb al-Jadīd, vol. 1 (1959; repr., Beirut, 1978), pp. 115–156; 'Alī Jawād al-Ṭāhir, *Mulāḥazāt 'ala Wafayāt al-A'yān* (Commentaries on the Obituaries of Illustrious Men), Mu'assasat al-Risāla (Beirut, 1977).

Samir Saul

AL-KINDĪ, Abū 'Umar Muḥammad Ibn Yūsuf (Fusṭāṭ, Egypt, A.D. 897–Fusṭāṭ, A.D. 961), Egyptian historian (not to be confused with the earlier Baghdad philosopher Abu Yūsuf Ya'qūb Ibn Isḥāq). After a thorough grounding in the traditional disciplines, al-Kindī became one of the leading *'ulamā'* (scholars) and *muḥaddithūn* (religious traditionists). As a historian, his renown rests on two important works detailing the lives and deeds of the governors and judges of Egypt. The first was entitled *Tasmiyat Wulāt Miṣr* (A Listing of the Governors of Egypt) but has since been known as *Umarā' Miṣr* (The Princes of Egypt). The author arranged Egyptian history within the framework of a chronological enumeration of the careers of successive governors from the Muslim conquest in A.D. 641 to 946. Someone else continued the manuscript to A.D. 973. Each section concerning a governor contained biographical material as well as accounts of noteworthy events of the period. Al-Kindī relied on various transmitters of historical traditions but especially on Ibn 'Abd al-Ḥakam (q.v.), and his book served in turn as a source for al-Maqrīzī's (q.v.) *Khiṭaṭ*. He followed the same method in *Tasmiyat Quḍāt Miṣr* (A Listing of the Judges of Egypt), or *Akhbār Quḍāt Miṣr* (Chronicles of the Judges of Egypt). Starting with the conquest of Egypt, the study ended in A.D. 861 but was carried to 1033 by others. In place of events, the author described cases and landmark legal decisions made by the various judges. The book was therefore an important source of information on the evolution of Islamic jurisprudence and the social history of Egypt. No other works by al-Kindī are extant, but some authors have referred to additional writings by him. His *Khiṭaṭ* of Fusṭāṭ was significant for placing al-Kindī in the line of practitioners of the *khiṭaṭ* genre, following Ibn 'Abd al-Ḥakam and preceding al-Maqrīzī and Ibn Duqmāq. *Kitāb al-Khandaq wa'l-Tarāwīḥ* (The Book of Moats and Relief) dealt with the defense of Fusṭāṭ in A.D. 683 against the Banī Amiyya. In *Kitāb al-Jund al-Gharbī* (The Book of the Western Army), al-Kindī wrote about the Arab tribes and their conquests in Africa. Finally, he related the history of Fusṭāṭ's Mosque of 'Amr in *Kitāb Masjid Ahl al-Rāya* (The Book of the Mosque of the People) and prepared a biography of al-Sarī Ibn al-Ḥakam. *Faḍā'il Miṣr* (The Excellences of Egypt), often attributed to al-Kindī, was really the work of his son and bore the same title as the opening chapter of Ibn 'Abd al-Ḥakam's *Futūḥ*.

Bibliography: Muḥammad 'Abd Allah 'Inān, *Miṣr al-Islāmiyya wa Ta'rīkh al-Khiṭaṭ al-Miṣriyya* (Islamic Egypt and the History of the Egyptian Khiṭaṭ), Dār al-Kutub (Cairo, 1931), on the *khiṭaṭ* genre; idem, *Mu'arrikhū Miṣr al-Islāmiyya wa Maṣādir al-Ta'rīkh al-Miṣrī* (Historians of Islamic Egypt and Sources of Egyptian History), Maṭba 'at Lajnat al-Ta'līf wa'l-Tarjama wa'l-Nashr (Cairo, 1969), pp. 21–33; Ḥasan Aḥmad Maḥmūd, *al-Kindī al-Mu'arrikh* (al-Kindī the Historian), al-Dār al-Miṣriyya li'l-Ta'līf wa'l-Tarjama (Cairo, n.d.).

Samir Saul

AL-MAS'ŪDĪ, Abū'l-Ḥasan 'Ali . . . (Baghdad, c. A.D. 896–Fusṭāṭ, Egypt, A.D. 956), Arab historian. Too little is known about the life of one of the major historians of early Islam. What is certain, however, is that from A.D. 915 until the end of his life, al-Mas'ūdī was constantly traveling. He journeyed far and wide, visiting, among other places, Persia, the Caspian Sea region, India, Zanzibar, and Arabia. He settled at times in Egypt, at other times in Syria. Neither the purpose of these sojourns nor al-Mas'ūdī's occupation is known beyond doubt. Religious or political motives have been adduced in view of his Twelver Shī'ite beliefs. He appears to have defrayed the costs of his voyages by engaging in trade. None of these suppositions has been positively corroborated, and the desire to learn may be the key to the author's peripatetic life. Al-Mas'ūdī placed history in its geographic framework and made it encompass all civilizations known to him. He was endowed with a particularly inquisitive mind, untrammeled by ethnic or religious preconceptions. He brought to Muslim historiography a novel outlook based on empirical investigation and gave it the well-defined task of finding meaning in the collected factual material. Al-Ya'qūbī (q.v.) had traveled also, but his fieldwork was neither as searching nor as systematic. Not only did al-Mas'ūdī widen the scope of historical writing by including non-Muslim territories, but he also viewed history as a field admitting of theoretical concerns. He approached it with the presuppositions of Greek, Indian, and Persian philosophy, a manner unlike that of his predecessors. The third century of Islam confirmed the considerable evolution of the *umma* (community) from an Arab-dominated to a pluralist empire, the home of a universal Arabic-language culture. The advent of foreign influences created a rift between traditionalists intent on upholding revealed religion and rationalists advocating the integration of the methodology of philosophy and natural science in Islamic thought. Whereas al-Ṭabarī (q.v.) contributed to the crystallization of classical historiography, al-Mas'ūdī sought to go beyond the manner of the *muḥaddith* (religious traditionist). The latter rested on the *isnād* (chain of transmitters or authorities), and the accounts that ensued were disjointed and eschewed explanations. He perceived that inquiry, rather than repetition or imitation, would yield significant results in terms of clarifying the historical process.

To al-Mas'ūdī were attributed thirty-six works in all fields, only three of which have survived. The universal history entitled *Akhbār al-Zamān* . . . (Chronicles of the Times and of the Ravages Which Time Has Wrought upon Past Nations, Ancient Generations, and Desolate Kingdoms, A.D. 943–947) filled thirty volumes, but only the first has been found. Its contents may be surmised from numerous references in the author's other works. Starting with the creation, it appears that it dealt with the pre-Islamic period and then with Islam. The most ample work to survive in complete form is *Murūj al-Dhahab wa Ma'adin al-Jawhar* (Meadows of Gold and Mines of Gems) (A.D. 947). Part 1 presents some views on the methodology of historical research and examines the work of other historians. Al-Mas'ūdī was the first important Muslim author to do this. Particularly evident was the attention he paid to the geography, history, way of life, and so on of non-Muslim peoples. *Murūj* truly aimed at universality. The second part concerns Islamic history from the beginning to A.D. 947. The originality of the approach was that, contrary to other writers who referred to non-Muslim peoples largely as a prelude to the rise of the *umma*, al-Mas'ūdī did not neglect them after the coming of Islam. His attitude toward them was free from censure; he tried to observe them on their own terms and as they in fact appeared. For instance, his accounts of the Byzantine Empire, with whom the Islamic world was chronically at war, demonstrated relative impartiality as well as curiosity. As for the treatment of his material, al-Mas'ūdī moved away from the annalistic arrangement. For ancient cultures, he followed a thematic method of dividing his text. For the Muslim period, he adopted sometimes a dynastic, sometimes a topical, structure. There was, however, no uniformity, and the organization of the book seemed slipshod, especially since digressions from the subject at hand abounded. Such shortcomings should perhaps be considered as the price paid by a nascent empirical mind for the satisfaction of discovery. The *isnād* were less prominent, in view of al-Mas'ūdī's interest in obtaining information from direct observation or original sources rather than from tradition. *Kitāb al-Tanbīh wa'l-Ishrāf* (The Book of Notification and Supervision) was much shorter but took the subject to A.D. 956. Conceived along the same lines as *Murūj*, it combined geographical and historical material in the framework of a universal history. There was evidence that al-Mas'ūdī wanted it to be a sort of synopsis of his other books. The contents of the three works overlapped, but none was meant as an abridgment of the other. Instead, the author revised, edited, or completed the various accounts contained in each version. As a representative of the philosophic, analytical methodology in Muslim historiography, al-Mas'ūdī observed patterns in the rise and fall of states, governed by the presence or disappearance of the spirit of inquiry and critical thought. In his view, a basic antinomy opposed scientific research and obedience to tradition throughout history.

Bibliography: Jawād 'Alī, "Mawārid Ta'rīkh al-Mas'ūdī" (Sources of al-Mas'ūdī's History), *Sumer* no. 20 (1964): 1–48; Baron Carra de Vaux, "Note sur un ouvrage attributé à Maçoudi," *Journal asiatique*, n.s., 7 (1896): 133–144; Tarif Khalidi, *Islamic Historiography: The Histories of Mas'ūdī* (Albany, 1975); S. Maqbūl Aḥmad, "The Travels of . . . al-Mas'ūdī," *Islamic Culture*, no. 28 (1954): 509–524; S. Maqbūl Ahmad and A. Rahmān, *Al-Mas'ūdī Millenary Commemoration Volume* (Aligarh, 1960); Ahmad M. H. Shboul, *Al-Mas'ūdī and His World: A Muslim Humanist and His Interest in Non-Muslims* (London, 1979).

Samir Saul

AL-MAQRĪZĪ, Taqī'l-Dīn Aḥmad (Cairo, 1364–Cairo, 1442), Egyptian historian–chronicler and government official. Al-Maqrīzī was a leading figure in a group whose writings made the fifteenth century an important era for historiography in Egypt and the Muslim world as a whole. A student of Ibn Khaldūn (q.v), he was the teacher of Ibn Taghrī Birdī (q.v.), al-Sakhāwī (q.v.), and Ibn Ḥajar (q.v.), among others. His assorted literary output was immense, filling more than one hundred large volumes, of which thirty-six have survived. Al-Maqrīzī was not writing at the request of persons of high station but to spread knowledge. Like other premodern authors, he generally was not aiming at explaining social phenomena but at recording them. However, the fact that he was relatively independent induced him to look beyond the tales about rulers, their lives, and their wars and to pay attention to social and political structures, economic data, ways of life, customs, crafts, and so on. His books thus furnished a rich, indeed an indispensable, lore on medieval Egypt. With respect to method, al-Maqrīzī, like his peers, relied on others for periods preceding his own and made original contributions primarily in connection with events he himself witnessed. In both cases, he displayed great industry and sound judgment in selecting his material and arranging it. Finally, following in the footsteps of Ibn ʻAbd al-Ḥakam (q.v.) and al-Kindī (q.v.), al-Maqrīzī focused on the history of one country, namely Egypt, although he did not neglect classic subjects such as universal history, as in *al-Khabar ʻan al-Bashar* (Chronicle about Humanity), or general Islamic history, as in *Imtāʻ al-Asmāʻ* . . . (Delight of the Ears . . . , a *sīra*, or biography, of the Prophet). His chief work was the massive two-part historical geography entitled *al-Mawāʻiẓ wa'l-Iʻtibār fī Dhikr al-Khiṭaṭʻ wa'l-Áthār* (Admonitions and Regard in a Relation on the Districts and Antiquities) (1417–1439). Known as al-Maqrīzī's *Khiṭaṭ*, it was a model of the *khiṭaṭ* genre, which approached history by way of the topography of a country. In the preface, the author enumerated eight points in which he discussed his purpose (to give comprehensive information), the title (*khiṭaṭ* being preferable to annals or biographies), the book's usefulness (the rapid education of the reader), its level (that of a reader familiar with the traditional and rational branches of learning), the author, the nature of the book, its structure, and its sources (copying, reports from knowledgeable people, and personal observation). After providing an introduction on the geography and the history of Egypt, al-Maqrīzī proceeded to a minute study of the large cities and their districts, history, and physical appearance. The book was replete with detailed descriptions of everything from markets to the customs of the Copts. The author went to considerable pains to obtain information and organize it.

Several works on the history of Egypt were meant by al-Maqrīzī to be a continuation of the *Khiṭaṭ*: *Al-Bayān wa'l-I'rāb* . . . (The Statement and the Declaration . . . , on the Islamic conquest), *ʻAqd Jawāhir* . . . (Tying the Contents . . . , on Fusṭāṭ), *Ittiʻāẓ al-Ḥunafā* . . . (Advice to Believers . . . , on the Fāṭimids until [487 H.]), and *al-Sulūk li-Maʻrifat Duwal al-Mulūk* (Paths toward Knowledge of the Kings' Dynasties, on the Ayyūbids and Mamlūks from 1174 to 1441). A major text, in four substantial parts, *al-Sulūk* remains a basic source on politics, economics, culture, and personalities in the ninth century. As elsewhere, al-Maqrīzī relied on others for the past but provided a wealth of original information about his own time. The chronicle was divided into the reigns of the sultans, each reign being broken down year by year and terminating with obituaries of notables. Al-Maqrīzī prepared two biographical dictionaries on famous Egyptians. *Kitāb al-Muqaffā* . . . (The Book of Rhyming . . .), encompassing personalities from the earliest times, was conceived as a vast collection of eighty volumes, but only sixteen appeared. The second, *Durar al-ʻUqūd al-*

Farīda... (Pearls of the Unique Necklaces...), in three volumes, contained only contemporaries. Al-Maqrīzī's interest in social and economic questions was noteworthy. He wrote *Shudhūr*... (Fragments..., on Islamic coins), *al-Akyāl* ... (Measures..., on weights and measures), *Naḥl*... (Bees..., on bees and wax production), *al-Maqāṣid*... (Intentions..., on minerals), and *Izāla*... (Removing..., on music). *Ighātha al-Umma bi-Kashf al-Ghumma* (Remedy to the Nation to End Its Grief) was a short essay elicited by the crisis of 1393–1405. The author wrote a history of famines in Egypt and their effects. He even analyzed the country's social structure by dividing it in seven classes. Seeking causes, he found them not in the weather but in administrative abuses, such as the debasement of the currency due to the introduction of copper. He made proposals for stabilization through the use of gold and silver.

Bibliography: Muḥammad 'Abd Allah 'Inān, *Mu'arrikhū Miṣr al-Islāmiyya wa Maṣādir al-Ta'rīkh al-Miṣrī* (Historians of Islamic Egypt and Sources of Egyptian History), Maṭba'at Lajnat al-Ta'līf wa'l-Tarjama wa'l-Nashr (Cairo, 1969), pp. 85–104; *Dirāsāt 'an al-Maqrīzī* (Studies on al-Maqrīzī), al-Hay'a al-Miṣriyya al-'Āma li'l-Ta'līf wa'l-Nashr (Cairo, 1971), this collection contains the excellent introductions of J. al-Shayyāl to some of al-Maqrīzī's works; Jean-Claude Garcin, "Al-Maqrizi," in Charles-André Julien et al., eds., *Les Africains*, vol. 9 (Paris, 1977), pp. 197–223; A. R. Guest, "A List of Writers, Books, and Other Authorities Mentioned by al-Maqrīzī in his *Khiṭaṭ*," *Journal of the Royal Asiatic Society* 34 (June 1902): 103–126; Muḥammad Muṣṭafa Ziyāda, *al-Mu'arrikhūn fī Miṣr fi'l-Qarn al-Khāmis 'Ashr al-Milādī (al-Qarn al-Tāsi' al-Hijrī)* (Historians in Egypt in the Fifteenth Century A.D. [Ninth Century H.]), 2d ed., Maṭba'at Lajnat al-Ta'līf wa'l-Tarjama wa'l-Nashr (Cairo, 1954), pp. 3–17.

Samir Saul

MISKAWAYH, Abū'Ali Aḥmad... (Rayy? Persia, 942/947?–Isfahān? 1030), Persian physician, philosopher, and historian. Born in a family of recent converts to Islam—Miskawayh may himself have been the first among them—he was reared in an environment still permeated with ancient Zoroastrian beliefs. From 962 to 1004 he was in the service of the Buwayhids in Baghdad as court secretary (*kātib*) and became an accomplished courtier. He especially came under the protection of their vizirs and was employed as librarian by Ibn al-'Amīd. From that vantage point he garnered a rich harvest of observations and impressions he was to ponder and put to use in his historical work. Miskawayh's turn of mind was decidedly philosophical, and he had a thorough grounding in the "Greek disciplines." In fact, with the exception of his well-known historical opus *Tajārib al-Umam* (The Experiences of Nations), all of Miskawayh's writings were in the domain of *falsafa*. *Tajārib* itself was cast in an unmistakable ethical mold, its normative approach and didactic intent confirmed throughout. Dedicated to their ruler 'Aḍud al-Dawla, the six volumes of text took the historical account to A.D. 980. For the periods before A.D. 918 the author relied on the annals of al-Ṭabarī (q.v.) and followed a similar mode of arrangement of his material, authentification through the *isnād* (chain of authorities), and so on. For the following years, his basic source of information was his own experience as well as testimony from officials and courtiers he had befriended. The *isnād* was omitted after A.D. 952. Unlike earlier Muslim historians, Miskawayh was not a *muḥaddith* (religious traditionist) or *'ālim* (scholar). He paid less attention to caliphs or to establishing the validity of traditions and the credentials of other learned men than to effective rulers and the practical problems of statecraft. Being a *kātib*, his concerns revolved around court life, administrative and financial affairs, military events, and political activity. Social, cultural, or religious matters received lesser emphasis. Not content to record facts, he sought coherence and meaning in history. He tried to make historical occurrences intelligible by explaining them in terms of cause and effect. Considering that he wrote history for the benefit of rulers and administrators, his purpose was pragmatic, namely, to educate them to fulfill their duties through the use of lessons (*'ibar*) drawn from the past. History became synonymous with the teaching of philosophy by examples, and ethical criteria governed his choices and judgments. Relegated to the background, his Shī'ī beliefs did not interfere with a secular attitude toward history and incredulity toward extraordinary tales. Like that of Thucydides (q.v.), Miskawayh's outlook was rational and bent on discovering the permanent verities of human nature. The strong psychological content of his view of causation derived from a consistent search for the motives of human behavior rather than for interrelationships between events. Miskawayh was guided by a basic norm, that of the ideal state governed by the principles of reason. His concentration on political affairs and the upper classes led him to disregard the rest of society. He tended to be partial to his Buwayhid patrons and too reliant on information provided by their officials. Although *Tajārib* had great value for the events Miskawayh witnessed during the Buwayhid rule of Iraq and Persia, its treatment of other areas was inadequate.

Bibliography: H. F. Amedroz, ''The Tajārib al-Umam of Abu 'Ali Miskawaih,'' *Islam* 5 (1914): 335–357; Mohammed Arkoun, ''Ethique et histoire d'après les Tajārib al-Umam,'' in *Essais sur la pensée humanisme musulmane* (Paris, 1973), pp. 51–86; idem, *L'humanism arabe au IVe/Xe siècle: Miskawayh, philosophe et historien* (Paris, 1982); M. S. Khan, ''The Eye-Witness Reporters of Miskawayh's Contemporary History,'' *Islamic Culture* 38, no. 4 (October 1964): 295–313; idem, ''Miskawayh and Arabic Historiography,'' *Journal of the American Oriental Society*, no. 89 (1969): 710–730; idem, ''Miskawayh and Ṯābit ibn Sinān,'' *Zeitschrift der Deutschen Morgenländischen Gesellschaft*, no. 117 (1967): 303–317.

Samir Saul

AL-NARSHAKHĪ, Abū Bakr Muḥammad Ibn Ja'far (Narshakh, near Bukhārā, A.D. 899–? A.D. 959), Persian historian. The Book of Sam'ānī mentions his date of birth (889) and date of death (959). While some scholars (Lerh, Schefer, Minorksy, Barthold) believe that one at least is accurate, R. Frye thinks that the fragment has nothing to do with al-Narshakhī. Little is known about his life, but he is noteworthy because of his contribution to the local history of Muslim Asia. He authored one work entitled *Tārīkh-i Bukhārā* (*The History of Bukhārā*), written in A.D. 943/944 (348 H.) and devoted to Nūḥ Ibn Naṣr of the

Sāmānid dynasty. The Arabic original has been lost. A Persian abridgment was prepared in 1128 by Abū Naṣr Aḥmad al-Qubāvī. In 1178 the book was revised and enlarged by Muḥammad Ibn Ẓufar, with insertions by Abu'l-Ḥasan al-Nīshāpūrī. In the thirteenth century an anonymous author supplemented it with a description of events up to the year 1220. Apart from political history starting in the seventh century and biographies, al-Narshakhī provided information on the topography, architecture, economy and coinage of Bukhārā and the surrounding area, on the Abrūī and al-Muqanna' uprisings, on Zoroastrianism, Buddhism, Christianity and the spread of Islam, all in a clear and straightforward manner.

Bibliography: Richard W. Bulliet, "City Histories in Medieval Iran," *Iranian Studies* 1, no. 3 (Summer 1968): 104–109; V. Minorsky, "Narshakhī, Abū Bakr Muḥammed B. Dja'far," *The Encyclopaedia of Islam* vol. III/2 (Leiden: Brill, 1936), p. 846.

T. M. Kalinina

AL-QALQASHANDĪ, Abū'l-'Abbās (Qalqashanda, Qalyūbiyya Province, Egypt, 1355–Cairo, 1418), Egyptian government official and historian. After a thorough education in the traditional disciplines, al-Qalqashandī entered the Diwān al-Inshā' in 1387. Being the chancery of the Mamlūk state, this body was responsible for keeping official records, conducting administrative business, drafting diplomatic correspondence, applying protocol, and acting in general as the secretarial bureau of the government. Its staff of *kuttāb* (secretaries, scribes) had to be knowledgeable in political usage as well as in a wide range of subjects bearing on the country's administration. Between 1402 and 1411 al-Qalqashandī prepared a monumental compendium of information essential to secretaries of the Diwān entitled *Ṣubḥ al-A'shā fī Ṣinā'at al-Inshā'* (The Enlightenment of Those Who Are in the Dark about the Skill of Letter Writing). The fourteenth and fifteenth centuries are viewed as the age of the *mawsū'a* (encyclopedia) in different fields, such as linguistics, philology, history, and rhetoric. Among the best known were Ibn Manẓūr's *Lisān al-'Arab* (The Language of the Arabs), al-Nuwayrī's (d. 1332) *Nihāyat al-Arab fī Funūn al-Adab* (The Ultimate Goal in the Arts of Belles-Lettres), and al-'Umarī's (d. 1348) *Masālik al-Abṣār fī Mamālik al-Anṣār* (The Routes of Insight into the Fortunes of Kingdoms) on geography. Al-Qalqashandī's was an administrative manual, wherein he sought to provide bureaucrats with models of documents and samples of letters they could use in their work. The author thought of the most varied circumstances a secretary might face and expounded on the knowledge he would need in the domains of grammar, proverbs, the Qur'ān, tradition, and so on. A long section was devoted to the demonstration of proper Arabic calligraphy. More ambitious seemed the author's aim to encompass and systematize all relevant facts on the geography, history, and institutions not only of Egypt but also of the neighboring countries. The result was a highly detailed reference work and an indispensable source for students of the Mamlūk state. Although the economic, social, and cultural life of the period was treated, the emphasis remained on matters pertaining to political rule and organization. The outlook throughout was utilitarian. Inspired by Ibn Qutayba's (d. 889) manual *'Uyūn al-Akhbār* (Eyes on the Events; literally, of the News), the author also relied on numerous sources, among them the books of Ibn al-Athīr (q.v.), al-Ṣūlī, al-Nu'mān, al-'Askarī, and al-Ḥalabī. In 1409 al-Qalqashandī wrote *Nihāyat al-Arab fī Ma'rifat Ansāb al-'Arab* (The Ultimate Goal in the Knowledge of the Lineage of the Arabs), a large work on the genealogy of the Arabs before the advent of Islam, later supplemented by a history of the pre-Islamic Arab tribes entitled *Qalā'id al-Jumān fī Qabā'il al-'Arab* (Necklaces of Pearls with Reference to the Tribes of the Arabs). His *Ma'āthir al-Ināfa fī Ma'ālim al-Khilāfa* (The Pitfalls of Refutation about the Characteristics of the Caliphs, 1416) was a study of the caliphate, its meaning, and its history, with special emphasis on the 'Abbāsid period.

Bibliography: Aḥmad 'Izzat 'Abd al-Karīm et al., *Abu'l-'Abbās al-Qalqashandī wa Kitābuh "Ṣubḥ al-A'shā"* (Abu'l-'Abbās al-Qalqashandī and His Book "Ṣubḥ al-A'shā"), al-Hay'a al-Miṣriyya al-'Āma li'l-Kitāb (Cairo, 1973); 'Abd al-Laṭīf Ḥamza, *Al-Qalqashandī fī Kitābih Ṣubḥ al-A'shā: 'Ardun wa Taḥlīl* (Al-Qalqashandī in His Book Ṣubḥ al-A'shā: Exposition and Analysis), al-Mu'assasat al-Miṣriyya al-'Āma . . . (Cairo, 1962); C. E. Bosworth, "A Maqāma on Secretaryship: Al-Qalqashandī's al-Kawākib al-Durriyya fi'l-Manāqib al-Badriyya," *Bulletin of the School of Oriental and African Studies* 27 (1964): 291–298; Gaston Wiet, "Les classiques du scribe égyptien au XVe siècle," *Studia Islamica* 18 (1963): 41–80.

Samir Saul

AL-SAKHĀWĪ, Shams al-Dīn (Cairo, 1427–Madīna, 1497), religious traditionist (*muḥaddith*) and historian. Al-Sakhāwī was a neighbor of Ibn Ḥajar al-'Asqalānī (q.v.) in his youth and later became his student. After training in the principal fields of learning, such as religious tradition (*ḥadīth*), Islamic jurisprudence (*fiqh*), Qur'ān exegesis (*tafsīr*), literature, history, and so on, he left Egypt at age twenty-two and traveled widely in the Ḥijāz and Syria for purposes of study. Even after he returned to teach, he journeyed six more times to Mecca for extended periods. Not unlike his contemporaries, al-Sakhāwī left a prodigious volume of writings, and this production occurred in the last thirty years of his life. More than one hundred titles of books and treatises could be attributed to him in his two main fields of interest: *ḥadīth* and history. The latter alone should be of concern here. A distinguishing feature of al-Sakhāwī's approach was its polemical character, for the author directed trenchant criticism at some of his peers. However, his censure of al-Maqrīzī (q.v.) did not prevent him from contributing a supplement to the latter's *al-Sulūk*, entitled *al-Tibr al-Masbūk fī Dhayl al-Sulūk* (The Molding of Raw Metal in the Complement to the Sulūk). Starting one year after the terminal point of al-Maqrīzī's book, these annals covered the years 1442 to 1454—it was said to extend to 1495—in the history of Egypt. Events were presented chronologically, even month by month, and each year concluded with the necrologies of famous persons. Most of al-Sakhāwī's historical work was biographical. His magnum opus was a monumental twelve-volume dictionary that he completed in a remarkably short time (c. 1485 to c. 1492). Entitled *al-Daw' al-Lāmi' fī A'yān al-Qarn al-Tāsi'* (Resplendent Light concerning Eminent People of the Ninth Century), it comprised thorough and, on the whole, reliable biographies; but some of the author's comments were acerbic and often marred by petulance and readiness to disparage. His pen inflicted wounds on several contemporaries. He and al-Suyūṭī (q.v.) engaged in acrimonious controversy in which personal antipathy intensified scholarly disagreements. One element of novelty in *al-Daw' al-Lāmi'* was the fact that volume 12 contained, solely, entries on famous women of Islam. Al-Sakhāwī's *al-Dhayl 'ala Raf' al-Iṣr* (The Complement to the Raf' al-Iṣr) continued a collection of biographies of judges started by Ibn Ḥajar al-'Asqalānī. The latter's life was told in *al-Jawāhir wa'l-Durar fī Tarjamat Shaykh al-Islām Ibn Ḥajar* (The Gems and the Pearls in the Biography of Shaykh al-Islām Ibn Ḥajar, 1467), that of another Shaykh al-Islām in *Tarjamat al-Nawawī* (Biography of al-Nawawī), and that of the notables of the fourteenth and fifteenth centuries in *al-Shāfī min al-Alam fī Wafayāt al-Umam* (The Healer of Ache about Obituaries of the Nations). Al-Sakhāwī's disputatious manner was perhaps the product of a desire to defend the prerogatives of the learned order of *'ulamā'* against intrusions by men of action or officials who took advantage of their positions in government to write history. Since the subject was no more than an ancillary discipline to *ḥadīth* studies, al-Sakhāwī also strove to overcome the skepticism of religious quarters—in other words, his own milieu—about its very utility. *Al-I'lān bi'l-Tawbīkh li-man Dhamm Ahl al-Ta'rīkh* (The Public Rebuke of the Critics of the Historians, 1492) represented a survey, set in didactic terms, of Islamic historiography, evaluating its contributions and highlighting its achievements.

Bibliography: Muḥammad 'Abd Allah 'Inān, *Mu'arrikhū Miṣr al-Islāmiyya wa Maṣādir al-Ta'rīkh al-Miṣrī* (Historians of Islamic Egypt and Sources of Egyptian History), Maṭba'at Lajnat al-Ta'līf wa'l-Tarjama wa' l-Nashr (Cairo, 1969), pp. 127–141; A. J. Arberry, *Sakhawiana* (London, 1951); William Popper, "Sakhāwī's Criticism of Ibn Taghrī Birdī," *Studi Orientalistici in Onore di Giorgio Levi Della Vida*, vol. 2 (Rome, 1956), pp. 371–389; Muḥammad Musṭafa Ziyāda, *al-Mu'arrikhūn fī Miṣr fi'l-Qarn al-Khāmis'Ashr al-Milādī (al-Qarn al-Tāsi' al-Hijrī)* (Historians in Egypt in the Fifteenth Century A.D. [Ninth Century H.]), 2d ed., Maṭba'at Lajnat al-Ta'līf wa'l-Tarjama wa'l-Nashr (Cairo, 1954), pp. 39–45.

Samir Saul

AL-SUYŪṬĪ, Jalāl al-Dīn (Cairo, 1445–Rawḍa Island, Cairo, 1505), religious scholar, grammarian, and historian. Al-Suyūtī was an exemplar of the order of the *'ulamā'* (learned men). After a thorough education in the traditional disciplines, he went to the Ḥijāz for further training. He was a student of Ibn Ḥajar al-'Asqalānī (q.v.) and al-Kāfiyajī. Al-Suyūṭī typified the *'ulamā'* of his epoch in two other respects, namely, in his attempt to master all branches of learning and in his staggering productivity, 561 titles. Most of them represented commentaries, compilations, extracts, or abridgments in the domain of religious tradition (*ḥadīth*), treatises on Islamic jurisprudence (*fiqh*), Qur'an exegesis (*tafsīr*), and glosses on texts about Arabic grammar or rhetoric. His historical writings alone are discussed here. This polygraph had a particularly abrasive, immodest, and ambitious personality. He offended others and earned their enmity by sharp attacks on them or their work. Charges of plagiarism, dishonesty, or ignorance were common and created considerable animosity among scholars of the period. Like his colleagues, al-Suyūṭī felt the sting of remarks by al-Sakhāwī (q.v.)—as well as by others—and replied in kind in *al-Kāwī 'ala Ta'rīkh al-Sakhāwī* (A Caustic Text on al-Sakhāwī's Historical Work). His history of Egypt, *Ḥusn al-Muḥāḍara fī Akhbār Miṣr wa'l-Qāhira* (Agreeable Lecture on the History of Egypt and Cairo), followed the pattern for contemporary works of that nature. It combined history with geography, biography, and aspects of the development of Egyptian civilization. The author relied on thirty sources, such as Ibn 'Abd al-Ḥakam (q. v.), al-Kindī (q.v.), al-Qadā'ī, al-Zubairī, al-Maqrīzī (q. v.), and Ibn Faḍl Allah. Volume 1 started with the creation, dealt with events year by year, and contained biographies of learned men. In volume 2 sultans, princes, and judges were presented, along with descriptions of schools, mosques, the Nile, and so on. Al-Suyūṭī's other major book, *Ta'rīkh al-Khulafā'* (History of the Caliphs), was more concerned with the lives and actions of the leaders than in the history of their reigns, their politics, or their wars. The author's general lack of interest in social and economic affairs was especially patent in that work. His criterion for judging the caliphs was basically religious, and he paid much attention to the *'ulamā'* and to religious studies. Strongly biased against the Fāṭimids, the author showed partiality in favor of the 'Abbāsids—who reigned in Cairo—and indifference toward the Umayyāds in Andalusia. Other fifteenth-century historians ignored the 'Abbāsid caliphs and cared only for the Mamlūk sultans. *Al-Shamārīkh fī' 'Ilm al-Ta'rīkh* (Leafless Branches in the Discipline of History) was a short treatise on the utility of studying history and on chronology according to the lunar calendar. Al-Suyūṭī wrote *Badā'i' al-Zuhūr fī Waqā'i' al-Duhūr* (Wondrous Blossoms in the Developments of the Ages), a world history, as well as a biography of the sultan Qāytabāy, a history of the city of Asyūṭ, and many books of *ṭabaqāt* (biographies of generations or classes of persons, including one on women). Among the latter was a collection of one hundred biographies of contemporaries, notable men and women in Egypt, Syria, and the Muslim world, entitled *Naẓm al-'Iqyān fī A'yān al-A'yān* (The Arrangement of Unruly Elements among the Eminent of the Eminent).

Bibliography: Muḥammad 'Abd Allah 'Inān, *Mu'arrikhū Miṣr al-Islāmiyya wa Maṣādir al-Ta'rīkh al-Miṣrī* (Historians of Islamic Egypt and Sources of Egyptian History), Maṭba'at Lajnat al-Ta'līf wa'l-Tarjama wa'l-Nashr (Cairo, 1969), pp. 142–151; *Jalāl al-Dīn al-Suyūṭī,* Proceedings of a symposium held in Cairo, March 6–10, 1976, al-Hay'a al-Miṣriyya al-'Āma li'l-Kitāb (Cairo, 1978); Muḥammad Muṣṭafa Ziyāda, *al-Mu'arrikhūn fī Miṣr fī'l-Qarn al-Khāmis 'Ashr al-Milādī (al-Qarn al-Tāsi' al-Hijrī)* (Historians in Egypt in the Fifteenth Century A.D. [Ninth-Century H.]), 2d ed., Maṭba'at Lajnat al-Ta'līf wa'l-Tarjama wa'l-Nashr (Cairo, 1954), pp. 56–68; E. M. Sartain, *Jalāl al-Dīn al-Suyṭī*, 2 vols. (Cambridge, Eng., 1975).

Samir Saul

AL-ṬABARĪ, Abū Ja'far . . . (Āmul, Ṭabaristān, now in Iran, A.D. 839–Baghdād, A.D. 923), Muslim *mufassir* (Qur'ān commentator), *muḥaddith* (religious traditionist), *faqīh* (religious jurist), and historian. Al-Ṭabarī was the chief figure in the historiography of third-century Islam, one whose magnum opus became a major point of reference for later historians. He epitomized the social category of learned men. In common with most of them, his primary domain of interest lay in the Muslim branches of study, history being in fact an ancillary activity. However, the methodology he employed and the scope of his historical compendium endowed it with the aura of definitiveness for generations of Muslim historians. Al-Ṭabarī gathered material during his education in various centers such as Rayy, Baghdād, Baṣra, Kūfa, and Fusṭāṭ. He then settled in Baghdād to lead the life of a scholar and teacher. Having inherited land in Ṭabaristān, he was of independent means and could afford to remain outside official employ to devote himself to learning. While his frugality and indefatigable diligence were proverbial, his religious attitude aroused controversy. Suspected erroneously of Shī'ite tendencies, he was in fact a pillar of Sunni orthodoxy but rejected the rigid Ḥanbalī interpretations in favor of those of the Shāfi'i school. Al-Ṭabarī took an interest in numerous subjects but especially in commentary of the Qur'ān, religious tradition, jurisprudence, and history. Only some of the twenty-eight works he authored have survived. They include his two principal texts in exegesis and history. *Jāmi' al-Bayān fi Tafsīr al-Qur'ān* (A Collection of Explanations on the Interpretation of the Qur'ān) contained methodical commentaries on Qur'ānic verses based on reports dating from the time of Muḥammad and authenticated by the method of *isnād* (chain of authorities). The author compiled the scholarship of his predecessors to produce an invaluable anthology from material that would otherwise have been lost. He then applied the methodology of the *Tafsīr* in a voluminous history of the world entitled *Ta'rīkh al-Rusūl wa'l-Mulūk* (History of the Prophets and Kings). Al-Ṭabarī collected different versions of the same event, presented them separately, and appended to each one its *isnād*. He withheld judgment on the substance of the accounts, confining his erudition to establishing the validity of the chain of transmitters.

Rigorous, wholesale resort to the methodology of *ḥadīth* was al-Ṭabarī's contribution to historiography. It constituted an important step in the direction of the systematization of historical writing through the application of the more developed criteria of verification prevalent in *ḥadīth*. Al-Ṭabarī's quest for accuracy was combined with the search for exhaustiveness, since he tried to integrate and supersede in *Ta'rīkh* the work of previous scholars. He thus synthesized past historical knowledge in a single work of encylopedic dimensions. Future generations were provided with a storehouse of information, meticulously recorded and highly detailed. The *Ta'rīkh* became the classic starting point that later writers supplemented, abridged, or reproduced. Faced with the immensity of the material he had gathered, especially for the period following the rise of Islam, al-Ṭabarī organized it year by year. In that way, the annalistic method was introduced in Muslim historiography and imitated by others such as Miskawayh (q.v.) and Ibn al-Athīr (q.v.). Al-Ṭabarī's text appeared disjointed but displayed an awareness of the necessary chronological order of facts. A universal history, the *Ta'rīkh* started with the creation and then delved into antiquity and the Persian past. By far the greater part, arranged annalistically, was devoted to the history of Islam from its beginning to A.D. 915. The author's perspective was unmistakably Iraqi, reflecting that of the 'Abbāsid central government of the *umma* (community). He neglected areas remote from Baghdād and lacked the universalist outlook of historians like al-Mas'ūdī (q.v.). He laid the most emphasis on political affairs, kings, leaders, and wars but omitted social and economic facts. *Ta'rīkh* represented the apex of classical Muslim historiography. It confirmed the demise of the tradition of the *khabar* (chronicle) told by a *rāwī* (storyteller) and the advent of *ta'rīkh* (history) composed by the *'ālim* (scholar). The next stages were the gradual abandonment of the *isnād* and the replacement of the annalistic by the dynastic order.

Bibliography: Aḥmad Muḥammad al-Ḥūfī, *Al-Ṭabarī*, Maṭābi' al-Ahrām al-Tijāriyya (Cairo, 1970); Jawād 'Ali, "Mawārid Ta'rīkh al-Ṭabarī" (Sources of al-Ṭabarī's Ta'rīkh), *Majallat al-Majma' al-'Ilmī al-'Irāqī* (Journal of the Iraqi Institute of Sciences) 1 (1950): 143–231; 2 (1951): 135–190; Joseph Dahmus, *Seven Medieval Historians* (Chicago, 1982), pp. 83–125; "Konkordanz zwischen Tabari's Annalen und Ibn Miskawaih's Taǧārib el-Umam," *Islam* 2 (1911): 105–114.

Samir Saul

IBN TAGHRĪ BIRDĪ, Abū'l-Maḥāsin (Cairo, 1409?–Cairo, 1470), historian of Egypt. Ibn Taghrī Birdī belonged to the governing caste of Mamlūks. His father was a "Rūmī" ("Greek," possibly from Anatolia) bought by the sultan and later named to leading positions in the army and to the vice-royalty of Damascus. One of the historian's sisters married Sultan al-Nāṣir Ibn al-Ẓāhir. Ibn Taghrī Birdī himself possessed considerable wealth. His background was both military and scholarly, and he was as familiar with horsemanship or music as with history. A hunting companion of Sultan Barsbāy, he became an intimate of Sultan Jaqmaq. Indeed, his interest in history took shape in the context of palace life, particularly as a result of hearing al-'Aynī read his works to Barsbāy. Ibn Taghrī Birdī could be considered a court historiographer, for, as he averred, he wrote for himself as well as for his prominent friends. He did not thereby surrender his critical faculties, having no doubt profited from the teachings of the master he revered, al-Maqrīzī (q.v.). After the latter's death in 1442 and al-'Aynī's in 1451, Ibn Taghrī Birdī emerged as the leading historian in Egypt. Of the twelve titles attributed to him, seven survived. His first major work, *al-Manhal al-Ṣāfī wa'l-Mustawfī ba'd al-Wāfī* (The Clear Spring and the Very Complete Book after the Complete One), was a biographical dictionary covering the period from 1248 to 1458 and possibly intended to complement al-Ṣafadī's *Al-Wāfī bi'l-Wafayāt* (The Complete Book of Obituaries, 1363). In fact, the book was a history of Mamlūk sultans and leading *amīrs* arranged alphabetically, for scholars and other personalities received less ample entries. The author relied on authorities such as al-Ṣafadī, al-Dhahabī (q.v.), al-Maqrīzī, al-ʻAynī, and al-Birzālī. Ibn Taghrī Birdī wrote two other historical works. In *al-Nujūm al-Zāhira fī-Mulūk Miṣr wa'l-Qāhira* (The Shining Stars among the Kings of Egypt and Cairo), he narrated the history of Egypt from the Muslim conquest to 1468. Following al-Maqrīzī's death, he decided to pursue the latter's *Sulūk* and wrote *Ḥawādith al-Duhūr fī Maḍa'l-Ayyām wa'l-Shuhūr* (Events of the Ages over the Days and the Months) to cover the years 1441 to 1469 more fully than in *al-Nujūm*. The author structured his accounts around the succession of sultanates, dividing the reigns by years and concluding them with the necrologies of important personages. Like other historians of his age, he extracted from his predecessors' books and abstained from evaluating the substance of the different or conflicting versions he reproduced of an event. Although Ibn Taghrī Birdī delved, as he proposed in the introduction to *al-Nujūm*, into matters such as the geographic background, urban civilization, and socioeconomic information, his primary concern lay with the struggles for political power. He wrote the history of the Mamlūk military aristocracy and of the institutions of government. His work was valuable on the one hand because of his association with the rulers and on the other hand because he did not fawn to them in his books. The books' weakness was revealed less because of the author's bias than because of the relatively limited range of his main subject. If Ibn Taghrī Birdī showed sternness in his criticism of individuals, he himself was not spared by contemporaries such as al-Sakhāwī (q.v.), who accused him of plagiarism, shallowness, and insufficient command of Arabic. Apart from abridgments of his main books and works on literature, he also wrote *Nuzhat al-Ra'y fī'l-Ta'rīkh* (Rambling Opinions on History), *Mawrid al-Laṭāfa fī man Wali al-Salṭana wa'l-Khilāfa* (The Purveyor of Refinement about Those Entrusted with the Sultanate and the Caliphate), and *al-Baḥr al-Zākhir fī' 'Ilm al-Awā'il wa'l-Awākhir* (The Overflowing Sea of Knowledge about Ancestors and Contemporaries), all on the history of Egypt.

Bibliography: *Al-Mu'arrikh Ibn Taghrī Birdī* (The Historian Ibn Taghrī Birdī), al-Hay'a al-Miṣriyya al-ʻĀma li'l-Kitāb (Cairo, 1974); Emile Amar, "La valeur historique de l'ouvrage biographique intitulé Al'-Manhal al-Sāfī," *Mélanges Hartwig Derenbourg (1844–1908)*, Ernest Leroux, ed. (Paris, 1909), pp. 245–254; Aḥmad Darrāj, "La vie d'Abū'l-Maḥāsin Ibn Taghrī Birdī et son oeuvre," *Annales Islamologiques* 9 (1972): 163–181; William Popper, "Sakhāwī's Criticism of Ibn Taghrī Birdī," *Studi Orientalistici in Onore di Giorgio Levi Della Vida*, vol. 2 (Rome, 1956), pp. 371–389; Gaston Wiet, *Les biographies du Manhal Safi*, Mémories présentés a l'Institut d' Egypte, vol. 19 (Cairo, 1932); idem, "L'historien Abūl-Maḥāsin," *Bulletin de l'Institut d'Egypte* 12 (1929–1930): 89–105.

Samir Saul

AL-YAʻQŪBĪ, Abū'l-ʻAbbās Aḥmad (? ?–? A.D. 897), Arab historian and geographer. At the end of a childhood spent in Iraq, al-Yaʻqūbī went to Armenia and eventually entered the court of the Ṭāhirids in Khurāsān. He journeyed to India and then settled in Egypt where he served as a government official. At least seven works have been attributed to him, only three of which are extant.

The first, the *Ta'rīkh* (History), was a universal history reaching the year A.D. 872. Volume 1 dealt with pre-Islamic times. Starting with the Hebrews, it encompassed ancient Mesopotamia, India, Persia, Greece, China, Abyssinia, and finally the pre-Islamic Arab Ḥijāz. Volume 2 was devoted to the history of Islam. Although the subject of the *Ta'rīkh* somewhat overlapped that of al-Ṭabarī's (q.v.) annals, the two texts differed in certain important respects. Al-Ya'qūbī divided his account according to reigns rather than year by year. He largely dispensed with the *isnād* (chain of authorities), preferring instead to fuse the several *akhbārs* (chronicles) into a continuous narrative. To achieve that result, he was induced to exercise judgment, compare his sources, and complete them. Finally, as a Shī'ī, his 'Alid sympathies caused him to throw a different light on certain events and to cover others that orthodoxy neglected. In view of its universalist perspective, its concern for non-Islamic lands, and the range of its sources, the *Ta'rīkh* constituted an important stage in Muslim historiography. Al-Ya'qūbī wrote an essay entitled *Mushākalat al-Nās li-Zamānihim* (The Adaptation of Men to their Time) in which he surveyed the way of life, customs, and mores of the upper classes since the rise of Islam, while providing some economic data. He is best known as one of the earliest writers on geography. His *Kitāb al-Buldān* (Book of Countries, A.D. 889–890) was intended as a guide for travelers or perhaps as a reference work for state officials. As he stated in the introduction, the idea came to him from his past travels, and he had gathered information during his trips. The author did not pretend to produce an exhaustive study. Instead, he chose to provide concise, factual descriptions, and his attention to statistical data was noteworthy. Accuracy being his objective, he generally withheld opinion and displayed laudable skepticism toward fanciful tales. Starting with Baghdad—to which he gave particular notice—al-Ya'qūbī directed his sight to all known parts of the world. The book was divided in four sections, representing the cardinal points. The agriculture, industry, topography, ethnography, and archaeology of foreign lands were among the subjects he included in *Kitāb al-Buldān*. It marked the rise of a formal category of geographical literature, sober, succinct, and unmixed with bias or fantasy.

Bibliography: T. M. Johnstone, "An Early Manuscript of Ya'kūbī's Ta'rīkh," *Journal of Semitic Studies* 2, no. 2 (April 1957): 189–195; J. Kramers, "La littérature géographique classique des musulmans," *Analecta Orientalia* 1 (1954): 172–204; William Guy Millward, "A Study of al-Ya'qūbī with Special Reference to His Alleged Shī'a Bias" (Ph.D. diss., Princeton University, 1962).

Samir Saul

YĀQŪT, Ibn 'Abd Allah . . . (Byzantine Anatolia, 1179–Aleppo, 1228), Muslim geographer, historian, and biographer. Captured in his youth, Yāqūt was sold as a slave to a wealthy merchant of Baghdad. His master provided him with an education in the basic Muslim disciplines, freed him at the age of twenty, and employed him on trading missions. Following his former owner's death, he took to traveling for himself to engage in the commerce of manuscripts and to gather information for the books he was preparing. Repeated journeys took him to several important centers in Iraq, Persia, Syria, and Egypt. Yāqūt's epoch was one of the decline of Arab culture, particularly in Iraq and Syria. External attacks by crusaders and Mongols combined with profound changes within Islam, resulting in the coming to the fore of the Seljūqid Turkish element. As often happened at the twilight of an era, the learned tended to concern themselves with putting together compendia of contemporary knowledge. Whether they did so on account of the petering out of inquiry and creative activity or from the urge to hand down a heritage, the product took the shape of immense encyclopedias rendering accessible the erudition then attained. However, the biographical genre was a constant in all periods of Muslim civilization. In his later scholarly life, Yāqūt was largely self-taught, perhaps an indication of the dearth of great masters. His works were based on the accumulated stock of written sources. He brought to his task a methodical mind, and his great contributions were the exhaustiveness of his approach, the consistency of his search for accuracy, and the orderly manner of organizing his material. Several of his works have not survived. Of those that have, two were particularly noteworthy. Comparable to Ibn Khallikān's (q.v.) later dictionary, *Kitāb Irshād al-Arīb ilā Ma'rifat al-Adīb* (Book of Guidance for the Resourceful toward Learning about the Man of Letters), known as the *Mu'jam al-Udabā'* (Dictionary of Men of Letters), presented biographical notices of litterateurs, poets, philologists, and so on in alphabetical order. The portraits were less crisp than Ibn Khallikān's but equally interspersed with telling anecdotes and more complete. The preparation of Yāqūt's other magnum opus, *Mu'jam al-Buldān* (Dictionary of Countries), began in 1212 and continued until the author's death. Geographical literature was held in high esteem in Muslim culture. Arising from the growth of commerce and the postal service, the need to administer an expanding *umma* (Islamic community), and the necessity to travel for reasons such as the pilgrimage or education, the genre known as the *masālik wa'l-mamālik* (routes and kingdoms) became an established domain of study. The extent of the evolution of geographical knowledge in Islam may be measured by comparing the *Mu'jam* to al-Ya'qūbī's (q.v.) *Kitāb al-Buldān*. Of massive scope, Yāqūt's gazetteer, the premier compilation on geography in medieval Islam, aimed at comprehensiveness. It included topographical information but supplemented it with historical, biographical, and literary details. Despite some errors and an occasional juxtaposition of contradictory data, Yāqūt produced a meticulous condensation of considerable amounts of knowledge drawn from many fields. Arranged alphabetically, the *Mu'jam* was preceded by an elaborate introduction in which the author presented the object and organization of his book. The purpose—to correct the mistakes of his contemporaries in the nomenclature of countries—seemed modest but led him to expand his criticism from etymology to issues such as climate and cosmography. Yāqūt also left a book on the genealogies of Arabs and a dictionary of geographic names.

Bibliography: Ṣalāḥ al-Dīn al-Munajjid, *A'lām al-Ta'rīkh wa'l-Jughrāfia' ind al-'Arab* (Noted Arab Historians and Geographers), Dār al-Kitāb al-Jadīd, vol.1 (1959; repr., Beirut, 1978), pp. 59–89; Abū'l-Futūḥ Muhammad al-Tawānisī, *Yāqūt al-Ḥamawī: al-*

Jughrāfiyyun, al-Raḥḥālun, al-Adībun (Yāqūt al- Ḥamawī: The Geographer, the Traveler, the Man of Letters), al-Hay'a al-Misriyya al-'Ama li'l-Ta'lif wa'l-Nashr (Cairo, 1971); Hartwig Derenbourg, "Les Croisades d'après le dictionnaire de Yakout," *Centenaire de l'Ecole des Langues Orientales Vivantes, 1795–1895* (Paris, 1895), pp. 71–92; F. Justus Heer, *Die Historischen und Geographischen Quellen in Jacut's Geographischem Worterbuch* (Strasbourg, 1898); I. U. Krachkovsky, *Ta'rīkh al-Ādāb al-Jughrāfī al-'Arabī* (The History of Arabic Geographical Literature), Lajnat al-Ta'līf wa'l-Tarjama, vol. 1 (Cairo, 1963–1965), pp. 335–344, a translation by Ṣalāḥ al-Dīn Hāshim of *Istoria Arabskoi Geograficheskoi Literatury* (Moscow and Leningrad, 1957); D. S. Margoliouth, "A Hitherto Undiscovered Volume of Yaqut's *Dictionary of Learned Men*," *Islamica* 1 (1925): 100–105; J. T. Reinaud, "Notice sur les dictionnaires géographiques arabes," *Journal Asiatique* 16 (August-September 1860): 85–86.

Samir Saul

AL-ZAYYĀNĪ, Abū'l-Qāsim (Fās, Morocco, 1734/1735–Fās, 1833), Moroccan historian and state official. Although al-Zayyānī had undergone a traditional education at the mosque and the *medersa*, he stood outside the mold of the Maghribī learned circles. His travels outside Morocco and the practical experience he acquired in politics gave greater breadth to his vision of events while placing a distinguishable personal stamp on his works. Of relatively modest Berber origins, al-Zayyānī became a *kātib* (scribe, secretary) at the sultan's court as a result of the knowledge he had gained on an eventful and prolonged pilgrimage to Mecca. Despite the jealousies he aroused among rivals, he was quickly promoted to various new functions, assigned to special missions by the ruler, and even named governor of certain towns. His career was tumultuous and interspersed with periods of disgrace followed by rapid ascension. Longing for tranquility, he would return to office only at the express summons of the sovereign. Not only did al-Zayyānī have ample occasion to travel within Morocco, but he was designated in 1786 to be ambassador to the Sublime Porte in Constantinople and undertook the same voyage in 1793 on a personal basis. The information he gathered on his sojourns found its way into his works. Of the fifteen titles credited to him, thirteen fell within the general provinces of history and geography. Al-Zayyānī was unique in neglecting subjects related to Muslim religious tradition, as well as in adopting a less-than-reverent attitude toward highly regarded personages.

His first work, *al-Turjumān al-Mu'rib 'an Duwal al-Mashriq wa'l-Maghrib* (The Plain-Speaking Interpreter on the Dynasties of the East and the West), was a universal history in the manner of the classical historians like al-Ṭabarī (q.v.) and Ibn al-Athīr (q.v.). Planned during his trip to Turkey, the book was written in 1792–1793 and brought up to date in 1813. Set in twenty chapters, it opened with the creation, discussed succinctly the ancient civilizations, surveyed with surprising brevity the Islamic era, and devoted considerable attention to the Ottomans. At that point the first part of the book ended. Much more detailed, the second part dealt with the history of the dynasties of the Maghrib since the arrival of Islam and was arranged in annalistic form. The author made use of a large quantity of administrative documents to which he obtained access in his official capacity. His reliance on the works of previous historians can be deemed modest. Moreover, his style, direct and measured, shunned ornate expressions, bombast, or florid rhyming. *Al-Turjumān* was noteworthy for breaking with the tradition of Moroccan historiography and encompassing more than North African history. The author's perspective extended not only to the Islamic past but also to contemporary happenings in Europe. On the other hand, guided as he was by personal curiosity, his treatment of the material was uneven and his selection of subjects not exhaustive. His conclusion, for example, offered a lengthy account of his travels and the cities he visited. *Al-Bustān al-Zarīf fī Dawlat Mawlāy 'Alī al-Sharīf* (The Lovely Garden in the Reign of Mawlāy 'Alī al Sharīf) was limited to the reigns of Sīdī Muḥammad b. 'Abd Allah and Mawlāy Sulaymān. Of higher literary value, it also demonstrated greater critical sense than *al-Turjumān*, especially concerning the character of individuals. As for his third major work, *al-Turjumāna al-Kubra allatī Jama'at Akhbār al-'Ālam Barran wa Baḥran* (The Larger Interpretation Which Combines Information on the World, both Dry Land and Maritime), completed in 1818, it represented a supplement to the two other works. Mainly a geography treatise based on data collected during his travels, it also contained particulars on a variety of different subjects, including history. Al-Zayyānī was alone among Moroccan historians in his concern for geography. He strove to achieve accuracy and generally succeeded. Although he may be considered the historian of the 'Alawite dynasty, he did not restrict himself to political events but took an interest in social reforms and economic developments.

Bibliography: A. Graulle, "Le *Boustān Adh-Dharīf* d'Az-Ziyānī," *Revue du monde musulman* 24 (1913): 311–317; R. Le Tourneau, "Al-Zayyānī, historien des Sa'diens," *Etudes d'orientalisme dédiées à la mémoire de Lévi-Provençal,* vol. 2 (Paris, 1962), pp. 631–637; *idem*, "Histoire de la dynastie sa'dide: Extrait de *al-Turǧumān al-mu'rib 'an duwal al-Mašriq wal Magrib* d'Abū al-Qāsim b. Aḥmad b. 'Ali b. Ibrāhīm al-Zayyānī," *Revue de l'Occident musulman et de la Méditerranée*, no. 23 (1977), pp. 7–109; idem, "La naissance du pouvoir sa'dien vue par l'historien al-Zayyānī," *Mélanges Louis Massignon*, vol. 3 (Damascus, 1957), pp. 65–80; E. Lévi-Provençal, *Les historiens des Chorfa* (Paris, 1922), pp. 142–199; G. Salmon, "Un voyageur marocain à la fin du XVIIIe siècle, la riḥla d'az -Zyāny," *Archives marocaines* 2 (1905): 330–340.

Samir Saul

Great Historians: Islamic (Ottoman)

ÂLİ, Mustafa bin Ahmed (Gallipoli, 1541–Jidda, 1600), Ottoman bureaucrat, litterateur, and historian. Âli trained in Gallipoli and Istanbul for a religious career as a professor or *kadĭ* (judge), but in 1560–1561 he entered scribal service at the court of Prince Selim (reigned 1566–1574 as Selim II), where he hoped that his literary talent and command of Arabic, Persian, and Turkish would win him rapid promotion. Âli subsequently served as secretary to the military governors of Damascus and Bosnia, and in 1578 he entered the central financial bureaucracy; he spent much of the rest of his life as a supervisor of provincial finances and district governor. Âli's career under four sultans, beginning with Süleyman the Lawgiver (1520–1566), added to his considerable knowledge the direct experience of Ottoman government in nearly every part of the empire. In Aleppo in 1581 Âli wrote most of the *Nuṣḥat üs-selâṭîn* (Counsel for Sultans), the prototype of the distinctively Ottoman *nasihatname* ("advice for rulers"). In this work, addressed to Sultan Murad III (1574–1595), Âli rejected the indirection and didactic tales set in bygone eras conventional to the Islamic *Fürstenspiegel*; instead, he used contemporary examples drawn from personal experience to expose the financial waste, irresponsibility, and administrative disorganization that he saw to be overtaking the Ottoman Empire. Âli called upon the sultan to assume his responsibilities to preserve the realm and the dynastic mandate through adherence to the principles of justice (*adâlet*) inherent in both *seri'at* (Islamic holy law) and *kanun*, the imperial customs and regulations established by the Ottoman house. Âli was the first articulator of a historiographical orientation common to later political commentators that endowed *kanun* with high symbolic content as the embodiment of the Ottoman commitment to justice, the efficacy of which was the measure of dynastic legitimacy and which used the image of a sixteenth-century "classical age" as the measure of subsequent imperial successes and failures. For Âli, the cardinal tenets of *adâlet* were protection of the rights of the taxpaying subjects and of the ruling class through enforcement of the law, cultivation of an ethic of service to the state, and adherence to the principles of regularity and meritocracy. For all the pragmatism of its specific recommendations, the *Counsel* reflects Âli's personal sense of failure to advance as much as it does his conviction, expressed in fearless exposé, that the imperial commitment to justice was genuine.

Âli became increasingly preoccupied with observing his society and with preserving the cosmopolitan literary and political culture it had created against what he saw as an apocalyptic decline of moral and intellectual standards, and this preoccupation led him to both encyclopedism and an Ottoman sociology. In 1587 he wrote *Menâḳīb-ĭ hünerverân* (The Artists' Exploits), a biographical dictionary of calligraphers and painters, and also the *Ḳavâ'id ül-mecâlis* (Etiquette of Salons), a semisatirical study of the mores of upper-class Istanbul. In 1592 (1000 A.H.) Âli began the *Künh ül-aḫbâr* (Essence of Histories), a universal history and Ottoman chronicle that occupied the remaining years of his life. By his own account Âli used some 130 written works as well as the personal sources afforded him by his long involvement with the leading figures of the time. He sought to present Ottoman history as part of a broader Islamic historical continuum and also to situate it within the more specific Turco-Mongol matrix and frontier conquest environment from which the Ottoman state derived its most distinctive political forms; he saw the empire as the product of a dual heritage, the one universal and the other regional. Âli's overall approach to the history of his own time is similar to that of his early mentor and model Celâlzâde (q.v.), although his broader scope and personal disenchantment with Ottoman society made Âli a more critical and philosophical historian. In expressing his own vision of the Ottoman historical experience Âli framed what has remained until the twentieth century the standard division of imperial history into "early principality" (1300–1453), "classical"(1453–1566), and "postclassical" ("decline") periods. Âli's explicit intent was to create in Turkish, a new language of polite Islamic letters, a compendium of all historical knowledge necessary to the educated or semieducated Ottoman that would equal in literary and historiographical quality the more prestigious Arabic and Persian exemplars of the genre; the *Essence* is a statement of Ottoman cultural maturity.

Because of its comprehensive and critically synthetic treatment of both the events and the sources of Ottoman history (Âli used sources no longer extant and interpreted them with the same pragmatic logic that informed the *Counsel*), and because of the biographies of major political and cultural figures that Âli added to his account of each reign (for Âli, history lay as much in the cultivation of human potential through learning and literature as in military and administrative efficiency), the *Essence* became the single most important source for pre-seventeenth-century history used by later Ottoman historians. The ideas that underlay his history, particularly his view of legitimate sovereignty in the dynastic state as a function of justice and ruling-class solidarity rather than of heredity and religion, also had a significant impact and paved the way for the Ottoman reception in the seventeenth century of the historical philosophy of Ibn Khaldūn (q.v.), with whom Âli shared striking similarities of approach. Âli articulated his conception of the cyclical nature of dynastic power in an immensely popular digest of the *Essence* entitled *Fuṣûl-i ḥall ve 'aḳd* (Seasons of Sovereignty), in which he explicated political morality (only vigilant attention to preservation of equity and responsible sovereign authority can protect against the inevitable decline that seizes a house when it comes to take its power for granted) through examples drawn from the rise and fall of thirty-two Islamic dynasties. In the last two years of his life Âli composed two further works that testify to the originality of his historiographical temperament. *Ḥâlât ül-Ḳâhire min el-'âdât iẓ-ẓâhire* (Conditions of Cairo concerning Her Actual Circumstances) describes the Egypt of 1599 in rich detail and catalogues the effects of Ottoman administration during the thirty years since Âli had last been there. The *Mevâ'id ün-nefâ'is fî ḳavâ'id il-mecâlis* (Tables of Delicacies on the Etiquette of Salons) illuminates Âli's vision of a moral degeneration overtaking all dimensions of Ottoman society in the last quarter of the sixteenth century through more than one hundred short articles that treat various aspects of contemporary social, political, and institutional life with an intimacy and directness unparalleled in Ottoman letters.

Bibliography: Nihal Atsĭz, *Âli Bibliografyasĭ* (Âli's Bibliography) (Istanbul, 1968); Franz Babinger, *Die Geschichtsschreiber der Osmanen und ihre Werke* (Leipzig, 1927); Cornell H. Fleischer, *Bureaucrat and Intellectual in the Ottoman Empire: The Historian Mustafa Âli (1541–1600)* (Princeton, N. J., 1986); idem, "Royal Authority, Dynastic Cyclism, and 'Ibn Khaldûnism' in Sixteenth-Century Ottoman Letters," *Journal of Asian and African Studies* 18, nos. 3–4 (1983): 198–220; Andreas Tietze, *Muṣṭafā 'Ālī's Counsel for Sultans of 1581*, 2 vols. (Vienna, 1978–1982); idem, *Muṣṭafā 'Ālī's Description of Cairo of 1599* (Vienna, 1975).

Cornell Fleischer

ASHIKPASHAZADE, Sheykh Ahmed Ashiki (? 1400–Istanbul, post–1494), Ottoman warrior, dervish, and chronicler. Ashikpashazade's *Tevarikh-i Al-i Osman* (Gestes of the House of Osman) is one of the major sources for early Ottoman history and is a literary monument in its own right. Ashikpashazade was a scion of one of Anatolia's most brilliant and saintly Muslim families; his patronymic Ashiki displayed his pride as the great-grandson of the mystic poet Ashik Pasha (1272–1333). Ashikpashazade took part in numerous Ottoman campaigns during the first half of the fifteenth century; in later life he lived near a mosque he had founded in Istanbul and worked on his chronicle. It is a prose work of some length, covering the Ottomans from their thirteenth-century origins until the end of the fifteenth century. The chronicle survives in at least fifteen manuscripts, many of which reflect Ashikpashazade's own revisions; there is much debate over the authorship, number, and order of the different recensions. Between the chapters are short recapitulatory verses; the prose text itself is elliptical, tightly compressed, and often conversational (with questions and answers reminiscent of an oral reading before an audience). Besides his own personal experiences and those of informants, Ashikpashazade used two written major sources. For the period to 1422 he used a version of the *Anonymous Chronicles* (edited by Friedrich Giese, 1922). For the period to the 1390s he used a book of events that he had found, as a young man, in the possession of

Yakhshi Fakih, the son of Orkhan's *imam*; thus Ashikpashazade had at his disposal a source only once removed from the earliest Ottoman heyday. The sources complement each other: Yakhshi Fakih's book focused on Anatolia, and the *Anonymous Chronicles* have a special interest in Balkan matters. The rough manner in which Ashikpashazade joined together the texts he found allows the modern reader to distinguish an earlier point of view or a different account of an episode. Although Ashikpashazade saw his Ottoman patrons as worthy of the highest praise, his failure to edit his sources reveals rulers somewhat more pragmatic and cosmopolitan than the single-minded warriors for the faith to whom his life was dedicated. His work was nonetheless popular and far from a scholarly compilation; numerous folk tales and stories revealing his heroes' sanctity enliven his account. If he is in any way reminiscent of a medieval European chronicler, it is Joinville: informal and discursive, openly critical of the "novelties" in society since his youth, blaming errors on the ruler's advisors rather than on the leader himself. Ashikpashazade's book was a major source for the later, more subtle court chroniclers of the Ottomans: Neshri, Sa'düddin, and Âli (qq.v.) all made great use of his version of the dynasty's past. They did not use him unwisely, for even though he was no great analyst and his chronology is often weak, he provided an intelligent eyewitness version to more than two generations of history and also preserved a unique set of reminiscences about the earliest years of the Ottoman enterprise.

Bibliography: Friedrich Giese, ed., *Die Altosmanische Chronik des Ašikpašazade* (Breslau, 1929; repr. Osnabrück, 1972); Richard Kreutel, trans., *Vom Hirtenzelt zur Hohen Pforte* (Graz, 1959).

Rudi Paul Lindner

CELÂLZÂDE, Muṣṭafâ Çelebi (known as Koca Nişancĭ) (Tosya, c. 1490–Istanbul, 1567), Ottoman statesman, littérateur, and historian. Trained in Istanbul for a religious career, Celâlzâde in 1516 became a chancery secretary of the Imperial Council (Dîvân-ĭ hümâyûn), where his literary skill in Arabic, Persian, and Turkish won him rapid promotion. Celâlzâde was appointed chief secretary (*Re'îs ül-küttâb*) in 1525 after serving as confidential secretary to Grand Vezir İbrahim Paşa, and he became chancellor (*Nişancĭ*) in 1534; he remained in this office until his retirement in 1557 and held it again from 1566 until his death. As chancellor to the centralizing Sultan Süleyman the Lawgiver (1520–1566) Celâlzâde established many of the protocols used by the Ottoman chancery for centuries thereafter, and he played a major role in the codification of dynastic law (*kanun*) that gave Süleyman his sobriquet. Celâlzâde's *Ṭabaḳât ül-memâlik ve derecât ül-mesâlik* (The Classification of the Lands and Gradations of the Ways) was the product of his years of retirement, although he composed portions of the work during his thirty years as chancellor. Celâlzâde planned the *Ṭabaḳât* as an Ottoman dynastic history accompanied by a systematic exposition of the geographical and governmental structure of the empire, but he was apparently able to complete only the final section of the projected whole, that treating the reign of Sultan Süleyman until 1557. Celâlzâde drew his information from his own intimate experience with the events of these years and from the personal and documentary sources to which his privileged position gave him access. Stylistically, the work marks a high point in the early period of development of Ottoman prose, being written in a high chancery style distinguished by its use of rhymed prose punctuated by poetry, chronograms, Qur'ānic quotations, and whole documents that Celâlzâde drew up as chancellor. Celâlzâde was a historiographical as well as literary innovator in that he based his presentation on the causal and logical interrelationship of events rather than on the more strictly annalistic format favored by most of his predecessors and contemporaries. His history reflects the perspective of a statesman possessing a vision of imperial greatness and moved by a more generalized growing Ottoman awareness that the empire had attained both unprecedented political power and cultural maturity. Celâlzâde's contemporary regnal history depicted the age of Süleyman as the peak of Ottoman development and so laid the foundation for later Ottoman idealization of that reign. Although his breadth of vision and ideological purpose occasionally took precedence over concern for strict factual accuracy (his other known historical work, *Selîmnâme* [Geste of Selim], is a yet more explicitly literary attempt to polish the slightly tarnished image of Süleyman's father Selim the Grim [1512–1520], who had rebelled against his own father, Bayezid II), the *Ṭabaḳât* became the single most important source for the reign used by later universal and dynastic historians such as Âli (q.v.) and Pečevi (q.v.), both because of the unimpeachable authority accorded its author and because of its stature as a literary model.

Bibliography: Franz Babinger, *Die Geschichtsschreiber der Osmanen und ihre Werke* (Leipzig, 1927); Petra Kappert, *Geschichte Sultan Süleymān Ḳānūnīs von 1520 bis 1557: ''Ṭabaḳāt ül-Memālik ve Derecāt ül-Mesālik'' von Celālzāde Muṣṭafā, genannt Ḳoca Nişāncī* (Wiesbaden, 1981); İ. H. Uzunçarşīlī, ''Onaltīncī asīr ortalarīnda yaşamīş olan iki büyük şahsiyet—Tosyalī Celâlzâde Mustafa ve Salih Çelebiler'' (Two Great Personalities of the Midsixteenth Century—Mustafa Çelebi and Salih Çelebi, Sons of Celal of Tosya), *Belleten* 22, no. 87 (1958): 393–441.

Cornell Fleischer

KÂTIB ČELEBI (also known by his professional title, Hadji Khalife) (Istanbul, 1609–Istanbul, 1657), Ottoman historian. Kâtib Čelebi combined his familiarity with the inner workings of the state bureaucracy and personal involvement with affairs of state gained through the day-to-day performance of his clerical duties and his periodic assignment to various parts of the empire with a remarkably wide-ranging and profound knowledge of naturalistic phenomena derived from his own immersion in reading, reflection, and disciplined study with scholars of his time. The scope of his contributions in literature, history, philosophy, geography, and the bibliographic sciences are ample testament to the universality of his intellectual interests. Among his lesser works, several were devoted to the history and institutional, cultural, and religious development of the European countries of his day. Autobiographical details about his family, education, and professional life are provided by him in his own works, especially in the conclusion to the *Mizan al-hakk* (The Balance of Truth). Born into a family already associated with state service through his father, Abd Allah, and member of the sultan's palace corps of swordbearers, Kâtib Čelebi was provided with an education befitting the son of a high-ranking government official and was encouraged by his father to pursue his training in the classical Arabic religious and philosophical texts and to achieve mastery of the more practical skills necessary for a career as a clerk in a government bureau. Accordingly, in 1623 his formal education was temporarily interrupted, and at his father's behest he entered state service as a clerical trainee in the office of Anatolian revenue accounts. Between 1624 and 1634 he pursued his career in public affairs. During the second period of his life he settled in Istanbul, and after an initial period of intense study with various learned men of the capital he resigned his post at the state treasury and devoted his energies exclusively to writing. Although the help of the Shaykh al-Islam secured him a sinecure in another office of the state treasury, which provided him with a modest income, his duties interfered little with his scholarly work.

Most of his immense scholarly output dates from the last decade of his life. Among his works of a strictly historical nature, the following deserve special mention: the *Takvim al-tevarih*, a genealogical and chronological table of world history completed in 1648 (Istanbul, 1733); the *Destur al-amel li islah al-halel*, a reform treatise on the subject of state finances written in 1653 (Istanbul, 1863): the *Tuhfat al-kibar fi asfar al-bihar*, a naval history containing the account of developments in the Ottoman-Venetian war over Crete until 1656 written in 1656 (Istanbul, 1729); the Arabic *fezleke*, a universal history to the year 1639 with an introduction presenting Čelebi's philosophy of history and concept of the historian's task; and the Turkish *fezleke*, a detailed chronicle of Ottoman history covering the years 1591 to 1655 (2 vols., Istanbul, 1870).

Bibliography: Franz Babinger, *Die Geschichtsschreiber der Osmanen und Ihre Werke* (Leipzig, 1927), pp. 195–203; Orhan Saik Gokyay, "Kâtib Čelebi," *Encyclopaedia of Islam*, vol. 2 (Leiden, 1978), pp. 760–762.

Rhoads Murphey

PEČEVI, Ibrahim (Pecs, 1574–? 1649?), Ottoman historian. Pečevi was a member of a prominent family with connections in Ottoman Bosnia and the Danubian provinces, and in his history of the Ottoman Empire between 1520 and 1640 he was most attracted to the European parts of the empire. Although his major work purports to be a comprehensive history of the empire to the end of Murad IV's reign (1617–1639), in the two-volume Istanbul edition of 1866 only the final two hundred pages are, in fact, devoted to the events after the reign of Mehmed III (d. 1603). Although his account of Süleyman I's reign (1520–1566) is based primarily on the writings of earlier historians, in particular Mustafa Celâlzâde (q.v.), Pečevi's account is nonetheless valuable, since he added to his sources a great deal of his own analysis and interpretation. Distanced by nearly a century from the events and personalities of Süleyman's time, he was perhaps better able to offer objective judgments than those with a more direct involvement in the events. As evidence of Pečevi's effort to present an even-handed account of events that took place before his time, one might point to his full-scale incorporation in Ottoman translation or paraphrase of foreign (presumably Hungarian) accounts describing Süleyman's conquests. In relating events closer to his own time, Pečevi did not shrink from presenting the facts as he saw them, even when they reflected poorly on the Ottoman administration. For instance, he openly criticized the scorched-earth policy carried out by Ottoman forces in Hungary under the command of the Grand Vizir Koca Sinan Pasha in 1593–1594 and deplored its effects on the civilian population. He portrayed Nicholas Palfy, one of the Ottomans' chief adversaries in their ongoing conflict with the Hapsburgs, as "able and intelligent." His appreciation of the complexity of historical events and his recognition that the aftereffects were often as significant as the more immediate consequences make his history a valuable source for the interpretation of Ottoman history apart from its importance as a storehouse of information about Pečevi's own time. An insight into the method of historical composition he followed is his account of Süleyman I's capture of the fortress of Istolni Belgrad (Hungarian: Székesfehérvár) in 1543, which may be divided into three fairly distinct sections. Section one summarizes in typical *ruzname* style the day-to-day unfolding of events and incorporates a reference to Celâlzâde's history; section two, an account of official appointments and other matters after the conquest, seems to be based on oral information and on-the-spot investigations carried out by Pečevi himself; and section three, devoted to a highly anecdotal physical description of the town, is clearly based on Pečevi's own knowledge and experience, which he acquired as governor between 1632 and 1635. On the last page, after apologizing to his readers for again indulging in such a lengthy digression, he returned to the main thread of his narrative.

Bibliography: Franz Babinger, *Die Geschichtsschreiber der Osmanen und Ihre Werke* (Leipzig, 1927), pp. 192–195.

Rhoads Murphey

SA'DÜDDİN bin Hasan Can (known as Hoca Efendi) (Istanbul, 1536/1537–Istanbul, 1599), Ottoman scholar, statesman, and historian. Sa'düddin's father, Hasan Can, and his grandfather, Ḥāfiẓ Muḥammad Iṣfahānī, were Iranian emigrés to the Ottoman capital, where Hasan Can became an intimate of Sultan Selim I (1512–1520). Sa'düddin studied religious sciences under prominent scholars of the day, including the chief jurisconsult (*Şeyh ül-islâm*) Ebüssu'ûd; as the latter's advanced student Sa'düddin became a candidate for a teaching position (*mülâzim*) in 1555–1556. After nearly twenty years of progress through ever more prestigious professorial posts, Sa'düddin was appointed preceptor (*hoca*) of Prince Murad, who shortly thereafter succeeded his father, Selim II (1566–1574), on the Ottoman throne as Murad III (1574–1595). Sa'düddin retained the position of royal preceptor under Murad's son Mehmed III (1595–1603) and in 1598 added to it the office of chief jurisconsult, an appointment that gave him virtual control of the entire Ottoman learned hierarchy of professors and judges. As the trusted advisor of two sultans, Sa'düddin played a central role in affairs of state, particularly foreign relations, for a quarter of a century. A poet and prolific translator of Arabic and Persian works into Turkish, Sa'düddin was a preeminent patron of learning and literature to whom even his critics dedicated books. Like his contemporaries Celâlzâde (q.v.) and Âli (q.v.), Sa'düddin was an early master, or even creator, of high Ottoman prose, which drew heavily upon Arabic and Persian vocabulary and rhetorical forms. Having translated the Persian universal history of Muṣliḥ al-dīn Lārī (d. 1571) into Ottoman Turkish for presentation to the palace, Sa'düddin became aware of the deficiencies of extant histories of the Ottoman dynasty, an important number of which (such as the *Hasht Bihisht* [Eight Paradises] of Idrīs-i Bidlīsī [d. 1520]) were written in an ornate Persian style no longer fully accessible to an increasingly Turcophone literary society and were often summary, uncritical, inaccurate, and incomplete, since most did not extend beyond the reign of Bayezid II (1481–1512). He planned his *Tâc üt-tevârîh* (Crown of Histories) as a comprehensive dynastic history that would reflect, in its clarity, literary quality, and accuracy, the newly acquired political and cultural prestige of the Ottoman house. Although Sa'düddin intended to bring his account through the reign of Süleyman (1520–1566) and apparently wrote portions of this section, the political activities that absorbed him after he presented the *Crown* to Murad III in 1575 prevented completion of this project, and so the history ends with the death of Selim I. Sa'düddin drew upon some ten written works as well as firsthand accounts transmitted by his courtier father, whose anecdotes about the conquering sultan Selim he incorporated into a separate *Selîmnâme* (Geste of Selim). Sa'düddin subjected both the accounts and the interpretations of his historiographical predecessors to critical scrutiny and did not hesitate to disagree with them. In dividing his history into individual regnal periods followed by short biographies of the major figures of each reign, Sa'düddin at once brought Ottoman historical writing into closer structural accord with the Arabic and Persian literary traditions that inspired Ottoman literati of the sixteenth century and provided a formal model that probably inspired his contemporary, the encyclopedic historian Âli. Âli adopted a similarly critical attitude toward his sources and said of Sa'düddin's contribution to the development of Ottoman historical writing that "he cut the die in marble." The *Crown of Histories* immediately became the authoritative dynastic history of the pre-Süleymanic era, although it was not "official" in that it was neither commissioned nor substantially supported by the palace, and the work was circulated and copied within the author's own lifetime. It became the major source for pre-sixteenth-century Ottoman history used by later historians, and in the seventeenth century a number of "continuations" of the *Crown* appeared, most notably the dynastic history of Hasan Beyzâde (d. 1636).

Bibliography: Münir Aktepe, "Hoca Sa'deddin Efendi'nin *Tacü't-tevarih*'i ve bunun zeyli hakkında" (On the *Crown of Histories* of Hoca Sa'düddin and Its Continuation), *Türkiyat Mecmuası* 13 (1958): 101–116; Franz Babinger, *Die Geschichtsschreiber der Osmanen und ihre Werke* (Leipzig, 1927); Barbara Flemming, "Khōdja Efendi," *Encyclopaedia of Islam*, 2d ed. (Leiden, 1960-); Cornell H. Fleischer, *Bureaucrat and Intellectual in the Ottoman Empire: The Historian Mustafa Âli (1541–1600)* (Princeton, N. J., 1986); Şerafeddin Turan, "Sa'd-ed-Din," *İslam Ansiklopedisi* (Encyclopedia of Islam) (Istanbul, 1940-).

Cornell Fleischer

SHARAF-HAN IBN SHAMSADDIN BIDLISI (Karakhrud, February 25, 1543–? 1603/1604?), Kurdish tribal leader and historian. Sharaf-han was descended from an aristocratic family that had long provided the leaders of the Kurdish Ruzaki tribal federation and the hereditary rulers of Bidlis. Brought up at the court of Shah Tahmasp (1524–1576), he received a typical Persian classical education. He showed a predilection for history and as a young man conceived the ambitious plan of writing a general history of the Kurdish tribes and their ruling dynasties. Continuous administrative and military service for the shahs of Iran and the Ottoman sultans, however, left little time for study and writing. He rose rapidly in the Iranian governing hierarchy, becoming emir of emirs of the Kurdish tribes of Iran in 1576. Out of favor after the death of Tahmasp in that year, he joined the Ottomans at the beginning of a new war with Iran. For his military services in the Caucasus the sultan rewarded him with the title Sharaf-han and recognized his hereditary possession of Bidlis. Sharaf-han withdrew from all official duties in 1596 to devote himself to the writing of his history.

He divided *Sharaf-name*, a title of his own choosing, into two main parts. The first recounted in detail the history of the Kurdish tribes and their chiefs, and the second, called *Khatimah*, provided a year-by-year history of the Ottoman and Iranian dynasties between the thirteenth and the end of the sixteenth centuries. His aim in adding this "Conclusion" was to place the Kurds in their proper historical setting. He used a large variety of sources. Well read in Persian and Arabic historiography, notably, al-Wakidi and al-Baladhuri, he drew valuable information also from official documents, tribal legends, and the accounts of eyewitnesses still living, all supplemented by the recollections of what he himself had seen and done. He wrote in Persian and carefully followed the canons of medieval Persian historiography. Although his style exhibits the mannerisms characteristic of the genre, he strove to give a realistic account of men and events. The reliability of his work as a historical source is enhanced by the fact that it was not an official court history. Feeling no constraints to defend the policies of Ottoman and Iranian rulers or to flatter them unduly, Sharaf-han could be relatively objective. His attitude, moreover, was that of a Kurdish aristocrat intent upon revealing unknown facts about his people and showing that, in effect, a Kurdistan existed. Such a theme was highly original for the time. Until then the history of the Kurds had been available only piecemeal in the writings of many authors from various countries. Sharaf-han's work was the first general history of the Kurds. It remains the most important single source about their medieval history and contains valuable information about the history of Iran in the sixteenth century.

Bibliography: F. B. Charmoy, *Chèref-nameh ou fastes de la nation kourde par Chèref-ou'ddine, prince de Bidlîs*, 2 vols. (St. Petersburg, 1868–1875), French translation; E. I. Vasil'eva, ed., *Sharaf-han ibn Shamsaddin Bidlisi, Sharaf-name*, 2 vols. (Moscow, 1967–1976), Russian translation; V. Véliaminof-Zernof, ed., *Scheref-nameh ou Histoire des Kourdes, Text persan*, 2 vols. (St. Petersburg, 1860–1862).

Keith Hitchins

SILAHDÂR (Findikli Mehmed aga) (Findikli, 1658–Istanbul, 1724), Ottoman historian. Silahdâr was enrolled in the corps of imperial gardeners in 1677 and in the following year was appointed to the corps of imperial halberdiers. From this time until his retirement from active government service in 1703, when he attained the high rank of chief swordbearer (*silahdâr*) to the new sultan Ahmed III, he held a number of important positions in the palace inner service as one of the wards of the sultan's personal household. Findikli Mehmed's personal and professional background and the perspective and factual content of his histories mark a substantive change in the craft of history writing in the Ottoman Empire. He gave proportionally greater weight than previous historians to behind-the-scenes disputes between various factions in the state administration and to details about the transfer of power. Close proximity to the person of the sultan gave him direct access to a whole range of information only sketchily related in other histories. Consequently, he was able to present in his history the full text of important documents, including incoming correspondence, proposals by foreign envoys at the Ottoman court, and the responses of the sultans to foreign heads of state. These papers, together with accounts of state council deliberations and consultations with senior statesmen, added to the sheer bulk of detail he provided on other matters and have earned the work an important place in the evolution of Ottoman historiography and have entitled its author to rank among its most significant practitioners.

The portion of Findikli Mehmed's history covering the period 1655–1695, which is usually referred to as the *Zeyl-i fezleke* and is a continuation of Kâtib Čelebi's (q.v.) account covering the period 1591–1655, is followed by a detailed history of the reign of Mustafa II (1695–1703) and a summary catalogue of major events during the first part of the reign of Ahmed III until the Serbian uprising of 1721, which is known as the *Nusretname*. Apart from being important for the internal history of the Ottoman Empire during the second half of the seventeenth century, his work has a particular value for diplomatic history and international relations after the Ottoman defeat at Vienna in 1683. For example, the activities of Zülfikar efendi during his four-year tenure as Ottoman envoy to the Hapsburg court during the intermittent peace negotiations in 1688–1692 are related in detail in nearly three hundred pages of text.

Bibliography: Franz Babinger, *Die Geschichtsschreiber der Osmanen und Ihre Werke* (Leipzig, 1927), pp. 253–254; Ahmed Refik, *Alimler ve Sanatkarlar* (Istanbul, 1924), pp. 228–255.

Rhoads Murphey

Great Historians: Italian

BARONIO, Cesare (or BARONIUS) (Sora, 1538–Rome, 1607), Italian ecclesiastical historian. In 1561, he earned a doctorate in law in utroque (civil and ecclesiastical law) at the University of Rome. Ordained a Catholic priest in May 1564, he was created a cardinal on June 5, 1596. The following year, he was appointed a Vatican librarian. He served on various commissions as a historian in the political activity of the Papacy (see, for example, *Paraenesis ad Rem Publicam Venetam* [Instruction for the Republic of Venice]). His specific field was the history of the Catholic Church, and his first work was the revision and correction of *Martyrologium romanum* (Roman Martyrology) published in Rome in 1583. The second edition which contained notes was published in Rome in 1586. This work, which represents the beginning of a Catholic hagiography built on a critical historical foundation, made Baronio known throughout Europe.

At the age of 20, Baronio began the research that would serve as the foundation for his master work, the *Annals*. In Germany, at about the same time, Matthias Flavius (q.v.), a strict follower of Martin Luther (1483–1546), and his associates (Johan Wigand, Matthias Hudex, Thomas Holthuter) began a history of the Church which was completed in 1574. The third edition was printed in Nurnberg in 1757 as *Centuriae Madgeburgenses* [Magdenburg Centuries], and since then it has been known by this title. Vlacic, with great scholarship, aimed to prove historically the truth of the Reformation and Luther's doctrine against the theological claims of the Church of Rome. In an Augustinian manner, *Centuries* conceived history as the eternal struggle between the forces of good and evil, God and the devil. History is, consequently, the history of God's will.

Philip Neri, detecting the germ of historical scholarship in Baronio, directed him to write a history of the Church. The result was twelve volumes of *Annales ecclesiatici* (Ecclesiastical Annals), edited in 1588–1607. They covered the period of time from the beginning of Christianity to 1198. As a Catholic reply to *Centuries*, the *Annals* were soon translated into Italian, French, Polish, and German. In 1756 the *Annals* reached the twenty-first edition.

Baronio is certainly an exponent of the Counter-Reformation (see the dedicatory letter to Sixtus V in the first volume of the *Annals*: "praesertim contra novatores nostri temporis, pro sacrarum traditionum antiquitate ac S. Romanae

Ecclesiae potestate'' [especially against the innovators of today in defense of the antiquity of the sacred traditions and of the authority of the Roman Church]). His apologetic sense of history was mitigated by an unfailing love for the truth, attested by the title of the work replacing the first one, *Historia ecclesiastica controversa* (A Disputed Church History).

Baronio distinguished between history (contemporaneous events) and annals (past events). In the *Annals*, he not only examined what happened but also took into account the reasons and motives (''sed et qua ratione quove consilio''). With utmost respect for the truth, he read innumerable sources, investigated coins, inscriptions, and whatever else yielded information. The manuscripts and all the corrections were done in his own writing. He considered it a sacrilege to alter a document even to the slightest degree. Hence, one may find a discontinuity in the narrative, repetitions, and a scrupulous accuracy in the chronology. Although it appears that Baronio was intent on considering historical events from the point of view of papal primacy, he did not hesitate to recognize that the so-called Donation of Constantine was a spurious document. Probably composed in the eighth century, the document was allegedly a legal grant of Emperor Constantine by which he handed over to Pope Sylvester I rulership over Rome and all provinces in Italy (See vol. 12 of *Annals*). The contemporary Pope Paul V believed that the document was authentic. For the same love for historical truth, Baronio incurred the hostility of the Benedictine Order (he denied that Gregory the Great belonged to their Order) and of Spain (because he denied the so-called ''Apostolic Legacy'' or ''Sicilian Monarchy'' vindicated by Spain). There was even an attempt to submit the *Annals* to the Inquisition.

Although Baronio is not exempt from inaccuracies, which one can expect from a pioneer and from his historical situation in the controversy between Reformers and Catholics, nevertheless it must be said that Baronio represents the precursor in the Catholic Church of the critical method applied to history. His distinguished pupil, the historian Richard Simon (1638–1712), applied the historical method to the Bible and is considered the father of Biblical criticism in the Catholic field.

Bibliography: All manuscripts of Baronio are located in Biblioteca Vallicelliana and Biblioteca Casanatense in Rome. A complete bibliography of books, manuscripts, and articles on Baronio is found in *Cesare Baronio: Scritti vari*, Sora, 1963. See also H. Jedin, *Lexikon für Theologie und Kirche*, Vol. 1, pp. 1270–1272; A. Molien, *Dictionnaire d'Histoire et de Géographie ecclésiastiques*, vol. 6, pp. 871–882; and A. Pincherle, *Dizionario biografico degli Italiani*, vol. 6, Rome, 1964, pp. 470–478.

Francesco Turvasi

BIONDO, Flavio (Forli, c. 1392–Rome, June 14, 1463), Italian Renaissance historian and papal official. Biondo's father was a notary in the Romagna, and he followed in that profession after receiving a humanist education in Forli. He served in various secretarial positions in several North Italian cities where he came into contact with some prominent humanists. In 1432 he entered the Roman

Curia and was especially favored by Pope Eugenius IV who used him on several missions. He stayed with the Curia when it went into exile in Florence in 1434 where he was a prominent figure at the Council of Florence. While in Florence, Biondo became familiar with the major Florentine humanists, especially Leonardo Bruni who acted as a model for his historical writing. Under Pope Nicholas V, Biondo fell from favor and left the Curia. He returned at the end of Nicholas' reign but never recovered his former influence. His last years were difficult financially, and he used the dedications to his writings as a means of supplementing his income. He married and had ten children, which limited his advance in the papal service. Biondo was one of the major historians of the Renaissance and his works enjoyed European-wide fame. His major history was the *Historiarum ab inclinatione Romani Imperii decades* (first issued in 1453 covering the period from 412 to 1441). Biondo broke with medieval providential history in telling the story of the decline of Rome and its fall essentially in terms of human actors and institutions. Generally avoiding ideological and rhetorical flourishes, he gave a relatively clear and politically comprehensive description of the later Roman and medieval history. Not surprisingly propapal in his narrative, Biondo showed usually an even hand in his treatment of individuals and tried to avoid excessive moral judgments. The history provided a fundamental treatment of medieval history that showed a major conceptual advance over previous histories. Closely tied with Biondo's historical work was his study of the remains of ancient Rome. His contributions to archaeology were as fundamental as were those to medieval history. His *Roma instaurata* brought together classical literary and epigraphical sources and his own observations of Roman ruins. The work broke with the unhistorical confusion that marked medieval attributions of Roman cities and put on a new footing the identification of ancient ruins and their histories. Although there were many errors in Biondo's identifications, their superiority over all previous attempts provided the basis for later archaeological study by Roman humanists. Especially important was Biondo's dependence on documentary sources as a basis for clarifying names and locations. Related to the *Roma instaurata* was the *Italia illustrata*. Besides being a description of Italian geography, it offered historical and cultural information collected from a wide variety of sources. His *De origine et gestis Venetorum* (like several of his smaller works) provided a particular narrative. Biondo's last great undertaking was the *Roma triumphans*, which described the private and public worlds of the ancient Romans. Basically a close study of ancient terms, it offered a commentary on important texts. The diffusion and popularity of his writings make Biondo one of the most influential historians of the Renaissance and a fundamental figure in the development of a critical historical sense.

Bibliography: R. Fubini, in *Dizionario biografico degli Italiani* 10 (1968): 536–559; A. Mazzocco, "Some Philological Aspects of Biondo Flavio's *Rome Triumphans*," *Humanistica Lovaniensia* 28 (1979): 1–26; Dorothy M. Robathan, "Flavio Biondo's Roma Instaurata," *Medievalia et Humanistica*, n.s., 1 (1970): 203–215; Paolo Viti, "Umanesimo letterario e primato regionale nell' 'Italia illustrata' di F. Biondo," in *Studi filologici, letterari e storici in memoria di Guido Favati*, vol. 2 (Padua, 1977), pp. 711–732; Roberto Weiss, *The Renaissance Discovery of Classical Antiquity* (Oxford, 1969).

John F. D'Amico

BRUNI, Leonardo (Arezzo, 1374–Florence, 1444), Italian rhetorician and historian. Secretary of the papal chancellory (1405) and municipal chancellor of Florence (1416), Bruni wrote numerous rhetorical works of a political, moral, historical and critical nature that were greatly appreciated at the time and from obvious consequence for his contemporaries. They show sizeable influence of Italian communal democracy presented in such writings as *De tyranno* (*About the Tyrants*) by Coluccio Salutati (1400), Bruni's teacher and predecessor in the Florentine chancellory, or *De re publica* (*On the Commonwealth*) by Uberto Decembrio (1420). Commonly thought of as founder of the doctrine of civic humanism, a doctrine encompassing awareness of the active public role of the man of letters, Bruni was also a promoter of the principles of classical studies in the modern sense. An admirer of the ancient rhetorical historiography of Livy (q.v.) whom he tried to imitate and further. For thirty years, starting in 1414, Bruni articulated a vast compilation ordered by the Florentine Commune dealing with the Tuscan history, *Historia Florentini populi* (The History of the People of Florence, ed. 1914–1926). Extended with numerous digressions and commentaries, like those referring to the First Punic War, the wars against the Goths, the history of Byzantium and especially events of his time, the rhetorical compilation in which Bruni included fictitious discourses was meant rather to illustrate the author's civic ideas than to depict the historical past. Translated into Italian as early as 1449 by Donato Acciajuoli (ed. 1855–1860), it had a steady influence on the Italian humanist historiography including that of Machiavelli (q.v.).

Bibliography: Hans Baron, *Humanistic and Political Literature in Florence and Venice at the Beginning of the Quattrocento*, Cambridge, Mass., 1955; idem, *The Crisis of the Early Italian Renaissance. Civic Humanism and Republican Literature in an Age of Classicism and Tyranny*, Princeton N. J., 1966; idem, *From Petrarch to Leonardo Bruni: Studies in Humanistic and Political Literature*, Chicago, Ill., 1968; E. Santini, "La fortuna della Storia fiorentina di Leonardo Bruni nel Rinascimento" (The Fate of the Florentine Stories of Leonardo Bruni in the Age of the Renaissance), *Studi Storici*, 1911, no. 20, pp. 177–195; idem, "Leonardo Bruni Aretino e i suoi Historiarum Florentini Populi libri XII" (L. B. Aretino and His Twelve Books of Histories of the People of Florence), *Annali della Reale Scuola Superiore di Pisa*, 1910, no. 22; N. S. Struever, *The Language of History in the Renaissance*, Princeton, N. J., 1970; D. J. Wilcox, *The Development of Florentine Humanist Historiography in the XVth Century*, Cambridge, Mass., 1969.

Radu Constantinescu

COMPAGNI, Dino (Florence, c. 1260–Florence, 1324), Italian chronicler. A prominent citizen of Florence and contemporary of Dante, he played an important part in Tuscan history in an epoch of crisis and civil wars as a leader of the Republican Guelphs (White) who opposed the establishment of a French monarchic domination. After 1301 he withdrew from public life and dedicated himself to literary activity, producing, among other things, a *Cronaca delle cose occorenti ne'tempi suoi* (1310–1312) (Chronicle of the Events Which Occurred During His Life-Time, edited 1907–1916). The chronology of that writing of political recollections is uncertain and even the crucial events of 1289–1301 lack accuracy. Compagni's work is an apology rather than a chronicle proper, yet the literary quality is quite remarkable.

Bibliography: A. del Monte, "La storiografia fiorentina del Trecento" (Florentine Historiography of the 14th Century), *Bollettino dell'Istituto Storico Italiano e Archivio Muratoriano*, 1950, no. 62; P. G. Ricci, *Compagni e la prosa del Trecento* (Compagni and the 14th Century Italian Prose), Firenze, 1958; M. Luzi, *La città di Dino* (Dino's City), Firenze, 1963.

Radu Constantinescu

DENINA, Gerolamo (Revello, now Saluzzo, 1731–Paris, 1813), Italian historian. Denina was a true man of the Enlightenment, one of the many Italians who roamed Europe enlivening with their learning and wit the various courts to which they were invited. In his youth he broke away from the clerical provincialism of his native Piedmont and adopted the ideas of the Enlightenment. Travels to other parts of Italy, entry into the cosmopolitan society of the foreign ambassadors stationed in Turin, ties with many of the French *philosophes*, and contacts with English noblemen on the Grand Tour further contributed to his education. His first work, *Discorso su le vicende d'ogni letteratura* (A Discourse on the Development of Different Literatures, 1760) was translated into several languages and brought him a European reputation. Two years later he appended to it the *Discorso sulla letteratura italiana* (A Discourse on Italian Literature). In 1765 he turned to the study of history, in preparation for *Delle rivoluzioni d'Italia* (Italian Revolutions, 1768–1772), which used the rich collection of sources collected by Ludovico Muratori. The publication of the first volume further enhanced his reputation and earned him the favor of the king of Piedmont and the chair of rhetoric at Turin's Collegio superiore. The publication of the second volume was rewarded with a professorship in Italian and Greek eloquence at the University of Turin. The benevolence with which the first two volumes had been greeted, however, changed to sharp disapproval with the appearance of the third volume. In it Denina blamed Italy's decline on poor educational practices, a frivolous idle nobility, too many beggars, and an excessive number of priests and monks. Despite criticisms by the clergy, the king continued to support Denina and gave him permission to write a treatise suggesting reforms. Denina did this in *Dell'impiego delle persone* (On the Employment of People). The Piedmontese inquisitor, however, banned its publication. On a trip to Tuscany in 1777, Denina released the manuscript to a Florentine editor, in violation of Piedmontese law. As punishment, he was dismissed from the university and exiled to Vercelli. In 1782 he accepted the invitation of Frederick II to go to Prussia. In 1804 he moved to Paris when Napoleon offered him a post as librarian.

Among his later works, the history of western Italy (Savoy, Piedmont, Liguria, and part of Lombardy), *Istoria dell'Italia occidentale* (1809), was one of the first studies on the impact of the French Revolution on northern Italy. Of his many writings, the history of Italian revolutions enjoyed continued popularity among Italians through the Risorgimento.

Bibliography: "Carlo Denina," in *Illuministi italiani. Riformatori lombardi, piemontesi e toscani*, ed. Franco Venturi (Milan and Naples, 1958), pp. 701–753; C. Denina, *Delle rivoluzioni d'Italia*, 3 vols. (Turin, 1769); idem, *A Dissertation, Historical and Political, on the Ancient Republics of Italy*, an extract from *Rivoluzioni d'Italia*, with original notes and observations by John Langhorne (London, 1773); idem, *Essai sur les traces anciennes du caractère des Italiens modernes, des Siciliens, des Sardes, et des Corse; suivi d'un coup d'oeil sur le tableau historique, statistique et moral de la Haute Italie* (Paris, 1807); idem, *Tableau historique, statistique, et moral, de la Haute-Italie et des Alpes qui l'entourent; précédés d'un coup d'oeil sur le caractère des empereurs, des rois et autres princes qui ont régné en Lombardie, depuis Bellovèse et César jusqu'à Napoléon premier* (Paris, 1805); Vitilio Masiello, "Carlo Denina riformatore civile e storico della letteratura," *Belfagor*, no. 5 (1969): 501–546.

Emiliana Pasca Noether

GIANNONE, Pietro (Ischitella, Puglia, 1676–Torino, 1748), Neapolitan jurist and historian. Giannone dedicated himself to the study of the relationship between history and law. He was persecuted for his jurisdictionalist ideas and forced to flee to the court of Charles VI in Vienna from 1723 to 1734 and then to Venice and finally to Switzerland. In 1736 he was taken prisoner by the troops of the king of Sardinia who acted under orders from Rome. Giannone died in prison. His *Vita scritta da lui medesimo* (Autobiography), which remained unedited until 1890, is an excellent reconstruction of the life and times of its author. His major work, *l'Istoria civile del Regno di Napoli* (A Civil History of the Kingdom of Naples) was published in 1723. The work was translated immediately into English, French, and German, which brought Giannone much popularity. The work details the historical events of the Italian South from the time of the Romans to the seventeenth century. Giannone's thesis was that "civil history in the Catholic world could not be separated from Ecclesiastical history." The goal of this work was to reveal the abuses that the Roman Church used to damage the power of the state in the kingdom of Naples from the Emperor Constantine to Charlemagne, from the Angevin kings to the Spanish domination. The work documents the illegitimate nature of the ecclesiastical usurpation of power and underlines the political theses that champion the politcal authority of the state. Clearly, this theme contributed to the success that Giannone's work enjoyed in the eighteenth century in both the battle of the Neapolitan jurisdictionalists against the Roman Church and the antiecclesiastical polemics of the European Enlightenment. Giannone's book mobilized several anti-Curialist forces and thus led the Church into fierce persecution of its author. For a long time the *History* was not considered the spontaneous product of the genius of its author but rather the effort of a collective group of Neapolitan secular intellectuals. Even if Giannone's work gathered up the results of a long critical preparation and an inspiring motivation shared by the most advanced sector of the Neapolitan intelligentsia, there is no question that the merit of having conceived it, written it, edited and published it, can only be ascribed to Giannone himself, who paid dearly for his deep commitment. While Giannone was in Vienna he dedicated his time to a defense of his work in his *L'Apologia*, published posthumously in 1755. From 1733 to early 1736 he was engaged in a project of even wider scope, *Il Triregno* (unedited until 1895), a portrait and reconstruction of religious history divided into three parts: *Regno terreno* (Earthly Kingdom), *Regno celeste* (Heavenly Kingdom), and *Regno papale* (Papal Kingdom). The first book examines Judaism and its search for the earthly kingdom; the next book delves into the revolution Christianity espoused with regard to this concept, and finally Giannone examined and exposed the overturn of these ideas by the papacy in its quest to expand its temporal domination of the world. This work, which was nourished by the most advanced radical culture of Europe, not only denied completely the temporal power of the Church of Rome but also accepted doctrines and theories that were decidedly rationalistic and materialistic. Today *Il Triregno* is considered the most notable contribution given by Giannone to the European Enlightenment.

Bibliography: Mario Fubini, ed., *La cultura illuministica in Italia* (Turin, 1957), pp. 163–173; P. Giannone, *Epistolario*, ed. Pantaleo Minervini (Fasano di Puglia, 1983); *Pietro Giannone e il suo tempo*, Atti del convegno di studi nel tricentenario della nascita, ed. R. Ajello (Naples, 1980).

Vittorio Conti, translated by Ilia Salomone-Smith

GIOVIO, Paolo (Como, 1483–Florence, 1552), Italian ecclesiastic and historian. He studied medicine at Pavia and Padua and early in his career he practiced as a physician. Medicine, however, had only limited attractions, and he traveled through Italy closely observing people and places. He finally ended in Rome in 1512 where he was befriended by Leo X and Cardinal Giulio de'Medici (the future Clement VII). Leo provided him with a readership in philosophy at the University of Rome in 1514. He became especially close to Clement VII, whom he accompanied into Castel Sant'Angelo during the Sack of Rome (1527). The pope named him bishop of Nocera dei Pagani in 1528. In papal service he travelled through Italy and Europe observing men and events and collecting information for his historical and biographical writings. In 1551 he left Rome for Florence where he enjoyed the patronage of Duke Cosimo I.

Although he was one of the most popular historical writers of his day, there is an extent to which he was more an observer and commentator than a historian, and may indeed be called a journalist. The themes he chose to write on were diverse: a description of Britain, a commentary on the Turks since the Fall of Constantinople, and biographies of such notables as Leo X, Adrian VI, and Clement VII. Undoubtedly his most important work is his history of his own times *Historiarum sui temporis libri XLV* (first published 1550–1552). He read widely and discussed important events with the knowledgable in Rome. While he painted on a broad canvas, Giovio's history was not comprehensive. He ignored much which might cause scandal and never was able to deal effectively with causal relationships. While being uncritical of the powerful, Giovio's works were written in excellent Latin which to a great extent accounted for their popularity, aided by their rapid translation into Italian. Giovio did provide his own Italian version for his *Commentario delle cose di Turchi* in order to guarantee it broad diffusion. Despite their analytical limitation, Giovio's histories and biographies offer well-written narratives and function as factual compendia.

Bibliography: Federico Chabod, "Paolo Giovio," *Scritti sul Rinascimento*, Turin: Einaudi, 1967; *Pauli Iovii opera*, Rome: Istituto poligrafico dello Stato, 1956–1958; T. C. Price Zimmermann, "The publication of Paolo Giovio's Histories," *La Bibliofilia*, 74 (1972); idem, "Paolo Giovio and the Evolution of Renaissance Art Criticism," *Cultural Aspects of the Italian Renaissance: Essays in Honor of Paul Oskar Kristeller* (Manchester: University of Manchester Press, 1976).

John F. D'Amico

GUICCIARDINI, Francesco (Florence, 1483–Florence, 1540), Italian statesman, diplomat, and historian. Scion of an old aristocratic Florentine family and ambitious for fame, Guicciardini studied law. He joined the opposition to the republican government of Piero Soderini and supported the exiled Medici. Throughout his life Guicciardini was a fierce defender of his aristocratic class and interpreted history partially in conformity with this ideology. With artistocratic support Guicciardini advanced in government service including in 1511 an ambassadorship to King Ferdinand of Spain. Guicciardini joined the returned Medici forces in 1513. In 1516 Leo X (formerly Giovanni de'Medici) named him governor of Modena and then of Reggio. He performed his duties efficiently, partially relying on force and executions. In 1521 Leo made him commissioner of the papal army. Leo's successor, Adrian VI, removed him from office, but he returned to favor under Clement VII (another Medici) in 1523. Guicciardini's pro-Medici sympathies hurt him when the Medici were expelled once again in 1527. The new Florentine republic (1527–1530) accused him, unjustly, of corruption. When in 1530 the Medici returned to power, Guicciardini again found favor; Clement appointed him governor of Bologna. Guicciardini retired from papal service in 1533 and returned to Florence to advise Alessandro de'Medici, the city's new ruler of Florence. With Alessandro's assasination in 1537 Guicciardini supported Cosimo de'Medici in the hope of containing Medici power. Cosimo, however, outmaneuvered his advisers and consolidated his control over the government. He left government service in 1538 and devoted the remaining two years of his life to writing. Guicciardini possessed a first-class analytical mind. Like Machiavelli, he was obssessed with contemporary political events. More than Machiavelli, he successfully moved from political considerations to historical ones. Fiercely realistic, he sought to know the very basis of human action by searching for documentary evidence and focusing on details. As a consequence, he was one of the first historians to rely on archival materials and to provide a close narrative of events. History could not teach humans exactly what to do in new circumstances since all human deeds were unique and new circumstances never fully paralleled previous ones. But through the study of the past, one could learn certain generalized principles that were of value if used intelligently.

Guiccardini began his historical work in 1508 when he composed his *History of Florence* (Storie fiorentine), which he left incomplete. Years of service and observation of the great events of his day, best presented in his *Ricordi*, led him to recast the history of Florence into his masterpiece, the *Storia d'Italia* (begun in 1534). Unlike his previous work, the *Storia* covered all of Italy and took for its theme the terrible events that befell Italy as a result of the French invasion of 1494. In explaining his story, Guicciardini carefully recorded and analyzed events. People acted for selfish motives in his view, and the story he wrote was one that showed the human origins of the tragedy. Guicciardini displayed a particularly strong antipathy toward the papacy and its role in the loss of Italian independence. Whereas some historians before him had taken all of Italy as their subject (Flavio Biondo (q.v.) for example), Guicciardini informed his history with such deep knowledge and judicious judgments that it outranks all others in intellectual strength. Such a work naturally has been subject to a variety of historical judgments. Nevertheless, it stands as one of the great Renaissance contributions to modern historiography by transcending the stylistic conceits of the Latin writing humanists and by founding narrative on documentary material without fostering a present-minded emphasis on contemporary political questions.

Bibliography: Peter E. Bondanello, *Francesco Guicciardini* (Boston, 1976); Vittorio da Caprariis, *Francesco Guiccardini: dalla politica alla storia* (Bari, 1950); *Enciclopedia italiana*, Vol. 18 (Rome, 1934), pp. 244–249; Felix Gilbert, *Machiavelli and Guicciardini: Politics and History in Sixteenth Century Florence* (Princeton, N. J., 1965); Mark Phillips, *Francesco Guicciardini: The Historian's Craft* (Toronto, 1977); Roberto Ridolfi, *Vita di Francesaco Guicciardini* (Rome, 1960); *Storia d'Italia*, 5 vols., ed. Constantino Panigrada (Bari, 1929); *Storie fiorentine*, ed. Roberto Palmarocchi (Bari, 1931).

John F. D'Amico

JOACHIM OF FIORE (Celico, Italy, c. 1135—Fiore, Calabria, c. 1202), Italian monk, mystic theologian, and historian. Son of a notary in the court of the king of Sicily, Joachim first followed his father's profession. He left royal service and after a visit to the Holy Land decided to retire to a monastery. After some delay, he entered the Cistercian order, becoming abbot of the monastery of Corazzo in 1178. He left in 1184 to devote his time to writing. He founded his own strict order, St. John of Fiore, which was confirmed in 1204. Joachim became famous for his learning and holy life. However, his theories did receive criticism in his own day. Most of his sixteen treatises are on biblical topics. Joachim was essentially a biblical commentator and prophetic writer. His historical theory was an offshoot of these primary interests. In his view one must know history or, more accurately, salvation history to realize that the time of tribulations was at hand; hence the study of the past formed part of his apocalyptical vision of time. History was therefore to be used as an element in understanding the spiritual truth of Scripture. Joachim organized history according to a Trinitarian model. God reveals himself in history, and since there are three persons in the Trinity, so there are three epochs in history, the Age of the Father (Old Testament), the irenic Age of the Son (New Testament), and the Age of the Spirit to come. These three epochs like the Trinity itself ultimately form a harmonic unity. Joachim saw in the third period a time of spiritual fulfillment modeled on his view of the perfection of the monastic state. Joachim's spiritual and apocalyptical ideas were of great influence in his day, especially among the Spiritual Franciscans, and have appealed to subsequent philosophers of history.

Bibliography: Morton W. Bloomfield, "Joachim of Fiore: A Critical Survey of His Canon, Teaching, Sources, Biography, and Influences," *Traditio* 13 (1957): 249–311; Marjorie Reeves, *Joachim of Fiore and the Prophetic Future* (London, 1976); Delno C. West and Sandra Zimdaras-Swartz, *Joachim of Fiore: A Study in Spiritual Perception and History* (Bloomington, Ind., 1983).

John F. D'Amico

LIUTPRAND (Pavia, ante 920–Cremona, 972), Italian memorialist. Born of a family of courtiers of the Italian kings, he went to the palatine school in Pavia and in 931 was appointed to the chancellory of King Hugo of Provence. In his capacity as first chancellor of King Berengar he headed a diplomatic mission in Constantinople (949) but, falling from Queen Willa's grace, he had to take refuge at the court of German King Otto I (956). In Frankfurt in 958 he started writing a strange work, titled in pseudo-Greek, *Antapodosis* (Return, or Revenge). Its essential purpose was to pillory Berengar, but was carried away by the subject matter of the history of the decline and fall of the Carolingian Empire. Liutprand narrated the events between 887 and 931, in six books, using the old people's memories without being very particular about chronology. The memorialist's job (spanning 939 to 962) remained unfinished, as Berengar's removal left the author without a reason to continue and complete his polemic production. *Historia Ottonis* (The History of King Otto), covering five years (960–964) of the rule of his new master, comprises interesting details related to Otto's crowning as Roman Emperor (962) and Liutprand's participation in the synod that deposed Pope John XII (963). Becoming imperial adviser and Bishop of Cremona (962), he headed more diplomatic missions in Constantinople (968, 971), writing *Relatio de legatione Constantinopolitana* (Report of His Embassy to Constantinople), an acid and savory narration of his adventures during his first mission.

Bibliography: Johann Koder and Theodor Werner, *Liutprand von Cremona in Konstantinopel*, Vienna, 1980; Elisabeth Müller-Mertens, *Regnum Teutonicum*, Berlin, 1970.

Radu Constantinescu

MACHIAVELLI, Niccolò (Florence, 1467–Florence, 1527), Italian statesman, political philosopher, playwright, and historian. Following his family's tradition of political service, Machiavelli in 1492 entered the republican government, which followed the execution of Savonarola, as head of the second Chancery (which concerned foreign affairs). He served on several embassies: in 1500 to France; in 1503 to Rome; in 1504 to France again; in 1506 to Rome again; and in 1508 to Germany, a trip that resulted in his *Rapporto delle cose della Magna*. In 1510 a third trip to France resulted in the *Ritratto di cose di Francia*. His last diplomatic trip was to France in 1511. Machiavelli advanced with the rise to power of Piero Soderini as *gonfaloniere* in 1502. He succeeded in persuading Soderini to sponsor the establishment of a citizen militia to fight for Florence rather than depend on foreign mercenaries, in line with his theory that the decline of the Italian states was partially due to the use of foreigners rather than citizens to fight their battles. He successfully helped lead this militia in battle against Pisa in 1509. Unfortunately for Florence, Julius II attacked and entered Florence in 1512; the Medici family returned to power in the city. Machiavelli suffered with the return of the Medici, even being imprisoned for implication in a plot. Excluded from politics and financially in bad straits, Machiavelli withdrew from Florence to the countryside to live on his small farm at San Casiano. Machiavelli continued to correspond with friends in the hope that they could help him secure some post with the new government, but without success. Despite the adverse circumstances, he produced his most important works: the *Il Principe* (1513) and the *Discorsi sopra la prima deca di Tito Livio* (1513–1519). The pessimism about human deeds and goodness mark both works and reflect, in part, his lonely existence at San Casciano. Closely related to these works is his *Dell'arte della querra* (1521). Pessimism is also evident in his Italian plays, above all *La Mandragola* (1518). Machiavelli's fortunes improved when Cardinal Giulio de'Medici in control of Florence from 1520 appointed him Florence's official historian and to other civic posts. In 1525 Machiavelli presented Giulio (then Pope Clement VII) with the eight books of his *Istorie fiorentine*. Clement continued to use Machiavelli in other ways, including as a representative in the army. With the expulsion of the Medici in 1527 Machiavelli unsuccessfully sought favor with the new republic. He died shortly afterward.

Machiavelli was a political philosopher who found in history essential material for the development of his own ideas. History offered a series of *exempla* of men's action from which to draw lessons. This was possible because Machiavelli believed that human nature was a constant and that the past formed an analogue to the present. Well acquainted with ancient writers, he was especially fond of Plutarch and Livy because they offered material Machiavelli needed. His *Discorsi* on Livy shows his movement from history to political philosophy. More historical in form was his biography of Castruccio Castracani, the fourteenth-century tyrant of Lucca. He felt free to invent episodes in Castracani's life in order to make him a more dramatic example of political action. The most important of Machiavelli's historical writings was the official *Istorie fiorentine*, which he composed as official historian of Florence. As history, it is superior to the biography of Castracani in being more careful in its presentation of facts. Machiavelli cast his narrative in humanist form; he was especially dependent on Leonardo Bruni for the early history of Florence. But he organized his work to present a particularly political reading of the Florentine past. Once again, individuals are presented as examples of universal political actors or events as generalized situations and not as discrete events in Florentine history. Men and their actions are praised or condemned insofar as they approximated Machiavelli's political precepts. In a sense, therefore, the *Istorie fiorentine* is a relatively historical exposition of the theories found in *Il Principe* and the *Discorsi*.

Bibliography: Peter E. Bondanella, *Machiavelli and the Art of Renaissance History* (Detroit, 1973); Felix Gilbert, *Machiavelli and Guicciardini: Politics and History in Sixteenth-Century Florence* (Princeton N.J., 1965); Niccolò Machiavelli, *Arte della querra e altri scritti politici*, ed. Sergio Bertelli (Milan, 1961); idem, *Istorie Fiorentine*, ed. Franco Gaeta (Milan, 1962); idem, *Legazione e commissarie*, ed. Sergio Bertelli (Milan, 1964); Roberto Ridolfi, *Vita di Niccolò Machiavelli* (Rome, 1954).

John F. D'Amico

MURATORI, Ludovico Antonio (Vignola, 1672–Modena, 1750), librarian, archivist, and historian. Muratori's early education was with the Jesuits and then at the public school of Modena. In 1688 he took minor orders and received his degree in *utroque jure* (canonical and civil law). His dominant interests, however, were in history. In 1695 he became a priest and was nominated curator of the Ambrosian Library of Milan by Count Carlo Borromeo. In 1700 Muratori returned to Modena where Duke Rinaldo I d'Este named him the chief archivist of his court, a position that Muratori retained for the rest of his life. In Modena he designed a project to contact and bring together men of letters from all over Europe in order to bring about a renewal of intellectual life. His *Primi disegni della Repubblica letteraria d'Italia* (First Designs for a Literary Republic of Italy) appeared in 1703. He illustrated this early "outline" in his subsequent work of 1708 entitled *Riflessioni sopra il buon gusto nelle scienze e nella arti* (Reflections on Good Taste in the Sciences and the Arts). "Good taste" was clearly an indictment of the "Baroque" in literature, as well as in philosophy and history. Taste, he pointed out, could be acquired only with critical observation and analysis and then through the application of the historical method, all of which ultimately amounted to the refusal to accept authority where this had no relevance or validity. Given his fine genius for distinctions, it was not surprising that in that same year, 1708, Muratori became involved in a clash between the Holy See and the Este Court in a dispute over land rights in the Comacchio valley. Muratori defined sharp limits between the temporal as opposed to the spiritual powers of the papacy. Notwithstanding his clerical status, he courageously defended the right of the duke of Este in temporal affairs. Through his research and direct observations while traveling in Italy, Muratori had been convinced only too strongly and correctly that many of the litigious entanglements at the heart of disputes between canonical and civil rights were historically, if often obscurely, rooted in medieval confusion of these two areas of law. From 1723 to 1738 Muratori published twenty-four volumes of his monumental opus *Rerum italicarum scriptores* (Writers or Historians of Italian Affairs), a vast collection of writings, chronicles, and documents covering numerous centuries of Italian history. This huge work was derived from the inspiration of the erudite philosopher Gottfried Leibnitz, the court historian of the duke of Brunswick with whom Muratori was in corrspondence, and the methodological lessons learned from the critical Benedictine French "school." In preparing his extraordinary work Muratori sought help from many men of letters who in turn sent documents from a number of major archives throughout the Italian peninsula. In fact, he succeeded in establishing a network of authentic erudition, a sort of transregional and transnational "academy" of scholars, archivists, and historians who seemed to agree informally with Muratori's implicit premises that, despite all other only all-too-obvious divisions, the culture of Italy had a unitary character, and the culture of Europe, of the West, was likewise bound by common elements and experiences.

In *Rerum* Muratori did not simply collect and introduce archival documents; rather, he wrote an original historical narrative derived or woven directly from them. Among other things, he clearly and consistently distinguished between "profane" and "sacred" history. History constitutes an account of human events, but these events spring forth from geographic, social, and economic factors. In his vast narrative ranging through one thousand years, from about 500 to 1500, Muratori has the Middle Ages as his central focus. The history of ancient Rome was left as a sort of backdrop while he pursued and illustrated the successive appearance on the stage of Italian history of new peoples, new institutions, new "factual" developments, and alternatives of historical vicissitudes. Long before the nineteenth-century rediscovery of the problem, Muratori grappled with the question of the significance and influence of the Lombards in Italian history as against both the heritage of Rome and the hegemonic domination of the Franks and Charlemagne. This theme of contrasts was further pursued in subsequent works, particularly in *Antiquitatis Italicae Medii Aevi* (Ancient Italy in the Middle Ages) published from 1738 to 1742 in six volumes, a work that Muratori himself sought to translate into Italian. In a basic sense, this is Muratori's major work in which he reevoked all forms of Italian life from the fall of the Roman Empire to the incipient rise of the European nation–states. In it Muratori presented an original overview of customs, religion, the arts, commerce, and political institutions. Simultaneous to these "civil" works Muratori continued his search for enlightened religious thought. His principal works in this connection are *Della carità cristiana* (On Christian Charity, 1723); *Cristianesimo felice nelle missioni de' padri della Compagnia di Gesù nel Paraguai* (Happy Christianity in the Missions of the Fathers of the Company of Jesus in Paraguay, 1743); *Della regolata devozione de' cristiani* (On the Regulated Devotion of Christians, 1747), and others. The year before his death Muratori published a critical work on jurisprudence entitled *Dei difetti della giurisprudenza* (On the Defects of Jurisprudence). His moral and intellectual testament is contained in his writing entitled *Della pubblica felicità* (On Public Happiness), which deals with the reciprocal duties of princes and subjects, or the rulers and the ruled, of leaders and citizens, a sensitive subject much and variously treated in Italy from Machiavelli (q.v.) to Muratori and the eighteenth-century Italian Illuministi and later in Europe in the disquisitions of economic and social thinkers and political and civil philosophers and in the programs of reformers and revolutionaries. Rightly, Muratori's contemporaries considered this work an exemplary text of the committed "new intellectual" of the dawning era of the no less committed, if quite differently, Italian and European *philosophes*. Two and a half centuries of developments and radical innovations in the history of erudition, scholarship, and the human sciences have not dimmed the well-nigh universal homage that has been bestowed on Muratori. Singly and together, his major works such as the *Rerum*, the *Antiquitates*, and the *Annali d'Italia* (1738–1744) endure as unique milestones in the history of European historiography as well as in the intellectual and cultural history of Italy.

Bibliography: *Atti del Convegno Internazionale di Studi Muratoriani*, 4 vols., ed. Luigi Muratori (Modena, 1972); *Opere di Ludovico Antonio Muratori*, 2 vols., ed. Giorgio Falco and Fiorenzo Forti (Naples and Milan, 1964).

Eluggero Pii, translated
by Ilia Salomone-Smith

PAUL THE DEACON (Warnefrid) (Friuli, 724–Monte Cassino, 799), Lombard poet and historian. A descendant of Lombard "Austrian" aristocracy (Friuli-Venezia Giulia), Paul, son of Warnefrid, went to the palatine school in Pavia, where he was taught by Flavianus, the author of a compilation (of which only excerpts from the twelfth century were preserved) *De vestigiis et dogmate philosophorum* (Philosophical Traditions and Teachings of the Antiquity). Acceding to the position of royal secretary and archdeacon of the Patriarchate of Aquileja, Paul became the tutor of Adelperge, daughter of King Theodaris, whom he accompanied at the court of her husband, Duke Arichis of Benevent. There he wrote a chronological world history in verse (763) and a *Historia Romana* (Roman History) up to Justinian (763–773) in which he paraphrased Eutropius (q.v.) and took up where he left off. Conceived as a *Fürstenspiegel*, Paul's writing would later be extended with events up to 813 and appended to the *Tripartite Chronography* of Anastasius Silentiarius by Landulf (ante 1023). After the fall of the Lombard kingdom (774), Paul took refuge in Monte Cassino. His brother, Arichis, was put in jail for his participation in an uprising of the Friulan nobility against the Frank conqueror (776). Paul made demarches for his brother, leaving for the court of Charlemagne (783) where he was kept until 787. It was there that he wrote in verse a paraphrase of the lives of the Bishops of Metz for archchapelman Angilramn (*Historia episcoporum Mettensium*, The History of the Bishops of Metz), subserviently imitating Vergil. Back in Italy, he produced upon the request of Carolingian superintendent Wala, numerous poetic, didactic, rhetorical, liturgic, grammatical, and legal compilations that were used for centuries on end. His original historical oeuvre, however, remained in the Italian libraries without enjoying the same dissemination and popularity. It consisted of *Historia Langobardorum* (The History of the Lombards, 787). Unaccomplished, the history was interrupted at year 744. His model was Livy (q.v.) and his sources were: the Roman analysts of the era of decadence (Valois' Anonymus, the Continuator of Prosper of Aquitaine); the local historians of the seventh century (the Ravenna Cosmographer, Secundus of Trento, c. 607, *Succinta de Langobardorum gentis historiola* (Brief History of the Lombards) and *Origo gentis Langobardorum* (The Beginnings of the Lombard Nation), preserved in an 807–810 compilation); the Roman continuator of Malalas (c. 740), *Liber pontificalis* (Book of the Roman Popes); and, to a great extent, the oral tradition.

Bibliography: Domenico Bianchi, "L'elemento epico nella Historia Langobardorum," *Memorie Storiche Forogiuliesi*, 1934, no. 30, pp. 117–168; 1935, no. 31, pp. 1–73; 1936, no. 32, pp. 1–72; Antonio Crivelucci, "Per l'edizione della Historia Romanorum di Paolo Diacono" (For a New Edition of the Roman History of Paul the Deacon), *Bollettino dell'Istituto Storico Italiano e Archivio Muratoriano,* 1921, no. 40, pp. 7–103; Olga Dobiash-Rozhdestvenskaja, "L'Historie des Longobards. Comment fut-elle conçue et achevée," in *Classical and Medieval Studies in Honour of Edward Kennard Rand*, ed. L. W. Jones, New York, 1938, pp. 71–85; William D. Foulke, ed., *The History of the Longobards by Paul the Deacon*, New York, 1907.

Radu Constantinescu

PICCOLOMINI, Enea Silvio (Pienza, 1405–Ancona, 1464), Italian prelate and historian. In the gallery of great historians, Piccolomini occupies a unique place. At the end of a brilliant political and ecclesiastical career (secretary to the Council of Basel, secretary to Emperor Frederic III, bishop in 1448, cardinal in 1456), he became Pope Pius II in 1458. During his pontificate, he made efforts to organize a crusade against the Ottomans, and he died when about to depart on this mission. Piccolomini was a complete humanist, a fine representative of the Renaissance spirit, a man of the Church and of the world, an accomplished diplomat and scholar. He wrote poems on occasion and even a novel of romance. As a historian, this "international political agent" (Ed. Fueter) used his own experiences and memories, combining them in a direct and personal style that was far from humanist canons. Beginning with a history of the Council of Basel (*Commentarii de gestis basiliensis Concilii*, 1440), he continued with a biography of Frederic III, a history of Bohemia (*Historia Bohemica,* published posthumously in 1475), a history of Europe, and a geography (*Cosmographia*). His memoirs, *Commentarii,* written in twelve books near the end of his life, present his political and religious activities as pope until 1463. Although his work lacked a critical system and a conception of history, its spontaneity, its variety, and its information on the first century of the Renaissance make it an outstanding work.

Bibliography: *Enciclopedia italiana*, vol. 27, pp. 310–312; Georg Voigt, *Enea Silvio de Piccolomini, als Papst Pius II, und sein Zeitalter*, 3 vols. (1856–1863).

Lucian Boia

PLATINA, Batolomeo Sacchi (called Piadena or Platina) (? 1421–Rome, 1481), papal official and historian. Originally intent on a military career, Platina studied at Mantua and became a tutor to the children of Marquis Ludovico Gonzaga. He continued his own studies in Florence and then went to Rome as secretary to Cardinal Francesco Gonzaga. In Rome he entered the Curia as an apostolic abbreviator under Pope Pius II. Platina became an important intellectual figure in Rome, an especially prominent member of the Roman Academy, which functioned under the leadership of Pomponio Leto. The academy was dedicated to humanistic studies, especially the investigation of classical antiquities. It could border on the eccentric, as it did by changing all names of its members into classical approximations. It was, however, an important center for intellectual activities in Rome. Platina lost his Curial post when Paul II dissolved the College of Abbreviators in 1468. Platina called for a council against the pope's dissolution, a recourse specifically forbidden by papal decree, and he and other members of the academy were arrested on charges of treason and immorality. Although the charges had little basis in fact, the pope acted in the fear that there did exist a republican plot against him among some of the humanists. Through the intercession of several cardinals, the academicians were released. After Paul's death, Platina returned to papal favor and Sixtus IV appointed him papal librarian, a post he occupied with distinction until his death. Platina's most important work was the *Liber de vita Christi ac omnium pontificum,* and his reputation as a historian is based on it. It was completed in 1474 and dedicated to Sixtus IV. The *Liber* was a complete history of the papacy organized biographically from Peter to his own time. As papal librarian he had access to earlier histories and documentary materials; however, when he depended on medieval sources he tended to use them somewhat uncritically. For contemporary popes he is a more valuable source; not surprisingly, he was especially negative toward Paul II. Since Platina used a biographical format, there was little detailed analysis of institutions and the presentation of limited connectives among the biographies. He basically supported papal policies in his narrative although he was capable of criticizing individual popes for political or moral faults. Although not a great historical work, the *Liber* was the most comprehensive history of the papacy and the best until that time; it enjoyed great popularity through the Renaissance and the Reformation when it was used for polemical purposes. It was printed throughout the sixteenth century with additional biographies to keep it current.

Bibliography: *Liber de vita Christi ac omnium pontificum,* ed. G. Gaida, in *Rerum Italicarum Scriptores* 3, no. 1 (1913); Richard J. Palermino, "Platina's History of the Popes" (M. litt. thesis, University of Edinburgh, 1973).

John F. D' Amico

SARPI, Paolo (Venice, 1552–Venice, 1623), Venetian theologian, philosopher, and historian. After making his profession that of a member of the Servites in 1575, Sarpi rose rapidly to high office within his order, becoming provincial (1579), procurator-general (1585–1588), and vicar-general (1599–1604). Roman

Church authorities rejected him three times for an Episcopal appointment, which played a part in the extreme dislike of the *curia* found in his later work. Sarpi transcended the confines of his order when he was appointed the official theological adviser of the Venetian government on January 28, 1606. In a series of important position papers he offered reasons supporting the Venetian stand against Pope Paul V in the interdict crisis, attacking secular power of the papacy, and defending the jurisdictional claims of Venice. He was ex-communicated, and the pope demanded his extradition to the Roman inquisition, which the Venetian government refused. An unsuccessful attempt on his life in 1607 strengthened his antipapal and anticurial views together with a particular distrust of the Jesuit order. Despite their prominence it would be erroneous to see in Sarpi only a polemicist against Rome. He was an extraordinarily complex and in many respects contradictory thinker. Explaining the shape of his thought has proven an elusive enterprise even to perceptive modern scholars since all of the pieces of the puzzle simply do not fit. Sarpi was a many-sided intellectual with wide-ranging interests including politics, ethics, the natural sciences, and mathematics on a level that elicited even Galileo's favorable comments. His private meditations, *Pensieri* (ed. Gaetano and Luisa Cozzi [Turin, 1976]), remain the object of disagreement among scholars since they defy categorization, showing skeptical, antireligious, even atheistic elements. How far he went in his Protestant sympathies is uncertain despite recent arguments that he was for all practical purposes a conservative Calvinist or a Zwinglian. His contacts with Protestants resulted in important epistolary exchanges especially after 1610. He was influenced by Gallican writers like Gentillet and apologists of the Church of England in his hostile views of the papacy.

Among Sarpi's historical writings are treatises with specific arguments on specific problems, among the most important of which are histories of the Interdict, of the Inquisition, and of Benefices. His great historical work for which he is remembered is the *Istoria del Concilio Tridentino* (History of the Council of Trent), published by the ex-bishop of Spolato, Marco Antonio de Dominis, in London in 1619. Put on the Index of prohibited books the same year, it reached a wide European readership through translations into five languages within the following decade. Its refutation by Sforza Pallavicino, *Istoria del Concilio di Trento* (Rome, 1656–1657), proved of little effect. Sarpi's work was later used by writers of the seventeenth century and the Enlightenment. One of its striking characteristics is his careful crafting of the council's history from documents and accounts available to him, many of which are presented verbatim and at length. To Sarpi, that history was "the Iliad of our times," tragic in the triumph of papal autocracy aided by the Jesuits and destructive of that structure of the Church envisioned by Marsilius of Padua, conciliarism, and Gallicanism, which he championed. Sarpi exposed many unedifying events that took place behind the scenes, especially compromises that had little to do with true reform of the Church as he desired it. That his work was tendentious is beyond discussion, but he did not write his history as a personal attack. Methodologically, it stands between humanist didactic narrative and the evolving genre of detailed, scholarly, and documented histories of the eighteenth century. His understanding of the role played by institutions rather than individuals in history gives his work a distinctly modern flavor.

Bibliography: Sarpi's works are most accessible in these editions: "*History of Benefices" and Selections from "History of the Council of Trent*," ed. Peter Burke (New York, 1967); *Istoria del Concilio Tridentino*, 2 vols., ed. Corrado Vivanti (Turin, 1974); *Lettere ai Gallicani*, ed. Boris Ulianich (Wiesbaden, 1961); *Lettere ai Protestanti*, 2 vols., ed. M. D. Busnelli (Bari, 1931); *Opere*, ed. Gaetano and Luisa Cozzi (Milan, 1969); *Scritti giurisdizionalistici*, ed. G. Gambarin (Bari, 1958). The old edition of his work is *Opere*, 8 vols. (Helmstadt, actually Verona, 1761–1768). On Sarpi see Giovanni Getto, *Paolo Sarpi* (Florence, 1967); David Wootton, *Paolo Sarpi* (Cambridge, Eng., 1983), with bibliography.

Elisabeth G. Gleason

TIRABOSCHI, Gerolamo (Bergamo, 1731–Modena, 1794). Italian historian of literature. One of the major erudites of the eighteenth century, Tiraboschi followed in the footsteps of Apostolo Zeno and Ludovico Muratori (q.v.). Inspired by Muratori, Tiraboschi determined to do for Italian literature what Muratori had done for history. A member of the Jesuit order, Tiraboschi taught at the Brera school in Milan and also served as its librarian. His first work was a three-volume collection of medieval monastic sources, *Vetera humiliatorum monumenta* (1766–1768). In 1770 Duke Francesco III called him to Modena as director of the Estense library, a post held by Muratori from 1700 to 1750. Two years after Tiraboschi's arrival in Modena, he began to publish the *Storia della letteratura italiana* (History of Italian Literature, 1772–1781). Immediately successful, the *Storia* was reprinted at Turin, Venice, Florence, and Milan and in abridged editions in French, English, and German. The *Storia* was followed by the *Vita del conte Fulvio Testi* (Life of Count Fulvio Testi, 1780); *Biblioteca modenese, o notizie varie della vita e delle opere degli scrittori natii negli stati del . . . duca di Modena, con un appendice de' professori di musica* (Modenese Encyclopedia, or Information on the Life and Works of Writers Born in the States of the Duke of Modena, 1786); *Memorie storiche modenesi* (Historical Notes on Modena, 1793–1794). At the same time, Tiraboschi edited the *Nuovo giornale de' letterati d'Italia* (New Journal of Italian Men of Letters, 1773–1790) and compiled the *Dizionario topografico-storico degli stati estensi* (Topographical-Historical Dictionary of the Este States, Published Posthumously, 1824–1825).

Tiraboschi's major achievement remains the fourteen-volume *Storia della letteratura italiana*. Some critics found it long on erudition and short on analysis. Ugo Foscolo called it "an organized . . . archive of materials . . . [and] documents . . . to serve as a basis for a literary history of Italy." A century later, however, Francesco De Sanctis, the great nineteenth-century literary critic, dubbed Tiraboschi "the Muratori of Italian literature," a designation that would have pleased the Jesuit scholar. One of the major products of eighteenth-century Italian scholarship, Tiraboschi's *Storia* ranks with Muratori's contributions to Italian historiography. Inspired by a desire to make known Italy's cultural achievements, Tiraboschi wrote the history of Italian literature from early times to the eighteenth century. For Tiraboschi, literature and culture were one and the same. Thus he wrote not only the history of literature but about the development of science and institutions and about painting, sculpture, and architecture. What emerged from Tiraboschi's pages was a veritable *Kulturgeschichte* of the Italian people. Volumes 7 and 8, probably the best, covered every aspect of the Italian Renaissance and in many ways anticipated *Die Kultur der Renaissance in Italien* (1860) by the Swiss historian Jakob Burckhardt. In sum, the *Storia* is a work of scrupulous scholarship, brightened by flashes of remarkable insight.

Bibliography: *In commemorazione di Girolamo Tiraboschi*, Modena, 1933–1934; G. Tiraboschi, various works in different editions.

Emiliana Pasca Noether

VALLA, Lorenzo (Rome, 1405/1407–Rome, 1457), Italian humanist. He led a venturesome and precarious life, as roving teacher of liberal arts, in Venice, Piacenza, Pavia, Milan, Genoa, and Florence, never ceasing to aspire after the position of papal secretary, which he finally got in 1448. As secretary of King Alfonso of Naples, he drew up a *Historia Ferdinandi regis Aragoniae* in 1445–1446, which is less of a biography and more of a panegyric. Inclined to the rationalist criticism of superstitions, legends, and errors that were accepted at least as useful if not as true by his contemporaries, Valla was repeatedly persecuted by lay and church authorities, a fact that gave him the posthumous aura of martyr of exact science. Actually, Valla shared almost all prejudices of his time and was ahead of his time only due to his successful effort to restore the written and spoken Latin to the purity and elegance of the classical one (*De elegantia linguae Latinae*, Refined Turns of the Latin Speech, 1444). His epicurean orientation (*De vero bono*, About True Mirth, 1430) and rationalist thinking (*De libero arbitrio*, On Free Will, 1439) earned for him, after his death, the valuation of Erasmus and Luther who, each in his own way, saw him as a forerunner. Valla had anyway the merit to have spurred the free investigation of Bible history (*In Novum Testamentum adnotationes*, Notes on the New Testament, 1449, edited in 1505 by Erasmus), of the church (*Apologia ad Eugenium Pontificem Maximum*, Apology to Pope Eugenius the IVth, 1444–1445), and of the papacy itself (*De falso credita et ementita Constantini donatione,* About the False and Deceitful Gift of Italy to the Pope by Constantine the Great, 1440, ed. 1967). His pioneer work of criticism of textual errors proved very useful in the following centuries of historiographic study, especially *Emendationes VI librorum T. Livii de secundo bello Punico* (Improvements of the False Readings in the Six Books of Livy Upon the Second Carthaginese War, 1447).

Bibliography: G. Antonazzi, "Lorenzo Valla e la Donazione di Costantino nel secolo XV" (Lorenzo Valla and the Donatio Constantini in the 15th Century), *Rivista per la Storia della Chiesa in Italia*, 1950, no. 4; *Opera omnia* (Complete Works), ed. Eugenio

Garin, 2 vols., Turin, 1962; S. J. Camporeale, *Lorenzo Valla. Umanesimo e teologia* (Lorenzo Valla: Humanism and Theology), Firenze, 1972; G. Zippel, "Lorenzo Valla e le origini della storiografia umanista a Venezia" (Lorenzo Valla and the Origins of Humanistic Historiography in Venice), *Rinascimento*, 1950, no. 7.

Radu Constantinescu

VASARI, Giorgio (Arezzo, 1511–Florence, 1574), Italian painter and writer of biographies. He learned painting (1528–1535) and architecture (1535–1539) in Florence and Rome in the studios of Michelangelo's and Andrea del Sarto's pupils. He travelled all over Italy to get an education and especially to make a living when his usual protectors of the Medici family left the capitals of Tuscany or Latium. As an artist he was no better than the common obscure mural painters of the previous century. His chief works are the deeds of Pope Paul III painted on the walls of the palace della Cancellaria in Rome (1546) and the historical and allegoric murals in Palazzo Vecchi (1554) and Galleria degli Uffizzi in Florence (1560). In 1547 he compiled for Paolo Giovio (q.v.) a collection of biographies of the plastic artists from Ciambue and Giotto to Michelangelo. When Giovio gave up the editing of the planned history of the Renaissance art, Vasari published the biographies in 1550 under the title *Le vite de'più eccelenti pittori, scultori e architetti* (The Lives of the Best Painters, Sculptors and Architects). His sources were the technical recommendations and theoretical considerations of Ghiberti, Ghiralandajo, Rafael, and Antonio Filarete's treatise on architecture and especially various local oral traditions, which he reproduces *in extenso*, word by word, sometimes in *oratio recta*. A second edition, in 1568, comprised the biographies of Michelangelo's pupils. Founder, along with Vespasiano da Bisticci, of the history of the arts, Vasari built his work upon the idea of steady progress of aesthetic achievements, defined by the specific baroque criteria of technical progress, agglomeration of graphic space, multiplication of realistic details, and pathetic expressiveness. He was equally the first author that extended the concept of the Renaissance systematically to the arts. Other writings that he left unaccomplished or remained in manuscript were edited only in our century: *Il libro delle ricordanze* (Memory Book), 1927, 1930 and *Zibaldone* (Journal), 1927, especially in the magazine *Il Vasari* put out in Arezzo since 1927. His other theoretical works were re-edited in 1878–1885.

Bibliography: K. Frey, *Der literarische Nachlass Giorgio Vasaris*, Munich, 1923–1930; A. Moschetti, *Giorgio Vasari*, Torino, 1935; *Le vite*, ed. R. Bettarin, 3 vols., Firenze, 1966–1971.

Radu Constantinescu

VETTORI, Francesco (Florence, 1474–Florence, 1539), Italian statesman and historian. Vettori's father, Piero, held important political posts, and Francesco wrote a biography in his honor. In 1503 Francesco Vettori embarked on his political career, beginning in the Collegio de'Dodici and becoming podesta of Castiglion Aretino in 1505. In 1507 he was appointed ambassador to Emperor Maximilian I. He recorded his observation in his *Viaggio in Alamagna*, in which he praised the good qualities of the German people. He was succeeded by Niccolo Machiavelli. He returned to Florence in 1509. In 1511 he represented Florence at the Schismatic Council of Pisa. In 1512 he took part in the coup that returned the Medici to power. He was sent to Rome as orator in 1513 and was there when Giovanni de'Medici was elected pope as Leo X. Although at first suspicious of Vettori's service to the republic, the Medici came to value his service. Vettori even helped arrange the release of Machiavelli from prison for anti-Medicean activities. He returned to Florence in 1515 where he was close to Lorenzo, duke of Urbino. He advised the duke on political and military matters and even helped arrange his marriage to Madeleine de Boulogne. In honor of his patron he composed his biography. Upon the Duke's death he became an adviser to Cardinal Giulio de'Medici (Pope Clement VII in 1525). He composed a *discorso* for the pope on the question of a league between the pope, the Venetians, and the emperor. With the Sack of Rome in 1527 and the temporary eclipse of the Medici, Vettori associated with representatives of other prominent citizens in trying to establish a republic dominated by the wealthy families, but without success. He withdrew from political service and began work on his *Sommario della Istoria d'Italia*. He returned to public service during the seige of Florence in 1529 where he formed part of the embassy to Clement in order to arrange a compromise with the pope. However, this proved impossible and Vettori decided to remain with the pope rather than return to Florence. When the Medici forces reestablished control of the city, Vettori was active in hunting out their enemies. In his *Pareri* he recommended that the city be governed by a duke with a small body of advisers. He had little success, however, in trying to move Duke Alessandro to act wisely. After the murder of Alessandro, Vettori was instrumental in bringing Cosimo de'Medici to power as the new duke. Like his fellow Florentine Francesco Guicciardini (q.v.), he underestimated the independent will of Cosimo. He was deeply affected by the execution of several of his friends, especially Filippo Strozzi, who had tried to overthrow the new ducal regime in 1537. Vettori retired from office in 1538 and died the next year.

Vettori was a friend of Machiavelli and Guicciardini and, like them, he developed a realistic, if not cynical, view of recent Italian history that had a decided influence on how he wrote his own history, *Sommario della Istoria d'Italia* (1511–1527). Like his two friends he had participated in important political events and had had the opportunity to observe how the rulers of Italy had misused their power to destroy its independence. He was at odds both with the secular rulers such as Piero Soderini, the leader of republican Florence, and with the ecclesiastical powers such as the Medici popes. The sad truth for Vettori was that politics could lead to no vision of a good government. Basically, there were only excesses and supressions of one group by another. Thus for Vettori, history had essentially a political meaning, teaching the pervasiveness of evil, tyranny, and the foolishness of people. He did, however, on occasion present his facts in such a way as to support certain republican or pro-French political values. Ultimately for Vettori, as for Machiavelli and in a different manner for Guicciardini, history is politics, and its theme is one of missed opportunities or incompetence or evil.

Bibliography: *Enciclopedia italiana*, vol. 35 (Rome, 1934), pp. 179–280; Giuseppe Giacalone, *Il viaggio in Alamagna di F. Vettori e il miti del Rinascimento* (Siena, 1982); Rosemary Devonshire Jones, *Francesco Vettori: Florentine Citizen and Medici Servant* (London, 1972); idem, "Some Observations on the Relations between Francesco Vettori and Niccolo Machiavelli during the Embassy to Maximilian I," *Italian Studies* 23 (1968): 93–113; Francesco Vettori, *Scritti storici e politici*, ed. Enrico Niccolini (Bari, 1972).

John F. D'Amico

VICO, Giovan Battista or Giambattista (Naples, 1668–? 1744), philosopher, jurist, man of letters, and, above all, historian. Vico lived and worked, with brief absences in the Vatolla, in the city of Naples. His "personality" is strictly bound with the modes in which his thought has been interpreted. Unlike many other world cultural-historical figures, with the possible exception of Friedrich Nietzsche, the combination of richness and complexity of thought, of the clarity of substantive intelligence and the quasi-obscurity of ways of expression, the millennially diachronic influence of his self-admitted four master-guides—Plato, Tacitus (q.v.), Bacon (q.v.), and Grotius (q.v.)—and the relatively synchronic character of his ideal antagonists, chief creators of new world-views that Vico ultimately fiercely combatted in his magnum opus on the "new science" (*La Scienza Nuova*, 1725; 1729; 1744)—all of these things and more contributed to the rise and continue to sustain (despite or perhaps because of the growth of the already incredibly voluminous exegetical literature on his mind, thought, and works) what must be called an exasperatingly challenging "Vico problem." On the one hand, his autobiography (*Vita scritta da sè medesimo*), which was first published in 1728, does not really help to clarify the ambiguities in his intellectual formation, what with his strong bonds with the legacy of the past of his Italian, European, and universalist culture and at the same time the unmistakable "projections," particularly in his major work, into a multiplicity of unexplored fields of vision and new areas for historical understanding. Thus it seems that his autobiography is rather the ideal history of an intellectual reflection on what he had done and what he felt was still to be done in delving into the world of history and not the history of the formation of an intellectual. On the other hand, there are the continual revisions, additions, innovations, contradictions, inquiries, and reevaluations of the whole or parts of his work so that Vico—who had been known by only a handful of local Neapolitan disciples (but Goethe had almost accidentally become an adopted companion!) during the eighteenth century—in the early nineteenth century was "discovered" by Michelet and thereafter became such an integral and active intellectual force that at the beginning of twentieth century Benedetto Croce called Vico "the nineteenth century *in germe*." But the phrase had hardly been launched with all of its implications than he began and has continued to be hailed culturally as "the twentieth century *in germe*." That is, the precursor of nineteenth-century Romanticism, idealism, historicism, and the philosophy of history became the ''anticipator'' and early ''explorer'' of the modern sciences of ethnology, anthropology, the psychology of religions, sociology, psychology, and even psychoanalysis. Year after year two very different Institutes of Vico Studies, one in Naples and the other in New York, issue ''bulletins'' and new publications that deepen and expand the realm of Vichian intellectual influence. This exceptional ''fortune'' of Vico's historical fame ironically underlines the contrast with his professional struggles and modest life in late seventeenth- and eighteenth-century Naples. He was the sixth of seven children of a modest bookseller, and in his own turn he came to have a family of six children by a very humble woman of the people. His education consisted of early exposure and soon rebellion against first the Jesuits, and in due time the no doubt ''sterile'' university courses of his day. At an early age Vico became an autodidact who, almost incredibly, managed to occupy the chair of eloquence or elocution at the University of Naples from 1699 to 1742. In 1735 his modest university stipend was increased through a small pension derived from the honorific title of regius professor of history conferred upon him by the new king of Naples, Carlo of Bourbon.

Vico wrote a series of occasional pieces in both connections, but it was only in the biennium, 1708–1710, that he ''read'' and eventually published his ''orations'' *De nostri temporis studiorum ratione* (On the Reason for the Studies of Our Times) and *De antiquissima italorum sapientia* (On the Ancient Wisdom of the Italians). In these pieces Vico first advanced the typical criterion of the convertibility of the *verum* and the *factum*. The nexus *verum–factum*, though perhaps not completely original with him as a concept, was first formulated as we know it by Vico. His real originality consisted in his transfer of it ''from natural things to civil human things'' and his extension of it to the world of philology and historical erudition. The conceptual nucleus upon which the Vichian ''project'' is founded is now patent and clarified: Humans know only that which they do or make. But it is necessary to define and refine the method of ascertaining and comprehending how the *factum* can lead to the *verum*. Vico thus unveiled the symmetry between the work of God and the work of humans, revealing each of them as as a creator, but he accentuated the latter for many obvious reasons as well as to emphasize the finiteness of human work. His biography of Antonio Carafa (*De rebus gestis Antonii Caraphei*) appeared in 1716, and it is notable for, among other things, both the substantive treatment it contains of European history during the last decades of the seventeenth century and the methodological inclusion of Grotius as the fourth (after Plato, Tacitus, and Bacon) of his master–guides. In 1725 Vico published the first edition of his *Scienza nuova* of which the full title was *Principi di una scienza nuova dintorno alla natura delle nazioni, per la quale si ritruovano i orincipi di altro sistema del diritto naturale delle genti*; its textual structure and span were revised in the second (1729) and also in the third (1744) editions. In all three editions the ''*scienza nuova*'' is history. The ''new science'' based, as Vico said, upon the ''nature of nations'' and ''the principles of the natural right of peoples'' is opposed to the "older" or other "sciences" on the premise that "this civil world has certainly been made by men, wherefrom can be found the principles within the modifications of our own human mind."

Vico read the events of the past, that is, the course of history, through the stages he observed in its development: the age of the gods, with its domination of "*senso*," the senses; the age of the heroes, with fantasy and imagination prevailing; and the age of people, with the prevalence of intellect and reason. Each stage has its own characteristic—in language, modes of expression, religion, state of families, forms of beliefs, types of money, and government. All are developmental stages of a nonlinear evolutionary process not necessarily involving "progress" but organic metamorphosis of historic structures of life, forms of the mind, visions of the world, and, at some point, a fine balance between freedom and reason before a "great change" germinates "times of trouble," convulsive events, anarchic rebellions, and catastrophic blows of destiny and a *ricorso* brings a "new beginning" in the history of societies, peoples, and nations. Thus it is obvious that for Vico the movement of history is driven by a cyclical rhythm, and at the end of the third stage a degenerated "age of men" is mysteriously transformed into an obscure, if pristine, new "age of the gods." Of the societies and civilizations of the past, only the Hebrews have been exempt from this "destiny"—and just as Machiavelli excluded Moses from his judgment on the nature of power, Vico excluded the Hebrews from the secular cycles of his *corsi–ricorsi*. Such is the schematic outline of the novel vision of history that the Vichian "new science" left as a rich and complex legacy to future generations of philosophers; thinkers in the social and psychological sciences; theoreticians of the origins and nature of language, the arts, and systems of politics and society; historians, novelists, and poets; students of myths and symbolic forms; and a succession of bold new seekers of the *verità effettuale* of human vicissitude in history, all of whom at some time, in some fashion, have found Vico's *Scienza nuova* a unique, if often elusive, stupendously inspiring guidebook.

Bibliography: Robert Crease, *Vico in English* (Atlantic Highlands, N. J., 1978); Benedetto Croce and Fausto Nicolini, *Bibliografia vichiana*, 2 vols. (Naples and Milan, 1947–1948); Maria Donzelli, *Contributo alla bibliografia vichiana (1948–1970)* (Naples, 1983); Max Harold Fisch and Thomas Goddard Bergin, eds., *The Autobiography of Giambattista Vico* (Ithaca, N.Y., and London, 1975); Giorgio Tagliacozzo and Hayden V. White, eds., *Giambattista Vico: An International Symposium* (Baltimore, 1969). Since 1970 the Centro di Studi Vichiani of Naples has published a bulletin of publications and articles on Vico.

Eluggero Pii, in collaboration with A.W.S.;
translation by Ilia Salomone-Smith

VILLANI, Giovanni (Florence, c. 1275–Florence, 1348), Italian chronicler. A prominent citizen of his native city, he discharged numerous public and diplomatic missions as an important member of the party of black Guelphs who were allied with the French royalty against the Pope. Starting 1300 and until his death he compiled in twelve books a history of Florence (*Cronaca fiorentina*, Florentine Chronicle, ed. 1844–1847 and 1856–1861), from legendary times to 1346. The first part, spanning the period up to 1265, is a paraphrase of Ricordano Malispini's chronicle, while the second contains valuable historical information. Villani strived to do the job of an historian and not a chronicler, but was not always successful. However, the memoirs are lively and picturesque and his oeuvre served not only as an essential source for the historians of the centuries that followed but also as a model of historical prose in vulgate. Giovanni Villani's work was furthered by his brother Matteo (1285–1363), who produced ten more books covering the years 1348–1363 and by the latter's son, Filippo (d. 1405), who wrote one more book for the period up to 1364 and, in Latin, a *Liber de origine civitatis Florentiae et ejusdem famosis civibus* (Book About the Beginnings of the City of Florence and Its Famous Citizens).

Bibliography: E. Morghen, *Die Weltanschauung des Giovanni Villani*, Leipzig, 1927; idem, *La storiografia fiorentina del Trecento* (Florentine Historiography of the 14th Century), Firenze, 1958.

Radu Constantinescu

Great Historians: Japanese

ARAI Hakuseki (Edo, now Tokyo, 1657–Edo, 1725), Japanese historian and statesman. Son of an obscure masterless samurai, Arai, despite strained circumstances, devoted himself to learning and in 1683 was taken into service by a minor *daimyo* (feudal lord). But with the lord's downfall in 1685 Arai was again unemployed. He then joined the school of Kinoshita Jun'an, an outstanding Confucian scholar of the day, who in 1693 recommended him as tutor to Tokugawa Tsunatoyo, lord of Kôfu and nephew of the childless shogun. When Tokugawa was chosen to succeed as the sixth Tokugawa shogun, reigning as Ienobu (1709–1712), Arai accordingly served as Confucian lecturer and policy adviser to the new shogun, bringing a period of civilian administration often termed "the peaceful era of Shôtoku" (1711–1716). After the early death of Ienobu, and his infant successor in 1716, Arai devoted himself entirely to writing about history, politics, linguistics, and international relations. He set forth his idea of history in *Koshitsû* (Study of Ancient History, 1716): "History is the science of describing historical events based on actual facts, which give lessons to readers and call for their sincere reflection." As a student of the Zhu Xi school of Neo-Confucianism, he was a distinguished positivistic historian, whose methods of rigorous documentation were backed by his critical intellect and strict rationalism. In *Koshitsû* he denied the mythical conception of the "age of the gods," arguing that "gods are nothing but men." He wrote a history of ancient Japan as a history of the human world just when a countermovement was taking shape that accepted literally the accounts of the "age of the gods" in the *Kojiki* and *Nihon shoki* (see Ô no Yasumaro, Prince Toneri, and Motoori Norinaga). In *Tokushi yoron* (Obiter dicta on Reading [Japanese] History, 1712–1716), based on his lectures to Ienobu in 1712 on eighth- to seventeenth-century Japanese history, he discussed the rise of rule by the military class (*samurai*), proposing an original periodization of Japanese history that aimed to justify the legitimacy of warrior governance and the legitimacy of its apotheosis, the Tokugawa shogunate. Arai's most widely read book, *Oritaku shiba no ki* (Told Round a Brushwood Fire, 1716), is considered the first Japanese autobiography. Other historical works include *Hankanfu*, a narrated genealogy of 337 feudal lords (1702), and *Seiyô kibun* (Notes on What I Heard about the West [Europe], 1715), reporting what he learned of Europe from his conversations with Giovanni Battista Sidotti, a captured Jesuit priest.

Bibliography: Joyce Irene Ackroyd, "Arai Hakuseki: Being a Study of His Political Career and Some of His Writings, with Special Reference to the *Hankampu* [Hankanfu]" (Ph.D. diss., University of Cambridge, 1951); *Arai Hakuseki nikki* (Diary), 2 vols. (1952); *Arai Hakuseki zenshû* (Complete Works), 6 vols. (1905–1907); "*Hyô-chû oritaku shiba no ki*: Autobiography of Arai Hakuseki, a scholar, poet, historian, economist, moralist, and statesman of the Eighteenth Century, A.D.," trans. George William Knox, *Transactions of the Asiatic Society of Japan* 30, no. 2 (1902): 98–242; Ulrich Kemper, *Arai Hakuseki und seine Geschichtsauffasung: Ein Beitrah zur Historiographie Japans in der Tokugawa-Zeit* (1967); *Lessons from History: The Tokushi Yoron*, trans. Joyce Ackroyd (1982); Kate Wildman Nakai, "The Political Implications of Arai Hakuseki's Historiography: The Case of *Koshitsû*," in *Transactions of the International Conference of Orientalists in Japan* 26 (1981): 51–63; idem, *Shogunal Politics: Arai Hakuseki and the Premises of Tokugawa Rule*, Harvard East Asian Monographs (1988); idem, "Tokugawa Confucian Historiography: The Hayashi, Early Mito School, and Arai Hakuseki," in Peter Nosco, ed., *Confucianism and Tokugawa Culture* (Princeton, N. J., 1984), pp. 62–91; Herman Ooms, "Hakuseki's Reading of History," in *Monumenta Nipponica* 39, no. 3 (1984): 333–350; Saeki Shôichi, "The Autobiography in Japan," *Journal of Japanese Studies* 11, no. 2 (1985): 357–368; *Told Round a Brushwood Fire: The Autobiography of Arai Hakuseki*, trans. Joyce Ackroyd (1980).

Masayuki Sato

HANAWA Hokiichi (Musashi Province, now Saitama Prefecture, 1746–Edo, now Tokyo, 1821), Japanese historian and historiographer. Son of a farmer in the hinterland of Edo, Hanawa became blind at age five and went to Edo to master acupuncture, a common craft of the blind. But he was set on a career in scholarship and studied *Kokugaku* (national learning, the study of the native classical tradition; see Motoori Norinaga), Japanese history, classics, and ancient institutions, relying on his extraordinary powers of memory. He believed that the study of the past must be based on reliable historical materials, established through careful textual criticism and then pursued with academic sincerity. Realizing the need for a classified collection of reliable texts of Japanese classics and historical documents, he planned publication of the *Gunsho ruijû* (Classified Collection of Japanese Classics and Documents) in 1779, issuing the first volume in 1786. In 1793 he received aid from the shogunate to found the Wagaku Kôdansho (Institute for Japanese Studies), where he continued compiling and publishing the *Gunsho ruijû*. The first series, 1,270 titles in 530 volumes, was completed in 1819; the second series, 2,103 titles in 1,150 volumes, appeared in 1822, after Hanawa's death. *Gunsho ruijû* includes documents from ancient times to the early seventeenth century, classified according to Hanawa's schema into twenty-five categories: Shintôism, emperors, official appointments, genealogies, biographies, official posts, ordinances, public affairs, apparel, literature, letters, poetry, linked-verse poetry, stories, diaries, travelogues, music, football (a court pastime), falconry, pastimes, food and drink, battles, warriors,

Buddhism, and miscellaneous. The classification system is in itself a system of Japanese studies by historical materials. This was the greatest collection of historical source materials in Japan, reaching high standards of bibliographic and philological scholarship, and remains today one of the major reference works for historians, as well as being a forerunner of numerous important modern collections and compendia of historical source materials, particularly the *Dai Nihon shiryô* (Historical Sources of Great Japan, 1900–), *Dai Nihon komonjo* (Historical Documents of Great Japan, 1901–), and other series of the *Shiryô Hensanjo* (Historiographical Institute) founded in 1869 by the Japanese government. From 1789 Hanawa also joined in the compilation of *Dai Nihon shi* (History of Great Japan, 1657–1906), a project founded by Tokugawa Mitsukuni (q.v.). He also compiled *Keiyô shô* (Collection on Foreign Affairs, 1811) and *Shiryô* (Historical Sources, 430 vols., 1808–1821). His conviction that the historian should let historical sources speak for themselves laid the foundation for much subsequent historical scholarship in Japan, where the tradition of extensive quotation of primary sources, even to the point of using a chronological sequence of historical documents as a history—as in the series *Dai Nihon shiryô*—remains strong.

Bibliography: *Gunsho ruijû*, 1st ser., 30 vols. (1959–1960); *Gunsho ruijû* 2d ser., 86 vols. (1957–1972); Onko Gakkai, ed., *Hanawa Hokiichi kenkyû* (Studies on Hanawa Hokiichi) (1981); idem (Society for Hanawa Hokiichi Studies), ed., *Onko sôshi* (Collected Studies on Hanawa Hokiichi), 21 vols. (1932–1965); Ota Yoshimaru, *Jinbutsu sôsho*, vol. 37, *Hanawa Hokiichi* [Biography] [Library of Biographies series] (1966); Sakamoto Tarô, *Koten to rekishi* (Classics and History) (1972).

Masayuki Sato

HAYASHI Razan (Kyoto, 1583–Edo, now Tokyo, 1657), Japanese historian, philosopher, and government adviser. Son of a tradesman, Hayashi entered the Zen monastery as a youth but left to study the rationalized Chinese metaphysics of the Zhu Xi Neo-Confucian school of interpretation of the Chinese classics. In 1605 he entered service with Tokugawa Ieyasu (1542–1616), founder of the Tokugawa shogunate (1603–1867), commencing a lifelong career as house scholar and brain trust for the first four shoguns. He worked for the establishment of the Tokugawa regime as ideologue, propagandist, and drafter of legislation and diplomatic correspondence. In 1630 he founded a school in Edo for the teaching of Zhu Xi's doctrines, which by the end of the eighteenth century were to become state orthodoxy. This school, later named the Shôheikô, in time became the shogunal Confucian academy, although it never had complete doctrinal control. As a historian, Razan compiled the *Kan'ei shoke keizu den* (Kan'ei Period Genealogies of the [Warrior] Houses, 1641–1643) and launched compilation of the *Honchô tsugan* (Comprehensive Mirror of Japan, 1644–1670), both on shogunal orders, and he is sometimes called the Father of Tokugawa Historiography. *Honchô tsugan* was written in classical Chinese and covers the history of Japan from the earliest times to the early seventeenth century, incorporating the *Rikkokushi* (Six National Histories; see Prince Toneri) for the years to A.D. 887 but also delving into the succeeding seven centuries. However, Hayashi's attitude toward history, which is clear in this work, became an *idée fixe* for the remaining two centuries of the Tokugawa period. His conception was essentially Zhu Xi's idea that "when historical events are described as they really were, based on actual facts, the facts speak for themselves of virtues and vices." Hayashi's purpose in compiling his history was to record Japan's periods of war and peace, rise and fall, on the method of Si-ma Guang's (q.v.) *Zu-zi tung-jian* (Comprehensive Mirror for Aid in Government, 1065–1084) and to discuss the virtues and vices of sovereigns and subjects on the method of Zhu Xi's *Zu-zi tung-jian gang-mu* (Comprehensive Mirror . . . Condensed, with introduction by Zhu Xi, n.d.; later compiled by his students). Hayashi tried to establish the Confucian idea of history as a moral lesson and the method of historical compilation based on historical facts, a method that later developed as *kôshôgaku* (historical study based on textual criticism of historical documents). *Honchô tsugan* is little read today but was important as a signal that early modern Japanese historiography would take its models from Neo-Confucianism and as the first work of early modern Japanese historiography not bound by the speculative approaches to history characteristic of medieval Japanese historiography (see Jien; Kitabatake Chikafusa (q.v.)). It encouraged the monumental Mito historical project of Tokugawa Mitsukuni's *Dai Nihon shi* (History of Great Japan, 1657–1906), which was a major ideological force in the middle and late Tokugawa period.

Bibliography: *Hayashi Razan bunshû* (Works of Hayashi Razan), 2 vols. (1930; repr., 1979); *Honchô tsugan* (Comprehensive Mirror of Japan), 18 vols. (1918–1920); Hori Isao, *Hayashi Razan* (Jinbutsu Sosho [Library of Biography]), vol. 18 (1964); Ishida Ichiro, "Hayashi Razan no shisô" (The Thought of Hayashi Razan), in *Nihon Shisô Taikei* ([Compendium of Japanese Thought]. vol. 28: *Fujiwara Seika: Hayashi Razan* [Writings of Fujiwara Seika and Hayashi Razan], ed. Ishide and Kanaya Osamu (1975), pp. 471–489; Kate Wildman Nakai, "Todugawa Confucian Historiography: The Hayashi, Early Mito School, and Arai Haduseki," in Peter Nosco, ed., *Confucianism and Tokugawa Culture* (Princeton, N. J., 1984), pp. 62–91; Ozawa Eiichi, *Kinsei shigaku shisôshi kenkyû* (Studies in the Intellectual History of Early-Modern Historiography) (1974); Ryusaku Tsunoda, Wm. Theodore de Bary, and Donald Keen, comps., *Sources of Japanese Tradition* (1958), pp. 350–361.

Masayuki Sato

JIEN (Kyoto, 1155–Ômi Province, now Shiga Prefecture, 1225), Japanese historian, philosopher of history, poet, court noble, and Buddhist cleric. Jien was the son of imperial regent Fujiwara Tadamichi and the younger brother of imperial regent Kujô Kanezane. The Fujiwara were the most distinguished and powerful noble family of the age, monopolizing the highest offices of state, as well as the right to provide consorts to the imperial line. Jien took orders at the age of thirteen in Enryakuji, the headquarters of the Tendai sect of Buddhism. Favored by his noble birth and family connections, he won rapid promotions, becoming

Zasu (archbishop of the Tendai sect) in 1192 and *Daisôjô* (chief prelate of Japan) in 1203. He is the first philosopher of history in Japan. Living in an age of political upheaval, as the hereditary civil nobility were losing secular political power to a provincial warrior aristocracy, Jien established close relations with the warrior elite, as well as with the nobility of which he was a leading member. He sought Japan's future in a reconciliation between the warriors and the nobility. This idea eventually found historical expression in his major work, *Gukanshô* (Notes of the Views of a Fool, 1220). The work comprises seven volumes: annals of the emperors (1–2); a narrative history of Japan (3–6); and his philosophy of history (7). Jien's most important concept in interpreting history is expressed in the term *dôri* (reason; principle), a manifold concept that here should be understood fundamentally as an idea of historical inevitability based on Buddhist ideas of history. This is not mere fatalism but an idea including arguments on historical causality and the importance of human factors, of a rule of the individual in history. He explained historical processes in terms of the state of development of *dôri* and proposed his own periodization. This enabled him to explain the change of regime in his own age, from nobles to warriors, as a natural expression of *dôri* imminent in the causal process of history. He so desired his history to be interpreted impartially that he published it anonymously and was identified as the author only in 1920 by the historian Miura Hiroyuki. It is generally assumed that his publication of *Gukanshô* was intended to discourage the retired emperor Gotoba (reigned 1183–1198; d. 1239) from attempting a military overthrow of warrior rule and restoration of direct imperial rule, an attempt that would be doomed, in Jien's schema, as contrary to *dôri*. Despite the importance of his philosophical conception of history and historical process, Jien is sometimes purposeful and illogical in explaining historical developments. *Gukanshô* is read by Japanese historians, along with Kitabatake Chikafusa's (q.v.) *Jinnô shôtôki*, as a great statement of a philosophy of history in medieval Japan.

Bibliography: W. G. Beasley, "Japanese Historical Writing in the Eleventh to Fourteenth Centuries," in Beasley and E. G. Pulleyblank, eds., *Historians of China and Japan* (1961), pp. 229–244; *The Future and the Past: A Translation and Study of the Gukanshô*, trans. and intro. by Delmer M. Brown and Ichirô Ishida (1979); Charles Hilton Hambrick, "The *Gukanshô*," *Japanese Journal of Religious Studies* 5, no. 1 (1978): 37–58; idem, "Gukanshô: A Religious View of Japanese History" (Ph.D. diss., University of Chicago Divinity School, 1971); James Armstrong Harrison, ed. and trans., *New Light on Early and Medieval Japanese Historiography* (1960); *Nihon Koten Bungaku Taikei* [Compendium of the Classics of Japanese Literature], vol. 86: *Gukanshô*, ed. Okami Masao and Akamatsu Toshihide (1967); Taga Munehaya, *Jien* (Life of Jien), Jinbutsu Sôsho Library of [Japanese] Biography, vol. 15 (1959).

Masayuki Sato

KITABATAKE Chikafusa (? 1293–Yamato Province, now Nara Prefecture, 1354), Japanese historian, philosopher of history, and major political and military figure in early fourteenth-century Japan, a period of dynastic schism. Born in a noble family that had served the Daikakuji line of emperors for three generations,

Kitabatake placed himself at the service of Emperor Godaigo (reigned 1318–1339), who rewarded him with confidence and high rank and office. In 1336, after the failure of the Kenmu Restoration, Godaigo's attempt to recover power from the warrior class and reinstitute direct imperial rule, Kitabatake aided Godaigo in establishing a separate imperial court (the Southern Dynasty) in Yoshino (near modern Nara). But he was defeated by the Muromachi shogunate (1336–1573), which supported the rival Northern dynasty. Kitabatake is best remembered as the author of *Jinnô shôtôki* (Chronicle of the True Descent of the Divine Sovereigns, c. 1339), which he wrote at Oda Castle in Hitachi (now Ibaraki Prefecture, east of Tokyo), while holding the castle against the enemy. Kitabatake struck his main theme for the entire work in his famous opening line: "Great Japan is the land of the gods," asserting that Japan is a land founded by the gods, that it is a land maintained by the blessings of an unbroken lineage of divinely descended emperors, and that legitimate successors to the imperial throne must succeed and be invested with virtue by historically established procedures. Kitabatake's intention in this is to justify the legitimacy of the Southern dynasty of emperors. *Jinnô shôtôki* covers Japanese history from the age of the gods and the birth of the Japanese islands to Kitabatake's own time. His style resembles that of an annals of the imperial reigns, in that he discussed the merits and demerits of each emperor or empress, their reigns, and the political background to each imperial succession on both a realistic and a moralistic basis, founded on his knowledge of Chinese historical precedents, Confucianism, Buddhism, and Shintoism. Shintô, the indigenous Japanese religion, contrasts with the dominant Buddhist-oriented, pessimistic vision of continuing historical decline, showing instead a constructive, optimistic view of history. He put the dynamics of history in a moral perspective that takes constancy as a given and declines as temporary and correctible, a position implying that the setbacks of the Southern court were themselves corrigible and that the Southern line would at some point recover power from the Muromachi shoguns and the rival Northern imperial line. It is now believed that Kitabatake wrote *Jinnô shôtôki* to persuade warrior leaders in the eastern provinces to support the Southern dynasty, as well as to instruct Emperor Gomurakami (reigned 1339–1368), Godaigo's son and successor.

Although Kitabatake's work had great contemporary political implications, of greater importance is his method of approach to Japanese history through an examination of the imperial successions and their political background. There he pursued a critical analysis showing that virtuous emperors produced prosperous reigns and transmitted the throne to their posterity, whereas emperors who lacked virtue lost the support of their subjects and were deprived of the throne, with succession passing to another member of the imperial family who possessed true virtue. The moral implication of this, *shôri* (right reason), is the nucleus of Kitabatake's theory of "legitimacy." He also noted that the legitimate occupant of the imperial throne must possess the imperial regalia—sword, jewel, and mirror—and argued that the Southern line, which held the regalia, was legitimate, whereas the Northern line were usurpers. (The regalia were transferred to the Northern line in 1392, ending the schism; all subsequent emperors were of the Northern line.) Debate over this theory of "imperial legitimacy" played an important role in the development of Japanese history and historiography. Kitabatake's criteria for determining legitimate imperial succession were adopted by the editors of *Dai Nihon shi* (History of Great Japan, 1657–1906; see Tokugawa Mitsukuni). *Jinnô shôtôki* was long treated as a canonical text of imperial loyalism for nationalist scholars in the later Tokugawa period (see Rai San'yô), and the legitimacy of the Southern dynasty became state orthodoxy from 1911 until after World War II. Apart from having political implications, *Jinnô shôtôki* occupies an important place in the development of speculative, theoretical considerations of Japanese history: Kitabatake placed his own time in the context of history and contemplated the meaning of "now" in historical terms. His work is regarded as a great landmark in the philosophy of history in medieval Japan, along with Jien's (q.v.) *Gukanshô* (1220), which is based on Buddhist ideas of history. Kitabatake wrote other works of history, including *Shokugenshô* (On Ranks and Titles in Japanese History, 1340), but none has been as influential as *Jinnô shôtôki*.

Bibliography: W. G. Beasley, "Japanese Historical Writing in the Eleventh to Fourteenth Centuries," in Beasley and E. G. Pulleyblank, eds., *Historians of China and Japan* (1961), pp. 229–244; *A Chronicle of Gods and Sovereigns: Jinnô Shôtôki of Kitabatake Chikafusa*, trans H. Paul Varley (1980); John Armstrong Harrison, ed., *New Light on Early and Medieval Japanese Historiography* (1960); *Nihon Koten Bungaku Taikei* [Compendium of Classics of Japanese Literature], vol. 87: *Jinnô shôtôki*, ed. Iwasa Tadashi (1965); H. Paul Varley, *Imperial Restoration in Medieval Japan* (1971).

Masayuki Sato

MOTOORI Norinaga (Matsuzaka, 1730–Matsuzaka, 1801), Japanese historian, classical scholar, and philologist. Motoori was the son of a wealthy wholesale merchant in cotton goods. Besides taking lessons in Chinese medicine, he studied both Chinese and Japanese classics in Kyoto, 1752–1757. He returned home in 1757, and although a medical practitioner by vocation, he began an intensive study of the Japanese classics, on which subjects he later began to lecture informally at his residence. Motoori was the scholar who brought the philological study of Japanese classics to its culmination, through which work he mainly searched for the true spirit of the ancient Japanese, undistorted and unembellished by (alien) Buddhism and Confucianism. The Kokugaku (national learning; the textual and exegetical study of Japanese classical histories, literatures, and poems) movement emerged in seventeenth-century Japan, in rivalry with Confucianistic Chinese studies, the dominant academic school at that time. Awakened to the importance of antiquity studies by Ogyû Sorai (q.v.) (1666–1728), sinologist and founder of philological studies of ancient Chinese texts, and by the philological method applied to the Japanese classics by Keichû (1640–1702), founder of Kokugaku, during his six year's stay in Kyoto, Motoori later established his own scholarship—*Kogaku* (ancient studies)—based on a critical adoption of the works and methods of the above two scholars. In 1764, inspired by Kamo no Mabuchi (1697–1769), a Kokugaku scholar and devotee of the "ancient Japanese spirit," Motoori began annotation of the *Kojiki* (Record of Ancient Matters) compiled by O no Yasumaro in A.D. 712, which took him thirty-five years to complete. The fruit of those labors, *Kojiki den* (Annotation of the Records of Ancient Matters, 1790–1822) in forty-four volumes, is his magnum opus, as well as the monumental work of the Kokugaku school. The significance of this achievement cannot be overemphasized: the language of the *Kojiki*, though a form of Japanese, was so archaic and obscure that the meaning of the text had been lost, until Motoori's explications recovered it; thereafter, it became a canonical text in modern Shintô nationalism. Motoori's attitude toward learning was to approach the classics himself, rather than to draw the classics to him, as is clear in this passage: "Classical learning is a study of illuminating the ancient things as they were by direct examination of the classical texts themselves, leaving the subsequent theories aside." His methodological premise was that word, deed, and mind showed themselves linked together but that among the three, word was the most important, because the deeds of the ancients, bequeathed in history, were put into words; "word is tantamount to deed." By elucidating the meanings and expressions of the ancient words, Motoori eventually aimed to throw light on the minds of the ancients and on facts as they were. That was why Motoori chose *Kojiki*: The work contained the records of archaic Japanese language and descriptions of the bounteous life of the ancient Japanese under the gods and their emperor descendants, without reference to moralistic principles, and so was more valuable than *Nihon shoki* (Chronicle of Japan, A.D. 720), the oldest official history of Japan, which was written in classical Chinese (see Prince Toneri). The choice also reflected his sense of revulsion for Chinese ways of thinking and the moralistic Chinese outlook.

Through all of Motoori's works, annotation characterizes his philological method: "When your study advances to a certain degree,—it shall be your next work to annotate the ancient texts: It contributes in every respect to the advancement of your study to make annotation" (Bibliographical studies and text critique were natural byproducts of the process of annotation). But he went too far in identifying what was written in the histories with the facts that actually happened in history and in expounding his vision of the path of duty based on those facts, for he then stepped from the world of learning into the world of faith. In his learning, these two contradictory ideas were unified: an objective and rigorous philological method and an attitude of faith toward ancient Japan. The former contributed to the development of Japanese philology and later produced historians such as Hanawa Hokiichi (q.v.). The latter was elaborated by Hirata Atsutane as the ideological character of nationalism and later used as an ideological frame-work for the emperor-centered nationalism of nineteenth- and twentieth-century Japan. Motoori also proposed a literary theory, developed in his annotational study *Genji monogatari* (Tale of Genji) written by Murasaki

Shikibu (fl. c. 1000) in the early eleventh century, the world's first novel. As opposed to the dominant moralistic Confucian interpretation of literature, Motoori argued that the main object of a novel lay in awakening a sense of pathos, of human feeling, as *mono no aware* (pathos of things and nature); his theory is still seen as a cardinal rule in understanding Japanese literature. Motoori taught more than five hundred students and published more than ninety-one titles in 263 volumes. His works on history include *Tama kushige* (A Fancy Comb Box, 1790) on national administration; *Tama katsuma* (A Basket of Fine Mesh, 1795–1812) on miscellaneous topics of history, literature, and so on; *Ui yamabumi* (First Walk in the Mountains, 1799), a prolegomena to learning; *Gyoju gaigen* (Resentment on Handling Barbarians, 1796) on the history of foreign relations; *Shinreki kô* (On the True Calendar, 1789); *Kokugô kô* (On the Name of a Country, 1787); and *Shokuki rekichô shôshi kai* (Annotation of the Imperial Edicts in *Chronicle of Japan, Continued,* 1803).

Bibliography: H. D. Harootunian, "The Consciousness of Archaic Form in the New Realism of Kokugaku," in Tetsuo Najita and Irwin Scheiner, eds., *Japanese Thought in the Tokugawa Period: Methods and Metaphors* (1978), pp. 63–104; Kobayashi Hideo, *Motoori Norinaga* (Motoori Norinaga) (1977); Maruyama Masao, *Studies in the Intellectual History of Tokugawa Japan* (1974); Matsumoto Shigeru, *Motoori Norinaga: 1730–1801* (1970); *Motoori Norinaga zenshû* (Complete Works), 22 vols. (1968–77); Muraoka Tsunetsugu, *Motoori Norinaga* (Motoori Norinaga), rev. ed. (1928); Sagara Tôru, *Motoori Norinaga* (Motoori Norinaga) (1978); Wolfgang Wernecke, "Moto'ori Norinaga, intellektueller Vertreter der sich entwickelnden burgerlichen Kultur im feudalabsolutischen Japan" (76–71) (1976): 309–319; Yoshikawa Kôjirô, *Motoori Norinaga* (Motoori Norinaga) (1977).

Masayuki Sato

Ô no Yasumaro (? ?–Nara, A.D. 723), Japanese historian and court official of the early Nara period (A.D. 710–794). Ô no Yasumaro is thought to be the son of Ô no Homuji, who distinguished himself in service to the victors in the Jinshin Disturbance of A.D. 672, a major struggle for succession to the imperial throne. Of Ô no Yasumaro's career little is known besides his promotions in court rank and office, honors received, and his work as a historian. In 1979 a coffin and bronze epitaph were unearthed in Nara, recording his name, his place of residence, court rank and title, and his death date. In A.D. 711, on order of Empress Genmei (reigned A.D. 707–715), he transcribed the oral recitations of the court chanter Hieda no Are, who had committed the *Teiki* (Imperial Genealogies) and *Kyûji* (Old Words) to memory. These transcriptions Ô no Yasumaro compiled as the *Kojiki* (Record of Ancient Matters, A.D. 712) in three volumes, Japan's oldest extant work of history. The *Kojiki*, along with the *Nihon shoki* (also known as *Nihongi*, Chronicle of Japan, A.D. 720), are the most important literary sources for the study of archaic (pre-Nara) Japanese history, as well as for the early development of Japanese historiography. *Kojiki* covers Japan's "history" from the mythical "age of the gods" to the early seventh century and contains stories such as the creation of Heaven and earth, the genealogies of the gods and a record of their doings, and the procreation of the Japanese islands by the primordial deity–couple, as well as an imperial genealogy and legends of the acts of heroes from the legendary founding emperor, Jinmu, to the reign of Empress Suiko (A.D. 593–628). Compiled when the Japanese were just beginning to master the Chinese language, Chinese scholarship, and Chinese canons of historiography, as well as to develop an orthography for their own language, the *Kojiki* was intended to justify the origin and history of imperial authority (only secured in the Jinshin Disturbance) and make the Japanese imperial line legitimate by clothing it with an aura of divine ancestry and antiquity and to elucidate the genealogical relations among the powerful clans in reference to the central figure of the emperor. It is in the *Kojiki* that we find the earliest extant form of the myths claiming imperial descent from the sun goddess Amaterasu Omikami.

In style the *Kojiki* is a monumental epic of the Japanese people, a mixture of genealogical and narrative presentation, written in a special form of mixed *kanbun* (classical Chinese) that mingles Chinese readings and grammar with the use of Chinese characters to render the phonetic or morphemic values of the archaic Japanese language. Consequently, the *Kojiki* is in a language unique to itself and is extremely difficult to decipher. Although the physical text survived continuously, its meaning was lost until the monumental work of Motoori Norinaga (q.v) (1730–1801), who, awakened to the importance of antiquity by the work of Ogyû Sorai (q.v), recovered the language of the *Kojiki* and the meaning of the text by application of the philological ideas of Keichû (1640–1701), a founder of the Kokugaku (national learning, as distinct from ''Chinese'' learning) school. Thereafter, the *Kojiki* was gradually transformed into a nationalistic religious text, the literal, fundamentalistic interpretations of which were in part responsible for the rise of the emperor-centered nationalism of nineteenth- and early twentieth-century Japan. On the other hand, modern scholarship, especially that of Tsuda Sôkichi, has shed much critical light on the *Kojiki* from an academic viewpoint. Since World War II the *Kojiki* has been dissected by manifold scholarly disciplines, including mythology, ethnology, folklore studies, linguistics, and history, as a valuable source for the history of ancient Japan. Ô no Yasumaro is also believed to have participated with Prince Toneri in the compilation of the *Nihon shoki*.

Bibliography: *Kojiki*, trans. and anno. by Donald L. Philippi (1968); *Kojiki; or, Records of Ancient Matters*, 2d ed., trans. Basil Hall Chamberlain, with notes by W. G. Aston (1918); *La mitologia giaponese: seconda il I libro del Koziki*, Rafaele Pettazzoni, prefazione introd. e note (1929); *Le Kojiki (Chronique des choses anciennes)*, Masumi et Maryse shibata, introduction, traduction integrale, et notes (1969); Masao Yaku, *The Kojiki in the Life of Japan* (1969); *Nihon Shisô Taikei Kojiki* (Compendium of Japanese Thought), vol. 1, ed., Aoki Kazuo, Ishimoda Shô, Kobayashi Yoshinori, and Saeki Arikiyo (1982).

Masayuki Sato

OGYÛ Sorai (Edo, now Tokyo, 1666–Edo, 1728), Japanese historian, Confucian philosopher, and political theorist. Son of a physician to the shogun, at fourteen Ogyû moved to Kazusa Province (now Chiba Prefecture) with his exiled father and stayed there for twelve years, absorbed in study. On returning to Edo, he entered the service of Yanagisawa Yoshiyasu, the shogun's intimate and chief adviser, in 1696 and in this capacity sometimes served as an unofficial brain trust for the shogun. In 1709 he started a private academy, Ken'en, where he educated many disciples who came to be known as the Ken'en school. Among his most important works are *Yakubun sentei* (Aids to Translation, 1711); *Ken'en zuihitsu* (Miscellaneous Writings of Ken'en, 1714); *Bendô* (Distinguishing the Way, 1717?); *Benmei* (On Distinguishing Names, 1717?); *Rongo chô* (Commentaries on the *Analects* of Confucius, 1718?); *Taiheisaku* (A Policy for Great Peace, 1719?–1722?); *Seidan* (Discourses on Government, 1727?); *Sorai sensei tômonsho* (Master Sorai's Letters in Response to Questions, 1727); and *Gakusoku* (Instructions for Students, 1727). One of the greatest men of ideas and letters in early modern Japan, Sorai was a firm historicist, his conception of history best expressed in this passage: "Since it is the extending of our hearing and vision that we call scholarship, scholarship reaches its pinnacle in history" (*Sorai sensei tômonsho*). He was not so much a writer of history as a great interpreter of history, which was the primary concern and the focus of study and work for most scholars in early modern Japan. To "learn history" was not to explore the facts of the past per se but rather to become conversant with the historical books of the successive Chinese dynasties and to make them thoroughly and completely one's own.

Most scholars in early modern Japan could be called historians in some sense, because even those Chinese classics that were not overtly "historical" were filled with reference to historical events, rather than with abstractions, which the scholar then had to interpret and from which he had to extract meaning. On the necessity of such interpretive history, Sorai stated that "the path into scholarship is a knowledge of one's letters, and for this one should employ the study of history . . . . For [histories] contain the facts of the successive dynasties, the Way for governing the country, the facts of the [great] military campaigns and the goings-on of the world at peace, as well as the accomplishments of loyal ministers and dutiful officials. Rather than [merely] hearing about Principle [governing the world], nothing will move one like observing the effects [of actions and events, through reading history]" (*Taiheisaku*). Believing that the mere reconstruction of the facts of the past was not the first purpose of history, Sorai cast his net widely in works ancient and modern as the basis of his many works. Most were overtly on subjects in philosophy, politics, or linguistics, but underlying all of them his ideas about the interpretation of history are clearly visible. This is also explicit in his definition of his own scholarship as that of *Fukko gaku* (classical study through a return to the original ancient texts rather than studying the later commentaries). His methodology of returning to original texts encouraged a concern for philology and linguistics, techniques necessary for the recovery of the meaning of ancient texts in their own time, which provoked a transformation of historical methodology in eighteenth- and nineteenth-century Japan (see Motoori Norinaga [q.v.]. Sorai opposed the Neo-Confucian idea that the purpose of history was moralistic, to encourage good and punish evil (see Arai Haduseki [q.v.]). Rather, his view of history is summed up in the phrase "actions speak louder than words."

Bibliography: Olof Lidin, *The Life of Ogyû Sorai: A Tokugawa Confucian Philosopher* (1973); idem, trans., *Ogyû Sorai: Distinguishing the Way (Bendô)* (1970); idem, trans., *Ogyû Sorai's Journey to Kai in 1706: A translation of the Kyôchûkikô* (1983); Masao Maruyama, *Studies in the Intellectual History of Tokugawa Japan* (1975); J. R. McEwan, *The Political Writings of Ogyû Sorai* (1962); Richard Minear, trans., "Ogyû Sorai's Instructions for Students: A Translation and Commentary," *Harvard Journal of Asiatic Studies* 36 (1976): 5–81; *Ogyû Sorai zenshû* (Complete Works) (1973-); Samuel Hideo Yamashita, "Nature and Artifice in the Writings of Ogyû Sorai (1666–1728)," in Peter Nosco, ed., *Confucianism and Tokugawa Culture* (Princeton, N. J., 1984), pp. 62–91.

Masayuki Sato

TOKUGAWA Mitsukuni (Mito, 1628–Hitachi, 1700), Japanese historian, historical compiler, and feudal lord. Grandson of Tokugawa Ieyasu, founder of the Tokugawa shogunate (1603–1867), Tokugawa Mitsukuni became second lord of the Mito domain (reigned 1661–1690). Laying great stress on civil administration, he won fame as a benevolent ruler, a reputation he enjoys today in popular lore. A devotee of the Zhu Xi school of Neo-Confucianism, he made himself a master of learning, employing as his teacher Zhu Shun-shui, a scholar who fled China at the fall of the Ming dynasty (1368–1644) rather than serve a new dynasty. Tokugawa's greatest historical work was launching the *Dai Nihon shi* (History of Great Japan, 1657–1906), a monumental work of early modern Japanese historical scholarship that involved dozens of scholars over two and a half centuries and had immense influence thereafter on both Japanese historical scholarship and ideology (see Kitabatake Chikafusa [q.v.]). As set forth in Mitsukuni's epitaph, "He [made manifest] the legitimacy of the Imperial Line, discussed the rights and wrongs (committed by) subjects, collected [these facts], and established himself as an authority." His intention in compiling the *Dai Nihon shi* was to define the relations of sovereign and subjects in Japanese history from the Neo-Confucian viewpoint of history as a moral lesson, in rivalry with *Honchô tsugan* (Comprehensive Mirror of Japan, 1644–1670), compiled by Hayashi Razan (q.v.) on shogunal order. In 1657 he established the Historical Bureau in Edo, to which he invited many distinguished historians. The bureau was renamed the *Shôkôkan* (Hall of Elucidation [of the Past] and Consideration [of the Future]) and was moved to Mito in 1829. The history is written in *kanbun* (classical Chinese) and is organized in the style of Chinese standard history (*zheng-shi*), epitomized in Si-ma Qian's (q.v.) *Shi-ji* (Records of the Grand Historian, c. 92–89 B.C.), comprising four parts: imperial annals, tables, treatises, and biographies.

On the premise that historical research should be carried out on the basis of accurate historical materials, Tokugawa concentrated his efforts on locating, gathering, and accumulating historical materials, criticizing them textually, and ascertaining accurate historical evidence. In this effort, he even sent inquiries overseas, seeking information from Chosön (Yi dynasty Korea) and probably from Qing (China) as well on Japanese who were known to have traveled abroad in prior centuries. Tokugawa attached great importance to objectivity in historical description, to narrating historical events, as it were, without editorializing, and indicated his sources in each article. Since the focus was constantly on the clarification of imperial legitimacy and of moral rectitude as mirrored in historical events themselves, the Mito historical project started by Tokugawa had a great impact on the Tokugawa-period rediscovery of the emperor as the center of Japanese loyalty. Tokugawa himself is said to have decided to adopt the position of Kitabatake Chikafusa's *Jinnô shôtôki* (Chronicle of the True Succession of the Divine Sovereigns, 1339), that in the dynastic schism of the midfourteenth century the Southern line was legitimate, and the Northern line were usurpers, a choice he was forced to by the Confucian principle that "In Heaven there are not two suns; on earth there are not two kings" (*Zhou-li* [Book of Rites]). When the state reviewed public school textbooks in 1911, this position became state orthodoxy and remained so until after World War II. Both in this manner, through force of intellect and evidence, in decisions on matters of historical interpretation, and by producing a large number of distinguished historians and scholars, including Hanawa Hokiichi (q.v.), who are collectively known as the Mito school, Tokugawa's historical project had a far-reaching influence on the movement for the restoration of imperial rule in the midnineteenth century and on the direction of Japanese ideology and historiography well into the twentieth century.

Bibliography: W. G. Beasley and Carmen Blacker, "Japanese Historical Writing in the Tokugawa Period (1603–1868)," in Beasley and E. G. Pulleyblank, eds., *Historians of China and Japan* (1961), pp. 245–263; *Dai Nihon shi* (History of Great Japan), 17 vols. (1928–1929); *Mito Gikô zenshû* (Complete Works of Mito Gikô [Tokugawa Mitsukuni]), 3 vols., ed. Tokugawa Kuniyuki (1970); Kate Wildman Nakai, "Tokugawa Confucian Historiography: The Hayashi, Early Mito School, and Arai Hakuseki," in Peter Nosco, ed., *Confucianism and Tokugawa Culture* (Princeton, N. J., 1984), pp. 62–91; Fritz Opitz, "Tokugawa Mitsukuni: ein Staatsmann der frühen Edo-Zeit," in Lydia Brill and Ulrich Kemper, ed., *Asien: Tradition und Fortschrift; Festschrift für Horst Hammitzsch zu seinen 60* (1971), pp. 458–467; Herschel Webb, "What Is *Dai Nihon shi?" Journal of Asian Studies* 19, no. 2 (1960): 135–150.

Masayuki Sato

TONERI, Prince (Asuka, A.D. 676–Nara, A.D. 735), Japanese historiographer, imperial prince, and court official of the early Nara period (A.D. 710–794). Toneri was the fifth son of Emperor Tenmu (reigned, A.D. 672–686). As a leading member of the imperial family, he took an active role in administration in the 710s, a period of unrest and power struggle between the imperial family and court nobility. In A.D. 720 he rose to the post of Chidajô kanji, the highest ministerial post, and assumed political leadership of the imperial family. His son, Prince Ôi, was enthroned as Emperor Junnin (reigned A.D. 758–764). In A.D. 720 Toneri, as chief compiler, presented to the court the completed *Nihon shoki* (also known as *Nihongi*, Chronicles of Japan), in thirty volumes, including one genealogical chart. Compilation commenced in A.D. 681 on Tenmu's orders. *Nihon shoki* is the oldest official history of Japan, the first of the six official histories known collectively as the *Rikkokushi* (Six National Histories), that covers the history of Japan from the mythical creation of the world to A.D. 887. *Nihon shoki* covers the period from the ''Age of the Gods'' to the end of the reign of Empress Jitô (A.D. 686–697), in chronological order, in annalistic form. As a leading political figure, Toneri took this work, a state history of Japan, not merely as a chronicle of the emperors and the imperial household but as an enterprise of national importance. Since the imperial house had over the last century been actively unifying Japan and building a centralized, imperial state on the Tang Chinese model, Toneri used the history as a forum to establish Japanese national identity and consciousness, symbolized in the use of the word *Nihon* (Japan) in the title. In these terms, *Nihon shoki* is in marked contrast to the *Kojiki* (Record of Ancient Matters, A.D. 712) completed eight years earlier under Ô no Yasumaro (q.v), in response to the Empress Genmei's order of A.D. 711. Whereas the *Kojiki* is a transcription of oral traditions in form, and a complex mixture of Chinese and Japanese in its language, *Nihon shoki* employed the style of the imperial chronicle, written in pure classical Chinese and modeled on the chronicle format (Chinese, *ji*; Japanese, *ki*) of Chinese historiography. There is some debate as to whether Toneri originally intended to complile a *Nihon sho* (Book of Japan), following the style of Chinese standard history (*zheng-shi*) in the full four-part format of the classified history (*Ji-chuan-ti*: imperial annals, tables, treatises, biographies), and only completed the *ki (ji* in Chinese; imperial annals) section; or whether he intended only to compile an imperial chronicle (*Nihongi*) from the start. Besides using the *Teiki* and *Kyûji* on which the *Kojiki* was based, Toneri also collected a wide range of other source materials, including Chinese and Korean histories, as well as diaries and notes of court officials and Buddhist priests.

Toneri's attitude toward the compilation was objective: when various accounts existed, he enumerated them and left the judgment to his readers. However, it still contains embellished narratives and inaccurate dates. Unlike Ô no Yasumaro's *Kojiki*, *Nihon shoki* attempts to assign precise dates to most events after the mythic founding of the Japanese empire by the ''first emperor'' Jinmu, purportedly on the lunar New Year's Day, 660 C., to underscore the antiquity of Japanese history. Although unreliable in its earlier chapters, *Nihon shoki's* veracity increases toward the later period. It has been read and studied widely by intellectuals since its compilation, with abundant commentaries appearing from the thirteenth century on; academic research began in the Edo period (1603–1868), and modern critical study began in the early twentieth century, with the work of Tsuda Sôkichi. However, after the Meiji Restoration (1868), the *Nihon shoki* was used politically to justify the emperor-centered nationalism that underlay the rise of Japanese imperialism until the end of World War II. After the *Nihon Sandai jitsuroku* (Veritable Records of the Three Reigns in Japan, A.D. 901), last of the *Rikkokushi*, the practice of officially sanctioned imperial cult lapsed until the Meiji period (1868–1912), although the ideal survived. (See Hayashi Razan [q.v.]; Tokugawa Mitsukuni [q.v.].) Official historiography and historical compilation formed the central core around which Japanese history and historical studies developed, in marked contrast to the traditions of European historiography.

Bibliography: *Japanische Annalen, A.D. 592–697*, trans. Karl Florenz (1935); *Japanische Mythologie*, trans. Karl Florenz (1901); *Kronika Japan*, trans. Kyuiti Nohara (1935); *Nihon Koten Bungaku Taikei* (Compendium of Classics of Japanese Literature), vols. 67, 68: *Nihon Shoki*, ed. Sakamoto Tarô et al., (1967); *Nihongi, Chronicles of Japan from the Earliest Times to A.D. 697*, trans. W. G. Aston (1896; repr., 1972); G. W. Robinson, "Early Japanese Chronicles: The Six National Histories," in W. G. Beasley and E. G. Pulleyblank, eds., *Historians of China and Japan* (1961), pp. 213–228.

Masayuki Sato

Great Historians: Jewish

JOSEPHUS, Flavius (Jerusalem, c. A.D. 38–Rome? c. A.D. 100), Jewish historian. Josephus' writings are unquestionably the most important source for the history of the Jews during the turbulent years of the first century A.D. Josephus lived among Pharisees, Sadducees, and Essenes and thus possessed firsthand knowledge of the three main Jewish sects of the period. He was well educated and knew Hebrew, Aramaic, and Greek. Josephus was intimately involved in the events he related; he served as an emissary of the Jews to Rome (A.D. 64) and as commander in Galilee during the Jewish revolt against Rome (A.D. 66–67). After the war he settled in Rome, became a citizen, and, under the patronage of the emperors, wrote his vast corpus of material. All of his extant writings are in Greek and were intended mainly for the non-Jewish world of the Roman Empire. Josephus' first book was *The Jewish War* (c. A.D. 78), presenting in great detail the aforementioned revolt. Although certain biases may be detected, the account is generally credible and is remarkable for its drawing on the author's personal participation and observation of the events described. Josephus' next work, his longest, was *Jewish Antiquities* (c. A.D. 94), chronicling the history of Judaism, from God's creation of the world to the author's own period. As such, much of this work parallels the Bible, which naturally served as a prime source. Other sources include various Hellenistic writers, both Jewish and non-Jewish, and haggadic traditions that very often resurface in later rabbinic collections. Josephus' last two books, both much shorter than the first two, were written as retorts to other writers. *Life* (c. A.D. 94), which appeared as an appendix to *Jewish Antiquities*, is an autobiography that responds to the accusation of Justus of Tiberias that the historian was anti-Roman. *Against Apion* (c. A.D. 98) refutes the anti-Jewish rhetoric of Apion of Alexandria and upholds Judaism as a morally and ethically superior religion. Collectively, these works make Josephus the most important Jewish historian of the premodern era. Without him our knowledge of the first century B.C. to first century A.D. period of Jewish history would be extemely poor. Ironically, however, Josephus had little impact on later generations of Jews. First, many of his coreligionists considered him a traitor and pro-Roman. Second, his books are in Greek, a language that only a few Jews continued to use after the Greco-Roman period. (Actually, *The Jewish*

War appeared first in Aramaic, but this original was soon lost.) Fortunately, his writings were preserved by the Church, which considered them a valuable source on the epoch that produced nascent Christianity.

Bibliography: H. W. Attridge, "Josephus and His Works," in M. E. Stone, ed., *Jewish Writings of the Second Temple Period* (Aasen, Netherlands, 1984), pp. 185–232; L. H. Feldman, *Josephus and Modern Scholarship, 1937–1980* (Berlin, 1984); H. St. J. Thackeray, R. Marcus, and L.H. Feldman, *Josephus*, Loeb Classical Library (Cambridge, Mass., 1926–1965).

Gary A. Rendsburg

Great Historians: Korean

AN Chŏng-bok (? 1712–? 1791), Korean historian. An Chŏng-bok was a student of Yi Ik, leader of the *sirhak* (practical learning) movement. Although he sometimes served in government posts, including that of county magistrate and the office of tutor to the crown prince, An Chŏng-bok is widely known for his innovative historical scholarship. Identified with the School of Practical Learning that gained prominence in the eighteenth and nineteenth centuries, he authored several important books, such as *Imgwan Chŏng'yo* (Magistrates' Handbook) and *Yŏlcho t'onggi* (Comprehensive Record of Successive Reigns [of the Yi Dynasty]). As many of his friends and associates accepted or became interested in Catholicism, he wrote *Ch'ŏnhak ko* (Critique of Catholicism) and *Ch'ŏnhak mundap* (Questions and Answers on Catholicism) criticizing Christianity from the Neo-Confucian standpoint. He is best known, however, for his historical work *Tongsa kangmok* (Outline of Korean History). Completed in 1778, *Tongsa kangmok* gives a full chronological treatment of Korean history from the legendary founding of Korea by Tan'gun (traditionally dated as 2333 B.C.) to the fall of Koryŏ (founded A.D. 918) in 1392. As the title suggests, An Chŏng-bok used Ju Xi's *Zi-zhi tong-jian gang-mu* (Outline of [Si-ma Guang's, q.v.] *Comprehensive Mirror for Aid in Government*) as a model and applied the Neo-Confucian principle of the rectification of names in his narration of history. He wrote in the preface: "The great principle all historians should adhere to is to establish clearly the legitimate lines in dynastic succession, to render a strict account of rebels and usurpers, to distinguish right from wrong, to extol and reward the virtues of loyalty and fidelity, and to provide clear chronicles of laws and institutions." For An Chŏng-bok, history was not only an aid to government but also an instrument of moral lessons for posterity. Based on painstaking research, *Tongsa kangmok* comprises seventeen sections of main text and four separate sections of addenda. Of particular interest are the addenda, in which he gave a careful analysis of controversial issues in Korean history, such as the lengendary founders Tan'gun and Kija and the geographical boundaries of various historical states, demonstrating his acumen as a historian.

Bibliography: Kim Ch'ŏl-chun, "Tongsa kangmok," in *Han'guk ŭi myŏnqjo* (Great Books of Korea) (Seoul 1969); Kim Sa-ŏk, "An Chŏng-bok ŭi yŏksagwan kwa kŭŭi choguk yŏksa p'yŏnsa e taehayŏ'' (On An Chŏng-bok's View of History and His Compilation of the History of the Fatherland), *Yŏksa Kwahak* (Historical Science), nos. 5–6 (1965); Hwang Wŏn-gu, ''An Chŏng-bok: New Discovery of Korean History,'' *Korea Journal* 13, no. 1 (January 1973).

Yŏng-ho Ch'oe

IRYŎN (Kyŏngsan, 1206–? 1289), Korean historian. A noted Buddhist monk and scholar, Iryŏn received the title of great mentor of Sŏn (Zen) in 1259 and the national preceptor (*kuksa*) in 1283 under the Koryŏ dynasty (918–1392). Although he wrote many commentaries on Buddhism, he is best known for his historical work *Samguk yusa* (Memorabilia of the Three Kingdoms), which he compiled around 1281. Along with Kim Pu-sik's (q.v.) *Samguk sagi* (History of the Three Kingdoms, 1145), the *Samguk yusa* is the only extant history of Korea composed before the Yi dynasty (1392–1910). Because the *Samguk yusa* and the *Samguk sagi* cover the same period, from antiquity to the fall of the Silla dynasty in A.D. 935, and because they are the oldest extant histories of Korea, these two works have inevitably been compared and contrasted with each other. Whereas the *sagi* is an ''official history'' compiled under state sponsorship and strongly reflects the orthodox Confucian tradition, the *yusa* is the work of a private individual with a Buddhist world-view. Iryŏn made an exhaustive search of historical records and often made careful notes of the sources he used. What he did in the *yusa,* however, was not to write a systematic or comprehensive history but to record tales and anecdotes that are not included in the *Samguk sagi*. Divided into nine sections, the *Samguk yusa* records mostly founding myths, supernatural stories of historical incidents, and Buddhist accounts of various kinds. In contrast to Kim Pu-sik's rational approach to history, Iryŏn's *yusa* abounds in stories of wonders and miracles that defy rational explanation, beginning with the legend of Tan'gun, the mythical founder of Korea. These tales and stories nevertheless take us back to the world of folk beliefs, superstitions, legends, and myths in ancient Korea. *Samguk yusa* is also an invaluable source of ancient Korean literature since it records fourteen *hyangga* (old Korean songs) out of only twenty-five that have survived.

Bibliography: Ch'oe Nam-sŏn, ''*Samguk yusa* haeje (Introduction to *Samguk yusa*),'' *Kyemyŏng* (Enlightenment) 18 (1927); Kim T'ae-yŏng, ''*Samguk yusa* e poinŭn Iryŏn ŭi yŏksa insik e taehayŏ'' (On Historical Perception of Iryŏn as Reflected in *Samguk yusa*), in Yi U-sŏng and Kang Man-gil, eds., *Han'guk ŭi yŏksa insik* (Perceptions of History in Korea), vol. 1 (Seoul, 1977); Ilyŏn (Iryon), *Samguk Yusa: Legends and History of the Three Kingdoms of Ancient Korea,* trans. Tae-Hung Ha and Grafton K. Mintz (Seoul, 1972); Yi Ki-baek, ''*Samguk yusa* ŭi yŏksa chŏk ŭi'ŭi''(Historiographical Significance of *Samguk yusa*), in Yi U-sŏng and Kang Man-gil, eds., *Han'guk ŭi yŏksa insik* (Perceptions of History in Korea), vol. 1 (Seoul, 1977).

Yŏng-ho Ch'oe

KIM Pu-sik (? 1075–? 1151), Korean historian and official of the Koryŏ dynasty (918–1392). Kim Pu-sik was in charge of compiling the *Samguk sagi* (History of the Three Kingdoms). First published 1145, the *Samguk sagi* is the oldest extant history of Korea, covering the period from the legendary beginning of the Three Kingdoms period in 56 B.C. through the fall of Unified Silla in A.D. 935. This is also the only history that treats Korea's ancient history systematically and comprehensively. Compiled under state auspices, the *sagi* is official history, in the tradition of China's dynastic histories. Modeled on Si-ma Qian's (q.v.) *Shi-ji*, it comprises four parts—*pon'gi* (annals), *yŏnp'yo* (tables), *chi* (treatises), and *yŏlchŏn* (biographies). Intending to preserve accurate records of Korean history, Kim Pu-sik used some 123 historical sources, both Korean and Chinese, in compiling the *sagi*. One basic principle that guided him in the compilation of the *sagi* was to bring out "the good and wicked acts of rulers, the loyalty and evil-doing of subjects, the safety and perils of the state, and the peaceful and rebellious acts of the people," which he intended to provide lessons for posterity. This praise-and-blame concept of history well suited the Confucian Kim, who frequently injected his own moralistic assessments of historical issues into the text. Although, along with *Samguk yusa* (Memorabilia of the Three Kingdoms) by Iryŏn (q.v.), the *Samguk sagi* is one of Korea's two most important historical sources, Kim Pu-sik has come under severe criticism from nationalistic Korean historians in the twentieth century. They charge that he accepted a China-centered world-view in his approach to history, to the detriment of Korean interests, and that his Confucian rationalism led him to obliterate or misrepresent native Korean traditions to suit his own Confucian temperament. There are others, however, who defend Kim on the grounds that there is no clear evidence of obliteration or misrepresentation in the *sagi* and that whatever deficiencies may be found in the text are due more to the limited sources available to the author at the time of compilation than to any deliberate attempt on Kim's part to narrate history in a way distorted by his own world-view.

Bibliography: John C. Jamieson, "The *Samguk sagi* and the Unification Wars," (Ph.D. thesis, University of California, Berkeley, 1969); Kim Ch'ŏl-chun, "Koryŏ chunggi ŭi munhwa ŭisik kwa sahak ŭi sŏnggyŏk" (Cultural Consciousness and the Historiographical Character of Mid-Koryŏ), in Ye U-sŏng and Kang Man-gil, eds., *Han'guk ŭi yŏksa insik* (Perceptions of History in Korea) (Seoul, 1977); Ko Pyŏng-ik, "*Samguk sagi* e issŏso ŭi yoHksa sŏsul" (Historical Narration in the *Samguk sagi*), in Ye U-sŏng and Kang Man-gil, eds., *Han'guk ŭi yŏksa insik* (Perceptions of History in Korea) (Seoul, 1977).

Yŏng-ho Ch'oe

SO Kŏ-jŏng (? 1420–? 1488), Korean government official, writer, and historian. A successful candidate in the higher civil service examination in 1444 and in 1451 named doctor in the Hall of Worthies (Chiphyŏnjŏn), the royal institute for scholarly research founded by King Sejong (reigned 1418–1450), So Kŏ-jŏng served in various government posts until 1464, when he was concurrently appointed the director (*Taejehak*) of both the Office of Special Counselors (Hong-mungwan) and the Office of Royal Decrees (Yemungwan), the two most prestigious posts for men of literary reputation. Widely regarded as the foremost literary personality of his time, So Kŏ-jŏng compiled in 1478 the *Tongmunsŏn*

(Anthology of Korean Literature), a multivolume selection of poetry and prose written by Koreans in classical Chinese. In 1481 he was a member of the editorial board that compiled *Tongguk yŏji sŭngnam* (Geographical Survey of Korea), a work of great importance on historical, cultural, and economic geography. He then headed the editorial board for the compilation of *Tongguk t'onggam* (Comprehensive Mirror of Korea), which was completed in 1485; his fame as a historian is associated with this work. The *t'onggam*, modeled on the *zi-zhi tong-jian* (Comprehensive Mirror for Aid in Government) of Si-ma Guang (q.v.), the Song-dynasty Chinese historian, is the first overall history of Korea from its ancient beginning through the fall of the Koryŏ dynasty in 1392. It follows the annalistic (*p'yŏnnyŏn*) format. Because its compilation was sponsored by the state, the *t'onggam* is regarded as an "official history." Compiled at a time when Neo-Confucianism was on the rise, the *t'onggam* reflects strongly the Neo-Confucian approach to history, as in So's statement in the preface that one of the editorial principles he followed was "to punish evil and to reward good . . . so that mistakes of the past may become warnings for the future." Subscribing to the notion that Neo-Confucian morality was absolute and was universally valid at all times, the compilers of the *t'onggam* did not hesitate to apply their moralistic values in rendering judgment on past events, frequently inserting editorial statements in the form of "the historian comments that . . . " Based largely on other secondary works, the *t'onggam* is a distillation of general Korean history emphasizing the practical aspects of governmental affairs. As such, it records many precedents that could be used as a convenient aid both for monarchs and for state officials in their government duties.

Bibliography: Chŏng Ku-bok, "*Tongguk t'onggam* e taehan sahaksa chŏk koch'al" (Historiographical Examination of *Tongguk t'onggam*), *Han'guksa yŏn'gu* (Journal of Korean History) 21–22 (1978); Han Yŏng-u, *Chosŏn chŏn'gi sahaksa yŏn'gu* (Study of the History of Historiography in the Early Chosŏn Dynasty) (Seoul, 1981).

Yŏng-ho Ch'oe

Great Historians: Polish

BIELSKI, Marcin (original surname, Wolski) (Biała pod Pajączrem, c. 1495–Biała pod Pajączrem, 1575), man of letters, poet, and historian; one of the founders of literature in the Polish language; adherent of the Reformation. Mainly self-taught, Wolski availed himself of the library and personal contacts at the court of Piotr Kmita (c. 1477–1553), who established at Wiśnicz an important center of Renaissance culture. Next, after a longer stay in Cracow, Bielski settled in Biała (adopting thereafter the surname Bielski) about 1540 and dedicated himself to literary work. Not all his texts have been preserved. The earliest known is his translation (from Czech) of Burley's *Vitae philosophorum,* entitled by Bielski as *Żywoty filozofów, to jest mędrców nauk przyrodniczych* (Lives of Philosophers, That Is, Sages Versed in Natural Science, 1535), which was the first Polish collection of biographies of lay personalities and the first outline of a history of philosophy. Later, in 1551 he saw the appearance of his most important work, which contributed to Bielski's being treated as a historian (rather than a chronicler), namely, the comprehensive *Kronika wszystkiego świata* (Chronicle of the Whole World). It is worth noting that the second edition, dated 1554, was considerably expanded, which shows that the author worked on it intensively. In the old Polish literature the *Chronicle* is the only work (except for handbooks of history dating from the eighteenth century) of universal history (from the creation of the world until Bielski's time). It was a compilation from various chronicles in which the principle of criticism was not yet applied, and as such it did not rise above the level of analogous works in other European countries. Bielski was an excellent satirist with a fine sense of observation. He was the author of the first Polish morality play and also the first Polish man of letters interested in the life of the burghers. He was thus a pioneer in many fields, of which historiography was only one. He did not leave great works, but what he wrote has had its place in the history of Polish literature and historiography. He was imitated by his son Joachim (Biała, c. 1540–Cracow, 1599), royal secretary from 1588. He based his work on the book of his father's *Chronicle* that pertained to Poland; he revised it thoroughly, supplied addenda, and published it in 1597 as *Kronika Polska Marcina Bielskiego, nowo przez Joachima Bielskiego, syna jego wydana* (Marcin Bielski's Polish Chronicle Newly Edited by Joachim Bielski, His Son). It was written in the Roman Catholic spirit (Joachim Bielski having adopted Roman Catholicism in 1595) and that of the ideology of the gentry. That was why he erased all traces of the Protestantism of his father. His uncompromising opinions accounted for the fact that the circulation of his work was prohibited.

Bibliography: Henryk Barycz, "Bielski Joachim," in *Polski Słownik Biograficzny* (Polish Biographical Dictionary), vol. 2, no. 1 (1936), pp. 63–64; Ignacy Chrzanowski, "Bielski (pierwotne nazwisko: Wolski) Marcin," *Polski Słownik Biograficzny*, vol. 2, no. 1 (1936), pp. 64–66; idem, *Marcin Bielski Studia Literackie* (Marcin Bielski, Literary Studies) (Lvov, 1926).

Jerzy Topolski

DŁUGOSZ, Jan (Brzeźnica, 1415–Cracow, 1480). The greatest Polish historian of the late medieval period; one of the most eminent European historians of his times. Canon of Cracow (from 1436), statesman and diplomat, tutor of the sons of King Casimir Jagellonian (from 1467), archbishop of Lvov (he could not assume that office because of illness), Długosz was at first linked to the most eminent Polish statesman, Bishop (later Cardinal) Zbigniew Oleśnicki, and was inclined to defend the position of the Church in the political conflicts of his times, but then he gradually adopted the position of the king (that of the *raison d'état*). That evolution had an essential influence upon his principal work, *Historia Polonica* (History of Poland, 1455; also known as *Annales seu cronicae incliti Regni Poloniae*), in which the state, the royal dynasty, and the interests of the state (and not the Church and its interests), as was the case in the lay historiography of the Renaissance, was the axis of conceptualization. In his *History* Długosz covered the entire history of Poland from the oldest times to 1480. The work was based on ample Polish and foreign sources and also on the author's own observations and information he collected. But it was still dependent on the work of ancient authors, who at that time (and in the following centuries) provided rhetorical models and patterns. The history is valued highly by historians as a source of ample information not to be found in other medieval texts. As has been established, with reference to the genealogy of the Piasts (the earliest Polish dynasty), which requires precision, the number of new and reliable items of information exceeds one hundred and covers several dozen members of the family. The general introduction, which is a rare example of methodological self-consciousness in a medieval historian, forms an essential part of Długosz's work. Philosophically, Długosz referred to the ideas of the then prominent Cracow school of philosophy, which proclaimed the superiority of praxis over metaphysics and criticized scholastics. For Długosz, historiography had the same values as all other liberated arts. "It is known," he wrote, "that it brings to the human species no lesser advantages than philosophy does" and even greater ones (*Historia Polonica*). History confirms what philosophy teaches, verifies it, and forms practical principles that guide human life. It does so both for the educated and the common people. That democratism of Długosz's opinion was a specific novelty in early European humanism. Długosz interpreted practical considerations of the study of history as closely linked to the cognitive ones. Among the more general philosophical categories found in his work, the most important are those of time and nature. The natural order is visible directly in his narration, although in the background we still find divine Providence. But that confusion of the natural and the divine order, observable in Długosz, was proof of his freeing himself from medieval one-sided religious thinking. In addition to writing his *History,* Długosz wrote many minor works intended, above all, to preserve and extend the sources for the history of Poland. He instructed Stanisław Durink, a painter from Cracow, to reproduce on parchment, in color, the banners of the Teutonic Knights, seized by the Poles in the Battle of Grunwald and Tannenberg in 1410 (*Banderia Prutenorum*, The Banner of the Prussians, before 1466); he described the Polish coats-of-arms (*Insignia seu clenodia Regni Poloniae*, The Coats-of-Arms of the Kingdom of Poland, between 1455 and 1480); he also described the lives of Saint Stanislaus (1465) and Blessed Kinga (between 1471 and 1475) and drew several lists of Polish bishops and archbishops of Gniezno. As a coworker of Oleśnicki he described in detail the big landed property of the bishopric of Cracow (*Liber beneficiorum dioecesis Cracoviensis*, The Book of the Benefices of the Diocese of Cracow, started in 1470 and continued for several years). Today it is one of the most valuable sources of the economic, social, and Church history of the last Middle Ages in Poland.

Bibliography: J. Dąbrowski, *Dawne dziejopisarstwo polskie (do roku 1480)* (Old Historiography in Poland up to 1480) (Wrocław, Warszawa, and Kraków, 1964), pp. 189–240; *Dlugossiana, Studia historyczne w pięćsetlecie śmierci Jana Długosza* (Dlugossiana, Historical Studies on the Five Hundredth Anniversary of the Death of Jan Długosz) (Kraków, 1980); Fryderyk Papée, "Długosz Jan," in *Polski Słownik Biograficzny* (Polish Biographical Dictionary), vol. 5, no. 22 (1939), pp. 176–180.

Jerzy Topolski

KROMER, Marcin (Biecz, 1512–Lidzbark, 1589). Of burgher origin, elevated to nobility by King Sigismundus Augustus in 1552, Kromer was one of the most eminent representatives of culture and science under the Polish Renaissance, and he maintained lively contacts with outstanding European intellectuals of his times. He was a man of letters (he wrote in Latin and in Polish), diplomat, secretary to the king, bishop of Warmia, and historian. Connected with the Church of Rome, he also worked as secretary to Archbishop Piotr Gamrat and Cardinal Stanisław Hozjusz. He was one of the principal intellectual representatives of the Polish Counter-Reformation, superior to many others by his broad horizons and the dislike of dogmatism. He won international renown by publishing (1545–1552) six homilies of Johannes Chrysostomus, discovered in Bologna in an ancient codex. Before he took to writing history in the strict sense of the word, Kromer joined the anti-Protestant campaign with his apologetic and polemic writings. Writing in Polish and using that language in a simple and fine manner were at that time a novelty in Roman Catholic religious writing. His idea of writing the history of his country (which he developed c. 1545) won him the support and assistance of King Sigismundus Augustus. At the same time, upon instructions from the king, he organized the royal archives in Wawel Castle in Cracow, doing in that respect immense work that was very highly appreciated. His history of Poland, *De origine et rebus gestis Polonorum libri XXX* (The Origin and Acts of the Poles, in thirty books, Basel, 1555), was intended primarily for foreigners. The book became very popular (it had five Latin and one Polish edition in a short time) and contributed to an increased knowledge abroad of things Polish. The description of the history of Poland concentrates on positive features, but his narration is matter of fact and linguistically elegant. In his work there are many references to original sources (Kromer cited more than one hundred documents; he also availed himself of the chronicle of Gallus Anonymus and established the nationality of the latter). Kromer strove to make his narratives coherent and to bring out causal sequences of events. His work, while being largely a popular modification of Jan Długosz's (q.v.) *History,* has its individual character and a distinct conceptualization, in agreement with the new trends, although in both texts the problems of the state come to the fore. Until the times of Naruszewicz (q.v.) it was one of the principal synthetic treatments of the history of Poland. The Sarmatian theory of the ethnogenesis of the Slavs had a considerable response abroad. Another particularly valuable work of Kromer's is connected with *De origine*. It is a *sui generis* encyclopedia of old and contemporaneous Poland. It first circulated in copies, was offered to King Henri de Valois on his arrival in Poland, and was for the first time published without Kromer's authorization in 1575; it finally appeared in a complete version in 1589 (*Polonia sive de situ, populis, moribus, magistratibus et republica regni Polonici*, Poland; or, the Location, Peoples, Customs, Officials and Commonwealth of the Kingdom of Poland). It was translated into Spanish in 1588 and into German in 1741. The Polish-language version appeared only in 1853. In addition to writing other works, for instance on music, Kromer wrote a literary text describing the adventures of Finnish Prince John and Princess Catherine, who were persecuted by the mentally ill king of Sweden Eric XIV (*Historia prawdziwa o przygodzie żałosnej książęcia finlandzkiego Jana i królewny Katarzyny*, The True History of the Deplorable Adventure of the Finnish Prince John and Princess Catherine, 1570, 1571).

Bibliography: Henryk Barycz, "Kromer Marcin," *Polski Słownik Biograficzny* (Polish Biographical Dictionary), vol. 15, 2, no. 65 (1970), pp. 319–320; vol. 15, 3, no. 66 (1970), pp. 321–325.

Jerzy Topolski

NARUSZEWICZ, Adam (Pińszczyzna, near Łahiszyn, 1733–Janów, 1796), Polish historian. About 1750 Naruszewicz assumed the position of professor of theology and philosophy at the academy in Vilna. Before 1758 he started lecturing on poetics, history, and geography at the Collegium Nobilium in Warsaw and teaching history in the Knights' School. He started his own scholarly work by translating ancient authors and editing literary texts. For his own literary production he was called "Polish Horace." King Stanislaus Augustus Poniatowski availed himself of his assistance in the formulation of political texts. Naruszewicz was an advocate of reforms and in that respect represented the progressive standpoint of the royal party. It was also the king who inspired him to write a history of the Polish nation. The carrying out of that task gave him the name of the Father of Modern Polish Historiography, of which he was the most eminent representative in its Enlightenment version. He expounded the methodological assumptions of his *Historia narodu polskiego* (A History of the Polish Nation [vols. 2–6, 1780–1786; vol. 1, 1824]) in the treatise *Memoriał względem pisania historii narodowej* (Memorandum on the Writing of National History, 1775). His point was to write a critical history that refers to reliable sources and is based on rationalist ideas. His *Historia* put those principles into effect for the first time on such a scale in Polish historiography. According to Naruszewicz, history was meant to clarify the causes and effects of historical facts and also to teach and educate readers. His synthesis had two axes: the state (monarchy) and the nation, which history had to serve: "strength for the State and happy existence for the nation)." Naruszewicz was still largely traditional in his conceptualization, although, for instance, his providentialism was always confronted with rationalism and the adoption of the standpoint of the Church (Naruszewicz was a bishop) mitigated by the interests of the state. He brought his *Historia* to 1386, but he left numerous source material (known as Naruszewicz's portfolios). Naruszewicz and his school are defined as representatives of the idea of monarchism and the state, which serves as the axis of synthesis and a lesson for society.

Bibliography: Kazimierz Bartkiewicz, *Obraz dziejów ojczystych w świadomości historycznej w Polsce doby oświecenia* (The Image of National History in the Historical Consciousness of the Poles in the Enlightenment Period) (Poznań, 1979); Andrzej Feliks Grabski, *Myśl historyczna polskiego oświecenia* (Historical Thought in the Polish Enlightenment) (Warszawa, 1976); J. Plat, "Adam Naruszewicz," in *Pqlski Słownik Biograficzny* (Polish Biographical Dictionary), vol. 22, 3, no. 94 (1977), pp. 554–651; Marian Henryk Serejski, *Adam Naruszewicz a Oświecenie w Polsce* (Adam Naruszewicz and the Enlightenment in Poland), in M. H. Serejksi, *Przeszłość a teraźniejszość: Szkice i studia historiograficzne* (The Past and the Present: Essays and Studies in Historiography) (Wrocław, Warszawa, Kraków, 1966), pp. 50–66.

Jerzy Topolski

STAROWOLSKI, Szymon (Stara Wola in Volhynia, 1588–Cracow, 1656), Polish writer and historian; representative of the then nascent critical (erudite) historiography in Poland, who enjoyed much renown abroad. Starowolski studied at the Academy of Cracow, where in 1618–1619 he lectured in the Faculty of Arts. But he mainly lived in the courts of magnates (those of Jan and later Tomasz Zamoyski; Anna Ostrogska; grand hetman of Lithuania Jan Karol Chodkiewicz, whose secretary he was in 1620–1624; and several others), in which connection he traveled extensively abroad. On taking holy orders (1639) he became connected with Jakub Zadzik, the bishop of Cracow, and in 1655 he became a canon in Cracow. Starowolski was a polyhistor and popularizer of knowledge. His activity *qua* historian was accompanied by publication of works on politics, economics, law, military art, and religious and moral matters (in Polish and Latin). With reference to history he was marked by general reflection of a methodological nature. In a special treatise, *Penu historicum* (1620), he extolled history as a subject that is indispensable for all human actions, whether theoretical or practical. He gave examples of what history contributes to practical life; science; in particular, theology; law; and medicine. He defended history against objections directed toward it by quoting examples from works of the best historians. In *Penu* we also find reflections on the definition of history and on general and particular branches of history, advice on what to read in history and in what order, and also advice on how to make notes from historical works (sources). In 1616 he published a history of the reign of King Sigismundus I (*De rebus Sigismundi primi*), in which he programmatically abstained from panegiricism. His collection of biographies of Polish writers (*Scriptorum Polonorum Hecatontas*, 1625), completed with a collection of biographies of orators (*De claris oratoribus Sarmatiae*, 1626), can be treated as the first outline of the history of Polish literature. Starowolski also collected inscriptions on graves (*Monumenta Sarmatorum*, 1655). Special mention is due to his encyclopedic description of contemporaneous Poland (*Poloniae sive status Rei Publicae description*). He was a clever observer of what was going on around him in the country; he criticized social injustice and the egoistic policies of the magnates, which gave rise to his moralizing works and *Votum o naprawie Rzeczypospolitej* (A Voice on the Emendation of the Commonwealth, 1625).

Bibliography: Henryk Barycz, *Z epoki renesansu, reformacji i baroku* (The Epoch of the Renaissance, the Reformation, and the Baroque) (Kraków, 1965), pp. 713–741; Feliks Bielak, ''Działalność naukowa S. Starowolskeigo'' (The Scholarly Activity of S. Starowolski), in *Studia i Materiały z Dziejów Nauki Polskiej* (Studies and Materials on the History of Science in Poland), vol. 5, no. 1, pp. 201–237; Leszek Hajdukiewicz, *Historia Nauki Polskiej* (History of Polish Science), vol. 6, biographical index to vols. 1 and 2 (Wrocław, Warszawa, Kraków, and Gdańsk, 1974), pp. 643–644; Ignacy Lewandowski, *Recepcja rzymskich kompendiów historycznych w dawnej Polsce* (Reception of Roman Historical Compendia in Old Poland) (Poznań, 1976); Henryk Piętka, *Poglady filozofi-czno-prawne Szymona Starowolskiego* (Szymon Starowolski's Opinions on the Philosophy of Law) (Warszawa, 1925).

Jerzy Topolski

Great Historians: Portuguese

BARROS, João de (Viseu? 1496–Santiago de Litém, Pombal, 1570), Portuguese historian and civil servant in Portugal, namely, commercial agent at the "Casa da Guiné" and "Casa da India." Barros had a share in the economic exploitation of Brazil (Maranhão), acting in partnership with two of Brazil's *capitães-mores* (governors). He wrote on literature, moral and social philosophy, grammar, and history. His great historical work was *Asia* (vol. 1, 1552–1615; vol. 2, 1623; vol. 3, 1752; vol. 4, 1777–1778; and so on) in periods of four decades, devoted to the Portuguese arrival and settlement in Asia from 1498 to 1538. Only the first three decades were published in his lifetime, but *Asia* was considered so important that another historian, Diogo do Couto, continued it on royal command up to 1600 (decades four to twelve). Barros conceived history in a typical Renaissance way, as a rhetorical and moral construction, evading or concealing real truth whenever it contradicted his views and aims. He also served the interests of the royal institutions and their allies, the Church and the aristocracy. Nonetheless, his work had a major impact on his time and was translated into Italian (1561–1562). It is still used as a valuable source of information, besides its linguistic and rhetorical interest. It is considered a masterpiece in Portuguese literature.

Bibliography: António Baião, *Documentos Inéditos sobre João de Barros* (Coimbra, 1917); Hernâni Cidade, Introduction to the *Décadas* (Lisboa, 1945–1946); António José Saraiva, *Para a História da Cultura em Portugal*, vol. 2 (Lisboa, 1962); António José Saraiva and Óscar Lopes, *História da Literatura Portuguesa*, 13th ed. (Lisboa, 1985).

A. H. de Oliveira Marques

LOPES, Fernão (Lisbon? 1380?–Lisbon? 1459?), Portuguese chronicler. Very little is known about Lopes' education, and his biographers think that his literary culture was acquired in the Royal Library, where he could read chivalry novels, chronicles, and the works of Aristotle, Saint Augustine, Seneca, Cicero, and Petrarch. The first document on his life is dated 1418, when he became "chief-guard of the deeds" in Tombo Tower, in Lisbon's castle. He was a clerk between 1418 and 1454, when he retired, but in 1434 he was instructed to write the chronicles of the Portuguese kings. For this work he was granted a life pension, raised by King Afonso the Fifth from fourteen thousand to twenty thousand "reais". As a "general notary" he wrote the infant D. Fernando's will in 1439. There is no certainty about the order in which he wrote his chronicles. We only know that in 1443 he was writing the *Crónica de D. João I* (Chronicle of John the First). As a chronicler, he was replaced by Gomes Eanes de Zurara in 1452. The last document concerning Fernão Lopes is a permission by King Afonso the Fifth to disinherit an illegitimate grandson. Only in the eighteenth century were the two chronicles of Pedro the First and D. Fernando published by Francisco Manuel Trigoso de Aragão Morato in volume 4 of *Collecção de livros inéditos da história portuguesa* (Collection of Unpublished Books on Portuguese History [Lisbon, 1796]). The first part of the Chronicle of John the First was published in 1915 by Braamcamp Freire. In 1946 and 1949 the first and the second parts of this chronicle were printed in Oporto, with a preface by António Sérgio. Unfortunately, this was not a critical and diplomatic edition as the first one was. In the prologue of this chronicle, Fernão Lopes affirmed "the certainty of the stories" he told, preferring the "plain truth to the embellished falsity." He intended to narrate only those facts recognized by all as true: "otherwise, we would keep silent, not to write false things." All his effort was then directed to putting in order "the naked truth," but at the same time he was an artist, the first great master of Portuguese prose. From the literary point of view, some scenes described by Fernão Lopes—such as the murder of Maria Teles in the Chronicle of D. Fernando or the revolution of 1383–1385, the Aljubarrota battle, and the personification of Lisbon in the Chronicle of John the First—are included in all anthologies. He was a great narrator, narrating in such a way as to place the reader among historical characters, for example, in the description of the Lisbon siege. Paying a great deal of attention to social groups, Fernão Lopes always wrote in terms of social opposition: noblemen/citizens or villains, important people/common people, and so on. It was a pleasure for him to describe the mob, and he even tried some sort of collective psychology, such as when he showed how the mob is risen or how it can be controlled. He emphasized the importance of rumors, the need of a leader, and the presence of women. Sometimes the mob is violent and this violence is marvellously described in the murder of the bishop of Lisbon. In his narrative there is even a philosophy of action, when he analyzed the intentions of his personages, when he made explicit the reasons or motives of the agents. As far as his sources are concerned, he did not omit those who had narrated the same facts before him, but he clearly preferred the official sources kept in Tombo Tower or the ecclesiastical sources in monasteries and churches and even the oral testimonies of the contemporaries.

Bibliography: Aubrey F. G. Bell, *Fernam Lopez* (Oxford, 1921); William Bentley, "Fernão Lopes and His Predecessors: Study of a Little Known Ms. in the Lisbon National Library," *Revista de História* 14 (1925); Augusto Botelho da Costa Veiga, "Fernão Lopes: Alguns elementos para o estudo de seus processos de investigação histórica" (Fernão Lopes: Some Elements for the Study of His Procedures in Historical Research), in *Congresso do Mundo Português*, vol. 2 (Lisbon, 1940); Gonçalves Cerejeira, *Do valor histórico de Fernão Lopes* (On the Historical Value of Fernão Lopes) (Coimbra, 1925); Agostinho de Campos, *Fernão Lopes*, 3 vols. (Lisbon, 1921–1922); A. H. de Oliveira Marques, "Fernão Lopes," in *Dicionário de História de Portugal* (Dictionary of Portuguese History), vol. 2, ed. Joel Serrão (Lisbon, 1965); Maria Lũcia Perrone de Faro Passos, *O herói na crónica de D. João I, de Fernão Lopes* (The Hero in the Chronicle of John the First, by Fernão Lopes) (Lisbon, 1974); Edgar Prestage, *The Chronicles of Fernão Lopes and Gomes Eanes de Zurara* (Watford, England, 1928); M. Rodrigues Lapa, *Froissart e Fernão Lopes* (Lisbon, 1930); Peter E. Russel, *As fontes de Fernão Lopes* (The Sources of Fernão Lopes), Portuguese translation (Coimbra, 1941).

Maria Beatriz Nizza da Silva

Great Historians: Roman

AMMIANUS MARCELLINUS (Antiochia, about A.D. 330–Rome? c. A.D. 400). As a Hellenized Syrian, Ammianus Marcellinus belonged to the municipal aristocracy in Antiochia. He had a brilliant military career (beginning A.D. 350), serving in a cavalry detachment of the imperial guard and then as officer of the general staff. He was one of General Ursicinus's personal attendants during the wars against the Persians. He also took part in the great campaign in the Orient, led in A.D. 363 by Emperor Julian. After the death of this emperor, Ammianus Marcellinus left the army, traveled a lot, and finally settled in Rome, where he wrote his historical work covering a period to about A.D. 400. This work, in thirty-one books, bore the title *Ammiani Marcellini rerum gestarum libri* (Ammianus Maecellinus's Books about Accomplished Deeds). It is, in fact, a history of the Roman Empire that continues Tacitus' (q.v.) work and covers a period extending from A.D. 96 to 378, as the author himself pointed out (31, 16, 9). We possess only Books 14–31, which give an account of the Roman events having occurred since A.D. 353. Thus it is obvious that Ammianus dwelled upon the historical events he had personally witnessed or could have witnessed. Ammianus Marcellinus conscientiously accumulated documentary material, using the works of other historiographers but also resorting to his direct experience or that of some other eyewitnesses especially military men, as well as to the reports drawn up by them during the battles and maneuvers. Repeatedly, this historian expressed the wish to render as accurately as possible the historical truth (for instance, 14, 6, 2). He put forth extremely valuable information about the historical events occurring in the fourth century A.D. about the evolution of the sociopolitical structures and about the morals of various peoples: Sarmatians, Huns, Gauls, Thracians, and so on. Ammianus condemned the tendency manifest with the abbreviators and biographers to stick to trifling details, irrelevant to political life in the Roman Empire (26, 1, 1). He was also a moralist who passed severe judgment on the shortcomings of his contemporaries. He wrote as *miles quondam et Graecus* (once a soldier and a Greek, 31, 16, 9), animated by an almost religious devotion to the military oath by his loyalty to Rome, which he glorified exultantly; and by his belief in the virtues of the monarchic political system. Ammianus believed in Rome's eternity and was optimistic about its future. He was not a Christian; yet he pleaded for religious toleration. His work stands out as a synthesis between the Hellenic culture and mentality, also perceptible in his methods of reconstituting history and Roman pagan customs. Ammianus' main hero is Emperor Julian, whom he regarded as the representative of the empire's destiny, as the almost perfect monarch. He ascribed to him a great number of virtues and turned Julian's feats, presented in a novelistic manner, into the weighty part of his work. Nevertheless, on several occasions Ammianus Marcellinus proved to have been endowed with a profound historical frame of mind. Although he was influenced by Tacitus, he thought and expressed his thoughts in an original manner. He employed a sophisticated language and an elaborate style, which were both a result of the fact that he did not express himself in his mother tongue and because of the inner psychological contradictions that characterized him. Ammianus Marcellinus was the last great Roman historian.

Bibliography: N.J.E. Astin, *Ammianus on Warfare: Investigation into Ammianus' Military Knowledge*, Collection Latomus 165 (Brussels, 1979); Pierre-Marie Camus, *Ammien Marcellin. Témoin des courants culturels et religieux à la fin du IV-e siècle* (Paris, 1967); K. Rosen, "Studien zur Darstelungskunst und Glaubwürdigkeit des Ammianus Marcellinus" (Diss., Rhenish Friedrich-Wilhelm Univ., Bonn, 1970); Guy Sabbah, *La méthode d'Ammien Marcellin. Recherches sur la construction du discours historique dans les Res Gestae* (Paris, 1979); E. A. Thompson, *The Historical Work of Ammianus Marcellinus* (Cambridge, Eng., 1947).

Eugen Cizek

AUGUSTINE, Saint (Aurelius Augustinus) (Thagaste, now Souk-Ahras, A.D. 354–Hippo Regius, now Bône, A.D. 430), Roman theologian and philosopher of history from North Africa. A student at Thagaste, Roman Numidia (A.D. 361), Madauros (A.D. 365–366), Carthage (A.D. 370), Saint Augustine was later a private teacher at Thagaste (A.D. 373) and Carthage (A.D. 374) and a professor of rhetoric at Rome (A.D. 383) and Milan (A.D. 384). He was converted to Christianity (A.D. 386) and baptized by Saint Ambrose, bishop of Milan (A.D. 387). He was then consecrated bishop of Hippo (A.D. 395). Originally Berber or Punic-speaking, Augustine became a master of Latin in writing and public disputation at first in philosophy but later in the cause of Christian orthodoxy. From A.D. 387 to 400 his writing was mainly against the Manichaeans as a philosopher of being, from A.D. 400 to 412 against the Donatists as a doctor of the Church, and from A.D. 412 to 430 against the pagans and Pelagians as theologian of history and champion of Grace. In spite of his heavy pastoral duties and poor health, Augustine wrote a tremendous number of books on many subjects with authority and originality, contributing to the creation of a new thought system for Western Christendom. In the early Middle Ages he was honored as being "post Apostolos omnium ecclesiarum magister" (after the apostles, teacher of all the churches) and was named first of the four "Great Doctors of the West," along with Saint Ambrose, Jerome, and Pope Saint

Gregory the Great. Only two of Augustine's numerous works have a direct historical bearing, namely, the *Confessiones* (The Confessions of Saint Augustine), A.D. 397; and *De Civitate Dei* (The City of God), A.D. 413–427.

The *Confessions* represents a spiritual autobiography, correctly detailing the major milestones in his life but rendered in the form of a prayer or monologue addressed to God. In addition, it contains the first extended treatment of a philosophy of time (Bk.11, Chs. 11–28): Time itself springs from God who is permanent and unchanging in "steadfast," "ever stable," "ever present" eternity and "decrees times future and those past." The nature of time is such that it is always changing "toward nonbeing," so that even the most obviously real present is virtually impossible to measure and must be defined as occupying "no space." Yet even the apparently unreal future and past exist in prophecy and in history. The future is seen in prophecy, and "those who narrate past events . . . perceive them by their minds." The reality of time is difficult to grasp because it is changing so fast, and only "passing time" may be measured. But time cannot be measured in the concrete conception of the movement of "sun, moon, and stars." Since time is, in essence, a process, it is "nothing more than distention . . . of mind itself." The mind then, synthesizes the process of the change of the future into the present and of the present into the past: "it looks forward, it considers, it remembers." It is the "impression" that passing things make upon the mind that gives the measure of time. Augustine declared his discourse on the nature of time a "most intricate riddle," and the problem of the measurement of time "most clear and familiar, but again . . . very obscure and a new task." It was characteristic of him to move from the obvious commonsense position to the deeply philosophical and mystical.

The City of God was, in part, a polemic against the pagans who argued, after the sack of Rome by Alaric the Visigoth in A.D. 410, that the event was the result of the neglect of the city's traditional gods following the adoption of Christianity. He devoted the first ten books to this challenge of the pagans, based on the opposition of "the City of God" and "the earthly city," which "are at present inextricably intermingled, one with the other." Accordingly, Rome, as well as other kingdoms and empires in all history before and after Christianity, has tended toward the one or the other and so toward destruction or well-being. In the following twelve books, Augustine detailed "the origins, history, and destiny of the respective cities, earthly and heavenly." The end or destiny of the earthly, ungodly city of Babylon is "everlasting punishment"; the end of the City of God, the terrestrial Jerusalem, the eternal City of God, is "everlasting life" and entry into "that Kingdom without end, the real goal of our present life." The peculiar contribution of Augustine was the introduction of the doctrines of original sin, grace, and predestination to the interpretation of history. According to Augustine, the sin committed by Adam and Eve "was so great that it impaired all human nature," imposing on it "a propensity to sin and a necessity to die." Out of this situation, a predestined few, of the City of God, have been saved "by the gratuitous grace of God." Human history, then, is already charted to a predestined end, and human action is not based on rational decisions, since all humanity is subject to a nature marred by sin and desire.

When he died in A.D. 430, the city of Hippo was under siege by the Vandals, and the Roman Empire had come to an end. Augustine passed on the legacy of antiquity in the package of Christian theology and philosophy.

Bibliography: Vernon J. Bourke et al., eds., *Saint Augustine: The City of God* (New York, 1958); Henri Marrou, *Saint Augustine and His Influence through the Ages* (New York, 1960).

E. J. Alagoa

AURELIUS VICTOR, Sextus (Africa, about A.D. 320/330–Rome, c. A.D. 390). Aurelius Victor came from a modest family living in Roman Africa. Yet he was a brilliant student and had a brilliant career. In A.D. 361 he met Emperor Julian, joined his court, and became governor of the province of Pannonia Secunda. At the end of the century, he became prefect of Rome. His historical work bears the title *Historiae abbreuiatae* (Abridged Histories), but it is generally known under the title *Caesares* and was written between A.D. 358 and 360. In this work elements of biography and epitome interweave. In the forty-two chapters, Aurelius Victor presented in fact the history of the Roman Empire from Augustus to Emperor Constantine, living at the end of the fourth century A.D., in short biographical inset portraits describing the emperors. He was the most brilliant abbreviator. He understood the psychology of the Caesars, as well as their finance policy or the functioning of institutions. Thus he pointed out the primary importance of the institutional reforms undertaken by Diocletianus (39,4) and later on by Constantine (41,17) or the essence of the principality set up by Augustus (1,1). He grasped the essential part played by the three forces that brought about the evolution of the Roman monarchy: the emperor, the army, and the Senate. Aurelius Victor expressed the ideology of the pagan circles, which had supported Julian. He remained partially true to the biographical structures and headings worked out by Suetonius (q.v.). He employed Suetonius' model creatively and originally. One of his imitators, conventionally called Pseudo-Aurelius Victor, abridged and resumed his work to the death of Emperor Theodosius (A.D. 395) under the title *Epitome de Caesaribus* (Epitome about the Caesars). In this epitome, built on another work of the same type, one can find some details that Aurelius Victor had not mentioned in his authentic work. In spite of all this, Pseudo-Aurelius Victor was endowed with less insight than his model.

Bibliography: H. W. Bird, "A Historical Commentary on Sextus Aurelius Victor's Liber de Caesaribus XVIII to XLII" (Diss., University of Toronto, 1972); Pierre Dufraigne, Introduction to Aurelius Victor, *Livre des Césars* (Paris, 1975), pp. 7–62; C.E V.

Nixon, "A Historical Study of the Caesares of Sextus Aurelius Victor" (Diss., University of Michigan, 1971).

Eugen Cizek

CASSIUS DIO (Cassius Dio Cocceianus) (also called Dio Cassius) (Nikaia or Nicaea, Bithynia, A.D. 163/164–Nikaia, c. A.D. 235). Cassius Dio's descent is probably from a family of Roman colonists who, under the impact of the Hellenic environment, assumed the Greek habits and ways of life. His father, Cassius Apronianus, was a Roman senator. Cassius Dio himself is the outcome of the overlapping of two traditions, one Roman, the other Greek. He studied in Italy and later had a brilliant senatorial career; he was appointed governor of various provinces (Africa, Dalmatia) and in A.D. 229 was elected a Roman consul, in the reign of the emperor Severus Alexander, who held him in high esteem. He is the author of a huge historical work, *Rhômaiké historía* or *Rhômaiká* (The Roman History), written in Greek and relying on heavy documentary evidence that he gathered during a period lasting from A.D. 197 to 207. Writing it took him fifteen years, from A.D. 207 to 222; in this long lapse of time Cassius Dio was the author of eighty other books. In the preface to this work (excerpt 2), Dio explicitly stated his intention to write a complete history of Rome, the other peoples in the Roman Empire being only scarcely mentioned, just from the point of view of their coming into contact with Roman power. The first fifty books set forth the events in royal and republican Rome. The rest of the work dealt with the empire, its golden age, which, according to Dio, extended to Marcus Aurelius' death (A.D. 180), and the last books focused on its "iron age," which covered a period between Commodus' reign and A.D. 219. Out of this work there survived only Books 36–54, presenting the end of the republic and the setting up of the principality, beginning with 68 B.C., as well as large excerpts from Books 55–60, dealing with the period A.D. 9–45, and from Books 79–80. Also some other scarce passages have been preserved as well. The entire work was summed up in the eleventh and twelfth centuries by two Byzantines, Xiphilinos and Zonaras. Their two summaries are not so mechanically conceived as some historians suggest. Cassius Dio was hostile to autocracy pushed to the extreme, as Commodus had been, and assumed a senatorial mentality. In the speeches he ascribed to Agrippa and Maecenas as pieces of advice given to Augustus, as well as in other excerpts in the work (52, 2–40; 53, 17 and 33), Cassius Dio showed himself in favor of an absolute monarchy, full of respect toward the Senate, and relatively moderate in general. Cassius Dio imagined Roman monarchy as a universal empire. But the historical parts dealing with the empire show the tendency of being structured as biographies of the Caesars. Biased toward sustained moralizing, Cassius Dio drew out of every event an ethical conclusion. In spite of his enthusiastic admiration of Thucydides (q.v.), Cassius Dio did not possess the former's insight in analyzing the historical process. He did not understand many important events, as for instance the advent of Christianity or the threat the barbarians represented to the Roman Empire. In exchange, he spoke of miracles, omens, and quaint anecdotes. Nevertheless, Cassius Dio put forward important information, often unique, about certain periods and aspects of Roman history, including Emperor Traianus' wars (the beginning of the second century A.D.). Although he deeply admired the sober language of the Atticists, Cassius Dio wrote a romantic history in a style often influenced by rhetoric. This history is sometimes pathetic and obviously created under the impact of Hellenic historiography, in its turn indebted to the models of Greek tragedy. Cassius Dio was endowed with a real narrative talent.

Bibliography: Michael Hammond, "The Significance of the Speech of Maecenas in Dio Cassius Book LII," *Transactions of American Philological Associations* 63 (1932): 82–102; Bernd Manuwald, *Cassius Dio und Augustus. Philologische Untersuchungen zu den Büchern 45–46 des Dionischen Geschichtswerkes* (Wiesbaden, 1979); Fergus Millar, *A Study of Cassius Dio* (Oxford, 1964); Cesare Questa, "Tecnica biografica e tecnica annalistica nei libri LII-LVIII di Cassio Dione," *Studi Urbinati* 31 (1957): 37–53.

Eugen Cizek

CAESAR, Gaius Iulius (Rome, 101 B.C.–Rome, 44 B.C.). Caesar was a member of the Julia family, an ancient patrician *gens* (clan) that claimed to descend from Iulius, Aeneas' son and, consequently, Venus's grandson. But this family had not had too deep an influence on Roman political life. Caesar's aunt was the widow of Marius, the general and political leader of the democratic faction (*populares*). In 63 B.C. Ceasar became *pontifex maximus* (high priest), head of the Roman religion, and in 60 B.C., together with Pompey and Crassus, he set up the first triumvirate—a verbal political agreement with a view to rule over Rome. In 59 B.C. he was elected a consul and between 58 and 50 B.C. he conquered the whole of Gaul for the benefit of Rome. In a civil war of large proportions that broke out in 49 B.C., he defeated Pompey and the republicans several times (49–45 B.C.). Once a dictator and unique ruler of Rome, he initiated the transformation of the Roman republic into a monarchy following the Hellenic model. He was murdered in the Senate on March 14th, 44 B.C., by a group of conspirators. He distinguished himself as a brilliant writer, the author of speeches, poems, encyclopedic works, and pamphlets. Caesar was the first Roman author of memoirs that are extant. These memoirs give an account of his military campaigns, and probably even before Caesar's death they had already constituted a unitary corpus of war papers. Later on, they furnished the subject matter for two works: *Commentarii de bello Gallico* (Commentaries on the Gallic War) in seven books, probably written in the autumn of 52 B.C., and to which Caesar's first lieutenant in Gaul, Hirtius, added the eighth book, and *Commentarii de bello ciuili* (Commentaries on the Civil War) in three books, presenting the beginning of the war against the republicans and ending with the year 48 B.C. This last work was probably published in 45 B.C. or even at the beginning of 44 B.C. For his memoirs, Caesar closely consulted military reports and, in general, war records. He adopted a rationalistic, even, epicurean, outlook on history. He not only depicted the battles but also presented and analyzed the morals and institutions of the peoples the Romans fought with: the Gauls, the Germanics, and the Britons. Caesar tried to recount his military campaigns from a totally objective point of view. He spoke about himself in the third person, and described the events in a particularly lucid manner. Nevertheless, this seeming objectivity veiled a skillful distortion of facts, sometimes even of space and time in order to highlight Rome's interests and to glorify, without giving the impression of doing so, Caesar's military initiative. The tendency toward a biased historical representation fully manifested itself in the memoirs about the Civil War, where Caesar laid the blame for its start on his adversaries. Caesar's style is remarkable for its particular sobriety, its deliberate simplicity, and the judicious balance of the various parts of speech in a sentence, which prompted Cicero's admiration.

Bibliography: F. E. Adcock, *Caesar as Man of Letters* (Cambridge, Eng., 1966); G. Pascucci, "Interpretazione linguistica e stilistica del Cesare autentico," *Aufstieg und Niedergang der römischen Welt*, vol. 1, no. 3 (Berlin, 1973), pp. 488–522; *Présence de César*, Collection of studies, ed. Raymond Chevalier (Paris, 1985); Michel Rambaud, *L'art de la déformation historique dans les Commentaires de César* (Paris, 1952; 2d ed., 1966).

Eugen Cizek

CATO, Marcus Porcius (called Maior, the Old, or the Censor) (Tusculum, 234 B.C.–Rome, 149 B.C.). Cato was a *homo nouus* (a new man); that is, he belonged to a simple plebeian family, out of which no member had yet risen to become a magistrate in Rome. He distinguished himself during the Second Punic War, at the end of the third century B.C. This enabled him to join the Roman magistrates, and in 195 B.C. he was elected a consul and a censor for a period of eight years, beginning with 184 B.C. While in charge of the latter office, he was noted for his sternness and moral intransigence. He was an enlightened conservative, devoted to the republican ideals and Italic tradition. He carried on a rich literary activity, especially as an orator and author of encyclopedic works. Between 168 B.C. and 149 B.C., the date of his death, he wrote *Origines* (Origins), a work in seven volumes, written and issued in installments. At the same time, *Origines* represented the first Roman historical work written in Latin and the first monograph, for Cato gives up the method of annalistically presenting the events. Only several excerpts have remained out of this work. In the first three books, Cato recounted the legends about the foundation of several Italic cities, while the rest of the work was a kind of chronicle of the events the author himself had witnessed, beginning with the Punic Wars and ending in 151 B.C. Cato made frequent references to the laws, customs, and institutions of the Italic peoples and even to those alien to the peninsula. His work is pervaded by a strong feeling of patriotism equally Roman and Italic. Rome stands out as the main center of Italic virtues, which Cato praised. A fervent republican, opposing the personalization of Roman political life, Cato mentioned no Roman general in *Origines*. His hero is anonymous Italy. He expressed his ideas in a sober, severe language, still rough and archaic.

Bibligraphy: Sylvie Agache, "Caton, le Censeur, les fortunes d'une légende," *Colloque Histoire de l'historiographie. Clio* (Paris, 1980), pp. 71–107; A. E. Astin, *Cato the Censor* (Oxford, 1978).

Eugen Cizek

CORNELIUS NEPOS (Ticinum, 99 B.C.–Rome, c. 24 B.C.). Cornelius Nepos came from a family belonging to the equestrian order. He spent most of his life in Rome, where he played a minor political role. Yet he frequented the intellectual and political society of the first century B.C. and struck up friendships with Caesar (q.v.), Cicero, Atticus, Hortensius, Varro, and others. He led a quiet life devoted to a rich literary activity, especially where erudition was concerned. He is the author of a chronology and of several geographical works, poems, letters, and especially biographies. He is the first Roman biographer whose work has partially survived. Besides covering Cicero's and Cato's (q.v.) lives, he wrote a large collection of biographies, *De uiris illustribus* (About Illustrious Men). In its initial and complete version, this volume dealt with certain important scholars, as well as with certain outstanding military and political figures. There have been preserved two biographies presenting the lives of two Roman historians, Cato and Atticus, respectively, as well as the section dwelling on several foreign military men. There are included Hannibal's Hamilcar's, Miltiades', Themistocles', Aristides', Alcibiades', and others' biographies. There also remained a preface and a short note mentioning the Persian and Macedonian kings. Generally, Cornelius Nepos presented his characters as paradigms of high moral conduct and bravery, even if they had a number of shortcomings and a life full of tribulations. He looked for virtues comparable with the Roman ones out of Italy's borders. Some inadvertences slipped in among his biographical data. He presented certain episodes in the life of his characters, but he also described the morals and manners of certain foreign peoples. Sometimes he inserted the presentation of his characters' virtues in the chronological account of their lives, but at other times he devoted to them a special part within the narrative. He also recounted various anecdotes. He made use of a simple, sober, and at times even crude language, although he resorted to certain rhetorical effects in order to praise his heroes.

Bibliography: Karl Büchner, "Humanitas. Die Atticus-Vita des Cornelius Nepos," *Gymnasium* 36 (1949): 100–121; V. d'Agostino, "La vita Corneliana di Tito Pomponio Attico," *Rivista di Studi Classici* 10 (1962): 1–16; Edna Jenkinson, "An Introduction to Latin Biography," *Latin Biography*, ed. T. A. Dorey (London, 1967), pp. 1–13.

Eugen Cizek

CURTIUS RUFUS, Quintus (? first century A.D.). The dates of Curtius Rufus' birth and death are unknown. It is generally supposed that he published *De rebus gestis Alexandri Magni libri decem* (ten books about Alexander the Great's Deeds)—a biography uncommonly large for antiquity and lacking the standardized rules of the genre; a biography devoted to Alexander, the famous Macedonian conqueror—after Emperor Gaius-Caligula's death and during Claudius' reign. The first two books and the beginning of the third were lost, so the biographical narrative, in its present form, recounts the events that took place between 333 B.C. and Alexander's death. Curtius Rufus resorted to the plentiful literary documentation concerning Alexander and made up a fictionalized presentation, mostly exulting, of his character's deeds. Yet he acknowledged his flaws. Curtius Rufus proved to be a fervent supporter of the monarchic political system. He also described the morals and manners of the countries conquered by Alexander, as for instance India (Bk. 8, 9, and 14). He employed a colorful, picturesque style, meant to impress the reader. Sometimes he was dramatic, looking for rhetorical effects.

Bibliography: S. Dosson, *Études sur Quinte-Curce, sa vie et son oeuvre* (Paris, 1887); D. Korzeniewski, *Die Zeit des Curtius Rufus* (Köln, 1959); E. I. McQueen, "Quintus Curtius Rufus," *Latin Biography*, ed., T. A. Dorey (London, 1967), pp. 17–43.

Eugen Cizek

EUTROPIUS, Flavius (? A.D. fourth century). Both the dates of this historian's birth and death are unknown, as well as his birthplace, although he was probably a native of the Greek-Levantine area of the Roman Empire. He joined the pagan circles that supported Emperor Julian and accompanied the latter in the expedition against the Persians in A.D. 363. As a high official, he later attended other emperors, such as Valens, and in A.D. 387 he became a consul. Of his works we have an epitome, in ten books, bearing the title *Breuiarium historiae Romanae* or *Breuiarium ab Urbe Condita* (Abstract of Roman History or Abstract from the Foundation of the City), which epitomizes the whole history of Rome to A.D. 364. In this work, Eutropius summarized the data furnished by Livy and other Roman historians, who wrote in a historical period closer to his time. In this very compressed epitome—a genuine digest—Eutropius showed no poignant interest in the causality and profound analysis of historical phenomena. He gave an account of the events observing the established clichés, although he was biased by the mentality of the pagan political circles that had supported Emperor Julian. When presenting Constantine's reign, Eutropius made no mention of his conversion to Christianity. The history of the Roman Empire is structured in short biographical inset portraits of the emperors. Even the dense historical narrative Eutropius devoted to the republic abounds in anecdotes; yet in the emperors' biographies one can easily detect the characteristics of Suetonius's (q.v.) biographical technique: headings devoted to the origins of the Caesars, their private lives, their military skill, their inner policy, their rough portraits —morals, level of culture, literary taste, and so on. The deaths of the Caesars and the duration of their reigns are also evoked here. They are either praised or condemned at the end of their biographical presentations. Thus, just like Aurelius Victor (q.v.) in *Breuiarium* Eutropius blended epitome with biography. He employed very crude language and a sober, classic, even dry style.

Bibliography: G. Bonamente, "Eutropio e la tradizione pagana su Constantino," in *Scritti storico-epigrafici in memoria di Marcello Zambelli* (Rome, 1978), pp. 17–59; N.

Scivoletto, "La civilitas del IV secolo e il significato del Breviarium di Eutropio," *Giornale Italiano di Filologia* 24 (1970): 14–45.

Eugen Cizek

FABIUS PICTOR, Quintus (Rome, end of the third century B.C.–? beginning of the second century B.C.). Fabius Pictor was the first famous Roman historiographer. That is why he was called Father of Roman History. He belonged to a well-known patrician *gens* (clan) and held mostly religious offices in Rome. He wrote his work in Greek, as did the other historiographers of his generation who were younger than he. This enabled him to use a more expressive and literary language than Latin, which was at that time in a primitive phase of development, and to fight against the pro-Carthaginian propaganda of some contemporary Greek historiographers. Fabius Pictor's intention was to plead Rome's cause with the Mediterranean reading public. He wrote an annalistic chronicle (annals) with an unknown title, presenting the history of Rome in a strictly chronological order. The entire work as such was lost, but there still remain a number of references and even excerpts—twenty-eight—included in the works of certain Greek and Roman authors, such as Polybius (q.v.) and Titus Livius Livy (q.v.). Fabius Pictor's chronicle began with Aeneas' arrival in Italy; the foundation of Rome, the legend of which was thus told; and the reigns of the seven kings, whose number and succession to the throne were finally cleared up due to this work; it concluded with the end of the Second Punic War (201 B.C.). Fabius Pictor thereby contributed to the folk tradition concerning the foundation of Rome, and he dwelled upon recent events, especially the Punic Wars. He laid the blame for the start of these wars on Hannibal's family, on its ambition and thirst for absolute power in Carthage and the Eastern Mediterranean. Fabius Pictor defended the cause of Roman expansion but nevertheless showed genuine interest in reconsidering the morals and manners, as well as the institutions, of the various peoples in the empire. His style certifies his search for dramatic and rhetorical effects.

Bibliography: Krister Hanell, "Zur Problematik der älteren römischen Geschichtsschreibung," *Histoire et historiens dans l'antiquité, Fondation Hardt*, vol. 4 (Vandoeuvres and Geneva, 1956), pp. 147–170 (pp. 161–170 about Fabius Pictor); Dieter Timpe, "Fabius Pictor und die Anfänge der römischen Historiographie," *Aufstieg und Niedergang der römischen Welt*, vol. 1, no. 2 (Berlin and New York, 1972), pp. 928–969.

Eugen Cizek

FLORUS, Lucius Annaeus (Hispania or Africa, c. A.D. 78–Rome, A.D. second century). Florus taught rhetoric in Tarraco, today Tarragona, and then settled in Rome, where he attended Emperor Hadrian's court. He wrote short, light, and amusing poems; a dialogue that survived but partially about Virgil (as a rhetorician and a poet); and a historical epitome. One cannot be sure whether there was just one Florus. There could have been more authors of literary works bearing the same name, of which only one could have been the writer of the epitome in two books, probably bearing the title *Tabella*, in fact an abstract of Roman history. Florus wrote a short presentation of Rome's history until Augustus' military campaigns, dwelling on the civil and expansionist wars led by the Romans. He drew his inspiration especially from Livy's (q.v.) work, but he also resorted to other sources. Florus spoke highly of the Romans, whom he set forth as a remarkable people (*Tabella*, Bk. 1, preface, 3). The Romans went through four ages: infancy, youth, robust maturity—until 43 B.C.—and then old age—until the Antoninuses' reign. Trajan was said to have restored to the empire its ancient vigor (*Tabella*, Bk. 1, preface, 3). According to Florus, Hadrian continued Trajan's work. Generally, Florus condemned Rome's enemies but acknowledged the valor of the Macedonians and the Iberians (*Tabella*, Bk. 1, 28, 33). He supplied some valuable information and details regarding the history of Rome, although he was no profound philosopher and was not concerned with historical causality. He presented the episodes in such a way that one could discern in their structure both dramatic patterns and rhetorical influences. His language is pathetic, striving for rhetorical effects.

Bibliography: Eugen Cizek, ''Observatii asupra compoziţiei şi stilulu din opera lui Florus'' (Notes on Pattern Structure and Style in Florus's Work), *Analele Universităţii C. I. Parhon*, seria *Stiinţe sociale, Filologie* 15 (1959): 451–463; Paul Jal, Introductory Study and Notes on Florus, *Oeuvres*, 2 vols. (Paris, 1967), pp. 9–171; Paola Zancan, *Floro e Livio* (Padova, 1942).

Eugen Cizek

HISTORIA AUGUSTA (Scriptores Historiae Augustae) (? A.D. fourth/fifth century). Historia Augusta is a collection of biographies describing the lives of the emperors living in the second and third centuries. The manuscripts bear the title *Vitae diuersorum principum et tyrannorum a diuo Hadriano usque ad Numerianum* (The Lives of Various Princes and Tyrants from the Divine Hadrian to Numerianus). On the basis of some vague hint in Emperor Tacitus' biography (Bk. 10, 3), two conventional titles were suggested in the seventeenth century for this work: *Historia Augusta* (The Augustan History) and *Scriptores Historiae Augustae* (The Writers of the Augustan History). According to its text, *Historia Augusta* is indebted to several authors, of whom some lived at the end of the third century A.D. and others at the beginning of the following century. Starting with Hermann Dessau, modern scientists proved that we are faced with a literary forgery of great proportions, since the whole collection was written by a sole unknown author who published it at the end of the fourth century or the beginning of the following one. This author was up to a point faithful to the model of Suetonius's (q.v.) biography, dwelling upon the emperors' private lives, anecdotes, and picturesque gossip. Nevertheless, *Historia Augusta* compresses numerous details that illustrate the political and social life of the Roman Empire in the second and third centuries A.D. For Rome and its provinces, *Historia Augusta* represents a source of major importance. The author of this collection of imperial biographies shared the traditionalistic political and religious ideals that animated the circles that supported Emperor Julian and that fought for the pagan resurrection at the end of the fourth century A.D. Like Ammianus Marcellinus (q.v.), this writer was a firm believer in Rome's eternal existence. The author of the *Augustan History*'s style is fluent, often colorful, and seeking rhetorical effects.

Bibliography: *Emperors and Biography: Studies in the Historia Augusta* (Oxford, 1971); Johannes Straub, *Studien zur Historia Augusta* (Bern, 1952); Karl-Heinz Stubenrauch, "Kompositionsprobleme der Historia Augusta. Einleitungen, der verlorene Anfang" (Diss., Georg August University, Göttingen, 1982); Sir Ronald Syme, *Ammianus Marcellinus and the Historia Augusta* (Oxford, 1968).

Eugen Cizek

IORDANES (? A.D. sixth century). A Romanized Ostrogoth, Iordanes published two historical works in the middle of the sixth century A.D. (c. A.D. 551). In *Getica* he made a summary of the history of the Goths, previously drawn up by Cassiodorus. Iordanes spoke highly of the Goths and pleaded for the reconciliation between the Goths and the Romans. He mistook the Goths for the Getae, whom he presented as the forefathers of the Goths contemporary with him. Yet, thoroughly knowing the Danubian regions, Iordanes furnished valuable information about the history of the Getae, as well as of the Huns, Sarmatians, and other peoples. In *Romana* Iordanes intended to complete an abstract of world history. This abstract began with Adam but also set forth the evolution of the republic and of the Roman monarchy. The author often appeared to be indebted to the new authorities that ruled over the Eastern Roman Empire, that is, the empire governed from Constantinople, and assumed the Christian outlook on history. This work also contained valuable historical information. Since he knew the real situation of the Danubian peoples, Iordanes pointed out that, during his reign, Emperor Aurelianus had withdrawn from Dacia only the military forces, that is, the legions (*Romana*, 217).

Bibliography: Roxana Iordache, "La confusion Gètes-Goths dans les *Getica* de Jordanès," *Corollas Philolgicas in Honorem Josephi Guillen Cabanero* (Salamanca, Spain, 1983), pp. 317–337; Zoe Petre, "À propos des sources de Jordanès, Getica 39–41 et 67–72," *Études d'historiographie*, ed. Lucian Boia (Bucharest, 1985), pp. 39–51; N. Wagner, *Getica. Untersuchungen zum Leben des Iordanes und zur frühen Geschichte des Goten* (Berlin, 1967).

Eugen Cizek

LIVY, Titus Livius (Patavium, now Padova, 59/57 B.C.–Patavium, 19/17 B.C.). Born in Cisalpine Gaul, which was not yet part of Italy, Livy was a Roman citizen, representing the first generation in his family to bear this title. Unlike most of the Roman historians, Livy was a "cabinet" writer, lacking an authentic political experience. Although he was on friendly terms with Augustus, he held no significant political office in Rome and spent most of his life in Patavium, where he carried on his activity in his own study, surrounded by his family. He is the author of a vast literary creation, consisting, among other things, of dialogues on the history of philosophy. Yet his major work remains *Ab Urbe condita* (Since the Foundation of the City [Rome]), one of the most extensive historiographic works in antiquity, in 142 books—but Livy had envisaged his work to contain at least 150 books, recounting the history of Rome since its foundation and even before that, to A.D. 9. This work set forth a vast historical canvas, supposedly divided by the author into unequal parts, comprising 5, 10, or 15 books. Of *Ab Urbe condita* we have only Books 1–10 and 20–45, several summaries of the other books, and some scarce fragments. Probably, Livy toiled all of his life on this work, from 31 B.C. until his death. For sources, he relied on a great number of earlier works, as for instance those written by Fabius Pictor (q.v.), Cato (q.v.), Valerius Antias, Claudius Quadrigarius, and Polybius (q.v.). He grouped the various versions supplied by his sources so as to sketch an original historical canvas. Concerned with the history of the Roman people, whom he named several times *princeps populus* (the ruling people) or *praeualens populus* (the chief or prevailing people), in the general preface to his work, Livy, at the beginning of the first book, advocated his intention to cover *uita* (life), *mores* (morals), *uiri* (men), and *artes* (concrete means), through which the life of the Roman people had come into being (general preface, Bk. 9). In analyzing the causality of the historical process, Livy laid a certain stress on the transcendental factors—fate and the gods—but he considered that Rome's evolution had been determined mostly by the people's vices and virtues. The worship of the ancient set of values secured the glory of Rome and its grandeur, which led Livy to assert that *nulla unquam res publica nec maior nec sanctior nec bonis exemplis ditior tuit* (no other state has ever been more powerful or sacred, or richer in good examples; general preface, Bk. 11). Wishing to glorify the history of Rome, Livy distorted certain events of the past, amplifying the qualities of the Romans. Nevertheless, he dwelled on the crisis of the Roman republic occurring in the last century of its existence, as well as the virtues and morals of other peoples. Livy was a republican and a conservative, inclined to present the patricians in a favorable light when recounting the beginnings of the republic; yet he understood the necessity to set up the monarchy in Rome and supported Augustus' policy. Generally, the narrative structure pervades his work, so that analysis and story are closely interwoven. Livy was a narrator endowed with an exceptional talent. But within the narrative, he looked for the inner implications of events, the psychological motivation. He employed a fluent, ample style, working with images that nowadays are furnished by the cinemascope. His writing is often indebted to the vocabulary of poetry, being at the same time profoundly classical.

Bibliography: Henry Bornecque, *Tite-Live* (Paris, 1933); T. J. Luce, *Livy: The Composition of His History*, (Princeton, N.J., 1977); Michel Rambaud, "Exemples de déformation historique chez Tite-Live. Le Tessin, la Trébie, Trasimène," *Colloque. Histoire et historiographie. Clio*, ed. R. Chevalier (Paris, 1980), pp. 109–126; P. G. Walsh, *Livy: His Historical Aims and Methods* (Cambridge, Eng., 1961).

Eugen Cizek

OROSIUS, Paulus (Tarraco, now Tarragona, Spain, or Bracara, now Braga, Portugal, c. A.D. 390– ? fifth century). A Christian priest in Hispania, after A.D. 414 Orosius frequented St. Augustine (Augustinus) in Africa. The place and date of his birth and death are unknown. He was the author of two theological works—polemics directed against the heretics—and of a vast historical work, *Aduersum paganos libri septem* (Seven Books against the Heathens), completed in A.D. 417. This work represents a history of the world, profoundly Christian in attitude, in which the author blends information from the Old Testament with events in the history of Rome and some other Mediterranean states. Orosius opposed the accusations brought by the heathens against Christianity, which they blamed for the troubles that befell Rome at the beginning of the fifth century. He demonstrated that the whole history of humanity has been strewn with calamities. Orosius assumed the contemporary Christian outlook on history, which postulates that divinity, not people, forge history. Providence punishes people for their errors, while the good things it bestows on them are the outcome of its own generosity (Bk. 2, 3, 5). Orosius advocated collaboration with the barbarians within a federation ruled by Rome. He named *Romania* the unity of peoples that live or could live within the borders of the Roman Empire. Orosius furnished interesting information about Roman history. His style was clear, classic, but full of pathos.

Bibliography: E. Corsini, *Introduzione alle storie di Orosio* (Torino, 1968).

Eugen Cizek

POMPEIUS TROGUS (Gallia Narbonensis, first century B.C.–Rome, beginning of the first century B.C.). Pompeius belonged to a Romanized Gaul family. His grandfather fought under Pompey's arms and his family received Roman citizenship during this famous general's rule, hence the writer's gentilitial name, Pompey. He wrote works of natural science and encyclopedic studies but, above all, a huge history of the world, *Historiae Philippicae* (Philippic Histories), in forty-four books. But there remain only some excerpts and an abbrevation by Justin, probably written in the second century A.D. Pompeius Trogus' narrative initially presented the history of the Orient and then that of Greece and Macedonia. The last books focused on the history of the Parthians and the Romans until Augustus' victory over the Celt–Iberians in 20 B.C. Pompeius Trogus reconstituted the Mediterranean routes but adopted a theory favoring the transfer of world supremacy from the Assyrians to the Medians and then to the Persians and finally to the Macedonians. His work focused on Macedonia during Philip II's reign. Nevertheless, Pompeius Trogus was no anti-Roman. For him, Rome represented *caput totius mundi* (the head of the whole universe, Bk. 43, 1–2), the heir to the Macedonians' power. Yet against the background of Roman historiography, which had a profoundly national character, for the historians put forth the deeds of the Romans in a favorable light, Pompeius Trogus is one of the first and in fact one of the few authors of histories of the world. In his summary—actually an epitome—Justin quoted mostly the picturesque fragments from Pompeius Trogus' work. It seems that Pompeius Trogus was a disciple of Sallustius's (q.v.) style, abundant in rhetorical effects and pathetic accents.

Bibliography: J. S. Pedergast, "The Philosophy of History of Pompeius Trogus," (Diss. University of Illinois, 1961); Otto Seel, *Eine römische Weltgeschichte: Studien zum Text der Epitome des Iustinus und zur Historik des Pompeius Trogus* (Erlangen, West Germany, 1972).

Eugen Cizek

SALLUSTIUS, Gaius Sallustius Crispus (Amiternum, 86 B.C.–Rome, 35 B.C.) Sallustius came from a family that belonged to the equestrian order. He was educated in Rome in the atmosphere of the civil war, which opposed Marius' supporters to Sulla's. He was involved in political activity as a member of the democratic faction of the *populares*; he rose in the ranks of a Roman magisterial career; and Caesar (q.v.), whose supporter he became, sent him in 46 B.C. to *Africa Noua* (New Africa) as governor of that province. After Caesar's death, Sallustius retired from political activity in favor of a wealthy existence—darkened by the civil war, which affected him deeply—devoted to writing. Several works have been attributed to him: an anti-Ciceronian pamphlet and especially two *Epistulae ad Caesarem senem de re publica* (Letters to Old Caesar about the State), in which Sallustius humbly advised the dictator to restore the morality and political balance. In any case, he is the author of two monographs, *De coniuratione Catilinae* (About Catilina's Conspiracy) consisting of sixty-one chapters, issued between 43 and 41 B.C. and tackling the events that had taken place in 63–62 B.C., especially Lucius Sergius Catilina's actions against the institutions of the Roman republic; and *De bello Iugurthino* (About the War against Iugurtha) in 114 chapters, dealing with the Romans' conflict with the last Numidian king and issued in 40 B.C. These short works have survived, but from the *Historiae* (Histories), a work written by Sallustius after 40 B.C. and containing five books, only few fragments have been saved. In this last work he recounted the events that had taken place in Rome before the preliminaries of Catilina's conspiracy, that is, from 78–67 B.C. In his monographs, Sallustius selected out of Roman history (*De coniuratione Catilinae*, 4, 2) two episodes that he considered mostly significant. In these monographs, one can find a real system of thought, based on a moralizing attitude toward the world. According to Sallustius, the fate, that is, the progress of events, changes with morals (*De coniuratione Catilinae*, 2, 5). Catilina stands for the inner evil and Iugurtha for the outer evil, which struck at the basis of the republic. At the same time, Catilina also symbolizes the vices of the Roman nobility (a social category that monopolized the political offices and which he blamed for bringing about the crisis of the Roman Empire). A devoted republican, although he had joined Caesar's supporters, Sallustius deeply detested the *nobilitas* (nobility) and considered that *ambitio* (the thirst for power) and *auaritia* (the greed for wealth) consumed the Roman republic after it had destroyed Carthage in the middle of the second century B.C. Iugurtha had become dangerous for Rome because of the incapacity and corruption of the noble generals who had fought against him at the beginning of the war. Only Marius, the republican general of humble origin, had been able to defeat Iugurtha. During this war, for the first time the self-pride of the nobility was challenged *(De bello Iugurthino* 5, 1). Clear minded, Sallustius noticed many significant phenomena and their consequences, mused over the human condition and the historiographer's status, and, especially in the philosophical prefaces to his monographs, manifested himself as a competent expert in human psychology and offered the reading public interesting geographical digressions. He was a skilful portraitist, sketching mostly characters, as for instance, Catilina's famous portrait (*De coniuratione Catilinae*, 5), as well as Iugurtha's, Marius' Caesar's, Cato's, and others. He was influenced by the Greek historian Thucydides (q.v.). He expressed himself in a concise, dense, colorful language based on a rich vocabulary and particularly well-chosen words. Sallustius changed the obsolete language of the Latin historiography into an artistic literary vehicle of high value.

Bibliography: Karl Büchner, *Sallust* (1960); Antonio La Penna, *Sallustio e la rivoluzione romana* (Milan, 2nd ed., 1968); (3d ed. 1973); Kurt Latte, *Sallust* (Leipzig, 1935); Sir Ronald Syme, *Sallust* (Berkeley, Calif., 1964); Étienne Tiffou, *Essai sur la pensée morale de Salluste à la lumière de ses prologues* (Paris, 1974).

Eugen Cizek

SUETONIUS, Gaius Suetonius Tranquillus (Ostia, or Hippo Regius, c. A.D. 69/75–Hippo Regius, c. A.D. 130). Son of an officer belonging to the equestrian order, Suetonius pursued a "knight's" career, at times enjoying Pliny the Younger's protection. After A.D. 117 he held important offices in imperial central administration, becoming the chief secretary with the prince's correspondence in Latin. He fell into disgrace in A.D. 122 and retired from a public career. He is the author of a great number of antiquarian works, written in Latin and Greek, that have been lost. In A.D. 113 he published the biographies of several scholars—historians, orators, philosophers, poets, and so on—under the title *De uiris illustribus* (About the Famous Men), of which we have only some biographical notes on grammarians and rhetoricians grouped under the title *De grammaticis et rhetoribus* (About Grammarians and Rhetoricians). This work abounds in biographical data and anecdotes, with the qualities and shortcomings being generally favorable to the scholars and unfavorable concerning the Caesars, whose biographies Suetonius published probably in A.D. 121–122 with the title *Vitae duodecim Caesarum* (The Lives of the Twelve Caesars). All Caesars, from Julius Caesar to Domitian, are presented here. Suetonius toiled conscientiously and studied enormously for these biographies. He seems to have been generally in favor of a moderate monarchic absolutism. Often malicious, Suetonius debunked the image of the Caesars, recounting anecdotes that exemplified the less honorable aspects of their existence. He presented the Caesars' public activities but especially their private lives. In almost every biography Suetonius evoked the good and the evil, the vices and the virtues. Only the degree of vice or virtue differed from one biography to another. Suetonius presented certain stages in the Caesars' lives chronologically, until the time of their coming to the throne and, at the end of the biographies, their deaths. But the most important part in these biographies is played by the ''eidological'' sector, where the character of the respective Caesar is put forth. Suetonius definitively standardized the rules of the ancient biographical writings, presenting successively the family background, the date and place of birth, the stages of a career, the virtues, the vices, a short portrait, and the death of the character. These rules, subtly handled by Suetonius, were taken over by biographers writing in the late centuries of antiquity. That is how Suetonius' biographical model came into being. He seldom passed judgments on the facts he presented in the generally sober, even dry narrative, written in a classic style and a language similar to the one used in chanceries. Disciple of the philosophy of the New Academy, which searched for probabilities and not absolute truths and gave a chance to every divergent explanation of facts, Suetonius found in this way an alibi and also speculated about the readers' judgment. Although he favored the picturesque gossip, Suetonius sometimes furnished valuable details about political life and daily existence or about the mentality of the imperial court. His work, which represents an important source of the study of historical events occurring in the first century A.D., skillfully completes Tacitus' (q.v.) creation.

Bibliography: Eugen Cizek, *Structures et idéologie dans les Vies des douze Césars de Suétone* (Bucharest and Paris, 1977); Francesco Della Corte, *Suetonio, eques Romanus*, 1st ed., 1958; 2d ed. 1967); Jacques Gascou, *Suétone historien* (Rome, 1984); Bohumila Mouchova, *Studie zu Kaiserbiographien Suetons* (Prague, 1968); Wolf Steidle, *Sueton und die antike Biographie* (Munich, 1st ed., 1951; 2d ed., 1963).

Eugen Cizek

TACITUS, Publius Cornelius (Gallia Narbonensis, c. A.D. 57–Rome, c. A.D. 120). Tacitus was probably born in Vasio or Forum Iulii, in Gallia Narbonensis (now the South of France), and his father was an imperial procurator in Gallia Belgica. Therefore, Tacitus must have come from a family belonging to the equestrian order, so he was a *homo nouus* (new man), the first one in his family to hold senatorial magistracies. He had been reared sternly, with his education molding his superego, which repressed all of his strong drives. From Pliny the Younger's letters one can infer that Tacitus was hard working, self-exacting, and conscientious. He rose through the ranks in a senatorial career and became consul in A.D. 97 and proconsul (senatorial governor) of the province of Asia between A.D. 112 and 114. He also held sacerdotal offices, so he gained a rich political experience. Hadrian's coming to the throne in A.D. 117 and the doing away with Avidius Negrinus and some other generals affected him deeply and marked his last work. He wrote a series of lawyer's speeches, which have been lost, and *Dialogus de oratoribus* (Dialogue about Orators), published in A.D. 105 and preserved until now, dealing with the themes of oratory and their relationship with poetry and the monarchic political system. In this work, Tacitus pleaded for the absolute monarchy and asserted that oratory becomes futile in a state ruled by *sapientissimus et unus* (solely one person and a very clever one, *Dialogus*, 40–41). At the end of A.D. 97 Tacitus published *Agricola*, a complex biography in forty-six chapters, lacking the standardized rules of the genre and comprising a funeral encomium of his father-in-law, a satire directed against Emperor Domitian, and an ethnographic description of Britain, where Iulius Agricola had been governor. In A.D. 98 or 99 he published a complex monograph, *Germania*, also consisting of forty-six chapters, in which the author, describing and praising the Germans' morals, implicitly satirized the moral dissolution of the Romans living at the time. Between A.D. 110 and 111 Tacitus published *Historiae* (Histories), a chronicle of the year A.D. 68–69 and of the Flavian emperors' reigns (A.D. 69–96). It is not known precisely how many books this work had; only the first four books survived and the beginning of the fifth, that is, the narrative covering the events between A.D. 69 and 70. Here Tacitus was more optimistic than in his previous minor historical works, but he feared that Hadrian might become his uncle Trajan's successor to the throne. It was probably under Hadrian, maybe after Tacitus' own death, that his most important work was published. This work, dealing with the Julio-Claudian emperors (A.D. 14–68), is generally called *Annales* (Annals) and contained sixteen rather than eighteen books, covering a period until A.D. 66, when Tacitus probably had to interrupt his narrative. The surviving fragments are Books 1–6, dealing with Emperor Tiberius, and Books 11–16, dealing with certain periods in Claudius' and Nero's reigns. In *Annales*, Tacitus appeared to be more disappointed than in *Historiae*. He skillfully employed the annalistic structure for the period until his time, rigidly organized in the works of his predecessors. To develop his great historical works, he consulted many literary sources and documents, to which he brought about a profoundly original interpretation.

Tacitus was also a historian, a philosopher, and a brilliant politologist. He manifested his interest in the deep motivation of events, *ratio causaeque* (the structure and causes of phenomena), which he opposed to the obvious facts of any situation (*Historiae*, 1, 4, 1). He searched for them in the human soul as well as in the political phenomena, which he considered from a moral point of view, according to good and evil, moral sanity and disease. Tacitus borrowed from Polybius (q.v.) the trichotomy of causal factors, as he differentiated the cause from the pretext and outset of events. Tacitus supported the antidogmatic philosophy of the New Academy, which was in quest of probabilities and not of absolute truth. That is why Tacitus often supplied more explanations, of which he picked one as his favorite, but he also left to the others the possibility of being accepted by the reader. Tacitus turned out to be a great psychologist, able to fathom the human soul. He was at the same time a judge and a brilliant witness to humanity. Nevertheless, he did not leave aside the civilization factors that he studied attentively. Often, when he alluded to the past, Tacitus assumed a senatorial mentality. He sometimes blamed the Senate, but in keeping with this mentality. Yet he urged the conscientious serving of the Roman state, because although the *principes* (princes) were mortal, *res publica* (the state) was forever (*Annales*, 3, 6, 3). *Persona* (the social and political role well carried out), *dignitas* (dignity), *libertas* (freedom), and *disciplina* (discipline) are the main values Tacitus advocated. He was nostalgic about the ancient Roman republic, but he understood that a monarchy was the only political system feasible in Rome at the time. Endowed with penetrating insight, Tacitus noticed many significant historical phenomena such as new faces in the Senate; the continous ascension of the Italic and provincial élite; the transformations the army had gone through and its capacity to set up new emperors; the defensive tendencies in Roman foreign policy in the first century A.D.; the dialectics of foreign and home policy, for the animosities between enemies favored Rome's interests; the progressive consolidation of imperial absolutism; the risks and at the same time the special part played by dignified conduct in the first century A.D.; and the changes in Roman morals. Tacitus was not only a great historian but also one of the most remarkable artists in the history of world literature. He wrote his work in a concise, rich language and employed a solemn and at the same time fascinating vocabulary, based on rare words. The art of insinuation, brilliantly used, pervades his work.

Bibliography: Étienne Aubrion, *Rhétorique et histoire chez Tacite* (Metz, France, 1985); Eugen Cizek, *Tacit* (Tacitus) (Bucharest, 1974); Joseph Lucas, *Les obsessions de Tacite* (Leiden, 1974); R. Martin, *Tacitus* (London, 1981); Alain Michel, *Tacite et le destin de l'Empire* (Paris, 1966); Ettore Paratore, *Tacito*, 2d ed. (Milan, 1962); Sir Ronald Syme, *Tacitus* (Oxford, 1958); *Ten Studies in Tacitus* (Oxford, 1970).

Eugen Cizek

VELLEIUS PATERCULUS, Gaius (Capua, 20/19 B.C.–Rome, A.D. 31). Velleius came from a Campanian family of the equestrian order, who had always served the Romans. He joined the army, rose in the ranks of a magisterial career, and became praetor in A.D. 15. Velleius enjoyed Marcus Vinicius' protection and supported Seianus, the powerful prefect of the praetorians during Tiberius's reign. He probably died in A.D. 31 when Seianus' supporters were done away with. In A.D. 30 he published *Vellei Paterculi ad Marcum Vinicium libri duo* (Two Books Addressed to Marcus Vinicius), the first epitome (historical abstract) in Latin historiography that has been preserved. But unlike other authors of epitomes, Velleius did not make a summary of a previous historical work but of the whole history of the world. Following Pompeius Trogus' (q.v.) example, he did not confine his study to Roman history but dealt with world history, in which Rome's evolution represented the most important episode. Velleius defended Rome's interests, but unlike other historiographers of the time, he pleaded for Roman monarchy, especially for Tiberius and Seianus. He is the first Roman historiographer who, in a series of disgressions, analyzed the Latin and Greek cultures and languages (1, 5, 7; 16–18; 2, 9; 36; 66). He dwelled both on the history of literature as well as on the general history, dialectically organized in *genera* (genres) but also in styles that after youth and maturity became obsolete and have to be replaced. After the genre of the republic followed that of the empire, whose dialectics stopped at the summit it had reached during Tiberius' reign. Velleius Paterculus expressed his thoughts in a colorful, rhetorical, and concise manner, as a contemporary disciple of Sallustius (q.v.) and the new style, which was flourishing at the time.

Bibliography: Eugen Cizek, "L'image du renouvelement historique chez Velleius Paterculus," *Studii clasice* (Classical Studies) 14 (1972): 85–93; Joseph Hellegouarc'h, Introduction à Velleius Paterculus, *Histoire romaine*, vol. 1 (Paris, 1982), pp. 7–102; Italo Lana, *Velleio Patercolo o della propaganda* (Torino, 1952).

Eugen Cizek

Great Historians: Romanian

CANTACUZINO, Constantin (? c. 1640–Constantinople, 1716), Romanian historian and statesman. Cantacuzino studied at Adrianople and Constantinople (1665–1667) and then in Italy at the University of Padua (1667–1669). He played an important political role in Wallachia as high steward in the time of his brother Şerban Cantacuzino's rule (1678–1688) and especially under the rule of Constantin Brîncoveanu (1688–1714) when, as Brîcoveanu's chief counselor, responsible for the country's foreign policy, he attempted to achieve a balance between the Ottoman Empire, Austria, and Russia. Toward the end, however, he plotted against his sovereign, who was deposed and killed, and succeeded in putting his own son Ştefan on the throne (1714–1716); the two, however, were executed only two years later in Constantinople. High steward Cantacuzino was a humanist with a very wide culture; the agitation of political life prevented him from showing in writing all of his capacities. In 1700, in Padua, he printed an outstanding map of Wallachia. His principal work, however, is *Istoria Ţării Româneşti* (History of Wallachia), unfinished and anonymous (first published in 1858). Only in 1899 was N. Iorga able to prove that Cantacuzino was the author. In presenting the ancient period, the Roman conquest of Dacia, and the formation of the Romanian people (to the fifth century), the high steward showed, through rich documentation, critical spirit, and scrupulous interpretation of sources, an understanding of history much superior to that of the Wallachian chroniclers of his times. Rejecting simple narration, he concentrated on presenting and analyzing the principal problems. He saw the formation of the Romanian people as a result of the melting of autochthonous Dacians and Roman colonists (while his contemporaries Miron Costin [q.v.] and Dimitrie Cantemir [q.v.] insisted on a strictly Latin origin), and he maintained, using logical argumentation to support his view, that the Romanized population continued to exist after the withdrawal of Roman rule in the second half of the third century.

Bibliography: Virgil Cândea ''Le stolnic Constantin Cantacuzène,'' *Revue roumaine d'histoire* 4 (1966): 587–629; idem, *Stolnicul între contemporani* (The High Steward among His Contemporaries) (Bucharest, 1971).

Lucian Boia

CANTEMIR, Dimitrie (Iaşi, 1673–Dimitrievka, near Moscow, 1723), Romanian prince and historian. The son of Constantin Cantemir (1685–1693), prince of Moldavia, Dimitrie Cantemir studied at the "Great School" of the Patriarchate of Constantinople (1688–1691); he ruled Moldavia for a very short time after the death of his father in 1693; then he lived in the Ottoman Empire until 1710 when he was named prince of Moldavia by the Turks. Wishing to liberate his country from Ottoman domination, he allied himself with Czar Peter the Great of Russia, but the Russian and Moldavian forces were defeated in 1711 at Stănileşti, on the Prut River; Cantemir fled to Russia, where, until his death, he remained as a close advisor to the czar and a member of the Imperial Senate. A man of great culture, a polyglot, and an expert in Eastern civilization, Cantemir has left a rich and varied collection of works. After his early works, which were philosophical and theological, and his allegorical novel *Istoria hieroglifică* (Hieroglyphic History), written in 1705, his major writings, which were essentially historical, followed in succession. In *Descriptio Moldaviae* (finished in 1716; first edition published in German: *Beschreibung der Moldau*, 1769–1770, followed by a second edition in 1771 also in German) he gave a very well-drawn general presentation of Moldavia in terms of its geographical, political, ethnographical, and cultural aspects. His best-known work, written in Latin, was his history of the Ottoman Empire: *Historia incrementorum atque decrementorum aulae othomanicae*, finished in 1716 but published later, first in an English version (*The History of the Growth and Decay of the Ottoman Empire*, 2 vols. [1734–1735; 2d ed., 1756]) and then in French (*Histoire de L'Empire Othoman* [1743]) and in German (*Geschichte des Osmanischen Reiches* [1745]). The book was especially valuable because it described Ottoman civilization including more recent events, and it remained the principal source of information in this field until the publication of Josef Hammer's work, *Geschichte des Osmanischen Reiches*, 1827–1834. The central theme was the decline of the empire, from which the Christian states were supposed to benefit. In 1722 he published in Russian at Petersburg a work on Moslem religion. In it he presented a general picture of the spiritual values of the Orient. When he participated in the Russian expedition in the Caucasus, also in 1722, he gathered material for a geographic and historical work on the region, but he did not have time to write it. On Romanian history, he wrote a biography of his father (*Vita Constantini Cantemyrii*), published in Latin and Russian in 1783, and *Evenimentele Cantacuzinilor şi ale Brîncovenilor* (The Deeds of the Cantacuzino and Brîncoveanu Families, which told about the confrontation between those two families from Wallachia), published in Russian in 1772 and in German in 1783. His most ambitious work, however, is *Hronicul vechimii romano-moldo-vlahilor* (Chronicle of the Antiquity of the Romano-Moldavians and Wallachians), written in Romanian between 1719 and 1722 and published for the first time in Romanian in 1835–1836 and again in 1901. This well-documented work offers a reconstruction of the ancient period of Romanian history until the thirteenth century, emphasizing the pure Latin origin of the Romanians and adding numerous pieces of information on the continuity of Romanian population in the medieval period. Cantemir is the first great Romanian historian who through his contributions left his imprint on world culture.

Bibliography: Virgil Cândea, *Dimitrie Cantemir (1673–1723), 300th Anniversary of His Birth* (Bucharest, 1973); P. P. Panaitescu, *Dimitrie Cantemir: Viaţa şi opera* (Dimitrie Cantemir: Life and Works) (Bucharest, 1958).

Lucian Boia

COSTIN, Miron (? 1633–Roman, 1691), Romanian chronicler from Moldavia. A member of the high nobility, Costin studied in Poland at the Jesuit college in Bar; then he occupied important functions in Moldavia including that of chancellor (1675–1683). He was beheaded in 1691, accused of having participated in a plot against the ruling prince, Constantin Cantemir. Miron Costin is the most important Romanian chronicler, noteworthy for his erudition and literary talent. He was influenced by classical Latin literature, European humanist culture, and Polish historiography. His major work is *Letopiseţul Ţării Moldovei* (Chronicle of Moldavia), completed in 1675, which covers the period 1595–1661. There he continued the chronicle of Grigore Ureche (1590–1647), and it was followed (to 1743) by Ioan Neculce (1672–1745). His work is noteworthy for the value of the information it contains as well as for the beauty of its style and the dramatic character of its narrative. He also wrote *De neamul moldovenilor* (On the Moldavian People), the first work in Romanian historiography on the origin of the Romanian people, which he considered to be of Latin stock. In 1677 he wrote, in Polish, a chronicle of Moldavia and of Wallachia: *Chronica ziem Moldawskich y Multanskich*, in which he emphasized the formation of the Romanian people and the Romanian states. To prove that the Romanians are descended from Romans, he undertook a detailed comparison of Latin and Romanian languages (compiling a list of eighty-seven Latino-Romanian etymologies). Living in an unsettled and difficult period, Costin had a fatalistic concept of history ("it is not the times that are under the helm of man, but helpless man under the times"). In politics he was an admirer of the Polish system and supported the preponderance of the nobility in running the state.

Bibliography: Miron Costin, *Opere* (Works), 2 vols. (Bucharest, 1965); Enache Puiu, *Viaţa şi opera lui Miron Costin* (The Life and Works of Miron Costin) (Bucharest 1975).

Lucian Boia

Great Historians: Russian

LOMONOSOV, Mikhail Vassilyevich (Denisovka Village, Arkhangelsk Province, 1711–Petersburg, 1765), Russian scientist and writer. Born into a peasant family, at the age of nineteen Lomonosov left for Moscow where he enrolled in the Slavic-Greek-Latin Academy. He became a student of the university at the St. Petersburg Academy of Sciences in 1735. A year later the academy sent him to Marburg to take a theoretical course in mathematics, physics, and philosophy and to Freiburg to learn chemistry and mineralogy. Upon returning to Russia in 1741, he worked until the end of his days at the St. Petersburg Academy of Sciences, Russia's chief scientific center. He worked his way up from student to academician and was an ardent promoter of Russian science and culture. His name is linked with the opening, in 1755, of Moscow University. He was a remarkable materialist philosopher, who also worked fruitfully in physics, chemistry, astronomy, astrophysics, geology, mineralogy, geography, geochemistry, physical chemistry, mining, soil studies, technology, history, economics, literature, and linguistics. As a poet of great merit, he wrought changes in the theory of the Russian literary language. As a historian he produced a number of special studies dealing with Russia's past *(Drevneishaya Rossiiskaya istoriya ot nachala rossiiskogo naroda do konchiny v.k. Yaroslava Pervogo, ili do 1054 goda* [Russia's Earliest History from the Beginnings of the Russian Nation to the Death of Grand Prince Yaroslav I, or to 1054] and *Kratkiy Rossiisky letopisets* [Short Russian Chronicle]. As were many other enlighteners, he was an idealist in his interpretation of social phenomena and pinned his hopes on an enlightened monarch. But unlike many of his contemporaries, he contributed immensely to a correct evaluation of the people's role in history. He had great faith in the people's creative strength, and he respected and honored their defense of the Fatherland. He was the first to mark the early Slavs' high economic and cultural level and the independent development of the Old Russian State. In his *O razmnozhenii i sokhranenii rossiiskogo naroda* (On the Reproduction and Preservation of the Russian Nation, 1761) he denounced serfdom. Foreign contemporaries such as Voltaire (q.v.), Leonard Euler, and Benjamin Franklin highly valued the Russian savant. In 1760 he was made an honorary member of the Swedish Academy of Sciences, and in 1763, of the Bologna Academy.

Bibliography: M. T. Belyavsky, *M. V. Lomonosov—nash pervyi universitet. K 250-letiyu so dnya rozhdeniya M. V. Lomonosova, 1711–1961* (Lomonosov—The First Russian University. In honor of his 250th Birthday, 1711–1961) (Moscow, 1961); B. B. Kudryavtsev, *Mikhail Vassilyevich Lomonosov* (Moscow, 1961); A. A. Morozov, *M. V. Lomonosov: Put k zrelosti, 1711–1741* (M. V. Lomonosov: The Road to Maturity, 1711–1741) (Moscow and Leningrad, 1962).

M. D. Kurmachev

NESTOR (? c. 1050–Kiev, 1120), early Russian chronicler and hagiographer; from age seventeen a monk at the Pechera Monastery (near Kiev) where he lived and worked for more than forty years until his death; a deacon. Nestor's historical records, *Povest vremennykh let* (A Tale of Bygone Years), written in Old Russian, was completed toward the end of his life (1013–1015). The original manuscript survived in fragments and is known to us from fourteenth-sixteenth century copies. The *Tale* narrates the history of the state of Rus and its origins as can be seen from the full title of the chronicles: *A Tale of Bygone Years, Whence Comes Russia, Who Was the First to Reign in Kiev and How Did the Russian State Emerge*. An authority on Russian chronicles, A. A. Shakhmatov, proved that this composition was not the first Russian chronicle to originate in Kiev. Nestor drew on his predecessor's (Ioanne, father superior of the Pechors Monastery) work of 1093–1905, *Nachalny Svod* (Primary Code), which highlighted the developments in Russia in the tenth and eleventh centuries as well as on many other sources, including the Byzantine Chronicle by Georgius Monachus (Amartol), Russia's Treaties with the Byzantine Empire in the tenth and eleventh centuries, *A Tale about the Origin of the Slavonic Alphabet*, and folk legends. Using these sources Nestor portrayed the origin and development of Rus. The history of the country that formerly began with the settlement of Slavic tribes in Eastern Europe was now related to world history through the biblical traditions about Noah's sons. In fact, *A Tale of Bygone Years* is an introduction to Nestor's chronicles. It provides a historical and geographical insight into the early history of Slavic tribes and their settlement in Europe, the origin of the Slavonic alphabet, the leading role of the Polyan tribe, and Kiy's dynasty, which preceded the dynasty of the Varangian prince invited by Novgorod. A critical assessment of sources and logic in selection of arguments to support his own judgments were not alien to Nestor's Christian pragmatic historicism. Writing on Russia's history of the ninth to eleventh century when the state was threatened with political fragmentation, he concentrated on Russia's unity and the role of her Kievan leaders. The idea of national unity permeating his work made it an outstanding piece of historiography and literature, a manual for all Russian historians of the thirteenth to sixteenth century. In the 1080s, before the *Tale*, Nestor had authored two hagiographies: *Readings on the Life and Death of Boris and Gleb, Brothers of Prince Yaroslav the Wise*, and *The Life of Theodosi (Father Superior and a Founding Father of the Pechera Monastery)*. Although these compositions follow the traditional patterns and show the author's excellent literary background, they also throw light on the activities of Kievan Russia's princes and, along with general topics, contain valuable information on everyday and public customs and activities of that time.

Bibliography: For the text of the *Tale* and its (modern) Russian translation, see *Pamyatniki literaturi drevnei Rusi, XI-pervaya polovina XII v* (Literary Monuments of Early Russia, Eleventh-First Half of Twelfth Century) (Moscow, 1978); for English translation and comments, see *The Russian Primary Chronicle, Laurentian Text*, The Mediaeval Academy of America, Publication no. 60, trans. and ed. S. H. Cross and O. P. Sherbowitz-Welzor (Cambridge, Mass., 1953); see also M. X. Aleshkovsky, *Povest vremennikh let: Sudba literaturnogo proizvedeniya v Drevnei Rusi* (A Tale of Bygone Years: The Destiny of a Literary Work in Early Russia) (Moscow, 1971); M. D. Priselkov, *Nestor-letopissets: Opyt istorico-literaturnoi kharakteristiki* (Chronicler Nestor: Experiment in Historical and Literary Description) (1923).

Y. N. Shchapov

TATISHCHEV, Vassily Nikitich (near Pskov, 1686–Boldino Village, Moscow Province, 1750), Russian statesman and historian. Tatishchev descended from a Smolensk family of nobility. Having finished the Moscow Engineering and Artillery School, in 1704 he entered military service and served in the Northern War. He traveled to Poland, Germany, and Sweden, carrying out diplomatic missions for Peter the Great. The years from 1720 to 1722 he spent in the Urals establishing state-owned enterprises and founding Ekaterinburg (now Sverdlovsk). After that he was given several important state posts. From 1734 to 1737 he served as governor of the Urals area and from 1741 to 1745 as governor of Astrakhan. Tatishchev was the first collector of historical sources—manuscripts, folk songs and legends, old maps, and so on. He prepared the first Russian historical source publication and put into circulation the texts of *Russkaya pravda* and *Sudebnik* (The Code of Laws) of 1550, supplemented with detailed commentaries. He launched ethnography, historical geography, and source studies in Russia and authored the first Russian encyclopedic dictionary *Leksikon* (Dictionary, three parts, 1793). He offered his own original classification of sciences in his *Razgovor dvukh pravitelei o polze nauk i uchilishch* (Discourse of Two Governors on the Benefit of Sciences and Schools, 1887). He regarded science as a means of self-perfection and self-cognition for the benefit of society. He wrote the first general history of his country, based on numerous Russian and foreign sources, entitled *Istoriya Rossiiskaya s samykh drevneishikh vremen* (History of Russia from the Earliest Times) in five volumes. Like all of his other works, it was published posthumously (1768–1848, 1962–1966). He was the first Russian historian to put forward the periodization of Russian history. Tatishchev rejected the providentialist point of view and as a rationalist connected the historical process with enlightenment. His was the first attempt in Russian historiography to reveal certain law-governed patterns of social development and to discover the reasons for the emergence of state power. He distinguished between three forms of government—monarchy, aristocracy, and democracy.

In his view, an autocratic monarchy was best suited for Russia. Later he came to be known as the Father of Russian History.

Bibliography: S. Blanc, *Un disciple de Pierre le Grand dans la Russie du XVIII siecle. V. N. Tatiscev (1686–1750)* (Lille, 1972); C. Grau, *Der Wirtschaftsorganisator, Staatsmann und Wissenschaftler Wasilij N. Tatiscev (1686–1750)* (Berlin, 1963); A. G. Kuzmin, *Tatishchev* (Moscow, 1981); *Ocherki istorii istoricheskoi nauki v SSSR* (Essays on the History of Historical Science in the USSR), vol. 1 (Moscow, 1955); A. I. Yukht, *Gosudarstvennaya deyatelnost V. N. Tatishcheva v 20-kh—nachale 30-kh godov XVIII veka* (Tatishchev's Statesmanship in the 1720s-Early 1730s) (Moscow, 1985).

R. A. Kireyeva

Great Historians: Serbian

BRANKOVIĆ, Count Djordje (Jenopolj, now Ineu, Romania, 1645–Cheb, now Czechoslovakia, 1711), Serbian historian and politician. Branković was educated in Alba Iulia by his brother Sava, the Transylvanian metropolitan. He entered the service of Prince Michail Apaffy (1661–1690) and was sent as interpreter to Constantinople (1663). On the way he met, in Edirne (Adrianople), the Serbian patriarch of Peč, Maksim, who, as Branković claimed later, bestowed upon him the title of Serbian despot. In 1668 Djordje accompanied his brother Sava to Moscow where they requested Russian support for the Serbian Church. During 1675–1677 Branković represented the Transylvanian prince in Constantinople. Involved, after his return, in a conspiracy against Prince Apaffy, Branković was arrested with his brother the metropolitan. In 1680 Djordje moved to Bucharest where the Wallachian prince Şerban Cantacuzino offered him hospitality. Branković persuaded the prince to approach the court in Vienna. The Austrian emperor Leopold tried to profit from Branković's alleged descent from the Serbian despots to involve the Serbs on the Austrian side in the coming war with the Turks in 1683. Branković was given the title of a Hungarian baron. In 1688 he obtained a written statement from the Serbian patriarch Arsenije III confirming Branković's descent from the despots. At that time the Austrian counteroffensive was moving toward the Balkans and Branković presented to Emperor Leopold a proposal to establish an "Illyrian kingdom" from the Adriatic to the Black Sea of which Branković was to be a despot under Austrian rule. The emperor only partially responded to the proposal. Branković was bestowed with the title of count of the Holy Roman Empire. However, the emperor was reluctant to found a Slavic state on his southern borders. Branković was sent to Transylvania to cooperate with the military command. In Orsova (Wallachia) he issued in 1689 a manifesto to the "peoples of Eastern and Northern Illyria, Thracia and Maesia" that he signed as despot of Upper and Lower Maesia, grand duke of the Holy Roman Empire, the ruler of Saint Sava's, Montenegro's, and Hercegovinian's duchies. His call for an uprising failed. Already seeming suspicious to the Austrians, who discovered his previous ties with the Russians and were angered by his independent action, Branković was arrested and sent to prison in Sibiu (October 1689). From there he was interned in Vienna (until

1703) and the fortress in Cheb, where he died in 1711. During his confinement in Vienna, Brankovic kept close contacts with the Serbian leaders who elected him despot at a meeting in Buda (1691). The Austrian authorities refused to approve the election. During imprisonment Branković wrote *Slaveno-Serbske Hronike* (Slavo-Serbian Chronicles), an opus of five volumes totaling 2,681 pages. His intention was to write a history from the creation of the world until his own time, but the primary goal was to prove his descendence from the last Serbian despots and the medieval Nemanjides. The first, unfinished volume comprised a universal chronicle of events until the coming of the Slavs to the Balkans. The next volumes dealt with Byzantine history and the history of the Romanian principalities and Turkey. The last volume, also not accomplished, covered his own time in a kind of memoir. The historical value of Branković's chronicles, with the exception of the last volume, are dubious. He had a solid knowledge of sources of which he found many in the Bucharest library of Constantine Cantacuzino, the brother of Prince Şerban. But he used sources uncritically. Some of his supplements are falsifications and inventions. The language and style were heavy and confusing. Chronicles were never published; the manuscript was stored in the library of the Patriarchate in Karlovci. They were later partially copied and published (Vuk Karadžić, Ilarion Ruvarac, Stojan Novaković). Their importance lies in the impact they had on the formation of modern Serbian nationalism through their patriotic message. They were used to justify and prove Serbian demands for national rights in the Hapsburg monarchy. The chronicles inspired later historians to make similar endeavors. J. Dobrovski thought them to be "the foundation of modern Serbian literature." Much later (in 1896) Ilarion Ruvarac rejected the legend of the Branković ties to the despots and subjected the chronicles to sharp criticism.

Bibliography: B. Djurdjev, B. Grafenauer, and J. Tadić, *Historija naroda Jugoslavije*, vol. 2 (Zagreb, 1959), pp. 820–825; Jovan Radonjić, *Grof Djordje Brankovic i njegovo vreme* (Beograd, 1911); N. Radojčić, "O Hronikama grofa Djordja Brankovića," in *Prilozi za književost, jezik, istoriju i folklor*, vol 6, Bk. 1 (Beograd, 1926), pp. 7–13; R. Samardžić, "Djordje Branković, Istorijske i političke osnove prvog srpskog programa," in *Pisci srpske istorije*, vol. 3 (Beograd, 1986), pp. 7–25.

Dimitrije Djordjevic

RAJIĆ, Jovan (Sremski Karlovci, 1726–monastery Kovilje, 1801), historian of Serbs and South Slavs. Rajić received his primary education in Serbian and Russian schools in Karlovci. He graduated from the high school in Komarom and Sopron (Hungry) and studied at the Spiritual Academy in Kiev (1753–56) under the famous theologian Teophan Prokopovich. After a brief journey to Moscow, Rajić returned to Karlovci but left again for Mount Athos, via Poland, the Romanian principalities, and Constantinople. Back home, he was ordained in the monastery of Kovilje (1772, Fruška Gora), where he spent the rest of his life as an archbishop. The contemporary Serbian intelligentsia in southern Hungary was influenced by Russian theology, rationalism, European historiography, and the historical legacy transferred to Hungary by the Serbian migration in 1690. In 1741 Hristifor Žefarović reproduced copperplates of the medieval Serbian and Bulgarian coats of arms; in 1765 Pavle Julinac published in Venice the first history of the Serbian people (*Kratkoe vvedenie v istoriju slaveno-serbskago naroda*), and Zaharije Orfelin (1726–1785) became the first editor of Serbian journals. Rajić espoused the ideas of pan-Slavism, Serbianism, and Enlightenment. A theologian by training, he wanted to protect Orthodoxy from Catholicism. His writing was based on previous works of Mavro Orbini (q.v.), Ritter Pavao Vitezović (q.v.), and other historians as well as sources he found in Kiev and especially in the Serbian monastery of Hilandar in Mount Athos, where he encouraged Father Paisii (q.v.) to write the history of the Bulgarian people. Working daily sixteen to seventeen hours, Rajić was extremely productive. Besides theological treaties, literary essays, and translations, his main work was the *Istoria raznih slavenskih narodov naipače Bolgar, Horvatov i Serbov* (The History of Various Slavic Peoples Especially Bulgars, Croats, and Serbs) in four volumes, published in 1794–1795. The intention was to present Serbian history as a part of the history of the South Slavs and closely connected to Russia. In the first volume Rajić dealt with the general Slavic and Bulgarian history; in the second he described the Croatian history (until the eighteenth century) and the Serbian past (until the 1371 Maritsa battle). In the third volume the period of Prince Lazar and the Serbian despots until the 1526 battle of Mohacz is exposed. The fourth volume concerns the history of the Serbs in Hungary and ends with the dissolution of the Patriarchate of Peć (1766).

The impact of Rationalism is visible in Rajić's writing. However, the historian was torn between rationalism, orthodoxy, Slavophilism, and Serbian legacy. As a rationalist he rejected the oral epic tradition; as an Orthodox monk he treated foreign and Catholic writers as enemies of his people. The composition of his study is often repetitious. He mechanically joined together contradicting sources, and his judgment was didactical and moralistic. He omitted sources he disliked. Imbued with patriotic and religious zeal he argued disdainfully with opponents. The language he used was a strange mixture of Church Slavonic and Russian; the style was heavy and pompous. However, in spite of these shortcomings, Rajić preserved and reproduced many sources that, without him, would have been lost forever. He was important by the influence he had on further generations of Serbian historians. The first volume of his history was reprinted in Russia and all four volumes in Buda in 1828. Johann Christian Engel (1770–1814) translated some parts in German, with a critical appraisal. Many abstracts were later also published. Until the 1860s Serbian historians focused upon Rajić. His history became a kind of bible of the Serbian national renaissance during the 1804–1813 uprising and inspired the historical writing of Vuk Karadžić. It served as a source of inspiration for painters, poets, and novelists who turned to the past during the period of romanticism. In that manner Rajić became the forerunner of modern Serbian historiography.

Bibliography: N. Radojčić, ''Srpski istoricar Jovan Rajić,'' in *Posebna izdanja SAN* 204 (Beograd, 1952); ''Položaj Jovana Rajića,'' in *Pisci srpske istorije*, vol. 1 (Beograd, 1976); Dimitrije Ruvarac, *Arhimandrit Jovan Rajić, 1726–1801*; Radovan Samardžić, ''Jovan Rajić, Vek prosvećenosti i srpski preobražaj.''

Dimitrije Djordjevic

Great Historians: Southeast Asian

AMIN, Enci' (? seventeenth century), Indonesian court scribe, poet, and historical writer. Enci' Amin was for many years secretary to the court of Goa (South Sulawesi, Indonesia) and is especially well known for his service to Sultan Hasanuddin (reigned 1653–1669). He possessed an intimate knowledge of the Makasarese ruling elite of his day, including leaders in the powerful trading community, and was responsible not only for writing or copying ordinary correspondence and taking notes at court meetings, but also for reading, copying, and lecturing about important contemporary Malay writings, both secular and religious, from throughout the archipelago. A contemporary of Syaich Yusuf of Makasar, a Sufi "saint" highly favored at court, Amin was a follower of a Wujudiyyah-type Sufi sect and an admirer of the poet Hamzah Fansuri. The single work by which Amin is known today is the *Syair Perang Mengkasar* (The Story of the Makasar War, 1670), in which he slyly described himself as "a clever fellow of rather small stature but well built . . . a man to be envied . . . graceful and attractive." The *Syair Perang Mengkasar* is a remarkable historical account, in traditional poetic form, of the war that the Makasarese fought with the Dutch between 1666 and 1667. Like other chroniclers of his time, Amin was required to entertain audiences with his work, praise his patron the sultan, and in general portray the court in the best light possible, but he also took seriously the duty of recording the events of the past. The work makes no claim to be objective; Amin viewed the conflict in black-and-white terms and was not inclined to say anything directly critical about his side. In the eyes of modern historians there are additional weaknesses: the underlying economic causes of the war receive little attention, for example, and military strategy is hardly considered, although it was in all likelihood very important to the outcome of the conflict. Yet the *Syair Perang Mengkasar* is factually very close to Dutch accounts, both contemporary and those composed later from documentary sources; in some respects Amin's details are superior. In addition, the *Syair Perang Mengkasar* is full of shrewd, vivid portraits of individuals and their emotions. Whether Amin's work is a representative piece of seventeenth-century Makasarese historical writing is uncertain, because few specimens of this genre are known. The *Syair Perang Mengkasar* is no less "historical" than the Malay *silsilah* and *hikayat* of its day, but it is possible that Amin deliberately borrowed from them to give his poetic text more historical content than the *syair* normally possessed in court writing, thereby contributing to Indonesian historiography a new and perhaps unique type of epic history.

Bibliography: Enci' Amin, *Sja'ir Perang Mengkasar*, ed. and trans. C. Skinner (The Hague, 1963).

William H. Frederick

BAJRA, Carik (Tumenggung Tirtawiguna) (? c. 1690s–? c. 1760s), Indonesian court secretary, poet, and chronicler. Few biographical details have been recorded about Carik Bajra, a well-known figure in Kartasura and Surakarta, Central Java, during the first half of the eighteenth century. He served the court of Mataram from an early age and in 1719 was given the title Tumenggung Tirtawiguna in recognition of his talent and position. In 1728, as secretary to the Javanese ruler, he participated in a diplomatic mission to Batavia (Jakarta), and in 1737 he made a similar trip and joined in signing a treaty with Dutch East India Company officials. Carik Bajra is popularly known as the author of numerous works from the culturally rich Kartasura period; the *Babad Kartasura* (History of Kartasura), *Damar Wulan*, *Sasana Prabu*, *Dasa Nama*, and many other poems, romances, and histories are ascribed to him. But his most famous contribution to Indonesian historiography is associated with the renowned *Babad Tanah Jawi* (The Javanese State Chronicles), of which he wrote two recensions, one in the 1720s and another after 1757. The *Babad Tanah Jawi* has been the object of much study, yet remains poorly understood compared to many other works of similar importance to Southeast Asian history. (There is no full translation from the original Javanese in any language, including modern Indonesian.) The original text of the *Babad Tanah Jawi* was probably written during the reign of Sultan Agung (1613–1645) to create a legitimizing, unifying historical background for the new state of Mataram. A subsequent version was written by Pangeran Adi Langu II early in the eighteenth century, by which time the Mataram ruling house, which was of comparatively modest social origin, had become firmly committed to a policy of heightening its prestige—especially in relation to the cultured noble families of Java's coastal region—by commissioning dynastic histories.

When Carik Bajra was asked to write his first recension of the *Babad Tanah Jawi*, his task was to show convincingly that in 1677 Sunan Mangkurat had rightly acceded to the throne and that his brother Pangeran Puger was entitled to succeed him. This was history with a clear political purpose. Carik Bajra's second assignment on the *Babad Tanah Jawi* required him not only to bring the chronicle up to date but to make the current ruler look as good as possible. Despite the justificatory aims and a tendency to use prophecies and supernatural events as explanations for events and policies, characteristics also found in later versions, the work remains a great deal more than an astounding piece of literature. Carik Bajra had access to and used court libraries and the range of documents stored in them; he may also have brought his own experiences to bear on his account of the recent past. Scholarship has shown that many sections describe events accurately, chronologically, and realistically. The suppositions that the Javanese cared little for their past or that the *Babad Tanah Jawi* is comprehensible only as sacral or "magical" writing are uncalled for. Carik Bajra's versions of the *Babad Tanah Jawi*, which unfortunately are known chiefly for their earliest portions describing legendary Java, exhibit in general a deft mixture of traditional Javanese literary convention and historical account as we might recognize it today, representing the classic form of the chronicles on which the later court historians of Java based their work and to which present-day scholars of Java must return for an understanding of the seventeenth and eighteenth centuries.

Bibliography: H. J. de Graaf, "Later Javanese Sources and Historiography," in Soedjatmoko et al., *An Introduction to Indonesian Historiography* (Ithaca, N.Y., 1964), pp. 119–136; Merle C. Ricklefs, "A Consideration of Three Versions of the *Babad Tanah Jawi*, with Excerpts on the Fall of Majapahit," *Bulletin of the School of Oriental and African Studies* 35, no. 2 (1972): 285–315; partial Dutch translation: J. J. Meinsma, *Babad Tanah Jawi in Proza. Javaansche Geschiedenis Loopende tot het Jaar 1647 der Javaansche Jaartelling* ('s-Gravenhage, 1903); partial modern Indonesian translation: Z. H. Sudibyo, *Babad Tanah Jawi* (Jakarta, 1980).

William H. Frederick

BODHIRANGSI, Mahathera (? late fourteenth century–? midfifteenth century), Thai Buddhist monk and chronicler. The Lanna Tai (Chiengmai) monk Bodhirangsi, about whom we have almost no biographical information, is known today as the author of two Pali works of uncertain date, the *Sihinganidana* (The Story of the Sihinga Buddha) and the *Camadevivamsa* (The History of Queen Camadevi). The latter is one of the best-known examples of *tamnan*, or Buddhist universal histories. Such works were written primarily with the idea of offering a guide to human activities by gleaning lessons from the past, and Buddhist values were to be imparted to the reader along with a description of events; only in this fashion would the history have meaning. The *Camadevivamsa*, like many other *tamnan*, was also written to emphasize to society the importance of continuity of community, especially as represented by Buddhism, and it seeks to explain how the famous Buddha image, and therefore Buddhism, came to the ancient kingdom of Hariphunjaya. It begins with the Buddha's prophecy of the founding of the city of Hariphunjaya, focuses on the early years of the kingdom in the seventh and eighth centuries, and ends with the discovery of the Buddha relic some three hundred years later. Bodhirangsi's interest did not lie in the pursuit of facts or in the discovery of historical laws but in confirming the interdependence of events and human behavior according to Buddhist moral principles. In this scheme of things, what was historically true did not necessarily matter, although accuracy in the historical material used was sought; the important thing was to draw the proper conclusions from appropriately selected examples; critical evaluation of evidence, including distinguishing between legend and actual event, was unimportant to the task at hand. Nevertheless, Bodhirangsi's work is of considerable interest to modern historians, both for what it suggests to us about the world-view of fifteenth-century Thai Buddhist society and because it is based at least in part on contemporaneous Thai inscriptions, from which Bodhirangsi occasionally quoted, and on eyewitness accounts, which are identified as such.

Bibliography: *Camadevivamsa*, modern Thai translation: *Ruanq Chammathewiwong, Phongsawadan Muang Hariphunchai* (Bangkok, 1921; repr. 1930, 1967); partial French translations: C. Notton, *Annales du Siam. Vol. 2: Chronique de La:pun, Histoire de la Dynastie Chamt'evi* (Paris, 1930); G. Coedès, "Documents sur l'histoire politique et réligieuse du Laos occidental," *Bulletin de l'Ecole Française d'Extrême-Orient* 25, nos. 1–2 (1925): 141–171; Anan Panjanapan, "Early Lan Na Thai Historiography: An Analysis of the Fifteenth- and Sixteenth-Century Chronicles" (M.A. thesis, Cornell University, 1976); *Sihinganidana*, French translation: C. Notton, *P'ra Buddha Sihinga* (Bangkok, 1933); David K. Wyatt, "Chronicle Traditions in Thai Historiography," in C. D. Cowan and O. W. Wolters, eds., *Southeast Asian History and Historiography* (Ithaca, N. Y., 1976), pp. 107–122.

William H. Frederick

HORATHIBODI, Phra (? eighteenth century), Thai court astrologer and compiler of chronicles. Little is known about this individual, who is the author of one of the earliest and best-known examples of the *phongsawadan* genre of Thai kingly histories, the *Phraratchaphongsawadan Krung Si Ayudhya chabap Luang Prasoet* (The Luang Prasoet Chronicle of Ayudhya), written during the reign of King Narai (1657–1688). *The Luang Prasoet Chronicle* so called after the individual who published the rediscovered work in 1907, departs from the earlier *tamnan* tradition of Buddhist histories. The author was not a monk, and the purpose was not to view events in a Buddhist framework but to record as accurately as possible—Phra Horathibodi used his astrologer's notebooks to record exact dates of events—activities and occurrences at the royal court. The language used was Thai, rather than the Pali of the *tamnan*. This historiographical change was not an indication that Buddhism had lost its importance in Thai society but that certain kinds of social change had taken place, among them the rise of a new and secular class of literati, and that a single, encompassing state had come into being. In addition, it seems likely that the appearance of Westerners, who frequently asked questions about the "real" and political history of Ayudhya, had some influence on the development of this sort of chronicle, although it cannot be said that the *phongsawadan* represented a Thai effort to imitate Western history writing. There are more than a dozen versions of the chronicles of Ayudhya, most produced in the early years of the Bangkok period, but nearly all seem to derive in some way from the Luang Prasoet recension. By the late nineteenth century Thai historiography had made another change, this time as a more direct result of Western influence, toward analytical history such as that first represented by the work of Prince Damrong Rajanubhab.

Bibliography: Charnvit Kasetsiri, "Thai Historiography from Ancient Times to the Modern Period," in Anthony Reid and David Marr, eds., *Perceptions of the Past in Southeast Asia* (Singapore, 1979), pp. 156–170; David K. Wyatt, "Chronicle Traditions in Thai History," in C. D. Cowan and O. W. Wolters, eds., *Southeast Asian History and Historiography* (Ithaca, N. Y., 1976), pp. 107–122; English translation: O. Frankfurter, "Events in Ayudhya from Chulasakaraj 686–966," *Journal of the Siam Society* 6, no. 3 (1909): 1–21.

William H. Frederick

KALA, U (Ava? c. 1678–? c. 1730?), Burmese historian. The son of a wealthy banker and a woman of noble background, U Kala had both the means and inclination to devote himself to a scholarly life. He is the first Burmese lay historian of whom we have record, traditional historical writing being generally the work of Buddhist monks or court ministers. U Kala's masterwork is the *Mahayazawingyi* (Great Royal Chronicle), probably completed in 1724, with a postscript describing the investiture of the heir apparent to the throne in 1729. This history, which begins with the creation of the world and proceeds to discuss the spread of Buddhism, the founding of the early Burmese kingdom of Srikshetra, and the story of dynasties until the reign of King Taninganwe (1714–1733), is the earliest existing Burmese chronicle except for Shin Thilawuntha's short *Yazawingyi* of 1520; comprising twenty-one volumes, it has never been published in its entirety, although several abridged versions exist. With the *Mahayazawingyi*, U Kala introduced to Burmese historiography a new attention to documentation and a preference for a unified historical view rather than a regional one. He assembled a wide range of materials from local oral legends to written sources and integrated them skillfully to form a single account. Over seventy primary sources are readily identifiable, and others such as records of the *hlutdaw* (royal council) and royal correspondence, to which U Kala had access, are incorporated as well. U Kala argued that a thoroughly reliable record of royal activities would serve present and future rulers as a guide to proper behavior, but he avoided what he seems to have considered the excessive moralizing and narrow outlook of his predecessors. Because U Kala came from a wealthy family with court connections and wrote in a period of comparative political tranquility, he did not find it necessary to glorify an insecure monarch or concern himself unduly with the possibility of royal reprisal for slights to the crown. The combination of simple, direct narrative—the substantial accuracy of which is demonstrable, at least for the portions dealing with the sixteenth to early eighteenth centuries—and a certain elegance of literary style make U Kala's *Mahayazawingyi* a true landmark in traditional Burmese historiography. Virtually all subsequent indigenous histories until the early twentieth century are founded upon it, and it is indispensable to Western scholars of the Burmese past. U Kala is also known to be the author of the *Yazawinlat*, an abbreviated version of the *Mahayazawingyi*, and of the *Yazawinchot*.

Bibliography: U Kala, *Mahayazawindaw Gyi*, 3 vols., ed. Pe Maung Tin, Saya Pwa, and Saya U Khin Soe (Rangoon, 1960–1961); Victor Lieberman, "How Reliable Is U

Kala's Burmese Chronicle? Some New Comparisons,'' *Journal of Southeast Asian Studies* 17, no. 2 (September 1986): 236–255.

William H. Frederick

LE Quy Don (? 1726–? 1784), Vietnamese philosopher and historian. An academic child prodigy who went on to become the outstanding Vietnamese intellectual of the eighteenth century, Le Quy Don placed first in the civil service examinations of 1752, traveled to China as an envoy of the Vietnamese court, and wrote perhaps as many as sixty books on a variety of philosophical and historical subjects. His most expansive work is undoubtedly the *Dai Viet Thong Su* (Complete History of Dai Viet, 50 vols., 1749), one of the most important works on Vietnamese history. It covers the Le dynasty from its beginning in 1428 to 1527 and includes biographies of prominent Mac family members as well as an extensive bibliography of historical sources. Because it was written as a ''private'' rather than an official court history, it is of particular interest to contemporary scholars. But Le Quy Don's historical outlook or philosophy, which was based on Neo-Confucian ideas, is more explicitly expressed in later works such as *Van Dai Loai Ngu* (Classified Discourse of the Library, 1773) and *Kien Van Tieu Luc* (Small Chronicle of Things Seen and Heard, 1777). He did not take a static view of existence but generally allowed for change and variation within a universal moral framework. When humanity cooperated spontaneously with the laws of nature, harmony was the result; when it did not, and when change violated unchanging morality, disaster was insured. He frequently seems to have been motivated by a concern that so much of Vietnam's history—in the sense of a knowledge of court rules, ceremonies, and other details of social organization—had disappeared and could not be recovered. But his chief interest lay in understanding the principles of social change, especially as they could be charted through an understanding of the historical evolution of, for example, civil service regulations, clothing, and rites. He was fascinated with the relationship between natural forms (*the*) and man-made rules (*le*). He did not hesitate to criticize when he thought criticism was deserved, and he showed great skepticism in all matters, especially those involving assumptions of Chinese superiority over Vietnamese civilization. In a famous passage Le Quy Don accepted the idea of a correspondence between the stars and earthly events but asked, if the ''great dome of the heavens was so immensely broad,'' what were astrological calculations based on and why did they seem to apply only to China? The chief difference between Le Quy Don's point of view and those of many Western contemporaries was that the latter generally assumed a difference between the principles on which society operated and those on which history, in the larger sense, proceeded. Le Quy Don saw only one source of moral authority and only one moral principle for both, and his histories made their judgments on this basis. Such a view, usually without the benefit of Le Quy Don's appreciation of the organic nature of change in history, prevailed among Vietnamese intellectuals until the end of the traditional order in Vietnam in the twentieth century.

Bibliography: Alexander Woodside, "Conceptions of Change and of Human Responsibility for Change in Late Traditional Vietnam," in David K. Wyatt and Alexander Woodside, *Moral Order and the Question of Change: Essays on Southeast Asian Thought* (New Haven, 1982), pp. 104–150; partial French translation of *Kien Van Tieu Luc*, Maurice Durand, "Le Quy Don: Notes des Choses Vues et Entendues," *Bulletin de la Société des Etudes Indochinoises*, n.s. 48 (1973): 51–116; modern Vietnamese translations: Hanoi, 1962; Saigon, 1963–1965.

William H. Frederick

LE Van Huu (? thirteenth century), Vietnamese scholar and historian. A civil-examination graduate of 1247, and for a time an official at the Han Lam academy, Le Van Huu was commissioned by the court to compile a comprehensive history of Vietnam from the time of Trieu Da (third century B.C.) to the end of the Ly dynasty in 1224. He presented his *Dai Viet Su Ky* (The Vietnamese Annals), in thirty volumes, in 1272. No copy of this important work (which probably was itself based heavily upon an earlier history) now exists, but it was the foundation for the subsequent compliations *Dia Viet Su Ky Toan Thu* (1479) by Ngo Si Lien, the *Viet Su Tian Thu* (1663) by Phan Cong Tru, and the *Dai Viet Su Ky Tuc Bien* (c. 1800) compiled under the supervision of Nguyen Quang Toan. Le Van Huu adhered to the classical Confucian historiographical tradition in which history was written for the edification of the ruler and the good of the realm, that is, for the moral and political lessons it might be made to yield. In Huu's own day the Tran court wanted to express in its historical outlook the idea of its rightful independence from China, then under Mongol rule and threatening the Vietnamese. Huu accomplished the purpose adroitly by acknowledging the efficacy of the classical Chinese model, but at the same time treating it as universal and therefore perfectly serviceable for Vietnam. Trieu Da, a Chinese adventurer who seized the Vietnamese throne and ruled from Canton, is treated by Huu as an ideal ruler on the Chinese pattern as well as an exemplary practitioner of independence. In recognizing imperial China and the principles on which it operated, Huu cleverly announced the launching of imperial Vietnam and indeed was able to do this in the very terms the Chinese understood and would have used to assert themselves. Thus rulers of the past who came in for special praise were those who had avenged Chinese attacks and in doing so upheld good Confucian political principles. Le Van Huu's treatment of Vietnam's past was also filled with frank criticisms of the Vietnamese court, for example, for not solving the troublesome matter of royal succession and for not curbing polygamous tendencies—in other words, for not sufficiently measuring up to Confucian ideals. Although Huu's ideas of historical change are not altogether clear, he was not inclined to suggest that the Vietnamese merely rest on a model such as that offered by Chinese civilization, however much it might be adapted to Vietnamese realities, but seems instead to have viewed Confucian historical understanding as requisite background for coping with ever-changing circumstances. This sense of dynamism and ongoing transition in the application of the lessons of the past was a characteristic that Le Van Huu passed down to many Vietnamese historians who followed in his footsteps.

Bibliography: O. W. Wolters, "Historians and Emperors in Vietnam and China: Comments Arising Out of Le Van Huu's History, Presented to the Tran Court in 1272," in Anthony Reid and David Marr, eds., *Perceptions of the Past in Southeast Asia* (Singapore, 1979), pp. 69–89; idem, "Le Van Huu's Treatment of Ly Than Ton's Reign (1127–1137)," in C. D. Cowan and O. W. Wolters, eds., *Southeast Asian History and Historiography* (Ithaca, N. Y., 1976), pp. 203–226.

William H. Frederick

PRAPAÑCA (? fourteenth century), Indonesian Buddhist official, court poet, and chronicler. Little is known of the personal life of this early Javanese historian. Prapañca may be the writer's sacerdotal name, his layman's name being Winada, or it may simply be a nom de plume. In any case, he bore the court title *mpu* (sir) and the honorific *sang*; he was a *rakawi* or official court poet, and also may have held the rank of *dharmadyaksa*, or religious superintendent, as did his father. He was probably about the same age as the ruler he served, King Hayam Wuruk (Rajasanagara), who ruled from 1350 to 1389. Prapañca is the author of a number of long poems known as *kakawin* and chronicles of various kinds but does not appear to have been considered in his day a distinguished poet. The work for which he is known today, the *Nagarakertagama* (The Kingdom Which Is Ordered According to Sacred Tradition), does not appear to have been famed in its own time and, at least in the opinion of scholars of Old Javanese literature, offers no evidence of special talent. Indeed, Prapañca's contemporary Mpu Tantular, whose works include the *Sutasoma* and *Arjuna Wiwaha*, came much closer to exemplifying existing ideals. Nevertheless, the *Nagarakertagama*, which was originally called the *Desawarnana* (Description of the Country) and later retitled by a Balinese scribe, has come to represent to later generations a unique source of information about Java in the fourteenth century.

The work was completed in 1365 and covers the years 1353–1364; it was not intended as a historical source of the type we are familiar with today and is widely understood to be a panegyric for Hayam Wuruk, whose favor Prapañca hoped to secure. Yet the term *panegyric* is not really suitable for most of the text, and it is possible that Prapañca also had in mind creating something fresh and historical, for the *Nagarakertagama* runs at odds with convention by presenting an unusually personal view of events. Although the form is poetic, Prapañca revealed in his approach that he was more scholar than poet: he mentioned his sources frequently and indicated when he was drawing on legends as opposed to other sources such as interviews or monastic records; he witnessed most of the events he described and frequently told his reader when he was or was not sharing firsthand information. These characteristics make this work the most valuable source extant on the history of the kingdom of Majapahit and have led one scholar to call it the starting point of Javanese historiography. We cannot be certain of the precise view of history Prapañca meant to exhibit in the *Nagarakertagama*. He did include a brief traditional chronicle, including an only partially accurate chronology of Javanese rulers, in the body of the text. Perhaps this was for convention's sake, and Prapañca inserted it clumsily. But in general Prapañca seems to aim at a work deliberately shorn of myth and literary prettification, deliberately descriptive and realistic. Like the famed Gajah Mada, Hayam Wuruk's powerful prime minister, Prapañca spoke of world conquest (*digwijaya*) and perhaps saw Majapahit's "real" history, as opposed to its legends and royal chronicles, as a more suitable model for the future. In this manner Prapañca may have attempted, in a gentle fashion, to update and reform the ways in which Majapahitan society gazed into the mirror of the past. If so, he was not, at least in the short run, successful, for we know of nothing remotely like it until certain Javanese works of the nineteenth century.

Bibliography: Th. G. Th. Pigeaud, trans., with commentary, *Java in the Fourteenth Century, a Study in Cultural History: The Nagara-kertagama by Rakawi Prapañca of Majapahit, 1365* A.D., 3d ed., 5 vols. (The Hague, 1962); P. J. Zoetmulder, *Kalangwan* (The Hague, 1974).

William H. Frederick

RATTANAPAÑÑA, Thera (? late fifteenth century–? mid-sixteenth century), Thai Buddhist monk and chronicler. An adherent of the New Ceylon School associated with Wat Pa Daeng in Chiengmai, Rattanapañña is known as the author of the famed *Jinakalamali* (The Sheaf of Garlands of the Epochs of the Conqueror), the most ambitious of a number of existing Pali *tamnan* or Buddhist universal histories. The work was completed in 1516–1517, although an addendum moves its story forward to 1527. The *Jinakalamali* presents the history of Buddhism from its origins in India and spread to Ceylon, to the introduction and expansion of the Sinhalese (Mahavira) form in Burma and Thailand, especially the kingdoms of Hariphunjaya, Sukothai, Ayuthia, and Lanna (Chiengmai). Rattanapañña used a wide variety of sources in compiling his account, among them the *Mulasasana* (The Origins of Buddhism) and the *Chronicle of Yonok*, building from them a narrative that is both strong in descriptive detail and aesthetically pleasing as a work of poetry. Its historical trustworthiness, especially in the sections dealing with Chiengmai, has been well established by later scholarship. A large number of place names and locations of Buddhist monuments, for example, can be identified from the text, and many historical names and dates can be verified in other sources. Because of its often precise descriptive qualities, it is useful as a source of information about social life in fifteenth- and sixteenth-century Thailand. Yet the *Jinakalamali* remains a *tamnan* of the traditional sort. It does not always distinguish between the clearly legendary or fantastic and the historical, and it views and teaches the past within the framework of Buddhist historical experience and Buddhist morals. In a final portion it becomes as well a kind of panegyric for the Lanna rulers Tilokaracha

(1441–1487) and Müang Kaeo (1495–1526), both supporters of the New Ceylon school, whose reigns are held up as examples for others to follow. Rattanapañña wrote in the epilogue, "Let all the lords of men who rejoice in unison in the performance of good deeds rule their subjects in accordance with the sacred word," thus leaving little doubt that the author did not consider even kings entirely above reproach or the need for moral and historical instruction.

Bibliography: Anan Ganjanapan, "Early Lan Na Thai Historiography: An Analysis of the Fifteenth- and Sixteenth-Century Chronicles" (M. A. thesis, Cornell University, 1976); Rattanapañña Thera, *The Sheaf of Garlands of the Epochs of the Conqueror*, trans. N. A. Jayawickrama (London, 1968).

William H. Frederick

TUN SERI LANANG, Bendahara Paduka Raja (also known as Tun Muhammad) (? late sixteenth century–? early seventeenth century), Malay statesman and chronicler. The son of Tun Ahmad, *temenggung* of Johor, and his wife, Tun Ganggang, Tun Seri Lanang was reared and educated in the shadow of the palace of the sultan of Johor. His principal tutor in language and literature was probably his maternal grandfather, Bendahara Seri Maharaja Tun Isap Misai, author of a (now lost) manuscript entitled *Anak Panak Sa-dasa*. Tun Seri Lanang is known to historians as the author of the principal recension of the *Sejarah Melayu* (Malay Annals), written between 1612 and 1615. There has been much debate about the various manuscripts of the *Sejarah Melayu*, their origin and authorship, but it is not unreasonable to believe that the recension in question, the earliest dated version (although the extant copy was made in the nineteenth century), was commissioned from Tun Seri Lanang by a certain Raja Abdullah, who had acquired a manuscript from Goa, Sulawesi, which needed expansion and improvement. Whatever the case, the *Sejarah Melayu* is generally considered the most important chronicle of the Malays, a masterpiece of classical Malay literature as well as of historical writing. It takes the form of a *hikayat* (story, account), or a collection of episodic accounts, and seeks to outline the genealogy of Malay kings and the details of ceremony and beliefs surrounding them; the overall purpose is to enlighten future generations, thereby insuring the continuity of the kingdom. Both the kingdom and its people are glorified, and rulers are praised and occasionally criticized according to the author's judgment. Almost certainly, too, the work was constructed as an entertainment, and there is not only plenty of drama and cleverness on display but also arresting portraits of a large cast of characters. The account begins with Alexander the Great (Raja Iskandar) and carries the story of Melaka to the time of Alauddin Riayat Shah, the first sultan of Johor, who began his reign in the early 1530s. As is the case with a great many other such Southeast Asian materials, from the point of view of modern, Western-style historiography, the *Sejarah Melayu* often appears more a collection of legends and folktales concerning the founding and subsequent rule of Melaka, many of them inaccurate or more incredible than history proper. Keeping the author's original aim in mind, however, the work is especially helpful today for its wealth of useful information about the Melakan court and the way in which its realm was governed, even if its chronology is not satisfactory. In this sense it, too, is, like any good history anywhere, a mirror of its time, place, and cultural setting.

Bibliography: C. C. Brown, trans., *Sejarah Melayu: or, Malay Annals* (Kuala Lumpur, 1970).

William H. Frederick

TWINTHINTAIKWUN MAHASITHU (? 1726–? 1806), Burmese court official and historian. A well-known scholar at the court of Bodowpaya (reigned 1781–1819), Twinthintaikwun Mahasithu was the most prominent of several individuals appointed in the 1790s to protect and reexamine the inscriptions of Amarapura. The king took a special interest in this endeavor because of his desire to check the veracity of tax, land, and labor records, a key to both political and economic consolidation of his rule. In 1798 Twinthintaikwun Mahasithu wrote the *Myanmayazawinthit*, sometimes styled *Mahayazawinthit* (New Chronicle), which criticized previous chronicles of Burma—especially that of U Kala (q.v.)—and attempted to correct both their facts and, to a lesser extent, their interpretations on the basis of the inscriptions and other sources he had assembled; he did not, however, question the aims or form of traditional historical writing. The *Myanmayazawinthit* is mentioned frequently in the *Glass Palace Chronicle* edited under the direction of the Monywe Hsayadaw, the important historical compilation of the Konbaung dynasty (1752–1885). Twinthintaikwun Mahasithu is also known as the author of *Alaung Mintayagyi Ayedawbon* (Narrative of King Alaungpaya, 180?), an account that is unusual because it occasionally has the character of a memoir.

Bibliography: Victor Lieberman, "How Reliable Is U Kala's Burmese Chronicle? Some New Comparisons," *Journal of Southeast Asian Studies* 17, no. 2 (September 1986): 236–255; modern Burmese edition: Twinthintaikwun Mahasithu, *Twinthin Myanma Yazawin Thit (Thwinthintaikwun's New Royal Chronicle of Burma)* (Rangoon, 1968).

William H. Frederick

WANNARAT (PHONNARAT), Somdet Phra (1735–c. 1800), Thai Buddhist monk, teacher, and chronicler. Little is known of Wannarat's early years, but he came to the attention of King Taksin (reigned 1767–1782) for bringing order to the *sangha* (Buddhist monastic order) in Phitsanulok during the first years of his reign. Wannarat became abbot of the Bangkok monastery eventually given the name Jetavana (Chettuphon), where he received the ecclesiastical title Vimaladhamma and was the teacher of Prince Paramanuchitchinorot. He lost his rank when he refused to recognize Taksin as a Buddha-to-be but was pardoned in 1782 by Rama I (reigned 1782–1809), who in 1794 bestowed on him the title Vanaratana (Wannarat). He was anything but a recluse and appears to have been equally comfortable advising the king on armaments and military strategy, negotiating with rebels, and compiling historical chronicles, for which he is best known. Wannarat authored a two-volume recension of the annals of Ayuthia (*Phraratchaphongsawadan Krung Kao*), but his most important work is the *Sangitiyavamsa* (Chronicle of the Buddhist Councils), also known as the *1789 Chronicle* from its date of composition. Although often classified as a *tamnan* (Buddhist universal history), this chronicle may also be seen as a modified *phongsawadan* (royal chronicle), of which it is the last great example. The *1789 Chronicle* was written at the command of Rama I, who chose Wannarat from among the four eminent monks laboring over a new version of the Buddhist *Tripitika*, which the king had commissioned; its purpose was to provide Rama I's 1788 Buddhist Council with a proper history and also to legitimate and record an auspicious beginning for the Chakri dynasty. Wannarat clearly had in mind as well the usual goal of instructing the monarch—then and in the future—that his success as a secular ruler depended heavily on his support for religion. Wannarat drew heavily on existing sources for his chronicle, especially the *Mahavamsa* and the *Jinakalamali* of Rattanapañña (q.v.), and there is little in it that the modern historian cannot find elsewhere; scholars have not found it to be noteworthy from the point of view of language or style. Yet the *1789 Chronicle* was an important work of its day and is a useful source from which to examine eighteenth-century Thai social and religious affairs and values. It is also perhaps the case that Wannarat, more than traditional authors of *tamnan*, was able to, and saw the need to, view the past beyond the confines imposed by Buddhist historiography. As a result, the *1789 Chronicle* seems to emphasize more than the works from which it is largely derived the idea that history offers humankind a way of learning from the past in order to improve the present and prepare for the future. Wannarat is also the author of *Nangsu Ruang Phraratchaphongsawadan* (Royal Chronicle, 1807), a history of Ayuthia from its foundation until after its destruction by the Burmese and the transition to Bangkok, which is based on an earlier work by Chaophraya Phiphitphichai.

Bibliography: Craig J. Reynolds, "Religious Historical Writing and the Legitimation of the First Bangkok Reign," in Anthony Reid and David Marr, eds., *Perspectives of the Past in Southeast Asia* (Kuala Lumpur, 1979), pp. 90–107; modern Thai translation of the *1789 Chronicle* by Phraya Pariyattithammathada, *Sangkhitiyawong, Phongsawadan Ruang Sangkhayana Phratham Phrawinai* (Chronicle of Buddhist Councils) (Bangkok, 1923); French translation: Georges Coedès, "Une Recension Palie des Annales d'Ayuthia," *Bulletin de l'Ecole Française d'Extrême-Orient* 14, no. 3 (1914).

William H. Frederick

YASADIPURA I, Raden Ngabei (? 1729–? 1803), Indonesian court poet and chronicler. The son of a high judiciary official in the kingdom of Kartasura, Central Java, Yasadipura studied religion and literature from the age of eight and at fourteen entered the service of Pakubuwana II (reigned 1726–1747), acting as a member of the king's guard. In the early 1740s the kingdom was thrown into turmoil by a Chinese revolt and the worsening struggle with the Dutch East India Company, and the capital was moved to present-day Surakarta (Solo). In such times Yasadipura rose in both political and literary stature, occupying the position of secretary to the king. After the signing of the Treaty of Giyanti with the Dutch in 1755, Surakartan life became more settled, and Yasadipura was able to occupy himself exclusively with literary pursuits. He was at the center of efforts to revive the heritage of Old Javanese literature, adapting or rewriting versions of classics for audiences of the late eighteenth century, among them the *Ramayana, Arjunawiwaha, Bratayuda, Dewaruci*, and *Serat Cabolek*. Sometimes considered to be evidence of a renaissance or "golden age" of Javanese writing, Yasadipura's literary activities tell us more clearly of an unsuccessful attempt to hang on to a tradition that in his day was poorly understood. Indeed, Yasadipura's own grasp of the Old Javanese language and of the traditional *sengkala* (chronogram) method of expressing dates was often shaky. After his death, Yasadipura's position at court was taken by his son R. Ng. Yasadipura II, whose own son, known as R. Ng. Ronggowarsito, later wrote as the last *pujangga* (court poet) of Surakarta. Yasadipura's chief work of history is the *Babad Giyanti* (History of Giyanti), written in the reign of Pakubuwana III (1749–1788). This was not an adaptation of an earlier text or texts but an original composition intended to chronicle the history of the Surakartan realm from the date of the move from Kartasura until 1755, based upon court documents and contemporary oral sources. The work is written in the *macapat* verse form, related to the classical *kakawin*. Most of the *Babad* recounts the war between Mangkubumi and Mas Said on the one hand and Pakubuwana III and the Dutch East India Company on the other hand for control of Java, and it is noteworthy for its largely accurate "insider's" view of events as well as for its surprisingly independent political position, considering its sponsor, for Yasadipura generally seems to have taken the side not of his master but of Mangkubumi, who as a result of the Treaty of Giyanti was established as the first ruler of a new, rival kingdom in Yogyakarta. Yasadipura I did not invent a new historical genre with his *Babad Giyanti*, but it would appear that he also did something more than merely copy old forms and reiterate old outlooks. Although the promise evident in this single, important work of history was never fully realized, it remains interesting for its interpretation of the period and for its potential as a line of historiographical development.

Bibliography: Merle C. Ricklefs, *Modern Javanese Historical Tradition* (London, 1978); Soebardi, "Raden Ngabehi Jasadipura I, Court Poet of Surakarta: His Life and Work," *Indonesia* 8 (October 1969): 81–102; Yasadipura I, *Babad Gijanti, Pratelan Namaning Tijang lan Panggenan* (Batavia, 1939).

William H. Frederick

Great Historians: Spanish

ALFONSO X, the Wise (Toledo, 1220–Seville, 1284), Spanish historian. Crowned king of Castille and Leon in 1252. Alfonso X, at an early age, began the legal-political works that later exerted great influence, works such as *Setenario, Fuero Real* (Royal Status-Law), *Espéculo* (Mirror), and *Partidas* (Divisions of the Law). At the same time he carried out important cultural work as protector of the development of all branches of knowledge officially cultivated in his kingdom. Especially in Seville and Toledo, he gathered a varied group of collaborators—Christians, Arabs, and Jews from the Peninsula and assorted foreigners. This team wrote the texts called Alphonsian. The king's task was to select the writers, direct the work, and provide for final revision. Thus many subjects emerged (history, jurisprudence, astrology, astronomy, classical and biblical accounts, physics, and philosophy) and were supported by a great variety of sources (Arab, classical, and high medieval). But the core of Alfonso's work was the dissemination of scientific knowledge and political thought through the use of Romance language, the vulgar language of Castille, which up to that moment had been used only for verbal communication, whereas Latin had been the written language. Beginning as a chronicler, Alfonso became more ambitious and innovative with the *Historia de España* (History of Spain), which was started around 1270. Here for the first time was recorded what was exclusively Spanish without any context of "universal history," the prevailing historiographical practice. For the first time, the concept of "Hispania" was extended to the boundaries of the Peninsula, without limiting the history to the kingdoms then ruled by Spaniards. For an unknown reason, perhaps because the tradition of universal history clashed with the more limited Peninsular concept, the *Historia de España* was abandoned. Simultaneously, Alfonso and his collaborators began the *General Estoria*, a universal history. Facts considered simultaneous were matched within the framework of an all-inclusive sacred history, "gentile history," and history of Spain from the beginning of biblical time.

Bibliography: "Alfonso X el Sabio. Centenario," *Historia* 16, no. 96 (1984); Francisco Lopez Estrada, "La Historia," *Historia* 16, no. 96 (1984): 60–66; Francisco Marcos Marín, "El desarrollo del castellano," *Historia* 16, no. 96 (1984): 67–70; Gonzalo Menéndez Pidal, "Como trabajaron las escuelas alfonsías," *N.R.F.M.* 5 (1951): 363–380;

Francisco Rico, *Alfonso el Sabio y la General Historia* (Barcelona, 1972); Nicasio Salvador Miguel, "El Intelectual," *Historia* 16, no. 96 (1984): 52–59; Julio Valdeón, "La època," *Historia* 16, no. 96 (1984): 46–52.

María Teresa Elorriaga Planes

DESCLOT, Bernat (? end of thirteenth century–? beginning of fourteenth century), Spanish historian. One of the most important Catalan chroniclers of the Middle Ages, Desclot belonged to a noble family. He received a solid and scholarly education, including knowledge of Arabic, which enabled him to hold a high post in the court of Pedro III (king of Aragon and Catalonia). We know of only one work by him: the *Crónica* (Chronicle). This, together with Jaime I's, Ramón Muntaner's (q.v.) , and Peter IV el Ceremonioso's work, form the so-called four great chronicles of the Catalan Middle Ages, or the "four pearls," as Morel Fatio would name them. Desclot's *Chronicle* starts with the union in 1137 of Catalonia and Aragon, alluding to a few previous events, and continues to the death of Pedro III the Great in 1285. Due to the diversity of manuscripts of this work, we know different titles: *Crónicas o conquestas de Catalunya, compostes é ordenades por en Bernat de Sclot o Libre del rey en Pere* and *De les histories de alguns comptes de Barcelona y reys de Aragó* (Chronicles or Conquests of Catalonia Composed and Ordered by Bernat de Sclot; or, The Book of King Pere and On the Histories of Certain Earls of Barcelona and Kings of Aragon), among others. Narrative is characterized by accuracy and critical reflection of facts. The author inserted several popular legends and attested to the events he participated in or witnessed; he also used official documents of the court and other sources now lost. He obtained, notwithstanding this diversity, a synthetic work with its own consistency, which earned him the reputation of a model chronicler, for in spite of the patriotism and dramatism occasionally guiding the narrative, he knew how to remain faithful to facts, which has gained for this work the status of a necessary reference in studies of these centuries. It was first published in Barcelona in 1616 by Rafael Cervera, who translated the Catalan original into Castilian.

Bibliography: *Crónica* (Chronicle), ed. and preface by M. Coll y Alentorn (Barcelona, 1982); *The Chronicle of the Reign of King Pedro III* . . . , 2 vols., trans., from the original Catalan text, and ed. Frank L. Critchlow (Princeton, N. J., 1928–1934); *Historia de la conquista de Mallorca* (History of the Conquest of Majorca) (Palma, 1957), notes and documents by José Mª Quadrado; *La leyenda del buen conde de Barcelona y la emperatriz de Alemania. Fragmento de la Crónica de Bernat Desclot* (The Legend of the Good Earl of Barcelona and the Empress of Germany. A Fragment of Bernat Desclot's Chronicle) (Barcelona, 1953), this legend has been studied by Lüdtke, Gaston Paris, Jean Calmette, Steinberg, J. Rubió, and M. Coll y Allentorn; *Los franceses en Cataluña en 1285* (The French in Catalonia in 1285) (Madrid, 1944), preliminary note by Joaquín Rodríguez de Arzúa; Jorge Rubió y Balaguer, *Consideraciones generales acerca de la historiografía catalana medieval y particular de la Crónica de Desclot* (General Considerations on Catalan Medieval Historiography, and in Particular on Desclot's Chronicle) (Barcelona, 1911).

Maria Teresa Elorriaga Planes

FERNÁNDEZ DE OVIEDO, Gonzalo (Madrid, 1478–Santo Domingo, 1557), Spanish historian. Fernández de Oviedo held several positions in the royal administration and was a chronicler of the Indies. Self-taught with a classical education, he wrote many works on a great variety of subjects, notably, *Oficios de la Casa Real* (Official documents from the Royal House) and *Batallas y Quinquagenas* (Battles and Quinquagenae, 1556). His main contribution was to be the first historian widely entering the discovery and colonization of America by Spaniards. His *Historia General y Natural de Indias* (General and Natural History of the Indies, 1519) consists of fifty volumes and has a geographical form of organization. Written on site, it is based on numerous official accounts and descriptions by persons participating in the events, although its main source was direct observation by the chronicler himself. It consists of an encyclopedic Americanist narrative where geographic, natural history, and anthropological descriptions are mixed with facts, with Plinius as a model and the most cited author therein. It provides the Spanish conquest with a historical-religious basis, observing native life from a religious point of view and emphasizing the Messianic character of the colonization. With the criteria of a true anthropologue, the author glimpsed the structural unity underlying each kind of culture and defined his idea of cultural backwardness or progress in accordance with moral rather than material criteria. His ethnological and ethnographical analysis, performed on a comparative basis and including countless cultural comparisons, provides an exact and detailed description of native family structures, everyday objects, and economic activity. His negative idea of the "Indian," which resulted in strong criticism by Bartolomé de Las Casas (q.v.), is based on the Aristotelian axiom concerning the relationship between rational plenitude and the knowledge of God. His correct description of the sociological and ethnic process of depopulation of the Antilles and the causes thereof is very important. An exact historian with high observation qualities and descriptive accuracy, besides being an excellent naturalist, Fernández de Oviedo had a concept of culture that was—if not evolutionist—one that established a historical border for progress.

Bibliography: Manuel Ballesteros, *Gonzalo Fernández de Oviedo* (Madrid, 1981).

Paloma Cirujano

FLOREZ, Enríque (Villadiego, 1702–Madrid, 1773), Spanish historian, priest, and theologian. A professor at the University of Alcala (1751). Florez started in 1742 the project of his main work, *Historia Sagrada* (Sacred History, 1747–1772), of which he published the first twenty-seven volumes and which other historians have continued up to the present. His was one of the most important ecclesiastical histories in Spain, offering the historical evolution of ancient dioceses. It is a geographical-historical study of Spain and the Church from the origins thereof, as well as on the location and extent of ancient dioceses. This work includes many documents on medieval history and geography, as well as a collection of the canons, and the compilation of ancient ecclesiastical law, together with many previously unpublished manuscripts and chronicles. His studies were based on sources amended by criticism. The encyclopaedic character of the work, containing geographical, chronological, epigraphic, numismatic, paleographical, archaeological and bibliographical data, mended many errors in Spain's civil and ecclesiastical history. From the methodological point of view he has been considered as a pioneer in Spanish historiographical scientism. His *Clave historial* (Historial Clue) was published in 1743, and the *Memoria de las Reinas Católicas* (Memoir of the Catholic Queens) in 1761, the latter being a genealogical history of the Royal House of Castile and Leon. Florez, with his upright interpretation of documents, his wide scholarship and his outstanding critical apparatus, is one of the historians whose work has remained valid up to the present.

Bibliography: Gregorio Martinez, *Biografía de Fray Enrique Florez* (Oviedo, Spain, 1972).

Paloma Cirujano

ISIDORE OF SEVILLE (Cartagena, ante 559–Seville, 636), Spanish encyclopaedist. Born in Visigoth Spain of a Roman family he deserted his native land after the Byzantines took it. Since his elder brother, Leander, acceded to the position of adviser to King Reccared, Isidore moved to Seville (578) where Leander was appointed bishop (587) and followed Leander in the see (600). A methodic and systematic philologist, Isidore made a point of passing through the melting pot of his classifications, series, and repertories of etymologies, excerpts, quotations, parallels, and symmetric examples, the whole cultural heritage of the ancient world. His chief oeuvre is *Origines* (Origins), an encyclopaedia organized by matters and disciplines, fitting the model offered by the fifth- and sixth-century school books which remained until the thirteenth century the most disseminated and referred to repertory of quotations, definitions, and bibliographic references. He also authored a *Historia mundi* (World History), from the Bible creation until 615 (625–627) in which, according to the model set by Augustine (q.v.), he identified the six days of the Creation with the six ages of the world (*aetates saeculi*) which, however, did not coincide with a universal empire that came into being, lived, and died, but with a new stage on the road to mankind's moral progress—the way Orosius, too, put it. Other historical writings: *Historia Gothorum, Vandalorum et Suevorum* (History of the Goths, Vandals, and Suevi, 625), constructed to the model of the earlier production by Maximus of Saragossa (c. 610) and continuing the collection of biographies of ecclesiastic writers drawn up in the fifth century by Gennadius of Marseilles under the title of *De viris illustribus* (On Famous Men). The latter writing would in turn be continued by Ildefonsus of Toledo (d. 667) and repeatedly re-edited or remade from the twelfth to fifteenth centuries by compilers like Sigebert of Gembloux (q.v.), Honorius of Autun, Anonymus of Melk, Hugo von Trimberg, and Johann Trithemius, among others.

Bibliography: Heinrich Philip, *Die historisch-geographischen Quellen in den Etymologiae des Isidorus von Sevilla* (Berlin, 1912–1913); *Miscellanea Isidoriana* (Isidorian Miscellany) (Rome, 1936); Juan Luis Romero, "San Isidoro de Sevilla. Su pensamiento historico-politico y sus relaciones con la Historia visigoda'' (Saint Isidore of Seville: His Political and Historical Thought and Its Relation to the Visigothic History), *Cuadernos para la Historia de Espana*, 1947, no. 8, pp. 5–71; *I caratteri del secolo VII° in Occidente* (Characters of the Seventh Century in Western Europe) (Spoleto, 1958).

Radu Constantinescu

MARIANA, F. Juan de (Talavera, 1536–Toledo, 1623), Spanish historian. Mariana received a solid humanistic education, mainly theological. At seventeen he entered the Society of Jesus where his main activity was teaching, which he did in several European cities until he returned to Spain in 1574 and settled in Toledo, where he worked as a synodal examiner and advisor to the Inquisition court. He was appointed royal chronicler in 1623 by Felipe IV. Mariana's *Historiae de rebus Hispaniae Libri XXV* is the first general history of Spain. A brilliant history in its time, it was the first attempt at conferring unity on the Spanish past. It was not conceived in Romance language, but in Latin, with its author's stated purpose that of allowing Spanish history to become known abroad. Its first edition (Toledo, 1592) included in twenty-five volumes the history of the Spanish nation from its origins to the death of Fernando V (1516), but the author subsequently extended his account to summaries of the events taking place until 1621. It was first published in Romance language in 1601 under the title *Historia General de España* (General History of Spain); many editions followed thereafter, to which additions were contributed by other historians, thus extending history of Spain to the date of publication. Thus the work of Mariana, as extended by his successors, lacked competitors for two centuries, and there were no other histories of the Spanish nation that could be compared to it: it was not until the first half of the nineteenth century that other historians undertook anew the task of writing a general history of Spain from its origins. The prevalence of this work for two centuries was the main reason for the countless criticisms it collected, for it is evident that it could not resist attacks arising from the subsequent development of historiography. Its opposers charged the author with mixing truth and tale, tradition and history, as well as with conveying false chronicles while omitting true ones. On the other hand, its main defenders, the Spanish historians of the central decades of the nineteenth century—who in the ideological field were living in an age of nationalistic passion and political centralism—attached great value to the work, based on its unitarian view of the national past, its patriotic values, and, certainly, the time in which it was written (from 1579 to 1584), a time of an absolute lack of knowledge of the techniques of modern historiography, as well as of archives, and a time of apogee for the Inquisition harshness, very much limiting development of science and dissemination of knowledge. But it is Georges Cirot who has finally rescued the image of Mariana and has to date produced the largest amount of clues for the understanding of the importance of his work. Mariana viewed history in the manner of Titus Livy (q.v.). He included vividness and drama in the narrative, physically and morally portrayed his characters, and took advantage of speech to inject his own political and moral ideas in order to educate both princes and subjects. On the other side, he was very conscientious when he had firsthand documents and was faithful to them. But a work on the history of Spain conceived for dissemination, written by a theologian, and lacking the usual procedures of a historian is bound to be limited to compilation, generally performed with dexterity, of the preceeding partial histories—Alfonso the Wise (q.v.), Ramón Muntaner's (q.v.), Estebande Garibay's—sometimes including mistakes due to the conveyance of false chronicles. He also made use of the ancient writers' passages on Spain. As for America, he let Francisco López de Gomara guide him. In summary, Mariana's historical work accounts for a man pervaded by his own time's humanism and guided by criticism, reason, and freedom.

Bibliography: Georges Cirot, *Étude sur l'historiographie espagnole. Mariana historien* (Bordeaux, 1905); Christian Hansen Roses, *Ensayo sobre el pensamiento político del P. J. de Mariana* (Santiago, 1959); Jaime Lluis y Navas Brusi, *Los estudios monetarios del P. Mariana* (Saragossa, 1960); Juan de Mariana, *Historia General de España . . .*, continued by Miniana and completed by Eduardo Chao, (Madrid, 1849); Francisco Pi y Margall, Preliminary speech to *Obras de Mariana, Biblioteca de Autores Españoles* (Madrid, 1854).

Maria Teresa Elorriaga Planes

MUNTANER, Ramón (Gerona, 1265–Ibiza, 1336), Spanish, medieval Catalan chronicler. While serving the different reigning branches in the Peninsula, Majorca, and Sicily, Muntaner played a leading role in the most significant military events that took place under the dynasty of Aragon. His participation in Roger de Flor's expedition to the East as an administrator for the "Great Company of Raiders" (Almogávares) stands out. He ended his life as governor of Ibiza. His *Chronicle* is the third one of the group that Morel Fatio called the "four pearls" of Catalan historiography. In the final years of the thirteenth century and first half of the fourteenth century, with few precedents, unlike Castile, a mature historiographical model written in vernacular Catalan was developed from the first moment in the crown of Aragon. Extensive general chronicles with a universal approach and compounding previous histories were written in Castile, whereas the crown of Aragon applied itself to ongoing narrative written in a lively, contemporary style. Besides Muntaner's *Chronicle*, the other three major chronicles are James I's, implying institutionalization of Catalan language by the monarch himself; that of Bernat Desclot (q.v.), a model of accuracy and impartiality; and the one by another sovereign, Peter IV, autobiographical, precise, and well supported with documentary evidence. Muntaner's *Chronicle* (Chronica, o descripció dels fets e hazanyes del Inclit Rey Don Jaume, primer Rey d'Aragó . . . e de molts de sos descendens—Chronicle or Description of the Feats and Heroic Deeds of the Illustrious King James, First King of Aragon . . . and of Many of His Descendants) consists of 298 chapters beginning with the birth of James the Conqueror in 1207 and ending with the reign of Alfonso the Benign in 1328. Covering all of the kings of the dynastic family of Aragon, most of the events therein were attended by Muntaner himself while in the service of this dynasty. Hence the two major features in his work are that it is a narrative of events witnessed by Muntaner himself, and with this narrative he attempted to set an example for future monarchs. The work is dedicated to the house of Aragon, members thereof being portrayed in an idealistic manner, and the author shows rivalry, even hatred, against the neighboring French monarchs. The style being lively and passionate, this work was written mainly to be listened to by an audience participating in the narrative of the feats therein. The author wrote in a brilliant Catalan influenced by the troubadours and chivalry books, but its contents are still a historical document for the knowledge of the Catalan-Aragonese Middle Ages.

Bibliography: B. Sánchez Alonso, *Historia de la historiografía española* (History of Spanish Historiography) (Barcelona, 1964); J. Miquel Sobre, *L'épica de la realitat: l'escriptura de R. Muntaner i Bernat Desclot* (The Epics of Reality: The Writings of R. Muntaner and Bernat Desclot) (Barcelona, 1978).

Juan Sisinio Pérez Garzón

ZURITA Y CASTRO, Jerónimo de (Saragossa, 1512–Saragossa, 1580), Spanish historian; first official chronicler of the kingdom of Aragon, a position created by the Cortes of Monzon in 1547. Born to a family belonging to the court entourage (his father was Fernando V and Carlos I's chamber physician), Zurita y Castro developed from 1537 a rising and comfortable bureaucratic career, serving important offices within the Inquisition. This gave him the chance to travel (Rome, Naples, Sicily, Holland, and so on), thus being able to collect notices and books for his work. Furthermore, Philip II, when appointing him chamber secretary in 1566, entrusted him with the direction of the collection of documents for the castle of Simancas. A result of his efforts to gather materials was his magnificent library, which later was to enrich El Escorial's. Besides other writings of a historical nature, all of them characterized by precision, Zurita's major work is *Annals of the Crown of Aragon* (Anales de la Corona de Aragón), on which he worked for thirty years, the last volume thereof being printed on the very year he died. It is the first general history of those territories, and it was adapted to the historiographic rules prevailing after the Renaissance, which reached their height in the Peninsula during the so-called Golden Century. The *Annals* are an accomplished example of what was then meant by historical research of a national whole. Directly based on documents, the critical use of sources—distorted at times only by literary and legendary tales—is the reason that it is still a true and reliable work. It already found in its time accusers and defenders, precisely due to its exhaustive details aimed at supporting the past on documents. It includes not only political history, but the evolution of institutions (justice, councils, monasteries, and so on), as well as the events involving major celebrities of the kingdom. The narrative, as suggested by the title itself, is organized on a yearly basis, and the chapters devoted to the different kingdoms of Aragon alternate therein, also including their relationship with the rest of the

Peninsular kingdoms. This year-by-year method determines the style and form thereof with a disorderly and careless appearance. On its turn, the concern about being firmly based on the sources makes the latter appear with a lack of narrative linking and a prolixity which renders its reading difficult.

Bibliography: C. Riba, *Jerónimo Zurita, primer cronista de Aragón* (Jerónimo Zurita, First Chronicler of Aragon) (Saragossa, 1946); Benito Sanchez Alonso, *Historia de la historiografía española* (History of Spanish historiography), 2d vol. (Madrid, 1944); A. Ubieto Arteta and Maria Pérez Soler, ed., *Anales de la corona de Aragón de J. Zurita* (Annals of the Crown of Aragon, by J. Zurita), 3 vols. (Valencia, 1967).

Juan Sisinio Pérez Garzón

Great Historians: Spanish American

DEL CAMPO Y RIVAS, Manuel Antonio (Cartago, Colombia, 1750–Mexico, 1830), Colombian historian. Son of Simón del Campo and Bárbara Rivas Asprilla, both of Spanish origin. Trained as a lawyer, he resided in Madrid during the 1780s. His major work, the *Compendio histórico de la fundación, progresos y estado de la ciudad de Cartago* (Historical Account of the Foundation, Progress and State of the City of Cartago) was written between 1799 and 1801 and published in Madrid in 1803. In 1812, del Campo y Rivas was appointed Judge to the Royal Audiencia of Mexico. The *Compendio histórico* . . . is divided into three parts: the civil history of Cartago, an account of great value for the study of American cities in the second half of the eighteenth century; the other two sections tell of a local miracle involving an image of the Virgin Mary venerated locally as Our Lady of Poverty. Apart from its informative value, del Campo y Rivas's work is important in that it shows the critical trend that the philosophy of Enlightenment brought to historical narrative. The miracle referred to in the book is described within the context of a cultural history of Cartago and not simply as a supernatural phenomenon. Also, in some of his digressions, del Campo y Rivas uses the word *mankind* in terms of the entire human race, and not merely, as was heretofore customary, as an equivalent word for Christendom.

Bibliography: German Posada, *Manuel del Campo y Rivas, cronista colombiano (1750–1830)* (Mexico, 1948).

Nikita Harwich Vallenilla

CLAVIJERO, Francisco Javier (Vera Cruz, Mexico, 1731–Bologna, Italy, 1787), Mexican Jesuit priest and historian. Son of Blas Clavijero and Maria Isabel Echegaray, both of distinguished Spanish origin, he studied at the Colegio de San Jerónimo and the San Ignacio Seminary, both in Puebla, joined the Jesuit order as a Noviciate of the Tepotzotlán monastery in 1748, and completed his formal education at the Jesuit College of Puebla. His instruction, however, was far more extensive and liberal than that of the vast majority of contemporary clerics. His father, a learned civil servant in the Spanish administration, taught him French and other European languages; he also learned the Indian language of Náhuatl and some reports suggest he knew twenty indigenous languages reasonably well. He had little interest in theology and studied instead many of the great writers of his time and from antiquity, including many whose works had been banned by the Church. Appointed Prefect of Studies of the San Ildefonso Seminary of Mexico City, he tried to apply his ideas on a more liberal education program by proposing a number of reforms which were not accepted. He therefore asked to be removed from his position, but this preoccupation with educational reform remained a permanent feature throughout his academic career. Ordained in 1754, he taught at the Colegio de San Gregorio, an institution that had been founded in the Mexican capital for the instruction of the native Indian population. At the same time, he devoted himself to the study of important documents and archaeological data referring to pre-Hispanic Mexico, which he found in the library of the adjoining Colegio de San Pedro y San Pablo. The idea soon emerged to collect and prepare these and other data for a major historical work. Appointed to teach at the Colegio de San Javier in Puebla and, later, in Valladolid (Michoacán), he was a member of the Colegio de Guadalajara faculty when the Jesuit order was expelled from Mexico in 1767. Clavijero was then exiled to Italy and settled in Bologna, where he dedicated his remaining years to historical study. The four-volume edition of his *Historia Antigua de Mexico* (The Ancient History of Mexico), originally published in Italian in Cesena (1780–1781), required ten years (1770–1780) for completion. His *Historia de la Antigua o Baja California* (History of Ancient or Lower California), also originally in Italian, was published in Venice in 1789, two years after his death. Both works, particularly the former, have been described as the first true history of New Spain. Unlike most of the colonial chroniclers, Clavijero not only dug deeply into the sources and with his knowledge of indigenous languages could consult material unavailable to others, but also showed a critical ability which he consistently applied. He set out to refute a dominant trend in the European historiography of his time concerning Spanish America which insisted upon denigrating the Spanish conquest and colonial rule. At the same time, he was determined to present a valid picture of pre-Hispanic cultures. He not only dealt with the narrative of events, but also included considerations on the social and demographic history of the native populations, the accuracy of which is presently being reconfirmed. Clavijero's balanced, objective approach was almost unique in his age and heightens the pioneering quality of his historical work.

Bibliography: Francisco Javier Clavijero, *Historia Antigua de Mexico* (Mexico: Porrua, 1945); Julio Le Riverend Brusone, *La Historia Antigua de Mexico del Padre Francisco Javier Clavijero* (Mexico, 1948).

Nikita Harwich Vallenilla

FERNANDEZ DE PIEDRAHITA, Lucas (Bogotá, 1624–Panamá, 1688), Colombian prelate and historian. Son of Domingo Hernandez de Soto y Piedrahita and Catalina Collantes. His mother was the granddaughter of the Peruvian princess Francisca Coya, niece of the Inca Huayna Capac. After graduating from the Jesuit College of San Bartolomé and receiving his doctoral degree from the Thomist University of Bogotá, he was ordained, served in the Indian curates of Fusagasugá and Paipa and, later, as treasurer of the Cathedral of Popayán. Appointed provisional governor of the Archbishopric of Bogotá (1654–1661), he was charged with irregularities while in office and sent to Spain for a hearing before the Royal Council of the Indies. During his six years of forced residence in the peninsula (1662–1668), he completed the manuscript of the first part of his major historical work, the *Historia general de las conquistas del Nuevo Reino de Granada* (General History of the Conquests of the New Kingdom of Granada). Finally exonerated from all charges, he was offered, in compensation, the position of bishop of Santa Marta, an appointment that was confirmed by the Pope. In 1676, he was promoted to the Bishopric of Panamá, but before he could leave Santa Marta, he was captured during a raid by English pirates and taken as hostage to Henry Morgan, governor of the island of Providencia, who decided on his release. Fernández de Piedrahita spent his last years in Panamá, where he strongly supported missionary and conversion activity among the Darien region Indian populations. The original edition of the *Historia general* was published in Antwerp in 1688. It was designed to be a two-volume study, but the second volume was either lost or never written. The history is divided into twelve books and continues up to 1563, but its main theme is the conquest of New Granada (Books 3 to 12). From his own account, Fernández de Piedrahita based his work on the manuscript of Gonzalo Jiménez de Quesada, the conqueror of New Granada, and used other chronicles such as the *Historia de Indias* (History of the Indies) by Juan de Castellanos and the *Décadas* . . . (Decades . . .) by Antonio de Herrera, all of which he was able to consult while in Spain. He freely admitted that his history was not a work conceived in primary documentation, but argued that its merit was in the updating of earlier chronicles. The first two books deal with the pre-Hispanic period, with particular emphasis on the Chibcha culture, including philosophical discussions on the morality and customs of the Chibchas, drawn from Fernández de Piedrahita's own experience. The conquest starts with the third book, featuring the foundation of Santa Marta by Rodrigo de Bastidas; other important episodes include Phillip Von Hutten's expedition, the foundation of Mérida (Venezuela), and the adventures of Lope de Aguirre. Fernández de Piedrahita also frequently insists on the moral teachings that can be drawn from historical knowledge. Enhanced with an elegant style, though sometimes not devoid of repetitions and digressions, the *Historia general* was the first attempt to clarify and explain, as impartially and truthfully as possible, the conquest of northern South America, and has served as a basic reference work for later studies of sixteenth-century Colombian history.

Bibliography: Carlos Felice Cardot, ed., *Venezuela en los Cronistas Generales de Indias* (Caracas: Academia Nacional de la Historia, 1962); Lucas Fernandez De Piedrahita, *Historia general de las conqusitas del Nuevo Reino de Granada* (Bogotá: Editorial Kelly, 1973).

Nikita Harwich Vallenilla

GARCILASO DE LA VEGA (Cuzco, Peru, 1539–Cordoba, Spain, 1616), Peruvian historian, also known as Garcilaso the Inca. Son of the Spanish captain Sebastian Garcilaso de la Vega y Vargas and of his common-law wife, the Inca princess Chimpu Ocllo, an alleged granddaughter of the emperor Tupac Inca Yupanqui and niece of the Inca Huayna Capac. He spent his early childhood in the care of his mother and her relatives, listening to tales of the pre-Hispanic Inca civilization. Around 1551, he was taken away to live with his father and was given the new family name of ''Gómez Suárez de Figueroa,'' which he used throughout his youth. Under the guidance of private tutors, he completed his formal education, learned Latin and Spanish, and became familiar with the uses of European culture. Shortly after his father's death, the young Garcilaso left Peru for Spain (1560) and settled in the town of Montilla, near Córdoba, in the house of his uncle Alonso de Vargas. He enlisted in the army and served as captain in several campaigns, particularly against the Granada moorish rebellion of 1570. Around 1574, he resigned from active service, and became involved in farming and horse breeding. In 1590, he left Montilla for Cordoba, where he spent the rest of his life, took minor religious orders and served as chief steward of the Immaculate Conception Hospital. His first historical work, *La Florida del Inca* (Florida of the Inca), written between 1586 and 1592 and published in Lisbon in 1605, attempted to tell the story of Hernando de Sotos's 1539 expedition to Florida. It relied mainly on the eyewitness account of Gonzalo Silvestre, one of the members of the expedition, whom Garcilaso had met on various occasions. The result also owed much to his own literary imagination in depicting scenes and situations in the style of the adventure novels of the time. Garcilaso's most famous work, however, is his two-part study of Peruvian history, presumbly written between 1592 and the time of his death, and published in Lisbon (1609, part one) and Córdoba (1617, part two). The first part of the book, under the title of *Comentarios Reales de los Incas* (Royal Commentaries of the Incas), was a history of the Inca and their empire before the Spanish conquest, based upon some of the earlier chronicles, particularly the account written in Latin by the Jesuit priest Blas de Valera, but also, and perhaps more importantly, on his own childhood memories. This latter aspect was of immeasurable importance to the work because of the personal feeling Garcilaso had for the land and people he was describing and because, instead of a Spanish chronicler, he was a mestizo writer of great literary talent who provided an often idealized but generally authoritative version of Peruvian pre-Colombian history from the native point of view. The second part of the work, entitled *Historia General del Peru* (General History of Peru), dealt with the Spanish conquest, the ten-year period of civil wars between the conquerers (1544–1554), and the viceregal reorganization of Peru under Francisco de Toledo (1569–1581). It did not have the compelling interest of the first part and is often unreliable in detail. However, despite its shortcomings, Garcilaso's work is still considered a major source for the study of early Peruvian history, and Garcilaso himself has become a symbol for the racial and cultural integration of Spanish America.

Bibliography: Julia Fitzmaurice-Kelly, *The Inca Garcilaso* (Oxford: Oxford University Press, 1921); Garcilaso De La Vega, *Royal Commentaries of the Incas*, 2 vols. (Austin: University of Texas Press, 1966); Aurelio Miro Quesada S., *El Inca Garcilaso y otros estudios garcilasistas* (Madrid: Ediciones Cultura Hispánica, 1971); Raul Porras Barrenechea, *El Inca Garcilaso de la Vega. 1539–1616* (Lima: Editorial Lumen, 1946); Luis Alberto Sanchez, *Garcilaso de la Vega, primer criollo* (Santiago de Chile: Editorial Ercilla, 1939); John Grier Varner, *El Inca. The Life and Times of Garcilaso de la Vega* (Austin: University of Texas Press, 1968).

Nikita Harwich Vallenilla

GUAMAN POMA DE AYALA, Felipe (San Cristobal de Suntunto?, Peru, between 1533 and 1545–? Peru, after 1615), Peruvian chronicler. He claimed descent, on his mother's side, from the Inca monarchy and through his father, Guaman Mallqui, from an ancient line of monarchs who ruled in the northern parts of Peru before the Inca domination. Guaman (falcon) and Poma (lion) may both be royal titles. He also claimed that, because his father had saved the life of Captain Luís Avalos de Ayala during the battle of Huarina (1547), he had come to use the latter's family name. Very little is known about his life. He appears to have accompanied, as an interpreter, the ecclesiastical visits of Cristóbal de Albórnoz to southern Peru (1565–1571). He probably also served as interpreter during the Third Lima Council (1583) and during the travels of Gabriel Solano de Figueroa to the Ayacucho region (1595). He is supposed to have attained the rank of town magistrate (teniente de corregidor). His last years were spent gathering information for a chronicle on the life and customs of ancient Peru that would also contain a series of rules on "good government." The manuscript was reportedly completed by 1615, but remained forgotten until it was discovered by the German philologist Richard Pietschmann in the Copenhagen Royal Library in 1908. The first facsimile edition was published in 1936, under the direction of Paul Rivet, by the Paris Ethnology Institute. The manuscript of the *Nueva corónica y buen gobierno* consists of 1,179 pages, including over one hundred full-page pen and ink drawings, which provide unparalled visual evidence of Peruvian life and manners during the time of the Inca and the early years of the conquest. It is the only illustrated Peruvian codex that is known so far. More than a quarter of the manuscript deals with conditions in Peru before the conquest and the work as a whole was intended as a bitter denunciation of the cruelty and oppression of Spanish rule. The text is confused and shows that the author was not altogether fluent in Spanish. Guaman Poma's conception of the past is influenced by both Andean and sixteenth-century European criteria regarding chronological sequences. Biblical myths and local legendary traditions are blended into a narrative that seeks to establish a parallel between both cultural worlds, in an attempt to articulate Andean pre-Hispanic history with the image of universal history, as seen through the teachings of the Catholic church. Special emphasis is also given to the notion of a world global order in which geographical references are used to justify an immutable spiritual and social structure of the universe. Of prime importance is Guaman Poma's representation of the Tawantinsuyu, the land of the "old order" Inca rulers, where "good government" was the norm. This mythical Golden Age did not last, and it was because its principles had been discarded that the Inca empire fell to the Spaniards. The final part of the work is an appeal for the re-establishment of "good government" in the Indies. While recognizing both the conquest and the Christian faith, Guaman Poma is critical of the abuses committed by the Spanish administration and provides specific proposals for the "recuperation" of the Andes and its native populations.

Bibliography: Luís M. Baudizzone, *Guaman Poma* (Buenos Aires: Editorial Nova, 1934); François Chevalier, "El códice ilustrado de Poma de Ayala," *Revista de Indias* Madrid, 1944, No 17; Felipe Guaman Poma De Ayala, *Nueva corónica y buen gobierno* (Caracas: Biblioteca Ayacucho nos. 75 and 76, 1980) 2 vols.; Georges Lobsiger, "Felipe Guaman Poma de Ayala," *Bulletin de la Société Suisse des Américanistes*, Geneva, March 1960, no 19; Guillermo Ludeña De La Vega, *La obra del cronista indio Felipe Guaman Poma de Ayala* (Lima: Editorial Nueva Encarnación, 1975); Juan M. Ossio, "La idea de la historia en Felipe Guaman Poma de Ayala," *Runa*, Lima, 1977, No. 1; Nathan Wachtel, "Pensamiento salvaje y aculturación: el espacio y el tiempo en Felipe Guaman Poma de Ayala y el Inca Garcilaso de la Vega," *Annales. Economies, Sociétés, Civilizations*, Paris, May–August 1971, Nos. 3–4.

Nikita Harwich Vallenilla

LAS CASAS, Bartolomé de (Seville, 1474–Madrid, 1566), Spanish missionary, administrator, and historian. Las Casas arrived in America in 1502 and made a notable career as a member of the Dominican Order attempting to remedy the exploitation of the Native Americans by their conquerors. A priest in Santo Domingo, then Cuba, he became bishop of Chiapas in Mexico in 1544. Later in his life he began the great works of history and polemics, which form the foundation of the "Black Legend" of the Spanish Conquest. Like other chroniclers, such as Gonzalo Fernandez de Oviedo (q.v.), Lopez de Gomara, or Cieza de Leon, Bartolomé included in his work passages on natural history and many observations on the culture of the Indians. Part of the battle with his peers was to have the Indians accepted as divinely created humanity and thus, as potential Christians, not liable to the status of slave or even infidel, like the Jews and Moors of Spain, nor liable to have their property seized in time of peace, for he insisted upon the Christian principle of restitution. Although he deserved his title as protector of the Indians for his efforts to reform the system of *encomiendas*, a paradox of his position was his recommendation that, instead of using the Indians for forced labor, African slaves were preferable. His multi-volume *Historia General de las Indias* (General History of the Indies, with introduction, 1561) was a general history including many of his writings since 1527, unpublished until 1875. In 1559 he wrote *Apologética historia sumaria* (Summary of the Historical Defense), which detailed his arguments and observations over many years on the physical and moral character of the Indians and their rights within the Spanish legal system. He also wrote the memorandum addressed to Emperor Charles V under the title *Brevisima relación de la destruyción de las*

Indias (Brief Report on the Destruction of the Indies, published in 1552). He produced lavish information about their religious customs in an attempt at what could be termed comparative cultural anthropology among the ancient Roman, Greek, Egyptain, Aztec, and Inca civilizations. Las Casas was among the first who exposed the colonial policy, and in the Americas he is considered one of the first indigenists.

Bibliography: Biblioteca de Autores Españoles, *Estudios lascasianos: IV centenario de la muerte de Fray Bartolomé de las Casas (1566–1966)*, Publicaciones de la Escuela de Estudios Hispanoamericanos, no. 175 (Seville, 1966); Bartolomé de las Casas, *Apologética historia sumaria*, ed. Edmundo O'Groman (Mexico City: 1967); idem, *Historia de las Indias* 2 vols., ed. Agustín Millares, with introductory essay by Lewis Hanke (Mexico City); Lewis Hanke, *Bartolomé de las Casas* (Buenos Aires, 1968), and his many books in English on las Casas; Walter Mignolo, ''Cartas, crónicas y relaciones del descubrimiento y la conquista,'' in Luis Ingio Madrigal, ed., *Historia de la literatura hispanoamericana, época colonial*, vol. 1 (Madrid, 1982), pp. 57–116; *Obras escogidas de fray Bartolomé de las Casas* (Madrid, 1958).

Paloma Cirujano

OVALLE, Alonso de (Santiago, Chile, 1601–Lima, Peru, 1651), Chilean Jesuit priest and historian. Educated in the Jesuit school of his native town, he completed his formal studies at the Colegio de Córdoba in Argentina. After joining the Jesuit order and being ordained, he was sent, as a missionary, to the small Negro settlements of the Province of La Plata, on the present Chilean-Argentinian border and was later sent to southern Chile to supervise the conversion of the Araucano and Mapuche Indian populations. As a missionary, he was vitally interested in education and soon became an authority on the subject. He was appointed Prefect of Studies of the Jesuit Colegio de San Francisco Javier in Santiago. Around 1643, on a visit to Europe, he was so appalled by the views commonly held on the situation of the Spanish American colonies that he decided to write a history of the region for the enlightenment of the European public and started collecting material for the book, which was published in Rome in 1646. As he was about to return to Chile, in 1647, news came of a disastrous earthquake that had destroyed Santiago and various other towns. Ovalle was then empowered by the Santiago City Council to deal with the Spanish crown in raising the funds necessary for reconstruction. Having completed his mission, both in Spain and in several other European countries, Ovalle was on his way back home when he fell ill and died. His major work, *Histórica relación del Reino de Chile y de las missiones y ministerios que ejercita en él la Compañia de Jesús* (Historical Relation of the Kingdom of Chile and of the Missions and Ministries Practiced in It by the Company of Jesus), was intended as a means to inform the European public about life in the Spanish American colonies and also to highlight the missionary activity of the Jesuit order in the New World. But it was also far more than a simple historical chronicle. Ovalle described in detail the colonial society, its culture and customs, geography, the crops produced, trade and crafts, and, in general, tried to be as comprehensive as possible. Helped by its author's lively literary style and by the interest it created as favorable propaganda for the Jesuits, the book was widely circulated throughout Europe and translated into English. It was first published in Chile in 1888 and was considered one of the founding reference works of Chilean historiography.

Bibliography: Alonso de Ovalle, *História relación del Reino de Chile y de las missiones y ministerios que ejercita en él la Compañia de Jesús* (Santiago, 1888); Francisco Antonio Encina, "Breve bosquejo de la literatura histórica chilena," *Atenea*, Santiago, 1949, Nos. 291–292.

Nikita Harwich Vallenilla

OVIEDO, Basilio Vicente de (Socota, Colombia, 1699–? 1765), Colombian historian. After completing his studies at the Jesuit College of San Bartolomé, in Bogotá, he was ordained in Popayán in 1726 and served as parish priest in various villages and towns of eastern New Granada (Colombia). His first-hand experiences served as reference material for a compilation titled *Pensamientos y noticias escogidas para utilidad de curas, del Nuevo Reino de Granada, sus riquezas y demás cualidades, y de todas sus poblaciones y curatos, con específica noticia de sus gentes y gobierno* (Selected Thoughts and Information for the Use of Priests, of the New Kingdom of Granada, Its Riches and Other Qualities, and of All Its Towns and Parishes, with Special Notice on Its Population and Government). The manuscript was completed by 1761, when its author presented it to the Viceroy Pedro Messia de la Cerda. Intended to be a sort of statistical vade mecum, the work remained unpublished. Of the eleven volumes that made up the original manuscript, ten were lost. The remaining text, published under the name of *Cualidades y riquezas del Nuevo Reino de Granada* (Qualities and Riches of The New Kingdom of Granada), is a mixture of natural and geographical descriptions, together with historical accounts of towns visited. Basilio Vicente de Oviedo insists on presenting facts, the accuracy of which he tries, insofar as possible, to verify. He also shows a marked interest in economic matters and is keen to relate the development of a particular town or region to the goods associated with it.

Bibliography: Carlos Felice Cardot, ed., *Venezuela en los Cronistas Generales de Indias* (Caracas: Academia Nacional de la Historia, 1962); Basilio Vicente De Oviedo, *Cualidades y riquezas del Nuevo Reino de Granada* (Bogotá: Biblioteca de Historia Nacional, 1930).

Nikita Harwich Vallenilla

OVIEDO Y BAÑOS, José de (Bogotá, 1671–Caracas, 1738), Venezuelan historian. Son of Juan Antonio de Oviedo y Rivas and Josefa de Baños y Sotomayor, both of distinguished Spanish ancestry. After his father's death in 1672, his mother returned to her hometown, Lima (Peru), where young José spent his early childhood. In 1686, he traveled to Caracas where he was placed under the protection of his maternal uncle, the illustrious and recently appointed Bishop Diego de Baños y Sotomayor, who supervised his formal education. Married in 1698 to Francisca Manuela de Tovar, who belonged to one of Caracas' leading patrician families, he was elected assistant mayor of the Caracas Municipal Council the following year. In 1703, he purchased the office of permanent alderman but resigned after a few months in office. Elected mayor in 1710 and again in 1722, he became directly involved in the administrative affairs of the Province of Venezuela. His acquaintance with the provincial archives, together with the study of various chronicles, particularly Fray Pedro Simón's *Noticias historiales*... (Historical notices...), as well as the knowledge his prominent social and economic position gave him of the personal inside histories of other leading families, enabled him to complete his major work, the *Historia de la conquista y población de la Provincia de Venezuela* (History of the Conquest and Population of the Province of Venezuela), the first part of which was published in Madrid in 1723 and covered the period from the discovery of Venezuela, during Columbus's third trip in 1498, up to 1600. The second part of the book, which was supposed to deal with the period from 1600 up to the early years of the eighteenth century, has been a matter of controversy. It is generally believed that the manuscript was completed, but was never published because it contained sensitive information on various prominent Caracas families and may have been destroyed intentionally during the first half of the nineteenth century. Written in an elegant, factual manner devoid of unnecessary stylistic flourishes, Oviedo y Baños' *Historia*... tries, insofar as possible, to present a balanced picture of the Spanish conquest. The Indian populations are referred to as "barbarians," but some of their leaders, particularly Guaicaipuro, are given credit for their brave resistance. Still considered a milestone in Venezuelan historiography, though recent studies have shown that Oviedo y Baños relied heavily on Fray Pedro Simón's previous account, the *Historia de la conquista*... has been one of the works most readily consulted, quoted, and copied by historians when dealing with the Venezuelan early Colonial period.

Bibliography: Angelina Lemmo, *Historiografía Colonial Venezolana* (Caracas: Universidad Central de Venezuela, 1977); Jose de Oviedo y Baños, *Historia de la conquista y población de la Provincia de Venezuela* (Madrid: Ediciones Atlas, Biblioteca de Autores Españoles, 1958); Caracciolo Parra Leon, *Analectas de Historia Patria* (Caracas, 1935).

Nikita Harwich Vallenilla

VELASCO, Juan de (Riobamba, Ecuador, 1727–Faenza, Italy, 1792), Ecuadorean Jesuit priest and historian. Son of Sargeant Major Juan de Velasco y López de Moncayo, who at that time was also mayor of Riobamba, and of Maria Pérez Petroche. After receiving his first degree from the Jesuit School of Riobamba (1743), Juan de Velasco was sent to the Seminary College of San Luís in Quito and, soon afterwards, joined the Jesuit order as a noviciate (1744). He took his vows in 1746 and pursued his academic career at the Colegio Máximo of Quito and at the San Gregorio Jesuit University where he obtained his doctoral degree in 1753. Ordained that same year, he was sent out on various teaching and missionary assignments, becoming fluent in Quechua and several other indigenous languages. He travelled widely throughout the territory of the Quito

Royal Audiencia, gathering notes and research material to be used in a major historical work he had been entrusted to write. In 1759, he taught at the Jesuit Colegio de Ibarra and, from 1762 on, at the Colegio de Popayán. Expelled from Latin America with the rest of the Jesuit order, Juan de Velasco left Ecuador in 1767 and was confined to residence in the small Italian town of Faenza, where he arrived, seriously ill, at the end of 1768. He was able, apparently, to save a substantial part of his books and notes, but his illness—an acute form of rhumatism—prevented him for nearly nine years from resuming his work. At the end of 1788, however, in a letter to Antonio Porlier, minister and secretary for the Indies to King Charles IV of Spain, he announced that he had completed a *History of the Kingdom of Quito* which he offered for publication. Polier acknowledged the offer and the manuscript was sent, but only to remain forgotten in the Royal Archives until the early 1840s when partial translations were published in Italian and in French; the first complete edition in Spanish was brought before the reading public between 1841 and 1844. The *Historia del Reino de Quito en la América Meridional* (History of the Kingdom of Quito in South America) was constructed from Velasco's own experience in Ecuador and from his knowledge of the indigenous pre-Hispanic society, but also from his reading of earlier chronicles (Garcilaso de la Vega [q.v.], López de Gómara, etc.).

The book is divided into three parts: natural, ancient, and modern history. The natural history offers a detailed description of the flora and fauna of the region; the ancient history starts out with the conquest of the mythical Scyri kingdom by the Inca empire, up to the consolidation of the Spanish conquest around 1550. The modern history extends from 1550 up to about 1760 and emphasizes the missionary activity then developed throughout the territory of present-day Ecuador. The author also provides valuable ethnographical data on the Indian populations of the period considered. Though the *Historia del Reino de Quito* has been criticized, particularly with regard to the "unscientific" value of the natural history section, and Velasco has been charged with gross inaccuracy in establishing a chronology of the Scyri dynasty—still a matter of controversy among scholars—it stands nonetheless as the first major contribution to the establishment of a specific Ecuadorean heritage and is considered the founding work of Ecuadorean historiography.

Bibliography: Leonidas Batallas, *Vida y Escritos del R. P. Juan de Velasco, S. J.*, 2nd edition. (Quito: Talleres Gráficos Nacionales, 1927); Gabriel Cevallos Garcia, *Historiadores ecuatorianos. Juan de Velasco* (Quito: Talleres Gráficos de Educación, 1958); Carlos Manuel Larrea, *El Padre Velasco y la Historia del Reino de Quito* (Quito, 1971); Juan de Velasco, *Historia del Nuevo Reino de Quito en la América Meridional* (Quito: Casa de la Cultura Ecuatoriana, 1977–1979), 3 vols.

Nikita Harwich Vallenilla

Great Historians: Swedish

LAGERBRING, Sven (Bosjökloster, Skåne, 1707–Lund, 1787), Swedish historian. Professor at the university of Lund from 1742, LagerBring, who before he was knighted in 1769 was called Sven Bring, and who thereafter called himself Sven LagerBring, was a versatile and independently minded historian. A law student, he was eligible in 1742 for professorships not only in history but also in *juris et moralium*. In addition, he was qualified in the area of constitutional studies and became a professor of history. He also devoted himself to the history of science and erudition, as well as local history, primarily dealing with his home province Skåne (Scania), which Sweden only a generation earlier had acquired from Denmark (LagerBring's ancestry was completely Danish). He edited historical documents dealing with Skåne, some of which benefited Lauritz Weibull in his critical studies of sources in the beginning of the twentieth century. LagerBring's many contacts with Danish intellectuals, and his refusal to designate Denmark as an archetypal "enemy" in his history writing, coupled with his unwavering royalism and his strong feeling of then being Swedish, later earned him a pioneer's label, "the first literary Scandinavian." LagerBring launched two larger projects, neither of which came to completion. The sole volume of *Historia literaria, eller inledning til wetnskapshistorien* (Historia Literaria, or Introduction to the History of Science), from 1748, deals with classical Greek science, and in later, smaller works he discussed, among other things, the so-called Cartesian struggles in Sweden during the seventeenth century, that is, the recurrent academic disputes on the respective virtues of Aristotelianism and Cartesianism. Although no more than a torso, his magnum opus is *Swea rikes historia* (The History of the Swedish Nation), in four parts, published, respectively, in 1769, 1773, 1776, and 1783. With the first chapters, in manuscript, of the fifth part, he reached the year 1463. During the 1770s he managed to publish one smaller and one larger abstract of his Swedish history, and that took his time and his strength away from—and also the economy out of—the larger task. In his Swedish history, LagerBring revealed himself as a man of the Enlightenment. He showed interest in a cultural history much like Voltaire's "l'esprit des moeurs," and this is part of his panoramic sketch of the resources and the conditions of the Swedish nation, reminiscent of the "political arithmetics'' in England from the turn of the century, 1700. He was also a rationalist–moralist, although he was relatively restrained, limiting his judgment to ''a personal view only.'' One of his critical assessments concerns the role of the Swedish nobility in the fifteenth century. In reproaching it for its narrow lust for power, as LagerBring saw it, he became known as the first representative of the so-called condemnation of the aristocracy (with the subsequent idealization of king and people) in Swedish history writing, in that sense being one of Erik Gustaf Geijer's predecessors. Some also found here a parallel to his own times, the so-called Age of Liberty in Sweden, when the ''Riksdag'' (Swedish Parliament), and its Four Estates, was quite influential and the kings were weak. LagerBring's credo for his history writing was ''truth is the life of history.'' This required of the historian that he account for his sources, choose the sources closest to the event, and, if necessary, use his critical reason to decide upon the quality of the information given. His relatively mature principles for using sources, together with his practices and his teachings, meant that for the first time one could talk of history writing in Sweden as a science.

Ragnar Björk

OLAUS MAGNUS (Linköping, 1490–Rome, Italy, 1557), Swedish cultural historian, cartographer, diplomat, and clergyman. The life of Olaus Magnus, as well as that of his older brother Johannes Magnus, was dominated by the opened and ever-widening rift within the Christian Church. The brothers were brought up and educated as Catholics, and they staunchly held on to their faith and their Church throughout their lives. For Olaus Magnus this meant a three-decade-long exile from Sweden, ending only with his death. He studied in Germany between 1510 and 1517. He attended the university of Rostock and probably also the Dominican school in Cologne. In 1523 Gustaf Eriksson Vasa became king in Sweden, and he effectively shook off Danish influence over Swedish internal affairs. During the following years the Reformation of the Church reached Sweden. The king continued to consolidate the nation and his own reign by stripping the Church of its financial assets in 1527. The Church leaders leaned in different directions spiritually, but the tendency was toward a defection from the pope. Since sharing a strong Swedish nationalist sentiment with Olaus Magnus and Johannes Magnus, the king had continued confidence in them, so far. In 1524 Olaus Magnus was sent on a diplomatic mission to Rome where he reported on the precarious situation of the Church in Sweden. In the years 1526–1527 he was commissioned by the king to negotiate with the Netherlands over trade problems. Meanwhile, his brother Johannes Magnus, archbishop since 1523, had to go into exile, and the brothers reunited in Danzig. In 1530 Olaus was deposed from his positions in the Church in Sweden, and his property was confiscated. During the following years in Poland, Olaus Magnus, incited by the Portuguese humanist Damianus a Goes, began work on a map with cultural and historical information on the Northern European sphere. Olaus Magnus left Danzig for Italy in 1537, and in 1539 his cartographical work *Carta Marina* was published in Venice with financial backing from Hieronimo Quirino. The map, covering not only northern Europe but also the eastern part of the Atlantic, is filled with images of natural wonders and the life of the people, and this cultural material is elaborated in commentaries to the Latin, Italian, and German editions of the map. Ever since their exile began, the brothers were indefatigably fighting for a restoration of the old church order in Sweden. In 1544 Johannes Magnus died in Rome, and Olaus was designated as his successor as archbishop of Sweden, although a Lutheran one had been appointed by the king in Sweden a decade earlier. After the failure of the meeting of the Church in Vicenza in 1538, the Tridentine meeting was finally assembled in 1545. Olaus Magnus was very active, as witnessed by his voluminous correspondence and his then strenuous efforts to have the many heretic German universities closed. He was also eager to save his homeland from the Lutherans. He then intensified the work, beginning with his map, to give an overall view of the peoples of the North, especially in Sweden, and their glorious past, thereby serving notice to the pope what important areas the Church now risked losing. In 1555 Olaus Magnus, in Rome, and in Latin, published his large work *Historia de gentibus septentrionalibus* (History of the Peoples of the North), with a huge number of illustrations. Although editions soon appeared in Italian, German, French, Dutch, and English, the first Swedish version did not appear until the beginning of the twentieth century. The twenty-two books of the history contain information on the nature and its wonders, on the natural resources, on the customs and virtues of the people, and on human endeavors of all kinds, not the least of them being the capacities of the Swedish people in warfare. In harmony with the work of Johannes Magnus, *Historia de omnibus Gothorum Sveonumque regibus* (History of All Gothic and Svea Kings), which Olaus had published in 1554, he emphasized the Gothic ancestry of the Swedish people. Olaus Magnus died in Rome in 1557, and, like his brother, he is buried in St. Peter.

Bibliography: G. Buschbell, ed., "Briefe von Johannes und Olaus Magnus," *Historiska handlingar* 28, no. 3 (1932); Hjalmar Grape, *Olaus Magnus—Forskare, Moralist, Konstnär* (Olaus Magnus—Researcher, Moralist, Artist) (Stockholm, 1970).

Ragnar Björk

Great Historians: Swiss

MÜLLER, Johannes von (Schaffhausen, 1752–Kassel, 1809), Swiss historian. He was the son of a priest coming from an old bourgeois family. After school in his native town, he learned theology and history of the church in Göttingen, where Ludwig Augustus Schlözer (q.v.) advised him to turn to history. It was at that time that his lifetime professional dilemma started. He was not fit for an ecclesiastic career. Although at twenty he was already a teacher in Greek in Schaffhausen, the born historian could not find a satisfactory position in Switzerland. The only university in Basel reserved its chairs for citizens of the city. Müller spent the years 1774–1780 as a private teacher in Geneva. The lectures delivered there were included in his posthumous book, *Vierzundzwanzig Bücher Allgemeiner Geschichten besonders der Europäischen Menschheit*. The tradition of Swiss world history had started with Isaak Iselin (1728–1782), a tradition which Müller continued in his own way, offering not only ideas related to the Enlightenment, but also facts: from the old oriental history to the contemporary one, from the battles for India to North American independence. No historical optimism results from it, only a leading thread of history, for "its plan is unknown, its way cannot be told." Müller considered that mankind's development was always disrupted by the wish for conquest and upsetting the balance. This is a leitmotiv of his historical thinking, which shows in his works *Reisen der Päpste* (1782) and *Darstellung des Fürstenbundes* (1787) with its introductory chapters "On Freedom" and "On Balance." When those writings came out, Müller was working on his chief oeuvre, *Die Geschichten der Schweizer* (1780), or—as the work was called since the second edition of its first volume—*Geschichten schweizerischer Eidgenossenschaft* (1786–1808), a work that covers the events up to 1489 from which other historians continued up to the nineteenth century. His work depicts the historical evolution of a small people with a common will; it is written in an archaic language that suited the classical taste of the time. Rousseau's influence on his youthful years was extended with the influence of Justus Möser (q.v.) and especially of Herder (q.v.), making him more sensitive to the peculiarities and beauties of the Middle Ages and the Christian religion. For his time he was the most appreciated German language historian, and had a powerful influence on the Swiss bourgeoisie. Through his writing, and through Schiller's play *Wilhelm Tell*, Swiss history acquired international significance. Teacher at the college in Kassel (1781), and librarian and adviser to the Archbishop of Mainz (1786), he was frightened away by the revolution which he regarded at first with reserve and later on resolutely rejected, just as he rejected the 1798 Swiss movement, decidedly placing himself at the Austrians' service. A court historian in Berlin and member of the academy there (1804), Minister of Culture of the Kingdom of Westphalia (1807), he passed away in 1809 in Kassel. While coping with his political and public duties, he also found time to articulate his chief work and contributed to the preservation of Switzerland's historical identity in an adverse period of its existence.

Bibliography: Edgar Bonjour, *Studien zu J. v. Müller*, Basel, 1957; Richard Feller and Edgar Bonjour, *Geschichtsschreibung der Schweiz vom Spätmittelalter zur Neuzeit*, vol. 2, Basel-Stuttgart, 1979, pp. 545–569; Karl Henking, *J. v. Müller*, 2 vols., Stuttgart-Berlin, 1909–28; Johannes von Müller, *Sämtliche Werke*, ed. Johann Georg Müller, 27 vols., Tübingen, 1810–19; *Briefe in Auswahl*, ed. E. Bonjour, Basel, 1954; Karl Schib, *J. v. Müller*, Schaffhausen, 1967.

Peter Stadler

TSCHUDI, Aegidus or Gilg (Glarus, 1505–Glarus, 1572), Swiss historian. Tschudi came from a leading family in the canton of Glarus, which he considered to belong to the nobility, and he occupied several important political offices in his home region, including, in 1558, the highest office, that of *Landamann*. In the following year he was sent as the ambassador of the Swiss Confederacy to the imperial court in Augsburg. His determined intervention for the Catholic cause, however, brought his canton and Switzerland to the brink of a war of religion, so he had to avoid his home region for several years. We know less about his education than about his political role. He probably never enjoyed a truly scholarly education, although for a short time in Basel he was a student of the respected humanist Henricus Glareanus. The latter probably stimulated him to write his first book, the only one that was published during his lifetime, the *Uralt wahrhafftig Alpisch Rhetia* (1538), which presents a combination of topography and history in the manner of the "Italia illustrata" or the "Germania illustrata" by Italian and German humanists. This interest is also found in his last work, the *Gallia comata* (Basel, 1758; repr. 1977), one of his very learned descriptions of ancient Switzerland and its surroundings from the Roman times to the High Middle Ages, more a collection of excerpts than a description, with a wealth of notices and inscriptions, but also rich historical and ethnographic material. This book already betrays his great diligence as a collector but also his dilettantism in making conjectures and comparisons. These two books could have earned him the highest reputation of a specialist.

What preserves Tschudi's fame today is his chief work, the *Chronicum helveticum*, a presentation of the whole of Swiss history from 1000 to 1470, the first book of its kind. This work was first published in 1734 to 1735 by the Basel professor Johann Rudolf Iselin; a critical new edition was undertaken in 1968.

The significance of this work rests in its being the crowning and culmination of the older Swiss chronicle method. There were many precursors who limited themselves to depicting history from the perspective of one city or one region and restricted themselves to a certain span of time. This holds for the Bern chroniclers, Justinger and his nephew Diebold Schilling's chronicle of Bern, or Petermann Etterlin's chronicle of Switzerland, to name only a few. Tschudi by no means knew all of them, because only a few had been published. In terms of scholarly achievement the Swiss chronicle published in 1548 by the Reformed clergyman Johannes Stumpf (1500–1577/1578) who had emigrated from Germany and with whom Tschudi had a stimulating correspondence despite differences in belief—he accused him of confessional one-sidedness—came closest or that of the reformer and historian Vadian from St. Gallen. With both he shared his antiquarian topographical understanding of history. These are some of the preconditions that gave rise to Tschudi's chronological *chef d'oeuvre*. Its significance rests for one in the comprehensive formulation of the theme that traces the history of the Swiss space from the medieval imperial period until the late Middle Ages and always keeps in mind the overall unity of this history with history in general.

In addition, Tschudi is known for his great achievement as a researcher in tracing documents of which many were preserved for posterity only through his efforts. In his determination to find evidence for everything, he at times supplemented and falsified documents or parts of documents—in the interest of a richer picture of the past but also in the interest of his own family's past. More important is his picture of the Swiss past and his legitimation of Swiss liberation. Tschudi was convinced that the latter did not constitute a revolt against the house of Hapsburg but a recreation of the old conditions, which he explained by the fact that the Swiss are directly descended from the old Helvetians. The Swiss Confederation thus did not originate in the Holy Roman Empire but stood as an equal entity beside it. Therefore, not the peasants, but rather the ''Ehrbarkeit,'' an elite comparable to the nobility, led the struggle for liberation. This view of history, in which humanism and patriotism are intertwined, has determined the tradition of Swiss school books until the twentieth century and has led Tschudi to the title of Father of Swiss History.

Bibliography: Richard Feller and Edgar Bonjour, *Geschichtsschreibung der Schweiz vom Spätmittelalter zur Neuzeit*, 2d ed., vol. 1 (Basel-Stuttgart, 1979), pp. 258–276, contains further listings of literature and also an extensive treatment of the older Swiss tradition of chronicles; Aegidius Tschudi, *Chronicum helveticum*, pt. 1, ed. Peter Stadler and Bernhard Stettler; pts. 2–5 (1970) and two supplementary vols., ed. Bernhard Stettler (Bern, 1968–1984).

Peter Stadler

INDEX OF HISTORIANS

SUBJECT INDEX

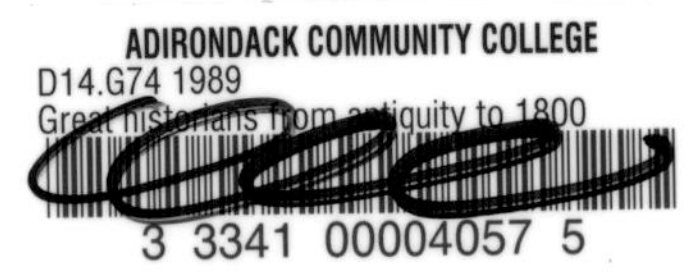